Frommer's®
New York City

My New York City
by Brian Silverman

NEW YORKERS ARE GREAT COMPLAINERS. WE LIKE TO BITCH AND MOAN.
And this is a good thing. Our grumbling keeps us on our toes.

We're also initially suspicious of the new—of invasions to our beloved landscape. When the twin towers of the World Trade Center were constructed, many of us saw them as a blight on the city's famous skyline. Compared with treasures like the Empire State Building and the Chrysler Building, they were abominations. Generations later, we mourn their loss not just because of the lives that went down with them, but because they'd become part of our spiritual landscape, symbols of our sheer brashness, our restless energy, our drive.

What makes New York a true original, however, is not one building or museum but the sum of it all, including the people. Las Vegas can create an instant New York on the strip, but it's a fantasy—you need New Yorkers to make New York. The city, and the spirit it embodies, just cannot be duplicated. I have no complaints about that.

Here are some of the places I like to go back to over and over. You won't want to miss them either.

© Eric Kampl/Index Stock

CENTRAL PARK (left) I'm very fortunate to live with my family near Central Park. It's like having our own personal nature preserve—except that we share it with thousands of others. Central Park is one of the best places in the city for people-watching, especially during summer. The parade of bikers, joggers, roller-bladers, and strollers is a source of endless amusement. And the park has so many routes I never get never bored. Pictured here is the Mall, with its wide walkway and overarching elms.

THE ROSE CENTER FOR EARTH AND SPACE (above) City icons don't develop overnight. But as soon as this giant glass cube opened 5 years ago, it was an instant hit. Inside, a four-story-high planetarium offers one of the most technologically advanced sky shows on the planet. This futuristic structure, draped in the largest suspended glass curtain wall in the U.S., is the perfect complement to the dusty dinosaurs inside the American Museum of Natural History, the building both share.

SUBWAY MUSICIANS (left) Most of us who live in New York spend a good deal of time taking the subways. It's the fastest and cheapest way to get around and not as complicated as it might seem. Rushing like rats through the stations to make connections, we're cheered on by sounds of music, even if we stop only long enough to drop a quarter in a cup. What makes the beat so special is that you never know when or where you'll hear it, or what it might be. Here a jazz duo has found an impromptu stage to show off their stuff.

CENTRAL PARK RESERVOIR (below) Also known as the Jacqueline Kennedy Onassis Reservoir, this is my favorite place for a jog. I'm not alone: The 1½-mile jogging track around the reservoir is packed with joggers in the morning and after work. What makes it so special are the views. As you circle east you see the stately apartment buildings of Fifth Avenue. From the north end you can see the Manhattan skyline to the south. The view west reveals the majestic Art Deco apartment buildings that line Central Park West.

GRAND CENTRAL STATION (above) No, it's not a planetarium, it's the "sky ceiling" in the main concourse of the magnificently restored Grand Central Station. The ceiling, lit greenish-blue, depicts the constellations of the winter sky above New York. Be careful staring up; you might get trampled by one of the thousands of commuters who rush through here each day. Grand Central is a pleasure even if you're not catching a train—you could spend hours shopping at the upscale food market, visiting the New York Transit Museum Store, noshing on the dining concourse, or slurping oysters at the landmark Oyster Bar.

LOUIS ARMSTRONG'S BATHROOM (right) This mirrored bathroom happens to be in the former house of jazz great Louis Armstrong. Armstrong could have lived anywhere, but he chose an unassuming house in the blue-collar neighborhood of Corona, Queens. Now a museum, the house has been preserved exactly as it was when his wife passed away in 1983.

© Serge Hambourg/Louis Armstrong House & Archives

© Angus Oborn/Lonely Planet Images

A FOODIE'S TOWN I admit it, I love food, and New York has tremendous variety. Other city greenmarkets are more convenient to my home, but none matches this one in **UNION SQUARE (left)**, not only for the scene but for the variety. The best time to visit is in the summer and fall, when the produce—apples, lettuces, corn, you name it—from local farms is bountiful. The dominant color on a brisk fall day? Pumpkin orange. When I want the best Southern fried chicken in the city, I head to the **M&G DINER (bottom left)** on 125th Street. Waiting on line for smoked fish at **ZABAR'S (upper right)** on a Sunday morning is an Upper West Side tradition. I love walking in Chinatown, where everything is right out on the street, from bootleg DVDs to boxes of ginseng. But what I love best about Chinatown are the countless restaurants, the vegetable markets, and the **FISH MARKETS (bottom right)**, where the catch is so fresh it's still flapping on ice.

© Dan Herrick/Lonely Planet Images

FLATIRON BUILDING (left) This architectural icon is one of the most recognizable structures in the world. It was built in 1902 to fill the awkward triangular property created by the intersection of Broadway and Fifth Avenue. Fronted with limestone and terra cotta, it measures just 6 feet across at its narrow end. It's a beauty to look at, but don't bother going inside; I've been there many times (my wife had an office there), and it's not worth the interminable wait for the outdated elevators.

YANKEE STADIUM (below) Rome may have its Colosseum, but New York has Yankee Stadium. There is no more famous sports arena in America than "The House that Ruth Built." You may be from Boston or Chicago and hate the Yankees, but don't hold that against Yankee Stadium. If you're here in the off-season, you can still go for a tour and wander amid the ghosts of all-time greats like Ruth, Gehrig, DiMaggio, and Mantle.

THE WALDORF-ASTORIA

The Waldorf-Astoria

WALDORF-ASTORIA (above) I'm a sucker for old-time, early-20th-century New York hotels. Thankfully, quite a few of these "grande dames" are still around. The Waldorf, comprising one square block and 1,000 rooms, just might be the grandest of them all. This is where kings stay when they come to town; where the president lays his head; and where Secret Service agents of all nationalities are a regular sight. The Waldorf also has fine shops, three restaurants, and four bars.

MUSEUM OF MODERN ART (right) The old MoMA was indistinguishable among the faceless towers on 53rd Street. Following a $425-million reno-vation, MoMA is now as close to a work of art as a museum can be—it's stunning both inside and out. Anyone who claims a love of modern art has to come here to enjoy one of the greatest collections of 20th-century art in the world.

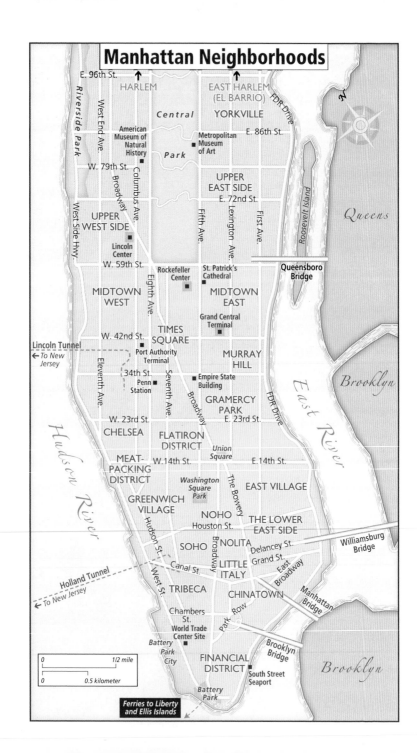

Central Park

Alice in Wonderland Statue **15**

Balto Statue **21**

The Bandshell **19**

Belvedere Castle **7**

Bethesda Terrace &
  Bethesda Fountain **17**

The Boathouse
  Restaurant **12**

Bow Bridge **9**

The Carousel **27**

The Central Park Zoo **24**

The Charles A. Dana
  Discovery Center **1**

Cleopatra's Needle
  (The Obelisk) **10**

Conservatory **14**

Conservatory Garden **1**

The Dairy Information
  Center **26**

Delacorte Clock **23**

Delacorte Theater **8**

Diana Ross Playground **5**

Hans Christian Andersen
  Statue **13**

Harlem Meer **1**

Hecksher Ball Fields **29**

Hecksher Playground **30**

Henry Luce
  Nature Observatory **7**

Imagine Mosaic **18**

Jacqueline Kennedy Onassis
  Reservoir **3**

Lasker Rink and Pool **1**

Loeb Boathouse **16**

The Mall **20**

North Meadow Ball Fields **2**

Pat Hoffman Friedman
  Playground **11**

The Pool **2**

Rustic Playground **22**

Shakespeare Garden **9**

Spector Playground **4**

Swedish Cottage
  Marionette Theatre **6**

Tavern on the Green **28**

Tisch Children's Zoo **24**

Wollman Rink **25**

ⓘ Information

Ⓜ Subway stop

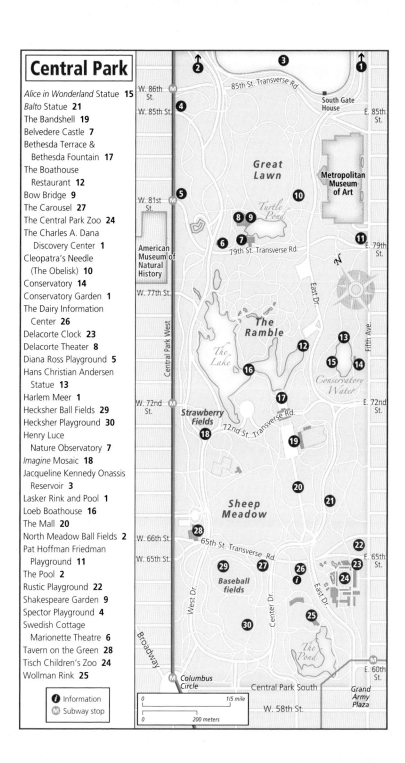

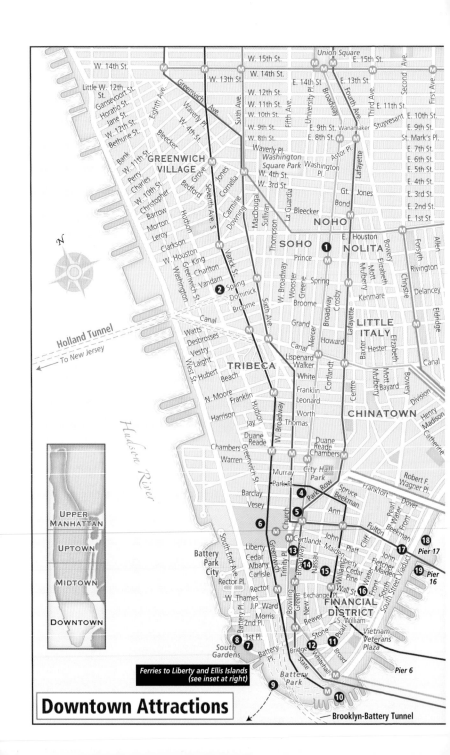

Downtown Attractions

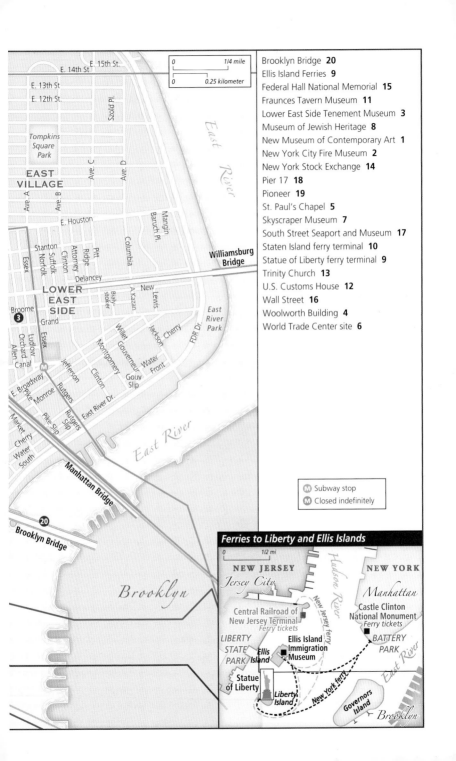

Brooklyn Bridge **20**
Ellis Island Ferries **9**
Federal Hall National Memorial **15**
Fraunces Tavern Museum **11**
Lower East Side Tenement Museum **3**
Museum of Jewish Heritage **8**
New Museum of Contemporary Art **1**
New York City Fire Museum **2**
New York Stock Exchange **14**
Pier 17 **18**
Pioneer **19**
St. Paul's Chapel **5**
Skyscraper Museum **7**
South Street Seaport and Museum **17**
Staten Island ferry terminal **10**
Statue of Liberty ferry terminal **9**
Trinity Church **13**
U.S. Customs House **12**
Wall Street **16**
Woolworth Building **4**
World Trade Center site **6**

Midtown Attractions

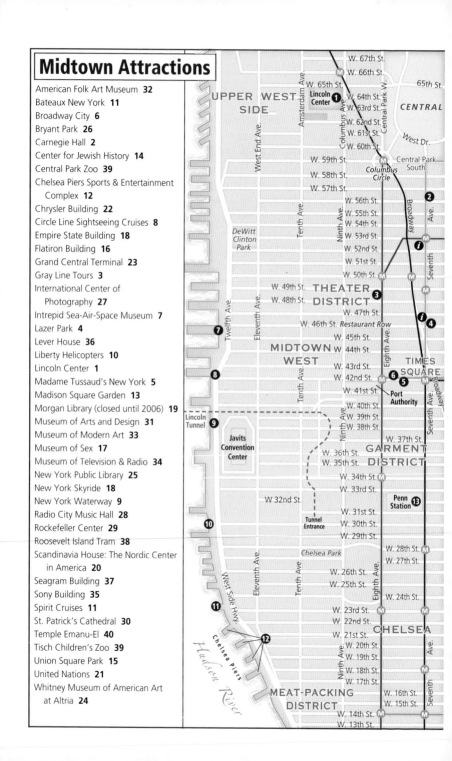

American Folk Art Museum **32**
Bateaux New York **11**
Broadway City **6**
Bryant Park **26**
Carnegie Hall **2**
Center for Jewish History **14**
Central Park Zoo **39**
Chelsea Piers Sports & Entertainment
    Complex **12**
Chrysler Building **22**
Circle Line Sightseeing Cruises **8**
Empire State Building **18**
Flatiron Building **16**
Grand Central Terminal **23**
Gray Line Tours **3**
International Center of
    Photography **27**
Intrepid Sea-Air-Space Museum **7**
Lazer Park **4**
Lever House **36**
Liberty Helicopters **10**
Lincoln Center **1**
Madame Tussaud's New York **5**
Madison Square Garden **13**
Morgan Library (closed until 2006) **19**
Museum of Arts and Design **31**
Museum of Modern Art **33**
Museum of Sex **17**
Museum of Television & Radio **34**
New York Public Library **25**
New York Skyride **18**
New York Waterway **9**
Radio City Music Hall **28**
Rockefeller Center **29**
Roosevelt Island Tram **38**
Scandinavia House: The Nordic Center
    in America **20**
Seagram Building **37**
Sony Building **35**
Spirit Cruises **11**
St. Patrick's Cathedral **30**
Temple Emanu-El **40**
Tisch Children's Zoo **39**
Union Square Park **15**
United Nations **21**
Whitney Museum of American Art
    at Altria **24**

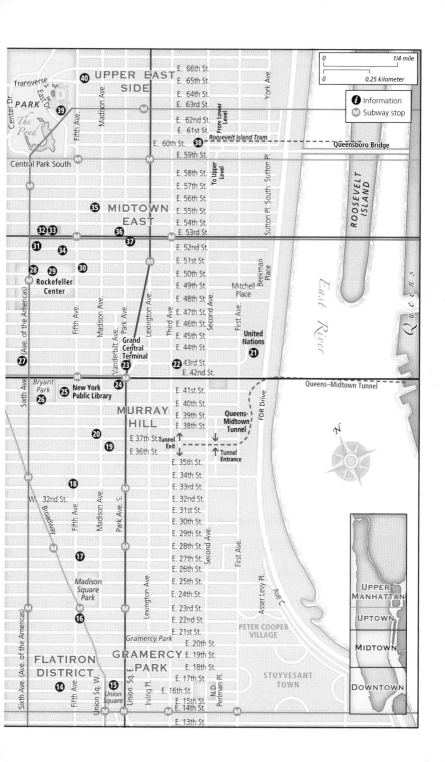

UPPER EAST SIDE

E. 66th St.
E. 65th St.
E. 64th St.
E. 63rd St.
E. 62nd St.
E. 61st St.
E. 60th St.
E. 59th St.

Central Park South

PARK
The Pond

Transverse
Center Dr.
East Dr.

Fifth Ave.
Madison Ave.
York Ave.

From Lower Level
Roosevelt Island Tram
Queensboro Bridge

E. 58th St.
E. 57th St.
E. 56th St.
E. 55th St.
E. 54th St.
E. 53rd St.
E. 52nd St.
E. 51st St.
E. 50th St.
E. 49th St.
E. 48th St.
E. 47th St.
E. 46th St.
E. 45th St.
E. 44th St.
E. 43rd St.
E. 42nd St.

To Upper Level

MIDTOWN EAST

ROOSEVELT ISLAND

East River

Queens

Rockefeller Center

Grand Central Terminal

United Nations

Sutton Pl. South
Sutton Pl.
Beekman Place
Mitchell Place
Second Ave.
First Ave.
Third Ave.
Lexington Ave.
Park Ave.
Vanderbilt Ave.
Madison Ave.
Fifth Ave.
Sixth Ave. (Ave. of the Americas)

Bryant Park
New York Public Library

MURRAY HILL

E. 41st St.
E. 40th St.
E. 39th St.
E. 38th St.
E. 37th St. Tunnel Exit
E. 36th St.
E. 35th St.
E. 34th St.
E. 33rd St.
E. 32nd St.
E. 31st St.
E. 30th St.
E. 29th St.
E. 28th St.
E. 27th St.
E. 26th St.
E. 25th St.
E. 24th St.
E. 23rd St.
E. 22nd St.
E. 21st St.
E. 20th St.
E. 19th St.
E. 18th St.
E. 17th St.
E. 16th St.
E. 15th St.
E. 14th St.
E. 13th St.

Queens-Midtown Tunnel

FDR Drive

Tunnel Entrance

Madison Square Park

Gramercy Park

FLATIRON DISTRICT

GRAMERCY PARK

W. 32nd St.
Broadway
Madison Ave.
Park Ave. S.
Lexington Ave.
Union Sq. W.
Union Sq. E.
Irving Pl.
N.D. Perlman Pl.
Asser Levy Pl.
First Ave.
Second Ave.
Avenue C

PETER COOPER VILLAGE

STUYVESANT TOWN

Union Square

40 39 38 35 36 37 32 33 31 34 28 29 30 27 25 26 24 23 22 21 20 19 18 17 16 14 15

0   1/4 mile
0   0.25 kilometer

i Information
Ⓜ Subway stop

UPPER MANHATTAN
UPTOWN
MIDTOWN
DOWNTOWN

N

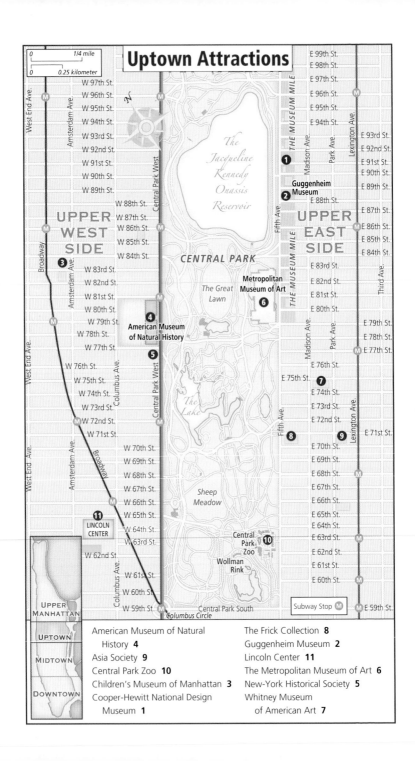

Uptown Attractions

Subway Stop Ⓜ

American Museum of Natural History **4**
Asia Society **9**
Central Park Zoo **10**
Children's Museum of Manhattan **3**
Cooper-Hewitt National Design Museum **1**

The Frick Collection **8**
Guggenheim Museum **2**
Lincoln Center **11**
The Metropolitan Museum of Art **6**
New-York Historical Society **5**
Whitney Museum of American Art **7**

Frommer's®

New York City

2006

by Brian Silverman

Here's what the critics say about Frommer's:

"Amazingly easy to use. Very portable, very complete."
—*Booklist*

"Detailed, accurate, and easy-to-read information for all price ranges."
—*Glamour Magazine*

"Hotel information is close to encyclopedic."
—*Des Moines Sunday Register*

"Frommer's Guides have a way of giving you a real feel for a place."
—*Knight Ridder Newspapers*

Wiley Publishing, Inc.

About the Author

Brian Silverman, who is also the author of *Frommer's New York City from $90 a Day* and *New York City For Dummies,* has written about travel, food, sports, and music for publications such as *Saveur, Caribbean Travel & Life, Islands, American Way,* the *New Yorker,* and *The New York Times.* He is the author of several books including *Going, Going, Gone: The History, Lore, and Mystique of the Home Run* (HarperCollins), and co-editor of *The Twentieth Century Treasury of Sports* (Viking Books). Brian lives in New York, New York, with his wife and two sons.

Published by:

Wiley Publishing, Inc.

111 River St.
Hoboken, NJ 07030-5774

ISBN 13: 978-0-7645-9546-2
ISBN 10: 0-7645-9546-6

Editor: Lorraine Festa
Special thanks to Alexis Flippin
Production Editors: Donna Wright and Katie Robinson
Cartographer: Roberta Stockwell
Photo Editor: Richard Fox
Production by Wiley Indianapolis Composition Services

Front cover photo: Chrysler Building
Back cover photo: The Lake at Central Park

For information on our other products and services or to obtain technical support, please contact our Customer Care Department within the U.S. at 800/762-2974, outside the U.S. at 317/572-3993 or fax 317/572-4002.

Wiley also publishes its books in a variety of electronic formats. Some content that appears in print may not be available in electronic formats.

Manufactured in the United States of America

5   4   3   2   1

Contents

List of Maps   vi

What's New in New York City   1

1 The Best of the Big Apple   4

1 Most Unforgettable Travel
Experiences 4

2 Best Events .6

3 Best Museums 6

4 Best New York City Structures 7

5 Best Parks .7

6 Best Places to Take the Kids 7

7 Best Places to Stroll 7

8 Best Things to Do for Free
(or Almost) 8

9 Best Offbeat Experiences 8

10 Best Way to Spend a Day
in a Borough 9

11 Best Splurge Hotels 9

12 Best Moderately Priced Hotels 10

13 Best Hotels for Families 10

14 Best Incentives for
Hotel-Hopping 10

15 The Most Unforgettable Dining
Experiences 11

16 Best New Restaurants 11

17 Best Bites for All Appetites 12

18 Best Shopping 13

19 Best Culture & Nightlife 14

2 A Traveler's Guide to New York's Architecture   15

by Lisa Torrance Duffy

1 New York Architecture 15

3 Planning Your Trip to New York City   27

1 Visitor Information 27

2 Money 28

3 When to Go 29

*New York City Calendar
of Events* .30

4 Travel Insurance 37

5 Health & Safety 38

6 Specialized Travel Resources 40

7 Planning Your Trip Online 44

*Frommers.com: The Complete Travel
Resource* .46

8 The 21st-Century Traveler 47

*Where to Check Your E-mail in
the City That Never Sleeps* 48

Online Traveler's Toolbox 50

9 Getting There 51

*AirTrains: Newark & JFK—The Very
Good & the Not-So-Very Good* 54

Flying with Film & Video 60

10 Packages for the Independent
Traveler 61

11 Escorted General-Interest Tours 62

12 Recommended Books & Films 63

4 For International Visitors 65

1 Preparing for Your Trip 65
  Size Conversion Chart 71
2 Getting to the U.S. 72

3 Getting Around the U.S. 73
  *Fast Facts: For the International
Traveler* 74

5 Suggested NYC Itineraries 80

1 The Best of New York City
in 1 Day .80
2 The Best of New York City
in 2 Days 83

3 The Best of New York City
in 3 Days 86

6 Getting to Know New York City 89

1 Orientation 89
  *Manhattan's Neighborhoods
in Brief* 92
  Manhattan Address Locator 102
  NYC Experiences to Avoid 106

2 Getting Around 109
  *Subway Stops for New York's
Top Attractions* 110
3 Playing It Safe 117
  Fast Facts: New York City 118

7 Where to Stay 122

1 South Street Seaport &
the Financial District 126
2 TriBeCa & Lower East Side 128
3 SoHo 129
4 Greenwich Village &
the Meat-Packing District 131
  Plenty of Room at the Inn 132
5 Chelsea 134

6 Union Square, the Flatiron
District & Gramercy Park 135
7 Times Square & Midtown West . . .139
  Hotel Row 144
  Family-Friendly Hotels 149
8 Midtown East & Murray Hill 150
9 Upper West Side 160
10 Upper East Side 165

8 Where to Dine 168

1 Restaurants by Cuisine 170
2 Financial District, South Street
Seaport & TriBeCa 174
3 Chinatown 178
4 Lower East Side 179
  Ice-Cream Fever 180
5 SoHo & Nolita 182

6 The East Village & NoHo 185
7 Greenwich Village & the
Meat-Packing District 186
  *Dining Zone: The Meat-Packing
District* 188
8 Chelsea 190
  The Prime Cut 194

9 Union Square, the Flatiron District
& Gramercy Park 195

*The Hole Truth: NY's Best
Bagels* 198

10 Times Square & Midtown West . . .199

Pizza, New York–Style 204

The New York Deli News 206

11 Midtown East & Murray Hill 207

Family-Friendly Restaurants 210

12 Upper West Side 211

Food Splurge 214

Breakfast, Not Brunch 220

13 Upper East Side 221

14 Harlem .223

15 The Outer Boroughs 224

The Soul of Harlem 226

9   Exploring New York City   230

1 Sights & Attractions by
Neighborhood 230

2 The Top Attractions 239

*World Trade Center Site
(Ground Zero)* 251

3 More Manhattan Museums 251

*Art for Art's Sake: The Gallery
Scene* 258

*Get Set: New York's Best
Movie Locations* 264

4 Skyscrapers & Other Architectural
Highlights 267

Not Your Ordinary Attractions 269

In Search of Historic Homes 270

Downtown Relics 271

5 Places of Worship 272

6 Central Park & Other
Places to Play 275

7 Organized Sightseeing Tours 286

Offbeat New York Tours 290

8 Talk of the Town: TV Tapings 292

9 Especially for Kids 294

10 Highlights of the Outer
Boroughs 297

11 Spectator Sports 306

10   Shopping   308

1 The Top Shopping Streets
& Neighborhoods 308

2 The Big Department Stores 315

3 Shopping A to Z 318

Murder, They Wrote 322

Chocolate City 329

11   New York City After Dark   344

1 All the City's a Stage:
The Theater Scene 344

*Kids Take the Stage:
Family-Friendly Theater* 348

*More Dramatics Venues
Worth Seeking Out* 350

2 Opera, Classical Music
& Dance .352

3 Major Concert Halls
& Landmark Venues 356

*Park It! Shakespeare, Music
& Other Free Fun* 360

4 Live Rock, Jazz, Blues & More 362

5 Cabaret .369

6 Stand-Up Comedy 370

7 Bars & Cocktail Lounges 371

Cocktails Alfresco 372

Late-Night Bites 376

The New York Dive Experience . . .378

Checking into Hotel Bars 380

8 Dance Clubs & Party Scenes 383

9 The Gay & Lesbian Scene 385

Appendix A: A Brief History of New York City   388

Appendix B: Useful Toll-Free Numbers & Websites   390

Index   393

General Index 393

Accommodations Index 403

Restaurant Index 403

List of Maps

New York Metropolitan Area   5

New York Architecture   17

The Best of NYC in 1 Day   81

The Best of NYC in 2 Days   85

The Best of NYC in 3 Days   87

Manhattan Neighborhoods   93

Downtown Accommodations   127

Midtown, Chelsea & Gramercy Park Accommodations   136

Uptown Accommodations   162

Financial District, TriBeCa, Chinatown & Little Italy Dining   175

Lower East Side, SoHo, Nolita & East Village Dining   181

Greenwich Village/Meat-Packing District Dining   187

Midtown, Chelsea, Flatiron District & Gramercy Park Dining   192

Uptown Dining   212

Harlem Dining   225

Downtown Attractions   232

Midtown Attractions   234

Uptown Attractions   236

Harlem Attractions   238

Central Park   276

Brooklyn Heights   303

Broadway Theaters   345

Lincoln Center   357

An Invitation to the Reader

In researching this book, we discovered many wonderful places—hotels, restaurants, shops, and more. We're sure you'll find others. Please tell us about them so we can share the information with your fellow travelers in upcoming editions. If you were disappointed with a recommendation, we'd love to know that, too. Please write to:

Frommer's New York City 2006
Wiley Publishing, Inc. • 111 River St. • Hoboken, NJ 07030-5774

An Additional Note

Please be advised that travel information is subject to change at any time—and this is especially true of prices. We therefore suggest that you write or call ahead for confirmation when making your travel plans. The authors, editors, and publisher cannot be held responsible for the experiences of readers while traveling. Your safety is important to us, however, so we encourage you to stay alert and be aware of your surroundings. Keep a close eye on cameras, purses, and wallets, all favorite targets of thieves and pickpockets.

Frommer's Star Ratings, Icons & Abbreviations

Every hotel, restaurant, and attraction listing in this guide has been ranked for quality, value, service, amenities, and special features using a **star-rating system.** In country, state, and regional guides, we also rate towns and regions to help you narrow down your choices and budget your time accordingly. Hotels and restaurants are rated on a scale of zero (recommended) to three stars (exceptional). Attractions, shopping, nightlife, towns, and regions are rated according to the following scale: zero stars (recommended), one star (highly recommended), two stars (very highly recommended), and three stars (must-see).

In addition to the star-rating system, we also use **seven feature icons** that point you to the great deals, in-the-know advice, and unique experiences that separate travelers from tourists. Throughout the book, look for:

Finds	Special finds—those places only insiders know about
Fun Fact	Fun facts—details that make travelers more informed and their trips more fun
Kids	Best bets for kids and advice for the whole family
Moments	Special moments—those experiences that memories are made of
Overrated	Places or experiences not worth your time or money
Tips	Insider tips—great ways to save time and money
Value	Great values—where to get the best deals

The following **abbreviations** are used for credit cards:

AE	American Express	DISC	Discover	V	Visa
DC	Diners Club	MC	MasterCard		

Frommers.com

Now that you have the guidebook to a great trip, visit our website at **www.frommers.com** for travel information on more than 3,000 destinations. With features updated regularly, we give you instant access to the most current trip-planning information available. At Frommers.com, you'll also find the best prices on airfares, accommodations, and car rentals—and you can even book travel online through our travel booking partners. At Frommers.com, you'll also find the following:

- Online updates to our most popular guidebooks
- Vacation sweepstakes and contest giveaways
- Newsletter highlighting the hottest travel trends
- Online travel message boards with featured travel discussions

What's New in New York City

In 2005, New York City made a big pitch to host the 2012 Olympic Games. As this book went to press, the winner was announced: London, England! If you want my two cents, I didn't think we needed an extra incentive to attract tourists, especially one that would have cost millions and disrupted city life for at least a month. No, New York has it all—it definitely didn't need more.

Here are some other recent changes that took place in the Big Apple:

GETTING AROUND NYC   Bad news on the subway front: In 2005 rates increased on the 7-day **MetroCard** from $20 to $24 and the 30-day card went from $70 to $76.

ACCOMMODATIONS   The biggest hotel news in New York was the closing of the legendary **Plaza Hotel.** There had been much controversy and debate between the city and the new owner, Elad Properties, about the Plaza's fate; whether it would ever reopen as the major hotel it once was or become a very ornate condominium. At press time, a compromise was reached: Elad Properties will convert much of the hotel into condominiums, but agreed to retain 348 of the Plaza's original 805 rooms as hotel rooms. The owner also agreed to keep the Palm Court, Oak Bar, and Grand Ballroom open for use by the public.

The other major hotel closing was the **Mayflower** on Central Park West. At press time, the fate of the **Stanhope,** on Fifth Avenue across from the Metropolitan Museum of Art, was very much up in the air with a new owner also leaning heavily toward a conversion to condos.

The **Gramercy Park Hotel** shut its doors in 2005, but only temporarily while new owner Ian Schrager (Hudson Hotel, Morgan's, the Royalton) renovates the place where the Beatles stayed in 1964. Let's just hope he leaves the groovy, lobby lounge intact.

On the flip side, numerous hotels debuted in late 2004 and 2005. The arrival of the Meat-Packing District's **Hotel Gansevoort,** 18 Ninth Ave. (© 212/206-6700), was the most anticipated, and that hotel is thriving.

Built from the ground up, the new **Hotel on Rivington** is located in the heart of the Lower East Side at 107 Rivington St. (© 212/475-2600). Its glass tower, offering unparalleled downtown views of the city, rises high above historic tenement houses that were once home to millions of immigrants.

The former Doral Park Avenue, at 70 Park Ave., was taken over by the Kimpton Hotel group and thoroughly remodeled and redesigned. It's appropriately called **70 Park Avenue** (© 877/707-2752). The former Gorham, 136 W. 55th St., also underwent a total renovation and is now called **The Blakely** (© 212/245-1800). Just down the block from the Blakely, the old Majestic hotel was gutted and transformed into **The**

Dream, 210 W. 55th St. (© 212/247-2000), where there is a Deepak Chopra healing center, Ayurvedic spa, and a fish tank in the lobby that you have to see to believe.

Across town, the Doubletree brand of Hilton hotels purchased the **Metropolitan,** 569 Lexington Ave. (© 212/752-7000), and poured $35 million into it, restoring the hotel to its early 1960s glory when it was designed by architect Morris Lapidus, better know for his Fontainbleau and Eden Roc hotels in Miami Beach.

RESTAURANTS Following a trend that began in 2003, a number of New York's white-gloved dining institutions continue to become history. In 2004, the traditional French restaurant **La Caravelle** shut its doors after 43 years.

Rocco's, the restaurant of the short-lived reality TV series *The Restaurant,* met a quick end when it closed in 2004.

Le Cirque 2000, the flamboyant second home for the rich and famous, has also closed its doors temporarily until it finds a new home.

One of New York's great settings to dine was at **Aquavit,** set in a West Side town house where there was a waterfall in the main dining room. Sadly, the town house was sold and the restaurant was forced to relocate to a colder, much more sterile place. The good news is that the food and service are as good as they were in the old locale. Now it's at 65 E. 55th St. (© 212/307-7311).

Fortunately, the opening of exciting new restaurants has far outnumbered the closings. The **Meat-Packing District** has become a dining mecca. Helping to establish the area as Food Central was the 2004 opening of the talented Jean-Georges Vongerichten's spin on Asian street food called **Spice Market** at 403 W. 13th St. (© 212/675-2322).

More innovative Asian restaurants include **Kittichai,** in the 60 Thompson Hotel, 60 Thompson St. (© 212/219-2000), where the food is as inventive as the breathtaking space in which it's served. The immensely talented chef Patricia Yeo opened **Sapa,** also in a stunning, open space at 43 W. 24th St. (© 212/929-1800); her menu is a sublime fusion of French and Vietnamese flavors. The best new Indian restaurant to open in the past year was **Devi,** 8 E. 18th St. (© 212/691-1300).

The Time Warner Center, at Columbus Circle, has become a food destination with a number of highly rated, and outrageously expensive restaurants including Thomas Keller's **Per Se** (© 212/823-9335), **V Steakhouse** (© 212/823-9500), Jean-Georges Vongerichten's take on meat and potatoes, and the Japanese **Masa** (© 212/823-9800), where prix-fixe meals begin at $300.

ATTRACTIONS After a 2-year $425-million renovation (and a temporary relocation to Queens), the **Museum of Modern Art,** 11 W. 53rd St. (© 212/708-9400), finally reopened its doors with an extra 40,000 square feet. It's bigger, better, and pricier ($20 admission!) than ever.

At press time, plans were in the works to remodel the 80th and 86th floors of the **Empire State Building.** But there just might be competition for New York's best views when, in late 2005, the Art Deco decks on the 69th and 70th floors of 30 Rockefeller Plaza reopen to the public, as **Top of the Rock,** after being closed for 17 years.

SHOPPING After being closed for 1 year because of bankruptcy, the most famous toy store in the world, **FAO Schwarz,** 767 Fifth Ave. (© 212/644-9400), reopened just in time for Christmas in 2004.

Other major openings include a smaller, more "downtown" branch of **Bloomingdale's** at 504 Broadway in SoHo (© **212/729-5900**), and a **Barney's Co-op** on the Upper West Side at 2151 Broadway (© **646/335-0978**).

NIGHTLIFE Featuring three spectacular new venues in the Time Warner Center, **Jazz at Lincoln Center** (© **212/258-9800**) is now the grandest showcase for jazz in the country.

1

The Best of the Big Apple

New York is the concentrate of art and commerce and sport and religion and entertainment and finance, bringing to a single compact arena the gladiator, the evangelist, the promoter, the actor, the trader and the merchant. It carries on its lapel the unexpungeable odor of the long past, so that no matter where you sit in New York you feel the vibrations of great times and tall deeds, of queer people and events and undertakings.

New York is nothing like Paris; it is nothing like London; and it is not Spokane multiplied by sixty, or Detroit multiplied by four. It is by all odds the loftiest of cities.

—E. B. White, *Here Is New York*

Novelist and essayist E. B. White wrote the words above more than 50 years ago, but his characterization of New York remains accurate today. And though the grandeur and importance of New York has not changed, the city is in a constant state of flux. In a way, New Yorkers have short attention spans. A restaurant, show, club, or store might be the hottest thing; a couple months later another has opened or been discovered and that once hot spot quickly becomes passé.

But not everything has to be new and hot for New Yorkers. We don't always appreciate change because that means we might have lost something we had come to love. New Yorkers respect the city's standards, the institutions that have been essential New York. What would we do without that reassuring sight of the Lady in the harbor; or the gleaming spire of the Empire State Building? Or the perfect pizza? Or a Sunday in Central Park? Or the rumbling of the trains beneath the earth? Or the sounds of jazz from a Village club? So while New York is ever-changing, its core remains the same. And we wouldn't have it any other way.

1 Most Unforgettable Travel Experiences

- **Sailing to the Statue of Liberty:** On Liberty Island in New York Harbor. If you have time to do only one thing on your visit to New York, sail to the Lady in the harbor. No other monument embodies the nation's, and the world's, notion of political freedom and economic potential more than Lady Liberty. It is also the ultimate symbol of New York, the personification of the city's vast diversity and tolerance. See p. 249.
- **Visiting the Empire State Building Observatory at Dusk:** Like the Statue of Liberty, the Empire State Building, once again the tallest building in New York, is one of the city's definitive icons. Arrive at dusk and watch the lights of the city come on. It's pure magic. See p. 242.
- **Walking the Brooklyn Bridge:** Manhattan has five major bridges connecting the island to other shores, and easily the most historic and most fascinating is the Brooklyn Bridge. For a close-up look at what was a marvel of civic engineering when it was built in 1883, and a true New

New York Metropolitan Area

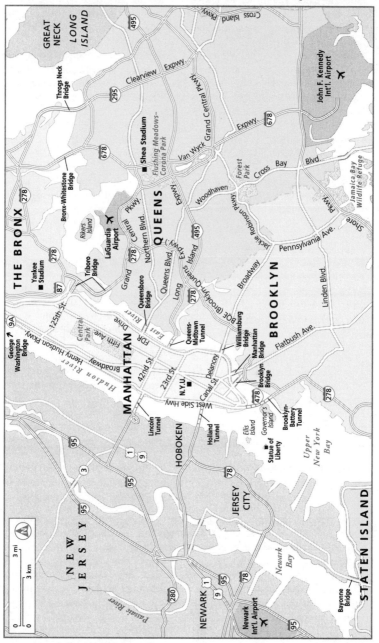

York experience, take the walk across the bridge from Manhattan to Brooklyn. See p. 241.

- **Taking the subway to Yankee Stadium for a Yankee game:** It doesn't sound very intriguing, does it? Good or bad, there's nothing like being crammed into a subway car packed with rabid Yankee fans. And it's an experience you'll not soon forget. See p. 251.
- **Jogging around the Central Park Reservoir:** Okay, you don't even have to jog it. You can walk the jogging path around the Jacqueline Kennedy Onassis Reservoir and take in the beauty of Central Park, the views of Central Park West, Fifth Avenue, and especially the skyline of midtown Manhattan. See p. 275.
- **Spending Sunday Morning in New York:** This might not sound so unforgettable, but to experience the city minus the noise and activity is something special. I've noticed quite a few tourists, usually jet-lagged Europeans, wandering the parks and streets early Sunday mornings.
- **Walking 125th Street:** Take a walk across this famous Harlem boulevard and your senses will be assaulted from the music, the variety of stores, the restaurants, the impromptu stalls selling everything from homemade CDs to fresh bean pies, the street prophets and musicians; the energy on this street is relentless.

2 Best Events

- **Best Parade: West Indian–American Day Carnival and Parade.** Held on Eastern Parkway in Brooklyn, this is the biggest parade in New York. The music (calypso, soca, reggae, and Latin), the amazing costumes, and the incredible Caribbean food make this an unforgettable experience. If you're lucky enough to be in town on Labor Day, don't miss it. See p. 34.
- **Best Street Festival: Ninth Avenue International Food Festival.** Held for one weekend (usually in the middle of May), this festival is the perfect illustration of the ethnic diversity in the city. You can taste foods from local restaurants and sample cuisines from Afghani to Peruvian. See p.32.
- **Best Time of Year to Come to New York: Summer.** Most people prefer the temperate days of fall to visit New York, and that's when the city is most crowded; but my personal favorite season is summer, when the streets are empty, restaurants and shows are easier to get into, and countless free outdoor cultural events abound.
- **Best Day to Come to New York: New Year's Day.** You've skipped the insanity of New Year's Eve and arisen fresh and sober. Get out on the town early; you have the city practically to yourself.

3 Best Museums

- **Best Overall Museum: American Museum of Natural History.** You can spend your entire visit to New York at this 4-square-block museum; there is that much to see. From the famed dinosaur halls to the Hall of Ocean Life, the Museum of Natural History houses the world's greatest natural science collection. See p. 239.
- **Best Art Museum: Metropolitan Museum of Art.** Not only the best art museum in New York, but the best in North America as well. The number of masterworks housed here is mind-boggling. See p. 244.

• **Best-Looking Museum: Museum of Modern Art.** Though the sight of the Guggenheim is the most memorable, MoMA's $450-million renovation makes it the classiest- and coolest-looking museum, inside and out, in town. See p. 245.

• **Best Home Posing as a Museum: The Louis Armstrong House Museum.** This unassuming house in Queens, was Satchmo's home for almost 30 years and it's been preserved almost exactly as it was at Armstrong's death in 1971. See p. 304.

4 Best New York City Structures

• **Best Historic Building: Grand Central Terminal.** Despite all the modern steel and glass skyscrapers in New York, there are still many historic marvels standing, and the best of those is this Beaux Arts gem. This railroad station, built in 1913, was remarkably restored in the 1990s to recapture its initial brilliance. Even if you don't have to catch a train, make sure you visit. See p. 244.

• **Best Skyscraper: The Chrysler Building.** There is no observation deck, but that's okay, this Art Deco masterpiece is best viewed from outside or from other observation decks like the Empire State Building. See. p. 268.

• **Most Impressive Place of Worship: Cathedral of St. John the Divine.** Construction began at this, the world's largest Gothic cathedral, in 1892 and it's still going on. But this is one structure that doesn't need finishing.

5 Best Parks

• **Best Park: Central Park.** One of the world's greatest urban refuges—a center of calm and tranquillity amongst the noise and bustle that is Manhattan. See p. 275.

• **Best Runner-Up Park: Riverside Park.** This 4-mile-long park along the picturesque Hudson River is a welcome alternative to the sometimes-overcrowded Central Park. See p. 283.

6 Best Places to Take the Kids

• **Central Park.** With its lovely carousel, a zoo, two ice-skating rinks, and numerous playgrounds and ball fields, Central Park is a children's wonderland. See p. 275.

• **Bronx Zoo Wildlife Conservation Park.** This is one of the great zoos in the world—and you don't have to be a kid to love it. See p. 297.

• *Intrepid* **Sea-Air-Space Museum.** Climbing through a retired battleship beats the playground any day. With real planes on deck and interactive exhibits inside, kids are never bored here. See p. 255.

7 Best Places to Stroll

• **The Upper West Side.** With museums, two great parks, some lovely old buildings and brownstones, inexpensive restaurants, and a real residential feel, this is my favorite neighborhood to stroll.

• **Greenwich Village.** With its historic streets, hidden cafes, cozy restaurants, and eccentric characters, Greenwich

Village is a constant, but pleasant, barrage on the senses.

- **Chinatown.** With the constant din of activity and the very crowded sidewalks, Chinatown might not seem like ideal strolling territory; but the neighborhood is so colorful, it's worth braving the mobs.

8 Best Things to Do for Free (or Almost)

- **Ride the Staten Island Ferry.** The Staten Island Ferry is used daily by thousands of commuters. Ride with them for a great view of the Statue of Liberty, Ellis Island, New York Harbor, and the skyline of lower Manhattan. You really can't beat the price. It's free. See p. 248.
- **Attend a Gospel Service.** All around New York you'll find Sunday gospel services, but for some special soul-stirring head to Harlem and the **Abyssinian Baptist Church** or Brooklyn and the **Brooklyn Tabernacle.** Services are free but when the basket is passed, don't be stingy. See p. 272 and 300.
- **Visit Free Museums.** Believe it or not, there are museums in New York that don't charge admission. Two of my favorites are the **National Museum of the American Indian** and the **Federal Hall National Memorial.** See. p. 261 and 271.
- **Take in a Game at the West 4th Street Basketball Courts,** West 4th Street and Sixth Avenue. I don't know what's more entertaining here—the showtime moves on the court or the inventive and constant trash talk that accompanies the games.

9 Best Offbeat Experiences

- **Visit the Little Italy of the Bronx.** Though it still qualifies, this experience, growing in popularity, is slowly becoming not so offbeat. With the demise of Little Italy in Manhattan, the area centered around Arthur Avenue, known as the Little Italy of the Bronx, is the place to go for old-fashioned Italian charm, food, and ambience. See p. 95.
- **Museum of Sex.** How many cities can claim their own Museum of Sex? Only in New York. But you must be 18 or older to enter. See p. 260.
- **Roosevelt Island Tram.** Impress your family and friends with a little known, but spectacular view of the New York skyline and take them for a ride on the Roosevelt Island Tram. During the 4-minute ride you will be treated to a gorgeous view down the East River and the east side skyline with views of the United Nations and four bridges: the Queensboro, Williamsburg, Manhattan, and Brooklyn bridges. On a clear day you might even spot Lady Liberty. See p. 248.
- **Bike Along the Hudson River.** If you are physically ambitious and walking is just not enough exercise for you, a good alternative is to rent a bike and ride the length of Manhattan via the work in progress, Hudson River Park. As of this writing, you can bike from Battery Park to Fort Tryon Park near the George Washington Bridge. However, there are detours along the way that occasionally take you on and off the paths. For bike rental information, see p. 280.
- **Ride the International Express.** The 7 train is sometimes known as the International Express. Take it out of

Manhattan and through the borough of Queens and you will pass one ethnic neighborhood after another, from Indian to Thai, from Peruvian to Columbian, from Chinese to Korean.

10 Best Way to Spend a Day in a Borough

- **In the Bronx:** Spend the morning at the **Bronx Zoo Wildlife Conservation Park** or the **Bronx Botanical Gardens** and then head to **Arthur Avenue,** the Little Italy of the Bronx (see "Best Offbeat Experiences," above, and p. 95), for an authentic Italian feast. See also p. 297 and 108.
- **In Brooklyn:** First take a look at what's showing at the always exciting **Brooklyn Museum,** and then get some fresh air with a stroll in nearby, lovely **Prospect Park.** Cap it off with a sandwich and a slice of cheesecake at **Junior's** on Flatbush Avenue. See p. 299, 301, and 228.
- **In Queens:** Take the 7 train, the **International Express** (see "Best Offbeat Experiences," above), to either the **Queens Museum of Art,** on the grounds of the 1964 World's Fair, or the **Louis Armstrong House Museum.** On your way back, stop for a meal at any number of ethnic restaurants you will find within close proximity of the 7 train. See also p. 305 and 304.

11 Best Splurge Hotels

- **Ritz-Carlton New York, Central Park,** 160 Central Park South (*©* **212/308-9100**). The combination of a great location, just across from Central Park, large well-outfitted rooms, typically excellent Ritz-Carlton service, and the magnificent restaurant **Atelier** (see below under "The Most Unforgettable Dining Experiences") make this Ritz extra special. See p. 139.
- **The Mercer,** 147 Mercer St. (*©* **888/918-6060** or 212/966-6060). The best of the hip, downtown hotels, the Mercer is located in the heart of SoHo. The high-ceilinged, loftlike rooms and suites, some with fireplaces and all with ceiling fans and luxurious bathrooms, are spectacular. See p. 129.
- **The Peninsula-New York,** 700 Fifth Ave. (*©* **800/262-9467** or 212/956-2888). The combination of Old World elegance and 21st-century technology is best realized in this practically perfect hotel. See p. 151.
- **St. Regis,** 2 E. 55th St. (*©* **212/753-4500**). Across the street from The Peninsula, the St. Regis offers unrivaled luxury—Louis XVI furniture, crystal chandeliers, and silk wall coverings—and impeccable service, including personalized butler service. See p. 152.
- **Trump International Hotel & Tower,** 1 Central Park West (*©* **212/299-1000**). Suites are huge and overlook Central Park. Service is so good they treat you like the Donald here. The great restaurant **Jean-Georges** offers room service and guests have use of an excellent fitness club and pool. See p. 160.
- **The Carlyle: A Rosewood Hotel,** 35 E. 76th St. (*©* **800/227-5737** or 212/744-1600). You are in rarefied territory when you stay in The Carlyle. Service is elegantly white-gloved and rooms are sumptuous. Many have incredible views of the city and Central Park. And don't forget the **Café Carlyle** for cabaret and **Bemelmans Bar** for a cocktail. See p. 165.

• **The Lowell,** 28 E. 63rd St. (© **212/ 838-1400**). Smaller and more intimate than the Carlyle, but the Lowell is just as elegant and romantic.

Rooms are all unique; many have fireplaces while some have good-size terraces. See p. 166.

12 Best Moderately Priced Hotels

• **The Lucerne,** 201 W. 79th St. (© **800/492-8122** or 212/875-1000). This is my favorite hotel on the Upper West Side and one of my favorites in New York. The homey, neighborhood feel of the hotel, combined with exceptional service, nicely sized, well-equipped rooms, and room service from **Nice Matin,** make this a very attractive midprice option. See p. 164.

• **Inn on 23rd Street,** 131 W. 23rd St. (© **877/387-2323** or 212/463-0330). You cannot do better than this charming inn for top-notch quality and extras. Rooms are rustic and originally designed but all have up-to-date

amenities. Breakfast is complimentary and served in a lovely library. See p. 134.

• **Sofitel New York,** 45 W. 44th St. (© **212/354-8844**). This relatively new hotel exudes Old World (French) elegance. And you should be able to score some very good weekend packages on the Internet. See p. 142.

• **Hotel Metro,** 45 W. 35th St. (© **800/ 356-3870** or 212/947-2500). You'll find very good deals and lots of extras at this conveniently located Midtown hotel that's popular with Europeans. See p. 146.

13 Best Hotels for Families

• **Hotel Beacon,** 2130 Broadway (© **800/572-4969** or 212/787-1100). Not only is this hotel a great deal—you can get good-size suites for so much less than you would pay in Midtown—the Upper West Side, with its parks, the Museum of Natural History, and fun, inexpensive restaurants, is also a great neighborhood for children. See p. 162.

• **Doubletree Guest Suites-Times Square,** 1568 Broadway (© **800/ 222-TREE** or 212/719-1600). This hotel boasts an entire floor of child-proof suites, complete with living rooms for spreading out and kitchenettes for preparing light meals. Also just a block from kid-friendly chain restaurants and the Toys "R" Us superstore. See p. 140.

14 Best Incentives for Hotel-Hopping

• **Best Hotel Suite: Townhouse Suite in the Kitano New York,** 66 Park Ave. (© **212/885-7000**). Each of the three one-bedroom suites built inside the landmark town house that is part of this hotel feature a long hallway leading to a sunken living room with original art, a state-of-the-art stereo system, and a tea maker with green tea. See p. 155.

• **Best Inexpensive Hotel Restaurant: Burger Joint** in **Le Parker Meridien,** 118 W. 57th St. (© **800/543-4300** or 212/245-5000). Discreetly hidden off the lobby, this sensational unnamed burger joint has been discovered by locals looking for cheap eats for their lunch break, so the lines are long, but worth it. The burgers are fabulous (see below under "Best Burger") and under $6. See p. 141.

- **Best Hotel Bar: Bemelmans Bar** in **The Carlyle,** 35 E. 76th St. (© **800/ 227-5737** or 212/744-1600). Named after book illustrator Ludwig Bemelmans, who created the *Madeline* books and painted the mural in the bar, this romantic and charming bar features white-gloved service and tremendous cocktails conceived by master mixologist Audrey Saunders. For more on Bemelmans, see p. 165.

- **Best Hotel for a Romantic Tryst: Hotel Elysée,** 60 E. 54th St. (© **800/ 535-9733** or 212/753-1066). This lovely old hotel, a favorite of mid-20th-century writers and actors, is discreetly dwarfed between two mammoth office buildings and is the perfect romantic hideaway in the middle of Manhattan. See p. 154.

15 The Most Unforgettable Dining Experiences

- **Chanterelle,** 2 Harrison St. (© **212/ 966-6960**). You'll be made to feel very special here from the impeccable, personalized service in a simple but lovely room to the exquisitely prepared food. Other restaurants try, but this is how it's supposed to be. See p. 174.

- **Eleven Madison Park,** 11 Madison Ave. (© **212/889-0905**). Higher praise has consistently gone to chef/ restaurateur Danny Meyer's other restaurants, Gramercy Park Tavern and Union Square Café, so this gem is often overlooked, which is a shame. It is a magnificent restaurant on every level. The Art Deco room is spectacular, the service almost otherworldly, and the food truly memorable. See p. 195.

- **The River Café,** 1 Water St., Brooklyn (© **718/522-5200**). Located at the foot of the Brooklyn Bridge in Brooklyn, there is no better dining view of Manhattan. Go at twilight as the lights of downtown begin to flicker on; it's a magical experience.

Though the food at restaurants with views is usually not very good, you won't be disappointed by the sophisticated fare prepared here. See p. 227.

- **Atelier,** in the Ritz-Carlton, Central Park, 50 Central Park South (© **212/ 521-6125**). This beautiful restaurant is one of the few in New York where you can actually converse with your companion. But you may want to forgo talk and just concentrate on the fantastic food. See p. 199.

- **Aquavit,** 65 E. 55th St. (© **212/307- 7311**). Though its new digs are not nearly as charming as its former town house setting, the service and the food are as good as ever. See p. 207.

- **Big Wong King,** 67 Mott St. (© **212/964-0540**). For the quintessential Chinatown experience. You'll share tables with Chinese families, order huge bowls of *congee* with fried crullers, plates of stir-fried vegetables, and heaping platters of roast pork and duck. I guarantee it will be an unforgettable dining experience. See p. 178.

16 Best New Restaurants

- **BLT Steak,** 106 E. 57th St. (© **212/ 752-7470**). Chef Laurent Tourendel has put his spin on the steakhouse and it's a winner. It's not your traditional

men's club steakhouse, but the meat is as good as I've had at any of those other testosterone-fueled red meat joints. See. p. 207.

• **Devi,** 8 E. 18th St. (© 212/691-1300). There are so many Indian restaurants in New York, I didn't think I could experience anything different in terms of Indian cuisine, but Devi's menu is an eye-opener and the food as flavorful as it gets. See p. 195.

• **Abboccato,** 136 W. 55th St. (© 212/265-4000). The newest addition from the owners of the excellent Molyvos and Oceana, Abboccato offers an exciting, rustic Italian menu. I'd go back just for another taste of the spaghettini with razor clams and mullet roe. See p. 200.

17 Best Bites for All Appetites

• **Best for Breakfast: Good Enough to Eat,** 483 Amsterdam Ave. (© 212/496-0163). They've been lining up on Amsterdam Avenue on weekend mornings for over 20 years to get a taste of chef/owner Carrie Levin's bountiful home-cooked breakfasts. But why wait in line? You're on vacation; go during the week. See p. 221.

• **Best for Brunch: Norma's,** at Le Parker Meridien hotel, 118 W. 57th St. (© 212/708-7460). Though I am not a devotee of brunch (see sidebar "Breakfast, Not Brunch," in chapter 8), I make an exception for Norma's. Traditional breakfast items are available but skip them and go for the creative interpretations, like the asparagus and seared rock lobster omelet. See p. 202.

• **Best Dessert: Fiamma Osteria,** 206 Spring St. (© 212/653-0100). There are many impressive pastry chefs in town, but few of them can top the remarkable Elizabeth Katz. Everything on Fiamma's "Dolci" menu is outstanding, but her *torta* (dark chocolate praline cake layered with hazelnut brittle) and *gianduja gelato* (hazelnut-flavored chocolate gelato) are as close to perfection as you can get. See p. 182.

• **Best Italian: Beppe,** 45 E. 22nd St. (© 212/982-8422). Restaurant critics don't give Beppe enough credit, but the mobs that pour into the place nightly know better. This is as close

to true Tuscan cuisine as you'll find outside of the Italy region. See p. 195.

• **Best Jewish Deli: Katz's Deli-catessen,** 205 E. Houston St. (© 212/254-2246). This is the choice among those who know their kreplach, knishes, and pastrami. No cutesy sandwiches named for celebrities here—just top-notch Jewish classics. See p. 182.

• **Best Burger: Burger Joint,** at Le Parker Meridien hotel, 118 W. 57th St. (© 212/708-7460). Who woulda thunk that a fancy hotel like Le Parker Meridien would be the home to a "joint" that serves great burgers at great prices? See p. 203.

• **Best Decadent Burger: db Bistro Moderne,** 55 W. 44th St. (© 212/391-2400). Daniel Boulud's creation is made with braised short ribs, foie gras, preserved black truffles, and minced sirloin and goes for a whopping $29. See p. 200.

• **Best Pizza: Patsy's Pizzeria,** 2287 First Ave. (© 212/534-9783). This great East Harlem pizzeria has been cranking out coal-oven pizza since 1932. You can also order by the slice here, but only do so if the pie is fresh out of the oven. See p. 205.

• **Best Seafood: Oceana,** 55 E. 54th St. (© 212/759-5941). You won't believe what chef Cornelius Gallagher can do with fish. His culinary creations look so good on the plate that they are worthy of museum status.

What's really remarkable is that the food tastes as good as it looks. See p. 208.

- **Best Steak: Strip House,** 13 E. 12th St. (© **212/328-0000**). Forget the cute play on words and the dizzying number of photos and artwork of old strippers and burlesque performers on the walls and concentrate on the red meat in front of you. Believe me, after a few bites, strippers and burlesque will be the last thing on your mind. See p. 189.
- **Best for Families: Virgil's Real BBQ,** 152 W. 44th St. (© **212/921-9494**). Located in kid-friendly Times Square, Virgil's, in a sense, is a theme restaurant, the theme being barbecue, but they do an excellent job smoking their meats. It's loud, colorful, and has great options for the children. See p. 202.
- **Best Cheap Meal: Gray's Papaya,** 2090 Broadway (© **212/799-0243**). Though the $2.45 "recession special"—two hot dogs and a fruit drink—is almost a $1 increase from the previous recession, it's still a bargain. But is it any good? Witness the lines out the door every day for lunch. See p. 218.
- **Best Ice Cream: Brooklyn Ice Cream Factory,** Fulton Ferry Landing Pier,

Brooklyn (© **718/246-3963**). The perfect reward after a brisk walk across the Brooklyn Bridge. Rich homemade ice cream with a view of the Manhattan skyline, a tough combination to beat. See p. 180.
- **Best Bagel: Absolute Bagels,** 2788 Broadway (© **212/932-2105**). They're not huge like some bagels these days, but they are always hot and cooked to perfection. See p. 198.
- **Best Soul Food: Charles' Southern Style Kitchen,** 2841 Eighth Ave. (© **877/813-2920** or 212/926-4313). Not only is this tiny Harlem restaurant the best soul food in the city, it's also the best buffet. For $9.95 on weekdays and $12 on weekends, the down-home offerings will tempt you to make an obscene amount of visits to the buffet line. See p. 226.
- **Best Restaurant Restroom: Sapa,** 43 W. 24th St. (© **212/929-1800**). You can tell a lot about a restaurant by its restrooms and Sapa's, with its bubbling pool, candles, and Chinese screens, are so immaculate and beautifully designed you might want to linger a little longer than you should. But then the very good grub prepared by chef Patricia Yeo might get cold and you wouldn't want that. See p. 196.

18 Best Shopping

- **Best Store: Saks Fifth Avenue.** Not as overwhelming as other department stores, Saks is consistently good. And don't miss those window displays at Christmas. See p. 318.
- **Best Clothes Store: Barney's.** This store is the pinnacle with prices to match. See p. 316.
- **Best Bookstore: Coliseum Books.** This book-lover's paradise is a mini-superstore (if there is such a thing)

with the heart of an independent. See p. 321.
- **Best Music Store: Tower Records.** A huge selection and frequent sales make this my personal favorite. See p. 340.
- **Best Shopping Zone: SoHo, NoHo, and NoLita.** All three neighborhoods are within easy walking distance of one another and feature the newest, trendiest boutiques. See p. 309.

19 Best Culture & Nightlife

- **Best Performance Space: Carnegie Hall.** You can find few greater performance spaces in the world than this one. Visually and acoustically brilliant, Carnegie Hall regularly attracts an amazing array of talent. See p. 357.
- **Best Free Cultural Event: Shakespeare in the Park.** Imagine Shakespeare performed by stars, under the stars, in Central Park. No wonder it has become a New York institution. See p. 360.
- **Best Children's Theater: Paper Bag Players.** For children ages 4–9, this group performs in the winter only and offers tales told in imaginative and original ways. See p. 348.
- **Best Jazz Club: Village Vanguard.** The acoustics and sight lines aren't great, but you can't do better for finding consistent, good-quality jazz. See p. 369.
- **Best Rock Club: Mercury Lounge.** This venue is intimate, but not obscure. The Merc is the best for hard-edged rock and roll. See p. 365.
- **Best Comedy Club: Gotham Comedy Club.** Comfortable and sophisticated, this is where the best come to hone their acts. See p. 370.
- **Best Pub: Ear Inn.** Located in an old hanger-on in chic SoHo, I hope it continues to survive amongst the lush lounges that surround it. See p. 373.
- **Best Dive Bar: Subway Inn.** Sure, I know you came to New York to go to a dive bar. Enter the Subway Inn, and it's as if you stepped into a 1940s moody film noir—minus the cigarette smoke, of course. See p. 379.
- **Best Bar With a View: Rise Bar,** in the Ritz-Carlton Battery Park Hotel. With views of Lady Liberty, New York Harbor, and incredible sunsets, this bar is worth seeking out even if you're not staying at the hotel. See p. 372.

2

A Traveler's Guide to New York's Architecture

by Lisa Torrance Duffy

New York City contains a wealth of architectural styles, from modest row houses to ornate churches to soaring skyscrapers. Constructed over 300 years, these buildings represent the changing tastes of the city's residents from Colonial times to the present. A brief look at the city's most popular styles provides a unique perspective on the city's past, present, and future.

For the locations of the buildings mentioned in this chapter, see p. 17.

1 New York Architecture

GEORGIAN (1700–76)

This style reflects Renaissance ideas made popular in England, and later in the United States, through the publication of books on 16th-century Italian architects. The most-studied Italian of this period was **Andrea Palladio** (1508–80), who had freely adapted classical Roman forms. Georgian houses are characterized by a formal arrangement of parts employing a symmetrical composition enriched with classical details, such as columns and pediments. In the United States, the style was seen as an appropriate expression of the relative prosperity and security of the colonies. It was a sharp contrast to the unadorned Colonial style that preceded it.

Georgian buildings share the following characteristics:

- A formal, symmetrical arrangement
- A roof with four uniformly pitched sides
- A *balustrade* (a railing with balusters, or posts)
- A central projecting pavilion topped by a *pediment* (a low-pitched triangular feature) and supported by colossal columns or *pilasters* (rectangular columns projecting only slightly from a wall)

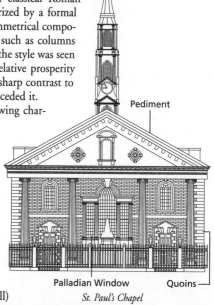

Pediment

Palladian Window   Quoins

St. Paul's Chapel

- A transom light above the front door
- Palladian windows (see illustration)
- *Quoins* (cornerstones in a distinctive material)
- Double-hung sash windows

St. Paul's Chapel, on Broadway between Vesey and Fulton streets (1764–66, Thomas McBean), the only pre-Revolutionary building remaining in Manhattan, is an almost perfect example of the Georgian style, with a pediment, colossal columns, Palladian window, quoins, and balustrade above the roof line (see illustration). Although it's a 20th-century reconstruction of a formal English house built here in 1719, **Fraunces Tavern,** 54 Pearl St., is another fine example of the style.

FEDERAL (1780–1820)

Lintel   Sash Window   Cornice

Side Light   Pilaster   Transom

Typical Federal Exterior

Federal was the first truly American architectural style. It was an adaptation of a contemporaneous English style called Adamesque, created by Scotsman **Robert Adam** (1728–92), which included ornate, colorful interior decoration. Federal combined Georgian architecture with the delicacy of the French rococo and the classical architecture of Greece and Rome. The overall effect is one of restraint and dignity, and may appear delicate when compared to the more robust Georgian style. Federal was popular with successful merchants throughout the cities and towns of the eastern seaboard. Its connection to the prosperous empires of Rome and Greece was seen as an appropriate reference for the young United States.

In New York, the Federal style was popular for row houses (see illustration) built after the 1811 creation of the city's grid pattern of avenues and streets. These houses often share the following features:

- A height of two or three stories
- Prominent end chimneys
- A red brick exterior
- A steeply pitched roof
- *Dormers* (upright windows projecting from a sloping roof) with pediments
- Double-hung sash windows, often with a flat *lintel* (horizontal member over a window, which carries the weight of the wall above it; commonly of stone)
- An elaborate doorway with sidelights and a fan or transom light (see illustration)
- Pilasters or columns flanking the doorway
- Delicate, exterior ornament of Roman origin, such as swags, urns, sheaths of wheat, and garlands
- A high basement

New York Architecture

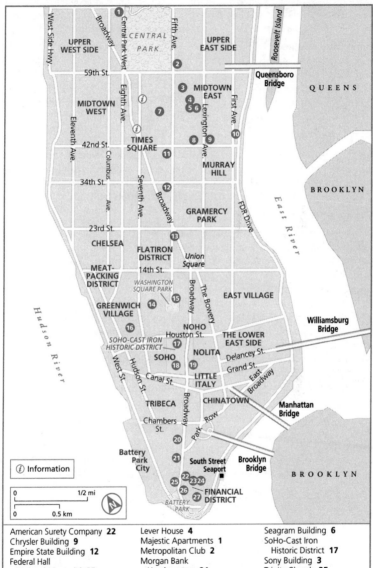

American Surety Company **22**
Chrysler Building **9**
Empire State Building **12**
Federal Hall
  National Memorial **23**
Flatiron Building **13**
Fraunces Tavern **27**
Grand Central Terminal **8**
Gunther Building **18**
Haughwout Store **19**
Jefferson Market Library **14**

Lever House **4**
Majestic Apartments **1**
Metropolitan Club **2**
Morgan Bank
  Headquarters **24**
New York Public Library **11**
Racquet and Tennis Club **5**
Radio City Music Hall **7**
Rockefeller Center **7**
The Row **15**
St. Paul's Chapel **21**

Seagram Building **6**
SoHo-Cast Iron
  Historic District **17**
Sony Building **3**
Trinity Church **25**
United Nations
  Headquarters **10**
U.S. Customs House **26**
West Village **16**
Woolworth Building **20**

Side Light   Fan Light   Side Light

Pilasters

Federal Doorway

In the **West Village,** near and along Bedford Street between Christopher and Morton streets, are more original Federal-style houses than anywhere else in Manhattan. House nos. 4 through 10 (1825–34) on Grove Street, just off Bedford, present one of the most authentic groups of late Federal–style houses in America. Notice the pedimented dormers and doors surrounded by pilasters and transom lights. Local carpenters created these buildings from plan books, probably published in England. In adapting the styles, they pared down the detail from the more delicate Adamesque in order to adapt to the needs— and pocketbooks—of their American merchant and craftsman clients.

GREEK REVIVAL (1820–60)

The Greek Revolution in the 1820s, in which Greece won its independence from the Turks, recalled to American intellectuals the democracy of ancient Greece and its elegant architecture, created around 400 B.C. At the same time, the War of 1812 diminished American affection for the British influence, including the still-dominant Federal style. With many believing America to be the spiritual successor of Greece, the use of classical Greek forms, particularly the Greek temple front, came to dominate residential, commercial, and government architecture. The style was so popular it came to be known as the National Style, and was used for numerous state capitols, as well as the U.S. Capitol in Washington, D.C.

Because ancient Greek structures did not use arches, the arched entrances and elliptical fanlights so popular in the Federal style were abandoned. The Greek Revival is most distinguished by a Greek temple front with the following:

• Classical orders specifying the use of three different column types: Corinthian, Ionic, or Doric (see illustration)

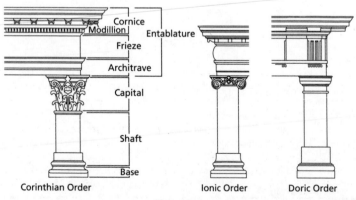

Cornice
Modillion
Entablature
Frieze
Architrave
Capital
Shaft
Base

Corinthian Order   Ionic Order   Doric Order

Classical Orders

- A full *entablature* (a set of roof parts, usually supported by a column, consisting of an architrave, frieze, and cornice)
- A low-pitch pediment
- White exteriors (it was not known at this time that ancient Greek buildings had been polychrome)

In New York, Grecian columns and orders were used mostly to decorate entrances on row houses, but whole buildings were also created. Perhaps the city's finest Greek Revival building is **Federal Hall National Memorial** (1834–42), at 26 Wall St., at Nassau Street, the site where George Washington took his presidential oath in 1789 (see illustration). The structure has a Greek temple front, with Doric columns and a simple pediment, resting on a high base, called a *plinth,* with a steep flight of steps.

The Row (1832–33, with later alterations), nos. 1 through 11 on Washington Square North, is an imposing block front of early-19th-century town houses. Note the stately entranceways with carved wooden and marble columns; the brickwork, called Flemish Bond, which alternates long and short brick in each row; and the Greek motifs, such as obelisks, lyres, and honeysuckle adornments, called *anthemia.*

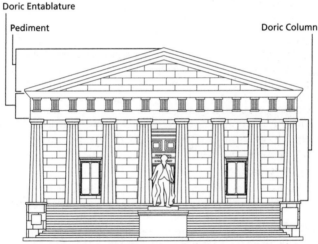

Federal Hall National Memorial

GOTHIC REVIVAL (1830–60)

The term *Gothic Revival* refers to a literary and aesthetic movement of the 1830s and 1840s that occurred in England and later in the United States. A pervasive current within this movement was known as Romanticism. Adherents believed that the wickedness of modern times could benefit with a dose of "goodness" presumed to have been associated with the Christian medieval past. Architecture was chosen as one of the vehicles to bring this message to the people. The revival style was used for everything from timber cottages to stone castles and churches. Some structures had only one or two Gothic features, most commonly a steeply pitched roof or pointed arches, whereas other buildings, usually churches, were accurate copies of English Gothic structures.

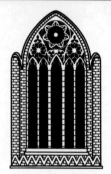

Gothic Window

A derivative style called **Victorian Gothic** (1860–90) became popular after the Civil War. Influenced by the writings of English theorist **John Ruskin** (1819–1900), this style is distinguished by contrasting colors of brick and stone in bold polychromatic patterns and decorative bands. This more freewheeling interpretation of the Gothic was well suited to the florid decorative approach of the late 19th century.

Gothic Revival is characterized by the following:

- Asymmetry
- Pointed arches
- Large pointed windows with tracery and colored glass (see illustration)
- Steeply pitched roofs
- A curvilinear gingerbread trim along the eaves (on houses)
- Towers
- *Battlements* (a fortified wall with alternate solid parts and openings; used for defense or a decorative motif)
- An overall picturesque quality

Trinity Church, at Broadway and Wall Street (Richard Upjohn, 1846), is one of the most celebrated, authentic Gothic Revival structures in the United States. Here you see all the features of a Gothic church: a steeple, battlements, pointed arches, Gothic tracery, stained-glass windows, *flying buttresses* (an external bracing system for supporting a roof or vault), and medieval sculptures. This was the tallest building in the area until the late 1860s.

The **Jefferson Market Library,** at 425 Sixth Ave. (Frederich Clarke Withers and Calvert Vaux, 1874–77), is a magnificent structure in the Victorian Gothic mode. Built as a courthouse, the asymmetrical structure sports striking bands of red brick and white stone, stained-glass windows, pointed arches, and a dramatic clock tower.

ITALIANATE (1840–80)

The architecture of Italy served as the inspiration for this building style, which could be as picturesque as the Gothic or as restrained as the classical. This adaptability made

---

Rival Revivals: Architectural Styles in the Late 19th Century

On the eve of the Civil War, the United States was a country of diverse tastes, interests, and cultures, and its differences were reflected in the country's architectural styles. During the latter half of the 19th century, several modes—including Victorian Gothic, Italianate, Renaissance Revivals, Second Empire, and even the exotic Moorish and Egyptian Revivals—coexisted. What these styles share is a certain eclecticism and picturesqueness. Mid-century architects reasoned that no age had produced the perfect architectural expression, so why not borrow freely from the best of the past and even mix different styles on the same building?

Although some of these styles were popular, none became dominant. In the 1870s in Chicago, technological advancements and imaginative design were coming together to create the world's first skyscrapers—*the* style that would one day dominate New York and the country's other urban areas.

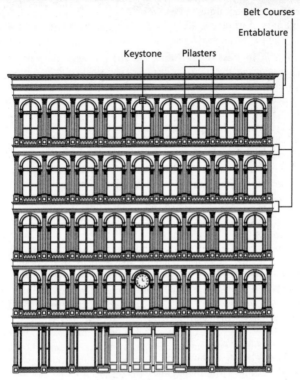

Haughwout Store

it immensely popular in the 1850s. In New York, the style was used for urban row houses and commercial buildings. The development of cast iron at this time permitted the inexpensive mass production of decorative features that few could have afforded in carved stone. This led to the creation of cast-iron districts in nearly every American city, including New York.

Italianate buildings often have a formal symmetry accentuated by pronounced moldings and decorative details. The commercial buildings resemble Italian palaces and tend to be rectangular buildings of several, spacious stories well suited to their original purposes as work spaces. The facades usually have the following features:

- A flat or low-pitched roof
- A bracketed cornice and an elaborate entablature
- Windows rounded at the top (flattened arches above windows are common, too)
- Large moldings over windows, called *hood moldings*
- Columns or pilasters flanking, or separating, windows
- Decorative keystones
- Quoins
- Balustrades

- Belt courses or entablatures at each story
- Vertical rows of windows and horizontal belt courses giving the building a very regular, compartmentalized look

New York's **SoHo–Cast Iron Historic District** has 26 blocks jammed with cast-iron facades, many in the Italianate manner. The single richest section is **Greene Street** between Houston and Canal streets. Stroll along here and take in building after building of sculptural facades. At Greene and Broome streets is the **Gunther Building** (Griffith Thomas, 1871), a fine example of the Italianate. The most celebrated building in SoHo is the **Haughwout Store** (John P. Gaynor, 1857), at the corner of Broadway and Broome streets, a New York version of a Venetian palace (now housing a Staples store, of all things). The handsome facade with cast iron on two sides has a window arrangement—two small, Corinthian columns supporting an arch over each window—based directly on a 15th-century, Italian design (see illustration).

EARLY SKYSCRAPER (1880–1920)

The invention of the skyscraper can be traced directly to the use of cast iron in the 1840s for storefronts, such as those seen in New York's SoHo. Experimentation with cast and wrought iron in the construction of interior skeletons eventually allowed buildings to rise higher. (Previously, buildings were restricted by the height supportable by their load-bearing walls.) In Chicago, important technical innovations—involving safety elevators, electricity, fireproofing, foundations, plumbing, and telecommunications—combined with advances in skeletal construction to create a new building type, the skyscraper. These buildings were spacious, cost-effective, efficient, and quickly erected—in short, the perfect architectural solution for America's growing downtowns.

Solving the technical problems of the skyscraper did not resolve how the building should look. Most solutions relied on historical precedents, including decoration reminiscent of the Gothic, Romanesque (a style characterized by the use of rounded arches), or Beaux Arts.

Other features of the early skyscrapers include the following:

- A rectangular shape with a flat roof
- Tripartite division of the facade, similar to that of a column, with a *base* (usually of two stories), *shaft* (midsection with a repetitive window pattern), and *capital* (typically an elaborate, terra-cotta cornice)
- Exterior expression of the building's interior skeleton through an emphasis on horizontal and vertical elements
- Use of *terra cotta,* a light and fireproof material that could be cast in any shape and attached to the exterior

New York's early skyscrapers relied heavily on historical decoration. A good early example in the Beaux Arts mode is the **American Surety Company,** at 100 Broadway (Bruce Price, 1895). The triangular **Flatiron Building,** at Fifth Avenue and 23rd Street (Daniel H. Burnham & Co., 1902), has strong tripartite divisions and Renaissance Revival detail. And, finally, the later **Woolworth Building** (Cass Gilbert, 1913), on Broadway at Park Place, dubbed the "Cathedral of Commerce," is a neo-Gothic skyscraper with flying buttresses, spires, sculptured gargoyles, and pointed arches.

SECOND RENAISSANCE REVIVAL (1890–1920)

Buildings in this style show a definite studied formalism. A relative faithfulness to Italian Renaissance precedents of window and doorway treatments distinguishes it from the much looser adaptations of the Italianate. Scale and size, in turn, set the Second Renaissance Revival apart from the first, which occurred from 1840 to 1890. The grand buildings of the Second Renaissance Revival, with their textural richness, well suited the tastes of New York's wealthy Gilded Age. The style was used for banks, swank town houses, government buildings, and private clubs.

Typical features include the following:

- A cubelike structure with a massive, imposing quality
- Symmetrical arrangement of the facade, including distinct horizontal divisions
- A different stylistic treatment for each floor; with different classical orders, finishes, and window treatments on each level
- Use of *rustication* (masonry cut in massive blocks and separated from each other by deep joints) on the lowest floor
- Quoins
- The indication of additional floors with small windows
- The mixing of Greek and Roman styles on the same facade (Roman arches and arcades may appear with Greek-style pedimented or straight-headed windows)
- A projecting cornice supported by large brackets
- A balustrade above the cornice

New York's Upper East Side has two fine examples of this building type, each exhibiting most of the style's key features: the **Racquet and Tennis Club,** 370 Park Ave. (McKim, Mead & White, 1918), based on the style of an elegant Florentine palazzo; and the **Metropolitan Club,** 1 East 60th St. (McKim, Mead & White, 1891–94).

BEAUX ARTS (1890–1920)

This style takes its name from the Ecole des Beaux-Arts in Paris, where a number of prominent American architects (including **Richard Morris Hunt** [1827–95], **John Mervin Carrère** [1858–1911], and **Thomas Hastings** [1860–1929], to name only a few) received their training, beginning around the mid–19th century. These architects adopted the academic design principles of the Ecole, which emphasized the study of Greek and Roman structures, composition, and symmetry, and the creation of elaborate presentation drawings. Because of the idealized origins and grandiose use of classical forms, the Beaux Arts in America was seen as the ideal style for expressing civic pride.

> **Impressions**
>
> *New York is the perfect model of a city, not the model of a perfect city.*
> —Lewis Mumford

Grandiose compositions, an exuberance of detail, and a variety of stone finishes typify most Beaux Arts structures. Particular features include the following:

- A pronounced cornice and ornate entablature topped by a tall parapet, balustrade, or attic story
- Projecting pavilions, often with colossal columns grouped in pairs
- Windows framed by freestanding columns, a sill with a balustrade, and/or entablatures with pediments or decorative keystones
- Grand staircases
- Grand arched openings
- Classical decoration: freestanding statuary, ornamental panels, swags, medallions
- A heavy *ashlar* (squared stone) base

New York has several exuberant Beaux Arts buildings, exhibiting the style's key features. The **New York Public Library,** at Fifth Avenue and 42nd Street (Carrère & Hastings, 1911), is perhaps the best example. Others of note are **Grand Central Terminal,** at 42nd Street and Park Avenue (Reed & Stem and Warren & Whetmore, 1903–13), and the **U.S. Customs House** (Cass Gilbert, 1907) on Bowling Green between State and Whitehall streets.

INTERNATIONAL STYLE (1920–45)

In 1932, the Museum of Modern Art hosted its first architecture exhibit, titled simply "Modern Architecture." Displays included images of International Style buildings from around the world, many designed by architects from Germany's Bauhaus, a progressive design school. The structures all shared a stark simplicity and vigorous functionalism, a definite break from historically based, decorative styles.

The International Style was popularized in the United States through the teachings and designs of **Ludwig Mies van der Rohe** (1886–1969), a German émigré based in Chicago. Interpretations of the "Miesian" International Style were built in most U.S. cities, including New York, as late as 1980. In the 1950s, erecting an office building in this mode made companies appear progressive. In later decades, after the International Style was a corporate mainstay, the style took on conservative connotations.

Features of the International Style as popularized by Mies include the following:

- A rectangular shape
- Frequent use of glass
- Balance and regularity, but not symmetry
- Horizontal bands of windows
- Windows meeting at corners
- Absence of ornamentation

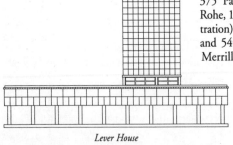

- Clear expression of the building's form and function (the interior structure of stacked office floors is clearly visible, as are the locations of mechanical systems, such as elevator shafts and air-conditioning units)
- Placement, or cantilevering, of buildings on tall piers

Two famous examples of this style in New York are the **Seagram Building,** at 375 Park Ave. (Ludwig Mies van der Rohe, 1958), and **Lever House** (see illustration), 390 Park Ave., between 53rd and 54th streets (Skidmore, Owings & Merrill, 1952). The latter, designed by a firm that made "Miesian" architecture a corporate staple, is credited for popularizing the use of plazas and glass curtain walls. Another well-known example is the Secretariat

Lever House

building in the **United Nations** complex, at First Avenue and 46th Street (1947–53), designed by an international committee of architects.

ART DECO (1925–40)

Art Deco is a decorative style that took its name from a Paris exposition in 1925. The jazzy style embodied the idea of modernity. One of the first widely accepted styles not based on historic precedents, it influenced all areas of design from jewelry and household goods to cars, trains, and ocean liners.

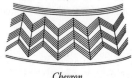

Chevron

Art Deco buildings are characterized by a linear, hard edge, or angular composition, often with a vertical emphasis and highlighted with stylized decoration. The New York zoning law of 1916, which required setbacks in buildings above a certain height to ensure that light and air could reach the street, gave the style its distinctive profile. Other important features include the following:

- An emphasis on geometric form
- Strips of windows with decorated *spandrels* (the horizontal panel below a window) that added to the sense of verticality
- Use of hard-edged, low-relief ornamentation around doors and windows
- Frequent use of black and silver tones
- Decorative motifs of parallel straight lines, zigzags, chevrons (see illustration), and stylized florals

Despite the effects of the Depression, several major Art Deco structures were built in New York in the 1930s, often providing crucial jobs. **Rockefeller Center** (Raymond Hood, 1932–40), a complex sprawling from 48th to 50th streets between Fifth and Sixth avenues, includes 30 Rockefeller Plaza, a tour de force of Art Deco style, with a soaring, vertical shaft and aluminum details. The **Chrysler Building,** Lexington Avenue at 42nd Street (William Van Alen, 1930), is a towering tribute to the automobile (see illustration). The Chrysler's needlelike spire with zigzag patterns in glass and metal is a distinctive feature on the city's skyline. The famous **Empire State Building,** Fifth Avenue at 34th Street (Shreve, Lamb & Harmon, 1931), contains a black- and silver-toned lobby among its many Art Deco features.

ART MODERNE (1930–45)

Art moderne strove for modernity and an artistic expression for the sleekness of the machine age. Unbroken horizontal lines and smooth curves visually distinguish it from Art Deco and give it a streamlined effect. It was popular with movie theaters, and was often applied to cars, trains, and boats to suggest the idea of speed.

The key features of art moderne buildings are as follows:

- A flat roof
- Soft or rounded corners

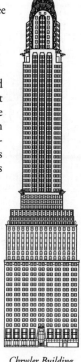

Chrysler Building

- Smooth wall finish without surface ornamentation
- Horizontal bands of windows creating a distinctive streamlined or wind-tunneled effect
- Ornamentation of mirrored panels, cement panels, and perhaps low-relief metal panels around doors and windows
- Aluminum and stainless steel for door and window trim, railings, and balusters
- Metal or wood doors may have circular windows or patterns with circular and angular outlines

The **Majestic Apartments,** at 115 Central Park West (Irwin S. Chanin, 1930), has futuristic forms and wide banks of windows that wrap around corners. **Radio City Music Hall,** on Sixth Avenue at 50th Street (Edward Durrell Stone and Donald Deskey, 1932), has a sweeping art moderne marquee.

POSTMODERN (1975–90)

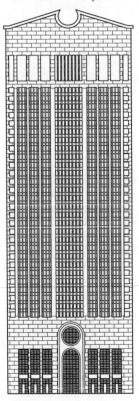

Sony Building

After years of steel-and-glass office towers in the International Style, postmodernism burst on the scene in the 1970s with the reintroduction of historical precedents in architecture. With many feeling that the office towers of the previous style were too cold, postmodernists began to incorporate classical details and recognizable forms into their designs—often applied in outrageous proportions.

Characteristics of postmodern skyscrapers tend to include the following:

- An overall shape (or incorporation) of a recognizable object, not necessarily associated with architecture
- Classical details, such as columns, domes, or vaults, often oversize and used in inventive ways
- A distinctive profile in the skyline
- A use of stone, rather than glass

The **Sony Building,** at 550 Madison Ave. (Philip Johnson/John Burgee, 1984), brings the distinctive shape of a Chippendale cabinet to the New York skyline. The **Morgan Bank Headquarters,** 60 Wall St. (Kevin Roche, John Dinkeloo & Assocs., 1988), resembles a classical column, with modern interpretations of a base, shaft, and capital. The base of the column mirrors in style the facade of the 19th-century building across the street.

3

Planning Your Trip to New York City

In the pages that follow, you'll find everything you need to know to handle the practical details of planning your trip in advance: airlines and area airports, a calendar of events, resources for those of you with special needs, and much more.

Note that there's no need to rent a car. Driving is a nightmare and parking is ridiculously expensive (or near to impossible in some neighborhoods). It's much easier to get around using public transportation, taxis, and your own two feet. If you're going to visit Aunt Erma on Long Island or you have some other need to travel beyond the five boroughs, call one of the major car-rental companies, such as **National** (© **800/227-7368;** www.nationalcar.com), **Hertz** (© **800/654-3131;** www.hertz.com), or **Avis** (© **800/230-4898;** www.avis.com), all of which have airport and Manhattan locations.

1 Visitor Information

For information before you leave home, your best source (besides this book, of course) is **NYC & Company,** the organization that fronts the New York Convention & Visitors Bureau (NYCVB), 810 Seventh Ave., New York, NY 10019. You can call © **800/NYC-VISIT** to order the **Official NYC Visitor Kit,** which contains the *Official NYC Guide* detailing hotels, restaurants, theaters, attractions, events, and more; a foldout map; a decent newsletter on the latest goings-on in the city; and brochures on attractions and services. It costs $5.95 to receive the packet (payable by credit card) in 7 to 10 days, $9.95 for rush delivery (3–4 business days) to U.S. addresses and international orders. (*Note:* I have received complaints that packages don't always strictly adhere to these time frames.)

You can also find a wealth of free information on the bureau's website, **www.nycvisit.com.** To speak with a travel counselor who can answer specific questions, call © **212/484-1222,** which is staffed weekdays from 8:30am to 6pm EST, weekends from 9am to 5pm EST.

For visitor center and information desk locations once you arrive, see "Visitor Information," in chapter 6.

FOR U.K. VISITORS The **NYCVB Visitor Information Center** is at 36 Southwark Bridge Rd., London, SE1 9EU (© **020/7202 6367**). You can order the Official NYC Visitor Kit by sending an A5-size self-addressed envelope and 72p postage to the above address. For New York–bound travelers in the London area, the center also offers free one-on-one travel-planning assistance.

2 Money

You never have to carry too much cash in New York, and while the city's pretty safe these days, it's best not to overstuff your wallet (although always make sure you have at least $20 in taxi fare on hand).

In most Manhattan neighborhoods, you can find a bank with **ATMs** (automated teller machines) every couple of blocks. The only places you may have some difficulty are in more far-flung neighborhoods, like the far East Village or far uptown in Harlem.

ATMS

The easiest and best way to get cash away from home is from an ATM. The **Cirrus** (© 800/424-7787; www.mastercard.com) and **PLUS** (© 800/843-7587; www.visa.com) networks span the globe; look at the back of your bank card to see which network you're on, then call or check online for ATM locations at your destination. Be sure you know your personal identification number (PIN) before you leave home and be sure to find out your daily withdrawal limit before you depart. Also keep in mind that many banks impose a fee every time a card is used at a different bank's ATM, and that fee can be higher for international transactions (up to $5 or more) than for domestic ones (where they're rarely more than $1.50). On top of this, the bank from which you withdraw cash may charge its own fee. To compare banks' ATM fees within the U.S., use www.bankrate.com. For international withdrawal fees, ask your bank.

You can also get cash advances on your credit card at an ATM. Keep in mind that credit card companies try to protect themselves from theft by limiting the funds someone can withdraw outside their home country, so call your credit card company before you leave home. Remember that you'll pay interest from the moment of your withdrawal, even if you pay your monthly bills on time.

TRAVELER'S CHECKS

Traveler's checks are something of an anachronism from the days before the ATM made cash accessible at any time. Traveler's checks used to be the only sound alternative to traveling with dangerously large amounts of cash. They are as reliable as currency, but, unlike cash, can be replaced if lost or stolen.

These days, traveler's checks are less necessary because most cities have 24-hour ATMs that allow you to withdraw small amounts of cash as needed. However, keep in mind that you will likely be charged an ATM withdrawal fee if the bank is not your own, so if you're withdrawing money every day, you might be better off with traveler's checks—provided that you don't mind showing identification every time you want to cash one.

You can get traveler's checks at almost any bank. **American Express** offers denominations of $20, $50, $100, $500, and (for cardholders only) $1,000. You'll pay a service charge ranging from 1% to 4%. You can also get American Express traveler's checks over the phone by calling © 800/221-7282; Amex gold and platinum cardholders who use this number are exempt from the 1% fee.

Visa offers traveler's checks at Citibank locations nationwide, as well as at several other banks. The service charge ranges between 1.5% and 2%; checks come in denominations of $20, $50, $100, $500, and $1,000. Call © 800/732-1322 for information. AAA members can obtain Visa checks without a fee at most AAA offices or by calling © 866/339-3378. **MasterCard** also offers traveler's checks. Call © 800/223-9920 for a location near you.

If you choose to carry traveler's checks, be sure to keep a record of their serial numbers separate from your checks in the event that they are stolen or lost. You'll get a refund faster if you know the numbers.

CREDIT CARDS

Credit cards are a safe way to carry money: They also provide a convenient record of all your expenses, and they generally offer good exchange rates. You can also withdraw cash advances from your credit cards at banks or ATMs, provided you know your PIN. If you've forgotten yours, or didn't even know you had one, call the number on the back of your credit card and ask the bank to send it to you. It usually takes 5 to 7 business days, though some banks will provide the number over the phone if you tell them your mother's maiden name or some other personal information.

3 When to Go

Summer or winter, rain or shine, there's always great stuff going on in New York City, so there's no real "best" time to go.

Culture hounds might come in fall, winter, and early spring, when the theater and performing arts seasons reach their heights. During summer, many of the top cultural institutions, especially Lincoln Center, offer free, alfresco entertainment. Those who want to see the biggest hits on Broadway usually have the best luck getting tickets in the slower months of January and February.

Gourmands might find it easiest to land the best tables during July and August, when New Yorkers escape the city on weekends. If you prefer to walk every city block to take in the sights, spring and fall usually offer the mildest and most pleasant weather.

New York is a nonstop holiday party from early December through the start of the new year. Celebrations of the season abound in festive holiday windows and events like the lighting of the Rockefeller Center tree and the Radio City Christmas Spectacular—not to mention those terrific seasonal sales that make New York a holiday shopping bonanza. However, keep in mind that hotel prices go sky high (more on that below), and the crowds are almost intolerable. If you'd rather have more of the city to yourself—better chances at restaurant reservations and show tickets, easier access to museums and other attractions—choose another time of year to visit.

MONEY MATTERS Hotel prices are more flexible than they've been in years, but New York hotels are by no means throwing a fire sale. Therefore, if money is a big concern, you might want to follow these rough seasonal guidelines.

Bargain hunters might want to visit in winter, between the first of the year and early April. Sure, you might have to bear some cold weather, but that's when hotels are suffering from the post-holiday blues, and rooms often go for a relative song—a song in this case meaning a room with a private bathroom for as little as $125. AAA cardholders could even do better in many cases (generally a 5%–10% savings, if the hotel offers a AAA discount). However, be aware that the occasional convention or event, such as February's annual Fashion Week, can sometimes throw a wrench in your winter savings plans.

Spring and fall are traditionally the busiest, and most expensive, seasons after holiday time. Don't expect hotels to be handing you deals, but you may be able to negotiate a decent rate.

The city is drawing more families these days, and they usually visit in the summer. Still, the prospect of heat and humidity keeps some people away, making July and the first half of August a significantly cheaper time to visit than later in the year; good hotel deals are often available.

At Christmas, expect to pay top dollar for everything. The first 2 weeks of December—the shopping weeks—are the absolute worst when it comes to scoring an affordable hotel room; that's when shoppers from around the world converge on the town to catch the holiday spirit and spend, spend, spend. But Thanksgiving can be a great time to come, believe it or not: Business travelers have gone home for the holiday, and the holiday shoppers haven't yet arrived. It's a little-known secret that most hotels away from the Thanksgiving Day Parade route have empty rooms sitting, and they're usually willing to make great deals to fill them.

WEATHER   Many consider that long week or 10 days that arrive each summer between mid-July and mid-August, when temperatures go up to around 100°F (38°C) with 90% humidity as New York's worst weather. But don't get put off by this—summer has its compensations, such as wonderful free open-air concerts and other events, as I've already mentioned—but bear it in mind. But if you are at all temperature sensitive, your odds of getting comfortable weather are better in June or September.

Another period when you might not like to stroll around the city is during

January or February, when temperatures are commonly in the 20s (below 0 Celsius) and those concrete canyons turn into wind tunnels. The city looks gorgeous for about a day after a snowfall, but the streets soon become an ugly, slushy mess. Again, you never know—temperatures have regularly been in the 30s and mild 40s (single digits Celsius) during the past few winters. If you hit the weather jackpot, you could have a bargain bonanza (see "Money Matters," above).

Fall and spring are the best times in New York. From April to June and September to November, temperatures are mild and pleasant, and the light is beautiful. With the leaves changing in Central Park and just the hint of crispness in the air, October is a fabulous time to be here—but expect to pay for the privilege.

If you want to know how to pack just before you go, check the Weather Channel's online 10-day forecast at **www.weather.com**; I like to balance it against CNN's online 5-day forecast at **www.cnn.com/weather**. You can also get the local weather by calling ✆ **212/976-1212.**

New York's Average Temperature & Rainfall

	Jan	Feb	Mar	Apr	May	June	July	Aug	Sept	Oct	Nov	Dec
Daily Temp. (°F)	38	40	48	61	71	80	85	84	77	67	54	42
Daily Temp. (°C)	3	4	9	16	22	27	29	29	25	19	12	6
Days of Precipitation	11	10	11	11	11	10	11	10	8	8	9	10

NEW YORK CITY CALENDAR OF EVENTS

The following information is always subject to change. Always confirm information before you make plans around a specific event. Call the venue or the NYCVB at ✆ **212/484-1222**, go to **www.nycvisit.com**, or pick up a copy of *Time Out New York* once you arrive in the city for the latest details.

January

New York National Boat Show. Slip on your Top-Siders and head to the

Jacob K. Javits Convention Center for the boat show, which promises a leviathan fleet of boats and marine products from the world's leading manufacturers. Call ✆ **212/984-7000,** or visit www.boatshows.com or www.javitscenter.com. First or second week in January.

Chinese New Year. Every year, Chinatown rings in its own New Year (based on a lunar calendar) with 2 weeks of celebrations, including parades with dragon and lion dancers, plus vivid costumes of all kinds. The parade usually winds throughout Chinatown along Mott, Canal, and Bayard streets, and along East Broadway. Call the NYCVB hot line at ℂ 212/484-1222 or the Asian American Business Development Center at ℂ 212/966-0100. Chinese New Year falls on January 29 in 2006 and it's the Year of the Dog.

Restaurant Week. Twice a year some of the best restaurants in New York offer three-course prix-fixe meals at almost affordable prices. At lunch, the deal is $20, while dinner is $30. Some of the participating restaurants in 2005 included stalwarts such as Capsouto Frères, Eleven Madison Park, Spice Market, and Aquavit. Call ℂ 212/484-1222 for info, or visit www.nyc visit.com. Late January.

February

Westminster Kennel Club Dog Show. The ultimate purebred pooch fest. Some 30,000 dog fanciers from the world over congregate at **Madison Square Garden** for the 130th "World Series of Dogdom." All 2,500 dogs are American Kennel Club Champions of Record, competing for the Best in Show trophy. Check the website www. westminsterkennelclub.org for further information. Tickets become available after January 1 through **Ticketmaster** (ℂ 212/307-7171; www.ticketmaster. com). February 13 to 14.

March

Triple Pier Antiques Show. The city's largest and most comprehensive antiques show takes place over 2 consecutive weekends, as more than 600 dealers exhibit their treasures, ranging from jewelry to home furnishings, on three piers along the Hudson River between 48th and 51st streets. **Pier 88** features 20th-century modern collectibles; **Pier 90** has all manner of

Americana, including country rustic, folk art, and Arts and Crafts; and **Pier 92** houses 18th- and 19th-century formal European antiques. Call ℂ 212/255-0020 for this year's dates, plus a calendar of additional shows. Usually mid-March, and again in mid-November.

St. Patrick's Day Parade. More than 150,000 marchers join in the world's largest civilian parade, as Fifth Avenue from 44th to 86th streets rings with the sounds of bands and bagpipes. The parade usually starts at 11am, but go extra early if you want a good spot. Call ℂ 212/484-1222. March 17.

April

New York International Auto Show. Here's the irony: You don't need a car in New York, yet this is the largest car show in the United States. Held at the Javits Center, many concept cars show up that will never roll off the assembly line but are fun to dream about nonetheless. Call ℂ 718/746-5300, or visit www.autoshowny.com or www. javitscenter.com. Early April.

Easter Parade. This isn't a traditional parade, per se: There are no marching bands, no baton twirlers, no protesters. Once upon a time, New York's gentry came out to show off their tasteful but discreet toppings. Today, if you were planning to slip on a tasteful little number—say something delicately woven in straw with a simple flower or two that matches your gloves—you will *not* be the grandest lady in this springtime hike along Fifth Avenue from 48th to 57th streets. It's more about flamboyant exhibitionism, with hats and costumes that get more outrageous every year—and anybody can join right in for free. The parade generally runs Easter Sunday from about 10am to 3 or 4pm. Call ℂ 212/484-1222. April 16.

Tribeca Film Festival. Conceived in 2002 by the unofficial mayor of TriBeCa, Robert DeNiro, the Tribeca Film Festival has grown in both popularity and esteem every year. In 2005, the 12-day festival featured over 250 films and included special events like a Family Festival Street Fair. Look for even more in 2006. Call ✆ **212/ 941-2400** or visit www.tribecafilm festival.org. Late April.

May

Bike New York: The Great Five Boro Bike Tour. The largest mass-participation cycling event in the United States attracts about 30,000 cyclists from all over the world. After a 42-mile ride through the five boroughs, finalists are greeted with a traditional New York–style celebration of food and music. Call ✆ **212/932-BIKE** (2453) or visit www.bikenewyork.org to register. First or second Sunday in May.

Ninth Avenue International Food Festival. Street fairs are part of the New York landscape each spring and summer, but this is one of the best. You can spend the entire day sampling sizzling Italian sausages, homemade pirogi, spicy curries, and an assortment of other ethnic dishes—if you can stomach it. Street musicians, bands, and vendors add to the festive atmosphere stretching along Ninth Avenue from 37th to 57th streets. Call ✆ **212/ 484-1222.** One weekend in mid-May.

Fleet Week. About 10,000 Navy and Coast Guard personnel are "at liberty" in New York for the annual Fleet Week at the end of May. Usually from 1 to 4pm daily, you can watch the ships and aircraft carriers as they dock at the piers on the west side of Manhattan, tour them with on-duty personnel, and watch some dramatic exhibitions by the U.S. Marines. Even if you don't take in any of the events, you'll know it's Fleet Week, because those 10,000 sailors invade Midtown in their starched white uniforms. It's wonderful—just like *On the Town* come to life. Call ✆ **212/ 245-0072,** or visit www.fleetweek. com (your best source for a full list of events) or www.intrepidmuseum.org. Late May.

June

Belmont Stakes. The third jewel in the Triple Crown is held at the **Belmont Park Race Track** in Belmont, Long Island. If a Triple Crown winner is to be named, it will happen here. For information, call ✆ **516/488-6000,** or visit www.nyracing.com/belmont. Early June.

Museum Mile Festival. Fifth Avenue from 82nd to 104th streets is closed to cars from 6 to 9pm as 20,000-plus strollers enjoy live music, from Broadway tunes to string quartets; street entertainers; and free admission to nine Museum Mile institutions, including the Metropolitan Museum of Art and the Guggenheim. Call ✆ **212/606-2296** or any of the participating institutions for details. Usually the second Tuesday in June.

Parades Around Town. During the summer there is a parade for almost every nationality or ethnicity. June is the month for (among others) the sometimes raucous but usually very colorful **Puerto Rican Day Parade** and the **Lesbian and Gay Pride Week and March,** where Fifth Avenue goes wild as the gay/lesbian community celebrates with bands, marching groups, floats, and plenty of panache. The parade starts on upper Fifth Avenue around 52nd Street and continues into the Village, where a street festival and a waterfront dance party with fireworks cap the day. Call ✆ **212/807-7433** or check www.hopinc.org. Mid- to late June.

SummerStage. A summer-long festival of outdoor performances in **Central Park,** featuring world music, pop, folk, and jazz artists ranging from Steve Earle to Craig David to Basement Jaxx to the New York Grand Opera (always performing Verdi) to the Chinese Golden Dragon Acrobats. Performances are often free, but certain events require purchased tickets (usually less than $30). Call ☎ **212/360-2756** or visit www.summerstage.org. June through August.

Shakespeare in the Park. The Delacorte Theater in **Central Park** is the setting for first-rate free performances under the stars—including at least one Shakespeare production each season—often with stars on the stage. For details, see "Park It! Shakespeare, Music & Other Free Fun," in chapter 11. Call ☎ **212/539-8750,** or visit www.publictheater.org. June through August.

Restaurant Week. Late June. (see "January," above).

July

Independence Day Harbor Festival and Fourth of July Fireworks Spectacular. Start the day amid the patriotic crowds at the Great July Fourth Festival in Lower Manhattan, and then catch Macy's great fireworks extravaganza (one of the country's most fantastic) over the East River (the best vantage point is from FDR Drive, which closes to traffic several hours before sunset). Call ☎ **212/484-1222,** or Macy's Visitor Center at 212/494-2922. July 4.

Lincoln Center Festival 2006. This festival celebrates the best of the performing arts from all over the world—theater, ballet, contemporary dance, opera, nouveau circus performances, even puppet and media-based art. Recent editions have featured performances by Ornette Coleman, the Royal Opera, the Royal Ballet, and the New York Philharmonic. Schedules are usually available in mid-March, and tickets go on sale in late May or early June. Call ☎ **212/546-2656,** or visit www. lincolncenter.org. Throughout July.

Midsummer Night's Swing. Dancing duos head to the **Lincoln Center Fountain Plaza** for romantic evenings of big-band swing, salsa, and tango under the stars to the sounds of top-flight bands. Dance lessons are offered with the purchase of a ticket. Call ☎ 212/875-5766, or visit www.lincoln center.org. July and August.

Mostly Mozart. World-renowned ensembles and soloists (Alicia de Larrocha and André Watts have performed in the past) are featured at this month-long series at **Avery Fisher Hall.** Schedules are usually available in mid-April, and tickets in early May. Call ☎ 212/875-5030 or 212/546-2656 for information, 212/721-6500 to order tickets, or visit www.lincoln center.org. Late July through August.

August

Lincoln Center Out of Doors. This series of free music and dance performances is held outdoors on the plazas of **Lincoln Center.** Call ☎ 212/875-5108 or 212/546-2656, or visit www.lincolncenter.org for this year's schedule (usually available in mid-July). Throughout August.

Harlem Week. The world's largest black and Hispanic cultural festival actually spans almost the whole month to include the Black Film Festival, the Harlem Jazz and Music Festival, and the Taste of Harlem Food Festival. Expect a full slate of music, from gospel to hip-hop, and lots of other festivities. Call ☎ **212/484-1222.** Throughout August.

New York International Fringe Festival. Held in a variety of tiny Lower East Side venues and park spaces for a mainly hipster crowd, this arts festival presents alternative as well as traditional theater, musicals, dance, comedy, and all manner of performance art, including new media. Literally hundreds of events are held at all hours over about 10 days. The quality can vary wildly (lots of performers use Fringe as a workshop to develop their acts and shows), and some performances really push the envelope. Nonetheless, you'd be surprised at how many shows are actually *good.* Call ℂ **888/FRINGE-NYC** or 212/279-4488, or visit www.fringenyc.org. Late August.

U.S. Open Tennis Championships. The final Grand Slam event of the tennis season is held at the Arthur Ashe Stadium at the USTA National Tennis Center, the largest public tennis center in the world, at **Flushing Meadows Park** in Queens. Tickets go on sale in May or early June. The event sells out immediately because many of the tickets are held by corporate sponsors who hand them out to customers. (It's worth it to check the list of sponsors to determine if anyone you know has a connection for getting tickets.) You can usually buy scalped tickets outside the complex (an illegal practice, of course), which is right next to Shea Stadium. The last few matches of the tournament are the most expensive, but you'll see a lot more tennis early on, when your ticket allows you to wander the outside courts and view several different matches. Call ℂ **888/OPEN-TIX** or 718/760-6200 well in advance; visit www.usopen.org or www.usta.com for additional information. Two weeks around Labor Day.

September

West Indian–American Day Parade. This annual Brooklyn event is New York's largest and best street celebration. Come for the extravagant costumes, pulsating rhythms (soca, calypso, reggae), bright colors, folklore, food (jerk chicken, oxtail soup, Caribbean soul food), and two million hip-shaking revelers. The route can change from year to year, but it usually runs along Eastern Parkway from Utica Avenue to Grand Army Plaza (at the gateway to Prospect Park). Call ℂ **212/484-1222** or 718/625-1515. Labor Day.

Broadway on Broadway. This free alfresco afternoon show features the songs and casts from virtually every Broadway production, performing on a stage erected in the middle of Times Square. Call ℂ **212/768-1560,** or visit www.timessquarebid.org and click on "Events." Sunday in mid-September.

New York Film Festival. Legendary hits *Pulp Fiction* and *Mean Streets* both had their U.S. premieres at the Film Society of Lincoln Center's 2-week festival, a major stop on the film fest circuit. Schedules in recent years have included advance looks at *The Sweet Hereafter, Rushmore,* and *All About My Mother.* Screenings are held in various Lincoln Center venues; advance tickets are a good bet always, and a necessity for certain events (especially evening and weekend screenings). Call ℂ **212/875-5600** for information, 212/875-5050 for tickets, or check out www.filmlinc.com. Two weeks from late September to early October.

BAM Next Wave Festival. One of the city's most important cultural events takes place at the **Brooklyn Academy of Music.** The months-long festival showcases experimental new dance, theater, and music works by both renowned and lesser-known international artists. Recent celebrated performances have included Astor Piazzolla's *Maria de Buenos Aires* (featuring Piazzolla disciple Gidon Kremer), the 25th anniversary of the Kronos Quartet, and choreographer Bill T. Jones's *We Set Out Early . . . Visibility Was Poor* (set to the music of Igor Stravinsky, John Cage, and Peteris Vask). Call © **718/636-4100** or visit www.bam.org. September through December.

October

Feast of St. Francis. Animals from goldfish to elephants are blessed as thousands of *Homo sapiens* look on at the **Cathedral of St. John the Divine.** A magical experience—pets, of course, are welcome. A festive fair follows the blessing and music events. Buy tickets in advance because they can be hard to come by. Call © **212/316-7540** or 212/662-7133 for tickets, or visit www.stjohndivine.org. First Sunday in October.

Ice-Skating. Show off your skating style in the limelight at the diminutive **Rockefeller Center** rink (© **212/332-7654;** www.rockefellercenter.com), open from mid-October to mid-March or early April (you'll skate under the magnificent Christmas tree for the month of Dec). In Central Park, try **Wollman Rink** on the east side of the park between 62nd and 63rd streets (© **212/439-6900;** www.wollman skatingrink.com), and **Lasker Rink,** midpark between 106th and 108th streets (© **917/492-3850**). Both Central Park skating rinks usually close in early April.

Greenwich Village Halloween Parade. This is Halloween at its most outrageous. You may have heard Lou Reed singing about it on his classic album *New York*—he wasn't exaggerating.

Drag queens and assorted other flamboyant types parade through the Village in wildly creative costumes. The parade route has changed over the years, but most recently it has started after sunset at Spring Street and marched up Sixth Avenue to 23rd Street or Union Square. Call the *Village Voice* Parade hot line at © **212/475-3333,** ext. 14044, visit www.halloween-nyc.com, or check the papers for the exact route so you can watch—or participate, if you have the threads and the imagination. October 31.

November

The Chocolate Show. This burgeoning 4-day event devoted solely to chocolate takes place each year about 2 weeks before Thanksgiving and is open to the public. The event is held at the Metropolitan Pavilion in Chelsea and features booths representing over 50 of the world's best chocolate makers, chocolate tastings, demonstrations by top pastry chefs, and activities for children. For more information call **866/CHOCNYC** or 212/889-5112 or visit the show's website, www.chocolate show.com. November 10 to 13 in 2005; call for 2006 dates.

New York City Marathon. Some 30,000 hopefuls from around the world participate in the largest U.S. marathon, and more than a million fans will cheer them on as they follow a route that touches on all five New York boroughs and finishes at Central Park. Call © **212/423-2249** or 212/860-4455, or visit www.nyrrc.org, where you can find applications to run. First Sunday in November. November 6 in 2005, November 5 in 2006.

Radio City Music Hall Christmas Spectacular. A rather gaudy extravaganza, but lots of fun nonetheless. Starring the Radio City Rockettes and a cast that includes live animals (just try to picture the camels sauntering in the Sixth Ave. entrance!). After undergoing an extensive restoration, spectacular Radio City itself is a sight to see. For information, call ☎ 212/247-4777 or visit www.radiocity.com; buy tickets at the box office or via Ticketmaster's **Radio City Hot Line** (☎ 212/307-1000), or visit www.ticketmaster.com. Throughout November and December.

Triple Pier Antiques Show. The city's largest antiques show takes place over 2 consecutive weekends, usually just before Thanksgiving; for details, see "March," above. Call ☎ 212/255-0020 or visit www.antiqnet.com/Stella for this year's dates.

Macy's Thanksgiving Day Parade. The procession from Central Park West and 77th Street and down Broadway to Herald Square at 34th Street continues to be a national tradition. Huge hot-air balloons in the forms of Rocky and Bullwinkle, Snoopy, Underdog, the Pink Panther, Bart Simpson, and other cartoon favorites are the best part of the fun. The night before, you can usually see the big blow-up on Central Park West at 79th Street; call in advance to see if it will be open to the public again this year. Call ☎ 212/484-1222, or Macy's Visitor Center at 212/494-2922. November 24 in 2005, November 23 in 2006.

Big Apple Circus. New York City's homegrown, not-for-profit performing-arts circus is a favorite with children and everyone who's young at heart. Big Apple is committed to maintaining the classical circus tradition with sensitivity, and only features animals that have a traditional working relationship with humans. A tent is pitched in **Damrosch Park** at **Lincoln Center.** Call ☎ 212/268-2500, or visit www.bigapple circus.org. November through January.

The Nutcracker. Tchaikovsky's holiday favorite is performed by the New York City Ballet at **Lincoln Center.** The annual schedule is available from mid-July, and tickets usually go on sale in early October. Call ☎ 212/870-5570, or go online to www.nycballet.com. Late November through early January.

Lighting of the Rockefeller Center Christmas Tree. The annual lighting ceremony is accompanied by an ice-skating show, singing, entertainment, and a huge crowd. The tree stays lit around the clock until after the new year. Call ☎ 212/332-6868 or visit www.rockefellercenter.com for this year's date. Late November or early December.

December

Holiday Trimmings. Stroll down festive Fifth Avenue and you'll see a 27-foot sparkling snowflake floating over the intersection outside **Tiffany's,** the **Cartier** building ribboned and bowed in red, wreaths warming the necks of the **New York Public Library**'s lions, and fanciful figurines in the windows of **Saks Fifth Avenue** and **Lord & Taylor.** Madison Avenue between 55th and 60th streets is also a good bet; **Sony Plaza** usually displays something fabulous, as does **Barney's New York.** Throughout December.

Christmas Traditions. In addition to the **Radio City Music Hall Christmas Spectacular** and the New York City Ballet's staging of **The Nutcracker** (see "November," above), traditional holiday events include *A Christmas Carol* at **The Theater at Madison Square Garden** (☎ 212/465-6741 or www.the garden.com, or ☎ 212/307-7171 or www.ticketmaster.com for tickets), usually featuring a big name to draw in the crowds. At **Avery Fisher Hall** is the National Chorale's singalong performances of Handel's *Messiah* (© **212/875-5030;** www.lincolncenter.org) for a week before Christmas. Don't worry if the only words you know are "Alleluia, Alleluia!"—a lyrics sheet is given to ticket holders. Throughout December.

Lighting of the Hanukkah Menorah. Everything is done on a grand scale in New York, so it's no surprise that the world's largest menorah (32 ft. high) is at Manhattan's **Grand Army Plaza,** Fifth Avenue and 59th Street. Hanukkah celebrations begin at sunset, with the lighting of the first of the giant electric candles. December 26 in 2005, December 16 in 2006.

New Year's Eve. The biggest party of them all happens in **Times Square,** where hundreds of thousands of raucous revelers count down in unison the year's final seconds until the new lighted ball drops at midnight at 1 Times Square. This one, in the cold surrounded by thousands of very drunk revelers, is definitely a masochist's delight. Call © **212/768-1560,** 212/484-1222, or visit www.timessquarebid.org. December 31.

***Runner's World* Midnight Run.** Enjoy **fireworks** followed by the New York Road Runners Club's annual run in **Central Park,** which is fun for runners and spectators alike; call © **212/860-4455** or visit www.nyrrc.org. December 31.

Brooklyn's fireworks celebration. Head to Brooklyn for the city's largest New Year's Eve **fireworks** celebration at Prospect Park; call © **718/965-8999** or visit www.prospectpark.org. December 31.

New Year's Eve Concert for Peace. The Cathedral of St. John the Divine is known for its annual concert, whose past performers have included the Manhattan School of Music Chamber Sinfonia, Tony award–winning composer Jason Robert Brown *(Parade),* American soprano Lauren Flanigan, and the Forces of Nature Dance Company. Call © **212/316-7540** for information, 212/662-2133 for tickets, or go online to www.stjohndivine.org. December 31.

4 Travel Insurance

Check your existing insurance policies and credit card coverage before you buy travel insurance. You may already be covered for lost luggage, canceled tickets, or medical expenses.

The cost of travel insurance varies widely, depending on the cost and length of your trip, your age and health, and the type of trip you're taking, but expect to pay between 5% and 8% of the vacation itself.

TRIP-CANCELLATION INSURANCE Trip-cancellation insurance helps you get your money back if you have to back out of a trip, if you have to go home early, or if your travel supplier goes bankrupt. Allowed reasons for cancellation can range from sickness to natural disasters to the State Department declaring your destination unsafe for travel. (Insurers usually won't cover vague fears, though, as many travelers discovered who tried to cancel their trips in Oct 2001 because they were wary of flying.) In this unstable world, trip-cancellation insurance is a good buy if you're getting tickets well in advance—who knows what the state of the world, or of your airline, will be in 9 months? Insurance policy details vary, so read the fine print—and especially make sure that your airline or cruise line is on the list of carriers covered in case of bankruptcy. A good resource is **"Travel Guard Alerts,"** a list of companies considered high-risk by Travel Guard International (see website below).

Protect yourself further by paying for the insurance with a credit card—by law, consumers can get their money back on goods and services not received if they report the loss within 60 days after the charge is listed on their credit card statement.

Note: Many tour operators, particularly those offering trips to remote or high-risk areas, include insurance in the cost of the trip or can arrange insurance policies through a partnering provider, a convenient and often cost-effective way for the traveler to obtain insurance. Make sure the tour company is a reputable one, however: Some experts suggest you avoid buying insurance from the tour or cruise company you're traveling with, saying it's better to buy from a "third party" insurer than to put all your money in one place.

For more information, contact one of the following recommended insurers: **Access America** (© 866/807-3982; www.accessamerica.com), **Travel Guard International** (© 800/826-4919; www.travelguard.com), **Travel Insured International** (© 800/243-3174; www.travelinsured.com), and **Travelex Insurance Services** (© 888/457-4602; www.travelex-insurance.com).

MEDICAL INSURANCE Most health insurance policies cover you if you get sick away from home—but check, particularly if you're insured by an HMO.

LOST-LUGGAGE INSURANCE On domestic flights, checked baggage is covered up to $2,500 per ticketed passenger. On international flights (including U.S. portions of international trips), baggage coverage is limited to approximately $9.07 per pound, up to approximately $635 per checked bag. If you plan to check items more valuable than the standard liability, see if your valuables are covered by your homeowner's policy, get baggage insurance as part of your comprehensive travel-insurance package, or buy Travel Guard's "BagTrak" product. Don't buy insurance at the airport, as it's usually overpriced. Be sure to take any valuables or irreplaceable items with you in your carry-on luggage, as many valuables (including books, money, and electronics) aren't covered by airline policies.

If your luggage is lost, immediately file a lost-luggage claim at the airport, detailing the luggage contents. For most airlines, you must report delayed, damaged, or lost baggage within 4 hours of arrival. The airlines are required to deliver luggage, once found, directly to your house or destination free of charge.

5 Health & Safety

WHAT TO DO IF YOU GET SICK AWAY FROM HOME

If you get sick, consider asking your hotel concierge to recommend a local doctor—even his or her own. This will probably yield a better recommendation than any 800 number would. There are also several walk-in medical centers, like **DOCS at New York Healthcare,** 55 E. 34th St., between Park and Madison avenues (© **800/673-3627**), for nonemergency illnesses. The clinic, affiliated with Beth Israel Medical Center, is open Monday through Thursday from 8am to 8pm, Friday from 8am to 7pm, Saturday from 9am to 3pm, and Sunday from 9am to 2pm. The **NYU Downtown Hospital** offers physician referrals at © **888/698-3362.** You can also try the emergency room at a local hospital. Many hospitals also have walk-in clinics for emergency cases that are not life-threatening; you may not get immediate attention, but you won't pay the high price of an emergency room visit. We list hospitals and emergency numbers under "Fast Facts: New York City," p. 118.

Avoiding "Economy Class Syndrome"

Deep vein thrombosis, or as it's know in the world of flying, "economy-class syndrome," is a blood clot that develops in a deep vein. It's a potentially deadly condition that can be caused by sitting in cramped conditions—such as an airplane cabin—for too long. During a flight (especially a long-haul flight), get up, walk around, and stretch your legs every 60 to 90 minutes to keep your blood flowing. Other preventative measures include frequent flexing of the legs while sitting, drinking lots of water, and avoiding alcohol and sleeping pills. If you have a history of deep vein thrombosis, heart disease, or other condition that puts you at high risk, some experts recommend wearing compression stockings or taking anticoagulants when you fly; always ask your physician about the best course for you. Symptoms of deep vein thrombosis include leg pain or swelling, or even shortness of breath.

If you suffer from a chronic illness, consult your doctor before your departure. For conditions like epilepsy, diabetes, or heart problems, wear a **Medic Alert identification tag** (© 888/633-4298; www.medicalert.org), which will immediately alert doctors to your condition and give them access to your records through Medic Alert's 24-hour hot line.

Pack **prescription medications** in their original containers in your carry-on luggage. Also bring along copies of your prescriptions in case you lose your pills or run out. Don't forget an extra pair of contact lenses or prescription glasses.

If you have dental problems, a nationwide referral service known as **1-800-DENTIST** (© 800/336-8478) will provide the name of a nearby dentist or clinic.

For domestic trips, most reliable health-care plans provide coverage if you get sick away from home. Bring your insurance ID card with you when you travel. For travel abroad, you may have to pay all medical costs upfront and be reimbursed later. See "Medical Insurance," under "Travel Insurance," above. Pack **prescription medications** in your carry-on luggage, and carry prescription

medications in their original containers, with pharmacy labels—otherwise they won't make it through airport security.

STAYING SAFE

The FBI consistently rates New York City as one of the safest large cities in the United States and it remains one of the safest, but it is still a very large city and crime most definitely exists here. Here are a few tips for staying safe in New York. For more, see "Playing it Safe" in chapter 6.

Trust your instincts, because they're usually right.

You'll rarely be hassled, but it's always best to walk with a sense of purpose and self-confidence. Don't stop in the middle of the sidewalk to pull out and peruse your map.

Anywhere in the city, if you find yourself on a deserted street that feels unsafe, it probably is; leave as quickly as possible.

If you do find yourself accosted by someone with or without a weapon, remember to keep your anger in check and that the most reasonable response (maddening though it may be) is not to resist.

6 Specialized Travel Resources

TRAVELERS WITH DISABILITIES

Most disabilities shouldn't stop anyone from traveling. There are new options and resources out there all the time, and New York is more accessible to travelers with disabilities than ever before. The city's bus system is wheelchair friendly, and most of the major sightseeing attractions are easily accessible. Even so, **always call first** to be sure that the places you want to go to are fully accessible.

Most hotels are ADA-compliant, with suitable rooms for wheelchair-bound travelers as well as those with other disabilities. But before you book, **ask lots of questions based on your needs.** Many city hotels are housed in older buildings that have had to be modified to meet requirements; still, elevators and bathrooms can both be on the small side, and other impediments may exist. If you have mobility issues, you'll probably do best to book one of the city's newer hotels, which tend to be more spacious and accommodating. At **www. access-able.com** (see below), you'll find links to New York's best accessible accommodations (click on "World Cities"). Some Broadway theaters and other performance venues provide total wheelchair accessibility; others provide partial accessibility. Many also offer lower-priced tickets for theatergoers with disabilities and their companions, though you'll need to check individual policies and reserve in advance.

GENERAL TRAVEL INFORMATION

Many travel agencies offer customized tours and itineraries for travelers with disabilities. **Flying Wheels Travel** (② 507/ 451-5005; www.flyingwheelstravel.com) offers escorted tours and cruises that emphasize sports and private tours in minivans with lifts. **Accessible Journeys** (② **800/846-4537** or 610/521-0339; www.disabilitytravel.com) caters specifically to slow walkers and wheelchair travelers and their families and friends.

Organizations that offer assistance to travelers with disabilities include the **MossRehab** (www.mossresourcenet.org), which provides a library of accessible-travel resources online; **SATH (Society for Accessible Travel & Hospitality** (② 212/ 447-7284; www.sath.org; annual membership fees: $45 adults, $30 seniors and students), which offers a wealth of travel resources for all types of disabilities and informed recommendations on destinations, access guides, travel agents, tour operators, vehicle rentals, and companion services; and the **American Foundation for the Blind (AFB)** (② 800/232-5463; www.afb.org), a referral resource for the blind or visually impaired that includes traveling with Seeing Eye dogs.

Access-Able Travel Source (② 303/ 232-2979; www.access-able.com) is another excellent online source, offering extensive access information and advice for traveling around the world with disabilities. You'll find relay and voice numbers for airlines and car-rental companies on their user-friendly site, as well as links to New York's best accessible accommodations, attractions, transportation, tours, local medical resources and equipment repair, and much more.

Avis Rent a Car has an "Avis Access" program that offers such services as a dedicated 24-hour toll-free number (② **888/ 879-4273**) for customers with special travel needs; special car features such as swivel seats, spinner knobs, and hand controls; and accessible bus service.

CITY-SPECIFIC   INFORMATION

Hospital Audiences, Inc. (② 212/ 575-7676; www.hospitalaudiences.org) arranges attendance and provides details about accessibility at cultural institutions as well as cultural events adapted for people with disabilities. Services include "Describe!," which allows visually impaired theatergoers to enjoy theater events; and the invaluable **HAI Hot Line** (© 212/ 575-7676), which offers accessibility information for hotels, restaurants, attractions, cultural venues, and much more. This nonprofit organization also publishes *Access for All,* a guidebook on accessibility, available by calling © 212/575-7663 or by sending a $5 check to 548 Broadway, 3rd floor, New York, NY 10012-3950.

Another terrific source for travelers with disabilities who are coming to New York City is **Big Apple Greeter** (© 212/ 669-8159; www.bigapplegreeter.org). All of its employees are extremely well versed in accessibility issues. They can provide a resource list of agencies that serve the city's community with disabilities, and sometimes have special discounts available to theater and music performances. Big Apple Greeter even offers one-to-one tours that pair volunteers with visitors with disabilities; they can even introduce you to the public transportation system if you like. Reserve at least 1 week ahead.

For more information specifically targeted to travelers with disabilities, the community website **iCan** (www.ican online.net) has destination guides and several regular columns on accessible travel. Also check out the quarterly magazine **Emerging Horizons** ($14.95 per year, $19.95 outside the U.S.; www. emerginghorizons.com); **Twin Peaks Press** (© 360/694-2462; http://home. pacifier.com/~twinpeak), offering travel-related books for travelers with special needs; and *Open World Magazine,* published by the Society for Accessible Travel and Hospitality (see above; subscription $13 per year, $21 outside the U.S.).

GETTING AROUND   Express Shuttle USA (© 800/451-0455 or 212/315-3006; www.graylinenewyork.com) operates minibuses with lifts from Newark airports to Midtown hotels by reservation; arrange pickup 3 or 4 days in advance. **Olympia Trails** (© 877/894-9155 or 212/964-6233; www.olympia

bus.com) provides service from Newark Airport, with half-price fares for travelers with disabilities (be sure to prepurchase your tickets to guarantee the discount fare, as drivers can't sell discounted tickets). Not all buses are appropriately equipped, so call ahead for the daily schedule of accessible buses (press "0" to reach a real person).

Taxis are required to carry people who have folding wheelchairs and guide or therapy dogs. However, don't be surprised if they don't run each other down trying to get to you; even though you shouldn't have to, you may have to wait a bit for a friendly (or fare-desperate) driver to come along.

Public buses are an inexpensive and easy way to get around New York. All buses' back doors are supposed to be equipped with wheelchair lifts (though the city has had complaints that not all are in working order). Buses also "kneel," lowering their front steps for people who have difficulty boarding. Passengers with disabilities pay half-price fares ($1). The **subway** isn't yet fully wheelchair accessible, but a list of about 30 accessible subway stations and a guide to wheelchair-accessible subway itineraries is on the MTA website. Call © 718/596-8585 for bus and subway transit info or go online to www.mta.nyc.ny.us/nyct and click on the wheelchair symbol.

You're better off not trying to rent your own car to get around the city. But if you consider it the best mode of transportation for you, **Wheelchair Getaways** (© 800/642-2042 or 800/344-5005; www.wheelchair-getaways.com) rents specialized vans with wheelchair lifts and other features for travelers with disabilities throughout the New York metropolitan area.

FAMILY TRAVEL

If you have enough trouble getting your kids out of the house in the morning, dragging them thousands of miles away may seem like an insurmountable challenge. But family travel can be immensely rewarding, giving you new ways of seeing the world through smaller pairs of eyes.

For more extensive recommendations, you might want to purchase a copy of *Frommer's New York City with Kids,* an entire guidebook dedicated to family visits to the Big Apple.

Good bets for the most timely information include the "Weekend" section of Friday's *New York Times,* which has a whole section dedicated to the week's best kid-friendly activities; the weekly *New York* magazine, which has a full calendar of children's events in its listings section; and *Time Out New York,* which also has a great weekly kids section with a bit of an alternative bent. The *Big Apple Parents' Paper* is usually available, for free, at children's stores and other locations in Manhattan; you can also find good information from the folks behind the paper at **www.parentsknow.com**.

The first place to look for **babysitting** is in your hotel (better yet, ask about babysitting when you reserve). Many hotels have babysitting services or will provide you with lists of reliable sitters. If this doesn't pan out, call the **Baby Sitters' Guild** (© **212/682-0227**; www.baby sittersguild.com). The sitters are licensed, insured, and bonded, and can even take your child on outings.

Familyhostel (© **800/733-9753**; www.learn.unh.edu/familyhostel) takes the whole family, including kids ages 8 to 15, on moderately priced domestic and international learning vacations. Lectures, field trips, and sightseeing are guided by a team of academics.

Recommended family travel Internet sites include **Family Travel Forum** (www.familytravelforum.com), a comprehensive site that offers customized trip planning; **Family Travel Network** (www. familytravelnetwork.com), an award-winning site that offers travel features,

deals, and tips; **Traveling Internationally with Your Kids** (www.travelwith yourkids.com), a comprehensive site offering sound advice for long-distance and international travel with children; and **Family Travel Files** (www.thefamily travelfiles.com), which offers an online magazine and a directory of off-the-beaten-path tours and tour operators for families.

How to Take Great Trips with Your Kids (The Harvard Common Press) is full of good general advice that can apply to travel anywhere.

SENIOR TRAVEL

Mention the fact that you're a senior when you make your travel reservations. Although all of the major U.S. airlines except America West have canceled their senior discount and coupon book programs, many hotels still offer discounts for seniors. In most cities, people over the age of 60 qualify for reduced admission to theaters, museums, and other attractions, as well as discounted fares on public transportation.

New York subway and bus fares are half-price ($1) for people 65 and older. Many museums and sights (and some theaters and performance halls) offer discounted admittance and tickets to seniors, so don't be shy about asking. Always bring an ID card, especially if you've kept your youthful glow.

Many hotels offer senior discounts; **Choice Hotels** (which include Comfort Inns, some of my favorite affordable Midtown hotels; see chapter 7, "Where to Stay"), for example, gives 30% off their published rates to anyone over 50, provided you book your room through their nationwide toll-free reservations number (that is, not directly with the hotels or through a travel agent). For a complete list of Choice Hotels, visit **www.hotel choice.com**.

Members of **AARP** (formerly known as the American Association of Retired

Persons), 601 E St. NW, Washington, DC 20049 (© 888/687-2277 or 202/434-2277; www.aarp.org), get discounts on hotels, airfares, and car rentals. AARP offers members a wide range of benefits, including *AARP: The Magazine* and a monthly newsletter. Anyone over 50 can join.

Many reliable agencies and organizations target the 50-plus market. **Elderhostel** (© 877/426-8056; www.elderhostel.org) arranges study programs for those aged 55 and over (and a spouse or companion of any age) in the U.S. and in more than 80 countries around the world. Most courses last 5 to 7 days in the U.S. (2–4 weeks abroad), and many include airfare, accommodations in university dormitories or modest inns, meals, and tuition. **ElderTreks** (© 800/741-7956; www.eldertreks.com) offers small-group tours to off-the-beaten-path or adventure-travel locations, restricted to travelers 50 and older. **INTRAV** (© 800/456-8100; www.intrav.com) is a high-end tour operator that caters to the mature, discerning traveler, not specifically seniors, with trips around the world that include guided safaris, polar expeditions, private-jet adventures, and small-boat cruises down jungle rivers.

Recommended publications offering travel resources and discounts for seniors include the quarterly magazine *Travel 50 & Beyond* (www.travel50andbeyond.com); *Travel Unlimited: Uncommon Adventures for the Mature Traveler* (Avalon); *101 Tips for Mature Travelers,* available from Grand Circle Travel (© 800/221-2610 or 617/350-7500; www.gct.com); *The 50+ Traveler's Guidebook* (St. Martin's Press); and *Unbelievably Good Deals & Great Adventures That You Absolutely Can't Get Unless You're Over 50* (McGraw-Hill), by Joann Rattner Heilman.

GAY & LESBIAN TRAVELERS

Gay and lesbian culture is as much a part of New York's basic identity as yellow cabs, high-rises, and Broadway theater. Indeed, in a city with one of the world's largest, loudest, and most powerful gay and lesbian populations, homosexuality is squarely in the urban mainstream. So city hotels tend to be neutral on the issue, and gay couples shouldn't have a problem; for particularly gay-friendly accommodations, see "Best for Gay & Lesbian Travelers" under "Best Hotels," in chapter 1. You'll also want to see "The Gay & Lesbian Scene," in chapter 11 for nightlife suggestions.

The International Gay and Lesbian Travel Association (IGLTA; © 800/448-8550 or 954/776-2626; www.iglta.org) is the trade association for the gay and lesbian travel industry, and offers an online directory of gay- and lesbian-friendly travel businesses; go to their website and click on "Members."

Many agencies offer tours and travel itineraries specifically for gay and lesbian travelers. **Above and Beyond Tours** (© 800/397-2681; www.abovebeyondtours.com) is the exclusive gay and lesbian tour operator for United Airlines. **Now, Voyager** (© 800/255-6951; www.nowvoyager.com) is a well-known San Francisco–based gay-owned and operated travel service. **Olivia Cruises & Resorts** (© 800/631-6277 or 510/655-0364; www.olivia.com) charters entire resorts and ships for exclusive lesbian vacations and offers smaller group experiences for both gay and lesbian travelers.

All over Manhattan, but especially in neighborhoods like the **West Village** (particularly Christopher St., famous the world over as the main drag of New York gay male life) and **Chelsea** (especially Eighth Ave., from 16th to 23rd sts., and W. 17th to 19th sts., from Fifth to Eighth aves.), shops, services, and restaurants have a lesbian and gay flavor. The **Oscar Wilde Bookshop,** 15 Christopher St. (✆ **212/255-8097;** www.oscarwilde books.com), is the city's best gay and lesbian bookstore, and a good source for information on the city's gay community. The **Lesbian and Gay Community Services Center** is at 208 W. 13th St., between Seventh and Eighth avenues (✆ **212/620-7310;** www.gaycenter.org). The center is the meeting place for more than 400 lesbian, gay, and bisexual organizations. You can check the online events calendar, which lists hundreds of happenings—lectures, dances, concerts, readings, films—or call for the latest. Their site offers links to additional gay-friendly hotels and guesthouses in and around New York, plus tons of other information; the staff is also exceedingly friendly and helpful in person or over the phone.

Other good sources for lesbian and gay events are *HX* (www.hx.com), the *New York Blade* (www.nyblade.com), *Next* (www.nextnyc.com), and the *Village Voice* (www.villagevoice.com)—all free weeklies that you can pick up in appropriate bars, clubs, stores, and sidewalk boxes throughout town. You'll also find lots of information on their corresponding websites. The glossy weekly *Time Out New York* (www.timeoutny.com) boasts a terrific gay and lesbian section. The Lesbian and Gay Community Services Center (see above) publishes a monthly guide listing dozens of events (also listed on its website).

In addition, there are lesbian and gay musical events, such as performances by the **New York City Gay Men's Chorus** (✆ **212/242-1777;** www.nycgmc.org); health programs sponsored by the **Gay Men's Health Crisis (GMHC;** ✆ **800/ AIDS-NYC** or 212/807-6655; www. gmhc.org); the **Gay & Lesbian National Hot Line** (✆ **212/989-0999;** www. glnh.org), offering peer counseling and information on upcoming events; and many other organizations.

The following travel guides are available at most travel bookstores and gay and lesbian bookstores, or you can order them from **Giovanni's Room** bookstore, 1145 Pine St., Philadelphia, PA 19107 (✆ **215/923-2960;** www.giovannisroom. com): *Frommer's Gay & Lesbian Europe,* an excellent travel resource; *Out and About* (✆ **800/929-2268** or 415/644-8044; www.outandabout.com), which offers guidebooks and a newsletter ($20/year; 10 issues) packed with solid information on the global gay and lesbian scene; *Spartacus International Gay Guide* (Bruno Gmünder Verlag; www.spartacusworld.com/gayguide/) and *Odysseus: The International Gay Travel Planner* (Odysseus Enterprises Ltd.), both good, annual English-language guidebooks focused on gay men; the *Damron* guides (www.damron.com), with separate, annual books for gay men and lesbians; and *Gay Travel A to Z: The World of Gay & Lesbian Travel Options at Your Fingertips* by Marianne Ferrari (Ferrari International; P.O. Box 35575, Phoenix, AZ 85069), a very good gay and lesbian guidebook series.

7 Planning Your Trip Online

SURFING FOR AIRFARES

The "big three" online travel agencies, **Expedia.com, Travelocity.com,** and **Orbitz.com** sell most of the air tickets bought on the Internet. (Canadian travelers should try expedia.ca and Travelocity.ca; U.K. residents can go to expedia.co.uk and opodo.co.uk.) Each has different business deals with the airlines and may offer different fares on the same flights, so it's wise to shop around. Expedia and Travelocity will also send you **e-mail notification** when a cheap fare becomes available to your favorite destination. Of the smaller travel agency websites, **SideStep** (www. sidestep.com) has gotten the best reviews from Frommer's authors. It's a browser add-on that purports to "search 140 sites at once," but in reality only beats competitors' fares as often as other sites do.

Also remember to check **airline websites,** especially those for low-fare carriers such as Southwest, JetBlue, AirTran, WestJet, or Ryanair, whose fares are often misreported or simply missing from travel agency websites. Even with major airlines, you can often shave a few bucks from a fare by booking directly through the airline and avoiding a travel agency's transaction fee. But you'll get these discounts only by **booking online:** Most airlines now offer online-only fares that even their phone agents know nothing about. For the websites of airlines that fly to and from your destination, go to "Getting There," p. 51.

Great **last-minute deals** are available through free weekly e-mail services provided directly by the airlines. Most of these are announced on Tuesday or Wednesday and must be purchased online. Most are only valid for travel that weekend, but some (such as Southwest's) can be booked weeks or months in advance. Sign up for weekly e-mail alerts at airline websites or check mega-sites that compile comprehensive lists of last-minute specials, such as **Smarter Travel** (www.smartertravel.com). For last-minute trips, **site59.com** and **last minutetravel.com** in the U.S. and **last minute.com** in Europe often have better air-and-hotel package deals than the major-label sites. A website listing numerous bargain sites and airlines around the world is **www.itravelnet.com**.

If you're willing to give up some control over your flight details, use what is called an **"opaque" fare service** like **Priceline** (www.priceline.com; www.priceline.co.uk for Europeans) or its smaller competitor **Hotwire** (www.hotwire.com). Both offer rock-bottom prices in exchange for travel on a "mystery airline" at a mysterious time of day, often with a mysterious change of planes en route. The mystery airlines are all major, well-known carriers—and the possibility of being sent from Philadelphia to Chicago via Tampa is remote; the airlines' routing computers have gotten a lot better than they used to be. But your chances of getting a 6am or 11pm flight are pretty high. Hotwire tells you flight prices before you buy; Priceline usually has better deals than Hotwire, but you have to play their "name your price" game. If you're new at this, the helpful folks at **BiddingForTravel** (www.bidding fortravel.com) do a good job of demystifying Priceline's prices and strategies. Priceline and Hotwire are great for flights within North America and between the U.S. and Europe. But for flights to other parts of the world, consolidators will almost always beat their fares. *Note:* In 2004 Priceline added non-opaque service to its roster. You now have the option to pick exact flights, times, and airlines from a list of offers—or opt to bid on opaque fares as before.

For much more about airfares and savvy air-travel tips and advice, pick up a copy of *Frommer's Fly Safe, Fly Smart* (Wiley Publishing, Inc.).

SURFING FOR HOTELS

Shopping online for hotels is generally done one of two ways: by booking through the hotel's own website or through an independent booking agency (or a fare-service agency like Priceline; see below). These Internet hotel agencies have multiplied in mind-boggling numbers of late, competing for the business of millions of consumers surfing for accommodations around the world. This competitiveness can be a boon to consumers who have the patience and time to shop and compare the online sites for good deals—but shop they must, for prices can vary considerably from site to site. And

Frommers.com: The Complete Travel Resource

For an excellent travel-planning resource, we highly recommend **Frommers.com** (www.frommers.com), voted Best Travel Site by *PC Magazine*. We're a little biased, of course, but we guarantee that you'll find the travel tips, reviews, monthly vacation giveaways, bookstore, and online-booking capabilities thoroughly indispensable. Among the special features are our popular **Destinations** section, where you'll get expert travel tips, hotel and dining recommendations, and advice on the sights to see for more than 3,500 destinations around the globe; the **Frommers.com Newsletter,** with the latest deals, travel trends, and money-saving secrets; our **Community** area featuring **Message Boards,** where Frommer's readers post queries and share advice (sometimes even our authors show up to answer questions); and our **Photo Center,** where you can post and share vacation tips. When your research is done, the **Online Reservations System** (www.frommers.com/book_a_trip) takes you to Frommer's preferred online partners for booking your vacation at affordable prices.

keep in mind that hotels at the top of a site's listing may be there for no other reason than that they paid money to get the placement.

Of the "big three" sites, **Expedia** offers a long list of special deals and "virtual tours" or photos of available rooms so you can see what you're paying for (a feature that helps counter the claims that the best rooms are often held back from bargain booking websites). **Travelocity** posts unvarnished customer reviews and ranks its properties according to the AAA rating system. Also reliable are **Hotels.com** and **Quikbook.com**. An excellent free program, **TravelAxe** (www.travelaxe.net), can help you search multiple hotel sites at once, even ones you may never have heard of—and conveniently lists the total price of the room, including the taxes and service charges. Another booking site, **Travelweb** (www.travelweb.com), is partly owned by the hotels it represents (including the Hilton, Hyatt, and Starwood chains) and is therefore plugged directly into the hotels' reservations systems—unlike independent online

agencies, which have to fax or e-mail reservation requests to the hotel, a good portion of which get misplaced in the shuffle. More than once, travelers have arrived at the hotel, only to be told that they have no reservation. To be fair, many of the major sites are undergoing improvements in service and ease of use, and Expedia will soon be able to plug directly into the reservations systems of many hotel chains—none of which can be bad news for consumers. In the meantime, it's a good idea to **get a confirmation number** and **make a printout** of any online booking transaction.

In the opaque website category, **Priceline** and **Hotwire** are even better for hotels than for airfares; with both, you're allowed to pick the neighborhood and quality level of your hotel before offering up your money. Priceline's hotel product even covers Europe and Asia, though it's much better at getting five-star lodging for three-star prices than at finding anything at the bottom of the scale. On the down side, many hotels stick Priceline guests in their least desirable rooms. Be sure to go to the BiddingforTravel website (see above) before bidding on a hotel room on Priceline; it features a fairly up-to-date list of hotels that Priceline uses in major cities. For both Priceline and Hotwire, you pay upfront, and the fee is nonrefundable. *Note:* Some hotels do not provide loyalty program credits or points or other frequent-stay amenities when you book a room through opaque online services.

The vast number of hotels in New York means that there's plenty of competition for your business, so sometimes the best place to find a deal is to go directly to the hotel's website.

8 The 21st-Century Traveler

INTERNET ACCESS AWAY FROM HOME

Travelers have any number of ways to check their e-mail and access the Internet on the road. Of course, using your own laptop—or even a PDA (personal digital assistant) or electronic organizer with a modem—gives you the most flexibility. But even if you don't have a computer, you can still access your e-mail and even your office computer from cybercafes.

WITHOUT YOUR OWN COMPUTER

It's hard nowadays to find a city that *doesn't* have a few cybercafes. Although there's no definitive directory for cyber-cafes—these are independent businesses, after all—two places to start looking are at **www.cybercaptive.com** and **www.cyber cafe.com**.

Aside from formal cybercafes, most **youth hostels** nowadays have at least one computer you can get to the Internet on. And most **public libraries** across the world offer Internet access free or for a small charge. Avoid **hotel business centers** unless you're willing to pay exorbitant rates.

Most major airports now have **Internet kiosks** scattered throughout their gates. These kiosks, which you'll also see in shopping malls, hotel lobbies, and tourist information offices around the world, give you basic Web access for a per-minute fee that's usually higher than cybercafe prices. The kiosks' clunkiness and high price means they should be avoided whenever possible.

To retrieve your e-mail, ask your **Internet Service Provider (ISP)** if it has a Web-based interface tied to your existing e-mail account. If your ISP doesn't have such an interface, you can use the free **mail2web** service (www.mail2web.com) to view your home e-mail. For more flexibility, you may want to open a free, Web-based e-mail account with **Yahoo! Mail** (http://mail.yahoo.com). (Microsoft's Hotmail is another popular option, but Hotmail has severe spam problems.) Your home ISP may be able to forward your e-mail to the Web-based account automatically.

If you need to access files on your office computer, look into a service called **GoToMyPC** (www.gotomypc.com). The service provides a Web-based interface for you to access and manipulate a distant PC from anywhere—even a cybercafe—provided your "target" PC is on and has an always-on connection to the Internet (such as with Road Runner cable). The service offers top-quality security, but if you're worried about hackers, use your own laptop rather than a cybercafe to access the GoToMyPC system.

WITH YOUR OWN COMPUTER

Wi-Fi (wireless fidelity) is the buzzword in computer access, and more and more hotels, cafes, and retailers are signing on as wireless "hot spots" from where you can get high-speed connection without cable wires, networking hardware, or a phone line (see below). You can get Wi-Fi connection one of several ways. Many

Where to Check Your E-mail in the City That Never Sleeps

The **Times Square Visitors Center,** 1560 Broadway, between 46th and 47th streets (© 212/768-1560; daily 8am–8pm), has computer terminals that you can use to send e-mails courtesy of Yahoo!; you can even send an electronic postcard with a photo of yourself home to Mom.

Open 24/7 in the heart of Times Square, **easyInternetCafé** ⚝, 235 W. 42nd St., between Seventh and Eighth avenues (© 212/398-0775; www.easy everything.com), is the first stateside branch of a worldwide web of Internet cafes. Boasting 15-inch flatscreen monitors and a superfast T-3 connection, this mammoth place makes accessing the Internet cheap through the economy of scale: Access is available for $1, and the length of access time that buck buys you fluctuates depending on the occupancy at the time you log on. This will generally work out to the cheapest Web time you can buy in the city.

CyberCafe (www.cyber-cafe.com)—in Times Square at 250 W. 49th St., between Broadway and Eighth Avenue (© 212/333-4109), and in SoHo at 273 Lafayette St., at Prince Street (© 212/334-5140)—is more expensive at $6.40 per half-hour, with a half-hour minimum (you're billed $3.20 for every subsequent 15 min.). But their T1 connectivity gives you superfast access, and they offer a full range of other cyber, copy, fax, and printing services.

FedEx Kinko's (www.kinkos.com) charges 30¢ per minute ($15 per hour) and is open at 100 Wall St., at Water Street (© 212/269-0024); near City Hall at 105 Duane St., between Broadway and Church Street (© 212/406-1220); 250 E. Houston St., between avenues A and B (© 212/253-9020); 21 Astor Place, between Broadway and Lafayette Street in the Village (© 212/228-9511); 245 Seventh Ave., at 24th Street (© 212/929-2679); 60 W. 40th St., between Fifth and Sixth avenues (© 212/921-1060); 221 W. 72nd St., at Broadway (© 212/362-5288); and about a billion other locations around town. If you want to do some advance planning, check the website for the location nearest your hotel before you leave home.

---

laptops sold in the last year have built-in Wi-Fi capability (an 802.11b wireless Ethernet connection). Mac owners have their own networking technology, Apple AirPort. For those with older computers, an 802.11b/**Wi-Fi card** (around $50) can be plugged into your laptop. You sign up for wireless access service much as you do cellphone service, through a plan offered by one of several commercial companies that have made wireless service available in airports, hotel lobbies, and coffee shops, primarily in the U.S. (followed by the U.K. and Japan). **T-Mobile Hotspot** (www.t-mobile.com/hotspot) serves up wireless connections at more than 1,000 Starbucks coffee shops nationwide. **Boingo** (www.boingo.com) and **Wayport** (www.wayport.com) have set up networks in airports and high-class hotel lobbies. IPass providers (see below) also give you access to a few hundred wireless hotel lobby setups. Best of all, you don't need to be staying at the Four Seasons to use the hotel's network; just set yourself up on a nice couch in the lobby. The companies' pricing policies can be byzantine, with a variety of monthly, per-connection, and per-minute plans, but in general you pay around $30 a month for limited access—and as more and more companies jump on the wireless bandwagon, prices are likely to get even more competitive.

There are also places that provide **free wireless networks** in cities around the world. To locate these free hotspots, go to www.personaltelco.net/index.cgi/WirelessCommunities.

If Wi-Fi is not available at your destination, most business-class hotels throughout the world offer dataports for laptop modems, and a few thousand hotels in the U.S. and Europe now offer free high-speed Internet access using an Ethernet network cable. You can bring your own cables, but most hotels rent them for around $10. **Call your hotel in advance** to see what your options are.

In addition, major Internet Service Providers (ISP) have **local access numbers** around the world, allowing you to go online by simply placing a local call. Check your ISP's website or call its toll-free number and ask how you can use your current account away from home, and how much it will cost.

If you're traveling outside the reach of your ISP, the **iPass** network has dial-up numbers in most of the world's countries. You'll have to sign up with an iPass provider, who will then tell you how to set up your computer for your destination(s). For a list of iPass providers, go to www.ipass.com and click on "Individual Purchase." One solid provider is **i2roam** (www.i2roam.com; ✆ **866/811-6209** or 920/235-0475).

Wherever you go, bring a **connection kit** of the right power and phone adapters, a spare phone cord, and a spare Ethernet network cable—or find out whether your hotel supplies them to guests.

USING A CELLPHONE
ACROSS THE U.S.

Just because your cellphone works at home doesn't mean it'll work elsewhere in the country (thanks to our nation's fragmented cellphone system). It's a good bet that your phone will work in major cities. But take a look at your wireless company's coverage map on its website before

---

Digital Photography on the Road

Many travelers are going digital these days when it comes to taking vacation photographs. Not only are digital cameras left relatively unscathed by airport X-rays, but with digital equipment you don't need to lug armloads of film with you as you travel. In fact, nowadays you don't even need to carry your laptop to download the day's images to make room for more. With a **media storage card,** sold by all major camera dealers, you can store hundreds of images in your camera. These "memory" cards come in different configurations—from memory sticks to flash cards to secure digital cards—and different storage capacities (the more megabytes of memory, the more images a card can hold) and range in price from $30 to over $200. (**Note:** Each camera model works with a specific type of card, so you'll need to determine which storage card is compatible with your camera.) When you get home, you can print the images out on your own color printer or take the storage card to a camera store, drugstore, or chain retailer. Or have the images developed online with a service like **Snapfish** (www.snapfish.com) for something like 25¢ a shot. See "Flying with Film & Video," p. 60.

Online Traveler's Toolbox

Veteran travelers usually carry some essential items to make their trips easier. Following is a selection of handy online tools to bookmark and use.

- **Airplane Seating and Food.** Find out which seats to reserve and which to avoid (and more) on all major domestic airlines at www.seatguru.com. And check out the type of meal (with photos) you'll likely be served on airlines around the world at www.airlinemeals.com.
- **Visa ATM Locator** (www.visa.com), for locations of PLUS ATMs worldwide, or **MasterCard ATM Locator** (www.mastercard.com), for locations of Cirrus ATMs worldwide.
- **Intellicast** (www.intellicast.com) and **Weather.com** (www.weather.com). Gives weather forecasts for all 50 states and for cities around the world.
- **Mapquest** (www.mapquest.com). This best of the mapping sites lets you choose a specific address or destination, and in seconds, it will return a map and detailed directions.
- **Subway Navigator** (www.subwaynavigator). Download subway maps and get savvy advice on using subway systems in dozens of major cities around the world.
- **Time and Date** (www.timeanddate.com). See what time (and day) it is anywhere in the world.
- **Entertainment** *New York* magazine's website (www.nymetro.com) and the free weekly newspaper's website (www.villagevoice.com) have good coverage of arts and events.

heading out—T-Mobile, Sprint, and Nextel are particularly weak in rural areas. If you need to stay in touch at a destination where you know your phone won't work, **rent** a phone that does from **InTouch USA** (© 800/872-7626; www.intouchglobal.com) or a rental-car location, but be aware that you'll pay $1 a minute or more for airtime.

If you're venturing deep into national parks, you may want to consider renting a **satellite phone ("satphones"),** which are different from cellphones in that they connect to satellites rather than ground-based towers. A satphone is more costly than a cellphone but works where there's no cellular signal and no towers. Unfortunately, you'll pay at least $2 per minute to use the phone, and it only works where you can see the horizon (that is, usually

not indoors). In North America, you can rent Iridium satellite phones from **Road-Post** (www.roadpost.com; © 888/290-1606 or 905/272-5665). InTouch USA (see above) offers a wider range of satphones but at higher rates.

If you're not from the U.S., you'll be appalled at the poor reach of our **GSM (Global System for Mobiles) wireless network,** which is used by much of the rest of the world (see below). Your phone will probably work in most major U.S. cities; it definitely won't work in many rural areas. (To see where GSM phones work in the U.S., check out www.t-mobile.com/coverage/national_popup.asp.) And you may or may not be able to send SMS (text messaging) home—something Americans tend not to do anyway, for various cultural and technological reasons. (International budget travelers like to send text messages home because it's much cheaper than making international calls.) Assume nothing—call your wireless provider and get the full scoop. In a worst-case scenario, you can always rent a phone; InTouch USA delivers to hotels.

9 Getting There

BY PLANE

Three major airports serve New York City: **John F. Kennedy International Airport** (© 718/244-4444) in Queens, about 15 miles (1 hr. driving time) from Midtown Manhattan; **LaGuardia Airport** (© 718/533-3400), also in Queens, about 8 miles (30 min.) from Midtown; and **Newark International Airport** (© 973/961-6000) in nearby New Jersey, about 16 miles (45 min.) from Midtown. Information about all three airports is available online at **www. panynj.gov**; click on the "All Airports" tab on the left.

Even though LaGuardia is the closest airport to Manhattan, it has a hideous reputation for flight delays and terminal chaos, in both ticket-desk lines and baggage claim. Hopefully, airport officials will have rectified the problems by the time you fly, but you may want to use JFK or Newark instead. (JFK has the best reputation for timeliness among New York–area airports.)

Almost every major domestic carrier serves at least one of the New York–area airports; most serve two or all three. Among them are **America West** (© 800/327-7810; www.americawest. com), **American** (© 817/967-2000; www. aa.com), **Continental** (© 800/525-3273; www.continental.com), **Delta** (© 800/ 221-1212; www.delta.com), **Northwest** (© 800/225-2525; www.nwa.com), **US Airways** (© 800/428-4322; www.us airways.com), and **United** (© 800/864-8331; www.united.com).

In recent years, there has been rapid growth in the number of start-up, no-frills airlines serving New York. You might check out Atlanta-based **AirTran** (© 800/AIRTRAN; www.airtran.com); Chicago-based **ATA** (© 800/225-2995; www.ata.com); Denver-based **Frontier** (© 800/432-1359; www.flyfrontier.com); Milwaukee- and Omaha-based **Midwest Airlines** (© 800/452-2022; www. midwestairlines.com); or Detroit-based **Spirit Airlines** (© 800/772-7117; www. spiritair.com). The JFK-based cheap-chic airline **jetBlue** ✈ (© 800/JETBLUE; www.jetblue.com) has taken New York by storm with its low fares and classy service to cities throughout the nation. The nation's leading discount airline, **Southwest** (© 800/435-9792; www.iflyswa. com), flies into MacArthur (Islip) Airport on Long Island, 50 miles east of Manhattan.

Tips Choosing Your NYC–Area Airport

It's more convenient to fly into Newark than Kennedy if your destination is Manhattan, and consider that fares to Newark are often cheaper than those to the other airports. Newark is particularly convenient if your hotel is in Midtown West or downtown. Taxi fare into Manhattan from Newark is roughly equivalent to the fare from JFK—both airports now have AirTrains in place (see "Transportation to & from the New York–Area Airports," below), but the AirTrain to Newark from Manhattan is quicker.

Most major international carriers also serve New York; see chapter 4, "For International Visitors," for details.

TRANSPORTATION TO & FROM THE NEW YORK–AREA AIRPORTS

Since there's no need to rent a car in New York, you're going to have to figure out how you want to get from the airport to your hotel and back.

For complete transportation information for all three airports (JFK, LaGuardia, and Newark), call **Air-Ride** (© 800/247-7433), which offers recorded details on bus and shuttle companies and private car services registered with the New York and New Jersey Port Authority 24 hours a day. Similar information is available at **www.panynj.gov/airports**; just click on the airport at which you'll be arriving.

The Port Authority also runs staffed Ground Transportation Information counters on the baggage-claim level in each terminal at each airport, where you can get information and book on all manner of transport once you land. Most transportation companies also have courtesy phones near the baggage-claim area.

Generally, travel time between the airports and Midtown Manhattan by taxi or car is 45 to 60 minutes for JFK, 20 to 35 minutes for LaGuardia, and 35 to 50 minutes for Newark. Always allow extra time, though, especially during rush hour, peak holiday travel times, and if you're taking a bus.

SUBWAYS & PUBLIC BUSES For the most part, your best bet is to stay away from the MTA when traveling to and from the airport. You might save a few dollars, but subways and buses that currently serve the airports involve multiple transfers, and you'll have to drag your luggage up and down staircases. On some subways, you'd be traveling through undesirable neighborhoods. Spare yourself the drama.

The only exception to this rule that I feel somewhat comfortable with is the subway service to and from JFK, which connects with the new AirTrain (see the box "AirTrains: Newark & JFK—The Very Good & the Not-So-Very Good," below). The subway can actually be more reliable than taking a car or taxi at the height of rush hour, but *a few words of warning:* This isn't the right option for you if you're bringing more than a single piece of luggage or if you have a sizable family in tow, since there's a good amount of walking and some stairs involved in the trip, and you'll have nowhere to put all those bags on the subway train. And *do not* use this method if you're traveling to or from the airport after dark or too early in the morning—it's just not safe. For additional subway information, see "Getting Around," in chapter 6.

TAXIS Despite significant rate hikes in 2004, taxis are still a quick and convenient way to travel to and from the airports. They're available at designated taxi stands outside the terminals, with uniformed dispatchers on hand during peak hours at JFK and LaGuardia, around the clock at Newark. Follow the GROUND TRANSPORTATION or TAXI signs. There may be a long line, but it generally moves pretty quickly. Fares, whether fixed or metered, do not include bridge and tunnel tolls ($3.50–$4) or a tip for the cabbie (15%–20% is customary). They do include all passengers in the cab and luggage—never pay more than the metered or flat rate, except for tolls and a tip (from 8pm–6am, a $1 surcharge also applies on New York yellow cabs). Taxis have a limit of four passengers, so if there are more in your group, you'll have to take more than one cab. For more on taxis, see "Getting Around," in chapter 6.

- **From JFK:** A flat rate of $45 to Manhattan (plus tolls and tip) is charged. The meter will not be turned on and the surcharge will not be added. The

An Airport Warning

Never accept a car ride from the hustlers who hang out in the terminal halls. They're illegal, don't have proper insurance, and aren't safe. You can tell who they are because they'll approach you with a suspicious conspiratorial air and ask if you need a ride. Not from them, you don't. Sanctioned city cabs and car services wait outside the terminals.

flat rate does not apply on trips from Manhattan to the airport.

- **From LaGuardia:** $17 to $27, metered, plus tolls and tip.
- **From Newark:** The dispatcher for New Jersey taxis gives you a slip of paper with a flat rate ranging from $30 to $38 (toll and tip extra), depending on where you're going in Manhattan, so you'll have to be precise about your destination. New York yellow cabs aren't permitted to pick up passengers at Newark. The yellow-cab fare from Manhattan to Newark is the meter amount plus $15 and tolls (about $45–$55, perhaps a few dollars more with tip). New Jersey taxis aren't permitted to take passengers from Manhattan to Newark.

PRIVATE CAR & LIMOUSINE SERVICES Private car and limousine companies provide convenient 24-hour door-to-door airport transfers for roughly the same cost of a taxi. The advantage they offer over taking a taxi is that you can arrange your pickup in advance and avoid the hassles of the taxi line. Call at least 24 hours in advance (even earlier on holidays), and a driver will meet you near baggage claim (or at your hotel for a return trip). You'll probably be asked to leave a credit card number to guarantee your ride. You'll likely be offered the choice of indoor or curbside pickup; indoor pickup is more expensive, but makes it easier to hook up with your driver (who usually waits in baggage claim bearing a sign with your name on

it). You can save a few dollars if you arrange for an outside pickup; call the dispatcher as soon as you clear baggage claim and then take your luggage out to the designated waiting area, where you'll wait for the driver to come around, which can take anywhere from 10 minutes to a half-hour. Besides the wait, the other disadvantage of this option is that curbside can be chaos during prime deplaning hours.

Vehicles range from sedans to vans to limousines and tend to be relatively clean and comfortable. Prices vary slightly by company and the size of car reserved, but expect a rate roughly equivalent to taxi fare if you request a basic sedan and have only one stop; toll and tip policies are the same. (**Note:** Car services are not subject to the flat-rate rule that taxis have for rides to and from JFK.) Ask when booking what the fare will be and if you can use your credit card to pay for the ride so there are no surprises at drop-off time. There may be waiting charges tacked on if the driver has to wait an excessive amount of time for your plane to land when picking you up, but the car companies will usually check on your flight beforehand to get an accurate landing time.

I've had the best luck with **Carmel** (© **800/922-7635** or 212/666-6666) and **Legends** (© **888/LEGENDS** or 888/534-3637; www.legendslimousine. com); **Allstate** (© **800/453-4099** or 212/333-3333) and **Tel-Aviv** (© **800/ 222-9888** or 212/777-7777) also have reasonable reputations. (Keep in mind,

AirTrains: Newark & JFK—The Very Good & the Not-So-Very Good

First the very good: A few years back, a new rail link revolutionized the process of connecting by public transportation to New York's notoriously underserved airport: the brand-new **AirTrain Newark,** which now connects Newark Airport with Manhattan via a speedy monorail/rail link.

Even though you have to make a connection, the system is fast, pleasant, affordable, and easy to use. Each arrivals terminal at Newark Airport has a boarding station for the AirTrain, so just follow the signs once you collect your bags. All AirTrains head to **Newark International Airport Station,** where you transfer to a **NJ Transit** train. NJ Transit will deliver you directly to New York Penn Station at 33rd Street and Seventh Avenue, where you can pick up a cab to your hotel.

The trip from my apartment on Manhattan's Upper West Side to the Newark Alitalia terminal was under a half-hour and only cost me $14 ($12 for the AirTrain link via Penn Station plus $2 for the subway to get to Penn Station). That's a savings of at least $35 if I took a cab, not to mention the time I saved. NJ Transit trains run 2 to 3 times an hour during peak travel times (once an hour during early and late hours); you can check the schedules on monitors before you leave the airport terminal, and again at the train station. Tickets can be purchased from vending machines at both the air terminal and the train station (no ticket is required to board the Air-Train). The one-way fare is $11 (children under 5 ride free). (On your return trip to the airport, the AirTrain is far more predictable, time-wise, than subjecting yourself to the whims of traffic.)

Note that travelers heading to points beyond the city can also pick up Amtrak and other NJ Transit trains at Newark International Airport Station to their final destination.

though, that these services are only as good as the individual drivers—and sometimes there's a lemon in the bunch. If you have a problem, report it immediately to the main office.)

These car services are good for rush hour (no ticking meters in rush-hour traffic), but if you're arriving at a quieter time of day, taxis work fine.

PRIVATE BUSES & SHUTTLES

Buses and shuttle services provide a comfortable and less expensive (but usually more time-consuming) option for airport transfers than do taxis and car services.

Super Shuttle serves all three airports; **New York Airport Service** serves JFK and LaGuardia; **Olympia Trails and Express Shuttle USA** serves Newark. These services are my favorite option for getting to and from Newark during peak travel times because the drivers usually take lesser-known surface streets that make the ride much quicker than if you go with a taxi or car, which will virtually always stick to the traffic-clogged main route.

The familiar blue vans of **Super Shuttle** (© 212/258-3826; www.supershuttle.

Now the not so very good: After years of anticipation and $1.9 billion, AirTrain JFK opened late in 2003. Though you can't beat the price—$7 if you take a subway to the AirTrain, $12 if you take Long Island Rail Road—you won't save much on time getting to the airport. From Midtown Manhattan, the ride is approximately 90 minutes and the connections are murky. Only a few lines connect with the AirTrain: the A, E, J, and Z; the E, J, Z to Jamaica Station and Sutphin Blvd.–Archer Ave. Station, and the A to Howard Beach/JFK Airport Station. The MTA is working hard to clear up the confusion, and though they are contemplating adding connections to the AirTrain in Lower Manhattan sometime in the next decade, there's not much they can do now to speed up the trip

A word of warning for both AirTrains: If you have mobility issues, mountains of luggage that will make connections difficult, or a bevy of small children to keep track of, skip the AirTrain. You'll find it easier to rely on a taxi, car service, or shuttle service that can offer you door-to-door transfers.

For more information on AirTrain Newark, call ✆ **888/EWR-INFO** or go online to **www.airtrainnewark.com**. For connection details, click on the links on the AirTrain website or contact **NJ Transit** (✆ **800/626-RIDE; www.njtransit.com**) or **Amtrak** (✆ **800/USA-RAIL; www.amtrak.com**).

For more information on AirTrain JFK, go online to www.airtrainjfk.com. For connection details, click on the links on the AirTrain website or the MTA site, www.mta.nyc.ny.us/mta/airtrain.htm.

com) serve all three area airports, providing door-to-door service to Manhattan and points on Long Island every 15 to 30 minutes around the clock. As with Express Shuttle, you don't need to reserve your airport-to-Manhattan ride; just go to the ground-transportation desk or use the courtesy phone in baggage claim and ask for Super Shuttle. Hotel pickups for your return trip require 24 to 48 hours' notice; you can make your reservations online. Fares run $15 to $19 per person, depending on the airport, with discounts available for additional persons in the same party.

New York Airport Service (✆ **718/ 875-8200;** www.nyairportservice.com) buses travel from JFK and LaGuardia to the Port Authority Bus Terminal (42nd St. and Eighth Ave.), Grand Central Terminal (Park Ave. between 41st and 42nd sts.), and to select Midtown hotels between 27th and 59th streets, plus the Jamaica LIRR Station in Queens, where you can pick up a train for Long Island. Follow the GROUND TRANSPORTATION signs to the curbside pickup or look for the uniformed agent. Buses depart the airport every 20 to 70 minutes (depending on your departure point and destination)

If You're Flying into Islip Airport on Southwest

Southwest Airlines flies into the New York area via Long Island's Islip MacArthur Airport, 50 miles east of Manhattan. If you're on one of these flights, here are your options for getting into the city:

Colonial Transportation (℗ 631/589-3500; www.colonialtransportation.com), **Classic Transportation** (℗ 631/567-5100; www.classictrans.com), and **Legends** (℗ 888/LEGENDS or 888/534-3637; www.legendslimousine.com) will pick you up at Islip Airport and deliver you to Manhattan via private sedan, but expect to pay about $125 plus tolls and tip for door-to-door service. Be sure to arrange for it at least 24 hours in advance.

For a fraction of the cost, you can catch a ride aboard a **Hampton Jitney** coach (℗ 631/283-4600; www.hamptonjitney.com) to various drop-off points on Midtown's east side. The cost is $27 per person, plus a minimal taxi fare from the terminal to the Hampton Jitney stop. Hampton Jitney can explain the details and arrange for taxi transport.

Colonial Transportation (℗ 631/589-3500; www.colonialtransportation.com) also offers regular shuttle service that traverses the 3 miles from the airport to the Ronkonkoma Long Island Rail Road Station, where you can pick up an LIRR (Long Island Rail Road) train to Manhattan. The shuttle fare is $5 per person, $1 for each additional family member accompanying a full-fare customer. From Ronkonkoma, it's about a 1½-hour train ride to Manhattan's Penn Station; the one-way fare is $12 at peak hours, $8.25 off-peak (half-fare for seniors 65 or older and kids 5–11). You can also catch the Suffolk County Transit bus S-57 between the airport and the station daily except Sundays for $1.50. Trains usually leave Ronkonkoma once or twice every hour, depending on the day and time. For more information, call ℗ 718/217-LIRR or visit **www.mta.nyc.ny.us/lirr**.

For additional options and the latest information, call **631/467-3210** or visit **www.macarthurairport.com**.

---

between 6am and midnight. Buses to JFK and LaGuardia depart the Port Authority and Grand Central Terminal on the Park Avenue side every 15 to 30 minutes, depending on the time of day and the day of the week. To request direct shuttle service from your hotel, call the above number at least 24 hours in advance. One-way fare for JFK is $15, $27 round-trip; to LaGuardia it's $12 one way and $21 round-trip.

Olympia Airport Express (℗ 212/964-6233; www.olympiabus.com) provides service every 15 to 30 minutes (depending on the time of day) from Newark Airport to Penn Station (the pickup point is the northwest corner of 34th St. and Eighth Ave., and the drop-off point is the southwest corner), the Port Authority Bus Terminal (on 42nd St. between Eighth and Ninth aves.), and Grand Central Terminal (on 41st St. between Park and Lexington aves.). Passengers to and from the Grand Central Terminal location can connect to Olympia's Midtown shuttle vans, which service select Midtown hotels. Call for the exact schedule for your return trip to the airport. The one-way fare runs $12, $20 round-trip; seniors and passengers with disabilities ride for $6.

Getting to the Other Boroughs & 'Burbs

If you're traveling to a borough other than Manhattan, call **ETS Air Service** (📞 **718/221-5341**) for shared door-to-door service. For Long Island service, call **Classic Transportation** (📞 **631/567-5100**; www.classictrans.com) for car service, or **JFK Flyer** (📞 **516/766-6722**) for bus service. For service to Westchester County or Connecticut, contact **Connecticut Limousine** (📞 **800/472-5466** or 203/878-2222; www.ctlimo.com) or **Prime Time Shuttle of Connecticut** (📞 **800/ 377-8745**; www.primetimeshuttle.com).

If you're traveling to points in New Jersey from Newark Airport, call **Olympic Limousine** (📞 **800/822-9797** or 732/938-4300) for Ocean and Monmouth counties; the **Airporter** (📞 **800/385-4000** or 609/587-6600; www.goairporter.com) to Middlesex and Mercer counties, plus Bucks County, Pennsylvania; or **State Shuttle** (📞 **800/427-3207** or 973/729-0030; www.stateshuttle.com) for destinations throughout New Jersey.

Additionally, **New York Airport Service** express buses (📞 **718/875-8200**; www.nyairportservice.com) serve the entire New York metropolitan region from JFK and LaGuardia, offering connections to the Long Island Rail Road; the Metro-North Railroad to Westchester County, upstate New York, and Connecticut; and New York's Port Authority, where you can pick up buses to points throughout New Jersey.

GETTING THROUGH THE AIRPORT

With the federalization of airport security, security procedures at U.S. airports are more stable and consistent than ever. Generally, you'll be fine if you arrive at the airport **1 hour** before a domestic flight and **2 hours** before an international flight; if you show up late, tell an airline employee and she or he will probably whisk you to the front of the line.

Bring a **current, government-issued photo ID** such as a driver's license or passport. Keep your ID at the ready to show at check-in, the security checkpoint, and sometimes even the gate. (Children under 18 do not need government-issued photo IDs for domestic flights, but they do for international flights to most countries.)

In 2003, the Transportation Security Administration (TSA) phased out **gate check-in** at all U.S. airports. And **e-tickets** have made paper tickets nearly obsolete. Passengers with e-tickets can beat the ticket-counter lines by using airport **electronic kiosks** or even **online check-in** from your home computer. Online check-in involves logging on to your airlines' website, accessing your reservation, and printing out your boarding pass—and the airline may even offer you bonus miles to do so! If you're using a kiosk at the airport, bring the credit card you used to book the ticket or your frequent-flier card. Print out your boarding pass from the kiosk and simply proceed to the security checkpoint with your pass and a photo ID. If you're checking bags or looking to snag an exit-row seat, you will be able to do so using most airline kiosks. Even the smaller airlines are employing the kiosk system, but always call your airline to make sure these alternatives are available. **Curbside check-in** is also a good way to avoid lines, although a few airlines still ban curbside check-in; call before you go.

Security checkpoint lines are getting shorter than they were during 2001 and

2002, but some doozies remain. If you have trouble standing for long periods of time, tell an airline employee; the airline will provide a wheelchair. Speed up security by **not wearing metal objects** such as big belt buckles. If you've got metallic body parts, a note from your doctor can prevent a long chat with the security screeners. Keep in mind that only **ticketed passengers** are allowed past security, except for folks escorting passengers with disabilities or children.

Federalization has stabilized **what you can carry on** and **what you can't.** The general rule is that sharp things are out, nail clippers are okay, and food and beverages must be passed through the X-ray machine—but that security screeners can't make you drink from your coffee cup. Bring food in your carry-on rather than checking it, as explosive-detection machines used on checked luggage have been known to mistake food (especially chocolate, for some reason) for bombs. Travelers in the U.S. are allowed one carry-on bag, plus a "personal item" such as a purse, briefcase, or laptop bag. Carry-on hoarders can stuff all sorts of things into a laptop bag; as long as it has a laptop in it, it's still considered a personal item. The TSA has issued a list of restricted items; check its website (www.tsa.gov/public/index.jsp) for details.

Airport screeners may decide that your checked luggage needs to be searched by hand. You can now purchase luggage locks that allow screeners to open and re-lock a checked bag if hand-searching is necessary. Look for Travel Sentry certified locks at luggage or travel shops and Brookstone stores (you can buy them online at www.brookstone.com). These locks, approved by the TSA, can be opened by luggage inspectors with a special code or key. For more information on the locks, visit www.travelsentry.org. If you use something other than TSA-approved locks, your lock will be cut off your suitcase if a TSA agent needs to hand-search your luggage.

FLYING FOR LESS: TIPS FOR GETTING THE BEST AIRFARE

Passengers sharing the same airplane cabin rarely pay the same fare. Travelers who need to purchase tickets at the last minute, change their itinerary at a moment's notice, or fly one-way often get stuck paying the premium rate. Here are some ways to keep your airfare costs down.

- Passengers who can book their ticket **long in advance,** who can **stay over Saturday night,** or who **fly midweek** or **at less-trafficked hours** may pay a fraction of the full fare. If your

---

Tips Don't Stow It—Ship It

If ease of travel is your main concern and money is no object, you can ship your luggage and sports equipment with one of the growing number of luggage-service companies that pick up, track, and deliver your luggage (often through couriers such as Federal Express) with minimum hassle for you. Traveling luggage-free may be ultraconvenient, but it's not cheap: One-way overnight shipping can cost from $100 to $200, depending on what you're sending. Still, for some people, especially the elderly or the infirm, it's a sensible solution to lugging heavy baggage. Specialists in door-to-door luggage delivery are **Virtual Bellhop** (www.virtualbellhop.com), **SkyCap International** (wwww.skycapinternational.com), **Luggage Express** (www.usxpluggageexpress.com), and **Sports Express** (www.sportsexpress.com).

Travel in the Age of Bankruptcy

Airlines go bankrupt, so protect yourself by **buying your tickets with a credit card,** as the Fair Credit Billing Act guarantees that you can get your money back from the credit card company if a travel supplier goes under (and if you request the refund within 60 days of the bankruptcy). **Travel insurance** can also help, but make sure it covers against "carrier default" for your specific travel provider. And be aware that if a U.S. airline goes bust mid-trip, a 2001 federal law requires other carriers to take you to your destination (albeit on a space-available basis) for a fee of no more than $25, provided you rebook within 60 days of the cancellation.

schedule is flexible, say so, and ask if you can secure a cheaper fare by changing your flight plans.

- You can also save on airfares by keeping an eye out in local newspapers for **promotional specials** or **fare wars,** when airlines lower prices on their most popular routes. You rarely see fare wars offered for peak travel times, but if you can travel in the off-months, you may snag a bargain.
- Search **the Internet** for cheap fares (see "Planning Your Trip Online," earlier in this chapter).
- **Consolidators,** also known as bucket shops, are great sources for international tickets, although they usually can't beat the Internet on fares within North America. Start by looking in Sunday newspaper travel sections; U.S. travelers should focus on the *New York Times, Los Angeles Times,* and *Miami Herald.* For less-developed destinations, small travel agents who cater to immigrant communities in large cities often have the best deals. *Beware:* Bucket shop tickets are usually nonrefundable or rigged with stiff cancellation penalties, often as high as 50% to 75% of the ticket price, and some put you on charter airlines, which may leave at inconvenient times and experience delays. Several reliable consolidators are worldwide and available on the Net. **STA Travel** is now the world's leader

in student travel, thanks to their purchase of Council Travel. It also offers good fares for travelers of all ages. **ELTExpress (Flights.com)** (© 800/TRAV-800;   www.eltexpress.com) started in Europe and has excellent fares worldwide, but particularly to that continent. It also has "local" websites in 12 countries. **FlyCheap** (© 800/FLY-CHEAP; www.1800fly cheap.com) is owned by package-holiday megalith MyTravel and so has especially good access to fares for sunny destinations. **Air Tickets Direct** (© 800/778-3447; www.air ticketsdirect.com) is based in Montréal and leverages the currently weak Canadian dollar for low fares; it'll also book trips to places that U.S. travel agents won't touch, such as Cuba.

I've gotten great deals on many occasions from **Cheap Tickets** (© 888/922-8849; www.cheap tickets.com) and **Council Travel** (© 800/226-8624; www.council travel.com). **The TravelHub** (© 888/AIR-FARE;   www.travelhub.com) represents nearly 1,000 travel agencies, many of whom offer consolidator and discount fares. Other reliable consolidators include **TFI Tours** (© 800/745-8000 or 212/736-1140; www.lowestairprice.com),   which serves as a clearinghouse for unused seats.

Flying with Film & Video

Never pack film—developed or undeveloped—in checked bags, as the new, more powerful scanners in U.S. airports can fog film. The film you carry with you can be damaged by scanners as well. X-ray damage is cumulative; the faster the film, and the more times you put it through a scanner, the more likely the damage. Film under 800 ASA is usually safe for up to five scans. If you're taking your film through additional scans, U.S. regulations permit you to demand hand inspections. In international airports, you're at the mercy of airport officials. On international flights, store your film in transparent baggies, so you can remove it easily before you go through scanners. Keep in mind that airports are not the only places where your camera may be scanned: Highly trafficked attractions are X-raying visitors' bags with increasing frequency.

Most photo supply stores sell protective pouches designed to block damaging X-rays. The pouches fit both film and loaded cameras. They should protect your film in checked baggage, but they also may raise alarms and result in a hand inspection.

You'll have little to worry about if you are traveling with **digital cameras.** Unlike film, which is sensitive to light, the digital camera and storage cards are not affected by airport X-rays, according to Nikon. Still, if you plan to travel extensively, you may want to play it safe and hand-carry your digital equipment or ask that it be inspected by hand. See "Digital Photography on the Road," p. 49.

Carry-on scanners will not damage **videotape** in video cameras, but the magnetic fields emitted by the walk-through security gateways and hand-held inspection wands will. Always place your loaded camcorder on the screening conveyor belt or have it hand-inspected. Be sure your batteries are charged, as you will probably be required to turn the device on to ensure that it's what it appears to be.

- Join **frequent-flier clubs.** Accrue enough miles, and you'll be rewarded with free flights and elite status. It's free, and you'll get the best choice of seats, faster response to phone inquiries, and prompter service if your luggage is stolen, your flight is canceled or delayed, or if you want to change your seat. You don't need to fly to build frequent-flier miles—**frequent-flier credit cards** can provide thousands of miles for doing your everyday shopping.
- For many more tips about air travel, including a rundown of the major

frequent-flier credit cards, pick up a copy of *Frommer's Fly Safe, Fly Smart* (Wiley Publishing Inc.).

BY CAR

From the **New Jersey Turnpike** (I-95) and points west, there are three Hudson River crossings into the city's west side: the **Holland Tunnel** (lower Manhattan), the **Lincoln Tunnel** (Midtown), and the **George Washington Bridge** (upper Manhattan).

From **upstate New York,** take the **New York State Thruway** (I-87), which crosses the Hudson on the Tappan Zee Bridge and becomes the **Major Deegan Expressway** (I-87) through the Bronx. For the east side, continue to the Triborough Bridge and then down the FDR Drive. For the west side, take the Cross Bronx Expressway (I-95) to the Henry Hudson Parkway or the Taconic State Parkway to the Saw Mill River Parkway to the Henry Hudson Parkway south.

From **New England,** the **New England Thruway** (I-95) connects with the **Bruckner Expressway** (I-278), which leads to the Triborough Bridge and the FDR Drive on the east side. For the west side, take the Bruckner to the Cross Bronx Expressway (I-95) to the Henry Hudson Parkway south.

Note that you'll have to pay tolls along some of these roads and at most crossings.

Once you arrive in Manhattan, park your car in a garage (expect to pay $20–$45 per day) and leave it there. Don't use your car for traveling within the city. Public transportation, taxis, and walking will easily get you where you want to go without the headaches of parking, gridlock, and dodging crazy cabbies.

BY TRAIN

Amtrak (© **800/USA-RAIL;** www. amtrak.com) runs frequent service to New York City's **Penn Station,** on Seventh Avenue between 31st and 33rd streets, where you can easily pick up a taxi, subway, or bus to your hotel. To get the best rates, book early (as much as 6 months in advance) and travel on weekends.

If you're traveling to New York from a city along Amtrak's Northeast Corridor—such as Boston, Philadelphia, Baltimore, or Washington, D.C.—Amtrak may be your best travel bet now that they've rolled out their new high-speed Acela trains, which will have replaced all the old Metroliners by the time you read this. The Acela Express trains cut travel time from D.C. down to 2½ hours, and travel time from Boston to a lightning-quick 3 hours.

10 Packages for the Independent Traveler

Before you start your search for the lowest airfare, you may want to consider booking your flight as part of a travel package. Package tours are not the same thing as escorted tours. Package tours are simply a way to buy the airfare, accommodations, and other elements of your trip (such as car rentals, airport transfers, and sometimes even activities) at the same time and often at discounted prices—kind of like one-stop shopping. Packages are sold in bulk to tour operators—who resell them to the public at a cost that usually undercuts standard rates.

One good source of package deals is the airlines themselves. Most major airlines offer air/land packages, including **American Airlines Vacations** (© 800/ 321-2121; www.aavacations.com), **Delta Vacations** (© 800/221-6666; www.delta vacations.com), **Continental Airlines Vacations** (© 800/301-3800; www.co vacations.com), and **United Vacations** (© 888/854-3899; www.unitedvacations. com). Several big **online travel agencies**—Expedia, Travelocity, Orbitz, Site59, and Lastminute.com—also do a brisk business in packages. If you're unsure about the pedigree of a smaller packager, check with the Better Business Bureau in the city where the company is based, or go online at www.bbb.org. If a packager won't tell you where they're based, don't fly with them.

Travel packages are also listed in the travel section of your local Sunday newspaper. Or check ads in the national travel magazines such as *Arthur Frommer's Budget Travel Magazine, Travel & Leisure,*

National Geographic Traveler, and *Condé Nast Traveler.*

Package tours can vary by leaps and bounds. Some offer a better class of hotels than others. Some offer the same hotels for lower prices. Some offer flights on scheduled airlines, while others book charters. Some limit your choice of accommodations and travel days. You are often required to make a large payment up front. On the plus side, packages can save you money, offering group prices but allowing for independent travel. Some even let you add on a few guided excursions or escorted day trips (also at prices lower than if you booked them yourself) without booking an entirely escorted tour.

Before you invest in a package tour, get some answers. Ask about the **accommodations choices** and prices for each. Then look up the hotels' reviews in a Frommer's guide and check their rates online for your specific dates of travel online. Finally, look for **hidden expenses.** Ask whether airport departure fees and taxes, for example, are included in the total cost.

11 Escorted General-Interest Tours

Escorted tours are structured group tours, with a group leader. The price usually includes everything from airfare to hotels, meals, tours, admission costs, and local transportation.

Many people derive a certain ease and security from escorted trips. Escorted tours—whether by bus, motor coach, train, or boat—let travelers sit back and enjoy their trip without having to spend lots of time behind the wheel or worrying about details. You know your costs up front; and there are few surprises. Escorted tours can take you to the maximum number of sights in the minimum amount of time with the least amount of hassle—you don't have to sweat over the plotting and planning of a vacation schedule. Escorted tours are particularly convenient for people with limited mobility. They can also be a great way to make new friends.

On the downside, an escorted tour often requires a big deposit up front, and lodging and dining choices are predetermined. You'll get little opportunity for serendipitous interactions with locals. The tours can be jam-packed with activities, leaving little room for individual sightseeing, whim, or adventure—plus they also often focus only on the heavily touristed sites, so you miss out on the lesser-known gems.

Before you invest in an escorted tour, ask about the **cancellation policy:** Is a deposit required? Can they cancel the trip if they don't get enough people? Do you get a refund if they cancel? If *you* cancel? How late can you cancel if you are unable to go? When do you pay in full? *Note:* If you choose an escorted tour, think strongly about purchasing trip-cancellation insurance, especially if the tour operator asks you to pay up front. See the section on "Travel Insurance," p. 37.

You'll also want to get a complete **schedule** of the trip to find out how much sightseeing is planned each day and whether enough time has been allotted for relaxing or wandering solo.

The **size** of the group is also important to know up front. Generally, the smaller the group, the more flexible the itinerary, and the less time you'll spend waiting for people to get on and off the bus. Find out the **demographics** of the group as well. What is the age range? What is the gender breakdown? Is this mostly a trip for couples or singles?

Discuss what is included in the **price.** You may have to pay for transportation to and from the airport. A box lunch may be included in an excursion, but drinks might cost extra. Tips may not be included. Find out if you will be charged if you decide to opt out of certain activities or meals.

Before you invest in a package tour, get some answers. Ask about the **accommodations choices** and prices for each.

Then look up the hotels' reviews in a Frommer's guide and check their rates for your specific dates of travel online. Finally, if you plan to travel alone, you'll need to know if a **single supplement** will be charged and if the company can match you up with a roommate.

12 Recommended Books & Films

For the definitive history of the birth of New York City to the end of the 19th century, there is no better read than *Gotham: A History of New York City to 1898,* by Edwin R. Burrows and Mike Wallace (Oxford University Press). Another recommended historical look at the growth of New York City, this one told in a breezy narrative tone, is *The Epic of New York City: A Narrative History,* by Edward Robb Ellis (Kodansha).

Luc Sante's *Low Life: Lures and Snares of Old New York* (Vintage Departures) details the bad old days of brothels, drug dens, and gambling saloons in New York in the early 20th century—it's a lively, fascinating read.

One of master biographer Robert Caro's early works, *The Power Broker: Robert Moses and the Fall of New York* (Random House), focuses on how the vision of master deal maker Robert Moses transformed New York to what it became in the second half of the 20th century.

In *The Great Bridge: The Epic Story of the Building of the Brooklyn Bridge* (Simon & Schuster), author David McCullough devotes his estimable talents to the story of the building of the Brooklyn Bridge.

The companion to the PBS Series (see below) *New York,* by Ric Burns, Lisa Ades, and James Sanders (Knopf) uses lavish photographs and illustrations to show the growth of New York City.

My all-time favorite book about New York is a children's classic called *This Is New York* (Universe Publishing), written and illustrated by M. Sasek in 1960. The book was recently reissued and, with an update added, as fresh as it was 45 years ago.

There are not many places as cinematic as New York City. Filmmakers sometimes think of the city as a character unto itself. The list of movies where New York plays a crucial role are too many to mention, but here are some of the top New York City movies, worth renting before you visit.

Possibly the best New York City promotional film is the musical **On the Town,** with Gene Kelly and Frank Sinatra, about three sailors with 24-hours leave spent exploring Gotham. Shot on location, all the landmarks captured in beautiful Technicolor.

Woody Allen is known as a New York filmmaker and proudly shoots all his films in the city. One of his best—and a good, but maybe a bit dated, look at neurotic New York—is *Annie Hall.*

Following in Woody Allen's footsteps are director Rob Reiner and writer Nora Ephron, who made *When Harry Met Sally.* It's sort of a poor-man's *Annie Hall,* but a gorgeous cinematic tribute to New York. The famous "orgasm scene" was filmed in **Katz's Delicatessen** (p. 182).

"I love this dirty town," says Burt Lancaster in the gritty, crackling *Sweet Smell of Success.* In the beautifully photographed black-and-white movie, Lancaster plays malicious gossip columnist J. J. Hunsecker, and Tony Curtis is perfectly despicable as the groveling publicist, Sidney Falco.

Another filmmaker always identified with New York is Martin Scorsese. He has made many films where New York played a central role, from *Mean Streets* to *Gangs of New York,* which was actually filmed in Italy. But the one film where New York is a character, and not a very flattering one, is *Taxi Driver.* The Academy Award–nominated 1976 movie about an alienated and psychotic taxi driver is tough and bloody, but to see images of seedy Times Square as it was before its recent reincarnation, there is no better film.

The best history of New York on video is the Ric Burns documentary *New York,* which aired on PBS. The seven-disc, 14-hour DVD (also available on VHS) is a must-see for anyone interested in the evolution of this great city.

4

For International Visitors

Now York's global media profile might make it appear familiar, but movies and TV, music videos, and news images distort as much as they reflect. The gap between image and reality can make certain situations puzzling for the foreign—or even the domestic—visitor. This chapter will help prepare you for the more common issues or problems that you may encounter.

1 Preparing for Your Trip

ENTRY REQUIREMENTS

Check at any U.S. embassy or consulate for current information and requirements. You can also obtain a visa application and other information online at the **U.S. State Department**'s website, at **www.travel.state.gov**.

VISAS The U.S. State Department has a **Visa Waiver Program** allowing citizens of certain countries to enter the United States without a visa for stays of up to 90 days. At press time, these included Andorra, Australia, Austria, Belgium, Brunei, Denmark, Finland, France, Germany, Iceland, Ireland, Italy, Japan, Liechtenstein, Luxembourg, Monaco, the Netherlands, New Zealand, Norway, Portugal, San Marino, Singapore, Slovenia, Spain, Sweden, Switzerland, and the United Kingdom. Citizens of these countries need only a valid passport and a round-trip air or cruise ticket in their possession upon arrival. If they first enter the United States, they may also visit Mexico, Canada, Bermuda, and/or the Caribbean islands and return to the United States without a visa. Further information is available from any U.S. embassy or consulate. Canadian citizens may enter the United States without visas; they need only proof of residence.

Citizens of all other countries must have (1) a valid passport that expires at least 6 months later than the scheduled end of their visit to the United States, and (2) a tourist visa, which may be obtained (with or without charge) from any U.S. consulate.

To obtain a visa, the traveler must submit a completed application form (either in person or by mail) with a 1½-inch-square photo, and must demonstrate binding ties to a residence abroad. Usually you can obtain a visa at once or within 24 hours, but it may take longer during the summer rush from June through August. If you cannot go in person, contact the nearest U.S. embassy or consulate for directions on applying by mail. Your travel agent or airline office may also be able to provide you with visa applications and instructions. The U.S. consulate or embassy that issues your visa will determine whether you are eligible to be issued a multiple- or single-entry visa and any restrictions regarding the length of your stay.

British subjects can obtain up-to-date visa information by calling the **U.S. Embassy Visa Information Line** (© **0891/200-290**) or by visiting the

"Visas to the U.S." section of the American Embassy London's website at www.usembassy.org.uk.

Irish citizens can obtain up-to-date visa information through the **Embassy of the USA Dublin,** 42 Elgin Rd., Dublin 4, Ireland (℃ 353/1-668-8777); or by checking the "Visas to the U.S." section of the website at http://dublin.us embassy.gov.

Australian citizens can obtain up-to-date visa information by contacting the **U.S. Embassy Canberra,** Moonah Place, Yarralumla, ACT 2600 (℃ 02/6214-5600), or by checking the U.S. Diplomatic Mission's website at http://us embassy-australia.state.gov/consular.

Citizens of **New Zealand** can obtain up-to-date visa information by contacting the **U.S. Embassy New Zealand,** 29 Fitzherbert Terrace, Thorndon, Wellington (℃ 644/472-2068), or get the information directly from the "Visas" section of the website at http://usembassy.org.nz.

MEDICAL REQUIREMENTS Unless you're arriving from an area known to be suffering from an epidemic (particularly cholera or yellow fever), inoculations or vaccinations are not required for entry into the United States. If you have a medical condition that requires **syringe-administered medications,** carry a valid signed prescription from your physician—the Transportation Security Administration (TSA) no longer allows airline passengers to pack syringes in their carry-on baggage without documented proof of medical need. If you have a disease that requires treatment with **narcotics,** you should also carry documented proof with you—smuggling narcotics aboard a plane is a serious offense that carries severe penalties in the U.S.

For **HIV-positive visitors,** requirements for entering the United States are somewhat vague and change frequently. According to the latest publication of *HIV and Immigrants: A Manual for AIDS Service Providers,* the Immigration and Naturalization Service (INS) doesn't require a medical exam for entry into the United States, but INS officials may stop individuals because they look sick or because they are carrying AIDS/HIV medicine.

If an HIV-positive noncitizen applies for a non-immigrant visa, the question on the application regarding communicable diseases is tricky no matter which way it's answered. If the applicant checks "no," INS may deny the visa on the grounds that the applicant committed fraud. If the applicant checks "yes" or if INS suspects the person is HIV-positive, it will deny the visa unless the applicant asks for a special waiver for visitors. This waiver is for people visiting the United States for a short time, to attend a conference, for instance, to visit close relatives, or to receive medical treatment. It can be a confusing situation. For up-to-the-minute information, contact **AIDSinfo** (℃ 800/448-0440, or 301/519-6616 outside the U.S.; www.aidsinfo.nih.gov) or the **Gay Men's Health Crisis** (℃ 212/367-1000; www.gmhc.org).

DRIVER'S LICENSES Foreign driver's licenses are mostly recognized in the U.S., although you may want to get an international driver's license if your home license is not written in English.

PASSPORT INFORMATION

Safeguard your passport in an inconspicuous, inaccessible place like a money belt. Make a copy of the critical pages, including the passport number, and store it in a safe place, separate from the passport itself. If you lose your passport, visit the nearest consulate of your native country as soon as possible for a replacement. Passport applications are downloadable from the websites listed below.

Note: The International Civil Aviation Organization has recommended a policy requiring that *every* individual who travels by air have a passport. In response, many countries are now requiring that children must be issued their own passport to travel internationally, where before those under 16 or so may have been allowed to travel on a parent's or guardian's passport.

FOR RESIDENTS OF CANADA

You can pick up a passport application at 1 of 28 regional passport offices or most travel agencies. Canadian children who travel must have their own passport. However, if you hold a valid Canadian passport issued before December 11, 2001, that bears the name of your child, the passport remains valid for you and your child until it expires. Passports cost C$85 for those 16 years and older (valid 5 years), C$35 for children 3 to 15 (valid 5 years), and C$20 for children under 3 (valid 3 years). Applications, which must be accompanied by two identical passport-size photographs and proof of Canadian citizenship, are available at travel agencies throughout Canada or from the central **Passport Office,** Department of Foreign Affairs and International Trade, Ottawa, ON K1A 0G3 (© **800/567-6868;** www.dfait-maeci.gc.ca/passport). Processing takes 5 to 10 days if you apply in person, or about 3 weeks by mail.

FOR RESIDENTS OF THE UNITED KINGDOM

To pick up an application for a standard 10-year passport (5-year passport for children under 16), visit the nearest Passport Office, major post office, or travel agency. You can also contact the **United Kingdom Passport Service** at © **0870/571-0410** or visit its website at www.passport. gov.uk. Passports are £33 for adults and £19 for children under 16, with another £30 fee if you apply in person at a Passport Office. Processing takes about 2 weeks (1 week if you apply at the Passport Office).

FOR RESIDENTS OF IRELAND

You can apply for a 10-year passport, costing €57, at the **Passport Office,** Setanta Centre, Molesworth Street, Dublin 2 (© **01/671-1633;** www.irlgov. ie/iveagh). Those under age 18 and over 65 must apply for a €12 3-year passport. You can also apply at 1A South Mall, Cork (© **021/272-525**) or over the counter at most main post offices.

FOR RESIDENTS OF AUSTRALIA

You can get an application from your local post office or any branch of Passports Australia, but you must schedule an interview at the passport office to present your application materials. Call the **Australian Passport Information Service** at © **131-232,** or visit the government website at www.passports.gov.au. Passports for adults are A$144 and A$72 for those under 18.

FOR RESIDENTS OF NEW ZEALAND

You can pick up a passport application at any New Zealand Passports Office or download it from their website. Contact the **Passports Office** at © **0800/225-050** in New Zealand, or 04/474-8100, or log on to www.passports.govt.nz. Passports are NZ$80 for adults and NZ$40 for children under 16.

CUSTOMS
WHAT YOU CAN BRING IN

Every visitor more than 21 years of age may bring in, free of duty, the following: (1) 1 liter of wine or hard liquor; (2) 200 cigarettes, 100 cigars (but not from Cuba), or 3 pounds of smoking tobacco; and (3) $100 worth of gifts. These exemptions are offered to travelers who spend at least 72 hours in the United States and who have not claimed them within the preceding 6 months. It is altogether forbidden to bring into the country foodstuffs (particularly fruit, cooked meats, and canned goods) and plants (vegetables, seeds, tropical plants, and the like). Foreign tourists may bring in or take out up to $10,000 in U.S. or foreign currency with no formalities; larger sums must be declared to U.S. Customs on entering or leaving, which includes filing form CM 4790. For more specific information regarding U.S. Customs and Border Protection, contact your nearest U.S. embassy or consulate, or the **U.S. Customs** office (© **202/927-1770** or www.customs.ustreas.gov).

WHAT YOU CAN TAKE HOME

U.K. citizens returning from a non-EU country have a customs allowance of: 200 cigarettes; 50 cigars; 250g of smoking tobacco; 2 liters of still table wine; 1 liter of spirits or strong liqueurs (over 22% volume); 2 liters of fortified wine, sparkling wine, or other liqueurs; 60cc (ml) perfume; 250cc (ml) of toilet water; and £145 worth of all other goods, including gifts and souvenirs. People under 17 cannot have the tobacco or alcohol allowance. For more information, contact HM Customs & Excise at © **0845/010-9000** (from outside the U.K., 020/8929-0152), or consult their website at www.hmce.gov.uk.

For a clear summary of **Canadian** rules, request the booklet *I Declare,* issued by the **Canada Customs and Revenue Agency** (© **800/461-9999** in Canada, or 204/983-3500; www.ccra-adrc.gc.ca). Canada allows its citizens a C$750 exemption, and, depending on the province you're entering, citizens aged over 18 or 21, are allowed to bring back, duty-free, 1 carton of cigarettes, 1 can of tobacco, 40 imperial ounces of liquor, and 50 cigars. In addition, you're allowed to mail gifts to Canada valued at less than C$60 a day, provided they're unsolicited and don't contain alcohol or tobacco (write on the package "Unsolicited gift, under $60 value"). All valuables should be declared on the Y-38 form before

departure from Canada, including serial numbers of valuables you already own, such as expensive foreign cameras. *Note:* The $750 exemption can only be used once a year and only after an absence of 7 days.

The duty-free allowance in **Australia** is A$400 or, for those under 18, A$200. Citizens age 18 and over can bring in 250 cigarettes or 250 grams of loose tobacco, and 1,125 milliliters of alcohol. If you're returning with valuables you already own, such as foreign-made cameras, you should file form B263. A helpful brochure available from Australian consulates or Customs offices is *Know Before You Go.* For more information, call the **Australian Customs Service** at © **1300/363-263,** or log on to www.customs.gov.au.

The duty-free allowance for **New Zealand** is NZ$700. Citizens over 17 can bring in 200 cigarettes, 50 cigars, or 250 grams of tobacco (or a mixture of all three if their combined weight doesn't exceed 250g); plus 4.5 liters of wine and beer, or 1.125 liters of liquor. New Zealand currency does not carry import or export restrictions. Fill out a certificate of export, listing the valuables you are taking out of the country; that way, you can bring them back without paying duty. Most questions are answered in a free pamphlet available at New Zealand consulates and Customs offices: *New Zealand Customs Guide for Travellers, Notice no. 4.* For more information, contact **New Zealand Customs,** The Customhouse, 17–21 Whitmore St., Box 2218, Wellington (© **0800/428-786** or 04/473-6099; www.customs.govt.nz).

HEALTH INSURANCE

Although it's not required of travelers, health insurance is highly recommended. Unlike many European countries, the United States does not usually offer free or low-cost medical care to its citizens or visitors. Doctors and hospitals are expensive, and in most cases will require advance payment or proof of coverage before they render their services. Policies can cover everything from the loss or theft of your baggage and trip cancellation to the guarantee of bail in case you're arrested. Good policies will also cover the costs of an accident, repatriation, or death. See "Travel Insurance" in chapter 3 for more information. Packages such as **Europ Assistance's "Worldwide Healthcare Plan"** are sold by European automobile clubs and travel agencies at attractive rates. **Worldwide Assistance Services, Inc.** (✆ **800/821-2828;** www.worldwide assistance.com) is the agent for Europ Assistance in the United States.

Though lack of health insurance may prevent you from being admitted to a hospital in nonemergencies, don't worry about being left on a street corner to die: The American way is to fix you now and bill the living daylights out of you later.

INSURANCE FOR BRITISH TRAVELERS Most big travel agents offer their own insurance and will probably try to sell you their package when you book a holiday. Think before you sign. **Britain's Consumers' Association** recommends that you insist on seeing the policy and reading the fine print before buying travel insurance. **The Association of British Insurers** (✆ **020/7600-3333;** www.abi.org.uk) gives advice by phone and publishes *Holiday Insurance,* a free guide to policy provisions and prices. You might also shop around for better deals: Try **Columbus Direct** (✆ **020/7375-0011;** www.columbusdirect.net).

INSURANCE FOR CANADIAN TRAVELERS Canadians should check with their provincial health plan offices or call **Health Canada** (✆ **613/957-2991;** www.hc-sc.gc.ca) to find out the extent of their coverage and what documentation and receipts they must take home in case they are treated in the United States.

MONEY

CURRENCY The U.S. monetary system is very simple: The most common **bills** are the $1 (colloquially, a "buck"), $5, $10, and $20 denominations. There are also $2 bills (seldom encountered), $50 bills, and $100 bills (the last two are usually not welcome as payment for small purchases). All the paper money was recently redesigned, making the famous faces adorning them disproportionately large. The old-style bills are still legal tender.

There are seven denominations of coins: 1¢ (1 cent, or a penny); 5¢ (5 cents, or a nickel); 10¢ (10 cents, or a dime); 25¢ (25 cents, or a quarter); 50¢ (50 cents, or a half dollar); the gold-colored "Sacagawea" coin worth $1; and, prized by collectors, the rare, older silver dollar.

Note: The "foreign-exchange bureaus" so common in Europe are rare even at airports in the United States, and nonexistent outside major cities. It's best not to change foreign money (or traveler's checks denominated in a currency other than U.S. dollars) at a small-town bank, or even a branch in a big city; in fact, leave any currency other than U.S. dollars at home—it may prove a greater nuisance to you than it's worth.

TRAVELER'S CHECKS Though traveler's checks are widely accepted, make sure that they're denominated in U.S. dollars, as foreign-currency checks are often difficult to exchange. The three traveler's checks that are most widely recognized—and least likely to be denied—are **Visa, American Express,** and **Thomas Cook.** Be sure to record the numbers of the checks, and keep that information in a separate place in case they get lost or stolen. Most businesses are pretty good about taking traveler's checks, but you're better off cashing them in at a bank (in small amounts, of course) and paying in cash. *Remember:* You'll need identification, such as a driver's

Travel Tip

Be sure to keep a copy of all your travel papers separate from your wallet or purse, and leave a copy with someone at home should you need it faxed in an emergency.

license or passport, to change a traveler's check.

CREDIT CARDS & ATMs   The following credit cards are the most widely used form of payment in the United States: **Visa** (Barclaycard in Britain), **MasterCard** (EuroCard in Europe, Access in Britain, Chargex in Canada), **American Express, Diners Club,** and **Discover.** There are, however, a handful of stores and restaurants that do not take credit cards, so be sure to ask in advance. Most businesses display a sticker near their entrance to let you know which cards they accept. (**Note:** Businesses may require a minimum purchase, usually around $10, to use a credit card.)

It is strongly recommended that you bring at least one major credit card. You must have a credit or charge card to rent a car. Hotels and airlines usually require a credit-card imprint as a deposit against expenses, and in an emergency a credit card can be priceless.

You'll find **automated teller machines (ATMs)** on just about every block in Manhattan. Some ATMs will allow you to draw U.S. currency against your bank and credit cards. Check with your bank before leaving home, and remember that you will need your personal identification number (PIN) to do so. Most accept Visa, MasterCard, and American Express, as well as ATM cards from other U.S. banks. Expect to be charged up to $3 per transaction, however, if you're not using your own bank's ATM.

One way around these fees is to ask for cash back at grocery stores that accept ATM cards and don't charge usage fees. Of course, you'll have to purchase something first.

ATM cards with major credit card backing, known as "debit cards," are now a commonly acceptable form of payment in most stores and restaurants. Debit cards draw money directly from your checking account. Some stores enable you to receive "cash back" on your debit-card purchases as well.

SAFETY

GENERAL SAFETY SUGGESTIONS

Tourist areas in Manhattan are generally safe, and the city has experienced a dramatic drop in its crime rate in recent years. Still, crime is a national problem, and U.S. urban areas tend to be less safe than those in Europe or Japan. You should always stay alert, use common sense, and trust your instincts. If you're in doubt about which neighborhoods are safe, don't hesitate to make inquiries with the hotel front desk staff or the local tourist office.

Avoid deserted areas, especially at night, and don't go into public parks after dark unless there's a concert or similar occasion that will attract a crowd.

Avoid carrying valuables with you on the street, and keep expensive cameras or electronic equipment bagged up or covered when not in use. If you're using a map, try to consult it inconspicuously— or better yet, study it before you leave your room. Hold onto your pocketbook, and place your billfold in an inside pocket. In theaters, restaurants, and other public places, keep your possessions in sight.

Always lock your room door—don't assume that once you're inside the hotel you are automatically safe and no longer need to be aware of your surroundings.

Size Conversion Chart

Women's Clothing

American	4	6	8	10	12	14	16
French	34	36	38	40	42	44	46
British	6	8	10	12	14	16	18

Women's Shoes

American	5	6	7	8	9	10
French	36	37	38	39	40	41
British	4	5	6	7	8	9

Children's Clothing

American	3	4	5	6	6X
French	98	104	110	116	122
British	18	20	22	24	26

Children's Shoes

American	8	9	10	11	12	13	1	2	3
French	24	25	27	28	29	30	32	33	34
British	7	8	9	10	11	12	13	1	2

Men's Suits

American	34	36	38	40	42	44	46	48
French	44	46	48	50	52	54	56	58
British	34	36	38	40	42	44	46	48

Men's Shirts

American	14½	15	15½	16	16½	17	17½
French	37	38	39	41	42	43	44
British	14½	15	15½	16	16½	17	17½

Men's Shoes

American	7	8	9	10	11		12	13
French	39½	41	42	43	44½	46	47	
British	6	7	8	9	10	11	12	

Hotels are open to the public, and in a large hotel, security may not be able to screen everyone who enters.

For more about personal security in Manhattan, see "Playing It Safe," on p. 117.

2 Getting to the U.S.

In addition to the domestic airlines listed in chapter 3, "Planning Your Trip to New York City," many international carriers serve John F. Kennedy International and Newark airports. **British Airways** (© **0845/77-333-77** or 0870/55-111-55 in the U.K., or 800/AIRWAYS in the U.S.; www.ba.com) has daily service from London as well as direct flights from Manchester and Glasgow. **Virgin Atlantic** (© **0870/380-2007** in the U.K., or 800/ 862-8621 in the U.S.; www.virgin-atlantic.com) flies from London's Heathrow to New York.

Canadian readers might book flights on **Air Canada** (© **888/247-2262;** www.aircanada.ca), which offers direct service from Toronto, Montreal, Ottawa, and other cities.

Aer Lingus flies from Ireland to New York (© **0818/365000** in Ireland, or 800/IRISH-AIR in the U.S.; www.aer lingus.ie). The following U.S. airlines fly to New York from most major European cities: **Continental** (© **0120/377-6464** in the U.K., or 800/523-3273 in the U.S.; www.continental.com), **United** (© **0845/ 844-4777** in the U.K., or 800/864-8331 in the U.S.; www.ual.com), **American** (© **0208/572-5555** or 0845/778-9789 in the U.K., or 800/433-7300 in the U.S.; www.aa.com), and **Delta** (© **0800/414-767** in the U.K., or 800/221-4141 in the U.S.; www.delta.com).

Qantas (© **13-13-13** in Australia, or 800/227-4500 in the U.S.; www.qantas.com.au) and **Air New Zealand** (© **0800/737-000** in New Zealand, or 800/262-1234 in the U.S.; www.airnewzealand.co.nz) fly to the West Coast and will book you straight through to New York City on a partner airline.

AIRLINE DISCOUNTS The smart traveler can find numerable ways to reduce the price of a plane ticket simply by taking time to shop around. For example, overseas visitors can take advantage of the APEX (Advance Purchase Excursion) reductions offered by all major U.S. and European carriers. For more money-saving airline advice, see "Getting There," in chapter 3. For the best rates, compare fares and be flexible with the dates and times of travel.

IMMIGRATION & CUSTOMS CLEARANCE Visitors arriving by air, no matter what the port of entry, should cultivate patience and resignation before setting foot on U.S. soil. Getting through immigration control can take as long as 2 hours on some days, especially on summer weekends, so be sure to carry this guidebook or something else to read. This is especially true in the aftermath of the World Trade Center attacks, when security clearances have been considerably beefed up at U.S. airports.

⟨Tips⟩ Prepare to Be Fingerprinted

Starting in January 2004, many international visitors traveling on visas to the United States will be photographed and fingerprinted at Customs in a new program created by the Department of Homeland Security called **US-VISIT**. Non–U.S. citizens arriving at airports and on cruise ships must undergo an instant background check as part of the government's ongoing efforts to deter terrorism by verifying the identity of incoming and outgoing visitors. Exempt from the extra scrutiny are visitors entering by land or those from 28 countries (mostly in Europe) that don't require a visa for short-term visits. For more information, go to the Homeland Security website at **www.dhs.gov/dhspublic**.

People traveling by air from Canada, Bermuda, and certain countries in the Caribbean can sometimes clear Customs and Immigration at the point of departure, which is much quicker.

3 Getting Around the U.S.

BY PLANE Some large airlines (for example, Northwest and Delta) offer travelers on their transatlantic or transpacific flights special discount tickets under the name **Visit USA,** allowing mostly one-way travel from one U.S. destination to another at very low prices. These discount tickets are not on sale in the United States and must be purchased abroad in conjunction with your international ticket. This system is the best, easiest, and fastest way to see the United States at low cost. You should obtain information well in advance from your travel agent or the office of the airline concerned, because the conditions attached to these discount tickets can be changed without advance notice.

BY TRAIN International visitors (excluding Canada) can also buy a **USA Rail Pass,** good for 15 or 30 days of unlimited travel on Amtrak (© **800/ USA-RAIL;** www.amtrak.com). The pass is available through many foreign travel agents. Prices in 2005 for a 15-day pass were $295 off peak, $440 peak; a 30-day pass costs $385 off peak, $550 peak. With a foreign passport, you can also buy passes at some Amtrak offices in the United States, including locations in San Francisco, Los Angeles, Chicago, New York, Miami, Boston, and Washington, D.C. Reservations are generally required and should be made for each part of your trip as early as possible. Regional rail passes are also available.

BY BUS Although bus travel is often the most economical form of public transit for short hops between U.S. cities, it can also be slow and uncomfortable— certainly not an option for everyone (particularly when Amtrak, which is far more luxurious, may offer similar rates). **Greyhound/Trailways** (©**800/ 231-2222**), the sole nationwide bus line, offers an **International Ameripass** that must be purchased before coming to the United States or by phone through the Greyhound International Office at the Port Authority Bus Terminal in New York City (© **212/971-0492**). The pass can be obtained from foreign travel agents and costs less than the domestic version. At press time, pass prices were as follows: 4 days ($149), 7 days ($209), 10 days ($259), 15 days ($299), 21 days ($359), 30 days ($399), 45 days ($449), or 60 days ($539). You can get more info on the pass at www.greyhound.com, or by calling © **212/971-0492** (14:00–21:00 GMT) and © **402/330-8552** (all other times). In addition, special rates are available for seniors and students.

BY CAR Unless you plan to spend the bulk of your vacation time in New York City, where walking is the best and easiest way to get around, the most cost-effective, convenient, and comfortable way to travel around the United States is by car. The interstate highway system connects cities and towns all over the country; in addition to these high-speed, limited-access roadways, there's an extensive network of federal, state, and local highways and roads. Some of the national car-rental companies include **Alamo** (© 800/327-9633; www.goalamo.com), **Avis** (© 800/331-1212; www.avis.com), **Budget** (© 800/527-0700;www.budget.com), **Dollar** (© 800/800-4000; www.dollar.com), **Hertz** (© 800/654-3131; www.hertz.com), **National** (© 800/227-7368; www.nationalcar.com), and **Thrifty** (© 800/367-2277; www.thrifty.com).

If you plan to rent a car in the United States, you probably won't need the services of an additional automobile organization. If you're planning to buy or borrow a car, automobile-association membership is recommended. The **American Automobile Association (AAA; ⓒ 800/222-4357; www.aaa.com)** is the country's largest auto club and supplies its members with maps, insurance, and, most important, emergency road service. The cost of joining runs from $63 for singles to $87 for two members, but if you're a member of a foreign auto club with reciprocal arrangements, you can enjoy free AAA service in America. See below for more information.

An inviolable rule of thumb for New York: Don't even think of driving within the city. Like many cities, New York has its own arcane rules of the road, confusing one-way streets, incomprehensible street-parking signs, and outrageously expensive parking garages. Public transportation—whether buses, subways, or taxis—will get you anywhere you want to go quickly and easily, and that's where you'll be most comfortable.

If you do drive to New York in a rental car, return it as soon as you arrive and rent another when you're ready to leave the city. Always keep your car doors locked. Never leave any packages or valuables in sight because thieves will break car windows. If someone attempts to rob you or steal your car, don't resist. Report the incident to the police department immediately.

FAST FACTS: **For the International Traveler**

Also see "Fast Facts: New York City," in chapter 6, for more New York City–specific information.

Automobile Organizations Auto clubs will supply maps, suggested routes, guidebooks, accident and bail-bond insurance, and emergency road service. The **American Automobile Association (AAA)** is the major auto club in the United States. If you belong to an auto club in your home country, inquire about AAA reciprocity before you leave. You may be able to join AAA even if you're not a member of a reciprocal club; to inquire, call AAA (ⓒ 800/222-4357). AAA is actually an organization of regional auto clubs; so look under "AAA Automobile Club" in the White Pages of the telephone directory. AAA has a nationwide emergency road service telephone number (ⓒ 800/AAA-HELP).

Business Hours Offices are usually open weekdays from 9am to 5pm. Banks are open weekdays from 9am to 3pm or later and sometimes Saturday mornings. Stores typically open between 9 and 10am and close between 5 and 6pm from Monday through Saturday. Stores in shopping complexes or malls tend to stay open late: until about 9pm on weekdays and weekends, and many malls and larger department stores are open on Sunday.

Currency & Currency Exchange See "Entry Requirements" and "Money" under "Preparing for Your Trip," earlier in this chapter.

Drinking Laws The legal age for purchase and consumption of alcoholic beverages is 21; proof of age is required and often requested at bars, nightclubs, and restaurants, so it's always a good idea to bring ID when you go out. In New York State, beer may be purchased in supermarkets.

Do not carry open containers of alcohol in your car or any public area that isn't zoned for alcohol consumption. The police can fine you on the spot. And nothing will ruin your trip faster than getting a citation for DUI (driving under the influence), so don't even think about driving while intoxicated.

Electricity Like Canada, the United States uses 110 to 120 volts AC (60 cycles), compared to 220 to 240 volts AC (50 cycles) in most of Europe, Australia, and New Zealand. If your small appliances use 220 to 240 volts, you'll need a 110-volt transformer and a plug adapter with two flat parallel pins to operate them here. Downward converters that change 220–240 volts to 110–120 volts are difficult to find in the United States, so bring one with you.

Embassies & Consulates All embassies are located in the nation's capital, Washington, D.C. Some consulates are located in major U.S. cities, and most nations have a mission to the United Nations in New York City. If your country isn't listed below, call for directory information in Washington, D.C. (© 202/555-1212), for the number of your national embassy.

The embassy of **Australia** is at 1601 Massachusetts Ave. NW, Washington, DC 20036 (© 202/797-3000; www.austemb.org). There are consulates in New York, Honolulu, Los Angeles, and San Francisco.

The embassy of **Canada** is at 501 Pennsylvania Ave. NW, Washington, DC 20001 (© 202/682-1740; www.canadianembassy.org). Canadian consulates are in Buffalo (NY), Detroit, Los Angeles, New York, and Seattle.

The embassy of **Ireland** is at 2234 Massachusetts Ave. NW, Washington, DC 20008 (© 202/462-3939; www.irelandemb.org). Irish consulates are in Boston, Chicago, New York, and San Francisco.

The embassy of **Japan** is at 2520 Massachusetts Ave. NW, Washington, DC 20008 (© 202/238-6700; www.embjapan.org). Japanese consulates are located in Atlanta, Kansas City, San Francisco, and Washington D.C.

The embassy of **New Zealand** is at 37 Observatory Circle NW, Washington, DC 20008 (© 202/328-4800; www.nzemb.org). New Zealand consulates are in New York, Los Angeles, Salt Lake City, San Francisco, and Seattle.

The embassy of the **United Kingdom** is at 3100 Massachusetts Ave. NW, Washington, DC 20008 (© 202/588-7800; www.britainusa.com/consular/embassy). British consulates are in Atlanta, Boston, Chicago, Houston, Los Angeles, New York, San Francisco, and Seattle.

Emergencies Call © 911 to report a fire, call the police, or get an ambulance anywhere in the United States. This is a toll-free call (which means that no coins are required at public telephones).

If you have a medical emergency that doesn't require an ambulance, you can walk into a hospital's 24-hour emergency room (usually a separate entrance). For a list of hospitals, see "Fast Facts: New York City," in chapter 6. Because emergency rooms are often crowded and waits are long, one of the walk-in medical centers listed under "What to Do If You Get Sick Away from Home" (under "Health & Safety," in chapter 3) might be a better option.

If you encounter serious problems, contact **Traveler's Aid International** (© 202/546-1127; www.travelersaid.org) to help direct you to a local branch.

This nationwide, nonprofit, social-service organization geared to helping travelers in difficult straits offers services that might include reuniting families separated while traveling, providing food and/or shelter to people stranded without cash, or even emotional counseling. If you're in trouble, seek them out.

Gasoline (Petrol) Petrol is known as gasoline (or simply "gas") in the United States, and petrol stations are known as both gas stations and service stations. Though prices are rising, gasoline costs much less here as it does in Europe (about $2 per gal. at press time), and taxes are already included in the printed price. One U.S. gallon equals 3.8 liters or 0.85 Imperial gallons.

Holidays Banks, government offices, post offices, and many stores, restaurants, and museums are closed on the following legal national holidays: January 1 (New Year's Day), the third Monday in January (Martin Luther King, Jr., Day), the third Monday in February (Presidents' Day, Washington's Birthday), the last Monday in May (Memorial Day), July 4th (Independence Day), the first Monday in September (Labor Day), the second Monday in October (Columbus Day), November 11 (Veterans' Day/Armistice Day), the fourth Thursday in November (Thanksgiving Day), and December 25 (Christmas). Also, the Tuesday following the first Monday in November is Election Day and is a federal government holiday in presidential-election years (held every 4 years, and next in 2008).

Legal Aid If you are "pulled over" for a minor infraction (such as speeding), never attempt to pay the fine directly to a police officer; this could be construed as attempted bribery, a much more serious crime. Pay fines by mail, or directly into the hands of the clerk of the court. If accused of a more serious offense, say and do nothing before consulting a lawyer. Here the burden is on the state to prove a person's guilt beyond a reasonable doubt, and everyone has the right to remain silent, whether he or she is suspected of a crime or actually arrested. Once arrested, a person can make one telephone call to a party of his or her choice. Call your embassy or consulate.

Mail If you aren't sure what your address will be in the United States, mail can be sent to you, in your name, c/o General Delivery at the main post office of the city or region where you expect to be. (Call © **800/275-8777** for information on the nearest post office.) The addressee must pick up mail in person and must produce proof of identity (driver's license, passport, and so on). Most post offices will hold your mail for up to 1 month, and are open Monday to Friday from 8am to 6pm, and Saturday from 9am to 3pm.

Generally found at intersections, mailboxes are blue with a red-and-white stripe and carry the inscription U.S. Mail. If your mail is addressed to a U.S. destination, don't forget to add the five-digit postal code (or zip code), after the two-letter abbreviation of the state to which the mail is addressed. This is essential to prompt delivery.

At press time, domestic postage rates were 22¢ for a postcard and 37¢ for a letter. For international mail, a first-class letter of up to ½ ounce costs 60¢ (46¢ to Canada and 40¢ to Mexico); a first-class postcard costs 50¢ (including Canada and Mexico); and a preprinted postal aerogramme costs 50¢.

Measurements See the chart on the inside front cover of this book for details on converting metric measurements to U.S. equivalents.

Newspapers & Magazines In addition to the *New York Times* and other city papers, many newsstands carry a selection of international newspapers and magazines. For major newspapers and magazines from around the world, visit **Universal News & Magazines,** at 234 W. 42nd St., between Seventh and Eighth avenues (🕾 **212/221-1809**), and 977 Eighth Ave., between 57th and 58th streets (🕾 **212/459-0932**); or **Hotalings News Agency,** 624 W. 52nd St., between Eleventh and Twelfth avenues (🕾 **212/974-9419**). Other good bets include the **Hudson** newsdealers, located in Grand Central Terminal, at 42nd Street and Lexington Avenue, and Penn Station, at 34th Street and Seventh Avenue.

Taxes The United States has no value-added tax (VAT) or other indirect tax at the national level. Every state, county, and city has the right to levy its own local tax on all purchases, including hotel and restaurant checks, airline tickets, and so on.

Telephone, Telegraph, Telex & Fax The telephone system in the United States is run by private corporations, so rates, especially for long-distance service and operator-assisted calls, can vary widely. Generally, hotel surcharges on long-distance and local calls are astronomical, so you're usually better off using a **public pay telephone,** which you'll find clearly marked in most public buildings and private establishments as well as on the street. Convenience grocery stores and gas stations always have them. Many convenience groceries and packaging services sell **prepaid calling cards** in denominations up to $50; these can be the least expensive way to call home. Many public phones at airports now accept American Express, MasterCard, and Visa credit cards. **Local calls** made from public pay phones in most locales cost either 25¢ or 35¢, but some locales charge 50¢. Pay phones do not accept pennies, and few will take anything larger than a quarter.

You may want to look into leasing a cellphone for the duration of your trip.

Most long-distance and international calls can be dialed directly from any phone. **For calls within the United States and to Canada,** dial 1 followed by the area code and the seven-digit number. **For other international calls,** dial 011 followed by the country code, the city code, and the telephone number of the person you are calling.

Calls to area codes **800, 888, 877,** and **866** are toll-free. However, calls to numbers in area codes **700** and **900** (chat lines, bulletin boards, "dating" services, and so on) can be very expensive—usually a charge of 95¢ to $3 or more per minute, and they sometimes have minimum charges that can run as high as $15 or more.

For **reversed-charge or collect calls,** and for person-to-person calls, dial 0 (zero, not the letter O) followed by the area code and number you want; an operator will then come on the line, and you should specify that you are calling collect, or person-to-person, or both. If your operator-assisted call is international, ask for the overseas operator.

For **local directory assistance** ("information"), dial 411; for long-distance information, dial 1, then the appropriate area code and 555-1212.

Telegraph and telex services are provided primarily by Western Union. You can bring your telegram into the nearest Western Union office (there are hundreds across the country) or dictate it over the phone (© **800/325-6000**). You can also telegraph money, or have it telegraphed to you, very quickly over the Western Union system, but this service can cost as much as 15% to 20% of the amount sent.

Most hotels have **fax machines** available for guest use (be sure to ask about the charge to use it). Many hotel rooms are even wired for guests' fax machines. A less expensive way to send and receive faxes may be at stores such as The UPS Store, a national chain of packing service shops. (Look in the Yellow Pages directory under "Packing Services.")

There are two kinds of telephone directories in the United States. The so-called **White Pages** list private households and business subscribers in alphabetical order. The inside front cover lists emergency numbers for police, fire, ambulance, the Coast Guard, poison-control center, crime-victims hot line, and so on. The first few pages will tell you how to make long-distance and international calls, complete with country codes and area codes. Government numbers are usually printed on blue paper within the White Pages. Printed on yellow paper, the so-called **Yellow Pages** list all local services, businesses, industries, and houses of worship according to activity, with an index at the front or back. (Drugstores/pharmacies and restaurants are also listed by geographic location.) The Yellow Pages also include city plans or detailed area maps, postal zip codes, and public transportation routes.

Time The continental United States is divided into **four time zones:** Eastern Standard Time (EST), Central Standard Time (CST), Mountain Standard Time (MST), and Pacific Standard Time (PST). Alaska and Hawaii have their own zones. For example, noon in New York City (EST) is 11am in Chicago (CST), 10am in Denver (MST), 9am in Los Angeles (PST), 8am in Anchorage (AST), and 7am in Honolulu (HST).

Daylight saving time is in effect from 1am on the first Sunday in April through 1am on the last Sunday in October, except in Arizona, Hawaii, part of Indiana (until April 2006, when it will begin observing DST), and Puerto Rico. Daylight saving time moves the clock 1 hour ahead of standard time.

For the correct local time in New York, dial © **212/976-1616**.

Tipping Tipping is so ingrained in the American way of life that the annual income tax of tip-earning service personnel is based on how much they should have received in light of their employers' gross revenues. Accordingly, they may have to pay tax on a tip you didn't actually give them.

Here are some rules of thumb:

In hotels, tip **bellhops** at least $1 per bag ($2–$3 if you have a lot of luggage) and tip the **chamber staff** $1 to $2 per day (more if you've left a disaster area for him or her to clean up, or if you're traveling with kids and/or pets). Tip the **doorman** or **concierge** only if he or she has provided you with some specific service (for example, calling a cab for you or obtaining difficult-to-get theater tickets). Tip the **valet-parking attendant** $1 every time you get your car.

In restaurants, bars, and nightclubs, tip **service staff** 15% to 20% of the check, tip **bartenders** 10% to 15%, tip **checkroom attendants** $1 per garment, and tip **valet-parking attendants** $1 per vehicle. Tip the **doorman** only if he has provided you with some specific service (such as calling a cab for you). Tipping is not expected in cafeterias and fast-food restaurants.

Tip **cab drivers** 15% of the fare.

As for other service personnel, tip **skycaps** at airports at least $1 per bag ($2–$3 if you have a lot of luggage) and tip **hairdressers** and **barbers** 15% to 20%.

Tipping ushers at movies and theaters, and gas-station attendants, is not expected.

Toilets You won't find public toilets or "restrooms" on the streets in most U.S. cities, but they can be found in hotel lobbies, bars, restaurants, museums, department stores, railway and bus stations, and service stations. Large hotels and fast-food restaurants are probably the best bet for good, clean facilities. If possible, avoid the toilets at parks and beaches, which tend to be dirty; some may be unsafe. Restaurants and bars in resorts or heavily visited areas may reserve their restrooms for patrons. Some establishments display a notice indicating this. You can ignore this sign or, better yet, avoid arguments by paying for a cup of coffee or a soft drink, which will qualify you as a patron. See "Restrooms" under "Fast Facts: New York City," in chapter 6.

5

Suggested NYC Itineraries

I've lived in New York for more than half my life and I still haven't seen it all. That's not because I don't want to; it's just that in New York there is so much to see. So it is understandable if you might feel a bit overwhelmed by all the options. Seeing the best of New York requires endurance, patience, perseverance, very good walking shoes, a $7 daily MetroCard Fun Pass (see chapter 6), and a good map of the New York city subway system. For some attractions— such as the Empire State Building or seeing a Broadway play—you should score tickets *before* you come to New York to avoid long lines or a disappointing shut-out. Besides your own two feet, the subway will be your best bet to cover the most ground. I will also recommend a few bus routes that will not only get you to some of New York's best attractions, but will also act as your own little tour bus where you'll see sights on the way.

1 The Best of New York City in 1 Day

If you want to have any chance of seeing the best of New York in just 1 day, you need to get an early start. You also need to have a plan of attack. You don't want to waste time zig-zagging across the city to various attractions. So I recommend taking New York in thirds. On the first third, we will concentrate on the best of Midtown Manhattan. *Start: Pier 83 on 42nd St.*

❶ Circle Line Sightseeing Cruise ★★
By starting your day on the water on this 2-hour half-island cruise, you'll get a very good overview of Manhattan. On the cruise you'll pass by the Statue of Liberty and Ellis Island, see the Lower Manhattan skyline, proceed up the East River where you will cruise under the Brooklyn, Manhattan, and Williamsburg bridges, and view the United Nations and the east side skyline, including the Empire State Building and Chrysler Building. See p. 286.

Take the M42 42nd Street crosstown bus to Fifth Avenue.

❷ New York Public Library ★★
You'll recognize this building by the lion sculptures guarding its gates. Step inside for more grandeur, especially the incredible, fully restored **Main Reading Rooms** where you might want to take a break and sit down and read the paper (if you have time). While you're here, take a look at the library's backyard, **Bryant Park.** If there are tents up, it means you're here during one of the two Fashion Weeks held yearly in the park. See p. 268.

❸ Grand Central Terminal ★★
Before stepping into this magnificent, working train station, take a look east

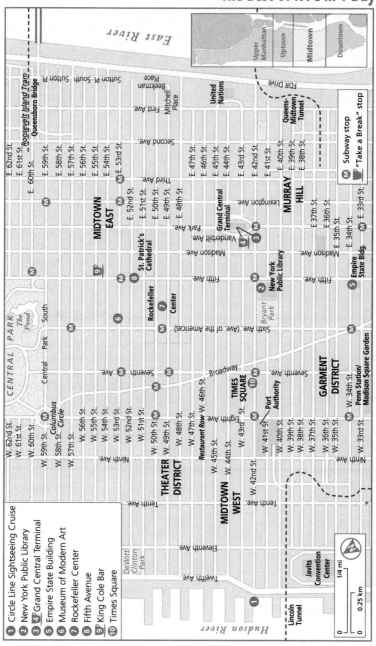

1 Circle Line Sightseeing Cruise
2 New York Public Library
3 4 Grand Central Terminal
5 Empire State Building
6 Museum of Modern Art
7 Rockefeller Center
8 Fifth Avenue
9 King Cole Bar
10 Times Square

M Subway stop

"Take a Break" stop

toward Lexington Avenue and then crane your neck up. You'll see my favorite skyscraper, the **Chrysler Building** 👁️👁️. Okay, now enter Grand Central, where approximately 500,000 commuters and subway riders dash through daily. I hope it's not rush hour . . . but even if it is, you really won't have to worry about colliding with a commuter; the building and the stupendous main concourse was constructed so cleverly that despite the perceived chaos, people rarely bump into each other. You'll want to spend hours examining the beautiful detail throughout the terminal, but you don't have hours to spare. A walk through the main concourse and a look at the sky ceiling will be evidence enough. See p. 244.

4️⃣ GRAND CENTRAL TERMINAL
You're hungry now and the choices in the Grand Central Terminal dining concourse are plentiful and very good. Chow down on everything from Indian food to pizza. Or opt for a heartier lunch at the legendary **Oyster Bar & Restaurant** or upstairs overlooking the concourse, a steak at **Michael Jordan's—The Steakhouse**. See p. 194.

5️⃣ Empire State Building 👁️👁️👁️
It's an 8-block walk down Fifth Avenue from Grand Central Station to the Empire State Building. Let's hope it's a beautiful day because I want your view from the top of this historic structure, the tallest building in New York, to be pristine. You already have your tickets (don't you?), so you don't have to wait at the ticket booth (see box on p. 243 for details). The elevator will zip you up to the 86th story observatory where you will get a panoramic view of Manhattan. See p. 242.

Take the B or D train uptown to Seventh Avenue. Walk east across 53rd Street.

6️⃣ Museum of Modern Art 👁️👁️
Yes, the $20 suggested admission is outrageous, but this is New York and you are slowly getting used to outrageous. And you'll forget about the admission charge once you peruse the exhibits in this recently renovated and expanded beautiful museum. Airy and expansive, with skylit, open galleries along with smaller, intimate rooms, the museum is one of a kind. See p. 245.

7️⃣ Rockefeller Center 👁️👁️
Just a short walk from MoMA is the famous Rockefeller Center complex. If you are here during the Christmas holidays, you'll fight the crowds for a glimpse of the famous Christmas tree and the skaters in the small rink below. If your timing is right, you might just be able to squeeze in the 70-minute NBC Studio Tour. If not, you'll see famous **Radio City Music Hall** 👁️ and **30 Rockefeller Center** 👁️ where, by the time you read this, you will be allowed to visit the newly opened observation deck on the 70th floor. Across the street you'll see the city's biggest Catholic church, **St. Patrick's Cathedral.** See p. 246.

8️⃣ Fifth Avenue
Is a street an attraction? When it's one of the most famous in the world, it is. Walk north up Fifth Avenue from Rock Center and pass big name stores like Saks Fifth Avenue, Henri Bendel, the NBA Store, Tiffany & Co., Cartier, Bergdorf Goodman, and FAO Schwarz, reopened after being closed for nearly a year. You'll also see the recognizable Trump Tower from the popular *Apprentice* series. At 59th Street you'll see the ornate Plaza Hotel, which, at press time, was fated to become part condominium, part hotel. Across the street, you'll see the southern end of Central Park. See p. 313.

☕ KING COLE BAR
Now would be a good time to rest your legs as well as your senses. Head back down a few blocks to the lounge at the St. Regis Hotel. This is where the Bloody Mary was supposedly invented, and it's the perfect place for a late afternoon or early evening cocktail. 2 E. 55th St., at Fifth Avenue. ✆ 212/744-4300. See p. 381.

⑩ Times Square

You've got tickets for a Broadway show, so before you head into the theater, this is your chance to see what Times Square is all about. The lights are blinding, the crowds are thick, and the noise is infernal, but that's Times Square. There's nowhere quite like it in the world. See p. 249.

2 The Best of New York City in 2 Days

On your second day, you'll head downtown and explore the city where it began. You'll wander through streets that are as old as any in New York, and some that are curiously towered by ultramodern, gleaming steel and glass skyscrapers. Again, you'll want to get a very early start because there is so much to see and always too little time. *Start: Subway: 1 or 9 to South Ferry or 4 or 5 to Bowling Green.*

❶ Statue of Liberty 👧👧👧

You saw Lady Liberty on your Circle Line half-island tour yesterday, but now you want to get up close and personal with her. Ferries leave from Battery Park every half-hour beginning at 8:30am. Once on Liberty Island you can take one of two tours. The Promenade Tour takes visitors through the monument lobby, past the original torch to the Statue of Liberty exhibit for a 20- to 30-minute ranger-guided tour and then outdoors to the lower promenade. The Observatory Tour incorporates the promenade tour and makes a visit to the pedestal observation platform where you can view the Statue's interior framework through a new glass ceiling portal. See p. 249.

❷ Ellis Island 👧👧

Your Statue of Liberty ferry ticket also includes a stop at Ellis Island; ferries to Ellis Island leave Liberty Island every half-hour. The Immigration Museum is one of the most touching in the city. Incredible, personal details of the immigrant experience are on display, from the smallest items, like personal letters and jewelry, to large battered valises. You could spend all day here, but you don't have time for that. Wander through the dramatic Registry room and you'll hear the echoes of hundreds of different languages of immigrants who came through these doors to a better life. See p. 242.

❸ Wall Street

The walk uptown to the heart of the Financial District is not a long one. Along the way you'll see various structures such as **Castle Clinton National Monument,** the remnants of a fort built in 1808 to defend New York Harbor against the British, and the very impressive **U.S. Customs House,** which houses the Museum of the American Indian, part of the Smithsonian Institution. Once on Wall Street, stop for a photo-op at the **Federal Hall National Memorial,** with the famous statue of George Washington in front, and the **New York Stock Exchange,** directly across the street. Unfortunately, the Exchange is no longer open for tours, but if you are a person of some significance they might let you ring the opening day's bell. See p. 250.

Take the free Downtown Connection bus that travels from Battery Park to South Street Seaport with stops along the way including one at Wall Street. See chapter 6 for details.

❹ South Street Seaport

Here the streets are really old—so old they are rough with cobblestones. This is a 17th-century landmark historic district with restored 18th- and 19th-century buildings still standing. The interesting South Street Seaport Museum will fill you in on more of the 11-square block's seafaring history. Also part of the Seaport complex is Pier 17, a historic barge that now is the home to various stores you probably are very familiar with. See p. 263.

Take the A or C at Broadway-Nassau Street toward Brooklyn and get off at High Street, the first stop in Brooklyn.

> **5️ GRIMALDI'S PIZZERIA**
> You are now in Brooklyn, and probably very hungry. You'll need nourishment for your next adventure, and where better than this famed pizzeria, in the shadow of the Brooklyn Bridge? 19 Old Fulton St., between Front and Water streets. ✆ 718/858-4300. See p. 204.

❻ Brooklyn Bridge ⭐⭐⭐

You have been well fed, so now you have the energy to make the approximately half-hour stroll back to Manhattan across one of the greatest suspended bridges in the world. The view of the Manhattan skyline is spectacular—make sure you have plenty of room in the card of your digital camera. See p. 241.

❼ Lower East Side Tenement Museum ⭐

You visited Ellis Island earlier in the day and learned about the immigrant's struggles to gain entry into this country. Now visit the prototype of a Lower East Side tenement where so many of those immigrants lived. The only way to see the museum is by guided tour, which takes

place every 40 minutes on weekdays and every half-hour on weekends. See p. 256.

Take the F or V train at Second Avenue and Houston Street two stops uptown to West 4th Street.

> **8️ IL LABORATORIO DEL GELATO**
> Just across the street from the Lower East Side Tenement Museum is a wonderful ice cream and gelato shop where you can experience a multitude of homemade ice cream and sorbet flavors. Pick up a cone or cup for the walk to the subway. 95 Orchard St., between Broome and Delancey streets. ✆ 212/343-9922. See p. 180.

❾ Washington Square Park

You are now in the center of Greenwich Village. And that neighborhood's bohemian tradition is best represented by this park and the characters that inhabit it. On the north end of the park you'll see a row of elegant late-19th-century town houses and the famous Washington Square Arch, patterned after the Arc de Triomphe in Paris. See p. 284.

❿ Union Square Park

About 10 blocks north of Washington Square Park you'll find this small, but very welcome bit of park. And if it is a Monday, Wednesday, Friday, or Saturday, you'll be in for a special treat because the city's best greenmarket, the **Union Square Greenmarket** ⭐⭐, will be the center of the park's activity. See p. 284.

> **11️ PETE'S TAVERN**
> A few blocks east of Union Square Park is Pete's Tavern, the city's oldest continually operating establishment. Look familiar? You may have seen it in an episode of *Seinfeld*, *Sex and the City*, or *Law & Order* or else on the big screen. Stop in for a pint to quench your thirst after that full day of walking. 129 E. 18th St. (at Irving Place). ✆ 212/473-7676. www.petestavern.com. Subway: L, N, R, 4, 5, 6, to 14th St./Union Sq. See p. 377.

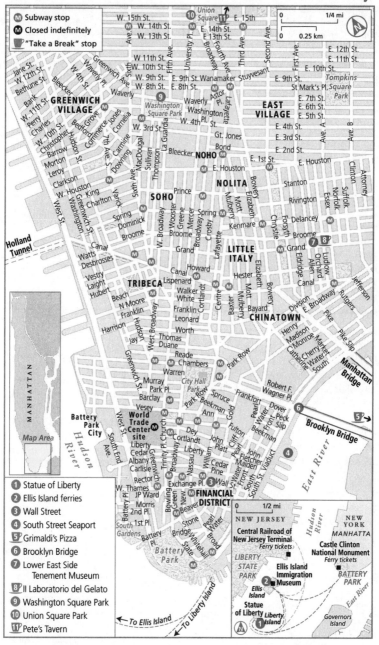

The Best of NYC in 2 Days

- Ⓜ Subway stop
- Ⓜ Closed indefinitely
- ☕ "Take a Break" stop

1 Statue of Liberty
2 Ellis Island ferries
3 Wall Street
4 South Street Seaport
5 Grimaldi's Pizza
6 Brooklyn Bridge
7 Lower East Side
   Tenement Museum
8 Il Laboratorio del Gelato
9 Washington Square Park
10 Union Square Park
11 Pete's Tavern

3 The Best of New York City in 3 Days

You've seen a sizable chunk of the best of Manhattan, but there's still plenty left to fill up a day. We haven't even gotten to some of the city's great museums, or that urban oasis called Central Park. We'll do all that and maybe even escape to the wilds of the Bronx before the day is done. If the weather's nice, plan on a picnic in Central Park. *Start:* B or C to 72nd Street.

❶ The Dakota

We'll start our day in front of this 1884-built apartment building. This was standing when the only thing around it was greenery. The building has a dubious past; it was here where Beatle great John Lennon lived (and where Yoko Ono still lives) and where he was shot and killed. Across the street in Central Park is a small patch of grass called **Strawberry Fields** ⭐, named in honor of the former Beatle; fans still gather here on the anniversary of his death, December 8. See p. 268.

❷ American Museum of Natural History ⭐⭐⭐

Don't try to cover too much ground at this 4-square-block museum; you'll be here all day. Pick a few of the highlights like the Fossils Halls where the dinosaurs reside, the Hall of Biodiversity, and the Culture Halls. On the 81st Street side of the building you'll find the **Rose Center for Earth and Space** where you can marvel at the beauty of the cosmos in the grand Hayden Planetarium. See p. 239.

❸ Central Park ⭐⭐⭐

From the Museum of Natural History, cross the street to Central Park and enter at 81st Street. Follow the path east, and just south of the Delacorte Theater you'll see Belvedere Castle. Climb to the top and soak in the view of the Park. To the north, you'll see the Great Lawn, site of so many big concerts, and beyond that the Jacqueline Kennedy Onassis Reservoir. To the south, you'll see the Lake with its rowboats (rent one if you have time) and the skyline of Manhattan. See p. 275.

> ☕ **A PICNIC IN THE PARK**
> If you didn't pack a picnic lunch today, stop in the Columbus Bakery (at 83rd St. and Columbus Ave.), just north of the Museum of Natural History, and get your lunch to go. Head over to the park and grab a bench, or better, if the weather is really nice, spread out a blanket and take in the sunshine.

❺ Metropolitan Museum of Art ⭐⭐⭐

Continuing east across Central Park, you'll hit Fifth Avenue and the Met. Like the Museum of Natural History, there is no way you could see all the Met has to offer in one short visit, but be sure to see the amazing Temple of Dendur, a gift from the Egyptian government, and the museum's collection of European paintings—including 37 Monets. There are various free (after the admission charge) museum highlight tours. They last an hour and will give you a pretty good overview of this great museum. See p. 244.

❻ Solomon R. Guggenheim Museum ⭐

Continuing on our minitour of Museum Mile, that stretch of artistic real estate that runs on upper Fifth Avenue, is the Guggenheim. You'll know it when you see it; there's nothing else like this Frank Lloyd Wright–designed museum anywhere, and now you have the chance to actually walk that spiraling rotunda. But get off the rotunda and take a look at some of the permanent collection that includes works by Picasso, Chagall, and

ST. NICHOLAS PARK

0   1/4 mi
0   0.25 km

HARLEM

W. 125th St.   E. 125th St.

MARCUS GARVEY PARK

Harlem River

THE BRONX

Yankee Stadium

BARNARD COLLEGE

COLUMBIA UNIVERSITY

EAST HARLEM

E. 116th St.

W. 115th St.
W. 114th St.
W. 113th St.
W. 112th St.
W. 111th St.

W. 114th St.
W. 113th St.

Cathedral of St. John the Divine ❼

Douglass Circle

Central Park North

Frawley Circle

Cathedral Pkwy.
W. 109th St.
W. 108th St.
W. 107th St.
W. 106th St.
W. 105th St.
W. 104th St.

E. 110th St.
E. 109th St.
E. 108th St.
E. 107th St.

Map Area

MANHATTAN

Harlem Meer

Lasker Rink & Pool

The Great Hill

Conservatory Garden

Museum of the City Of New York

W. 103rd St.

The Pool

North Meadow

East Meadow

CENTRAL PARK

97th St Transverse Rd.

W. 97th St.
W. 96th St.
W. 95th St.
W. 94th St.
W. 93rd St.
W. 92nd St.
W. 91st St.
W. 90th St.
W. 89th St.
W. 88th St.
W. 87th St.

Tennis Courts

Jacqueline Kennedy Onassis Reservoir

E. 96th St.
E. 95th St.
E. 94th St.
E. 93rd St.
E. 92nd St.
E. 91st St.
E. 90th St.
E. 89th St.
E. 88th St.
E. 87th St.
E. 86th St.

JOAN OF ARC PARK

Soldiers and Sailors Monument

Jewish Museum

Cooper-Hewitt Museum

Guggenheim Museum ❻

W. 86th St.

86th St Transverse Rd.

GREAT LAWN

Metropolitan Museum Of Art ❺

E. 85th St.
E. 84th St.
E. 83rd St.
E. 82nd St.
E. 81st St.

UPPER EAST SIDE

Children's Museum
W. 82nd St.
W. 81st St.
W. 80th St.
W. 79th St.

Hayden Planetarium

American Museum of Natural History ❷

Delacorte Theater

Belvedere Castle

Belvedere Lake

Obelisk

79th St Transverse Rd.

W. 77th St.
W. 76th St.
W. 75th St.
W. 74th St.
W. 73rd St.
W. 72nd St.

New York Historical Society

The Ramble

Conservatory Pond

The Lake

Boat House

❶ Strawberry Fields

UPPER WEST SIDE

Sheep Meadow

Bandshell

The Mall

East Green

Tavern on the Green

W. 66th St
W. 65th St

LINCOLN CENTER

65th St Transverse Rd.

Zoo

❶ The Dakota
❷ American Museum of Natural History
❸❹ Central Park
❺ Metropolitan Museum of Art
❻ Solomon R. Guggenheim Museum
❼ Cathedral of St. John the Divine
❽ M&G Diner
❾ Yankee Stadium

Klee. Or wander into the new Kandinsky Gallery for a good dose of the master's eye-opening works. See p. 247.

Take the M96 crosstown bus at Fifth Avenue and 97th Street west. Get off at Amsterdam Avenue and 96th Street and transfer to an uptown M11 or M7 bus. Get off at 110th Street.

❼ Cathedral of St. John the Divine ⓐ

On the east side of Amsterdam, you will see the world's largest Gothic cathedral. Construction began in 1892 and is still not yet finished. You can explore the inside of the huge cathedral on your own or opt for a public tour. If you're here at Easter time or during the Feast of St. Francis in October, don't miss the blessing of animals—where the creature congregation has been known to include an elephant or camel. See p. 273.

Take the M11 or M7 uptown bus to 125th Street.

---

⁸ M&G DINER

This is the place for first-rate soul food. If you are really hungry, don't hesitate to order the excellent pan-fried chicken. If all you want is a cup of coffee, a slice of homemade carrot cake would go perfectly with it. 383 W. 125th St., at St. Nicholas Avenue. ⓒ 212/864-7325. See p. 227.

Take the B or D train at 125th Street station uptown to the Bronx. Get off at 161st/River Avenue.

❾ Yankee Stadium ⓐⓐ

You come out of the subway station and you hear the din of the loudspeaker—maybe it's the voice of longtime Yankee announcer Bob Sheppard announcing the day's starting lineup. You are at the Big Ballpark in the Bronx. You've got your tickets already and if you arrive early enough, visit Monument Park in the outfield, open to the public when the gates open and up to 45 minutes prior to game time. See p. 251.

6

Getting to Know
New York City

This chapter gives you an insider's take on Manhattan's most distinctive neighborhoods and streets, tells you how to get around town, and serves as a handy reference to everything from personal safety to libraries and liquor.

1 Orientation

VISITOR INFORMATION

INFORMATION OFFICES

- The **Times Square Visitors Center,** 1560 Broadway, between 46th and 47th streets (where Broadway meets Seventh Ave.), across from the TKTS booth on the east side of the street (© **212/768-1560;** www.timessquarebid.org), is the city's top info stop. This pleasant and attractive center features a helpful info desk offering loads of citywide information. There's also a tour desk selling tickets for Gray Line bus tours and Circle Line boat tours; a Metropolitan Transportation Authority (MTA) desk staffed to sell MetroCard fare cards, provide public transit maps, and answer all of your questions on the transit system; a Broadway Ticket Center providing show information and selling full-price show tickets; ATMs and currency exchange machines; and computer terminals with free Internet access courtesy of Yahoo! It's open daily from 8am to 8pm.
- The New York Convention and Visitors Bureau runs the **NYCVB Visitor Information Center** at 810 Seventh Ave., between 52nd and 53rd streets. In addition to loads of information on citywide attractions and a multilingual counselor on hand to answer questions, the center also has interactive terminals that provide free touch-screen access to visitor information via Citysearch (www.citysearch.com), a guide to events, dining, and nightlife, and sell advance tickets to major attractions, which can save you from standing in long ticket lines once you arrive. (You can also buy CityPass using these; see the box on p. 240.) There's also an ATM, a gift shop, and a bank of phones that connect you directly with American Express card member services. The center is open Monday through Friday from 8:30am to 6pm, Saturday and Sunday from 9am to 5pm. For over-the-phone assistance, call © **212/484-1200,** or check online at www.nycvisit.com.

PUBLICATIONS

For comprehensive listings of films, concerts, performances, sporting events, museum and gallery exhibits, street fairs, and special events, the following are your best bets:

- The *New York Times* (**www.nytimes.com** or www.nytoday.com) features terrific arts and entertainment coverage, particularly in the two-part Friday "Weekend" section and the Sunday "Arts & Leisure" section. Both days boast full guides to the latest happenings in Broadway and Off-Broadway theater, classical music, dance, pop and jazz, film, and the art world. Friday is particularly good for cabaret, family fun, and general-interest recreational and sightseeing events.

- *Time Out New York* (www.timeoutny.com) is my favorite weekly magazine. Dedicated to weekly goings-on, it's attractive, well organized, and easy to use. *TONY* features excellent coverage in all categories, from live music, theater, and clubs (gay and straight) to museum shows, dance events, book and poetry readings, and kids' stuff. The regular "Check Out" section, unequaled in any other listings magazine, will fill you in on upcoming sample and closeout sales, crafts and antiques shows, and other shopping-related scoops. A new issue hits newsstands every Thursday.

- The free weekly *Village Voice* (www.villagevoice.com), the city's legendary alterna-paper, is available late Tuesday downtown and early Wednesday in the rest of the city. From classical music to clubs, the arts and entertainment coverage couldn't be more extensive, and just about every live music venue advertises its shows here.

Other useful weekly rags include the glossy *New York* magazine (www.newyork metro.com), which offers valuable restaurant reviews and whose listings section is a selective guide to city arts and entertainment; and the *New Yorker* (www.new yorker.com), which features an artsy "Goings On About Town" section at the front of the magazine. Monthly *Paper* (www.papermag.com) is a glossy alterna-mag that serves as good prep for those of you who want to experience the hipper side of the city.

CITY LAYOUT

Open the sheet map that comes with this book and you'll see that the city comprises five boroughs: **Manhattan,** where most of the visitor action is; the **Bronx,** the only borough connected to the mainland United States; **Queens,** where Kennedy and LaGuardia airports are located and which borders the Atlantic Ocean and occupies part of Long Island; **Brooklyn,** south of Queens, which is also on Long Island and is famed for its attitude, accent, and Atlantic-front Coney Island; and **Staten Island,** the least populous borough, bordering Upper New York Bay on one side and the Atlantic Ocean on the other.

When most visitors envision New York, they think of Manhattan, the long finger-shaped island pointing southwest off the mainland—surrounded by the Harlem River to the north, the Hudson River to the west, the East River (really an estuary) to the east, and the fabulous expanse of Upper New York Bay to the south. Despite the fact that it's the city's smallest borough (14 miles long, 2¼ miles wide, 22 sq. miles), Manhattan contains the city's most famous attractions, buildings, and cultural institutions. For that reason, almost all of the accommodations and restaurants suggested in this book are in Manhattan.

In most of Manhattan, finding your way around is a snap because of the logical, well-executed grid system by which the streets are numbered. If you can discern uptown and downtown, and East Side and West Side, you can find your way around pretty easily. In real terms, **uptown** means north of where you happen to be, and **downtown** means south, although sometimes these labels have vague psychographic meanings (generally speaking, "uptown" chic vs. "downtown" bohemianism).

Avenues run north–south (uptown and downtown). Most are numbered. **Fifth Avenue** divides the East Side from the West Side of town, and serves as the eastern border of Central Park north of 59th Street. **First Avenue** is all the way east and **Twelfth Avenue** is all the way west. The three most important unnumbered avenues on the East Side you should know are between Third and Fifth avenues: **Madison** (east of Fifth), **Park** (east of Madison), and **Lexington** (east of Park, just west of Third). Important unnumbered avenues on the West Side are **Avenue of the Americas,** which all New Yorkers call Sixth Avenue; **Central Park West,** which is what Eighth Avenue north of 59th Street is called as it borders Central Park on the west (hence the name); **Columbus Avenue,** which is what Ninth Avenue is called north of 59th Street; and **Amsterdam Avenue,** or Tenth Avenue north of 59th.

Broadway is the exception to the rule—it's the only major avenue that doesn't run uptown–downtown. It cuts a diagonal path across the island, from the northwest tip down to the southeast corner. As it crosses most major avenues, it creates **squares** (Times Sq., Herald Sq., Madison Sq., and Union Sq., for example).

Streets run east–west (crosstown) and are numbered consecutively as they proceed uptown from Houston (pronounced *House*-ton) Street. So to go uptown, simply walk north of, or to a higher-numbered street than, where you are. Downtown is south of (or a lower-numbered street than) your current location.

As I've already mentioned, Fifth Avenue is the dividing line between the **East Side** and **West Side** of town (except below Washington Sq., where Broadway serves that function). On the East Side of Fifth Avenue, streets are numbered with the distinction "East"; on the West Side of that avenue they are numbered "West." East 51st Street, for example, begins at Fifth Avenue and runs east to the East River, while West 51st Street begins at Fifth Avenue and runs west to the Hudson River.

If you're looking for a particular address, remember that even-numbered street addresses are on the south side of streets and odd-numbered addresses are on the north. Street addresses increase by about 50 per block starting at Fifth Avenue. For example, nos. 1 to 50 East are just about between Fifth and Madison avenues, while nos. 1 to 50 West are just about between Fifth and Sixth avenues. Traffic generally runs east on even-numbered streets and west on odd-numbered streets, with a few exceptions, such as the major east–west thoroughfares—**14th, 23rd, 34th, 42nd, 57th, 72nd, 79th, 86th,** and so on—which have two-way traffic. Therefore, 28 W. 23rd St. is a short walk west of Fifth Avenue; 325 E. 35th St. would be a few blocks east of Fifth.

Avenue addresses are irregular. For example, 994 Second Ave. is at East 51st Street, but so is 320 Park Ave. Thus, it's important to know a building's cross street to find it easily. If you don't have the cross street and you want to figure out the exact location using just the address, use the **Manhattan Address Locator,** later in this chapter.

Unfortunately, the rules don't apply to neighborhoods in Lower Manhattan, south of 14th Street—such as Wall Street, Chinatown, SoHo, TriBeCa, and the Village— since they sprang up before engineers devised this brilliant grid scheme. A good map is essential when exploring these areas.

STREET MAPS   You'll find a useful pullout map of Manhattan at the back of this book. There's also a decent one available for free as part of the **Official NYC Visitor Kit** if you write ahead for information (see "Visitor Information," in chapter 3); you can also pick it up for free at the visitor centers listed above.

> **Tips Getting Oriented**
>
> I've indicated the cross streets for every destination in this book, but be sure to ask for the cross street (or avenue) if you're ever calling for an address.
>
> When you give a taxi driver an address, always specify the cross streets. New Yorkers, even most cab drivers, probably wouldn't know where to find 994 Second Ave., but they do know where to find 51st and Second. If you're heading to the restaurant Aquavit, for example, tell them that it's on 55th Street between Madison and Park avenues. The exact number (in this case, no. 65) is given only for further precision.
>
> If you have only the numbered address on an avenue and need to figure out the cross street, use the **Manhattan Address Locator** on p. 102.

Even with all these freebies at hand, I suggest investing in a map with more features if you really want to zip around the city like a pro. **Hagstrom** maps are my favorites because they feature block-by-block street numbering—so instead of trying to guess the cross street for 125 Prince St., you can see right on your map that it's Greene Street. Hagstrom and other visitor-friendly maps are available at just about any good bookstore, including the Barnes & Noble and Borders branches around town; see chapter 10 for locations. You might also want to look for *The New York Map Guide: The Essential Guide to Manhattan* (Penguin), by Michael Middleditch, a 64-page book that maps the entire city, including attractions, restaurants, and nightlife spots.

Because there are always disruptions or changes in service, don't rely on any subway map that hasn't been printed by the Metropolitan Transit Authority; you can find out more on this in "Getting Around," later in this chapter.

MANHATTAN'S NEIGHBORHOODS IN BRIEF

Because they grew up over the course of hundreds of years, Manhattan neighborhoods have multiple, splintered personalities and fluid boundaries. Still, it's relatively easy to agree upon what they stand for in general terms—so if you stop a New Yorker on the street and ask them to point you to, say, the Upper West Side or the Flatiron District, they'll know where you want to go. From south to north, here is how I've defined Manhattan's neighborhoods throughout this book.

Downtown

Lower Manhattan: South Street Seaport & the Financial District At one time, this was New York—period. Originally established by the Dutch in 1625 (hence the city's original name, Nieuw Amsterdam), New York's first settlements sprung up here, on the southern tip of Manhattan island; everything uptown was farm country and wilderness. While all that's changed, this is still the best place in the city to search for the past.

Lower Manhattan constitutes everything south of Chambers Street.

Battery Park, the point of departure for the Statue of Liberty, Ellis Island, and Staten Island, is on the very south tip of the island. The **South Street Seaport,** now touristy but still a reminder of times when shipping was the lifeblood of the city, lies a bit north on the east coast; it's just south of the Brooklyn Bridge, which stands proudly as the ultimate engineering achievement of New York's 19th-century Industrial Age.

The rest of the area is considered the **Financial District,** but may be more famous now as **Ground Zero.** Until

Manhattan Neighborhoods

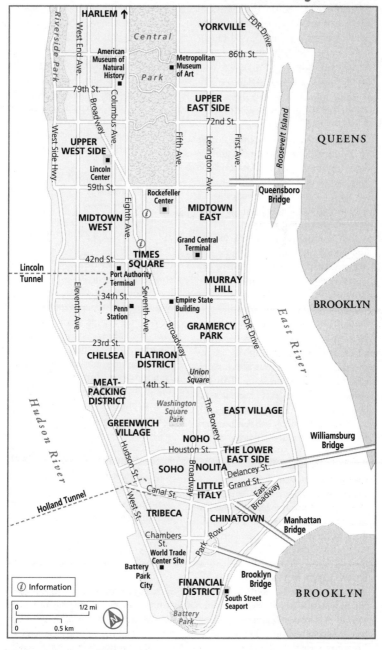

September 11, 2001, the Financial District was anchored by the **World Trade Center,** with the World Financial Center complex and residential Battery Park City to the west, and **Wall Street** running crosstown a little south and to the east. Construction has begun slowly on the new complex, but it will be years before its completion.

City Hall remains the northern border of the district, abutting Chambers Street (look for City Hall Park on the map). Most of the streets of this neighborhood are narrow concrete canyons, with Broadway serving as the main uptown–downtown artery.

Just about all of the major subway lines congregate here before they either end up in or head to Brooklyn. See "Getting Around," later in this chapter, for information on where to gather the latest subway information.

TriBeCa Bordered by the Hudson River to the west, the area north of Chambers Street, west of Broadway, and south of Canal Street is the *Tri*angle *Be*low *Ca*nal Street, or TriBeCa. Since the 1980s, as SoHo became saturated with chic, the spillover has been quietly transforming TriBeCa into one of the city's hippest residential neighborhoods, where celebrities and families quietly coexist in cast-iron warehouses converted into spacious, expensive loft apartments. Artists' lofts and galleries as well as hip antiques and design shops pepper the area, as do some of the city's best restaurants.

Robert DeNiro gave the neighborhood a tremendous boost when he established the TriBeCa Film Center, and Miramax headquarters gave the area further capitalist-chic cachet. Still, historic streets like White (especially the Federal-style building at no. 2) and Harrison (the complete stretch west from Greenwich St.) evoke a bygone, more human-scaled New York, as do a few holdout businesses and old-world pubs.

The main uptown–downtown drag is **West Broadway** (2 blocks to the west of Broadway). Consider the Franklin Street subway station on the 1/9 line to be your gateway to the heart of the action.

Chinatown New York City's most famous ethnic enclave is bursting past its traditional boundaries and has seriously encroached on Little Italy. The former marshlands northeast of City Hall and below Canal Street, from Broadway to the Bowery, are where Chinese immigrants arriving from San Francisco were forced to live in the 1870s. This booming neighborhood is now a conglomeration of Asian populations. It offers tasty cheap eats in cuisines from Szechuan to Hunan to Cantonese to Vietnamese to Thai. Exotic shops offer strange foods, herbs, and souvenirs; bargains on clothing and leather are plentiful. It's a blast to walk down Canal Street, peering into the myriad electronics and luggage stores and watching crabs cut loose

---

Downtown Revival

After September 11, 2001, the rebuilding process has been long and difficult for downtown New York, the area hardest hit economically by the terrorist attacks. But Lower Manhattan has so much to offer that the local community has united to revitalize and promote the area. The website for the Alliance for Downtown New York, Inc. (www.downtownny.com) is updated daily; check it for useful information on new developments and exciting downtown events.

Impressions

Can we actually "know" the universe? It's hard enough finding your way around Chinatown.

—Woody Allen

from their handlers at the exotic fish markets.

The Canal Street (J, M, Z, N, R, 6, Q, W) station will get you to the heart of the action. The streets are crowded during the day and empty out after around 9pm; they remain quite safe, but the neighborhood is more enjoyable during the bustle.

Little Italy Little Italy, traditionally the area east of Broadway between Houston and north of Canal streets, is a shrinking community today, due to the encroachment of thriving Chinatown. It's now limited mainly to **Mulberry Street,** where you'll find most restaurants, and just a few offshoots. With rents going up in the increasingly trendy Lower East Side, a few chic spots are moving in, further intruding upon the old-world landscape. The best way to reach Little Italy is to walk east from the Spring Street station, on the no. 6 line, to Mulberry Street; turn south for Little Italy (you can't miss the year-round red, green, and white street decorations).

The Lower East Side The Lower East Side boasts the best of both old and new New York: Witness the stretch of Houston between Forsyth and Allen streets, where Yoneh Shimmel's Knish Shop sits shoulder-to-shoulder with the city's newest art-house cinema— and both are thriving, thank you very much. Some say that the Lower East Side has come full circle: Hipster 20-somethings with Ivy League educations and well-honed senses of entitlement have been drawn back to the neighborhood their immigrant

grandparents worked their fingers to the bone to escape.

Of all the successive waves of immigrants and refugees who passed through this densely populated tenement neighborhood from the mid–19th century to the 1920s, Eastern European Jews left the most lasting impression here. The Jewish communities, which first popped up between Houston and Canal streets, east of the Bowery, are now just part of history. The neighborhood has experienced quite a renaissance over the last few years, and makes a fascinating itinerary stop for both nostalgists and nightlife hounds. Still, the blocks well south of Houston can be grungy in spots, so walk them with confidence and care after dark.

There are some remnants of what was once the largest Jewish population in America along **Orchard Street,** where you'll find great bargain hunting in its many old-world fabric and clothing stores still thriving between the club-clothes boutiques and trendy lounges. Keep in mind that the old-world shops close early on Friday afternoon and all day on Saturday (the Jewish Sabbath). The exponentially expanding trendy set can be found in the blocks between Allen and Clinton streets south of Houston and north of Delancey, with more new shops, bars, and restaurants popping up in the blocks to the east every day.

This area is not well served by the subway system (one cause for its years of decline), so your best bet is to take the F train to Second Avenue and walk east on Houston; when you see Katz's Deli, you'll know you've arrived. You can also reach the neighborhood from the Delancey Street station on the F line, and the Essex Street station on the J, M, and Z lines.

SoHo & Nolita No relation to the London neighborhood of the same name, **SoHo** got its moniker as an abbreviation of "*So*uth of *Ho*uston Street." This superfashionable neighborhood extends down to Canal Street, between Sixth Avenue to the west and Lafayette Street (1 block east of Broadway) to the east. It's easily accessible by subway: Take the N or R to the Prince Street station; the C, E, or 6 to Spring Street; or the F or V train to the Broadway-Lafayette stop (note that the B, D, and Q trains are not currently serving Broadway-Lafayette due to construction on the Manhattan Bridge).

An industrial zone during the 19th century, SoHo retains the impressive cast-iron architecture of the era, and in many places, cobblestone peeks out from beneath the street's asphalt. In the early 1960s, cutting-edge artists began occupying the drab and deteriorating buildings, soon turning it into the trendiest neighborhood in the city. SoHo is now a prime example of urban gentrification and a major New York attraction thanks to its impeccably restored buildings, fashionable restaurants, and stylish boutiques. On weekends, the cobbled streets and narrow sidewalks are packed with shoppers, with the prime action between Broadway and Sullivan Street north of Grand Street.

Some critics claim that SoHo is becoming a victim of its own popularity—witness the recent departure of art galleries and independent boutiques that fled to TriBeCa and Chelsea as well as the influx of suburban mall–style stores such as J. Crew, Victoria's Secret, and Smith & Hawken. However, SoHo is still one of the best shopping neighborhoods in the city, and few are more fun to browse. High-end street peddlers set up along the boutique-lined sidewalks, hawking silver jewelry, coffee-table books, and their own art. At night, the neighborhood is transformed into a terrific, albeit pricey, dining and barhopping neighborhood.

In recent years, SoHo has been crawling its way east, taking over Mott and Mulberry streets—and white-hot Elizabeth Street in particular—north of Kenmare Street, an area now known as **Nolita** for its *No*rth of *Li*ttle *It*aly location. Nolita is becoming increasingly well known for its hot shopping prospects, which include a number of pricey antiques and home design stores. Taking the 6 to Spring Street will get you closest by subway, but it's just a short walk east from SoHo proper.

The East Village & NoHo The **East Village,** which extends between 14th Street and Houston Street, from Broadway east to First Avenue and

---

Visiting the Lower East Side

The **Lower East Side Business Improvement District** operates a neighborhood visitor center at 261 Broome St., between Orchard and Allen streets (© **866/ 224-0206** or 212/226-9010), that's open daily from 10am to 4pm (sometimes later). Stop in for an Orchard Street Bargain District shopping guide (which they can also send you in advance), plus other information on this historic yet freshly hip 'hood. You can also find shopping, dining, and nightlife directories online at **www.lowereastsideny.com**.

Impressions

Nobody's going to come from the boondocks anymore and live in SoHo and be an artist. You can't afford to park there, let alone live there.

—Pete Hamill

---

beyond to Alphabet City—avenues A, B, C, and D—is where the city's real bohemia has gone. Once, flower children tripped along St. Marks Place and listened to music at the Fillmore East; now the East Village is a fascinating mix of affordable ethnic and trendy restaurants, upstart clothing designers and kitschy boutiques, punk-rock clubs (yep, still), and folk cafes. A half-dozen Off-Broadway theaters also call this place home.

The gentrification that has swept the city has made a huge impact on the East Village, but there's still a seedy element that some of you won't find appealing—and some of you will. Now yuppies and other ladder-climbing types make their homes alongside old-world Russian immigrants who have lived in the neighborhood forever, and the cross-dressers and squatters who settled here in between. The neighborhood still embraces great ethnic diversity, with strong elements of its Ukrainian and Irish heritage, while more recent immigrants have taken over 6th Street between First and Second avenues, turning it into a Little India.

The East Village isn't very accessible by subway; unless you're traveling along 14th Street (the L line will drop you off at Third and First aves.), your best bet is to take the 4, 5, 6, N, Q, R, or W to 14th Street/Union Square; the N or R to 8th Street; or the 6 to Astor Place and walk east.

Until 1998 or so, **Alphabet City** resisted gentrification and remained a haven of drug dealers and other unsavory types—no more. Bolstered by a major real estate boom, this way-east area of the East Village has blossomed. French bistros and smart shops have popped up on every corner. Nevertheless, the neighborhood can be deserted late at night, since it's generally the province of locals. It's far off the subway lines, so know where you're going if you venture out here.

The southwestern section of the East Village, around Broadway and Lafayette between Bleecker and 4th streets, is called **NoHo** (for *No*rth of *Ho*uston), and has a completely different character. As you might have guessed from its name, this area has developed much more like its neighbor to the south, SoHo. Here you'll find a crop of trendy lounges, stylish restaurants, cutting-edge designers, and upscale antiques shops. NoHo is fun to browse; the Bleecker Street stop on the no. 6 line will land you in the heart of it, and the Broadway-Lafayette stop on the F, V line will drop you at its southern edge.

Greenwich Village Tree-lined streets crisscross and wind, following ancient streams and cow paths. Each block reveals yet another row of Greek Revival town houses, a well-preserved Federal-style house, or a peaceful courtyard or square. This is "the Village," from Broadway west to the Hudson River, bordered by Houston Street to the south and 14th Street to the north. It defies Manhattan's orderly grid system with streets that predate it, virtually every one chockablock with activity, and unless you live here, it may be impossible to master the lay of the land—so be sure to take a map along as you explore.

The Seventh Avenue line (1, 2, 3, 9) is the area's main subway artery, while the West 4th Street stop (where the A, C, and E lines meet the F and V lines) serves as its central hub.

Nineteenth-century artists such as Mark Twain, Edgar Allan Poe, Henry James, and Winslow Homer first gave the Village its reputation for embracing the unconventional. Groundbreaking artists such as Edward Hopper and Jackson Pollack were drawn in, as were writers such as Eugene O'Neill, e. e. cummings, and Dylan Thomas. Radical thinkers from John Reed to Upton Sinclair basked in the neighborhood's liberal ethos, and beatniks Allen Ginsberg, Jack Kerouac, and William Burroughs dug the free-swinging atmosphere. Now, like so many neighborhoods, gentrification and escalating real-estate values conspire to push out the artistic element, but culture and counterculture still rub shoulders in cafes, internationally renowned jazz clubs, neighborhood bars, Off-Broadway theaters, and an endless variety of tiny shops and restaurants.

The Village is probably the most chameleon-like of Manhattan's neighborhoods. Some of the highest-priced real estate in the city runs along lower Fifth Avenue, which dead-ends at **Washington Square Park.** Serpentine **Bleecker Street** stretches through most of the neighborhood and is emblematic of the area's historical bent. The tolerant anything-goes attitude in the Village has fostered a large gay community, which is still largely in evidence around **Christopher Street** and Sheridan Square. The streets west of Seventh Avenue, an area known as the **West Village,** boast a more relaxed vibe and some of the city's most charming and historic brownstones. Three colleges—New York University, Parsons School of Design, and the New School for Social Research—keep the area thinking young.

Streets are often crowded with weekend warriors and teenagers, especially on Bleecker, West 4th, 8th, and surrounding streets, and have been known to become increasingly sketchy west of Seventh Avenue in the very late hours, especially on weekends. Keep an eye on your wallet when navigating the weekend throngs. Washington Square Park was cleaned up a couple of years back, but it's still best to stay out of the area after dark.

Midtown

Chelsea & the Meat-Packing District
Chelsea has come on strong in recent years as a hip address, especially for the gay community. A low-rise composite of town houses, tenements, lofts, and factories, the neighborhood comprises roughly the area west of Sixth Avenue from 14th to 30th streets. (Sixth Ave. itself below 23rd St. is actually considered part of the Flatiron District; see below.) Its main arteries are Seventh and Eighth avenues, and it's primarily served by the C or E and 1 or 9 subway lines.

The **Chelsea Piers** sports complex to the far west and a host of shops

---

(both unique boutiques and big names such as Williams-Sonoma), well-priced bistros, and thriving bars along the main drags have contributed to the area's rebirth. Even the Hotel Chelsea—the neighborhood's most famous architectural and literary landmark, where Thomas Wolfe and Arthur Miller wrote, Bob Dylan composed "Sad-Eyed Lady of the Low Land," Viva and Edie Sedgwick of Andy Warhol fame lived, and Sid Vicious killed girlfriend Nancy Spungeon—has undergone a renovation. You'll find a number of very popular flea markets set up in parking lots along Sixth Avenue, between 24th and 27th streets, on the weekends.

One of the most influential trends in Chelsea has been the establishment of far **West Chelsea** (from Ninth Ave. west) and the adjacent **Meat-Packing District** (south of West Chelsea, roughly from 17th St. to Little W. 12th St.) as the style-setting neighborhoods for the 21st century. What SoHo was in the '60s, this industrial west world (dubbed "the Lower West Side" by *New York* magazine) is today. New restaurants, cutting-edge shopping, and superhot restaurants pop up daily in the Meat-Packing District, while the area from West 22nd to West 29th streets between Tenth and Eleventh avenues is home to the cutting edge of today's New York art scene. The power of art can also be found at the Joyce Theater, New York's principal modern dance venue. This area is still seriously industrial and in the early stages of transition, however, and not for everyone. With galleries and bars tucked away in converted warehouses and former meat lockers, browsing can be frustrating, and the sometimes-desolate streets a tad intimidating. Your best bet is to have a specific destination (and an exact address) in mind, be it a restaurant, gallery, boutique, or nightclub, before you come.

The Flatiron District, Union Square & Gramercy Park These adjoining and at places overlapping neighborhoods are some of the city's most appealing. Their streets have been rediscovered by New Yorkers and visitors alike, largely thanks to the boom-to-bust dot.com revolution of the late 1990s; the Flatiron District served as its geographical heart and earned the nickname "Silicon Alley" in the process. These neighborhoods boast great shopping and dining opportunities and a central-to-everything location that's hard to beat. A number of impressive new hotels have been added to the mix over the last few years. The commercial spaces are often large, loft-like expanses with witty designs and graceful columns.

The **Flatiron District** lies south of 23rd Street to 14th Street, between Broadway and Sixth Avenue, and centers around the historic Flatiron Building on 23rd (so named for its triangular shape) and Park Avenue South, which has become a sophisticated new Restaurant Row. Below 23rd Street along Sixth Avenue (once known as the Ladies' Mile shopping district), mass-market discounters such as Filene's Basement, Bed Bath & Beyond, and others have moved in. The shopping gets classier on Fifth Avenue, where you'll find a mix of national names and hip boutiques. Lined with Oriental carpet dealers and high-end fixture stores, Broadway is becoming the city's home-furnishings alley; its crowning jewel is the justifiably famous ABC Carpet & Home, with eight floors of gorgeous textiles, housewares, and gifts on one side of Broadway, and an equally dazzling display of floor coverings on the other.

Union Square is the hub of the entire area; the N, R, 4, 5, 6, and L trains stop here, making it easy to reach from most other city neighborhoods. Long in the shadows of the more bustling (Times and Herald) and high-toned (Washington) city squares, Union Square has experienced a major renaissance in the last decade. Local businesses joined forces with the city to rid the park of drug dealers a few years back, and now it's a delightful place to spend an afternoon. Union Square is best known as the setting for New York's premier green market every Monday, Wednesday, Friday, and Saturday. In-line skaters take over the market space in the after-work hours. A number of hip restaurants rim the square, as do superstores such as the city's best Barnes & Noble superstore, and a Virgin Megastore.

From about 16th to 23rd streets, east from Park Avenue South to about Second Avenue, is the leafy, largely residential district known as **Gramercy Park.** The pity of the Gramercy Park district is that so few can enjoy the park: Built by Samuel Ruggles in the 1830s to attract buyers to his property in the area, it is the only private park in the city and is locked to all but those who live on its perimeter (the rule is that your windows have to overlook the park in order for you to have a key). Located at the southern endpoint of Lexington Avenue (at 21st St.), it is one of the most peaceful spots in the city. If you know someone who has a magic key, go there.

At the northern edge of the area, fronting the Flatiron Building on 23rd Street and Fifth Avenue, is another of Manhattan's lovely little parks, **Madison Square.** Across from its northeastern corner once stood Stanford White's original Madison Square Garden (in whose roof garden White was murdered in 1906 by possibly deranged, but definitely jealous, millionaire Harry K. Thaw). It's now majestically presided over by the massive New York Life Insurance Building, the masterful New York State Supreme Court, and the Metropolitan Life Insurance Company, whose tower in 1909 was the tallest building in the world at 700 feet.

Times Square & Midtown West
Midtown West, the vast area from 34th to 59th streets west of Fifth Avenue to the Hudson River, encompasses several famous names: Madison Square Garden, the Garment District, Rockefeller Center, the Theater District, and Times Square. This is New York's tourism central, where you'll find the bright lights and bustle that draw people from all over the world. As such, this is the city's biggest hotel neighborhood, with options running the gamut from cheap to chic.

The 1, 2, 3, 9 subway line serves the massive neon station at the heart of Times Square, at 42nd Street between Broadway and Seventh Avenue, while the F, V, B, D line runs up Sixth Avenue to Rockefeller Center. The N, R line cuts diagonally across the neighborhood, following the path of Broadway before heading up Seventh Avenue at 42nd Street. The A, C, E line serves the west side, running along Eighth Avenue.

If you know New York but haven't been here in a few years, you'll be quite surprised by the "new" **Times Square.** Longtime New Yorkers like to kvetch nostalgic about the glory days of the old peep-show-and-porn-shop Times Square that this cleaned-up, Disneyfied version supplanted. And there really is not much here to offer the native New Yorker. The revival, however, has been nothing short of an outstanding success for tourism. Grand old theaters have come back to life as

Impressions

I'm opposed to the redevelopment. I think there should be one neighborhood in New York where tourists are afraid to walk.

—Fran Lebowitz on the "new" Times Square

Broadway and children's playhouses, and scores of new family-friendly restaurants and shops have opened. Plenty of businesses have moved in— MTV studios overlook Times Square at 1515 Broadway, and *Good Morning America* has its own street-facing studio at Broadway and 44th Street. The neon lights have never been brighter, and Middle America has never been more welcome. Expect dense crowds, though; it's often tough just to make your way along the sidewalks.

Most of the great Broadway theaters light up the streets just off Times Square, in the West 40s just east and west of Broadway. At the heart of the **Theater District,** where Broadway meets Seventh Avenue, is the TKTS booth, where crowds line up daily to buy discount tickets for that day's shows.

To the west of the Theater District, in the 40s and 50s between Eighth and Tenth avenues, is **Hell's Kitchen,** an area that is much nicer than its ghoulish name and one of my favorites in the city. The neighborhood resisted gentrification until the mid-'90s, but has grown into a charming, less touristy adjunct to the neighboring Theater District. Ninth Avenue, in particular, has blossomed into one of the city's finest dining avenues; just stroll along and you'll have a world of great dining to choose from, ranging from American diner to sexy Mediterranean to traditional Thai. Stylish boutiques and bars have also popped up in this area in the last several years. Realtors have tried to rename the area Clinton, but locals

have held fast to the Hell's Kitchen moniker with delight.

Unlike Times Square, gorgeous **Rockefeller Center** has needed no renovation. Situated between 46th and 50th streets from Sixth Avenue east to Fifth, this Art Deco complex contains some of the city's great architectural gems, which house hundreds of offices, a number of NBC studios (including *Saturday Night Live, Late Night with Conan O'Brien,* and the famous glass-walled *Today* show studio at 48th St.), and some pleasing upscale boutiques (attention, shoppers: Saks Fifth Avenue is just on the other side of Fifth). If you can negotiate the crowds, holiday time is a great time to be here, as ice-skaters take over the central plaza and the huge Christmas tree twinkles against the night sky.

Along Seventh Avenue south of 42nd Street is the **Garment District,** of little interest to tourists except for its sample sales, where some great new fashions are sold off cheap to serious bargain hunters willing to scour the racks. Other than that, it's a pretty grim commercial area. Between Seventh and Eighth avenues and 31st and 33rd streets, **Penn Station** sits beneath unsightly behemoth **Madison Square Garden,** where the Rangers, Liberty, and the Knicks play. Taking up all of 34th Street between Sixth and Seventh avenues is **Macy's,** the world's largest department store; exit Macy's at the southeast corner and you'll find more famous-label shopping around **Herald Square.** The blocks around 32nd Street just west of Fifth Avenue have

Manhattan Address Locator

To locate avenue addresses, cancel the last figure, divide by 2, and add (or subtract) the key number below. The answer is the nearest numbered cross street, approximately.

Avenue A:	add 3	11th Avenue:	add 15
Avenue B:	add 3	Amsterdam Avenue:	add 59
Avenue C:	add 3	Columbus Avenue:	add 59 or 60
First Avenue:	add 3	Lexington Avenue:	add 22
Second Avenue:	add 3	Madison Avenue:	add 27
Third Avenue:	add 10	Park Avenue:	add 34
Sixth Avenue:	subtract 12	Park Avenue South:	add 8
Eighth Avenue:	add 9	West End Avenue:	add 59
Ninth Avenue:	add 13	York Avenue:	add 4
Tenth Avenue:	add 14		

Note special instructions for finding address locations on the following:

Fifth Avenue

63 to 108:	add 11	776 to 1286: cancel last figure of house
109 to 200:	add 13	number and subtract 18 (do not divide
201 to 400:	add 16	house number by 2)
401 to 600:	add 18	1310 to 1494: cancel last figure of house
601 to 775:	add 20	number. For 1310, subtract 20, and for every
		additional 20 street numbers, increase
		deduction by 1

Seventh Avenue

1 to 1800:	add 12	above 1800:	add 20

Broadway

Anything from 1 to 754 is south of 8th Street, and hence a named street.

756 to 846:	subtract 29	above 953:	subtract 31
847 to 953:	subtract 25		

Central Park West

Cancel last figure and add 60

Riverside Drive

Cancel last figure and

Up to 567:	add 72	568 and up:	add 78

developed into a thriving Koreatown, with midprice hotels and bright, bustling Asian restaurants offering some of the best-value stays and eats in Midtown.

Midtown West is also home to some of the city's most revered museums and cultural institutions, including **Carnegie Hall,** the **Museum of Modern Art, Radio City Music Hall,** and the *Intrepid* **Sea-Air-Space Museum,** to name just a few.

Midtown East & Murray Hill Midtown East, the area including Fifth Avenue and everything east from 34th to 59th streets, is the more upscale side of the Midtown map. This side of town is short of subway trains, served primarily by the Lexington Avenue 4, 5, 6 line.

Midtown East is where you'll find the city's finest collection of grand hotels, mostly along Lexington Avenue and near the park at the top of Fifth. The stretch of **Fifth Avenue** from Saks at 49th Street extending to the Plaza Hotel at 59th is home to the city's most high-profile haute shopping, including Tiffany & Co. and Bergdorf Goodman, but more midprice names such as Banana Republic and Liz Claiborne have moved their superstores in over the last 5 years or so. The stretch of 57th Street between Fifth and Lexington avenues is also known for high-fashion boutiques (Chanel, Hermès) and high-ticket galleries, but change is underway since names such as Levi's and Niketown squeezed in. You'll find plenty of spillover along **Madison Avenue,** a great strip for shoe shopping in particular.

Magnificent architectural highlights include the recently repolished **Chrysler Building,** with its stylized gargoyles glaring down on passersby; the Beaux Arts tour de force that is **Grand Central Terminal; St. Patrick's Cathedral;** and the glorious **Empire State Building.**

Far east, swank Sutton and Beekman places are enclaves of beautiful town houses, luxury living, and tiny pocket parks that look out over the East River. Along this river is the **United Nations,** which isn't officially in New York City, or even the United States, but on a parcel of international land belonging to member nations.

Claiming the territory east from Madison Avenue, **Murray Hill** begins somewhere north of 23rd Street (the line between it and Gramercy Park is fuzzy), and is most clearly recognizable north of 30th Street to 42nd Street.

This brownstone-lined quarter is largely a quiet residential neighborhood, most notable for its handful of good budget and midprice hotels. The stretch of Lexington Avenue in the high 20s is known as Curry Hill and has usurped the East Village's Little India as the destination for inexpensive, high-quality Indian and Pakistani food.

Uptown

Upper West Side North of 59th Street and encompassing everything west of Central Park, the Upper West Side contains **Lincoln Center,** arguably the world's premier performing arts venue; the new (in 2004) **Time Warner Center** with its upscale shops, such as **Hugo Boss, A/X Armani,** and **Sephora; Jazz at Lincoln Center;** the **Mandarin Oriental Hotel;** the gargantuan **Whole Foods Market,** and possibly the most expensive food court in the world, with restaurants such as **Per Se** and **Masa,** and **V, The Steakhouse.** The Upper West Side is also the home of the **American Museum of Natural History,** whose renovated Dinosaur Halls and magnificent new Rose Center for Earth and Space garner justifiably rave reviews. You'll also find a growing number of midprice hotels whose larger-than-Midtown rooms and nice residential location make them some of the best values—and some of my favorite places to stay—in the entire city.

Unlike the more stratified Upper East Side, the Upper West Side is home to an egalitarian mix of middle-class yuppiedom, laid-back wealth (lots of celebs and monied media types call the grand apartments along Central Park West home), and ethnic families who were here before the gentrification.

The neighborhood runs all the way up to Harlem, around 125th Street, and encompasses **Morningside Heights,** where you'll find **Columbia University** and the perennial construction project known as the **Cathedral of St. John the Divine.** But prime Upper West Side—the part you're most likely to explore—is the area running from Columbus Circle at 59th Street into the 80s, between the park and Broadway. North of 59th Street is where Eighth Avenue becomes Central Park West, the eastern border of the neighborhood (and the western border of Central Park); Ninth Avenue becomes Columbus Avenue, lined with attractive boutiques and cafes; and Tenth Avenue becomes Amsterdam Avenue, less charming than Columbus to the east and less trafficked than bustling Broadway (whose highlights are the gourmet megamarts Zabar's and Fairway) to the west; still, Amsterdam has blossomed into quite a happening restaurant and bar strip over the last couple of years. You'll find Lincoln Center in the mid-60s, where Broadway crosscuts Amsterdam.

Two major subway lines service the area: the 1, 2, 3, 9 line runs up Broadway, while the B and C trains run up glamorous Central Park West, stopping right at the historic Dakota apartment building (where John Lennon was shot and Yoko Ono still lives) at 72nd Street, and at the Museum of Natural History at 81st Street.

Upper East Side North of 59th Street and east of Central Park is some of the city's most expensive residential real estate. This is New York at its most gentrified: Walk along Fifth and Park avenues, especially between 60th and 80th streets, and you're sure to encounter some of the wizened WASPs and Chanel-suited socialites that make up the most rarefied of the city's population. Madison Avenue from 60th Street well into the 80s is the monied crowd's main shopping strip, recently

vaunting ahead of Hong Kong's Causeway Bay to become the most expensive retail real estate *in the world*—so bring your platinum card. You can also use it to stay at one of the neighborhood's remarkably luxurious hotels, such as the Carlyle or the Plaza Athénée, or to dine at four-star wonders such as Café Boulud and Daniel.

The main attraction of this neighborhood is **Museum Mile,** the stretch of Fifth Avenue fronting Central Park that's home to no fewer than 10 terrific cultural institutions, including Frank Lloyd Wright's **Guggenheim,** and anchored by the mind-boggling **Metropolitan Museum of Art.** But the elegant rows of landmark town houses are worth a look alone: East 70th Street, from Madison east to Lexington, is one of the world's most charming residential streets. If you want to see where real people live, move east to Third Avenue and beyond; that's where affordable restaurants and active street life start popping up.

A second subway line is in the works, but it's still no more than an architect's blueprint. For now, the Upper East Side is served solely by the crowded Lexington Avenue line (4, 5, 6 trains), so wear your walking shoes (or bring taxi fare) if you're heading up here to explore.

Harlem Harlem has benefited from a dramatic image makeover in the last few years, and with new restaurants, clubs, and stores is slowly becoming a neighborhood in demand.

Harlem is actually several areas. **Harlem proper** stretches from river to river, beginning at 125th Street on the West Side, 96th Street on the East Side, and 110th Street north of Central Park. East of Fifth Avenue, **Spanish Harlem** (El Barrio) runs between East 100th and East 125th streets. Harlem proper, in particular, is benefiting greatly from the revitalization that has swept so much of the city, with national-brand retailers moving in, restaurants and hip nightspots opening everywhere, and visitors arriving to tour historic sites related to the golden age of African-American culture, when great bands such as the Count Basie and Duke Ellington orchestras played the Cotton Club and Sugar Cane Club, and literary giants such as Langston Hughes and James Baldwin soaked up the scene. Some houses date from a time when the area was something of a country retreat, and represent some of the best brownstone mansions in the city. On **Sugar Hill** (from 143rd to 155th sts., between St. Nicholas and Edgecombe aves.) and **Striver's Row** (W. 139th St. between Adam Clayton Powell Jr. and Frederick Douglass boulevards) are a significant number of fine town houses. For cultural visits, there's the Morris-Jumel Mansion, the Schomburg Center, the Studio Museum, and the Apollo Theater.

You'll find 125th a fun place to shop with its mix of national chains like Old Navy standing side-by-side with emporiums of hip-hop fashion.

By all means, come see Harlem—it's one of the city's most vital, historic neighborhoods, and no other feels quite so energized right now. Your best bet for seeing all the sights is to take a guided tour (see "Organized Sightseeing Tours," chapter 9); if you head up on your own to sightsee, come in daylight. Don't wander thoughtlessly through Harlem, especially at night. If you head up after dark to a restaurant or nightspot, just be clear and confident about where you're going and stay alert.

Washington Heights & Inwood
Located at the northern tip of Manhattan, Washington Heights (the area from 155th St. to Dyckman St., with adjacent Inwood running to the tip) is home to a large segment of Manhattan's Latino community, plus an increasing number of yuppies who don't mind trading a half-hour subway commute to Midtown for much lower rents. **Fort Tryon Park** and **the Cloisters** are the two big reasons for visitors to come up this way. The Cloisters houses the Metropolitan Museum of Art's stunning medieval collection, in a building perched atop a hill, with excellent views across the Hudson to the Palisades. Committed off-the-beaten-path sightseers might also want to visit the **Dyckman Farmhouse,** a historic jewel built in 1783 and the only remaining Dutch Colonial structure in Manhattan.

The Boroughs

Manhattan is just one of the five boroughs that make up the very Big Apple. The others are Brooklyn, the Bronx, Queens, and Staten Island.

Brooklyn Brooklynites are quick to tell you that their borough is the fourth largest city in the United States. That's because this borough is about pride and attitude. And though it has been over 45 years since the team left, don't even talk to them about the Dodgers.

Brooklyn is also about neighborhoods and diversity; the borough is a pleasure to explore. Some of the highlights include New York's first historic district, **Brooklyn Heights,** with its elegant brownstones; the Promenade, with its spectacular view of Manhattan; and the romantic River Cafe. To get to Brooklyn Heights, take the A, C, F to Jay Street; the 2, 3, 4, 5 to Clark Street; or the N, R to Court Street.

Brooklyn's newest neighborhood is the creation called **DUMBO** (Down Under the Manhattan Bridge Overpass). What was once a scattering of warehouses is now a thriving artist's

Tips NYC Experiences to Avoid

New York has so much going for it, the good overwhelms the bad. But there is bad, and I'm not talking about the obvious. I'm talking about experiences that might be perceived as good, but take my word for it: They are not. So, despite what you have heard, the following are a few experiences you must do your best to avoid.

New Year's Eve in Times Square: You see the event on television every year, and now you're here. This is your chance to be one of the hundreds of thousands of revelers packed tightly together in the frigid cold to watch the ball drop. Don't do it! Despite the happy faces you see on television, the whole thing is a miserable experience and not worth the forced elation of blowing on a noisemaker at midnight with half a million others. And you won't find many New Yorkers here; we know better.

Three-Card Monte: When you see a crowd gathered around a cardboard box with one man flipping cards, madly enticing innocent rubes into his game, while another guy scans the crowd for undercover cops, keep on walking. Don't stop and listen to the dealer's spiel or think you can be the one to beat him at his game. You can't. Buy a lottery ticket instead; your odds are much better.

Horse-Drawn Carriage Rides: Pity those poor beasts of burden. They get dragged out in the heat (though not extreme heat) and cold (though not extreme cold) with a buggy attached to them just to give passengers the feel of an old-world, romantic buggy ride through Central Park. But the horses look so forlorn, as if it's the last thing they want to do. And they don't even get a cut of the generous take: $40 for a 20-minute ride, $60 for 45 minutes, excluding tip. If you want a slow, leisurely ride through Central Park, minus the ripe and frequent smell of horse poop, consider an alternative called Manhattan Rickshaw Company (© 212/604-4729). The beast of burden behind the rickshaw has two legs, and the rate is about $1 per minute.

Chain Restaurants: Oh yes; they're here, probably to stay—and most likely with more to come. I'm referring to those restaurants with familiar names

colony, with those former warehouses now converted into very expensive lofts. The main drag is **Washington Street,** and businesses are beginning to populate the area. It's here where you'll find **Jacques Torres Chocolate,** the **Brooklyn Ice Cream Factory,** and **Grimaldi's Pizza.** The best way to get to DUMBO is the F train to York Street or the A or C to High Street.

Brooklyn's hippest neighborhood (some say way past hip) is **Williamsburg.** In the early 1990s, artists began to flee Manhattan's high rents to live here among the Hispanic and Hasidic communities already there. Now, though, the hipsters have seen their once independent and inexpensive enclave being slowly transformed into SoHo/Brooklyn. There are a number of funky, youth-oriented boutiques here like Olive Garden, Applebee's, Red Lobster, and Domino's. When you begin to feel the pangs of hunger, ask yourself: Did I come to New York to eat exactly what I can eat in every city or town in this country? Or did I come here to experience what makes New York so unique? Well, that includes the amazing variety of unchained restaurants, from the coffee shops and diners to the bargain-priced ethnic cuisine and higher-end dining experiences. So bypass the old standards, and try something different and exciting. You won't regret it.

Electronics Stores: You might notice a wealth of electronics stores in and around Times Square, on Fifth Avenue, or wherever gullible tourists frequent. Many of the stores post banners advertising a GOING OUT OF BUSINESS sale. These guys have been going out of business since the Stone Age. That's the bait and switch; pretty soon you've spent too much money for not enough stereos or cameras or MP3 players. The people who work at these stores are a special breed of shark; they work you hard to take their deal. Don't even get close enough to let them sink their fangs into you because when they do, you're usually theirs for the taking.

The Feast of San Gennaro: At one time this was a distinct and genuine Italian feast (see the films *Godfather II* and *Mean Streets* for the Feast in the good old days). Its decline has pretty much coincided with the decline of Little Italy, a neighborhood that is just a shell of what it once was. Now the Feast, held annually for 2 weeks in September, is just an overblown and overcrowded street fair with bad food, cheap red wine, and games of chance you have no chance of winning.

Driving in the City: You have been warned already about driving in the city, but some people are stubborn and just can't give up the so-called freedom of maneuvering a car in heavy traffic, battling yellow cabs, and searching fruitlessly for a legal parking spot. With subways, buses, and your feet, New York has the best and fastest public transportation. A car is a luxury you want no part of.

along the neighborhood's main drag, **Bedford Avenue,** but Williamsburg is also the home of that venerable red meat institution, **Peter Luger.** The best train to take to get to Williamsburg from Manhattan is the L to Bedford Avenue.

Other emerging neighborhoods are **Carroll Gardens, Cobble Hill,** and **Boerum Hill. Smith Street** cuts

through all three and has become a booming restaurant destination. To get to Smith Street the best train is the F, with stops at either Carroll Street or Bergen Street.

Downtown Brooklyn off Flatbush Avenue is probably best known for **BAM,** the **Brooklyn Academy of Music.** You'll also find a number of chain department stores and one of the borough's most beloved landmarks, **Junior's,** the diner noted for its famous cheesecakes. Many trains converge in downtown Brooklyn at the Pacific Street/Atlantic Avenue station, including the 2, 3, 4, 5, M, N, Q, R, and W.

Park Slope is probably the heart of Brooklyn; it is here and in nearby Prospect Heights where you find the **Brooklyn Museum,** the **Brooklyn Botanical Gardens,** and **Prospect Park.** The 2, 3, 4, 5 trains to Grand Army Plaza will land you close to all of the above.

In its heyday during the early 20th century, **Coney Island** was to New York what South Beach is now to Miami. This was where everyone flocked to escape the heat and grime of a New York summer day. A few remnants of Coney Island's past remain, such as the long-defunct parachute ride. But during the summer you can still ride on one of the best roller coasters anywhere, the famous **Cyclone.** Coney Island is also the home of the **New York Aquarium** and the minor-league baseball team the Cyclones. To get to Coney Island, take the D or F to West 8th Street, Brooklyn.

The Bronx Perhaps the most famous destination in the Bronx, and next to Rome's Coliseum maybe one of the most celebrated sports arenas in the world, is **Yankee Stadium.** Even if you are a Yankee hater, you will be awed by the stadium. The 4, B, and D trains all stop there.

The Bronx is also the home of the United States' largest metropolitan animal park, the **Bronx Zoo,** and the national landmark **Bronx Botanical Gardens.** Both are wonders very worthy of an excursion from Manhattan. To get to the Bronx Zoo, you can take the 2 train to Pelham Parkway and walk to the Bronxdale entrance of the zoo. To get to the Botanical Gardens, you can take Metro-North from Grand Central Station to the Botanical Gardens station.

While visiting either the Bronx Zoo or the Botanical Gardens, stop at the Little Italy of the Bronx, **Arthur Avenue,** for a mouthwatering walk past meat markets, delis, vegetable stands, fish markets, cafes, and restaurants. To get to Arthur Avenue, take the 4 or D train to Fordham Road, and transfer to the 12 bus east or the 2 or 5 train to Pelham Parkway and the 12 bus west.

Queens Queens is the largest borough in New York and it's also the city's most ethnically diverse. There are more languages spoken in this 109 square miles than anywhere else on the planet. All that ethnicity translates into an adventurous eater's paradise. I've dined on Thai, Peruvian, Indian, Guyanese, Greek, Colombian, and Brazilian here, and I've barely scratched the surface. But there's more to Queens than just food.

Astoria, with its large Greek community, is also the home of the **American Museum of the Moving Image,** dedicated to the movies—film, video, and digital. To get to Astoria, take the N to Broadway.

Long Island City, directly across the river from Manhattan's Upper East Side is where you will find a number of museums including **Socrates Park,** the **Museum of African Art,** and the **P.S. 1 Contemporary Art Center.** The best train to take to get to Long Island City is the 7. The 7 train is really the heartbeat of Queens, also known as the International Express, running through one ethnic community after another; get off at just about any spot and you'll see signs in an assortment of languages. The 7 train will also take you to Flushing, where you'll find **Shea Stadium,** home of the Mets; the Louis Armstrong Stadium and the Arthur Ashe Stadium at **Flushing Meadow Park,** where the **U.S. Open** is held each September; and the **Queens Museum of Art** on the grounds of the 1964 World's Fair.

Staten Island Staten Island is the most remote of the boroughs and best reached by ferry. There is a suburban feel to the borough, making it a haven for commuters. The free **Staten Island Ferry** gets you to the borough. If you decide to spend time in Staten Island, take in a **Staten Island Yankees** minor-league baseball game. The stadium is within walking distance from the ferry and has lovely views of downtown Manhattan.

2 Getting Around

Frankly, Manhattan's transportation systems are a marvel. It's simply miraculous that so many people can gather on this little island and move around it. For the most part, you can get where you're going pretty quickly and easily using some combination of subways, buses, and cabs; this section will tell you how to do just that.

But between traffic gridlock and subway delays, sometimes you just can't get there from here—unless you walk. Walking can sometimes be the fastest way to navigate the island. During rush hours, you'll easily beat car traffic while on foot, as taxis and buses stop and groan at gridlocked corners (don't even *try* going crosstown in a cab or bus in Midtown at midday). You'll also see a whole lot more by walking than you will if you ride beneath the street in the subway or fly by in a cab. So pack your most comfortable shoes and hit the pavement—it's the best, cheapest, and most appealing way to experience the city.

BY SUBWAY

Run by the **Metropolitan Transit Authority (MTA),** the much-maligned subway system is actually the fastest way to travel around New York, especially during rush hours.

Tips Sidewalks of New York

What's the primary means New Yorkers use for getting around town? The subway? Buses? Taxis? Nope. Walking. They stride across wide, crowded pavements without any regard for traffic lights, weaving through crowds at high speeds, dodging taxis and buses whose drivers are forced to interrupt the normal flow of traffic to avoid flattening them. **Never take your walking cues from the locals.** Wait for walk signals and always use crosswalks—don't cross in the middle of the block. Do otherwise and you could quickly end up as a flattened statistic.

Always pay attention to the traffic flow. Walk as though you're driving, staying to the right. Pay attention to what's happening in the street, even if you have the right of way. At intersections, keep an eye out for drivers who don't yield, turn without looking, or think a yellow traffic light means "Hurry up!" as you cross. Unfortunately, most bicyclists seem to think that the traffic laws don't apply to them; they'll often blithely fly through red lights and dash the wrong way on one-way streets, so be on your guard.

For more important safety tips, see "Playing It Safe," later in this chapter.

Subway Stops for New York's Top Attractions

ATTRACTIONS	SUBWAY STOPS
MUSEUMS	
American Museum of Natural History	**B, C** to 81st Street
The Cloisters	**A** to 190th Street
Ellis Island	**4, 5** to Bowling Green or **N, R** to Whitehall Street
Guggenheim Museum	**4, 5, 6** to 86th Street
Intrepid Sea-Air-Space Museum	**A, C, E** to 42nd Street–Port Authority
Metropolitan Museum of Art	**4, 5, 6** to 86th Street
Museum of Modern Art	**E, V** to Fifth Avenue
HISTORIC BUILDINGS AND ARCHITECTURE	
Brooklyn Bridge	**4, 5, 6** to Brooklyn Bridge–City Hall
Chrysler Building	**4, 5, 6, 7, S** to Grand Central–42nd Street
Empire State Building	**B, D, F, V, N, R, Q, W** to 34th Street–Herald Square
Grand Central Terminal	**4, 5, 6, 7, S** to Grand Central–42nd Street
Rockefeller Center	**B, D, F, V** to 47–50th sts.–Rockefeller Center
Staten Island Ferry	**1, 9** to South Ferry (first five cars)
United Nations	**4, 5, 6, 7, S** to Grand Central–42nd Street
Yankee Stadium	**4, B, D** to 161st River Avenue–Yankee Stadium
NEIGHBORHOODS	
Chinatown	**6, J, M, Z, N, R, W** to Canal Street
Greenwich Village	**A, C, E, B, D, F, V** to West 4th Street
Times Square	**1, 2, 3, 7, N, R, W, S** to 42nd Street–Times Square
Wall Street	**4, 5** to Wall Street or **N, R** to Rector Street
CHURCHES	
Cathedral of St. John the Divine	**1** to Cathedral Parkway (110th St.)
St. Patrick's Cathedral	**B, D, F, V** to 47–50th sts.–Rockefeller Center or **E, V** to Fifth Avenue–53rd Street

Some 3.5 million people a day seem to agree with me, as it's their primary mode of transportation. The subway is quick, inexpensive, relatively safe, and pretty efficient, as well as being a genuine New York experience.

The subway runs 24 hours a day, 7 days a week. The rush-hour crushes are roughly from 8 to 9:30am and from 5 to 6:30pm on weekdays; the rest of the time the trains are relatively uncrowded.

PAYING YOUR WAY

The subway fare is $2 (half-price for seniors and those with disabilities), and children under 44 inches tall ride free (up to three per adult).

Tokens were phased out in 2003 and are no longer available. People now pay fares with the **MetroCard,** a magnetically encoded card that debits the fare when swiped through the turnstile (or the fare box on any city bus). Once you're in the system, you can transfer freely to any subway line that you can reach without exiting your station. MetroCards also allow you **free transfers** between the bus and subway within a 2-hour period.

MetroCards can be purchased from each station's staffed token booth, where you can only pay with cash; at the ATM-style vending machines now located in just about every subway station in the city, which accept cash, credit cards, and debit cards; from a MetroCard merchant, such as most Rite Aid drugstores or Hudson News at Penn Station and Grand Central Terminal; or at the MTA information desk at the Times Square Visitor Center, 1560 Broadway, between 46th and 47th streets.

MetroCards come in a few different configurations:

Pay-Per-Ride MetroCards can be used for up to four people by swiping up to four times (bring the whole family). You can put any amount from $4 (two rides) to $80 on your card. Every time you put $10 or $20 on your Pay-Per-Ride MetroCard, it's automatically credited 20%—that's one free ride for every $10, or 5 trips. You can buy Pay-Per-Ride MetroCards at any subway station; an increasing number of stations now have automated MetroCard vending machines, which allow you to buy Metro-Cards using your major credit card. MetroCards are also available from shops and newsstands around town in $10 and $20 values. You can refill your card at any time until the expiration date on the card, usually about a year from the date of purchase, at any subway station.

Unlimited-Ride MetroCards, which can't be used for more than one person at a time or more frequently than 18-minute intervals, are available in four values: the **daily Fun Pass,** which allows you a day's worth of unlimited subway and bus rides for $7; the **7-Day MetroCard,** for $24; and the **30-Day MetroCard,** for $76. Seven- and 30-day Unlimited-Ride MetroCards can be purchased at any subway station or from a MetroCard merchant. Fun Passes, however, cannot be purchased at token booths—you can only buy them at a MetroCard vending machine; from a MetroCard merchant; or at the MTA information desk at the Times Square Visitor Center. Unlimited-Ride MetroCards go into effect not at the time you buy them but the first time you use them—so if you buy a card on Monday and don't begin to use it until Wednesday, Wednesday is when the clock starts ticking on your MetroCard. A Fun Pass is good from the first time you use it until 3am the next day, while 7- and 30-day MetroCards run out at midnight on the last day. These MetroCards cannot be refilled; throw them out once they've been used up and buy a new one.

Tips for using your MetroCard: The MetroCard swiping mechanisms at turnstiles are the source of much grousing among subway riders. If you swipe too fast or too slow, the turnstile will ask you to swipe again. If this happens, *do not move to a different turnstile,* or you may end up paying twice. If you've tried repeatedly and really can't make your MetroCard work, tell the token booth clerk; chances are good, though, that you'll get the movement down after a couple of uses.

If you're not sure how much money you have left on your MetroCard, or what day it expires, use the station's MetroCard Reader, usually located near the station entrance or the token booth (on buses, the fare box will also provide you with this information).

To locate the nearest MetroCard merchant, or for any other MetroCard questions, call ℂ **800/METROCARD** or 212/METROCARD (212/638-7622) Monday through

Friday between 7am and 11pm, Saturday and Sunday from 9am to 5pm. Or go online to **www.mta.nyc.ny.us/metrocard**, which can give you a full rundown of MetroCard merchants in the tri-state area.

USING THE SYSTEM

As you can see from the full-color subway map on the inside back cover of this book, the subway system basically mimics the lay of the land aboveground, with most lines in Manhattan running north and south, like the avenues, and a few lines east and west, like the streets.

To go up and down the east side of Manhattan (and to the Bronx and Brooklyn), take the 4, 5, or 6 train.

To travel up and down the west side (and also to the Bronx and Brooklyn), take the 1, 2, 3, or 9 line; the A, C, E, or F line; or the B or D line.

The N, R, Q, and W lines first cut diagonally across town from east to west and then snake under Seventh Avenue before shooting out to Queens.

The crosstown S line, the Shuttle, runs back and forth between Times Square and Grand Central Terminal. Farther downtown, across 14th Street, the L line works its own crosstown magic.

Lines have assigned colors on subway maps and trains—red for the 1, 2, 3, 9 line; green for the 4, 5, 6 trains; and so on—but nobody ever refers to them by color. Always refer to them by number or letter when asking questions. Within Manhattan, the distinction between different numbered trains that share the same line is usually that some are express and others are local. **Express trains** often skip about three stops for each one that they make; express stops are indicated on subway maps with a white (rather than solid) circle. Local stops are usually about 9 blocks apart.

Directions are almost always indicated using "Uptown" (northbound) and "Downtown" (southbound), so be sure to know what direction you want to head in. The outsides of some subway entrances are marked UPTOWN ONLY or DOWNTOWN ONLY; read carefully, as it's easy to head in the wrong direction. Once you're on the platform, check the signs overhead to make sure that the train you're waiting for will be traveling in the right direction. If you do make a mistake, it's a good idea to wait for an express station, such as 14th Street or 42nd Street, so you can get off and change to the other direction without paying again.

The days of graffiti-covered cars are gone, but the stations—and an increasing number of trains—are not nearly as clean as they could be. Trains are air-conditioned (move to the next car if yours isn't), though during the dog days of summer the platforms can

---

Subway Service Interruption Notes

The subway map featured on the inside back cover of this book was as accurate as possible at press time, but service is always subject to change, so your best bet is to contact the **Metropolitan Transit Authority (MTA)** for the latest details; call © **718/330-1234** or visit **www.mta.nyc.ny.us**, where you'll find system updates that are thorough, timely, and clear. Once you're in town, you can also stop at the MTA desk at the **Times Square Visitors Center,** 1560 Broadway, between 46th and 47th streets (where Broadway meets Seventh Ave.) to pick up the latest subway map. (You can also ask for one at any token booth, but they might not always be stocked.)

Tips **For More Bus & Subway Information**

For additional transit information, call the Metropolitan Transit Authority's **MTA/New York City Transit's Travel Information Center** at © **718/330-1234.** Extensive automated information is available at this number 24 hours a day, and travel agents are on hand to answer your questions and provide directions daily from 6am to 9pm. For online information that's always up-to-the-minute current, visit **www.mta.nyc.ny.us.**

To request system maps, call the Customer Assistance Line at © **718/330-3322** (although realize that recent service changes may not yet be reflected on printed maps). Riders with disabilities should direct inquiries to © **718/596-8585;** hearing-impaired riders can call © **718/596-8273.** For MetroCard information, call © **212/638-7622** weekdays from 7am to 11pm, weekends 9am to 5pm, or go online to **www.mta.nyc.ny.us/metrocard.**

You can get bus and subway maps and additional transit information at most information centers (see "Visitor Information" in "Orientation," earlier in this chapter). A particularly helpful MTA transit information desk is located at the **Times Square Visitor Center,** 1560 Broadway, between 46th and 47th streets, where you can also buy MetroCards. Maps are sometimes available in subway stations (ask at the token booth), but rarely on buses.

---

be sweltering. In theory, all subway cars have PA systems to allow you to hear the conductor's announcements, but they don't always work well. It's a good idea to move to a car with a working PA system in case sudden service changes are announced that you'll want to know about.

For **subway safety tips,** see "Playing It Safe," below.

BY BUS

Less expensive than taxis and more pleasant than subways (they provide a mobile sightseeing window on Manhattan), MTA buses are a good transportation option. Their very big drawback: They can get stuck in traffic, sometimes making it quicker to walk. They also stop every couple of blocks, rather than the 8 or 9 blocks that local subways traverse between stops. So for long distances, the subway is your best bet; but for short distances or traveling crosstown, try the bus.

PAYING YOUR WAY

Like the subway fare, **bus fare** is $2, half-price for seniors and riders with disabilities, and free for children under 44 inches (up to three per adult). The fare is payable with a **MetroCard** or **exact change.** Bus drivers don't make change, and fare boxes don't accept dollar bills or pennies. You can't purchase MetroCards on the bus, so you'll have to have them before you board; for details on where to get them, see "Paying Your Way" under "By Subway," above.

If you pay with a MetroCard, you can transfer to another bus or to the subway for free within 2 hours. If you pay cash, you must request a **free transfer** slip that allows you to change to an intersecting bus route only (legal transfer points are listed on the transfer paper) within 1 hour of issue. Transfer slips cannot be used to enter the subway.

Tips   **Take a Free Ride**

The Alliance for Downtown New York's **Downtown Connection** offers a free bus service that provides easy access to important Downtown destinations, including Battery Park City, the World Financial Center, and South Street Seaport. The buses, which run daily from 10am to 8pm, make dozens of stops along a 5-mile route from Chambers Street on the West Side to Beekman Street on the East Side. For schedules and more information, call the Downtown Alliance at ℂ **212/566-6700**, or visit www.downtownny.com.

USING THE SYSTEM

You can't flag a city bus down—you have to meet it at a bus stop. **Bus stops** are located every 2 or 3 blocks on the right-side corner of the street (facing the direction of traffic flow). They're marked by a curb painted yellow and a blue-and-white sign with a bus emblem and the route number or numbers. Guide-A-Ride boxes at most stops display a route map and a hysterically optimistic schedule.

Almost every major avenue has its own **bus route.** They run either north or south: downtown on Fifth, uptown on Madison, downtown on Lexington, uptown on Third, and so on. There are **crosstown buses** at strategic locations all around town: 8th Street (eastbound); 9th (westbound); 14th, 23rd, 34th, and 42nd (east- and westbound); 49th (eastbound); 50th (westbound); 57th (east- and westbound); 65th (eastbound across the West Side, through the park, and then north on Madison, continuing east on 68th to York Ave.); 67th (westbound on the East Side to Fifth Ave. and then south on Fifth, continuing west on 66th St. through the park and across the West Side to W. End Ave.); and 79th, 86th, 96th, 116th, and 125th (east- and westbound). Some bus routes, however, are erratic: The M104, for example, starts at the East River, then turns at Eighth Avenue and goes up Broadway. The buses of the Fifth Avenue line go up Madison or Sixth and follow various routes around the city.

Most routes operate 24 hours a day, but service is infrequent at night. Some say that New York buses have a herding instinct: They arrive only in groups. During rush hour, main routes have "limited" buses, identifiable by the red card in the front window; they stop only at major cross streets.

To make sure that the bus you're boarding goes where you're going, check the map on the sign that's at every bus stop, get your hands on a route map (see "For More Bus & Subway Information," above), or **just ask.** The drivers are helpful, as long as you don't hold up the line too long.

While traveling, look out the window not only to take in the sights but also to keep track of cross streets so you know when to get off. Signal for a stop by pressing the tape strip above and beside the windows and along the metal straps, about 2 blocks before you want to stop. Exit through the pneumatic back doors (not the front door) by pushing on the yellow tape strip; the doors open automatically (pushing on the handles is useless unless you're as buff as Hercules). Most city buses are equipped with wheelchair lifts, making buses the preferable mode of public transportation for wheelchair-bound travelers; for more on this topic, see "Specialized Travel Resources," on p. 40. Buses also "kneel," lowering down to the curb to make boarding easier.

BY TAXI

If you don't want to deal with public transportation, finding an address that might be a few blocks from the subway station, or sharing your ride with 3.5 million other people, then take a taxi. The biggest advantages are, of course, that cabs can be hailed on any street (providing you find an empty one—often simple, yet at other times nearly impossible) and will take you right to your destination. I find they're best used at night when there's little traffic to keep them from speeding you to your destination and when the subway may seem a little daunting. In Midtown at midday, you can usually walk to where you're going more quickly.

Official New York City taxis, licensed by the Taxi and Limousine Commission (TLC), are yellow, with the rates printed on the door and a light with a medallion number on the roof. You can hail a taxi on any street. *Never* accept a ride from any other car except an official city yellow cab (private livery cars are not allowed to pick up fares on the street).

Lobbying by taxi drivers led to fare increases in 2004. The base fare on entering the cab is $2.50. The cost is 40¢ for every ⅕ mile or 40¢ per 2 minutes in stopped or very slow-moving traffic (or for waiting time). There's no extra charge for each passenger or for luggage. However, you must pay bridge or tunnel tolls (sometimes the driver will front the toll and add it to your bill at the end; most times, however, you pay the driver before the toll). You'll also pay a $1 surcharge between 4 and 8pm and a 50 cent surcharge after 8pm and before 6 am. A 15% to 20% tip is customary.

Forget about hopping into the back seat and having some double-chinned, cigar-chomping, all-knowing driver slowly turn and ask nonchalantly, "Where to, Mac?" Nowadays most taxi drivers speak only an approximation of English and drive in engagingly exotic ways. Always wear your seat belt—taxis are required to provide them.

The TLC has posted a **Taxi Rider's Bill of Rights** sticker in every cab. Drivers are required by law to take you anywhere in the five boroughs, to Nassau or Westchester counties, or to Newark Airport. They are supposed to know how to get you to any address in Manhattan and all major points in the outer boroughs. They are also required to provide air-conditioning and turn off the radio on demand, and they cannot smoke while you're in the cab. They are required to be polite.

You are allowed to dictate the route that is taken. It's a good idea to look at a map before you get in a taxi. Taxi drivers have been known to jack up the fare on visitors who don't know better by taking a circuitous route between point A and point B. Know enough about where you're going to know that something's wrong if you hop in a cab at Sixth Avenue and 57th Street to go to the Empire State Building (Fifth Ave. and 34th St.), say, and you suddenly find yourself on Ninth Avenue.

Tips Taxi-Hailing Tips

When you're waiting on the street for an available taxi, look at the **medallion light** on the top of the coming cabs. If the light is out, the taxi is in use. When the center part (the number) is lit, the taxi is available—this is when you raise your hand to flag the cab. If all the lights are on, the driver is off duty.

A taxi can't take more than four people, so expect to split up if your group is larger.

On the other hand, listen to drivers who propose an alternate route. These guys spend 8 or 10 hours a day on these streets, and they know them well—where the worst midday traffic is, where Con Ed has dug up an intersection that should be avoided. A knowledgeable driver will know how to get you to your destination quickly and efficiently.

Another important tip: **Always make sure the meter is turned on at the start of the ride.** You'll see the red LED readout register the initial $2 and start calculating the fare as you go. I've witnessed unscrupulous drivers buzzing unsuspecting visitors around the city with the meter off, and then overcharging them at drop-off time.

Always ask for the receipt—it comes in handy if you need to make a complaint or have left something in a cab. In fact, it's a good idea to make a mental note of the driver's four-digit medallion number (usually posted on the divider between the front and back seats) just in case you need it later. You probably won't, but it's a good idea to play it safe.

A taxi driver is obligated to take you to your desired destination. If a taxi driver is on duty but refuses to take you to your desired destination, write down the driver's name and medallion number and file a complaint with the Taxi and Limousine Commission.

For all driver complaints, including the one above, and to report lost property, call the 24-hour Consumer Hot Line at ℂ **212/NYC-TAXI.** For details on getting to and from the local airports by taxi, see "By Plane" under "Getting There," in chapter 3. For further taxi information—including a complete rundown of your rights as a taxi rider—point your Web browser to **www.ci.nyc.ny.us/taxi**.

BY CAR

Forget driving yourself around the city. It's not worth the headache. Traffic is horrendous, and you don't know the rules of the road (written or unwritten) or the arcane alternate-side-of-the-street parking regulations (in fact, precious few New Yorkers do). You don't want to find out the monstrous price of parking violations or live the Kafkaesque nightmare of liberating a vehicle from the tow pound. Not to mention the security risks.

If you do arrive in New York City by car, park it in a garage (expect to pay at least $25–$45 per day) and leave it there for the duration of your stay. If you drive a rental car in, return it as soon as you arrive and rent another on the day you leave. Just about all of the major car-rental companies, including **National** (ℂ **800/227-7368;** www.nationalcar.com), **Hertz** (ℂ **800/654-3131;** www.hertz.com), and **Avis** (ℂ **800/230-4898;** www.avis.com), have multiple Manhattan locations.

TRAVELING FROM THE CITY TO THE SUBURBS

The **PATH** (ℂ **800/234-7284;** www.panynj.gov/path) system connects urban communities in New Jersey, including Hoboken and Newark, to Manhattan by subway-style trains. Stops in Manhattan are at the World Trade Center, Christopher and 9th streets, and along Sixth Avenue at 14th, 23rd, and 33rd streets. The fare is $1.50.

Impressions
Traffic signals in New York are just rough guidelines.

—David Letterman

New Jersey Transit (© 800/772-2222; www.njtransit.com) operates commuter trains from Penn Station, and buses from the Port Authority at Eighth Avenue and 42nd Street, to points throughout New Jersey.

The Long Island Rail Road (© 718/217-LIRR; www.mta.nyc.ny.us/lirr) runs from Penn Station, at Seventh Avenue between 31st and 33rd streets, to Queens (ocean beaches, Shea Stadium, Belmont Park) and points beyond on Long Island, to even better beaches and summer hot spots like Fire Island and the Hamptons.

Metro-North Railroad (© 800/METRO-INFO or 212/532-4900; www.mta.nyc. ny.us/mnr) departs from Grand Central Terminal, at 42nd Street and Lexington Avenue, for areas north of the city, including Westchester County, the lovely Hudson Valley, and Connecticut.

3 Playing It Safe

Sure, there's crime in New York City, but millions of people spend their lives here without being robbed and assaulted. In fact, New York is safer than any other big American city, and is listed by the FBI as somewhere around 150th in the nation for total crimes. While that's quite encouraging for all of us, it's still important to take precautions. Visitors especially should remain vigilant, as swindlers and criminals are expert at spotting newcomers who appear disoriented or vulnerable.

Men should carry their wallets in their front pockets and women should keep constant hold of their purse straps. Cross camera and purse straps over one shoulder, across your front, and under the other arm. Never hang a purse on the back of a chair or on a hook in a bathroom stall; keep it in your lap or between your feet, with one foot through a strap and up against the purse itself. Avoid carrying large amounts of cash. You might carry your money in several pockets so that if one is picked, the others might escape. Skip the flashy jewelry and keep valuables out of sight when you're on the street.

Panhandlers are seldom dangerous and can be ignored (more aggressive pleas can firmly be answered, "Not today"). If a stranger walks up to you on the street with a long sob story ("I live in the suburbs and was just attacked and don't have the money to get home" or whatever), it's likely to be a scam, so don't feel any moral compulsion to help. You have every right to walk away and not feel bad. Be wary of an individual who "accidentally" falls in front of you or causes some other commotion, because he or she may be working with someone else who will take your wallet when you try to help. And remember: You *will* lose if you place a bet on a sidewalk card game or shell game.

Certain areas should be approached with care late at night. I don't recommend going to the Lower East Side, Alphabet City in the far East Village, or the Meatpacking District unless you know where you're going. Don't be afraid to go, but head straight for your destination and don't wander onto deserted side streets. The areas above 96th Street aren't the best, either (although they're improving almost by the day). Times Square has been cleaned up, and there'll be crowds around until midnight, when theater- and moviegoers leave the area. Still, stick to the main streets, such as Broadway or Ninth Avenue, Midtown West's newest restaurant row. The areas south of Times Square are best avoided after dark, as they're largely abandoned once the business day ends. Take a cab or bus when visiting the Jacob Javits Center on 34th Street and the Hudson River. Don't go wandering the parks after dark, unless you're going to a performance; if that's the case, stick with the crowd.

Impressions

I like it here in New York. I like the idea of having to keep eyes in the back of your head all the time.

—John Cale

If you plan on visiting the outer boroughs, go during the daylight hours. If the subway doesn't go directly to your destination, your best bet is to take a taxi. Don't wander the side streets; many areas in the outer boroughs are absolutely safe, but neighborhoods change quickly, and it's easy to get lost.

All this having been said, don't panic. New York has experienced a dramatic drop in crime and is generally safe these days, especially in the neighborhoods that visitors are prone to frequent. There's a good police presence on the street, so don't be afraid to stop an officer, or even a friendly-looking New Yorker (trust me—you can tell), if you need help getting your bearings.

SUBWAY SAFETY TIPS   In general, the subways are safe, especially in Manhattan. There are panhandlers and questionable characters like anywhere else in the city, but subway crime has gone down to 1960s levels. Still, stay alert and trust your instincts. Always keep a hand on your personal belongings.

When using the subway, **don't wait for trains near the edge of the platform** or on extreme ends of a station. During nonrush hours, wait for the train in view of the token booth clerk or under the yellow DURING OFF HOURS TRAINS STOP HERE signs, and ride in the train operator's or conductor's car (usually in the center of the train; you'll see his or her head stick out of the window when the doors open). Choose crowded cars over empty ones—there's safety in numbers.

Avoid subways late at night, and splurge on a cab after about 10 or 11pm—it's money well spent to avoid a long wait on a deserted platform. Or take the bus.

FAST FACTS: New York City

American Express   Travel service offices are at many Manhattan locations, including 1185 Sixth Ave., at 47th Street (✆ **212/398-8585**); at the New York Marriott Marquis, 1535 Broadway, in the eighth-floor lobby (✆ **212/575-6580**); on the mezzanine level at Macy's Herald Square, 34th Street and Broadway (✆ **212/ 695-8075**); and 374 Park Ave., at 53rd Street (✆ **212/421-8240**). Call ✆ **800/AXP-TRIP** or go online to **www.americanexpress.com** for other city locations or general information.

Area Codes   There are four area codes in the city: two in Manhattan, the original **212** and the new **646,** and two in the outer boroughs, the original **718** and the new **347.** Also common is the **917** area code, which is assigned to cellphones, pagers, and the like. All calls between these area codes are local calls, but you'll have to dial 1 + the area code + the seven digits for all calls, even ones made within your area code.

Business Hours   In general, **retail stores** are open Monday through Saturday from 10am to 6 or 7pm, Thursday from 10am to 8:30 or 9pm, and Sunday from noon to 5pm (see chapter 10). **Banks** tend to be open Monday through Friday from 9am to 3pm and sometimes Saturday mornings.

Dentists See "Health & Safety," in chapter 3.

Doctors For medical emergencies requiring immediate attention, head to the nearest emergency room (see "Hospitals," below). For less urgent health problems, New York has several walk-in medical centers, such as **DOCS at New York Healthcare,** 55 E. 34th St., between Park and Madison avenues (✆ **212/252-6001**), for nonemergency illnesses. The clinic, affiliated with Beth Israel Medical Center, is open Monday through Thursday from 8am to 8pm, Friday from 8am to 7pm, Saturday from 9am to 3pm, and Sunday from 9am to 2pm. The **NYU Downtown Hospital** offers physician referrals at ✆ **888/698-3362.**

Embassies & Consulates See "Fast Facts: For the International Traveler," in chapter 4.

Emergencies Dial ✆ **911** for fire, police, and ambulance. The **Poison Control Center** can be reached at ✆ **800/222-1222** toll-free from any phone.

Hospitals The following hospitals have 24-hour emergency rooms. Don't forget your insurance card.

Downtown: New York University Downtown Hospital, 170 William St., between Beekman and Spruce streets (✆ 212/312-5063 or 212/312-5000); **St. Vincent's Hospital and Medical Center,** 153 W. 11th St., at Seventh Avenue (✆ 212/604-7000); and **Beth Israel Medical Center,** First Avenue and 16th Street (✆ 212/420-2000).

Midtown: Bellevue Hospital Center, 462 First Ave., at 27th Street (✆ 212/252-94571); **New York University Medical Center,** 550 First Ave., at 33rd Street (✆ 212/263-7300); and **St. Luke's/Roosevelt Hospital,** 425 W. 59th St., between Ninth and Tenth avenues (✆ 212/523-4000).

Upper West Side: St. Luke's Hospital Center, Amsterdam Avenue and 113th Street (✆ 212/765-5454); and **Columbia Presbyterian Medical Center,** 622 W. 168th St., between Broadway and Fort Washington Avenue (✆ 212/305-2500).

Upper East Side: New York Presbyterian Hospital, 525 E. 68th St., at York Avenue (✆ 212/472-5454); **Lenox Hill Hospital,** 100 E. 77th St., between Park and Lexington avenues (✆ 212/434-2000); and **Mount Sinai Medical Center,** Fifth Avenue at 100th Street (✆ 212/241-6500).

Hot Lines The 24-hour **Rape and Sexual Abuse Hot Line** is ✆ 212/267-7273. The **Bias Crimes Hot Line** is ✆ 212/662-2427. The **LIFENET Hot Line** for suicide prevention, substance abuse, and other mental health crises is ✆ 800/543-3638. For **Mental Health and Alcoholism Services Crisis Intervention,** call ✆ 212/219-5599. You can reach **Alcoholics Anonymous** at ✆ 212/647-1680 (general office) or 212/647-1680 (intergroup, for alcoholics who need immediate counseling from a sober, recovering alcoholic). The **Domestic Violence Hot Line** is ✆ 800/621-4673. Other useful numbers include the **Crisis Help Line** ✆ 212/532-2400; the **Samaritans' Suicide Prevention Line** ✆ 212/673-3000; to locate local **police** precincts ✆ 646/610-5000 or 718/610-5000; **Department of Consumer Affairs** ✆ 212/487-4444; and **taxi complaints** at ✆ 212/NYC-TAXI or 212/676-1000. If you suspect your car may have been towed, call the **Department of Transportation TOWAWAY Help Line** at ✆ 212/869-2929.

Internet Centers See the box "Where to Check Your E-Mail in the City That Never Sleeps," on p. 48.

Libraries The **New York Public Library** is on Fifth Avenue at 42nd Street (© 212/930-0830). This Beaux Arts beauty houses more than 38 million volumes, and the beautiful reading rooms have been restored to their former glory. More efficient and modern, if less charming, is the mid-Manhattan branch at 455 Fifth Ave., at 40th Street, across the street from the main library (© 212/340-0833). There are other branches in almost every neighborhood; you can find a list online at **www.nypl.org**.

Liquor Laws The minimum legal age to purchase and consume alcoholic beverages in New York is 21. Liquor and wine are sold only in licensed stores, which are open 6 days a week, with most choosing to close on Sundays. Liquor stores are closed on holidays, and election days while the polls are open. Beer can be purchased in grocery stores and delis 24 hours a day, except Sunday before noon. Last call in bars is at 4am, although many close earlier.

Newspapers & Magazines There are three major daily newspapers: the *New York Times,* the *Daily News,* and the *New York Post.* For details on where to find arts and entertainment listings, see "Publications" under "Visitor Information" in "Orientation," earlier in this chapter.

If you want to find your hometown paper, visit **Universal News & Magazines,** at 234 W. 42nd St., between Seventh and Eighth avenues (© 212/221-1809), and 977 Eighth Ave., between 57th and 58th streets (© 212/459-0932); or **Hotalings News Agency,** 624 W. 52nd St., between Eleventh and Twelfth avenues (© 212/974-9419). Other good bets include the **Hudson** newsdealers, located in Grand Central Terminal, at 42nd Street and Lexington Avenue, and Penn Station, at 34th Street and Seventh Avenue.

Pharmacies **Duane Reade** (www.duanereade.com) has 24-hour pharmacies in Midtown at 224 W. 57th St., at Broadway (© 212/541-9708); on the Upper West Side at 2465 Broadway, at 91st Street (© 212/799-3172); and on the Upper East Side at 1279 Third Ave., at 74th Street (© 212/744-2668).

Police Dial © **911** in an emergency; otherwise, call © **646/610-5000** or 718/610-5000 (NYPD headquarters) for the number of the nearest precinct.

Restrooms Public restrooms are available at the visitor centers in Midtown (1560 Broadway, between 46th and 47th sts.; and 810 Seventh Ave., between 52nd and 53rd sts.). Grand Central Terminal, at 42nd Street between Park and Lexington avenues, also has clean restrooms. Your best bet on the street is Starbucks or another city java chain—you can't walk more than a few blocks without seeing one. The big chain bookstores are good for this, too. You can also head to hotel lobbies (especially the big Midtown ones) and department stores like Macy's and Bloomingdale's. On the Lower East Side, stop into the Lower East Side BID Visitor Center, 261 Broome St., between Orchard and Allen streets (open Sun–Fri 10am–4pm, sometimes later).

Salon Services Need a haircut or a manicure while you're here in town? Bold, bustling **Warren-Tricomi,** 16 W. 57th St., just west of Fifth Avenue (© 212/262-8899; www.warrentricomi.com), can meet all of your salon needs. For a dash of

My, what an inefficient way to fish.

Ring toss, good. Horseshoes, bad.

Faster! Faster! Faster!

We take care of the fiddly bits, from providing over 43,000 customer reviews of hotels, to helping you find our best fares, to giving you 24/7 customer service. So you can focus on the only thing that matters. Goofing off.

travelocity
You'll never roam alone.™

downtown style (and slightly lower prices), make an appointment at **Arte,** 284 Lafayette St., SoHo (📞 **212/941-5932**). If it's a good manicure or pedicure you need, visit **Pinky,** which has five locations on the Upper West Side, including 2050 Broadway, at 70th Street (📞 **212/362-9466**); 312 Columbus Ave., at 74th Street (📞 **212/787-0390**); and 2240 Broadway, at 80th Street (📞 **212/877-4992**).

Smoking Smoking is prohibited on all public transportation, in the lobbies of hotels and office buildings, in taxis, bars, restaurants, and in most shops.

Taxes **Sales tax** is 8.625% on meals, most goods, and some services, but it is not charged on clothing and footwear items under $110. **Hotel tax** is 13.25% plus $2 per room per night (including sales tax). **Parking garage tax** is 18.25%.

Time For the correct local time, dial 📞 **212/976-1616.**

Transit Information For information on getting to and from the airport, see "Getting There," in chapter 3, or call **Air-Ride** at 📞 **800/247-7433.** For information on subways and buses, call the **MTA** at 📞 **718/330-1234,** or see "Getting Around," earlier in this chapter.

Traveler's Assistance **Travelers Aid (www.travelersaid.org)** helps distressed travelers with all kinds of problems, including accidents, sickness, and lost or stolen luggage. There is an office on the second floor of the International Arrivals Building at JFK Airport (📞 **718/656-4870**), and one in Newark Airport's Terminal B (📞 **973/623-5052**).

Weather For the current temperature and next day's forecast, look in the upper-right corner of the front page of the *New York Times* or call 📞 **212/976-1212.** If you want to know how to pack before you arrive, point your browser to **www.cnn.com/weather** or **www.weather.com.**

7

Where to Stay

New York City may be the most expensive place to live in the United States. It only follows that hotel rates here will also be more expensive than most any other city in the country. So understanding that from the get-go will help you get over any notions that you might find rates comparable to those back home. That said, there are bargains out there at every price level; but a bargain in New York might be a king's ransom in Raleigh.

If you want to spend less than 100 bucks a night, you're probably going to have to put up with some inconveniences, such as sharing a hall bathroom with your fellow travelers. (Europeans seem to have a much easier time with this than do Americans.) If you want a room with standard amenities—such as a private bathroom or a real closet (rather than just a bar screwed to the wall)—plan on spending at least $150 a night or so. If you do better than that, you've landed a deal.

New York hotel rooms give everybody a whole new perspective on "small." Space is the city's biggest asset, and getting some costs. If you're traveling on a budget, don't be surprised if your room isn't much bigger than the bed that's in it and your cramped bathroom has a sink so small that it looks like it was manufactured for the Keebler elves. Even expensive rooms can be on the small side, or lack closet space, or have smallish bathrooms.

PRICE CATEGORIES & RACK RATES

The **rates** quoted in the listings below are "rack rates"—the maximum rates that a hotel charges for rooms. I've used these rack rates to divide the hotels into four price categories, ranging from "Very Expensive" to "Inexpensive," for easy reference. But rack rates are only guidelines, and there are often ways around them; see "Tips for Saving on Your Hotel Room," below.

The hotels listed below have provided us with their best rate estimates for 2006, and all quoted rates were correct at press time. Be aware, however, that **rates can change at any time.** Rates are always subject to availability, seasonal fluctuations, and plain old rate changes. It's smart to expect price shifts in both directions in late 2005 and 2006 as hoteliers adjust to new demand patterns.

PET POLICIES I've indicated in the listings below those hotels that generally accept pets. However, understand that these policies may have limitations, such as weight and breed restrictions; may require a deposit and/or a signed waiver against damages; and may be revoked at any time. Always inquire when booking if you're bringing Fluffy or Spike along— *never* just show up with a pet in tow.

TIPS FOR SAVING ON YOUR HOTEL ROOM

In the listings below, I've tried to give you an idea of the kind of deals that may be available at particular hotels: which ones have the best discounted packages, which ones offer AAA and other discounts, which ones allow kids to stay with Mom and Dad for free, and so on. But there's no way of knowing what the offers will be when you're booking, so also consider these general tips:

- **Ask about special rates or other discounts.** Always ask whether a room less expensive than the first one quoted is available, or whether any special rates apply to you. You may qualify for corporate, student, military, senior, or other discounts. Mention membership in AAA, AARP, frequent-flier programs, or trade unions, which may entitle you to special deals as well. Find out the hotel policy on children—do kids stay free in the room or is there a special rate?

- **Choose your season carefully.** Room rates can vary dramatically—by hundreds of dollars in some cases—depending on what time of year you visit. Winter, from January through March, is best for bargains, with summer (especially July–Aug) second best. Fall is the busiest and most expensive season after Christmas, but November tends to be quiet and rather affordable, as long as you're not booking a parade-route hotel on Thanksgiving weekend. All bets are off at Christmas-time—expect to pay top dollar for everything. For more on this subject, see "Money Matters" in "When to Go," in chapter 3.

- **Go uptown or downtown.** The advantages of a Midtown location are highly overrated, especially when saving money is your object. The subway can whisk you anywhere you want to go in minutes; even if you stay on the Upper West Side, you can be at the ferry launch for the Statue of Liberty in about a half-hour. You'll get the best value for your money by staying outside the Theater District, in the residential neighborhoods where real New Yorkers live, such as Greenwich Village, Chelsea, Murray Hill, or the Upper West Side. These are the neighborhoods where real New Yorkers hang out, too, so you won't want for good eats, nightlife, or Big Apple bustle.

- **Visit over a weekend.** If your trip includes a weekend, you might be able to save big. Business hotels tend to empty out, and rooms that go for $300 or more Monday through Thursday can drop dramatically, as low as $150 or less, once the execs have headed home. These deals are especially prevalent in the Financial District, but they're often available in tourist-friendly Midtown, too. Look in the Travel section of the Sunday *New York Times* for some of the best weekend deals. They're also often advertised on the hotel's website. Or just ask when you call.

- **Shop online.** Hotels often offer "Internet only" deals that can save you 10% to 20% over what you'd pay if you booked over the telephone. Also, hotels often advertise all of their available deals on their websites, so you don't have to rely on a reservation agent to fill you in. What's more, some of the discount reservations agencies (see below) have sites that allow you to book online. And consider joining the **Playbill Online Theater Club (www.playbillclub.com),** a free service that offers some excellent members-only rates at select city hotels, in addition to discounts on the-ater tickets. American Automobile Association members can often score the best dis-counts by booking at **www.aaa.com**. Travel search sites such as **Orbitz** (www. orbitz.com), **Microsoft Expedia** (www.expedia.com), **Priceline** (www.priceline. com), and **Travelocity** (www.travelocity.com) offer other discount options. Shop around. And if you have special needs—a quiet room, a room with a view—call the hotel directly and make your needs known after you've booked online.

- **Dial direct.** When booking a room in a chain hotel, you'll often get a better deal by calling the individual hotel's reservation desk rather than the chain's main number.

- **Make deals with the budget chains.** With a few exceptions, I have not listed budget chains in this chapter. In my opinion, they tend to lack the character and local feel that most independently run hotels have. And it's that feel, I believe, that is so much a part of the travel experience. Still, when you're looking for a deal, they can be a good option. Most hotels—particularly chains like Comfort Inn and Best Western—are market-sensitive. Because they hate to see rooms sit empty, they'll often negotiate good rates at the last minute and in slow seasons.

  You can also pull out all the stops for discounts at a budget chain, from auto-club membership to senior status. And you might be able to take advantage of corporate rates or discounted weekend stays. Most chain hotels let the kids stay with parents for free. Ask for every possible kind of discount; if you find that you get an unhelpful reservation agent, call back and try again. Of course, there's no guarantee.

  Two chains with franchises in Manhattan include **Best Western** (✆ 800/780-7234; www.bestwestern.com), though their rack rates for New York hotels are higher than you'd expect, and **Howard Johnson** (✆ 800/446-4656; www.hojo.com). There's a Best Western at South Street Seaport and at two Midtown locations, and a Howard Johnson on the Lower East Side. Check their websites for all the details.

  At these and other franchised hotels—such as the ones run by **Apple Core Hotels** (www.applecorehotels.com), a small management company that handles the **Comfort Inn Midtown,** the **Ramada Inn Eastside,** Manhattan's first **Red Roof** (p. 148), the **Super 8 Hotel Times Square,** and the new **La Quinta,** 7 W. 32nd St. (✆ 212/736-1600)—doubles can go for as little as $89. Check with the franchiser if you're not quoted a good advance-booking rate directly or through the management company's online reservations system; their global 800 and online reservations systems will often garner you a better rate, which might include a promotion—or, at minimum, an "Internet User's Rate" that's 10% lower than the standard.

  A good source for deals is **Choice Hotels** (✆ 877/424-6423; www.hotelchoice.com), which oversees Comfort Inn, Quality Hotel, and Clarion Hotel chains, all of which have Manhattan branches.

  Another hotel to try is the **Days Hotel Midtown,** 790 Eighth Ave., at 48th Street (✆ 800/321-7460 or 212/581-7000; www.daysinn.com).

- **Investigate reservations services.** These outfits usually work as consolidators, buying up or reserving rooms in bulk, and then dealing them out to customers at a profit. You can get 10% to 50% off; but remember, these discounts apply to rack rates—inflated prices that people rarely end up paying. You may get a decent rate, but always call the hotel direct to see if you can do better.

  Quikbook (✆ 800/789-9887 or 212/779-7666; www.quikbook.com) is probably the best of the bunch. Another good bet is **Hotel ConXions** (✆ 800/522-9991 or 212/840-8686; www.hotelconxions.com). You might also try the **Hotel**

⌒Tips **More Advice on Accommodations**

For an easy-to-scan introduction to the best of what the city has to offer, check out the Best Hotel categories in chapter 1. For extra help in choosing a location, take a close look at "Manhattan's Neighborhoods in Brief," in chapter 6.

And remember: All hotel rooms are subject to 13.25% tax plus $2 per night.

Reservations Network, also known as HotelDiscount!com (© **800/715-7666;** www.hoteldiscount.com).

Note: Never just rely on a reservations service or an online booking site. Do a little homework; compare the rack rates to the discounted rates being offered by the service to see what kind of deal they're actually offering. If you're being offered a stay in a hotel I haven't recommended, do more research to learn about it, especially if it isn't a reliable chain name like Holiday Inn or Hyatt. It's not a deal if you end up at a dump.

- **Avoid excess charges and hidden costs.** When you book a room, ask whether the hotel charges for parking. Use your own cellphone, pay phones, or prepaid phone cards instead of dialing direct from hotel phones, which usually have exorbitant rates. And don't be tempted by the room's minibar offerings: Most hotels charge through the nose for water, soda, and snacks. Finally, ask about local taxes and service charges, which can increase the cost of a room by 15% or more. If a hotel insists upon tacking on a surprise "energy surcharge" that wasn't mentioned at check-in or a "resort fee" for amenities you didn't use, you can often make a case for getting it removed.
- **Buy a money-saving package deal.** A travel package that combines your plane tickets and your hotel stay for one price may just be the best bargain of all. In some cases, you'll get airfare, accommodations, transportation to and from the airport, plus extras—maybe an afternoon sightseeing tour, or restaurant and shopping discount coupons—for less than the hotel alone would have cost had you booked it yourself. For more on this, see "Packages for the Independent Traveler," in chapter 3.
- **Rely on a qualified professional.** Certain hotels give travel agents discounts in exchange for steering business their way, so if you're shy about bargaining, an agent may be better equipped to negotiate discounts for you.
- **Consider B&B accommodations or an apartment.** If Big Apple hotels seem too expensive, or you'd just like something a little more like home, consider renting a room in a genuine New York apartment—or even an entire apartment. These accommodations can range from spartan to splendid, from a hosted bedroom in a private home to an unhosted, fully equipped apartment with multiple bedrooms. No matter what, you can pretty much guarantee that you'll get more for your money than if you book into a regular hotel. However, you need to be rather independent-minded to enjoy this option. For more, see the sidebar "Plenty of Room at the Inn," on p. 132.

The place to start is with **Manhattan Getaways** (© **212/956-2010;** www. manhattangetaways.com). Judith Glynn maintains a beautifully kept and managed network of bed-and-breakfast rooms (from $105 nightly) and unhosted apartments (from $135) around the city. There's a 3-night minimum stay, and credit cards are accepted. Another decent bet is **A Hospitality Company** (© **800/ 987-1235** or 212/813-2244; www.hospitalityco.com), which owns and manages 300 apartments around Manhattan starting at $139 a night, or $850 weekly for a basic studio. These are rather sparsely furnished apartments, and the company offers very little in the way of service (it took me 5 days to get my broken TV fixed when I was displaced from home by renovation), but the apartments are clean and do the trick. There's no minimum stay, and credit cards are accepted. Optional cleaning services are available for longer stays.

Additional agencies that can book you into a B&B room or a private apartment, with prices starting at $90 nightly, include **As You Like It** (© **800/277-0413** or 212/695-3404; www.furnapts.com); **Abode Apartment Rentals** (© **800/835-8880** or 212/472-2000; www.abodenyc.com); **City Sonnet** (© **212/614-3034;** www.citysonnet.com); **Manhattan Lodgings** (© **212/677-7616;** www.manhattan lodgings.com); and **New York Habitat** (© **212/255-8018;** www.nyhabitat.com). Be sure to get all details in writing and an exact total up front to avoid disappointments.

LANDING THE BEST ROOM

Somebody has to get the best room in the house. It might as well be you. You can start by joining the hotel's frequent-guest program, which may make you eligible for upgrades. A hotel-branded credit card usually gives its owner free Silver or Gold status in frequent-guest programs. Always ask about a corner room. They're often larger and quieter, with more windows and light, and they often cost the same as standard rooms. When you make your reservation, ask if the hotel is renovating; if it is, request a room away from the construction. Ask about nonsmoking rooms, rooms with views, rooms with twin, queen-, or king-size beds. If you're a light sleeper, request a quiet room away from vending machines, elevators, restaurants, bars, and discos. Ask for a room that has been most recently renovated or redecorated.

If you aren't happy with your room when you arrive, ask for another one. Most lodgings will be willing to accommodate you.

1 South Street Seaport & the Financial District

To locate the hotels in this section, see the map on p. 127.

VERY EXPENSIVE

Ritz-Carlton New York, Battery Park ★★★   Perfect on almost every level, the only drawback to this Ritz-Carlton is its remote downtown location. But that location, on the extreme southern tip of Manhattan, is also one of its strengths. Where else can you get, in most rooms anyway, magnificent views of New York Harbor from your bedroom—complete with telescope for close-ups of Lady Liberty? Where else can you have a cocktail in your hotel bar and watch the sun set over the harbor? And where else can you go for a morning jog around the Manhattan waterfront? This modern, Art Deco–influenced high-rise, which opened in 2002, differs from the English countryside look of most Ritz-Carlton properties, including its sister hotel on Central Park (p. 139), but that's where the differences end. You'll find the full slate of comforts and services typical of Ritz-Carlton here, from Frette-dressed feather beds to the chain's signature Bath Butler, who will draw a scented bath for you in your own deep soaking tub. Standard rooms are all very large and have huge bathrooms, while suites are bigger than most New York apartments. If you don't mind the location and the commute to Midtown and beyond, you won't find a more luxurious choice than this.

2 West St., New York, NY 10004. © **800/241-3333** or 212/344-0800. Fax 212/344-3801. www.ritzcarlton.com. 298 units. $350–$495 double; from $750 suite. Extra person 12 and over $50 (starting from $100 on club level). Check website for promotional weekend packages. AE, DC, DISC, MC, V. Valet parking $50. Subway: 4, 5 to Bowling Green. **Amenities:** Restaurant; lobby lounge for afternoon tea and cocktails, w/outdoor seating; 14th floor cocktail bar w/light dining and outdoor seating; state-of-the-art health club w/views; spa treatments; 24-hr. concierge; well-equipped business center w/24-hr. secretarial services; 24-hr. room service; dry cleaning/laundry service; Ritz-Carlton Club Level w/5 food presentations daily; technology butler and bath butler services. *In room:* A/C, TV w/pay movies and video games, dataport, minibar/fridge, hair dryer, safe, high-speed Internet connectivity, CD player, DVD w/surround sound in suites and Club rooms.

Downtown Accommodations

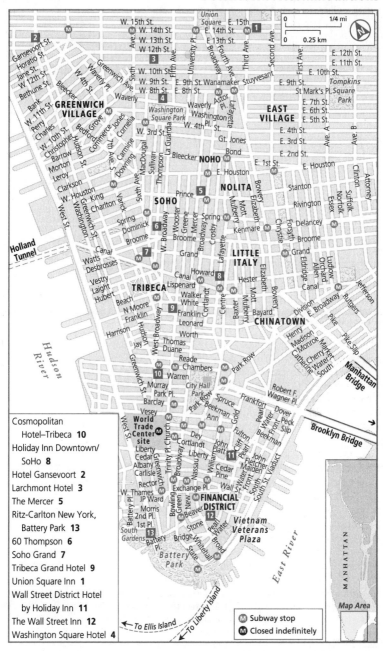

Cosmopolitan
  Hotel–Tribeca **10**
Holiday Inn Downtown/
  SoHo **8**
Hotel Gansevoort **2**
Larchmont Hotel **3**
The Mercer **5**
Ritz-Carlton New York,
  Battery Park **13**
60 Thompson **6**
Soho Grand **7**
Tribeca Grand Hotel **9**
Union Square Inn **1**
Wall Street District Hotel
  by Holiday Inn **11**
The Wall Street Inn **12**
Washington Square Hotel **4**

Ⓜ Subway stop
Ⓜ Closed indefinitely

← To Ellis Island
To Liberty Island

EXPENSIVE/MODERATE

Wall Street District Hotel by Holiday Inn ⋆   This is one of Lower Manhattan's most technologically advanced hotels. The comfortable queen-bedded rooms are stocked with everything an executive might need, including an 8-foot L-shaped workstation with desk-level inputs, dual-line portable phones, and the kind of office supplies you never bring but always need, such as paper clips and tape. About half of the rooms have PCs with Microsoft Word and Office applications and a CD drive. The top floor is dedicated to special SMART rooms, which feature Toshiba Satellite laptop computers (with carrying case), fax/printer/copiers, and other upgraded amenities, plus buffet breakfast. Room decor is chain standard all the way, but fresh and perfectly comfortable; an easy chair and ottoman expands seating options. Management is always staying on the cutting edge with such techno-toys as a "Pocket Concierge" plug-in in the lobby that allows you to download local information to your PDA; an ATM-style machine for one-touch credit card check-in (similar to a self-serve gas pump); and cellular connection services that allow you to forward your room calls to your cellphone. The staff prides itself on meeting the needs of its bullish guests, so expect to be well cared for.

15 Gold St. (at Platt St.), New York, NY 10038. ⓒ 800/HOLIDAY, 212/232-7800, or 212/232-7700. Fax 212/425-0330. www.holidayinnwsd.com or www.holiday-inn.com. 138 units. $139–$349 double; from $389 suite. Check for discounts galore (AAA, AARP, corporate, government, military), plus deeply discounted weekend rates and other specials. AE, DC, DISC, MC, V. Parking $24. Subway: 2, 3, 4, 5, A, C, J, M, Z to Fulton St./Broadway–Nassau St. Dogs up to 25 lb. accepted. **Amenities:** Restaurant; bar; exercise room and access to nearby health club; concierge; self-service business center; 24-hr. room service, delivery from 24-hr. deli; dry cleaning/laundry service; executive-level rooms; CD library. *In room:* A/C, TV w/pay movies/Internet access/Nintendo, standard dataport, minibar, coffeemaker, hair dryer, iron, safe, high-speed Internet connectivity, CD player.

The Wall Street Inn ⋆ *(Finds*   With the demise of the Regent Wall Street, this intimate hotel is now the preferred choice for those working on the Street. But it's also a good choice for visitors who don't want to work. This intimate, seven-story hotel is ideal for those who want a Lower Manhattan location without corporate blandness. The lovely early American interiors boast a pleasing freshness. The hotel is warm, comforting, and serene, and the friendly, professional staff offers the kind of personalized service you won't get from a chain. Rooms aren't huge, but the bedding is top-quality and all the conveniences are at hand. Rooms ending in "01" are smallest; seventh-floor rooms are best, as the bathrooms have extra counter space and whirlpool tubs.

Vacationers who don't mind the weekend quiet of Wall Street will find amazing deals once the execs go home: Rates can drop as low as $159 on weekend nights, and the staff will assign you the best available room when you check in.

9 S. William St. (at Broad St.), New York, NY 10004. ⓒ 212/747-1500. Fax 212/747-1900. www.thewallstreetinn. com. 46 units. $249–$450 double. Rates include continental breakfast. Ask about corporate, group, and/or deeply discounted weekend rates (as low as $159 at press time). AE, DC, DISC, MC, V. Parking $35–$40 nearby. Subway: 2, 3 to Wall St.; 4, 5 to Bowling Green. **Amenities:** Well-outfitted exercise room w/sauna and steam; concierge; business center; babysitting arranged; dry cleaning/laundry service; video library; common guest kitchen w/microwave. *In room:* A/C, TV/VCR, fax, fridge, hair dryer, iron, safe, high-speed Internet.

2 TriBeCa & Lower East Side

To locate the hotels in this section, see the map on p. 127.

VERY EXPENSIVE

Tribeca Grand Hotel ⋆   This sister to the **Soho Grand** (p. 130) is set on a triangular plot just south of SoHo; its decidedly retro brick-and-cast-iron exterior blends perfectly with the surrounding neighborhood.

Set along open atrium-facing corridors, the streamlined guest rooms boast generous built-in work space (with a Herman Miller Aeron chair) and state-of-the-art technology. But because the rooms face the atrium, noise levels can be a problem, so each room is equipped with a noise-dulling device. The rooms, however, definitely take a back seat to what's below: a dramatic eight-story atrium lobby, with its soaring proportions consumed by the very popular Church Lounge, an upscale lounge and restaurant.

2 Sixth Ave. (at White and Church sts.), New York, NY 10013. © 877/519-6600 or 212/519-6600. Fax 212/519-6700. www.tribecagrand.com. 203 units. From $339 double; from $699 suite. Promotional and Internet-only rates as low as $259 at press time; ask about corporate rates and value-added packages. AE, DC, DISC, MC, V. Parking $42. Subway: 1, 9 to Franklin St.; A, C, E to Canal St. Pets accepted. **Amenities:** Restaurant; lounge; fitness center; well-connected 24-hr. concierge; business center w/complete workstations; 24-hr. room service; same-day laundry and dry-cleaning; CD libraries; screening room; coffee, tea, and cocoa bar on each floor. *In room:* A/C, TV/VCR w/Internet access, fax/printer/copier, standard dataport, minibar, hair dryer, safe, high-speed Internet connectivity, CD player, iPods.

INEXPENSIVE

Cosmopolitan Hotel–Tribeca ⭐ *(Value* Hiding behind a plain-vanilla TriBeCa awning is one of the best hotel deals in Manhattan for budget travelers who prefer a private bathroom. Everything is strictly budget, but nice: The modern IKEA-ish furniture includes a work desk and an armoire (a few rooms have a dresser and hanging rack instead); for a few extra bucks, you can have a love seat, too. Beds are comfy, and sheets and towels are of good quality. Rooms are small but make the most of the limited space, and the whole place is pristine. The two-level minilofts have lots of character, but expect to duck on the second level. Management does a great job of keeping everything fresh and new. The TriBeCa location is safe, superhip, and subway-convenient. Services are kept at a bare minimum to keep costs down, so you must be a low-maintenance guest to be happy here.

95 W. Broadway (at Chambers St.), New York, NY 10007. © 888/895-9400 or 212/566-1900. Fax 212/566-6909. www.cosmohotel.com. 105 units. $129–$159 double. AE, DC, MC, V. Parking $20, 1 block away. Subway: 1, 2, 3, 9 to Chambers St. *In room:* A/C, TV, dataport, ceiling fan.

3 SoHo

To locate the hotels in this section, see the map on p. 127.

VERY EXPENSIVE

The Mercer ⭐⭐⭐ The best of the downtown, celebrity-crawling, hip and trendy hotels, the Mercer is a place where even those who represent the antithesis of hip (and I'm speaking personally) can feel very much at home. Though SoHo can be a bit over the top with its high-end boutiques, cutting-edge restaurants, and a constant parade of too serious fashionistas on the streets, it is still a very exciting place to be. And the corner of Mercer and Prince streets, the location of the hotel, is probably the epicenter of SoHo. Still, once inside the hotel there is a pronounced calm—from the postmodern library lounge and the relaxed Mizrahi-clad staff, to the huge soundproof loftlike guest rooms; the hotel is a perfect complement to the scene outside your big window. The Mercer is one of the few New York hotels with ceiling fans and even if you don't need to use them, they look very nice whirring above your extremely comfortable bed. The tile-and-marble bathrooms have a steel cart for storage, and an oversize shower stall or oversize two-person tub (state your preference when booking). Just off the lobby is the Kitchen restaurant, one of Jean-Georges Vongerichten's earlier endeavors that is still going strong.

147 Mercer St. (at Prince St.), New York, NY 10012. ℂ **888/918-6060** or 212/966-6060. Fax 212/965-3838. www. mercerhotel.com. 62 units. $410–$450 double; $530–$650 studio; from $1,200 suite. AE, DC, DISC, MC, V. Parking $35 nearby. Subway: N, R to Prince St. **Amenities:** Restaurant; lounge; food and drink service in lobby; free access to nearby Crunch fitness center; 24-hr. concierge; secretarial services; 24-hr. room service; dry cleaning/laundry service; video, DVD, and CD libraries. *In room:* A/C, TV/VCR, dataport, minibar, safe, wireless Internet access, CD player, ceiling fan.

60 Thompson ⚐   Some hotels have more comfortable rooms, others have better service, but few can match the all-around hipness of SoHo's 60 Thompson. A magnet for downtown celebs, 60 Thompson provides some excellent people-watching opportunities—in the Thom Bar and the gorgeous rooftop bar, A60. The chic, soft-toned accommodations, designed by the same designer who did Giorgio Armani's Central Park West apartment, are spacious but spare, while bathrooms are enormous and luxuriously coated in Italian marble. The hotel has 11 suites including the magnificent Thompson Loft, a duplex penthouse suite with amazing views, four-poster bed, and a fireplace that is a favorite of visiting rock groups. Room service is available from the fabulous **Kittichai** (p. 183).

This Thompson is a smoker-friendly hotel, so ask for a nonsmoking room or bring your air ionizer if the smell of stale cigarette smoke bothers you.

60 Thompson St. (btwn Broome and Spring sts.), New York, NY 10012. ℂ **877/431-0400** or 212/431-0400 Fax 212/431-0200. www.60thompson.com. 100 units. Doubles from $350; suites from $650. AE, DISC, MC, V. Valet parking $35. Subway: C, E to Spring St. **Amenities:** Restaurant; 2 bars; access to nearby health club; concierge; 24-hr. room service (limited menu 1–7am); nonsmoking rooms. *In room:* A/C, TV, minibar, hair dryer, iron, safe, high-speed Internet, DVD/CD player.

Soho Grand   When the Soho Grand opened in 1996 as the first major hotel in SoHo it immediately became one of the trendiest hotels in New York. But after nearly a decade and the opening of so many other hotels that followed in that chic tradition, the Soho Grand still retains its cool. The Grand Bar, located one level above the street, just a few feet from the check-in desk, with its sofas and comfy chairs, was one of the first "lounge bars" in New York and that too has remained a hot spot. Guest rooms, however, have not quite kept up with the times and could use a makeover; bathrooms are good-size but spare.

Make sure you ask for a nonsmoking room; the hotel attracts a hip, European crowd that enjoys a nicotine fix and the cigarette stench can linger well after the guests have departed. But you choose the Soho Grand more for the name and all that it implies rather than for comfort and service.

310 W. Broadway (at Grand St.), New York, NY 10013. ℂ **800/965-3000** or 212/965-3000. Fax 212/965-3244 (reservations) or 212/965-3200 (guests). www.sohogrand.com. 363 units. From $339 double; from $3,000 loft suites. Corporate, promotional, and Internet-only rates as low as $259; your travel agent may be able to do even better. AE, DC, DISC, MC, V. Parking $42. Subway: A, C, E, N, R, 1, 9 to Canal St. Pets accepted. **Amenities:** Restaurant; bar and lounge; fitness center; concierge; 24-hr. room service; dry cleaning/laundry service; nonsmoking rooms; butler's pantry w/complimentary coffee, tea, and hot chocolate on every floor. *In room:* A/C, TV/VCR, dataport, minibar, hair dryer, safe, CD player, iPods.

MODERATE

Holiday Inn Downtown/SoHo   This Holiday Inn is actually on the northern edge of Chinatown, but its just-off-SoHo location is perfect for hipsters who want access to the ultrachic scene without its high price tag. It's everything you'd expect from this good-value chain: clean, well outfitted, reliable, and comfortable. The guest rooms are standard but have everything you need. Doubles are a good-value bet for small families or sharing friends. You'll find Asian touches throughout the hotel—a nod to the brink-of-Chinatown location—and a well-respected Asian restaurant. Rack rates are high, but it's easy to snag a discount or score a room on the low end with advance booking.

138 Lafayette St. (at Howard St., 1 block north of Canal St.), New York, NY 10013. ℂ 800/HOLIDAY or 212/966-8898. Fax 212/941-5832. www.holidayinn-nyc.com. 227 units. $159–$259 double; $249–$329 junior suite. Extra person $20. Children 18 and under stay free in parent's room. Check for AAA, AARP, government, corporate, and other discounts. AE, DC, DISC, MC, V. Parking $27. Subway: 6, J, M, N, R, Q, W to Canal St. **Amenities:** Restaurant; bar; access to nearby health club; concierge; fax and copy service; room service (6:30am–11pm); dry cleaning/laundry service. *In room:* A/C, TV w/pay movies, fax (in most junior suites), dataport, coffeemaker, hair dryer, iron, CD player.

4 Greenwich Village & the Meat-Packing District

To locate the hotels in this section, see the map on p. 127.

EXPENSIVE

Hotel Gansevoort 🔏🔏   Built from the ground up by hotelier Henry Kallan (of New York's Hotel Giraffe and The Library) and opened in 2004, the Gansevoort became the first major hotel in the white-hot Meat-Packing district. And now, this sleek, 14-floor zinc-colored tower, with its open, sprawling clubby lobby, the very popular Jeffrey Chodorow–owned, Jeffrey Beers–designed restaurant **Ono** (p. 186), and the indoor/outdoor rooftop bar and pool (with music piped underwater), is the symbolic anchor of the district. Despite its potentially excessive trendiness, the Gansevoort offers, as do all of Henry Kallan's hotels, excellent, personable service. As well, rooms are good-size with comfortable furnishings in soft tones and high-tech amenities like plasma televisions and wireless Internet. Suites have a living room and separate bedroom and some have small balconies and bay windows. Corner suites offer adjoining guest rooms for families or larger parties. The generously sized bathrooms are done up in ceramic, stainless steel and marble and are impeccably appointed. In all the guest rooms and throughout the hotel, original art by New York artists is on display. At press time, the G Spa, a 5,000-square-foot spa and fitness center, was slated for a Fall 2005 opening.

By the time you read this, the Meat-Packing district might be on the outs, but you can be sure the Hotel Gansevoort is there to stay.

18 Ninth Ave. (at 13th St.), New York, NY 10014. ℂ 877/426-7386 or 212/206-6700. Fax 212/255-5858. www.hotel gansevoort.com. 187 units. From $395 double; from $625 suites. Parking $40. Subway: A, C, E to 14th St. Pet-friendly floors. **Amenities:** Restaurant; rooftop bar and lounge; indoor/outdoor pool; spa and fitness center; concierge; business center; 24-hr. room service; dry cleaning/laundry service; rooftop garden. *In room:* A/C, TV, dataport, minibar, hair dryer, iron, safe, wireless and high-speed Internet, voice mail, dual line telephones.

INEXPENSIVE

Larchmont Hotel 🔏🔏 *Value*   Well located on a beautiful tree-lined block in a quiet residential part of Greenwich Village, this is a wonderful European-style hotel. If you're willing to share a bathroom, it's hard to do better for the money. The entire place has an air of warmth and sophistication; the butter-yellow lobby even *smells* good. Each bright guest room is tastefully done in rattan and outfitted with a writing desk, a minilibrary of books, an alarm clock, a wash basin, and a few extras that you normally have to pay a lot more for, such as cotton bathrobes, slippers, and ceiling fans. Every floor has two shared bathrooms (with hair dryers) and a small, simple kitchen. The management is constantly renovating, so everything feels clean and fresh. What's more, those looking for a hip downtown base couldn't be better situated, since some of the city's best shopping, dining, and sightseeing—plus your choice of subway lines—are just a walk away. Book *well* in advance (the management suggests 6–7 weeks' lead time).

Plenty of Room at the Inn

When you think of accommodations in New York, you usually think big—tall, sturdy, monoliths with hundreds of rooms. You don't think of quaint antiques-laden guesthouses or inns where a home-cooked breakfast is served. But we all know New York is a diverse city and that diversity can be found in its accommodations, too. So if you want an alternative to the quintessential huge New York hotel and would prefer a taste of urban hominess where you might actually meet your innkeeper, here are a few options.

On the steep end of the economic scale, but definitely worth the price if authentic 19th-century Victorian romance is what you are seeking, is the fabulous **Inn at Irving Place** ⭐⭐. Housed in a 170-year-old town house, rates range from $325 to $495 and the rooms are all named after late-19th- or early-20th-century New Yorkers, many inspired by the works of Edith Wharton and Henry James. Complimentary breakfast is served each morning in Lady Mendl's parlor, where, if the weather is nippy, you'll find a comforting fire roaring. See p. 135 for a detailed review.

Breakfast prepared by culinary students of the New School is one of the highlights of the **Inn on 23rd Street** ⭐⭐⭐. Each of the inn's 14 rooms, which range from $179 to $359, were distinctly decorated by the personable owners, Annette and Barry Fisherman, with items they've collected from their travels over the years. See p. 134 for a detailed review.

The first home of the Gay Men's Health Crisis, an 1850 brownstone in the heart of Chelsea, is now the charming **Colonial House Inn**, 318 W. 22nd St., between Eighth and Ninth avenues (© 800/689-3779 or 212/243-9669; www. colonialhouseinn.com). This 20-room four-story walk-up caters to a largely gay and lesbian clientele, but everybody is welcomed equally and straight couples are a common sight. Some rooms have shared bathrooms; deluxe rooms have private bathrooms and some even have working fireplaces. There's also a roof deck with a clothing-optional area. Breakfast is included in the rates, which range from $80 to $125 for a shared bathroom or $125 to $140 for a deluxe room with private bathroom.

On the increasingly popular yet still very residential Upper West Side is the aptly named **Country Inn the City** ⭐, 270 W. 77th St., between Broadway and

27 W. 11th St. (btwn Fifth and Sixth aves.), New York, NY 10011. © 212/989-9333. Fax 212/989-9496. www.larchmonthotel.com. 58 units, all with shared bathroom. $70–$95 single; $90–$125 double. Rates include continental breakfast. Children under 13 stay free in parent's room. AE, MC, V. Parking $18 nearby. Subway: A, B, C, D, E, F, V to W. 4th St. (use 8th St. exit); F to 14th St. **Amenities:** Tour desk; fax service; room service (10am–6pm); common kitchenette. *In room:* A/C, TV, hair dryer, safe, ceiling fan.

Washington Square Hotel   Popular with a young international crowd, this affordable hotel sits behind a pretty facade facing Washington Square Park (historically Henry James territory, now the heart of New York University) in the heart of Greenwich Village. The lobby was recently renovated and is now a pleasant place for tea in the afternoon and cocktails in the evening. The rooms are tiny, but pleasant. Each

West End Avenue (© 212/580-4183; www.countryinnthecity.com). This 1891 town house has only four rooms but all are spacious, quaintly decorated, and equipped with full kitchens. Rates range from $150 to $230 and include breakfast items stocked in your refrigerator. But you're on your own here in many respects; there is no resident innkeeper and a maid services your room only every few days. Still, if you are the independent sort, the inn's charm makes it an excellent choice.

If you want the absolute genuine New York brownstone experience, there is only one place to go: Harlem. **The Bed and Breakfast Mont Morris,** 56 W. 120th St., at Lenox Avenue (© 917/617-4354; www.montmorris.com), is located in the middle of one of Harlem's most historic areas and not far from the bustle of 125th Street. The B&B offers four units, one on each floor, and a continental breakfast from the very good Settepani Bakery just down the block. Rates range from the very affordable $85 to $95.

Like Harlem, Brooklyn also boasts a number of historic districts with immaculately restored brownstones, some of which have been converted to inns. One of the most interesting is **Akwaaba Mansion,** 347 MacDonough St. (© 718/455-5958; www.akwaaba.com), a meticulously restored 1860s Italianate villa in Bedford-Stuyvesant, outfitted with Afrocentric elegance. Four suites are available in the 18-room home, each with private bathroom with either a claw-foot or a Jacuzzi tub ($150–$165 double)—including a hearty, Southern-style breakfast.

The historic neighborhood of Park Slope is the heart of brownstone Brooklyn, and home to **Bed & Breakfast on the Park,** 113 Prospect Park W. (© 718/499-6115; www.bbnyc.com). Housed in an 1895 Victorian town house across the street from Prospect Park, this inn has two beautifully outfitted shared-bathroom units ($125 or $150 double). A sumptuous breakfast is served in the formal dining room. Six more rooms with private bathrooms are available for guests who are willing to splurge.

comes with a firm bed, a private bathroom, and a small closet with a pint-size safe. It's worth paying a few extra dollars for a south-facing room on a high floor, since the others can be a bit dark. Bathrooms were also renovated, with the addition of granite counters. On-site is a very good restaurant and lounge, North Square Lounge, which even draws locals with its stylish design, well-priced cocktails and international bistro fare, and Sunday jazz brunch.

103 Waverly Place (btwn Fifth and Sixth aves.), New York, NY 10011. © 800/222-0418 or 212/777-9515. Fax 212/979-8373. www.wshotel.com. 160 units. $127–$141 single; $150–$179 double; $184–$204 quad. Rates include continental breakfast. Rollaway $20. Inquire about special rates and jazz packages. AE, MC, V. Parking $20 nearby. Subway: A, B, C, D, E, F, V to W. 4th St. (use 3rd St. exit). **Amenities:** Restaurant and lounge; exercise room; dry cleaning/laundry service. *In room:* A/C, TV, dataport, hair dryer, iron, safe, high-speed Internet access.

5 Chelsea

To locate the hotels in this section, see the map on p. 136.

MODERATE

Inn on 23rd Street ★★★ *(Finds)*   Behind an unassuming entrance in the middle of bustling 23rd Street is one of New York's true lodging treasures: a real urban bed-and-breakfast with as personal a touch as you will find anywhere. All 14 guest rooms are spacious. Each has a king or queen bed outfitted with a supremely comfy pillow-top mattress and top-quality linens, satellite TV, a large private bathroom with thick Turkish towels, and a roomy closet. Rooms have themes based on how they are designed; there's the Rosewood Room, with '60s built-ins; the elegantly Asian Bamboo Room; and Ken's Cabin, a large, lodgelike room with cushy, well-worn leather furnishings and wonderful Americana relics. I stayed in the Victorian suite where the decor curiously included framed Victorian-era dental tools. The Inn features a lovely library where the complimentary breakfast is served and where there is also an honor bar where you can make yourself a drink for cheaper than you would pay in any hotel in the city. Other perks include free high-speed Internet access in the rooms, wireless in the library, and wine and cheese served on Fridays and Saturdays. The only drawback is that the Inn is so comfortable and accommodating you might be tempted to lounge around inside all day instead of getting out there and seeing the town.

131 W. 23rd St. (btwn Sixth and Seventh aves.), New York, NY 10011. © 877/387-2323 or 212/463-0330. Fax 212/463-0302. www.bbonline.com/ny/innon23rd. 14 units. $175–$250 double; from $250 suite. Rates include continental breakfast. Extra person $20. Children under 12 stay free in parent's room. AE, DC, MC, V. Parking $20 nearby. Subway: F, 1, 9 to 23rd St. **Amenities:** Fax and copy service; cozy library w/stereo and VCR. *In room:* A/C, TV, dataport, hair dryer, iron, high-speed Internet access.

INEXPENSIVE

Also consider the intimate guesthouse the **Colonial House Inn** (© **800/689-3779** or 212/243-9669). For more information, see the sidebar "Plenty of Room at the Inn," above.

Chelsea Lodge ★★ *(Value)*   Housed in a lovely brownstone on a landmark block in the heart of Chelsea, this small hotel is utterly charming and a terrific value—arguably the best in the city for budget-minded travelers. Impeccable renovations have restored original woodwork to mint condition. The beds are the finest and best outfitted I've seen in this price category.

The only place with a similar grown-up sensibility for the same money is Greenwich Village's **Larchmont Hotel** (p. 131), but there, all bathroom facilities are shared; at Chelsea Lodge, each room has its own sink and in-room shower stall, so you only have to share a cute toilet room with your neighbors. I won't kid you—rooms are petite, the open closets are small, and beds are full-size (queens wouldn't cut it). But considering the stylishness, the amenities, and the great neighborhood, you'd be hard-pressed to do better for the money. Best for couples rather than shares. *Tip:* Try to book no. 2A, which is bigger than most, or one of the first-floor rooms, whose high ceilings make them feel more spacious.

318 W. 20th St. (btwn Eighth and Ninth aves.), New York, NY 10011. © **800/373-1116** or 212/243-4499. Fax 212/243-7852. www.chelsealodge.com. 22 units, all with semiprivate bathroom. $95 single; $110 double. AE, DC, DISC, MC, V. Parking about $20 nearby. Subway: 1, 9 to 18th St.; C, E to 23rd St. *In room:* A/C, TV, wireless Internet, ceiling fan.

6 Union Square, the Flatiron District & Gramercy Park

To find the hotels described in this section, see p. 136.

EXPENSIVE

Hotel Giraffe ★★   Located in the increasingly fashionable Madison Park area, this hotel is a real charmer with a very calm, intimate feel to it. Guest rooms are stylish, evoking an urban European character, with high ceilings, velveteen upholstered chairs, and original black-and-white photographs from the '20s and '30s. All the rooms are of a good size with high ceilings, while deluxe rooms and suites feature French doors that lead to small balconies with large windows and remote-controlled blackout shades. Bathrooms are spacious with plenty of marble counter space and glass-paneled doors, and all rooms have very generous marble-topped desks with free high-speed Internet. But what really separates this hotel from so many others are its services: A continental breakfast is included in the rate and served in the hotel's elegant lobby, where coffee, cookies, and tea are available all afternoon, and wine, cheese, and piano music are offered each evening. There is also a lovely rooftop garden—the perfect place for a glass of wine or morning coffee during warm weather.

365 Park Ave. South (at 26th St.), New York, NY 10016. ℂ 877/296-0009 or 212/685-7700. Fax 212/685-7771. www.hotelgiraffe.com. 73 units. $325–$425 double; from $425 1- or 2-bedroom suite; from $2,500 penthouse suite. Rates include continental breakfast and evening wine and cheese accompanied by piano music. Check website or ask about reduced rates (as low as $259 at press time). AE, DC, MC, V. Parking $28. Subway: 6 to 28th St. **Amenities:** Restaurant; 2 bars; complimentary access to nearby gym; concierge; business services; limited room service; dry cleaning/laundry service; rooftop garden; video and CD libraries. *In room:* A/C, TV/VCR, dataport, minibar, hair dryer, iron, safe, high-speed wireless Internet, CD player.

Inn at Irving Place ★★   If it weren't for the street noise outside—or the high-speed wireless Internet in your room—upon entering the Inn you would think you were suddenly transported to the 19th-century New York of the *Age of Innocence*. This 170-year-old town house offers antique charm more easily found in the Berkshires than in the heart of what used to be Dot.Com Alley of Manhattan. All rooms are spacious, with period antique furniture and art, nonworking fireplaces, and big bathrooms with pedestal sinks and brass fixtures, while the junior suites feature small, but luxurious sitting areas. The rooms are named for famous 19th-century New Yorkers such as Edith Wharton, O. Henry, and Washington Irving. The Madame Olenska (bonus points if you know who she was) junior suite features a king bed and a window nook overlooking Irving Place where you can curl up with a glass of sherry or a cup of tea. Breakfast in bed, tea served in your rooms, or in-room massages can all be easily arranged by the Inn's very helpful staff. And if the sugary sweetness of a bygone era begins to wear on you, venture downstairs for a blast of reality at Cibar, a very popular martini bar that features a DJ nightly.

56 Irving Place (btwn 17th and 18th sts.), New York, NY 10003. ℂ 800/685-1447 or 212/533-4600. Fax 212/533-4611. www.innatirving.com. 12 units. $325–$415 double; $475–$525 suite. Extra person $25. Rates include continental breakfast. 2-night minimum on weekends. AE, DC, MC, V. Parking $25–$30 nearby. Subway: N, R, 4, 5, 6 to 14th St./Union Sq. No children under 12. **Amenities:** 2 restaurants; lounge; access to nearby health club; concierge; 24-hr. room service; in-room massage; dry cleaning/laundry service; video and CD libraries. *In room:* A/C, TV/VCR, dataport, minibar, hair dryer, CD player, laptops and fax machines on request.

Midtown, Chelsea & Gramercy Park Accommodations

Affinia Dumont **31**
The Alex **43**
The Algonquin **42**
Americana Inn **35**
Belvedere Hotel **8**
The Benjamin **48**
The Blakely New York **3**
Broadway Inn **9**
Casablanca Hotel **12**
Chelsea Lodge **16**
City Club **41**
Colonial House Inn **15**
Doubletree Guest Suites-
    Times Square **11**
Doubletree Metropolitan Hotel **49**
Four Seasons Hotel New York **54**
Gershwin Hotel **23**
Habitat Hotel **53**
Hotel Chandler **26**
Hotel Elysée **50**
Hotel Giraffe **22**
Hotel Grand Union **30**
Hotel Metro **32**
Hotel Plaza Athénée **61**
Inn at Irving Place **19**
Inn on 23rd Street **20**
Iroquois Hotel **40**
The Kimberly **46**
The Kitano New York **33**
La Quinta Inn Manhattan **29**
Le Parker Meridien **55**
The Library Hotel **36**
The Lowell **59**
The Mansfield **37**
The Marcel **21**
The Melrose Hotel **60**
The Michelangelo **5**
Murray Hill Inn **25**
The Muse **44**
Novotel New York **4**
The Peninsula-New York **51**
The Phillips Club **1**
The Regency **58**
Red Roof Inn **28**
Ritz-Carlton New York,
    Central Park **56**
continues on opposite page

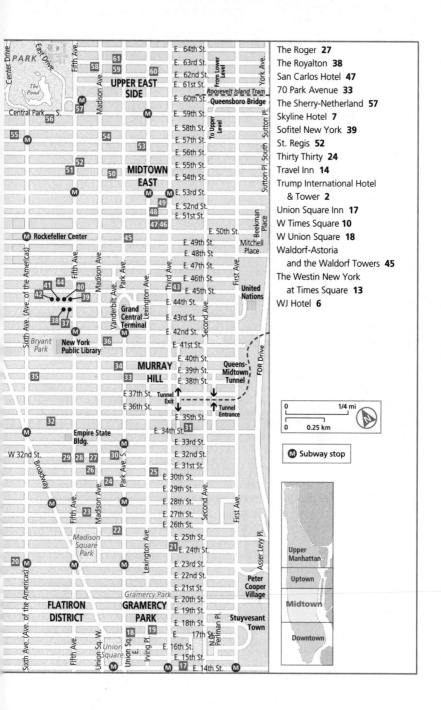

The Roger **27**
The Royalton **38**
San Carlos Hotel **47**
70 Park Avenue **33**
The Sherry-Netherland **57**
Skyline Hotel **7**
Sofitel New York **39**
St. Regis **52**
Thirty Thirty **24**
Travel Inn **14**
Trump International Hotel
   & Tower **2**
Union Square Inn **17**
W Times Square **10**
W Union Square **18**
Waldorf-Astoria
   and the Waldorf Towers **45**
The Westin New York
   at Times Square **13**
WJ Hotel **6**

W Union Square (★)   Überarchitect David Rockwell transformed the magnificent 1911 Guardian Life building overlooking leafy Union Square into a new gem, successfully fusing original Beaux Arts detailing with bold, clean-lined modernism and a relaxing, grown-up air. Rooms boast distinctive touches such as luminous mother-of-pearl counters in the bathrooms. Star chef Todd English's Mediterranean-accented Olives gets raves, and nightclub impresario Rande Gerber's dark and sultry Underbar is just downstairs.

201 Park Ave. South (at 17th St.), New York, NY 10003. (📞) **212/253-9119.** Fax 212/253-9229. www.starwood.com. $239–$550 double. Check website for specials. AE, DC, DISC, MC, V. Subway: N, R, W, 4, 5, 6 to Union Sq. **Amenities:** Restaurant; bar; fitness center; concierge; 24-hr. room service; laundry/valet services; video library. *In room:* A/C, TV/DVD, fridge, dataport, Internet access.

INEXPENSIVE

Gershwin Hotel (★) (*Kids*)   Nestled between Le Trapeze, an S&M club, and the Museum of Sex, and with its own glowing protruding horns as your landmark, the proximity to erotica is really just a coincidence. This creative-minded, Warhol-esque hotel caters to up-and-coming artistic types—and well-established names with an eye for good value—with its bold modern art collection and wild style. The lobby was recently renovated, and along with a new bar, Gallery at the Gershwin, much of the original art remains. The standard rooms are clean and bright, with Picasso-style wall murals and Philippe Starck–ish takes on motel furnishings. Superior rooms are best, as they're newly renovated, and well worth the extra $10; all have either a queen bed, two twins, or two doubles, plus a newish private bathroom with cute, colorful tile. If you're bringing the brood, two-room suites, or Family Rooms, are a good option.

The hotel is more service-oriented than you usually see at this price level, and the staff is very professional.

7 E. 27th St. (btwn Fifth and Madison aves.), New York, NY 10016. (📞) **212/545-8000.** Fax 212/684-5546. www.gershwinhotel.com. 150 units. $99–$189 double (usually less than $150); $189–$219 family room. Extra person $10. Check website for discounts, 3rd-night-free specials, or other value-added packages. AE, MC, V. Parking $25 3 blocks away. Subway: N, R, 6 to 28th St. **Amenities:** Bar; tour desk; babysitting; dry cleaning/laundry service; Internet access. *In room:* A/C, TV, dataport, hair dryer, iron.

The Marcel (★) (*Finds*)   Being budget-challenged doesn't mean you have to settle for boring. This Gramercy Park hotel offers high style and a super-hip scene at low, low prices. Thanks to designers Goodman Charlton, who love to infuse retro styles with futuristic freshness, the Marcel sits on the cutting edge style-wise. Fab faux *Mod Squad*–era Scandinavian stylings in the lobby lead to guest rooms boasting gorgeous blond-wood built-ins that make clever use of limited space, and a bold geometric cushioned headboard adds a downright luxurious flair. The designer furnishings and textiles look and feel expensive, even if the somewhat lumpy beds don't; still, budget travelers will be thrilled. Even if the service isn't fabulous or the little details aren't perfect, you should feel like you're getting a great deal here.

201 E. 24th St. (at Third Ave.), New York, NY 10011. (📞) **888/66-HOTEL** or 212/696-3800. Fax 212/696-0077. www. nychotels.com. 97 units. $125–$175 double. AE, DISC, MC, V. Parking $24. Subway: 6 to 28th St. **Amenities:** Restaurant; stylish lounge; all-day coffee and cappuccino bar; limited room service; dry cleaning/laundry service. *In room:* A/C, TV w/pay movies, dataport, hair dryer, iron, CD player.

Union Square Inn (★) (*Value*)   Situated a stone's throw east of Union Square, on the fringe of the energetic East Village, this unassuming little hotel is a welcome addition to the budget hotel scene. Rooms here aren't quite as cheap as those at its sister hotel, the Murray Hill Inn, but comforts are better quality; every room has a private bathroom, and everything feels fresh and new. Four standard rooms are tiny twins with trundle beds, and a handful in the deluxe category are spacious rooms with two double beds that can accommodate more than two if necessary. Most fall in the moderate category, with one double bed and little room to spare. All rooms boast quality mattresses and bedding, and pretty Italian-tile bathrooms. On the downside, the rooms lack views, open wall racks substitute for closets, most bathrooms have showers only, halls are narrow, and there's no elevator—but those are minimal sacrifices considering the low prices. Services are virtually nonexistent in order to keep costs down, but everything you'll need—from restaurants to dry cleaners to a slate of subway lines—is right at hand in the hip, central-to-everything location.

209 E. 14th St. (btwn Second and Third aves.), New York, NY 10003. ℭ 212/614-0500. Fax 212/614-0512. www.union squareinn.com or www.nyinns.com. 40 units. $90–$149 double. Extra person $20. Rates include basic continental breakfast. AE, MC, V. Parking $25 nearby. Subway: L to Third Ave.; 4, 5, 6, N, R to 14th St./Union Sq. **Amenities:** Coffee bar serving light meals; access to local fitness club. *In room:* A/C, TV, dataport.

7 Times Square & Midtown West

To find the hotels described in this section, see p. 136.

VERY EXPENSIVE

Ritz-Carlton New York, Central Park ★★★ *Kids* There's a lot to like about this hotel—from its enviable location overlooking Central Park to the impeccable and personable service—but what I like best is that this undoubtedly luxury hotel manages to maintain a homey elegance, and does not intimidate you with an overabundance of style.

Rooms are spacious and decorated in traditional, English-countryside style. Suites are larger than most New York City apartments. Rooms facing Central Park come with telescopes, and all have flatscreen TVs with DVD players; the hotel even has a library of Academy Award–winning films available. The marble bathrooms are also oversize and feature a choice of bathrobes, terry or linen, and extravagant Frederic Fekkai bath amenities.

For families who can afford the very steep prices, the hotel is extremely kid-friendly. Suites have sofa beds, and cribs and rollaway beds can be brought in. Children are given in-room cookies and milk. You can even bring your dog (under 60 lb.); if it rains, the pooch gets to wear a Burberry trench coat. Now that's homey elegance. While the kids and dogs are entertained, the older folks can be pampered with facials or massages at the Switzerland-based La Prairie spa, or dine at the spectacular **Atelier** (p. 199).

50 Central Park South (at Sixth Ave.), New York, NY 10019. ℭ 212/308-9100. Fax 212/207-8831. www.ritz carlton.com. 277 units. $650–$975 double; from $1,395 suite. Package and weekend rates available. AE, DC, DISC, MC, V. Parking $50. Subway: B, N, Q, R to 57th St. Pets under 60 lbs. accepted. **Amenities:** Restaurant; bar; lobby lounge for tea and cocktails; fitness center; La Prairie spa and facial center; concierge; complimentary Bentley limousine service; business center; 24-hr. room service; babysitting; overnight laundry/dry-cleaning; technology butler and bath butler services. *In room:* A/C, TV/DVD, dataport, minibar, hair dryer, iron, safe, high-speed Internet connectivity, telescopes in rooms w/park view.

EXPENSIVE

The Algonquin ★★ Is this a literary clubhouse or a hotel? The atmosphere in this 1902-built landmark building is so steeped in writer's lore that you'll feel guilty turning on the television instead of reading the latest issue of the *New Yorker* that's provided in the guest rooms. Or maybe the television will be a welcome respite from the barrage of witticisms and prose displayed throughout the hotel. Rooms can be extremely cramped but they are equipped with possibly the most comfortable, inviting beds in the city as well as 21st-century technology like high-speed Internet and flatscreen televisions. If you have a tendency toward claustrophobia, head to the plush lobby where you can sit in cushy chairs, sip exquisite (and expensive) cocktails, have a snack, or just read or play on your laptop (the lobby is Wi-Fi equipped). For a special splurge, stay in one of the roomy one-bedroom suites, where all that is missing to get you going on that novel you've been toying with is a manual Smith Corona typewriter.

Meals are served in the recently renovated and very celebrated Round Table Room, while the fabulous **Oak Room** (p. 370) is one of the city's top cabaret rooms, featuring such esteemed talents as Andrea Marcovicci and Julie Wilson. The publike Blue Bar is home to a rotating collection of Hirschfeld drawings that's well worth a browse.

59 W. 44th St. (btwn Fifth and Sixth aves.), New York, NY 10036. ⒸⒸ 888/304-2047 or 212/840-6800. Fax 212/944-1419. www.algonquinhotel.com. 174 units. $209–$499 double; from $309 suite. Check website or inquire about discounted rates or special package deals. AE, DC, DISC, MC, V. Parking $28 across the street. Subway: B, D, F, V to 42nd St. **Amenities:** 2 restaurants; lounge; bar; exercise room; concierge; limited room service; dry cleaning/laundry service. *In room:* A/C, TV w/pay movies, dataport, hair dryer, iron, safe, high-speed Internet.

The Blakely New York ★★ (Finds)

After a major renovation, the hotel formerly known as the Gorham bears little resemblance to its predecessor and now has a clubby, yet modern feel to it. Opened in 2004, the Blakely is an excellent small midtown hotel option. The rooms are all generously sized: None are smaller than 300 square feet and, if it matters to you, some have views of the City Center dome across the street. The dark cherrywood furniture helps perpetuate the clubhouse aura that is contrasted, happily, by very modern amenities such as flatscreen TVs and wireless Internet in all the rooms. Marble bathrooms are good-size and well appointed; bathroom suites have separate tubs and showers. The lobby, though redesigned after the renovation, remains small and can get hectic at times, but the staff is helpful and efficient. Off the lobby is the Italian restaurant Abboccato, also new in 2004, from the owners of Oceana and Molyvos.

136 W. 55th St. (btwn Sixth and Seventh aves.), New York, NY 10019. Ⓒ 212/245-1800. Fax 212/582-8332. www.blakelynewyork.com. 120 units. Double $225–$325; suites $245–$345. Check the website for packages and seasonal specials. AE, DISC, MC, V. Parking $33. Subway: N, R to 57th St. **Amenities:** Restaurant; complimentary access to nearby health club; concierge; 24-hr. room service. *In room:* A/C, TV, minibar/fridge, coffeemaker, iron/ironing board, safe, wireless Internet, CD/DVD player, microwave.

Doubletree Guest Suites-Times Square ★ (Kids)

For many, the location of this 43-story Doubletree, in the heart of darkness known as Times Square where just outside the hotel's entrance the streets will be constantly gridlocked, the bright neon will burn holes into your eye sockets, the noise level is ear-splitting, and where, lucky you, there is an Olive Garden across the street and a McDonald's next door, might offer a more Vegas-like experience than a true New York one. But, at times we all must make sacrifices for our children, and this Doubletree, location and all, is perfect for the kids. From the fresh-baked chocolate chip cookies given out upon arrival, the spacious, and affordable, suites big enough for two 5-year-olds to play hide-and-seek (as mine did), and the all-day children's room-service menu to the proximity to the gargantuan Toys "R" Us, the TKTS Booth, and other kid-friendly Times Square offerings, this Doubletree is hard to beat for families. Bathrooms have two entrances so the kids don't have to traipse through the parent's rooms and every suite has two televisions with Sony PlayStation so while Nickelodeon is on one, CNN is on the other.

1568 Broadway (at 47th St. and Seventh Ave.), New York, NY 10036. © **800/222-TREE** or 212/719-1600. Fax 212/921-5212. www.doubletree.com. 460 units. From $209 suites. Extra person $20. Children under 12 stay free in parent's suite. Ask about senior, corporate, and AAA discounts and special promotions. AE, DC, DISC, MC, V. Parking $35. Subway: N, R to 49th St. **Amenities:** Restaurant; lounge; fitness center; concierge; limited room service; babysitting; dry cleaning/laundry service. *In room:* A/C, 2 TVs w/pay movies and video games, dataport, minibar, fridge, wet bar w/coffeemaker, hair dryer, iron, safe, high-speed Internet connectivity, microwave.

Le Parker Meridien ★★ *Kids*   Not many hotels in New York can rival the attributes of this hotel: Its location on 57th Street, not too far from Times Square and a close walk to Central Park and the shopping of Fifth Avenue, is practically perfect; the 17,000-square-foot fitness center, called Gravity, features state-of-the-art equipment, a basketball and a racquetball court, a spa, and a rooftop pool; three excellent restaurants, including **Norma's** (p. 202), where breakfast is an art, and the aptly named **Burger Joint,** rated by many as the best hamburger in the city; a gorgeous, bustling lobby that also serves as a public space; and elevators with televisions that continuously show *Tom and Jerry* and *Rocky and Bullwinkle* cartoons, and Charlie Chaplin shorts that are a wonder for the kids. The spacious hotel rooms, though a bit on the Ikea side, have a fun feel to them, with hidden drawers and swirling television platforms, inventively exploiting an economical use of space. Rooms have wood platform beds with feather beds, built-ins that include large work desks, stylish Aeron chairs, free high-speed Internet, and 32-inch flatscreen televisions with VCR/CD and DVD players. The slate and limestone bathrooms are large, but unfortunately come only with shower. A stay at Le Parker Meridien is a New York experience in itself.

118 W. 57th St. (btwn Sixth and Seventh aves.), New York, NY 10019. © **800/543-4300** or 212/245-5000. Fax 212/307-1776. www.parkermeridien.com. 731 units. $420–$680 double; from $480 suite. Extra person $30. Excellent packages and weekend rates often available (as low as $225 at press time). AE, DC, DISC, MC, V. Parking $40. Subway: B, N, Q, R to 57th St. Pets accepted. **Amenities:** 2 restaurants; a burger joint; fantastic rooftop pool; fantastic fitness center and spa; concierge (2 w/Clefs d'Or distinction); courtesy car to/from Wall St.; full-service business center; 24-hr. room service; dry cleaning/laundry service. *In room:* A/C, 32-in. TV w/DVD/CD player, fax, dataport, minibar, hair dryer, iron, safe, Internet access.

The Michelangelo ★★ *Finds*   Owned by the Italian-based Starhotel, this is the group's only U.S. property and it offers a very welcome dose of Italian hospitality in the heart of New York. From the moment you enter the spacious lobby adorned with Italian marble, you feel as if you have suddenly departed from the rapid-fire sight and sound assault of nearby Times Square. Off the lobby is a nice lounge where coffee and cappuccino are served all day and a complimentary Italian breakfast of pastries and fruit is offered each morning. The rooms come in various sizes and are curiously decorated in three different styles: Art Deco, country French, and neoclassical. I prefer the country French, but whatever the style, the rooms are all of a good size and include marble foyers, Italian fabrics, king beds, and two television sets (one in the bathroom). The bathrooms are well maintained and feature deep whirlpool bathtubs. Limoncello, the hotel's Mediterranean restaurant, offers lunch, dinner, and an innovative breakfast (try the polenta pancakes). Service is helpful and friendly, creating a relaxed, casual atmosphere rare in many New York hotels.

152 W. 51st St. (btwn Sixth and Seventh Aves.), New York, NY 10019. © **800/237-0990** or 212/765-1900. Fax 212/541-6604. www.michelangelohotel.com. 178 units. From $395 double; from $595 suite. Rates include Italian breakfast. Visit website for (sometimes substantial) discounts. AE, DC, DISC, MC, V. Parking available 2 blocks away: $27

per day self-park, $40 per day valet. Subway: N, R to 49th St. **Amenities:** Restaurant; lounge; fitness center; concierge; complimentary morning limo service to Wall St.; 24-hr. room service; dry cleaning/laundry. *In room:* A/C, TV, fax, minibar, hair dryer, iron, safe, high- speed Internet.

The Muse ⊛ The beauty of the Muse is that it is a Times Square hotel that feels like it's miles away; an inspired oasis in the midst of the Vegas-like hokeyness, bustle, and noise that is now Times Square. In the intimate, mahogany-paneled lobby you will be personally checked in by a concierge and brought to your room by a bellman who will familiarize you with the amenities. But while he's doing that you might be marveling at the classical contemporary decor and not really paying attention. All the rooms are good-size with feather beds and custom linens. The bathrooms are sumptuous and well outfitted. Service is solid and anticipatory; you even get your own personalized business cards. My only complaint, and it's not one that is unusual in New York, was the cacophony of garbage trucks working on 46th Street before sunrise. Try to secure a back room if street noise is an issue.

130 W. 46th St. (btwn Sixth and Seventh aves.), New York, NY 10036. ⓒ **877/692-6873** or 212/485-2400. Fax 212/485-2900. www.themusehotel.com. 200 units. $229–$399 double; from $399 suite. AE, DC, DISC, MC, V. Parking $43. Subway: B, D, F, V to 42nd St. Pets accepted. **Amenities:** Restaurant; good fitness room; concierge; business services; limited room service; in-room massage; dry cleaning/laundry service. *In room:* A/C, TV w/pay movies, dataport, coffeemaker, hair dryer, iron, safe, high-speed Internet connectivity, CD player.

Sofitel New York ⊛⊛⊛ *(Finds* There are many fine hotels on the centrally located block of 44th Street between Fifth and Sixth avenues (see the sidebar "Hotel Row," on p. 144), but the newest (built in 2000) and best in this man's estimation is the soaring Sofitel. Upon entering the hotel and the warm, inviting lobby with check-in tucked off to the side, you wouldn't think you were entering a hotel that is less than 6 years old, which is one of the reasons why the hotel is so special. The designers have successfully melded modern, new world amenities with European old-world elegance. The rooms are spacious and ultracomfortable, adorned with art from New York and Paris. The lighting is soft and romantic; the walls and windows soundproof. Suites are extra-special, equipped with king beds, two televisions, and pocket doors separating the bedroom from a sitting room. Bathrooms in all rooms are magnificent, with separate showers and soaking tubs. Owned by the Accor Hotels & Resorts company of France, Sofitel reflects its heritage with a greeting of *bonjour* or *bonsoir* at reception; a unique gift shop with hard-to-find French products, including perfumes and cosmetics; and a stylish French restaurant called Gaby that bakes delicious croissants for breakfast.

45 W. 44th St. (btwn Fifth and Sixth aves.), New York, NY 10036. ⓒ **212/354-8844.** Fax 212/782-2480. www.sofitel. com. 398 units. $229–$429 double; from $359 suite. 1 child stays free in parent's room. AE, DC, MC, V. Parking $45. Subway: B, D, F, V to 42nd St. Pets accepted. **Amenities:** Restaurant; bar; exercise room; concierge; 24-hr. room service; dry cleaning/laundry service. *In room:* A/C, TV w/pay movies and Internet access, dataport, minibar, hair dryer, iron, safe, high-speed Internet connectivity, CD player.

The Westin New York at Times Square ⊛ *(Finds* This happy, welcome paradox is a high-tech, high-style, high-rise with a warm yet quirky personality. The warmth comes from the inside, from the extra-attentive staff, but the quirkiness is outside, realized in its odd, wavy exterior. The 10-color, mostly copper and blue, glass edifice looks more like a transplant from Miami Beach than something familiar to the New York City terrain. No wonder—the hotel was designed by the Miami-based architectural firm Arquitectonica. And if that isn't enough to distinguish itself, the hotel also boasts a beam of light that rises through an atrium, then up to the top of the 45-story tower and into the already well-illuminated sky of Times Square.

Though style is big here, there's plenty of substance, too. The rooms are spacious, with the Club Rooms and Suites being the biggest. All feature the same amenities, including Westin's truly celestial Heavenly Bed—a custom Simmons Beautyrest pillow-top mattress set dressed in layer upon layer of fluffy down and crisp white linen—and the signature Heavenly Bath, featuring the luxurious two-head shower. The hotel is located on very busy Eighth Avenue, taking up the block between 42nd and 43rd streets; rooms facing 42nd Street and Eighth can be loud. The hotel also features a state-of-the-art fitness center and spa, but surprisingly, there is a fee for guests to use the facility.

270 W. 43rd St. (at Eighth Ave.), New York, NY 10036. © **800/WESTIN-1**, 888/627-7149, or 212/201-2700. Fax 212/201-2701. www.westinnewyork.com. 863 units. $199–$539 double; $239–$579 suite. AE, DC, DISC, MC, V. Parking $38. Subway: A, C, or E to 42nd St. **Amenities:** Restaurant; bar; 2,500-sq.-ft. fitness center and spa ($10 per day, $30 per week); concierge and theater desk; business center; 24-hr. room service; dry cleaning/laundry service; currency exchange; internal access to E Walk, a 200,000-sq.-ft. entertainment and retail complex featuring a 13-movie theater. *In room:* A/C, TV w/pay movies, dataport, minibar, hair dryer, safe, high-speed Internet.

W Times Square ★

Who said Times Square hotels can't be hip? The W Hotel group, a subsidiary of Starwood Hotels & Resorts, bucked that trend by bringing a distinct downtown feel to the heart of Times Square. Take the elevator to the seventh floor to the ultramodern, loungelike lobby to check-in, where the only way to distinguish hotel employees from guests is the tiny "W" pin they wear. Otherwise, everyone is dressed in the dark tones of Kenneth Cole–designed "urban" attire. The lobby bar always seems to be busy—or maybe that's just the lounge music that plays continuously throughout all the hotel's public spaces. Most rooms boast magnificent views of the neon spectacle of Times Square, but all that neon means a very bright room; thankfully, the shades do a good job of blocking out most of that light at night and the double-paned windows keep the rooms surprisingly quiet. Standard rooms are compact, but roomy enough, with a big plexiglass desk, mirrors everywhere (is that good or bad?), a 27-inch TV, and the Westin (sister company of Starwood) Heavenly Bed. Bathrooms in the standard rooms are small and a bit clumsy, featuring a semi-open shower stall and a huge sink that takes up what little counter space there is. Suites are similarly designed and will get you an extra bathroom and a flatscreen television. The hotel's restaurant, Blue Fin, is highly rated for seafood, and The Whiskey, run by nightclub impresario Rande Gerber, is a popular drinks destination.

1547 Broadway (at 47th St.), New York, NY 10036. © **888/625-5144** or 212/930-7400. Fax 212/930-7500. www.whotels.com. 509 units. From $259 double; from $399 suite. AE, DC, DISC, MC, V. Parking $48. Subway: N, R to 49th St. Pets accepted. **Amenities:** Restaurant; 2 bars; fitness center and spa; concierge; 24-hr. room service; dry cleaning/laundry service. *In room:* A/C, TV w/DVD/CD, minibar, hair dryer, iron, safe, high-speed Internet.

MODERATE

Belvedere Hotel ★ *Kids* Here's another excellent choice from the Empire Hotel Group, the people behind the Upper West Side's Lucerne and Newton. Done with a sharp retro-modern-deco flair, the impressively stylish public spaces lead to sizable, comfortable, freshly renovated, and attractive rooms. Beds are nice and firm, bathrooms are smallish but very nice, and every room has a work desk and a pantry kitchenette with minifridge, sink, and microwave (BYO utensils or go plastic). Double/doubles are big

Hotel Row

There are hundreds of hotels in Manhattan, but most of them are spread out over a good chunk of real estate. There is, however, 1 block—West 44th Street, between Fifth and Sixth avenues—where the hotels stand practically side by side.

The block has a sophisticated, urbane, and literary feel to it, probably stemming from the presence of the 1902-built **Algonquin** ★★ (59 W. 44th St.; p. 139), where the *New Yorker* was born, where Lerner and Loewe wrote *My Fair Lady,* and—most famously—where some of the biggest names in 1920s literati, among them Dorothy Parker, met to trade boozy quips at the celebrated Algonquin Round Table.

Next to the Algonquin, at 55 W. 44th St., sits the 65-room Jeffrey Bilhuber–designed luxurious **City Club** (© 212/921-5500; www.cityclubhotel.com). The structure started out in 1904 as a gentlemen's club and saw many incarnations over the last century, but its latest life, as the ultrafashionable City Club, casts aside the usual style of the New York "boutique" property—cramped and minimalist decor that make a virtue of discomfort. City Club's modernist elements are tempered with traditional touches such as Queen Anne chairs, natural Frette linens, vintage books, chocolate marble, and Hermés bath products you'd be afraid to steal. This haven for mavens of fashion also is the home of one of Daniel Boulud's restaurant's, db Bistro Moderne (p. 200).

For many years there was a barbershop located adjacent to the lobby of the **Iroquois Hotel**, 49 W. 44th St. (© 212/840-3080; www.iroquoisny.com), called the Dumont Barbershop and Shoeshine. The shop's principal barber, Louis Fontana, used to notice a kid hanging out on the stoop of the hotel, which, at the time, was a men's residence. When Louie (as he was known by his regulars) asked the kid why he was hanging around the barbershop, the kid stuttered that he needed a haircut but couldn't afford one; he was an

enough for friends and small families who don't mind sharing, and your kids will love you for booking a room with Nintendo and on-screen Web access. Executive-level rooms and suites boast duvet-dressed down comforters, workstations with ergonomic chairs and task lighting, CD players, and plush robes. Whether or not you go executive, ask for a high floor (eight and above) for great views, which usually cost no more (ask when booking).

319 W. 48th St. (btwn Eighth and Ninth aves.), New York, NY 10036. © 888/HOTEL58 or 212/245-7000. Fax 212/245-4455. www.belvederehotelnyc.com. 400 units. $160–$450 double. AAA discounts available; check website for special Internet deals. AE, DC, DISC, MC, V. Parking $24 nearby. Subway: C, E to 50th St. **Amenities:** Restaurant; breakfast cafe; lounge; concierge; car-rental desk; self-service business center; dry cleaning/laundry service; coin-op laundry; executive-level rooms. *In room:* A/C, TV w/pay movies/video games/Internet access, dataport, wet bar w/microwave, fridge, coffeemaker, hair dryer, iron, safe.

Broadway Inn ★★ *Finds*   More like a San Francisco B&B than a Theater District hotel, this lovely, welcoming inn is a real charmer. The second-floor lobby sets the actor looking for work. "Kid, what's your name?" the legend goes. The kid answered, "James Dean." Big-hearted Louis gave him a haircut for free that day. That's a true story and part of the legend of the Iroquois Hotel. The 114-room hotel, after a full renovation some years ago, is now a member of the Small Luxury Hotels of the World and features a suite named after its former most famous resident.

Just next to the Iroquois, at 45 W. 44th St., is the **Sofitel New York** ★★★ (p. 142); from the appearance of the lobby and entrance, you might think you have entered a hotel built in the same era as the others. But take a look from across the street, at the glittering curved tower that was built less than 6 years ago. Despite its newness, the hotel blends in perfectly on historic Hotel Row.

Closer to Fifth Avenue and on the south side of the block at 12 W. 44th St. is **The Mansfield** ★ (© **800/255-5167** or 212/944-6050), which was built as a bachelor's residence in 1905 and, in keeping with the block's literary and artistic tradition, was once the home of poet W. B. Yeat's father. Now it's a 124-room hotel where cappuccino and cookies are available all day and there's an attractive library-style lounge called the "M" Bar that is a big draw with locals who work in the area.

Finally, and closer to Sixth Avenue at 44 W. 44th St., is the Ian Schrager–managed and Philippe Starck–designed, **Royalton** (© **800/635-9013** or 212/869-4400; www.ianschragerhotels.com). Though it is also set in an early-20th-century building, the feel is definitely late 1990s, with that minimalist Starck style. The solitary homage to the past is the presence of working fireplaces in 40 of the hotel's 169 rooms. In keeping with the block's artistic tradition, the Royalton is a favorite of music, fashion, and film types.

homey, easygoing tone with stocked bookcases, cushy seating, and cafe tables where breakfast is served. The rooms are basic but comfy, outfitted in an appealing neo-deco style with firm beds, good-quality linens and textiles, and nice bathrooms (about half have showers only). The whole place is impeccably kept. Two rooms have king beds and whirlpool tubs, but the standard doubles are just fine for two if you're looking to save some dough. If there are more than two of you, or you're staying a while, the suites—with pullout sofa, microwave, minifridge, and lots of closet space—are a great deal. The location can be noisy, but double-paned windows keep the rooms surprisingly peaceful; still, ask for a back-facing one if you're extra sensitive.

The inn's biggest asset is its terrific staff, who go above and beyond the call to make guests happy; they'll even give you a hot line number upon check-in so you can call while you're on the town for directions, advice, and other assistance. Service just doesn't get any better in this price range. This corner of the Theater District makes a great home base, especially for theatergoers. The inn has inspired a loyal following, so reserve early. However, there's no elevator in the four-story building, so over-packers and travelers with limited mobility should book elsewhere.

264 W. 46th St. (at Eighth Ave.), New York, NY 10036. (*C*) **800/826-6300** or 212/997-9200. Fax 212/768-2807. www. broadwayinn.com. 41 units. $109–$125 single; $149–$225 double; $239–$450 suite. Extra person $10. Children under 12 stay free in parent's room. Rates include continental breakfast. Check website for specials. AE, DC, DISC, MC, V. Parking $20 3 blocks away. Subway: A, C, E to 42nd St. **Amenities:** 2 neighboring restaurants where inn guests have special discounts; concierge; fax and copy service. *In room:* A/C, TV, dataport, fridge, hair dryer, iron.

Casablanca Hotel *(*★*) (Value*   A wealth of freebies—including breakfast; coffee, tea, and cookies all day; wine and cheese most evenings; free passes to a nearby health club with pool and sauna; and use of Internet-access PCs—make this stylish Moroccan-themed boutique hotel an excellent value. With vibrant mosaic tiles, warm woods and rattan, potted palms, and North African–themed art gracing the public spaces and guest rooms, the ambience is just right—all that's missing is Bogart and Bergman.

The rooms aren't big, but they're nicely outfitted with comfortable platform beds, ceiling fans, two-line phones, bathrobes, and double-paned windows for quiet. The bathrooms are gorgeous and even the smallest is spacious enough for an oversize shower (request a tub when booking if you want one). Rick's Cafe is one of the city's finest hotel guest lounges, boasting a serve-yourself cappuccino machine, a fireplace, a big-screen TV, and PCs with T1 connectivity. A tiled second-floor courtyard is also ideal for summer lounging, and the rooftop deck is a perfect vantage for watching the New Year's ball drop. The staff is attentive, and the ambitious manager is constantly at work improving the property. Book well ahead, as an increasing number of happy repeat guests and corporate clients fill this place up fast.

147 W. 43rd St. (just east of Broadway), New York, NY 10036. (*C*) **888/922-7225** or 212/869-1212. Fax 212/391-7585. www.casablancahotel.com. 48 units. $169–$265 double; from $295 suite. Rates include continental breakfast, all-day cappuccino, and weekday wine and cheese. Check website for Internet rates and other special deals (as low as $159 at press time). AE, DC, MC, V. Parking $25 next door. Subway: N, R, 1, 2, 3, 9 to 42nd St./Times Sq. **Amenities:** Cyber lounge; free access to New York Sports Club; concierge; business center; limited room service; dry cleaning/laundry service; video library. *In room:* A/C, TV/VCR, dataport, minibar, hair dryer, CD player, ceiling fan.

Hotel Metro *(*★★*) (Kids*   The Metro is the choice in Midtown for those who don't want to sacrifice either style or comfort for affordability. This lovely Art Deco–style jewel has larger rooms than you'd expect for the price. They're outfitted with smart retro furnishings, playful fabrics, fluffy pillows, and smallish but beautifully appointed marble bathrooms, and alarm clocks. Only about half the bathrooms have tubs, but the others have shower stalls big enough for two (junior suites have whirlpool tubs). The family room is an ingenious invention: a two-room suite that has a second bedroom in lieu of a sitting area; families on tighter budgets can opt for a roomy double/double.

The neo-deco design gives the whole place an air of New York glamour that I've not otherwise seen in this price range. A great collection of black-and-white photos, from Man Ray classics to Garbo and Dietrich portraits, adds to the vibe. The comfy, fire-lit library/lounge area off the lobby, where complimentary buffet breakfast is laid out and the coffeepot's on all day, is a popular hangout. Service is attentive, and the well-furnished rooftop terrace boasts a breathtaking view of the Empire State Building, and makes a great place to order up room service from the stylish—and very good—Metro Grill.

45 W. 35th St. (btwn Fifth and Sixth aves.), New York, NY 10001. (*C*) **800/356-3870** or 212/947-2500. Fax 212/ 279-1310. www.hotelmetronyc.com. 179 units. $165–$250 double; $175–$300 triple or quad; $175–$350 family room; $210–$400 suite. Extra person $25. 1 child under 14 stays free in parent's room. Rates include continental breakfast.

Check with airlines and other package operators for great-value package deals. AE, DC, MC, V. Parking $20 nearby. Subway: B, D, F, V, N, R to 34th St. **Amenities:** Restaurant; alfresco rooftop bar in summer; good fitness room; salon; limited room service; dry cleaning/laundry service. *In room:* A/C, TV, dataport, fridge, hair dryer, iron, high-speed Internet.

Novotel New York ⭐ *Kids*   Run expertly by the French company Accor (Sofitel, p. 142), this towering hotel on the northern fringe of Times Square, with its bilingual staff and a selection of foreign newspapers, attracts an international crowd. But domestic visitors shouldn't neglect what is a very good moderate option in one of the busiest parts of the city. The vast, sunny lobby on the seventh floor, with open views of Times Square, is the hotel's pride and joy; it is also the location of the underrated Café Nicole, where a sumptuous breakfast buffet is offered. Guest rooms, though pleasant and of a decent size, are currently more motel-like in decor. At press time, however, a major renovation to upgrade the rooms was soon to commence. Some have spectacular views of Times Square and/or the Hudson River and all are soundproof to keep out the bustle from below. Family-friendly, kids under 16 can stay free in their parent's room and eat free at Café Nicole (with some restrictions).

226 W. 52nd St. (at Broadway), New York, NY 10019. ✆ 212/315-0100. Fax 212/765-5365. www.novotel.com. 480 units. From $169 double. 2 children under 16 eat for free and stay free in parent's room. AE, DC, MC, V. Parking $23. Subway: B, D, E to Seventh Ave. Pets accepted. **Amenities:** Restaurant; bar; fitness room; concierge; limited room service; dry cleaning. *In room:* A/C, TV, minibar, hair dryer, high-speed and wireless Internet.

WJ Hotel ⭐   This is one of the few affordable hotels situated in the heart of my favorite Manhattan neighborhood for dining, Hell's Kitchen. The lobby has a warm and welcoming ambience, with a friendly, snappily attired staff and more than a dash of designer style. Snazzy red-carpeted halls lead to rooms that are *small*—don't say I didn't warn you—but very attractively outfitted in a palette of soft grays. Nice touches include platform beds with generous cushioned headboards and fluffy goose-down comforters. The gorgeous limestone-and-slate bathrooms are stylish and relatively spacious, although some have showers only. Score one of the 18 king rooms if you can; they're roomy and boast a pullout love seat as well as a Jacuzzi tub in the bathroom. The Japanese restaurant in the hotel is just a sample of some of the different ethnic cuisines you will find in the neighborhood.

318 W. 51st St. (btwn Eighth and Ninth aves.), New York, NY 10019. ✆ 212/246-7550. Fax 212/246-7622. www.wjhotel.com. 127 units. $159–$349 double. Rates include continental breakfast with Krispy Kreme doughnuts (subject to change at any time, so call before you count on it). Ask about special deals (from $99 at press time). AE, DC, DISC, MC, V. Parking $25 nearby. Subway: C, E to 50th St. **Amenities:** Restaurant; exercise room; limited room service. *In room:* A/C, TV w/pay movies/video games/Internet access, dataport, hair dryer, iron, safe.

INEXPENSIVE

Americana Inn ⭐ *Value*   The cheapest hotel from the Empire Hotel Group—the people behind the Belvedere, the Lucerne, and the Newton among other top-notch properties—is a star in the budget-basic category. Linoleum floors give the rooms a somewhat unfortunate institutional quality, but the hotel is professionally run and immaculately kept. Rooms are mostly spacious, with good-size closets, private sinks, and an alarm built into the TV; the beds are the most comfortable I've found at this price. Most rooms come with a double bed or two twins; a few can accommodate three guests in two twin beds and a pullout sofa or in three twins. One hall bathroom accommodates every three rooms or so; all are spacious and spotless. Every floor has a common kitchenette with microwave, stove, and fridge (BYO cooking tools and utensils, or go plastic). The five-story building has an elevator, and four rooms are accessible for travelers with disabilities. The Garment District location is convenient for Midtown sightseeing and shopping; ask for a back-facing room away from the street noise.

69 W. 38th St. (at Sixth Ave.), New York, NY 10018. ℂ **888/HOTEL-58** or 212/840-6700. Fax 212/840-1830. www.new yorkhotel.com. 50 units, all with shared bathroom. $75–$115 double. Extra person $10. Check website for specials (winter rates as low as $60 double). AE, MC, V. Parking $25–$35 nearby. Subway: B, D, F, V to 34th St. **Amenities:** Common kitchen. In room: A/C, TV, hair dryer (ask reception).

La Quinta Inn Manhattan ★ (Value

The newest of the Apple Core group's properties and the first and only La Quinta Inn in Manhattan is another excellent midtown budget choice. Housed in a 1904 Beaux Arts structure on the block known as Little Korea, La Quinta Inn offers standard motel amenities along with very motel-like prices. Like the other Apple Core properties, including the Red Roof Inn across the street, service is friendly and a continental breakfast adds to the value. The rooms are basic motel-room decor and size, but there's nothing wrong with that especially at these prices. Bathrooms are comparably small, but clean and well equipped. There's even a cozy rooftop bar that offers indoor and outdoor seating in the shadow of the majestic Empire State Building. And if you like Korean barbecue and dumplings, you won't have to travel far; the block is packed with some very good Korean restaurants.

17 W. 32nd St. (btwn 5th and 6th aves.), New York, NY 10001. ℂ **800/567-7720** or 212/790-2710. www.applecore hotels.com. 182 units. $89–$329 double (usually less than $159). Rates include continental breakfast. Children under 14 stay free in parent's room. AE, DC, DISC, MC, V. Parking $22. Subway: B, D, F, N, R, V to 34th St. **Amenities:** Breakfast room; bar; exercise room; concierge; business center; laundry service; dry cleaning. In room: A/C, TV w/pay movies and video games, dataport, coffeemaker, iron, wireless Internet.

Red Roof Inn ★★ (Value

Manhattan's first, and only, Red Roof Inn offers relief from Midtown's high-priced hotel scene. The hotel occupies a former office building that was gutted and laid out fresh, allowing for more spacious rooms and bathrooms than you'll usually find in this price category. The lobby feels smart, and elevators are quiet and efficient. In-room amenities—including coffeemakers and TVs with on-screen Web access—are better than most competitors', and furnishings are new and comfortable. Wi-Fi wireless Internet is available throughout the property. The location—on a bustling block lined with nice hotels and affordable Korean restaurants, just a stone's throw from the Empire State Building and Herald Square—is excellent.

Be sure to compare the rates offered by Apple Core Hotel's reservation line (the management company) and those quoted on Red Roof's national reservation line and website, as they can vary significantly. Complimentary continental breakfast adds to the good value.

6 W. 32nd St. (btwn Broadway and Fifth Ave.), New York, NY 10001. ℂ **800/567-7720**, 800/RED-ROOF, or 212/643-7100. Fax 212/643-7101. www.applecorehotels.com or www.redroof.com. 171 units. $89–$329 double (usually less than $159). Rates include continental breakfast. Children under 14 stay free in parent's room. AE, DC, DISC, MC, V. Parking $22. Subway: B, D, F, N, R, V to 34th St. **Amenities:** Breakfast room; wine-and-beer lounge; exercise room; concierge; business center; laundry service; dry cleaning. In room: A/C, TV w/pay movies and Internet access, dataport, fridge, coffeemaker, hair dryer, iron, wireless Internet, video games.

Skyline Hotel (Kids

This nice, newly renovated motor hotel offers predictable comforts and some uncommon extras—inexpensive storage parking ($8 per day) and a lovely indoor pool—that make it a very good value. A pleasant lobby leads to motel-standard rooms that were, thankfully, recently renovated, and are bigger than most in this price range. There are two room categories: standard, with two twin beds, and deluxe, with either a king bed with sofa or a queen bed. The deluxe with king and sofa is best for families. They boast decent-size closets, small work desks (in most), and

Family-Friendly Hotels

Lugging the kids to New York City can be a daunting experience. Finding a hotel that makes that experience, whether it is in the accommodations or in the amenities, a bit less daunting can be a huge help. Here are some of the city's best accommodations for families:

Belvedere Hotel (Midtown West; p. 143)   What kid wouldn't like in-room Nintendo and on-screen Web access? The pantry kitchen, with minifridge and microwave, also helps.

Doubletree Guest Suites-Times Square (Times Square; p. 140)   An entire floor of childproof suites, plus a Kids Club, for ages 3 to 12.

Gershwin Hotel (Flatiron District; p. 138)   High space-to-dollar ratio with the Family Room, a two-room suite.

Hotel Beacon (Upper West Side; p. 162)   In-room kitchenette, on-site laundromat, and spacious rooms all in a kid-friendly neighborhood—what more do you want?

Hotel Metro (Midtown West; p. 146)   The sitting rooms of the hotel's Family Room suites are smartly converted into second bedrooms.

Le Parker Meridien (Midtown West; p. 141)   Cartoons playing in the elevators, a great swimming pool, a very kid-friendly burger joint in the lobby, and spacious rooms and suites.

The Lowell (Upper East Side; p. 166)   Total luxe, but with the feel of a residential dwelling. Most units are equipped with kitchenette or fully equipped kitchen.

Novotel New York (Midtown West; p. 147)   Kids under 16 stay free in their parent's room and eat free at the hotel's beautiful Café Nicole.

The Regency (Midtown East; p. 156)   A big welcome by longtime kids' concierge Kaptain Kidz, with goodies for the children upon arrival.

Ritz-Carlton New York, Central Park (Midtown West; p. 139)   You'll pay dearly for it, but kids love the in-room cookies and milk.

Skyline Hotel and **Travel Inn** (Midtown West; p. 148 and p. 150)   Free parking, oversize rooms, and swimming pools (a rarity in affordable hotels).

double-paned windows that open to let fresh air in, and shut out a surprising amount of street noise when closed. Some rooms have brand-new bathrooms, but the older ones are still fine. Everything is very well kept. Another plus for the family is the pool, which has a nicely tiled deck and plush deck chairs, but it's only open limited hours, so call ahead if it matters.

725 Tenth Ave. (at 49th St.), New York, NY 10019. ℂ **800/433-1982** or 212/586-3400. Fax 212/582-4604. www.skylinehotelny.com. 230 units. $109–$179 standard; $139–$229 deluxe. Extra person $15. Children 14 and under stay free in parent's room. Check website or inquire about special rates (as low as $99 at press time). AE, DC, DISC, MC, V. Parking $8 (charge for in/out privileges). Subway: A, C, E to 50th St. Pets accepted with $200 deposit. **Amenities:** Restaurant; bar w/extensive beer list, big-screen TV, and live entertainment; indoor pool; Gray Line tour desk; Internet access in lobby. *In room:* A/C, TV w/pay movies/video games/high-speed Internet, dataport, hair dryer, iron, safe.

Travel Inn *(Kids)* Extras such as a huge outdoor pool and sun deck, a sunny and up-to-date fitness room, and absolutely free parking (with in and out privileges!) make the Travel Inn another terrific deal, similar to the one offered by the **Skyline Hotel** (see above). Like the Skyline, the Travel Inn may not be loaded with personality, but it does offer the clean, bright regularity of a good chain hotel—an attractive trait in a city where "quirky" is the catchword at most affordable hotels. Rooms are oversize and comfortably furnished, with extra-firm beds and work desks; even the smallest double is sizable and has a roomy bathroom, and double/doubles make great affordable shares for families. A total renovation over the last couple of years has made everything feel like new, even the nicely tiled bathrooms. Though a bit off the track, Off-Broadway theaters and great affordable restaurants are at hand, and it's just a 10-minute walk to the Theater District.

515 W. 42nd St. (just west of Tenth Ave.), New York, NY 10036. ℂ **888/HOTEL58,** 800/869-4630, or 212/695-7171. Fax 212/967-5025. www.newyorkhotel.com. 160 units. $105–$250 double. Extra person $10. Children under 16 stay free in parent's room. AAA discounts available; check website for special Internet deals. AE, DC, DISC, MC, V. Free self-parking. Subway: A, C, E to 42nd St./Port Authority. **Amenities:** Coffee shop; terrific outdoor pool w/deck chairs and lifeguard in season; fitness center; Gray Line tour desk; 24-hr. room service. *In room:* A/C, TV, dataport, hair dryer, iron.

8 Midtown East & Murray Hill

To find the hotels described in this section, see p. 136.

VERY EXPENSIVE

Affinia Dumont *(★★)* The Affinia Dumont is the perfect choice for fitness-focused guests: Instead of those basic New York City guide magazines stocked in the rooms, you get a choice of *Sports Illustrated, Shape,* or *Men's Fitness.* Plus, when you book a room, you can request a complimentary "Fit Kit" that will be prepared based on your needs for an in-room workout. But you might want to venture out and to the hotel's terrific fitness spa, complete with all the most advanced weights, cardio equipment, and massage and skin treatments. But even if you don't want to break a sweat during your stay, the hotel features amenities that make it a very attractive option. The spacious suites range from studios to two-bedrooms, and all include full kitchens, at least one 27-inch TV, a large desk with an ergonomic chair, the "Affinia Bed," with a custom-designed mattress and four-selection "pillow menu," and a minibar stocked with unusual options, such as health elixirs with names like Depth Recharger or Virtual Buddha. The hotel is a bit away from the center of Midtown, but still within easy walking distance to Herald Square shopping, the Empire State Building, Madison Square Garden, and Grand Central Station.

150 E. 34th St. (btwn Second and Third aves.), New York, NY 10016. ℂ **212/481-7600** or 212/320-8019. Fax 212/889-8856. www.affinia.com. 241 units. From $350 studio suite; from $450 1-bedroom suite; from $650 2-bedroom suite. AE, DC, MC, V. Valet parking $27. Subway: 6 to 33rd St. **Amenities:** Restaurant; health club and spa; fitness concierge; concierge; limited room service; coin-operated laundry; grocery shopping service. *In room:* A/C, TV/VCR, dataport, full kitchen, minibar, hair dryer, iron, safe, laptop-size safe, high-speed Internet, Fit Kit.

The Benjamin *(★★★)* From the retro sign and clock on Lexington Avenue to the high-ceilinged marble lobby, when you enter the Benjamin, it's as if you've suddenly stepped into the jazz era of New York of the 1920s. But once you get to your spacious room and notice the numerous high-tech amenities, such as Bose Wave radios, Internet browsers and video games for the TVs, high-speed Internet access, fax machines, ergonomic chairs and moveable workstations, you will know you are most definitely in the 21st century. Many of the amenities are geared toward business travelers, but why should they be the only ones to experience all this comfort and luxury? All rooms are airy, but the deluxe studios and one-bedroom suites are extra large. There are even a few one-bedroom suites with terraces. How many hotels can claim a "sleep concierge" or *guarantee* a good night's sleep? And don't forget the pillow menu featuring 11 options, including buckwheat and Swedish Memory, in which foam designed by NASA reacts to your body temperature. I chose the standard down pillow and did not have to exercise the guarantee. If you are a light sleeper, however, book a room off Lexington Avenue, which can get very busy most weeknights and mornings. Bathrooms feature Frette robes, TV speakers, and water pressure from the shower head strong enough to make you think you've just experienced a deep-tissue massage. The hotel also features a good fitness center and the Woodstock Spa and Wellness Center.

125 E. 50th St. (at Lexington Ave.), New York, NY 10022. © **888/4-BENJAMIN**, 212/320-8002, or 212/715-2500. Fax 212/715-2525. www.thebenjamin.com. 209 units. From $459 superior double; from $499 deluxe studio; from $559 suite. Call or check website for special weekend-stay offers. AE, DC, DISC, MC, V. Parking $35. Subway: 6 to 51st St.; E, F to Lexington Ave. **Amenities:** Restaurant; cocktail lounge; state-of-the-art exercise room; full-service spa; concierge; sleep concierge; business services; 24-hr. room service; dry cleaning/valet service. *In room:* A/C, TV w/pay movies/video games/Internet access, fax/copier/printer, dataport, kitchenette, minibar, coffeemaker, laptop-size safe, high-speed Internet connectivity, microwave, china.

Four Seasons Hotel New York ⭑⭑   Designed by überarchitect I. M. Pei, this modernist tower of honey-hued limestone rises 52 stories, making it the city's tallest hotel and providing hundreds of rooms with a view. As soon as you enter the soaring lobby, with its marble floors and backlit onyx ceiling, you'll immediately know this place is special. From the stellar service, only surpassed by the Ritz-Carlton hotels and Trump International, to the fantastic facilities, including a new luxurious spa, this hotel is a stunner.

The completely soundproof guest rooms are among the city's largest, averaging 600 square feet. Each is beautifully furnished in an understated but plush contemporary style and has an entrance foyer, a sitting area, an oversize oval desk with two leather chairs, custom built-ins, coffered ceilings, and massive windows (50% of which boast Central Park views). About two dozen of the priciest rooms also have terraces. The mammoth Florentine marble bathrooms have soaking tubs that fill in 60 seconds, and separate showers with pressure controls. Other special touches include goose-down pillows, Frette-made beds, oversize bath towels, and cushy robes, plus multidisk CD players in suites. But at these prices, why charge extra for Internet access?

57 E. 57th St. (btwn Park and Madison aves.), New York, NY 10022. © **800/819-5053**, 800/487-3769, or 212/758-5700. Fax 212/758-5711. www.fourseasons.com. 368 units. $625–$925 double; from $1,550 suite. Extra rollaway bed $50. Weekend rates from $555; also check for value-added packages and other deals. AE, DC, DISC, MC, V. Parking $42. Subway: N, R, 4, 5, 6 to 60th St. **Amenities:** Restaurant; bar w/evening entertainment; lobby lounge for afternoon tea and light fare; 5,000-sq.-ft. spa and fitness center w/whirlpool, steam, and sauna; children's program; concierge; courtesy limo; business center w/secretarial services; 24-hr. room service; in-room massage; babysitting; dry cleaning/laundry service w/1-hr. pressing. *In room:* A/C, TV w/pay movies, dataport, minibar, hair dryer, safe, high-speed Internet connectivity.

The Peninsula-New York ⭑⭑⭑   The paparazzi was waiting outside as I lugged my overnight bag into the hotel lobby and for a moment they contemplated an explosion of flashbulbs. It didn't take them long, however, to realize I was no celeb—just a fortunate soul spending a night at the marvelous Peninsula Hotel. Housed in a beauty of a landmark, Beaux Arts building, the Peninsula is the perfect combination of old-world charm and modern, state-of-the-art technology. Rooms are huge with plenty of closet and storage space, but best of all is the bedside control panel that allows you to regulate lighting, television, stereo, air-conditioning, and signal the DO NOT DISTURB sign on your door. Even though you really don't have to leave the comfort of your bed, eventually you will need to go to the bathroom and when you do, you'll not be disappointed. The huge marble bathrooms all have spacious soaking tubs with yet another control panel at your fingertips including the controls for, in most rooms, a television so you can watch while taking your bubble bath (now that's happy excess). The Peninsula also features one of the best and biggest New York hotel health clubs and spas, the rooftop Pen-Top Bar, and a faultless concierge desk. All this wonderfulness, however, doesn't come cheap, but if a splurge is what you want, you won't do much better than the Peninsula.

700 Fifth Ave. (at 55th St.), New York, NY 10019. ✆ **800/262-9467** or 212/956-2888. Fax 212/903-3949. www. peninsula.com. 239 units. $595–$760 double; from $960 suite. Extra person $50. Children under 12 stay free in parent's room. Winter weekend package rates from $410 at press time. AE, DC, DISC, MC, V. Valet parking $45. Subway: E, V to Fifth Ave. Pets accepted. **Amenities:** Restaurant; rooftop bar; library-style lounge for afternoon tea and cocktails; tri-level rooftop health club and spa w/treatment rooms, heated pool, exercise classes, whirlpool, sauna, and sun deck; 24-hr. concierge; business center; 24-hr. room service; in-room massage; babysitting; dry cleaning/laundry service. *In room:* A/C, TV w/pay movies, fax, minibar, hair dryer, laptop-size safe, wireless Internet, T1 Internet connectivity, complimentary "water bar" w/5 choices of bottled water.

The Sherry-Netherland ✮✮✮   One of New York's classic grand-dame hotels, this 1927-built beauty, from the ornate, marble and bronze lobby and the Italian Renaissance painted paneled elevators to room service from super elegant Harry Cipriani restaurant, the Sherry is pure old-school luxury. Though it's a big building, only 77 rooms are used for the hotel, the rest are private residential co-ops. Guest rooms vary in decor, but each is grandly proportioned with high ceilings, big bathrooms, and walk-in closets. The rooms are very spacious and every one features high-quality furnishings and art. About half are suites with kitchenettes that have a cooktop or microwave, often both. Bathrooms are huge and impeccably designed and outfitted. And with an enviable location at Fifth and 58th opposite Central Park and adjacent to the Plaza Hotel, most of the rooms have glorious views. Other perks include complimentary continental breakfast at Harry Cipriani, a welcoming box of Godiva chocolates, and complimentary soft drinks, water, and mineral water. And though the hotel is from a different, more refined era, it's not stuffy—the hotel's white-gloved elevator operator and I had a refreshing discussion about the Yankees' prospects for the upcoming season.

781 Fifth Ave. (at 59th St.), New York, NY 10022. ✆ **800/247-4377** or 212/355-2800. Fax 212/319-4306. www.sherry netherland.com. 77 units. $425–$625 double; from $550 1- and 2-bedroom suite. Children stay free in parent's room. Rates include continental breakfast at Cipriani. AE, DC, DISC, MC, V. Parking $40. Subway: N, R to Fifth Ave. Pets accepted. **Amenities:** Restaurant; fitness room; concierge; business center; salon; limited room service; in-room massage; babysitting; dry cleaning/laundry service; video library. *In room:* A/C, TV/VCR, fax, fridge w/free soft drinks, free high-speed Internet.

St. Regis ✮✮✮   When John Jacob Astor built the St. Regis in 1904, he set out to create a hotel that would reflect the elegance and luxury he was used to in hotels in Europe. Over a hundred years later, the St. Regis, now a New York landmark, still reflects that European splendor. Located on Fifth Avenue, and close to Rockefeller Center, St. Patrick's Cathedral, and Saks, this Beaux Arts classic is a marvel; antique furniture, crystal chandeliers, silk wall coverings, and marble floors adorn both the public spaces and the high-ceilinged, airy guest rooms. The suites are particularly ornate, some with French doors, four-poster beds, and decorative fireplaces. The marble bathrooms are spacious and feature separate showers and baths. In a nod to the future, plasma televisions were recently added in all the rooms, along with LCD screens in the bathrooms. Service is efficiently white-gloved and every guest is assigned a personal, tuxedoed butler, on call 24 hours to answer any reasonable requests. The hotel has a large fitness center and a spa that is the first in New York to offer the skin care line from the renowned Carita Spa of Paris. Afternoon tea is served daily in the Astor Court.

Even if the St. Regis is beyond your budget, take a walk through the sumptuous lobby and have a drink in the hotel bar, the world-renowned **King Cole Bar** (see "Checking into Hotel Bars," in chapter 11), birthplace of the Bloody Mary, and home to the famous *Old King Cole* mural by Maxfield Parrish.

2 E. 55th St. (at Fifth Ave.), New York, NY 10022. © 212/753-4500. Fax 212/787-3447. www.stregis.com. 256 units. $660–$735 double; from $1,150 suite. Check Internet for specials as low as $400 at press time. AE, DC, DISC, MC, V. Parking $42. Subway: E, F to Fifth Ave. **Amenities:** Restaurant; historic bar; tea lounge; fitness center and spa; concierge; 24-hr. room service; babysitting; laundry/valet service; 24-hr. butler service. *In room:* A/C, TV, minibar, hair dryer, safe, high-speed Internet connectivity, DVD/CD player.

EXPENSIVE

The Alex ⚔ The theme of the Alex hotel is serenity and comfort—a tough task when you are located in the middle of one of the busiest sections of Manhattan. But renowned designer David Rockwell, using his trademark economically sleek *moderne* style, has created a soothing and very glossy retreat. Each room features furniture designed exclusively for the hotel, such as the four mobile pieces—a chair, a low game table, a coffee table that rises to dining table height, and a nightstand. And all rooms, which range from large junior suites to one- and two-bedroom apartments, also feature state-of-the-art full kitchens with sub-zero refrigerators that are so cleverly designed it took this high-style innocent way too long to distinguish it from the other kitchen amenities. But you might choose to forgo the fridge and order room service from the hotel's Japanese-fusion restaurant, **Riingo** (p. 209).

Flat-panel televisions can also be found in each room and in the bathrooms, which feature rainforest showers and Frederic Fekkai products. Efficiency is the key word here, and the staff goes out of its way to make sure they meet the specific needs of each of the hotel's guests. My only real complaint is that in the Alex's search for efficiency, the workspace, hidden inside a closet, is much too small. But perhaps we shouldn't come here to work when there are all those toys and gadgets designed for play.

205 E. 45th St. (btwn Second and Third aves.), New York, NY 10017. © 212/867-5100. Fax 212/867-7878. www. thealexhotel.com. 203 units. From $299 double; from $349 suite. Check for Internet specials. AE, DC, DISC, MC, V. Parking $37. Subway: 4, 5, 6 to Grand Central. **Amenities:** Restaurant; fitness center; concierge; 24-hr. room service; laundry service. *In room:* A/C, TV, fridge, hair dryer, safe, high-speed Internet, DVD/CD player, microwave.

Hotel Chandler ⚔ Formerly called Le Marquis, this is one of the few boutique properties in Murray Hill. With its warm cherry woods and blue-glass light fixtures, the lobby has a comfortable contemporary look. In the back is a wonderful living room–style lounge that boasts a 40-inch flatscreen TV, books, board games, and sofas you can sink into. You'll find bigger guest rooms elsewhere, but the available space is beautifully filled with custom furnishings that include armoires and efficiently sized work desks. Every detail has incorporated such luxurious appointments as platform beds dressed in goose-down and Frette linens; DVD/CD/MP3 players; plush terry robes; and Aveda toiletries. The sparkling white-tiled bathrooms with their beveled blue-tile accents are magnificent. While having bathrooms with showers only is often seen as a liability in a hotel, double-wide stalls and luxurious rain-shower heads make these rooms more desirable than those with standard tub/shower combos (which are available, if you prefer). At press time, a restaurant was in the works.

12 E. 31st St. (btwn Fifth and Madison aves.), New York, NY 10016. © **866/628-7847** or 212/889-6363. Fax 212/889-6699. www.hotelchandler.com. 120 units. $199–$399 double. Check for seasonal specials (as low as $159 at press time). AE, DC, DISC, MC, V. Parking $35. Subway: B, D, F, V, N, R to 34th St. **Amenities:** Breakfast room serving morning buffet; all-day coffee bar in library lounge; cocktail lounge serving light fare; exercise room w/Finnish sauna; concierge; dry cleaning/laundry service; DVD and CD libraries. *In room:* A/C, TV w/pay movies/video games/high-speed Internet access, minibar, hair dryer, safe, DVD/CD/MP3 player.

Hotel Elysée ✦✦   This little romantic gem of a hotel in the heart of midtown might be easy to miss; it's dwarfed by modern glass towers on either side of it. But that it is so inconspicuous is part of the Elysée's immense romantic appeal. Built in 1926, the hotel has a storied past as the preferred address for artists and writers including Tennessee Williams, Jimmy Breslin, Maria Callas and Vladimir Horowitz (who donated a Steinway which still resides in the Piano Suite), John Barrymore, Marlon Brando, and Ava Gardner, who once had a tryst here with football legend Paul Hornung. The hotel still retains that sexy, discreet feel and now is run expertly by HK Hotels (The Giraffe, The Gansevoort, and The Library). Rooms were recently renovated and have many quirky features; some have fireplaces, others have kitchens or solariums and all are decorated in country-French furnishings. Good-size bathrooms are done up in Italian marble and are well outfitted. Off the gorgeous black and white marble-floored lobby is the legendary Monkey Bar (see chapter 11) and the restaurant, **The Steakhouse at the Monkey Bar.** On the second floor is the Club Room where a free continental breakfast is offered daily along with complimentary wine and cheese weekday evenings.

60 E. 54th St. (btwn Park and Madison aves.), New York, NY 10022. © **800/535-9733** or 212/753-1066. Fax 212/980-9278. www.elyseehotel.com. 101 units. Doubles from $295; suites from $425. Check the website for seasonal specials. Rates include continental breakfast and weekday evening wine and cheese. AE, DC, MC, V. Parking $26. Subway: E, V to Fifth Ave. **Amenities:** Restaurant; bar; free access to nearby gym; concierge; limited room service; dry cleaning/laundry service. *In room:* A/C, TV/VCR, dataport, minibar, hair dryer, iron, safe, wireless Internet.

The Kimberly ✦ *(Value*   Surprisingly good rates on suites here mean that you could be standing on your private balcony overlooking Manhattan for a lot less than you'd pay for a cell-like room in many other Midtown hotels. Most New Yorkers don't have it this good: These are full apartments with dining areas; living rooms with Oriental rugs; full-size, fully equipped kitchens complete with china and cookware; marble bathrooms; tons of closet space; and private unfurnished balconies (in all but eight suites)—it's all part of the package. The executive suites have a larger living space, but the standard one-bedrooms are just fine for most. The two-bedroom suites each have two bathrooms; you can choose between a configuration that adjoins the bedrooms or puts them at opposite ends of the apartment (great for couples traveling together). The 21 regular rooms are handsome and comfortable, too, with extra-nice bathrooms with deep tubs. Additional amenities include two-line phones and plush robes. The hotel may not be the most stylish place in town, but it's done in an attractive traditional style that's cozy and comfortable, and everything is in very good condition.

   A unique perk is complimentary boarding of a 75-foot yacht for a 3-hour sunset cruise (weekends May–Oct, weather permitting).

145 E. 50th St. (btwn Lexington and Third aves.), New York, NY 10022. © **800/683-0400** or 212/755-0400. Fax 212/486-6915. www.kimberlyhotel.com or www.worldhotels.com. 186 units. $259–$349 double; $299–$1,000

1-bedroom suite (including specialty suites); $459–$689 2-bedroom suite. Extra person $25. Children 17 and under stay free in parent's room. Check for deeply discounted off-season and weekend rates (as low as $199 at press time) as well as package deals. AE, DC, DISC, MC, V. Parking $30. Subway: 6 to 51st St.; E, F to Lexington Ave. **Amenities:** 2 restaurants; 2 bars; free access to fabulous New York Health & Racquet Club, w/pool, classes, racquetball courts, and indoor golf; concierge; room service (6am–11pm); in-room massage; babysitting; dry cleaning/laundry service; executive-level rooms. *In room:* A/C, TV w/pay movies and PlayStation, fax/copier, dataport, minibar, fridge, coffeemaker, hair dryer, iron, laptop-size safe, high-speed and wireless Internet.

The Kitano New York ★★★ *Finds*   Owned by the Kitano Group of Japan, this elegant Murray Hill gem offers a unique mix of East and West sensibilities. The marble and mahogany lobby, with its Y-shaped staircase and Botero bronze *Dog,* is one of the most attractive in New York. The hotel was first opened in 1973; in the mid-1990s, along with acquiring an 1896 landmark town house next door, the Kitano was fully renovated. If you're a very lucky (and wealthy) individual, you'll get the opportunity to stay in one of three one-bedroom town house suites, each with sunken living rooms, bay windows, and original, eclectic art. Or, if your sensibilities are Eastern-oriented, the hotel offers a Tatami suite, with tatami mats, rice paper screens, and a Japanese Tea Ceremony room. Most rooms are not quite that luxurious or unique, but all include tasteful mahogany furniture, soundproof windows, and, for a real taste of Japan, green tea upon arrival; marble bathrooms are large and have heated towel racks and removable shower heads. The sky-lit **Garden Café,** residing in the town house, offers contemporary American cuisine while **Hakubai** serves traditional multicourse Kaiseki cuisine. There's also an interesting gift shop in the lobby specializing in unique Japanese items. But best of all is the mezzanine-level bar where Wednesday through Saturday evenings it turns into the acclaimed **Jazz at the Kitano**.

66 Park Ave. (at 38th St.), New York, NY 10016. © 212/885-7000. Fax 212/885-7100. www.kitano.com. 149 units. $480–$605 double; from $715 suite. AE, DC, MC, V. Parking $31. Subway: 4, 5, 6, 7, S to Grand Central. **Amenities:** 2 restaurants; bar w/live jazz; access to a nearby health club; concierge; complimentary limo service to Wall St. on weekdays; limited room service; dry cleaning/laundry service. *In room:* A/C, TV, fax, dataport, hair dryer, iron, high-speed Internet, complimentary tea.

The Library Hotel ★★ *Finds*   New York is not Las Vegas, so I'm usually wary of the hotel as high concept, but in this case, the concept really works: a hotel located 1 block from the New York Public Library, each of whose 10 guest room floors is dedicated to 1 of the 10 major categories of the Dewey Decimal System. When I visited the hotel I was appropriately booked into a "Geography and Travel" room. There I was greeted with books such as *Barcelona,* by Robert Hughes, and *Bella Tuscany,* by Frances Mayes. The most disappointing thing about all those books is that I was only staying 1 night and didn't have the chance to read any of them. Still, there was something about having them by my bed; perhaps their soothing aura comforted me. Overall, the hotel has a pleasing, informal feel. Guest rooms, which come in three categories, petite (really small), deluxe, and junior suites, feature mahogany built-ins, generous desks, and immaculate marble bathrooms; all are extremely comfortable. The Library's public spaces—a reading room where weekday wine and cheese and a complimentary daily breakfast are served, a writer's den with a fireplace and flatscreen television, and a rooftop terrace—all help make the Library a welcome refuge in the heart of the city.

299 Madison Ave. (at 41st St.), New York, NY 10017. © 877/793-7323 or 212/983-4500. Fax 212/499-9099. www.libraryhotel.com. 60 units. $295–$425 double; $395 Love Room or junior suite; $740 2-room family suite. Rates include continental breakfast buffet, all-day snacks, and weekday wine and cheese. Inquire about corporate, promotional, and weekend rates (as low as $199 at press time). AE, DC, MC, V. Parking $28 nearby. Subway: 4, 5, 6, 7, S to

42nd St./Grand Central. **Amenities:** Restaurant; free access to nearby health club; business center; limited room service; dry cleaning/laundry service; video library of American Film Institute's Top 100 films. *In room:* A/C, TV/VCR, dataport, minibar, hair dryer, iron, laptop-size safe, high-speed Internet connectivity, CD player.

The Regency ⭐⭐ *(Kids)* Mirroring the elegance of Park Avenue and with its enviable location close to Central Park, Bloomingdale's, and the white-gloved shops of Madison Avenue, the Regency has long been a haven for celebrities and those who aspire to celebrity status. On one of my visits to the hotel, I saw New York Yankee outfielder Hideki Matsui amble through the glittering, marble-laden lobby. But even if you aren't on the cover of a magazine, a stay at the Regency might make you feel like a star. The guest rooms are all huge, featuring a king bed or two doubles, a large marble writing desk with an ergonomic chair, and a small eating table. The bathrooms, though not enormous, are equipped with terry-cloth robes and a small television. Suites are typically grandiose, ranging from the 450-square-foot Executive, with two bathrooms and French doors, to the Grand Suite, with two bedrooms and two marble bathrooms. Despite its elegance, the Regency is a surprisingly good choice for kids. Children under 18 stay free when sharing a room with their parents; rollaway beds are an additional $25 for the stay. Even pets get the special treatment, with the hotel providing services such as place mats with food and water bowls and a room service menu for pets. Complimentary homemade hot chocolate is served in the lobby in the winter months, replaced by lemonade in the summer. The hotel's restaurant, 540 Park Avenue, is one of the great power breakfast spots in the city, while **Feinstein's at The Regency** (p. 369) is considered the standard when it comes to cabaret.

540 Park Ave. (at 61st St.), New York, NY 10021. © 212/759-4100. Fax 212/826-5674. www.loewshotels.com. 351 units. $419–$499 double; from $539 suite. Children under 18 stay free in parent's room; additional $25 for rollaway bed. AE, DC, MC, V. Parking $49. Subway: 4, 5, 6, N, R to 59th St. Pets accepted. **Amenities:** 2 restaurants; cabaret; fitness center; children's program; concierge; 24-hr. room service; dry cleaning/laundry service. *In room:* A/C, TV w/VCR, dataport, minibar, hair dryer, iron, safe, high-speed Internet, CD player.

The Roger ⭐⭐ The swinging candy-colored lobby is a delicious entree to what appears to be a winner of a boutique hotel in the newly renovated incarnation of the Roger Williams Hotel in Murray Hill. In the smallish rooms, where the jewel tones from the lobby are echoed in the colorful bed quilts, you'll find the kind of amenities that have become de rigueur in upscale city hotels: flatscreen TVs, Egyptian cotton linens, Wi-Fi, all the lotions and potions your body requires, and great snacks. Of the 190 rooms and suites, 10% have been outfitted with private landscaped terraces. A floating granite staircase leads from the lobby to a mezzanine lounge, where you can breakfast in the morning and drink cocktails by candlelight at night.

131 Madison Ave. (at 31st St.), New York, NY 10016. © 888/448-7788 or 212/448-7000. Fax 212/448-7007. www. hotelrogerwilliams.com. 190 units. $235–$385 double. Rates include help-yourself breakfast pantry. AE, DC, DISC, MC, V. Subway: 6 to 28th St./Lexington Ave. **Amenities:** Lounge; fitness center; concierge; dry cleaning/laundry service; complimentary Wi-Fi; conference suite. *In room:* A/C, flatscreen TV, minibar, iron/ironing board, safe.

San Carlos Hotel ⭐ With the Waldorf=Astoria, W New York, the Benjamin, Doubletree Metropolitan, and a Marriott and Sheraton all within a 2-block radius, maybe it's a good thing that this unassuming, but charming gem gets a little lost among the giants. The hotel won't blow you away with an ornate lobby or a hip lounge or restaurant on its premises. What it provides is simple, relatively unadorned hominess. The standard rooms, which were recently renovated, are of a moderate size, but include a small pantry (suites come with kitchenettes), 27-inch flatscreen TV, and good-size work desks. What makes the hotel a cut above are the extras like complimentary continental breakfast, free high-speed Internet, and personable service.

150 E. 50th St. (btwn Lexington and Third aves.), New York, NY 10022. ✆ **800/722-2017.** Fax 212/688-9778. www.san carloshotel.com. 150 units. $300–$390 double; $460–$700 suites. Rates include continental breakfast. Check website for seasonal specials. AE, DC, MC, V. Parking $30. Subway: 6 to 51st St. **Amenities:** Fitness center; business center; dry cleaning/laundry service. *In room:* A/C, TV, minibar, fridge, hair dryer, iron/ironing board, safe, high-speed Internet, CD player, 2-line phone.

70 Park Avenue ✦

After a $19-million renovation, the San Francisco–based Kimpton Hotels's first foray into the New York market debuted in 2004. Formerly the Doral Park Avenue, this Murray Hill property underwent a complete renovation including design by the distinctive Jeffrey Bilhuber who, with his warm earth tones, has created a homey, residential feel. Albeit this is one home that is absolutely state-of-the-art, with 42-inch flatscreen televisions, MAINstage Music & Theater Sound System, and wireless Internet. And in keeping with Kimpton's New Age trademark, the hotel encourages environmental awareness (including guest recycling and water-saving programs) and guests get a yoga channel on their TVs.

The lobby is a beauty with a long wooden table that serves as the concierge station and a 14-foot limestone and sandstone fireplace. Guest rooms, though not overly large, are efficiently constructed with an economical use of space: Note the minibar tucked into a dresser and the mahogany armoire that serves as the closet. In the room where I stayed, there were five huge mirrors, which could be a good thing or a bad thing depending on your physical self-esteem. Bathrooms in standard rooms are a bit tight, but well outfitted, while a number of guest rooms offer two-person whirlpool spa tubs. On premises is the gorgeous Silverleaf Tavern.

70 Park Ave. (btwn 37th and 38th sts.), New York, NY 10016. ✆ **877/707-2752** or 212/973-2400. Fax 212/973-2401. www.70parkavenuehotel.com. 205 units. $325–$455 double; from $1,000 suites. AE, DC, DISC, MC, V. Valet parking $42. Subway: 4, 5, 6, 7, S to Grand Central. Pets accepted. **Amenities:** Restaurant; bar; access to nearby fitness center; concierge; 24-hr. room service; laundry service. *In room:* A/C, TV, dataport, minibar, hair dryer, iron, safe, wireless and high-speed Internet, DVD/CD player, cordless telephone, voice mail.

Waldorf=Astoria and the Waldorf Towers ✦✦✦

If you are looking for the epitome of old-school elegance, you can't do better than the Waldorf=Astoria. This massive 1-square-block Art Deco masterpiece is not only a hotel icon, it's a genuine New York City landmark. Here you'll find a lobby so big and grand, it's reminiscent of Grand Central Station, including having its own signature clock. With over 1,000 rooms, the pace can be hectic, and at times the lines for checking in might remind you of the post office. Thankfully, service here is much more efficient than the post office and it won't be long before you're in your room. And what rooms they are; no two the same, yet all are airy, with high ceilings, traditional decor, comfortable linens and beds, and spacious marble bathrooms, along with fax machines and high-speed Internet access. If you crave more luxury, book a room on the **Astoria** level, which features huge suites, deluxe bathroom amenities, access to the clubby Astoria Lounge for breakfast or afternoon hors d'oeuvres, and free entry to the hotel's fitness club (other guests pay a fee); for even more opulence, try a suite in the **Waldorf Towers,** where most rooms are bigger than New York City apartments.

One of three bars in the hotel, **Sir Harry's Bar,** off the lobby, is the main gathering spot for a pre- or post-dinner cocktail, but even better is the **Bull and Bear,** with its signature round mahogany bar, classic original cocktail creations, and celebrated steaks (see "The Prime Cut," in chapter 8). **Oscars,** which also has a bar, offers break-fast, lunch, and dinner, and **Inagiku** serves innovative Japanese cuisine.

301 Park Ave. (btwn 49th and 50th sts.), New York, NY 10022. © **800/WALDORF,** 800/774-1500, or 212/355-3000. Fax 212/872-7272 (Astoria) or 212/872-4799 (Towers). www.waldorfastoria.com or www.waldorf-towers.com. 1,245 units (180 in the Towers). Waldorf=Astoria $229–$485 double; from $349 suite. Waldorf Towers $329–$625 double; from $515 suite. Extra person $40. Children under 18 stay free in parent's room. Corporate, senior, seasonal, and weekend discounts may be available (as low as $189 at press time), as well as attractive package deals. AE, DC, DISC, MC, V. Parking $45. Subway: 6 to 51st St. **Amenities:** 3 restaurants; 4 bars; 3,000-sq.-ft. fitness center and excellent spa; concierge and theater desk; expansive 24-hr. business center; salon; 24-hr. room service; dry cleaning/laundry service; executive-level rooms. Tower rooms include butler service, Clefs d'Or concierge. *In room:* A/C, TV w/pay movies, fax/copier/printer, dataport, minibar, coffeemaker, hair dryer, iron, high-speed Internet connectivity (in executive-level rooms and suites). Waldorf Towers rooms include kitchenette or wet bar w/fridge, safe.

MODERATE

Doubletree Metropolitan Hotel ★ (Value) It might be the middle of January and the wind chills are below zero, but one look at the exterior of the Metropolitan and a walk inside the retro-cool lobby and you'll think you are in Miami Beach (ca. 1961). That's because the hotel was designed in 1961 by the renowned architect Morris Lapidus, the man responsible for Miami's legendary Fontainbleau and Eden Roc hotels. But in 1961, were you given fresh-baked chocolate chip cookies upon check-in? Most recently a Loews Hotel, in 2004 the Doubletree brand (cookies and all) took over the hotel and poured $35 million into renovations updating the Art Deco feel throughout the hotel. The lobby is now stocked with mod furniture where guests can lounge and surf the Internet on their laptops (the public places have wireless capability). Guest rooms are on the smallish side and even with the renovations (including LCD televisions), still have a cookie-cutter, motel feel to them, but the beds are, like other Doubletree properties, extremely comfortable guaranteeing the "Sweet Dreams by Doubletree Sleep Experience." The renovations and the exemplary Doubletree service are a huge improvement on what the hotel once was and now is a very good midpriced option in the middle of Manhattan.

569 Lexington Ave. (at 51st St.), New York, NY 10022. © **212/752-7000.** Fax 212/758-6311. www.metropolitanhotel nyc.com. 755 units. Rates $250–$350 single; $300–$450 double. Check website for specials as low as $199. AE, DC, MC, V. Parking $30 nearby. Subway: 6 to 51st St. or E, V to Lexington Ave. **Amenities:** Restaurant; bar; fitness center; concierge; business center; limited room service; barbershop; nail salon. *In room:* A/C, TV, hair dryer, iron, safe, high-speed Internet, 2-line telephone.

INEXPENSIVE

Habitat Hotel Marketed as "upscale budget," this hotel features rooms dressed to appeal to travelers who are short on funds but big on style. They're well designed in a natural palette accented with black-and-white photos. Everything is better quality and more attractive than in most hotels in this price range, from the firm mattresses to the plush towels to the pedestal sinks in every room. The bathrooms are all new; choose between shared (one for every three to four rooms), private, or a semiprivate minisuite (two rooms sharing an adjacent bathroom—great for friends traveling together).

The only downside—and it may be a big one for romance-seeking couples—is the sleeping accommodations. A few queens are available (at the highest end of the price spectrum, of course), but most of the double rooms consist of a twin bed with a pull-out trundle, which takes up most of the width of the narrow room when it's open. Despite that drawback, rates are attractive, especially for the rooms with shared bath-room, considering the *Metropolitan Home* mindset and the A-1 location. I prefer the private bathrooms at sister hotel **Thirty Thirty** (below), because they don't have the space limitations these have, but this hotel has a more thrilling location and a more exciting feel thanks to the popular restaurant and bar, Opia.

130 E. 57th St. (at Lexington Ave.), New York, NY 10022. (℃) **800/497-6028** or 212/753-8841. Fax 212/838-4767. www.habitatny.com. 330 units, about 40 with private bathroom. $75–$115 single or double with shared bathroom; $125–$185 single or double with private bathroom; $240–$270 minisuite (2 rooms with shared bathroom). Rates include continental breakfast. Call or check website for student rates and promotions (from $79 at press time). AE, DC, DISC, MC, V. Parking $25. Subway: 4, 5, 6 to 59th St.; E, F to Lexington Ave. **Amenities:** Restaurant/bar; tour desk. *In room:* A/C, TV, dataport.

Hotel Grand Union This centrally located hotel is big with budget-minded international travelers. A pleasant white-on-white lobby leads to clean and spacious rooms with nice extras that are uncommon in this price category, such as hair dryers and free HBO. Bad fluorescent overhead lighting, unattractive colonial-style furniture, and an utter lack of natural light dampen the mood—but considering the roominess, low rates, and excellent central-to-everything location, the Grand Union is a very good deal. Room no. 309, a nicely configured quad with two twins and a queen in a separate alcove, is a great bet for families. Most bathrooms have been freshly outfitted in granite or tile; ask for a newly renovated one to get the most for your money. The staff is helpful, there's a pleasant sitting room off the lobby, and an adjacent coffee shop is convenient for morning coffee or a quick burger.

34 E. 32nd St. (btwn Madison and Park aves.), New York, NY 10016. (℃) **212/683-5890.** Fax 212/689-7397. www. hotelgrandunion.com. 95 units. $120–$130 single or double; $140–$155 twin or triple; $165–$180 quad. Call or check website for special rates (as low as $90 at press time). AE, DC, DISC, MC, V. Parking $22 nearby. Subway: 6 to 33rd St. **Amenities:** Coffee shop; tour desk; fax service. *In room:* A/C, TV, dataport, fridge, hair dryer.

Murray Hill Inn Housed in a renovated five-story walk-up in a pleasant and quiet residential neighborhood, the Murray Hill Inn is shoestring basic—but there's no arguing with its cleanliness, which is key when judging accommodations in this price range. Rooms are tiny and outfitted with not much more than either one or two beds with motel-standard bedspread and furnishings, a wall rack, a phone, and a small TV; most rooms with shared bathroom also have private sinks (request one when booking). These Euro-style rooms share the in-hall bathrooms that are new and spotless. Some of the doubles have an alcove that can accommodate a third traveler on a cot if you're on an extra-tight budget. Rooms with private bathrooms are definitely the nicest; they're spacious, with new bathrooms and dataports on the telephones. Most also have pullout sofas that can accommodate an extra traveler or two. Don't expect much in terms of facilities beyond a pleasant (if tiny) lobby, plus a plain downstairs sitting area with a vending machine, an ATM, and a luggage-storage area. Services are kept to a bare minimum to keep costs down, but the staff is personable.

143 E. 30th St. (btwn Lexington and Third aves.), New York, NY 10016. (℃) **888/996-6376** or 212/683-6900. Fax 212/545-0103. www.murrayhillinn.com. 50 units, 10 with shared bathroom. $79–$85 double with shared bathroom; $89–$125 double with private bathroom; $95–$145 private deluxe. Extra person $15. Children under 12 stay free in parent's room. Ask about discounts and special rates (as low as $59 double with shared bathroom, $95 with private bathroom at press time). AE, MC, V. Parking about $25 nearby. Subway: 6 to 28th St. *In room:* A/C, TV, wireless Internet.

Thirty Thirty ⭐ Ⓥ𝑎𝑙𝑢𝑒 Thirty Thirty is just right for bargain-hunting travelers looking for a splash of style with an affordable price tag. The building—which formerly housed the well-known Martha Washington women's hotel and the legendary nightclub

Danceteria, where Madonna got her start—was gutted, renovated, and redone with brand-new everything.

The design-conscious tone is set in the loftlike industrial-modern lobby. Rooms are mostly on the smallish side, but do the trick for those who intend to spend their days out on the town rather than holed up here. They're done in a natural palette with a creative edge—purplish carpet, khaki bedspread, woven wallpaper—that comes together more attractively than you might expect. Configurations are split between twin/twins (great for friends), queens, and queen/queens (great for triples, budget-minded quads, or shares that want more spreading-out room). Nice features include cushioned headboards, firm mattresses, two-line phones, nice built-in wardrobes, and spacious, nicely tiled bathrooms. A few larger units have kitchenettes, great if you're staying in town for a while, as you'll appreciate the extra room and the fridge. No room service, but delivery is available from nearby restaurants.

30 E. 30th St. (btwn Madison and Park aves.), New York, NY 10016. ✆ **800/497-6028** or 212/689-1900. Fax 212/689-0023. www.thirtythirty-nyc.com. 243 units. $115–$145 double; $145–$195 double with kitchenette; $185–$245 quad. Call for last-minute deals, or check website for special promotions (as low as $99 at press time). AE, DC, DISC, MC, V. Parking $35 1 block away. Subway: 6 to 28th St. Pets accepted with advance approval. **Amenities:** Restaurant; concierge; dry cleaning/laundry service. *In room:* A/C, TV, dataport, hair dryer.

9 Upper West Side

To find the hotels described in this section, see p. 162.

VERY EXPENSIVE

Trump International Hotel & Tower ⭐⭐⭐   From the outside, it's the prototypical, not very attractive Trump creation—a tall, dark monolith, hovering over Columbus Circle and lower Central Park. But go inside and spend a night or two at the Trump International, experience services such as your own Trump Attaché, a personal concierge who will provide comprehensive services (your wish is their command); take advantage of such first-class facilities as the 6,000-square-foot health club with lap pool and a full-service spa; or order room service from the hotel's signature restaurant, the four-star Jean-Georges. Not only will you immediately dispel any prejudices you might have had toward The Donald, you might even begin to comprehend why someone would be willing to sell their soul for the chance to become the Master Builder's apprentice.

Guest rooms are surprisingly understated, with high ceilings and floor-to-ceiling windows, some with incredible views of Central Park and all with telescopes for taking in the view, and sumptuous marble bathrooms with Jacuzzi tubs. But if that's not enough—it certainly was for me—you also get two complimentary bottles of Trump water, complete with a picture of The Donald on each one. For a hotel this well run, you can forgive the man for his excesses.

1 Central Park West (at 60th St.), New York, NY 10023. ✆ **212/299-1000.** Fax 212/299-1150. www.trumpintl.com. 167 units. $595–$625 double; from $845 1- or 2-bedroom suite. Children stay free in parent's room. Check website for special rates (as low as $355 at press time) and package deals; also try booking through www.travelweb.com for discounted rates. AE, DC, DISC, MC, V. Parking $45. Subway: A, B, C, D, 1, 9 to 59th St./Columbus Circle. **Amenities:** Restaurant; spa and health club w/steam, sauna, and pool; Clefs d'Or concierge; staffed business center w/secretarial services; 24-hr. room service; in-room massage; babysitting; dry cleaning/laundry service; butler (personal attaché); CD library. *In room:* A/C, TV/VCR w/pay movies and video games, fax/copier/printer, dataport, minibar, coffeemaker, hair dryer, iron, laptop-size safe, high-speed Internet connectivity, DVD/CD player.

EXPENSIVE

The Phillips Club ⭐ Located in the heart of Lincoln Center, the Phillips Club was one of the first extended-stay hotels to open in Manhattan, but your stay doesn't have to be long to appreciate the hotel's many amenities. Offering spacious suites and one-bedroom apartments with full granite kitchens, the Phillips Club is less a hotel than a home away from home. The lobby is minimalist and maybe not as warm and welcoming as many hotels, but the staff is friendly and helpful. All units have that sophisticated New York City apartment feel and are equipped with big work desks with ergonomic chairs, sofa beds, and home entertainment centers; the nearby Tower Records store will even deliver videos to your room. The marble bathrooms are large, though not extravagant. There are washers and dryers on each floor, and though there is no restaurant on the premises, Balducci's, the gourmet grocery store located next door to the hotel, will deliver a full continental breakfast, sandwiches, or anything else they make to your room. Guests have access to the Reebok Sports Club/NY, one of the most exclusive and largest fitness clubs in Manhattan, which features 140,000 square feet of exercise space, including two basketball courts, an Olympic-size pool, and a 40-foot climbing wall. The apartment-like amenities make the hotel a good, though expensive, option for families or for anyone seeking a bit more control over their environment while visiting the city.

155 W. 66th St. (btwn Broadway and Amsterdam Ave.), New York, NY 10023. ℂ 212/835-8800. Fax 212/835-8850. www.phillipsclub.com. 173 units. $440 junior suite; $550 1-bedroom suite. AE, DISC, MC, V. Parking $30 nearby. Subway: 1, 9 to 66th St. **Amenities:** Delivery from local restaurants; free access to nearby Reebok Sports Club/NY; concierge; same-day laundry service. *In room:* A/C, 2 TVs/VCR/CD in living area, fax, full kitchen, iron, safe, Internet access.

MODERATE

In addition to the hotels below, also consider the romantic **Country Inn the City** ⭐, 270 W. 77th St., between Broadway and West End Avenue (ℂ **212/580-4183;** www.countryinnthecity.com), comprised of four self-contained units in a charming 1891 town house (see "Plenty of Room at the Inn," on p. 132).

Excelsior Hotel The recently renovated, newly elegant Excelsior almost gives the Lucerne (see below) a run for its money. Everything is fresh throughout the hotel, from the richly wood-paneled lobby to the supremely comfy guest rooms to the small but state-of-the-art exercise room. The chic residential location is across from the Museum of Natural History and just steps from Central Park. However, the staff doesn't quite live up to the Lucerne's impeccable example.

Freshly done in an attractive traditional style, the guest rooms boast high-quality furnishings, commodious closets, two-line phones, thick terry bathrobes, a work desk, free bottled water, and full-length dressing mirrors (a nice touch). The pretty new bathrooms are most impressive. The two-bedded rooms are large enough to accommodate budget-minded families (a few even have two queens), and suites feature pullout sofas and pants presses. The sunny museum-facing rooms are only worth the extra dough if a park view is really important to you, as all rooms are relatively bright and quiet. Housekeeping is impeccable throughout the hotel. On the second floor is a gorgeous library-style lounge with working fireplace, books, games, gorgeous leather seating, writing desks, and a large flatscreen TV with VCR and DVD player. All in all, a good midprice choice.

45 W. 81st St. (btwn Columbus Ave. and Central Park West), New York, NY 10024. ℂ **212/580-3972** or 212/362-9200. Fax 212/721-2994. www.excelsiorhotelny.com. 198 units. $159–$229 double; $259–$359 1-bedroom suite; $359–$549 2-bedroom suite. Extra person $20. Children 12 and under stay free in parent's room. Inquire about

Uptown Accommodations

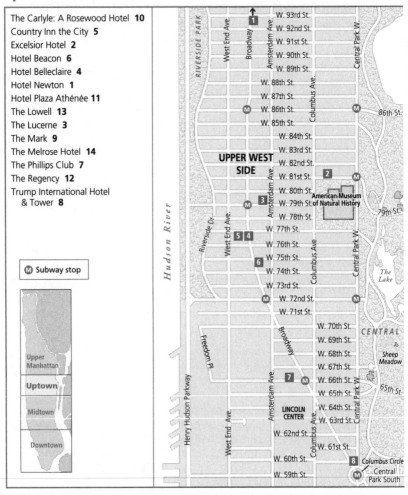

The Carlyle: A Rosewood Hotel **10**
Country Inn the City **5**
Excelsior Hotel **2**
Hotel Beacon **6**
Hotel Belleclaire **4**
Hotel Newton **1**
Hotel Plaza Athénée **11**
The Lowell **13**
The Lucerne **3**
The Mark **9**
The Melrose Hotel **14**
The Phillips Club **7**
The Regency **12**
Trump International Hotel & Tower **8**

ⓂSubway stop

Upper Manhattan
Uptown
Midtown
Downtown

seasonal rates and specials (winter rates can go as low as $129 double; $179 for suites). AE, DC, DISC, MC, V. Parking $27 nearby. Subway: B, C to 81st St./Museum of Natural History. **Amenities:** Breakfast room w/2 open-air decks and daily breakfast buffet; exercise room; concierge; dry cleaning/laundry service. *In room:* A/C, TV w/pay movies/video games/Internet access, fax/copier, dataport, hair dryer, iron, safe.

Hotel Beacon 🎯🎯 *(Kids)* *(Value)*   Okay, so you're not in Times Square or in trendy SoHo, but when you're at the Hotel Beacon, you're on the Upper West Side, and for families, you won't find a better location—or value. Close to Central Park and Riverside Park, the Museum of Natural History and Lincoln Center, and major subway lines, it's not like the Beacon is in a desolate spot. Rooms here are generously sized and feature a kitchenette, a roomy closet, and a new marble bathroom. Virtually all standard rooms feature two double beds, and they're plenty big enough to sleep a family on a

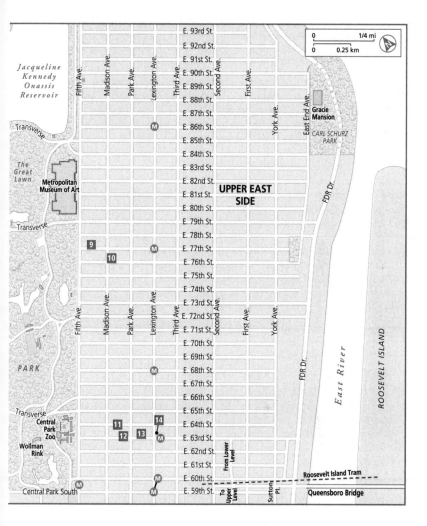

budget. The large one- and two-bedroom suites are some of the best bargains in the city; each has two closets and a pullout sofa in the well-furnished living room. The two-bedrooms have a second bathroom, making them well outfitted enough to house a small army—including my own. And the view from our room and many in the hotel is a true New York vista; the magnificent, turn-of-the-century Ansonia building, ballet dancers limbering up at a dance studio, and fresh fruit and vegetables constantly being replenished at Fairway market directly across the street. There's no room service, but a wealth of good budget dining options that deliver, along with excellent markets like the aforementioned Fairway, make the Beacon even more of a home away from home.

2130 Broadway (at 75th St.), New York, NY 10023. (© 800/572-4969 or 212/787-1100. Fax 212/724-0839. www. beaconhotel.com. 236 units. $205–$215 single or double; from $265 1- or 2-bedroom suite. Extra person $15. Children under 17 stay free in parent's room. Check website for special deals (doubles from $145; 1-bedroom suites as low as $195 at press time). AE, DISC, MC, V. Parking $29 1 block away. Subway: 1, 2, 3, 9 to 72nd St. **Amenities:** Coffee shop adjacent; access to health club in the building; concierge; dry cleaning/laundry service; coin-op laundry; fax and copy service; Internet center. *In room:* A/C, TV w/pay movies, kitchenette, hair dryer, iron, laptop-size safe.

The Lucerne ★★ *Finds*   This magnificent 1903 landmark building has had many incarnations over the years, including one as a dormitory for Columbia University students. But most recently it has been transformed into a luxury boutique hotel, and that transformation has been a triumph on many levels. As a longtime resident of the Upper West Side, I can easily say the Lucerne best captures the feel of that very special neighborhood. Service here is impeccable, especially for a moderately priced hotel; the attentive GM is on top of every detail and everything is fresh and immaculate. The rooms are all comfortable and big enough for kings, queens, or two doubles, with attractive bathrooms complete with travertine counters. Some of the rooms have views not only of the Hudson River, but of one of my favorite pubs, the Dublin House (see chapter 11). The suites are extra special here and include a kitchenette, a stocked minifridge, a microwave, and a sitting room with a sofa and extra television. The highly rated **Nice Matin** (p. 217) offers room service or breakfast, lunch, and dinner. But if you don't want to dine there, you can sample some of the neighborhood food at nearby Zabar's or H&H Bagels.

201 W. 79th St. (at Amsterdam Ave.), New York, NY 10024. © **800/492-8122** or 212/875-1000. Fax 212/579-2408. www.newyorkhotel.com. 250 units. $140–$270 double or queen; $160–$290 king or junior suite; $220–$410 1-bedroom suite. Extra person $20. Children under 16 stay free in parent's room. Continental breakfast additional $5 per person. AAA discounts offered; check website for special Internet deals. AE, DC, DISC, MC, V. Parking $25 nearby. Subway: 1, 9 to 79th St. **Amenities:** Restaurant; fitness center; business center; 24-hr. room service; dry cleaning/laundry service. *In room:* A/C, TV w/Nintendo and Internet access, dataport, coffeemaker, hair dryer, iron.

INEXPENSIVE
Hotel Belleclaire   This Beaux Arts hotel, which underwent a face-lift in 2004, boasts a great Upper West Side location and renovated, stylish guest rooms that are larger than most. The accommodations, though simple, do the job, and the management seems intent on pleasing. The rooms have small, freshly tiled bathrooms with tub/shower combos (six have roll-in showers to accommodate travelers with disabilities). Beds have cushioned headboards and there are nice fabric-covered cubes for modular seating; closets are small. The shared-bathroom units are the same but have in-room sinks and share hall bathrooms at a ratio of three to one. The family suite features two attached, semiprivate bedrooms with a bathroom, a minifridge, and a big walk-in closet. A perfectly decent choice in a first-class residential neighborhood.

250 W. 77th St. (at Broadway), New York, NY 10024. © **877/HOTEL-BC** (468-3522) or 212/362-7700. Fax 212/362-1004. www.hotelbelleclaire.com. 189 units, 39 with shared bathroom. $109 double with shared bathroom; $169–$189 double with private bathroom; $229 family suite. Ask about AAA, corporate, group, and other discounts. AE, DC, DISC, MC, V. Parking $25 nearby. Subway: 1, 9 to 79th St. **Amenities:** Access to nearby health club; tour desk; dry cleaning/laundry; fax. *In room:* A/C, TV w/pay movies and games, dataport, fridge, hair dryer, iron.

Hotel Newton ★ *Value*   Located on the burgeoning northern extreme of the Upper West Side, the Newton, unlike many of its peers, doesn't scream "budget" at every turn. As you enter the pretty lobby, you're greeted by a uniformed staff that's attentive and professional. The rooms are generally large, with good, firm beds, a work desk, and a sizable new bathroom, plus roomy closets in most (a few of the cheapest have wall racks only). Some are big enough to accommodate families, with two doubles or two queen beds. The suites feature two queen beds in the bedroom, a sofa in the sitting room, plus niceties such as microwave, minifridge, and iron, making them well worth the few extra dollars. The bigger rooms and suites have been upgraded with cherrywood furnishings, but even the older laminated furniture is much nicer than I usually see in this price range. The AAA–approved hotel is impeccably kept. The 96th Street express subway stop is just a block away, providing convenient access to the rest of the city, and the Key West Diner next door is a favorite for huge, cheap breakfasts.

2528 Broadway (btwn 94th and 95th sts.), New York, NY 10025. ☎ **888/HOTEL58** or 212/678-6500. Fax 212/678-6758. www.newyorkhotel.com. 110 units. $95–$160 double or junior suite. Extra person $10. Children under 15 stay free in parent's room. AAA, corporate, senior, and group rates available; check website for special Internet deals. AE, DC, DISC, MC, V. Parking $20 nearby. Subway: 1, 2, 3, 9 to 96th St. **Amenities:** 24-hr. room service. In room: A/C, TV, hair dryer.

10 Upper East Side

To find the hotels described in this section, see p. 162.

VERY EXPENSIVE

The Carlyle: A Rosewood Hotel ★★★ This 34-story grand dame towers over Madison Avenue majestically, perfectly epitomizing the old world, moneyed neighborhood where it stands. Service is white-glove (literally) and doormen actually wear bowler hats; the many celebrities or dignitaries, some with faces obscured by silk scarves, sip tea in the hotel's cozy Gallery. Guest rooms range from singles to seven-room suites, some with terraces and full dining rooms. All have marble bathrooms with whirlpool tubs and all the amenities you'd expect from a hotel of this caliber. The English manor–style decor is luxurious but not excessive, creating the comfortably elegant ambience of an Upper East Side apartment. Many apartments have breathtaking views of either downtown or the west side and Central Park; in 2005 during the Christo phenomenon, "The Gates," a two-bedroom suite with a perfect view of Central Park was booked for $6,000.

The lobby was renovated recently: The marble floors and columns, the original clock, and the Piranesi prints and murals were all restored and new features such as Baccarat light fixtures, a new reception desk, and an expanded concierge space added. The hotel's first-class restaurant, dumonet at The Carlyle, features excellent French fare while the supper club **Cafe Carlyle** (p. 369) is the place for first-rate cabaret. Charming **Bemelmans Bar,** named after children's book illustrator Ludwig Bemelmans, who created the Madeline books and painted the mural here (see "Checking into Hotel Bars," in chapter 11), is a wonderful spot for cocktails; there's live soft jazz Monday through Saturday evenings.

35 E. 76th St. (at Madison Ave.), New York, NY 10021. ☎ **800/227-5737** or 212/744-1600. Fax 212/717-4682. www.thecarlyle.com. 180 units. $495–$750 double; from $750 1- or 2-bedroom suite. AE, DC, MC, V. Parking $50. Subway: 6 to 77th St. Pets accepted. **Amenities:** 3 restaurants (including one of the city's best cabaret rooms); tearoom; bar; high-tech fitness room w/sauna, Jacuzzi, and spa services; concierge; 24-hr. room service; dry cleaning/laundry service; video library. In room: A/C, TV/VCR, fax/copier/printer, dataport, pantry kitchenette or full kitchen w/minibar, hair dryer, safe, CD player.

Hotel Plaza Athénée ★★★ This hideaway in New York's toniest neighborhood (the stretch of Madison Ave. in the 60s), is a mirror image of that elevated social strata; it's elegant, luxurious, and oozing with sophistication. With antique furniture, hand-painted murals, and the Italian marble floor that adorns the exquisite lobby, the Plaza

Athénée has a distinctly European feel. And in that tradition, service here is as good as it gets, with personalized check-in and attentive staff at every turn.

The rooms, which were recently renovated, come in a variety of shapes and sizes, and are all high-ceilinged and spacious; entrance foyers give them a real residential feel. They are designed in rich fabrics and warm colors that help set a tone that makes you want to lounge in your room longer than you should. The suites have so much closet space it made this New Yorker, used to miniscule apartment closets, very envious. All of the suites have chaises, which you don't see too often in New York hotels, and a few have terraces large enough to dine out on. The Portuguese marble bathrooms are outfitted with thick robes made exclusively for the hotel; put one on and you might never want to take it off. The lush, leather-floored lounge is appropriately called Bar Seine and is a welcome spot for a pre-dinner cocktail. The restaurant, Arabelle, receives high praise for its weekend brunch.

37 E. 64th St. (btwn Madison and Park aves.), New York, NY 10021. ℭ **800/447-8800** or 212/734-9100. Fax 212/772-0958. www.plaza-athenee.com. 149 units. $535–$675 double; from $1,200 suite. Check for packages and seasonal specials (as low as $359 at press time). AE, DC, MC, V. Parking $48. Subway: F to Lexington Ave. **Amenities:** Restaurant; bar; fitness center; Clefs d'Or concierge; business center; 24-hr. room service; dry cleaning/laundry service. *In room:* A/C, TV, fax, dataport, minibar, hair dryer, safe, high-speed Internet connectivity.

The Lowell ★★★ *Kids* The Lowell's style of luxury is best described as elegant, sophisticated 20th-century opulence. It has the feel of a residential dwelling; the lobby is small and clubby with first-rate European, old-world service. The rooms are the real treasures here; each different from the other and all very good-size. About two-thirds are suites with kitchenettes or fully equipped kitchens; some have private terraces and most have working fireplaces. In the rooms you'll also find nice big, cushy armchairs, lots of leather, interesting artwork, and porcelain figurines scattered about. Bathrooms are Italian marble and outfitted with Bulgari amenities. The Pembroke Room offers breakfast, including a hearty English breakfast and afternoon tea while the Post House is best known for their steaks. Located on a quiet, tree-lined street 1 block from Central Park and right in the middle of Madison Avenue shopping, the Lowell's location is ideal for those who want (and can afford) an urban retreat away from the midtown madness.

28 E. 63rd St. (btwn Madison and Park aves.), New York, NY 10021. ℭ **212/838-1400.** Fax 212/319-4230. www.lowellhotel.com. 68 units. $525–$585 doubles; from $785 suites. Ask about special packages and weekend and seasonal rates. AE, DC, MC, V. Parking $45. Subway: F, V to Lexington Ave. Pets under 15 lb. accepted. **Amenities:** 2 restaurants; tearoom; well-outfitted fitness room; 24-hr. concierge; limousine service; secretarial services; 24-hr. room service; babysitting; dry cleaning/laundry service; video library. *In room:* A/C, TV/VCR/DVD, fax/copier/dataport, minibar, hair dryer, wireless Internet, CD player.

The Mark ★★ Just a block separates the Mark from its chief hotel rival (the Carlyle) on that coveted stretch of Upper East Side real estate that comprises the boutiques of Madison Avenue and Museum Mile. Both feature impeccable service and comfort, but the Carlyle is more of a white-gloved grand dame, while the Mark prides itself on its motto, "no jacket, no tie, no attitude." Don't let that motto fool you, however, into thinking the Mark is one of those ultratrendy, shallowly hip downtown hotels; it is surprisingly and happily quite traditional. All the rooms are spacious, with high ceilings, and decorated in soft tones that give them a warm, homey feel. All have fax machines and most have kitchenettes. The suites vary in size and some have terraces, dining areas, and French doors. The bathrooms on the top floors have been newly renovated in marble, but I prefer the look of the familiar white and black tile bathrooms on the lower floors.

Off the small lobby is the intimate, cozy, and very popular **Mark's Bar** (see "Checking into Hotel Bars," in chapter 11), while Mark's restaurant, also off the lobby, is an underrated pleasure. On Mondays, sommelier Richard Dean conducts wine-class dinners. Afternoon tea at the Mark is a treat hosted by Tea Master Ringo Lo, who changes the tea menu daily, creating some amazingly exotic Asian-influenced concoctions in the process.

25 E. 77th St. (btwn Madison and Fifth aves.), New York, NY 10021. © **800/THEMARK** or 212/744-4300. Fax 212/744-2749. www.mandarinoriental.com/themark. 180 units. $545–$695 single or double; from $725 suite. Check for packages and seasonal specials (as low as $299 at press time). AE, DC, MC, V. Parking $45. Subway: 6 to 77th St. **Amenities:** Restaurant; bar; fitness center; concierge; free shuttle to Wall St. weekdays and theater district weekends; 24-hr. room service; dry cleaning/laundry service. *In room:* A/C, TV/VCR, fax, dataport, kitchenette, hair dryer, iron, safe, Internet access.

MODERATE

The Melrose Hotel ★ *Finds*   This was once the most famous hotel in New York—for women only and known as the Barbizon. It first admitted men in 1981, and in 2002, after a $40-million renovation, became the Melrose Hotel. The Barbizon was the first stop in New York for professional, educated women, including Joan Crawford, Grace Kelly, and Candice Bergen. Designed as an eclectic mix of Italian renaissance, Gothic, and Islamic architecture, this lovely old building, with its twin deco towers, stands out majestically amongst the glass and steel of its Upper East Side location. From a dorm-size petite room to a stately, sprawling tower suite, the range of rooms and the corresponding rates can also be considered eclectic. You can spend as little as $150 a night or as much as $1,700. All rooms, no matter the size, are well kept, offer plenty of light, and are equipped with all the basic amenities. Standard and superior rooms come with small workstations, while the magnificent (and very expensive) tower suites come with terraces, some as large as 500 square feet. There is a very good Equinox Fitness Club and Spa, with a nearly 60-foot-long pool on the premises; inexplicably, guests must pay an $18 fee daily to use it. The Library Bar in the lobby serves light snacks throughout the day and the hotel has a "Sign and Dine" program with some highly rated local restaurants. A few blocks from Bloomingdale's, Madison Avenue, and Central Park, the Melrose is a nice midrange alternative to other more pricey hotels in the area.

140 E. 63rd St. (at Lexington Ave.), New York, NY 10021. © **800/MELROSE** or 212/838-5700. Fax 212/888-4271. www.melrosehotel.com. 306 units. $239–$399 double; from $740 suite. Check website and Internet for packages and specials (as low as $150 at press time). AE, DC, MC, V. Parking $40. Subway: F to Lexington Ave. **Amenities:** Restaurant (breakfast only); "sign and dine" program w/local restaurants; bar (serving light meals); access to fitness center; 24-hr. room service; same-day laundry service. *In room:* A/C, TV, dataport, minibar, hair dryer, safe, high-speed Internet connectivity, CD player.

8

Where to Dine

Attention, foodies: Welcome to your mecca. Without a doubt, New York is the best restaurant town in the country, and one of the finest in the world. Other cities might have particular specialties, but no other culinary capital spans the globe so successfully as the Big Apple.

New Yorkers can be fickle: One moment a restaurant is hot; the next it's passé. So restaurants close with a frequency we wish applied to the arrival of subway trains. Always call ahead.

But there's one thing we all have to face sooner or later: Eating in New York isn't cheap. The primary cause? The high cost of real estate, which is reflected in what you're charged. Wherever you're from, particularly if you hail from the reasonably priced American heartland, New York's restaurants will seem *expensive*. Yet good value abounds, especially if you're willing to eat ethnic, and venture beyond tourist zones into the neighborhoods like Chinatown, the East Village, Harlem, and even the Upper West Side. Still, I've included inexpensive restaurants in every neighborhood, including some of the city's best-kept secrets, so you'll know where to get good value for your money no matter where you are in Manhattan.

RESERVATIONS

Reservations are always a good idea in New York, and a virtual necessity if your party is bigger than two. Do yourself a favor and call ahead as a rule of thumb so you won't be disappointed. If you're booking dinner on a weekend night, it's a good idea to call a few days in advance if you can.

Call *far* ahead for any special meal you don't want to miss—a month in advance is a good idea. Most top places start taking reservations exactly 30 days in advance, so if you want to eat at a hot restaurant at a popular hour—Saturday at 8pm, say, at Chanterelle—be sure to mark your calendar and start dialing 30 days prior at 9am. If you're booking a holiday dinner, call even earlier.

But if you didn't call well ahead and your heart's set on dinner at BLT Steak or Kittichai, don't despair. Often, early or late hours—between 5:30 and 6:30pm, or after 9pm—are available, especially on weeknights. And try calling the day before or first thing in the morning, when you may be able to take advantage of a last-minute cancellation. Or go for lunch, which is usually much easier to book without lots of advance notice. If you're staying at a hotel with a concierge, don't be afraid to use them—they can often get you into hot spots that you couldn't get into on your own.

Tips **The Best of the Best**

Check out my picks for New York's best dining in chapter 1.

> **Tips** **Make Reservations in Advance**
>
> **OpenTable (www.opentable.com)** allows you to book a reservation—and get
> an instant confirmation—over the Web at about 150 restaurants throughout
> Manhattan. You'll also find that an increasing number of restaurants offer
> online reservations through their own websites.

But What If They Don't *Take* Reservations?   Lots of restaurants, especially at the
affordable end of the price continuum, don't take reservations at all. One of the ways
they keep prices down is by packing people in as quickly as possible. Thus, the best
cheap and midprice restaurants often have a wait. Again, your best bet is to go early.
Often you can get in more quickly on a weeknight. Or just go knowing that you're
going to have to wait if you head to a popular spot; hunker down with a cocktail at
the bar and enjoy the festivities around you.

SMOKING POLICY
You cannot light up in any restaurant anywhere in the city.

TIPPING
Tipping is easy in New York. The way to do it: Double the 8.65% sales tax and *voilà!,*
happy waitstaff. In fancier venues, another 5% is appropriate for the captain. If the
wine steward helps, hand him or her 10% of the bottle's price.
  Leave $1 per item, no matter how small, for the checkroom attendant.

MORE SOURCES FOR SERIOUS FOODIES
Of course, New York has far more fabulous dining than I have room to discuss here—
although the listings below are enough to keep you fat and happy for a year, much less
the length of a vacation. But if you'd like a wider selection, a few very good sources
are available online or from your local bookstore.
  Your best online sources are **Citysearch (www.citysearch.com),** which runs a great
restaurant page that's updated weekly as part of its comprehensive offerings; **New York
Metro (www.newyorkmetro.com),** the online arm of the glossy weekly *New York;*
New York Today (www.nytoday.com), the *New York Times*'s arts and lifestyle site,
where you can access a database of the paper's stellar restaurant reviews; and the *Village Voice* **(www.villagevoice.com),** especially for the cheap eats reviews by Robert
Sietsema.
  The best online source for the serious foodie is **www.chowhound.com**, a national
website with message boards in local areas, including New York, where you can make
an inquiry about a certain restaurant, type of food, location, and so on, and within a
few hours, you might have five or more very informative responses.
  The *Zagat Survey,* which has made a name for itself rating restaurants based on
extensive diner surveys, maintains a searchable database of city restaurants at **www.
zagat.com**, so if you're willing to do your research before you leave home (or if you're
toting a laptop), there's no need to acquire a hard copy of the no-frills guide. They do,
however, charge a fee to access the online information. At press time, a year's subscription of Zagat online was $19.95 and a 30-day subscription was $3.95.
  If you do want a book reference to have on hand while you're in the city, I suggest
the colorful, reviewer-written *Time Out New York: Eating & Drinking* guide, which

I find to be more comprehensive, candid, and descriptive than Zagat's. If you don't feel the need for a big ol' book, stop at any newsstand for a copy of the slick weekly *Time Out New York,* whose "Eat Out" section always includes listings for *TONY*'s 100 Favorite Restaurants in every issue, as well as coverage of new openings and dining trends. Weekly *New York* magazine also maintains extensive restaurant listings in its listings section at the back of the magazine.

1 Restaurants by Cuisine

AFRICAN
La Marmite ✷ (Harlem, $, p. 224)

AMERICAN
See also "Contemporary American," below.
Artie's New York Delicatessen (Upper West Side, $, p. 206)
Big Nick's Burger and Pizza Joint ✷ (Upper West Side, $, p. 219)
Bubby's Pie Company ✷ (TriBeCa and Brooklyn, $$, p. 177 and 228)
Burger Joint ✷ (Midtown West, $, p. 203)
City Bakery ✷ (Flatiron District, $, p. 198)
Clinton St. Baking Company ✷ (Lower East Side, $, p. 182)
Cub Room ✷ (SoHo, $$$, p. 182)
Good Enough To Eat ✷ (Upper West Side, $, p. 221)
Little Pie Company (Midtown East, $, p. 209)
Moran's Chelsea (Chelsea, $$, p. 191)
Norma's ✷✷ (Midtown West, $$, p. 202)
The Odeon ✷ (TriBeCa, $$, p. 177)
P.J. Clarke's ✷ (Midtown East, $$, p. 209)
Prime Burger (Midtown East, $, p. 211)
Serendipity 3 (Upper East Side, $, p. 223)
Tavern on the Green (Upper West Side, $$$, p. 215)
Walker's (TriBeCa, $, p. 178)

ASIAN FUSION/PAN-ASIAN/PACIFIC RIM
The Biltmore Room ✷✷ (Chelsea, $$$, p. 190)
5 Ninth (Meat-Packing District, $$$, p. 188)
Nyonya ✷ (Chinatown, $, p. 179)
PlateNYC (Nolita/SoHo, $$, p. 184)
Spice Market (Meat-Packing District, $$, p. 188)

BARBECUE/SOUTHERN
Blue Smoke ✷ (Flatiron District, $$, p. 197)
Dinosaur Bar-B-Que ✷ (Harlem, $, p. 223)
Virgil's Real BBQ ✷✷ (Times Square, $$, p. 202)

BREAKFAST & BRUNCH
Absolute Bagels (Upper West Side, $, p. 198)
Artie's New York Delicatessen (Upper West Side, $, p. 206)
Balthazar (SoHo, $$, p. 183)
Barney Greengrass, the Sturgeon King (Upper West Side, $, p. 206)
Big Wong King ✷ (Chinatown, $, p. 178)
Bubby's Pie Company ✷ (TriBeCa and Brooklyn, $$, p. 117 and 228)
Clinton St. Baking Company ✷ (Lower East Side, $, p. 182)
Ess-A-Bagel (Midtown East, $, p. 198)
Florent (Meat-Packing District, $, p. 188)

Key to Abbreviations: $$$$ = Very Expensive $$$ = Expensive $$ = Moderate $ = Inexpensive

Good Enough to Eat ✿ (Upper West Side, $, p. 221)

Home ✿✿ (Greenwich Village, $$, p. 189)

Jean-Georges ✿✿✿ (Upper West Side, $$$$, p. 214)

Katz's Delicatessen ✿✿ (Lower East Side, $, p. 182)

Murray's Bagels (Greenwich Village, $, p. 198)

Norma's ✿✿ (Midtown West, $$, p. 202)

Pastis (Meat-Packing District, $$, p. 188)

Sylvia's (Harlem, $, p. 227)

Veselka ✿ (East Village, $, p. 186)

BRUNCH ONLY (WEEKENDS)
Some of these establishments serve brunch on Sunday only; check listings for specifics.

Celeste ✿✿ (Upper West Side, $, p. 219)

Fiamma Osteria ✿✿ (SoHo, $$$, p. 182)

Nice Matin ✿ (Upper West Side, $$, p. 217)

The Odeon ✿ (TriBeCa, $$, p. 177)

Tavern on the Green (Upper West Side, $$$, p. 215)

CHINESE

Big Wong King ✿ (Chinatown, $, p. 178)

New York Noodletown ✿✿ (Chinatown, $, p. 178)

CONTEMPORARY AMERICAN

Home ✿✿ (Greenwich Village, $$, p. 189)

Ouest ✿✿✿ (Upper West Side, $$$, p. 216)

The River Café (Brooklyn, $$$$, p. 227)

CONTINENTAL

Tavern on the Green (Upper West Side, $$$, p. 215)

FILIPINO

Ihawan (Queens, $, p. 229)

FRENCH

Aix ✿✿ (Upper West Side, $$$, p. 215)

Alain Ducasse (Midtown West, $$$$, p. 214)

Atelier ✿✿✿ (Midtown West, $$$$, p. 199)

Balthazar (SoHo, $$, p. 183)

Café Boulud ✿ (Upper East Side, $$$, p. 221)

Café des Artistes ✿ (Upper West Side, $$$$, p. 211)

Capsouto Frères ✿ (TriBeCa, $$$, p. 174)

Chanterelle ✿✿✿ (TriBeCa, $$$$, p. 174)

Daniel (Upper East Side, $$$$, p. 214)

db Bistro Moderne ✿ (Midtown West, $$$, p. 200)

Eleven Madison Park ✿✿✿ (Flatiron District, $$$, p. 195)

Florent (Meat-Packing District, $, p. 188)

Jean-Georges ✿✿✿ (Upper West Side, $$$$, p. 214)

Landmarc ✿✿ (TriBeCa, $$$, p. 176)

Le Bernardin (Midtown West, $$$$, p. 214)

Marseille ✿ (Midtown West, $$, p. 202)

Nice Matin ✿ (Upper West Side, $$, p. 217)

Paradou (Meat-Packing District, $$, p. 188)

Pastis (Meat-Packing District, $$, p. 188)

Sapa ✿✿ (Flatiron District, $$$, p. 196)

GERMAN

Knödel (Midtown East, $, p. 210)

GLOBAL

Voyage ✦✦ (Greenwich Village, $$, p. 190)

GOURMET SANDWICHES/ DELI/TAKEOUT

Absolute Bagels (Upper West Side, $, p. 198)

Artie's New York Delicatessen (Upper West Side, $, p. 206)

Barney Greengrass, the Sturgeon King (Upper West Side, $, p. 206)

Carnegie Deli (Midtown West, $, p. 206)

Eisenberg's Coffee Shop (Flatiron District, $, p. 198)

Ess-A-Bagel (Midtown East, $, p. 198)

Gray's Papaya (Upper West Side and Greenwich Village, $, p. 218)

H&H Bagels (Upper West Side and Midtown West, $, p. 198)

Junior's (Midtown East, $, p. 228)

Kalustyan's ✦ (Midtown East, $, p. 172)

Katz's Delicatessen ✦✦ (Lower East Side, $, p. 182)

Murray's Bagels (Greenwich Village, $, p. 198)

Nathan's Famous (Brooklyn, $, p. 228)

Second Avenue Deli (Lower East Side, $$, p. 206)

Stage Deli (Midtown West, $, p. 206)

GREEK

Molyvos ✦✦ (Midtown West, $$$, p. 201)

Onera ✦ (Upper West Side, $$, p. 218)

Thalassa ✦ (TriBeCa, $$$, p. 176)

Uncle Nick's (Midtown West, $, p. 205)

INDIAN

Brick Lane Curry House ✦ (East Village, $$, p. 185)

Cafe Spice Express (Midtown East, $, p. 209)

Devi ✦✦ (Flatiron District, $$$, p. 195)

Tamarind ✦✦ (Flatiron District, $$$, p. 196)

ITALIAN

Abboccato ✦✦ (Midtown West, $$$, p. 200)

Barbuto ✦ (Greenwich Village, $$, p. 189)

Bar Pitti ✦ (Greenwich Village, $, p. 190)

Becco ✦ (Midtown West, $$, p. 201)

Beppe ✦✦ (Flatiron District, $$$, p. 195)

Bread ✦ (Nolita/SoHo, $, p. 185)

Bread Tribeca ✦ (TriBeCa, $$, p. 177)

Caffè Roma (Little Italy, $, p. 178)

Carmine's ✦ (Upper West Side and Times Square, $$, p. 217 and 201)

Celeste ✦✦ (Upper West Side, $, p. 219)

'Cesca ✦✦ (Upper West Side, $$$, p. 215)

Dominick's (Bronx, $$, p. 226)

Ferdinando's Focacceria ✦ (Brooklyn, $, p. 228)

Ferrara (Little Italy, $, p. 178)

Fiamma Osteria ✦✦ (SoHo, $$$, p. 182)

Frankie and Johnnie's Pine Restaurant (Bronx, $$, p. 226)

Landmarc ✦✦ (TriBeCa, $$$, p. 176)

L'Impero ✦✦ (Midtown East, $$$, p. 208)

Lupa ✦✦ (SoHo, $$, p. 184)

Macelleria (Meat-Packing District, $$$, p. 188)

Mario's Restaurant (Bronx, $$, p. 226)

Nick's Family-Style Restaurant and Pizzeria ✦ (Upper East Side, $, p. 222)

Nonna ✦✦ (Upper West Side, $$, p. 217)

JAPANESE
Kai 🅀 (Upper East Side, $$$, p. 222)
Masa (Upper West Side, $$$$, p. 214)
Ono 🅀 (Meat-Packing District, $$$, p. 186)
Riingo 🅀 (Midtown East, $$$, p. 209)
Sapporo 🅀 (Midtown West, $, p. 204)

JEWISH DELI
Artie's New York Delicatessen (Upper West Side, $, p. 206)
Barney Greengrass, the Sturgeon King (Upper West Side, $, p. 206)
Carnegie Deli (Midtown West, $, p. 206)
Junior's (Midtown East, $, p. 210)
Katz's Delicatessen 🅀🅀 (Lower East Side, $, p. 182)
Second Avenue Deli (Lower East Side, $$, p. 206)
Stage Deli (Midtown West, $, p. 203)

KOREAN
Mandoo Bar 🅀 (Midtown West and Greenwich Village, $, p. 203)

LATIN AMERICAN/HISPANIC/ SOUTH AMERICAN
Flor de Mayo (Upper West Side, $, p. 219)
La Fonda Boricua 🅀 (Harlem, $, p. 224)
Suba 🅀 (Lower East Side, $$$, p. 179)

MEDITERRANEAN
Landmarc 🅀🅀 (TriBeCa, $$$, p. 176)
Savann 🅀 (Upper West Side, $$, p. 218)

MEXICAN/TEX-MEX/ SOUTHWESTERN
Dos Caminos (Flatiron District & SoHo, $$, p. 197)
El Paso Taqueria 🅀 (Harlem, $, p. 223)
Noche Mexicana 🅀 (Upper West Side, $, p. 221)
Pampano 🅀🅀 (Midtown East, $$$, p. 208)

Rosa Mexicano (Upper West Side, $$$, p. 216)

MIDDLE EASTERN
Afghan Kebab House (Midtown West, $, p. 203)
Kalustyan's 🅀 (Midtown East, $, p. 211)

PERUVIAN
La Pollada de Laura (Queens, $, p. 229)

PIZZA
Big Nick's Burger and Pizza Joint 🅀 (Upper West Side, $, p. 219)
Grimaldi's Pizzeria (Brooklyn, $, p. 204)
John's Pizzeria (Times Square, Greenwich Village, and Upper East Side, $, p. 204)
Lombardi's (Little Italy, $, p. 204)
Patsy's Pizzeria (Harlem, $, p. 205)
Totonno's Pizzeria Napolitano (Upper East Side and Brooklyn, $, p. 205)
Two Boots (Midtown East, $, p. 210)

PORTUGUESE
Pao! 🅀 (SoHo, $$, p. 184)

SCANDINAVIAN
Aquavit 🅀🅀🅀 (Midtown East, $$$, p. 207)

SEAFOOD
Christer's (Midtown East, $, p. 210)
Le Bernardin (Midtown West, $$$$, p. 214)
Lure Fishbar 🅀🅀 (SoHo, $$$, p. 183)
The Neptune Room 🅀 (Upper West Side, $$$, p. 216)
Oceana 🅀🅀🅀 (Midtown East, $$$, p. 208)
Oyster Bar & Restaurant 🅀 (Midtown East, $$, p. 211)

SOUL FOOD
Amy Ruth's (Harlem, $, p. 226)
Charles' Southern Style Kitchen 🅀 (Harlem, $, p. 226)

Copeland's (Harlem, $$, p. 226)
M&G Diner (Harlem, $, p. 227)
Miss Mamie's Spoonbread Too
(Harlem, $$, p. 227)
Sylvia's (Harlem, $, p. 227)

SPANISH
La Nacional 🐸🐸 (Chelsea, $$, p. 191)
Suba 🐸 (Lower East Side, $$$, p. 179)

STEAKS
Ben Benson's Steakhouse (Midtown
West, $$$, p. 200)
BLT Steak 🐸🐸🐸 (Midtown East,
$$$, p. 207)
Bull and Bear (Midtown East, $$$,
p. 194)
MarkJoseph (South Street Seaport,
$$$, p. 194)
Michael Jordan's–The Steak House 🐸🐸
(Midtown East, $$$, p. 194)
Nick & Stef's Steakhouse (Midtown
West, $$$, p. 194)
Peter Luger Steakhouse 🐸🐸 (Brooklyn,
$$$, p. 228)

Strip House 🐸🐸 (Greenwich Village,
$$$, p. 189)
Uncle Jack's Steakhouse 🐸 (Midtown
West, $$$, p. 201)
V Steakhouse (Upper West Side,
$$$$, p. 194)

THAI
Arunee Thai (Queens, $, p. 229)
Kittichai 🐸 (SoHo, $$$, p. 183)
Wondee Siam 🐸 (Midtown West,
$, p. 207)

UKRAINIAN
Veselka 🐸 (East Village, $, p. 186)

**VEGETARIAN/HEALTH-
CONSCIOUS**
Pure Food and Wine 🐸🐸 (Flatiron
District, $$, p. 197)

VIETNAMESE
Pho Viet Huong 🐸 (Chinatown, $,
p. 179)
Sapa 🐸🐸 (Flatiron District, $$$,
p. 196)

2 Financial District, South Street Seaport & TriBeCa

To find the restaurants reviewed below, see the map on p. 175.

VERY EXPENSIVE

Chanterelle 🐸🐸🐸 CONTEMPORARY FRENCH   One of New York's best "special occasion" restaurants mainly because, well, they treat you so special here. The dining room is a charmer with daily floral displays and an interesting modern art collection. Tables are far enough apart to give diners plenty of intimacy, something rare in many New York restaurants these days. Your server will work with you on you choices, paring items that go best together. The French-themed menu is seasonal and changes every few weeks, but one signature dish appears on almost every menu: a marvelous grilled seafood sausage. Cheese lovers should opt for a cheese course—the presentation and selection can't be beat. The wine list is superlative, yet expensive. Still, you don't come to Chanterelle on the cheap—you come to celebrate.

2 Harrison St. (at Hudson St.). ✆ **212/966-6960**. www.chanterellenyc.com. Reservations recommended well in advance. Fixed-price lunch $43; a la carte lunch $20–$27; 3-course fixed-price dinner $95; tasting menu $115. AE, DC, DISC, MC, V. Mon 5:30–11pm; Tues–Sat noon–2:30pm and 5:30–11pm. Subway: 1, 9 to Franklin St.

EXPENSIVE

For excellent steak, try **MarkJoseph,** 261 Water St., at Peck Slip (✆ **212/277-0020;** subway: 2, 3 to Fulton St.). For details, see the "The Prime Cut," on p. 194.

Capsouto Frères 🐸 FRENCH   In 1980, before the triangle below Canal Street was given the acronym TriBeCa, and before the neighborhood became rife with celebrities

Financial District, TriBeCa, Chinatown & Little Italy Dining

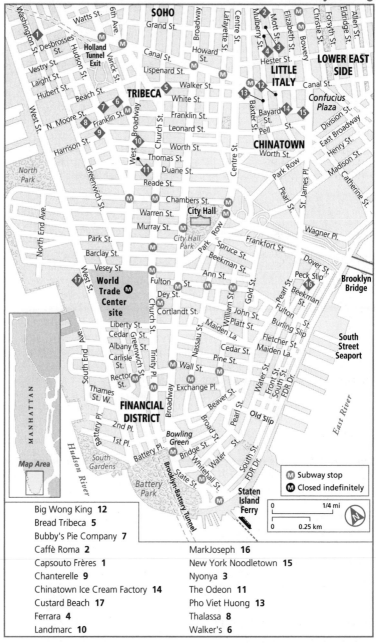

Big Wong King **12**
Bread Tribeca **5**
Bubby's Pie Company **7**
Caffè Roma **2**
Capsouto Frères **1**
Chanterelle **9**
Chinatown Ice Cream Factory **14**
Custard Beach **17**
Ferrara **4**
Landmarc **10**

MarkJoseph **16**
New York Noodletown **15**
Nyonya **3**
The Odeon **11**
Pho Viet Huong **13**
Thalassa **8**
Walker's **6**

and hip restaurants, Capsouto Frères opened. And through TriBeCa's amazing growth, its devastation after 9/11 and subsequent rebirth, Capsouto Frères has not only survived—a feat unto itself—but it has thrived with a loyal following. What accounts for the restaurant's longevity during all that tumult? Is it the simple, homestyle French cuisine served here: the famous soufflés, the spicy saucisson, the always reliable sole meunière, steak frites, or cassoulet; the warm, wood-floored, high-ceilinged always festive dining room; the gregarious and engaging hosts; the *freres* Jacques, Sammy, and Albert? Or is it a combination of all of the above? Whatever it is, it works. Sturdy and reliable Capsouto Frères offers a literal taste of what it what it was like before Robert DeNiro "discovered" TriBeCa.

451 Washington St. (at Watts St.). (✆ 212/966-4900. www.capsoutofreres.com. Reservations recommended. Lunch: Prix fixe $20; main courses $12–$24. Dinner: Prix fixe $35; main courses $15–$27. AE, DISC, MC, V. Tues–Fri noon–3:30pm; Sun–Thurs 6–10pm; Fri–Sat 6–11pm; brunch Sat–Sun noon–3:30pm. Subway: 1,9, A, C, E to Canal St.

Landmarc ★★ *Finds* MEDITERRANEAN   This cozy, intimate TriBeCa restaurant is too good to just be considered a neighborhood joint. Chef/owner Marc Murphy has put his own distinctive spin on this Italian/French rendition of a bistro. Here you'll find excellent smoked mozzarella and ricotta fritters alongside escargots bordelaise. It will be up to you to decide whether you imagine yourself in a Tuscan trattoria or a Provençal bistro. Or, you can mix and match cuisines. Try the pasta of the day accompanied by mussels with a choice of sauce—Provençal, Dijonnaise, or the comforting blend of shallots, parsley, and white wine. Steaks and chops are cooked over an open fire and the steaks are also offered with a variety of sauces; I had the hangar with a shallot bordelaise that complemented the meat perfectly. What keeps the neighbors pouring into Landmarc along with the excellent food are the remarkably affordable wines sold, not by the glass, but by the bottle or half bottle. Desserts are simple, small, and priced that way, with none more than $3. For a special treat or if you've brought the kids, ask for the cotton candy. Now you won't find that in a Tuscan trattoria.

179 West Broadway (btwn Leonard and Worth sts.). (✆ 212/343-3883. www.landmarc-restaurant.com. Reservations recommended. Main courses $15–$25. AE, DC, DISC, MC, V. Mon–Fri noon–5pm; daily 5:30pm–2am. Subway: 1,9 to Franklin St.

Thalassa ★ GREEK   Greek food is best when prepared simply with the freshest ingredients, especially fish, and Thalassa does a remarkable job living up to that standard. The variety of seafood is staggering; when I visited, the numerous options included fresh langoustines from Scotland, monstrous pound-and-a-half shrimp from Mexico, and a number of different oyster selections. For starters, the kataifi pastry-wrapped diver scallops with sheep's milk butter was a revelation, while the octopus, simply grilled with a red-wine vinaigrette, was as good as I've had west of Astoria. The main courses won't disappoint either; the pan-roasted Dover sole was delicately prepared and perfectly seasoned with a touch of olive oil and lemon, while the sea bream with slices of diver scallops layered on top was exceptional. The knowledgeable sommelier can help you select a Greek wine, of which there are many, from the restaurant's cellar, where a number of unusual and very good Greek cheeses are also stored. The restaurant is large; tables are spaced well enough apart for intimacy and service is attentive and pleasant.

197 Franklin St. (btwn Greenwich and Hudson sts.). (✆ 212/941-7661. www.thalassanyc.com. Reservations recommended. Prix-fixe lunch $20; prix-fixe dinner $30; main courses dinner $14–$28. AE, DC, DISC, MC, V. Mon–Thurs noon–2:30pm and 6–11pm; Fri–Sat 6pm–midnight; Sun 5–10pm. Subway: 1, 9 to Franklin St.

MODERATE

Bread Tribeca ⊛ NORTHERN ITALIAN   Bread Tribeca is one of the few restaurants in New York to feature the cuisine of Italy's Liguria region. What is Ligurian cuisine? Seafood is a big part of it and Bread Tribeca does a good job with its *fritto misto,* a mixture of fried fish (such as calamari, cod, and mussels) and vegetables; and its *zuppa de pesce,* assorted seafood in a saffron-tomato sauce. Homemade pastas are another trademark of Ligurian food, and at Bread Tribeca you'll find pansotti, ravioli-like dumplings served with a walnut sauce; and fresh taglierini, a spaghetti-like pasta that was slightly overwhelmed by the dense combination of haricots verts, potatoes, and a surprisingly subtle pesto. A wood-burning oven turns out excellent thin-crust pizzas and roasted meats and, like its sister restaurant (see Bread, p. 185), the breads are superb, including a remarkable combination of sardine, tomato, and peperoncini slathered on a baguette. Most of the tables are communal, so if the restaurant is crowded don't expect intimacy; and the 50-inch television above the bar that runs movies (when I was there last, *Chocolat*) is often a distraction, not a complement, to the food. On weekends, a deejay spins calming, low-key music to accompany the rustic food.

301 Church St. (at Walker St.). ☎ **212/334-8282.** www.breadtribeca.com. Reservations recommended. Main courses $13–$23 at dinner. AE, DC, DISC, MC, V. Sun–Thurs 11:30am–11pm; Fri–Sat 11:30am–midnight. Subway: A, C, E to Canal St.

Bubby's Pie Company ⊛ AMERICAN   You might have to wait on line to eat at Bubby's. You might get squeezed into a table perilously close to another couple. And you might have to talk very loud to maintain a conversation with your dining companion. But your level of discomfort will immediately subside as soon as you begin to consume Bubby's comfort food. Whether it is the slow-cooked pulled barbecue pork, the magnificent, lighter-than-air meatloaf, or the buttermilk-fried half chicken, coupled with sides like collard greens, sautéed spinach, macaroni and cheese, and baked beans, Bubby's dishes define comfort. Take Bubby's advice and save room for the desserts, especially the homemade pies; one taste of the chocolate peanut-butter pie immediately brought on happy childhood flashbacks. Breakfast is big here and lasts well into the middle of the day. On weekends, though, here in trendy TriBeCa, the wait for brunch can be very lengthy. Celebrities need comfort too and you might spot one or two at Bubby's seeking anonymity and down-home chow. Bubby's also has a branch across the river in the DUMBO neighborhood of Brooklyn.

120 Hudson St. (at N. Moore St.). ☎ **212/219-0666.** www.bubbys.com. Reservations recommended for dinner (not accepted for brunch). Main courses $2–$7 at breakfast, brunch, and lunch; $9–$19 at dinner. AE, DC, DISC, MC, V. Mon–Thurs 8am–11pm; Fri 8am–midnight; Sat 9am–4:30pm and 6pm–midnight; Sun 9am–10pm. Subway: 1, 9 to Franklin St. Bubby's Brooklyn: 1 Main St. (at Water St.). ☎ 718/222-0666. Subway: A, C to High St., F to York St.

The Odeon ⊛ AMERICAN BRASSERIE   For over two decades the Odeon has been a symbol of the TriBeCa sensibility; in fact, the restaurant can claim credit for the neighborhood's cachet—it was the first to lure artists, actors, writers, and models to the area below Canal Street before it was given its moniker. Why did they come? They came to drink, to schmooze, and to enjoy the hearty no-frills brasserie grub like the still-splendid country frisee salad with bacon, Roquefort cheese, and pear vinaigrette and the truffled poached egg, grilled skirt steak, *moules frites* (mussels with fries), and sautéed cod. Though the restaurant has not always been the celebrity magnet it was in its heyday of the 1980s, the food, drink, and that inviting, open, deco-ish room has withstood the test of time and has surpassed trendy to now claim well-deserved New York establishment status.

145 W. Broadway (at Thomas St.). ℂ **212/233-0507.** Reservations recommended. Main courses $9–$25 at lunch; $14–$28 at dinner (most less than $21); fixed-price lunch $20. AE, DC, DISC, MC, V. Mon–Fri noon–3am; Sat 11:30am–3am; Sun 11:30am–2am. Subway: 1, 2, 3, 9 to Chambers St.

INEXPENSIVE

For an inexpensive alternative in TriBeCa, consider the pub **Walker's** (see chapter 11), 16 N. Moore St., at Varick Street (ℂ **212/941-0142**), where you can get a very good burger and fries for less than $10.

3 Chinatown

To find the restaurants reviewed below, see the map on p. 175.

INEXPENSIVE

Big Wong King ⚘ CANTONESE   A couple years ago Big Wong was called New Big Wong, this year they want to be called Big Wong King. No matter. They will always be Big Wong and that's a good thing. Why mess with success? For over 30 years, Big Wong has been an institution for workers from the nearby courthouses and Chinese families who come to feast on *congee* (rice porridge) and fried crullers for breakfast (see "Breakfast, Not Brunch," on p. 220). They also come for the superb roasted meats, the pork and duck seen hanging in the window, the comforting noodle soups, and the terrific barbecued ribs. This is simple, down-home Cantonese food—lo mein, chow fun, bok choy in oyster sauce—cooked lovingly, and so very cheap. If you don't mind sharing a table, Big Wong is a must at any time of day.

67 Mott St. (btwn Canal and Bayard sts.). ℂ **212/964-0540.** Appetizers $1.50–$5; congee $1.50–$6; soups $3–$5; Cantonese noodles $5.25–$11. No credit cards. Daily 8:30am–9pm. Subway: N, R, 6 to Canal St.

New York Noodletown ⚘⚘ CHINESE/SEAFOOD   So what if the restaurant has all the ambience of a school cafeteria? I'm wary of an over-adorned dining room in Chinatown; the simpler the better I say. And New York Noodletown is simple, but the

---

Espresso Anyone?

With the increasing encroachment of Chinatown upon what was formerly Little Italy's turf, north of Canal Street, the neighborhood made so famous in movies such as *The Godfather* has lost much of its appeal. More importantly, the quality restaurants are gone. Though there are still many Italian restaurants, especially along Mulberry Street, there are none I can in good conscience recommend. Sadly, the street has become a tourist trap with waiters trying to lure customers off the streets by waving menus at them. I do, however, recommend the very appetizing combination of a dinner at Chinatown in an Asian restaurant followed by coffee and a pastry at one of Little Italy's *pasticcerie*. My favorite is **Caffè Roma,** 385 Broome St., on the corner of Mulberry (ℂ 212/226-8413); the cannoli (try the chocolate-covered) and tiramisu are spectacular. Open 8am to midnight daily. Another you might want to try is **Ferrara,** 195 Grand St., between Mott and Mulberry streets (ℂ 212/226-6150). Founded in 1892, the *pasticceria* claims to be America's first espresso bar. Cafe seating is available so you can enjoy instant sweet-tooth gratification. Open daily 8am to midnight (to 1am on Sat).

---

food is the real thing. Seafood-based noodle soups are spectacular as is the platter of chopped roast pork. Those two items alone would make me very happy. But I'm greedy and wouldn't leave the restaurant without one of its perfectly prepared shrimp dishes, especially the salt-baked shrimp. If you're lucky and your hotel has a good-size refrigerator, take the leftovers home—they'll make a great snack the next day. New York Noodletown keeps very long hours, which makes it one of the best late-night bets in the neighborhood, too.

28½ Bowery (at Bayard St.). ✆ 212/349-0923. Reservations accepted. Main courses $4–$13. No credit cards. Daily 9am–3:30am. Subway: N, R, 6 to Canal St.

Nyonya ⭐ *(Finds* MALAYSIAN You won't find many Malaysian restaurants in New York, but one of the few, and also one of the best, is Chinatown's Nyonya. This spacious, bustling restaurant designed like a south Asian tiki hut, offers efficient and friendly service, but it's the huge portions of exotic, spicy food that are the real treat. Coconut milk, curry, and chili pepper–laden dishes are staples of Malaysian cuisine and the norm at Nyonya. The Malaysian national dish, *roti canai* (an Indian pancake with a curry chicken dipping sauce), is outstanding. The noodle soups are meals in themselves; *prawn mee* (egg noodles, shredded pork, large shrimp in a spicy shrimp broth) is sinus-clearing, while the curry spareribs are nothing short of spectacular. Even the drinks and desserts are exotic, including *sooi pooi* drink (sour plum) and *pulut hitam* (creamy black glutinous rice with coconut milk). But vegetarians beware: There's not much on the menu for you here; most dishes are prepared in either a meat or fish broth.

194 Grand St. (btwn Mulberry and Mott sts.). ✆ 212/334-3669. Appetizers $2.25–$8; noodle soups $4.25–$6; main dishes $5.25–$16. No credit cards. Sun–Thurs 11am–11:30pm; Fri–Sat 11am–midnight. Subway: 6 to Spring St.

Pho Viet Huong ⭐ *(Value* VIETNAMESE Chinatown has its own enclave of Vietnamese restaurants and the best among them is Pho Viet Huong. The menu is vast here and needs intense perusing, but your waiter will gladly help you pare it down. The Vietnamese know soup and *pho,* a beef-based soup served with many different ingredients, is the most famous, but the hot and sour *canh* soup, with either shrimp or fish is the real deal. The small is more than enough for two to share while the large is more than enough for a large family. The odd pairing of barbecued beef wrapped in grape leaves is another of the restaurant's specialties and should not be missed while the *bun,* various meats and vegetables served over rice vermicelli, are simple, hearty, and incredibly inexpensive. You'll even find Vietnamese sandwiches here; French bread filled with ham, chicken, eggs, lamb, and even pâté. For the daring, there are the frogs' legs, but don't expect what you're used to at your friendly neighborhood French restaurant; these require patience and fortitude. All of the above is best washed down with an icy cold Saigon beer.

73 Mulberry St. (btwn Bayard and Canal sts.). ✆ 212/233-8988. Appetizers $4.50–$8.50; soups $4–$9; main courses $8.50–$15. AE, MC, V. Sun–Thurs 10am–10pm; Fri–Sat 10am–11pm. Subway: 6, N, R, Q to Canal St.

4 Lower East Side

EXPENSIVE

Suba ⭐ SPANISH With its eclectic, almost surreal design and innovative Latin cuisine, Suba is a sensualist's delight. Walking past the suave cocktail and tapas lounge and down the steel staircase to my table in the "grotto," a dining room surrounded by an illuminated pool, I thought I had stepped onto the set of the 1960s Peter Sellers

Ice-Cream Fever

It's an addiction. I have cravings that occur almost daily that are only satis-fied by a decadently sweet fix. Like so many others, I am an ice-cream junkie. But I am fortunate to live in New York, where I can fulfill this con-stant need with some of the finest quality stuff that can be found any-where. If you suffer as I do, here are some of the city's best sources to help get you through the day.

Brooklyn Ice Cream Factory, Fulton Ferry Landing Pier, Brooklyn (© **718/ 246-3963**). The best ice cream in New York can be found right over the Brooklyn Bridge. Everything is freshly made, including the hot fudge for your sundae.

Chinatown Ice Cream Factory, 65 Bayard St., between Mott and Elizabeth streets (© **212/608-4170**). In Chinatown, this is perfect after a spicy Chinese meal. The ice cream here features exotic Asian flavors like almond cookie, litchi, and an incredible green tea.

Cold Stone Creamery, 253 W. 42nd St., between Seventh and Eighth avenues (© **212/398-1882;** www.coldstonecreamery.com), and 1651 Second Ave., at 86th Street (© **212/249-7080**). This Arizona-based ice-cream fran-chise broke into the New York market in 2003 and I'm not complaining. No, the more options to satisfy my insatiable need, the better. At Cold Stone, or "Stone Cold" as I refer to them, the rich, "creamy" ice cream is mixed on a frozen granite stone and made into creations like "mud pie mojo," "coconut cream pie," and "our strawberry blonde."

Custard Beach, 2 World Financial Center (© **212/786-4707**). This is the best soft ice cream I've had since my summers down the shore.

Il Laboratorio del Gelato, 95 Orchard St., between Broome and Delancey streets (© **212/343-9922;** www.laboratoriodelgelato.com). Jon Snyder, the owner of this remarkable little ice-cream/gelato shop on the Lower East Side, creates sweet magic in his laboratory. I, for one, am willing to sacrifice in the name of science by taste-testing any of his new delicious concoctions.

movie *The Party.* The place is definitely groovy, but I wouldn't describe the food that way, especially the wonderful tapas, ceviches, and appetizers. The grilled sardines with red cabbage, beans, and guacamole, and a sliver of spicy chipotle sauce was a stand-out, but the appetizer I still dream about was the salty, flavorful Serrano ham, with goat cheese and quince paste layered on a black pepper tuiles. Entrees, though not the strength here, feature a delicate melding of flavors such as a chipotle-marinated tuna with an aioli on top of a pumpkin cake. Candles on the tables come in handy; you'll need them to read the menu in the dimly lit dining room. Or better, ask the very help-ful and knowledgeable waiters to order for you. Late at night a deejay spins Latin and world music and on Sundays there is live Flamenco.

109 Ludlow St. (at Delancey St.). © 212/982-5714. www.subanyc.com. Reservations suggested. Tapas $4–$12; ceviche $10–$12; main courses $24–$26. AE, DC, DISC, MC, V. Sun–Wed 6pm–midnight; Thurs 6pm–2am; Fri–Sat 6pm–4am. Subway: F to Delancey St.

Lower East Side, SoHo, Nolita & East Village Dining

Balthazar **14**	Kittichai **13**
Bread **16**	Lombardi's Pizza **15**
Brick Lane Curry House **3**	Lupa **4**
Clinton St. Baking Company **8**	Lure Fishbar **9**
Cub Room **10**	Pao! **11**
Dos Caminos Soho **5**	PlateNYC **6**
Fiamma Osteria **12**	Second Avenue Deli **1**
Il Laboratorio del Gelato **18**	Suba **17**
Katz's Delicatessen **7**	Veselka **2**

INEXPENSIVE

Clinton St. Baking Company ⭐ *Finds* AMERICAN   Though they are open all day, breakfast and desserts are best here. The blueberry pancakes with maple butter and the buttermilk-biscuit egg sandwich are worth braving the morning lines for, while the desserts, all homemade and topped with a scoop or two of ice cream from the Brooklyn Ice Cream Factory, are good any time of day.

4 Clinton St. (at Houston St.). ⓒ **646/602-6263.** Main courses $7–$14. No credit cards. Mon–Sat 8am–11pm; Sun 10am–6pm. Subway: F or V to Second Ave.

Katz's Delicatessen ⭐⭐ *Value* JEWISH DELI   Arguably the city's best Jewish deli. The motto is, "There's Nothing More New York Than Katz's," and it's spot-on. Founded in 1888, this cavernous, brightly lit place is suitably Noo Yawk, with dill pickles, Dr. Brown's cream soda, and old-world attitude to spare. But one word of caution: Katz's has become a serious tourist destination so if you see a big tour bus parked in front, you might be in for a long wait.

205 E. Houston St. (at Ludlow St.). ⓒ **212/254-2246.** Reservations not accepted. Sandwiches $2.15–$10; other main courses $5–$18. AE, MC, V ($20 minimum). Sun–Tues 8am–10pm; Wed–Thurs 8am–11pm; Fri–Sat 8am–3am. Subway: F to Second Ave.

5 SoHo & Nolita

To locate the restaurants reviewed below, see the map on p. 181.

EXPENSIVE

Cub Room ⭐ AMERICAN   You'll have to drag yourself from the Cub Room's inviting lounge and bar scene to the very attractive dining room, but you'll be glad you did. Not because you needed to get away from all the beautiful people at the bar, but because now you get to chow on chef Henry Meer's delectable creations. The menu changes seasonally, but whatever the season, the signature Cub Steak, a butter-roasted filet, is a must. If steak's not your thing, there are always fish options; I had a very good sautéed red snapper in an orange-brown butter emulsion. Another worthy signature dish is the pâté de campagne, a homemade rustic pâté that, chunky with bits of pork, is unforgettable. Service is friendly but not oversolicitous.

131 Sullivan St. (at Prince St.). ⓒ **212/677-4100.** www.cubroom.com. Reservations recommended. Main courses $24–$30. AE, DC, MC, V. Mon–Fri noon–10pm; Sat–Sun 11am–10pm. Subway: C, E to Spring St.

Fiamma Osteria ⭐⭐ MODERN ITALIAN   From Stephen Hanson (Blue Water Grill, Ruby Foo's, Dos Caminos), the Steven Spielberg of restaurateurs, comes his art-house effort, Fiamma Osteria, and this one wins all the awards. A Hanson trademark, the restaurant is beautifully designed, depicting a modern Northern Italian style with mirrors, lustrous red walls, leather chairs, and a glass elevator that can deposit you on any of the four floors, three for dining and one for the restrooms. But the decor here is surpassed by the sumptuous, modern Italian food prepared by executive chef Michael White. Start with an antipasti of grilled octopus in an olive vinaigrette sprinkled with ceci beans (chickpeas) and cooled by chopped mint leaves and then move on to a pasta or two; the *agnolini* (braised oxtail and beef shank ravioli) and the buffalo milk ricotta *tortelli* are both outstanding. We often tend to neglect Italian main courses in favor of pastas, but doing that here would be a mistake; the *orata* (grilled *daurade* with cranberry beans in a Manila clam broth), the pan-roasted cod with shrimp and broccolini, and the *nodino* (seared veal chop with sage and sweet-and-sour cipollini onions) are too good to pass up. Fiamma is blessed to have the services of pastry chef extraordinaire Elizabeth Katz; her dessert creations are really second to none. Her *torta*, a dark-chocolate praline cake layered with hazelnut brittle and gianduja gelato, is an absolute masterpiece. Dinner is a scene so don't expect intimacy, but lunch, with a similar menu, is a much more relaxed option.

206 Spring St. (btwn Sixth Ave. and Sullivan St.). ✆ 212/653-0100. Reservations recommended. Pasta $21–$24; main courses $25–$32. AE, DISC, MC, V. Mon–Sat noon–2:30pm; Mon–Thurs and Sun 5:30–11pm; Fri–Sat 5:30pm–midnight. Subway: C, E to Spring St.

Kittichai ✿ THAI   The hotel 60 Thompson (see chapter 7) and its public spaces are a magnet for people of the beautiful kind, and Kittichai, the restaurant that shares the hotel's address, more than reinforces that reputation. From the Thai silk and wood covered walls to the model-like servers to the luminous reflecting pool where candles float peacefully in the restaurant's center, everything is pristine at Kittichai. But don't let all that style intimidate you from trying the restaurant's inventive and very flavorful food. Kittichai offers Thai tapas and, of these, the fish cakes and the sesame-spiced chicken lollipops stand out. And even a vegetarian might be tempted by the chocolate back ribs appetizer. For the entrees, I was extremely content with the hearty short ribs in green curry while the clay pot prawns with vermicelli and prosciutto (that Thai staple) was like nothing I'd ever had in any other Thai restaurant. Despite the peaceful aura created by the design, Kittichai can reach high decibel levels, so be prepared.

60 Thompson St. (btwn Broome and Spring sts.). ✆ 212/219-2000. www.kittichairestaurant.com. Reservations recommended. Tapas $6–$10; appetizers $8–$14; main courses $14–$27. Sun–Thurs 6–11pm; Fri–Sat 6pm–midnight. Subway: C, E to Spring St.

Lure Fishbar ✿✿ SEAFOOD   I'm not big on ships, boats, or anything that rocks gently or otherwise in water. I tend to turn green. But the luxury yacht that is Lure Fishbar, a bit below street level in SoHo, is one boat I will gladly board and I don't even need a supply of Dramamine. Chef Josh Capon doesn't get too fancy with the seafood he offers and that's a good thing. He keeps his raw fish bar relatively simple, kind of like the American equivalent of sashimi (yes, sashimi is also available here). Some of the standout raw items include Nantucket bay scallops lightly marinated in ginger and yellowtail accompanied by a spicy jalapeño condiment. This is Manhattan, yet at Lure the New England clam chowder, flavored with smoked bacon and abundant with whole clams, is as good as I've had in New England. The fried calamari in a smoked chili glaze will immediately make you forget the generic fried calamari you've had in the past. Of the entrees, the grilled whole dourade, rubbed with chilis, herbs, and lime brings back very fond memories of fish barbecues on the beach. Save room for the fun desserts like the homemade ice-cream sandwiches. The restaurant is lively and loud; try for one of the roomy banquettes for ultracomfortable dining.

142 Mercer St. (at Prince St.). ✆ 212/931-7676. www.lurefishbar.com. Reservations recommended. Raw appetizers $12–$16; Main courses $24–$32. AE, DC, MC, V. Daily 11:30am–3:30pm; Sun–Wed 5:30–11pm; Thurs–Sat 5:30pm–midnight. Subway: N, R to Prince St.

MODERATE

Also consider the second outpost of hot Mexican **Dos Caminos Soho,** at 425 W. Broadway, at Houston (✆ **212/277-4300**).

Balthazar *(Value* FRENCH BISTRO   This French bistro might just win the award as the loudest restaurant in New York. But you'll need your sight more than your voice to stare at the never-ending parade of eye candy that populates the place, especially at the long mirrored bar where beautiful people get to admire their comely reflections.

Really, the best way to enjoy Balthazar is to come in the off hours—for breakfast, lunch, or a midday meal—to enjoy the excellent fare in a more relaxing environment. Weekend brunch is busy but enjoyable, but reservations are a must. Or just stop into the adjacent *boulangerie,* which sells fresh-baked breads, desserts, and sandwiches to go.

80 Spring St. (at Crosby St., 1 block east of Broadway). ⓒ 212/965-1785. Reservations highly recommended (some walk-ins accepted). Main courses $11–$20 at lunch (most less than $16); $12–$32 at dinner (most less than $21). AE, MC, V. Mon–Thurs 7:30am–1:30am; Fri–Sat 7:30am–2am; Sun 7:30am–midnight. Subway: 6 to Spring St.; N, R to Prince St.

Lupa 🌟🌟 *(Value* ROMAN ITALIAN   Since it first opened in late 1999, this Roman-style osteria has remained a hot ticket. For one, it's blessed with an impeccable pedigree: Among its owners is Mario Batali, the Food TV "Iron Chef" who has built a miniempire in the Manhattan restaurant world. Second, it offers high-quality food at good value—you can eat very well here and not have to max out your credit card. And finally, the food is consistently tasty—but don't expect big portions. That's part of the secret to the good value, but don't worry—you won't starve. The menu is thoughtful and creative, focusing on lusty Roman fare like ricotta gnocchi with sausage and fennel, or pork saltimbocca. Wines, too, have been thoughtfully chosen, and you can order a bottle from the extensive list or sample one of several varieties that come in a carafe. Here, perhaps more than at any other Batali enterprise, the service hits just the right notes: Servers are both warm and supremely knowledgeable. Make a reservation, or go early to snag one of the tables set aside for walk-ins.

170 Thompson St. (btwn Houston and Bleecker sts.). ⓒ 212/982-5089. www.luparestaurant.com. Reservations recommended. Primi $9–$15; secondi $16–$20. AE, MC, V. Mon–Fri noon–3pm and 5–11:30pm; Sat–Sun noon–2:45pm and 4:45–11:30pm. Subway: B, D, F, Q, A, C, E to W. 4th St.

Pao! 🌟 PORTUGUESE   New York has multiple restaurants of almost every ethnicity, yet there is a surprising scarcity of Portuguese eateries. Of the few, this cozy, comfortable charmer is the best. Pao!, which translates to bread, keeps it simple, and the results are pure and authentic. Start with *caldo verde,* traditional Portuguese soup, made with shredded kale, potatoes, and wonderfully smoky *linguica* (Portuguese sausage). The baked octopus salad, tender and soaked in a garlic/cilantro vinaigrette, rivals any I've had in numerous Greek restaurants, while the cod cakes, another Portuguese standard, are light and not too salty. The combination of pork and seafood might seem odd, but it's common in Portugal; Pao!'s pairing of pork and clams is an acquired taste—and one I've happily acquired. Salt cod is to Portugal as hamburgers are to the United States, and I'll take Pao!'s hearty *bacalhau a braz,* salt cod with egg, onion, and straw potatoes, over hamburger most any day. To complement the food, stick with a delicious Portuguese wine, from which there are many to choose. Desserts are egg-based and delicate; the soft pound cake with lemon egg custard filling is heavenly.

322 Spring St. (at Greenwich St.). ⓒ 212/334-5464. Reservations recommended. AE, DC, MC, V. Lunch $12–$14; dinner $17–$20. Mon–Fri noon–2:30pm; daily 6–11pm. Subway: C, E to Spring St.

PlateNYC *(Finds* LATIN-ASIAN FUSION   So far there have only been a handful of restaurants on this small stretch of boutique-driven real estate known as Nolita, but the numbers are growing and one of the more recent additions is PlateNYC. The restaurant, with its offerings of small plates of Latin and Asian fusion food, its creative, sake-infused cocktails, and its stylish space, including an enclosed garden patio, is a fitting complement to the neighborhood's style and verve. Though family-style platters are served here, stick with the small plates, appetizers, and bowls, starting with something from the raw bar like Kumomoto oyster shooters, and then move on to the ceviche tasting that changes daily, or the coconut shrimp skewed by sugar cane and served with a jalapeño cucumber dipping sauce. Bowls are also offered; the paella "Asian Style" with sweet Chinese sausage, shrimp, mussels, clams, edamame, and coconut jasmine rice was like no paella I've ever tasted. The food here is meant to share so the more the merrier—or join another party at a communal table. And, if you are in Nolita to shop during daytime hours, PlateNYC turns into Fashion/Plate NYC, a combination bar and boutique where you can nibble on chocolates or sip a "saktail" after perusing the racks of designer duds.

264 Elizabeth St. (btwn Houston and Prince sts.). (*) 212/219-9212. www.platenyc.com. Reservations recommended. Small plates $4–$8; appetizers $7–$11; bowls $9–$15; main courses $14–$21. AE, DC, MC, V. Sun–Thurs 5:30pm–midnight; Fri–Sat 5:30pm–2am; Sat–Sun 11:30am–3:30pm. Fashion/PlateNYC: Daily 11am–5pm. Subway: B, D, F, V to Broadway/Lafayette.

INEXPENSIVE

Also consider **Lombardi's Pizza,** 32 Spring St., between Mott and Mulberry streets, (*) **212/941-7994** (see "Pizza, New York–Style," p. 204).

Bread (*) ITALIAN   The older, yet smaller sibling of Bread Tribeca (p. 177) does bread like no other sandwich shop. The bread comes from Balthazar Bakery down the street, but it's what they do with it that makes this eatery so special. For example, they take a rustic ciabatta loaf, slather it with Sicilian sardines, Thai mayonnaise, tomato, and lettuce, and then turn it over to their panini press. The result is a gooey convergence of flavors that you will attempt to gobble down gracefully. It *will* fall apart, but that's okay; someone will be along very shortly with more napkins. Besides the spectacular sardine sandwich, the Italian tuna with mesclun greens and tomatoes in a lemon dressing and the fontina with grilled zucchini, eggplant, arugula, and tomato in a balsamic vinaigrette are also standouts. Really, there are no losers on the bread side of Bread's menu, which also includes salads, pastas, and "plates." The 32-seat restaurant is located in fashionably chic Nolita and if you are lucky you might even be treated by the sight of a breathtakingly thin model doing her best to keep the contents of one of Bread's sandwiches from staining her custom-made designer duds.

20 Spring St. (btwn Mott and Elizabeth sts.). (*) 212/334-1015. Reservations not accepted. Breads $7–$9; plates $6–$16. AE, DC, MC, V. Daily noon–midnight. Subway: 6 to Spring St.

6 The East Village & NoHo

To locate the restaurants reviewed below, see the map on p. 181.

MODERATE

Brick Lane Curry House (*) *Finds* INDIAN   The vibrancy of the traditional Indian restaurants, seemingly interconnected on the block of East 6th Street known as "Little India," has diminished over the years, but this relatively new addition has added some welcome vigor to the street. The food is so good at Brick Lane they don't even need the requisite sitar players to draw in customers. But beware: They don't compromise on their spice here. In fact, they might just have the hottest dish to be found in the city. It's a curry called "phaal" that requires a verbal disclaimer by the customer to not hold the restaurant liable for any physical or emotional damage incurred from eating the curry. And if you are able to finish it, the restaurant promises a bottle of beer on the house. But there is no need to blister your intestines; the other, less hazardous, curries will bring on a good enough sweat including the excellent Madras and the tangy Goan. Brick Lane's signature boti rolls, chicken tikka served in fresh baked bread, are special while the rassam soup of the day, a thin, clear soup that changes daily will help clear your sinuses even before you touch a curry. There are also a number of vegan items for those of you who desire such a thing.

306–308 E. 6th St. (btwn First and Second aves.). (C) 212/979-2900. www.bricklanecurryhouse.com. Reservations recommended. Appetizers $5–$9; curries $12–$17. AE, DC, MC, V. Sun–Thurs noon–11pm; Fri–Sat noon–1am. Subway: 6 to Astor Place.

INEXPENSIVE

Also consider the all-kosher **Second Avenue Deli,** 156 Second Ave., at 10th Street ((C) 212/677-0606), for kosher Jewish deli fare extraordinaire; for details, see "The New York Deli News" box on p. 206.

Veselka ⚘ UKRAINIAN DINER Whenever the craving hits for hearty Eastern European fare at old-world prices, Veselka fits the bill with fluffy and light (if that's possible) *pirogi* (small doughy envelopes filled with potatoes, cheese, or sauerkraut), *kasha varnishkes* (cracked buckwheat and noodles with mushroom sauce), stuffed cabbage, grilled Polish kielbasa, freshly made potato pancakes, and classic soups, like a sublime borscht. Breakfast is special here (see "Breakfast, Not Brunch," p. 220). If all you want is a burger, don't worry—it's a classic, too.

Despite the authentic fare, the diner is comfortable, modern, and appealing, with an artsy slant and delicious house-made desserts. No wonder Veselka surpasses its status as a popular after-hours hangout with club kids and other night owls to be a favorite at any hour.

144 Second St. (at 9th St.). (C) 212/228-9682. Reservations not accepted. Main courses $5–$13. AE, DC, DISC, MC, V. Daily 24 hr. Subway: 6 to Astor Place.

7 Greenwich Village & the Meat-Packing District

For more choices in the Meat-Packing District, see the sidebar "Dining Zone: The Meat-Packing District," below.

EXPENSIVE

Ono ⚘ JAPANESE Like other ventures by restaurateur Jeffrey Chodorow, Ono is no shrinking violet. It's big, brash, and when it opened in 2005 off the lobby of the Hotel Gansevoort, it became an instant scene. And if you can get past the circuslike atmosphere—the murals of tattooed body parts, the long, illuminated sushi bar, and the outdoor area where there are actually private cabanas—you'll find some surprisingly good and interesting dishes. The menu is vast and you'll definitely need help in ordering; my waiter suggested sticking to the "small" plates and sharing. So I shared the Kumamoto oyster shooter with wasabi and quail egg to start followed by the miso barbecued "tuna spare ribs" that was as close to pork as a fish could ever get. The Japanese-style rabata grill is one of Ono's stars. The grill and wooden skewers are brought to the table with your choice of meat, seafood, vegetables, or combos. I went with the kobe beef filet that was perfectly grilled. Eat quickly, however, because the heat from the grill is so intense your own sweat might drip onto your plate. Ono also features "o no rice" rolls, rolls without rice, and very hearty sashimi and nigiri. The restaurant encourages raucous communal, as opposed to intimate, dining so know that going in and you'll enjoy the show.

Greenwich Village/Meat-Packing District Dining

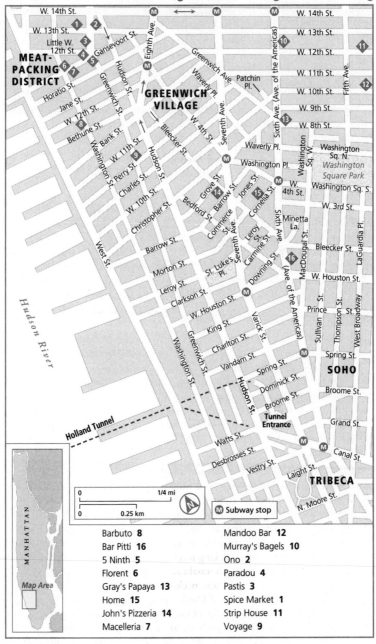

Barbuto **8**
Bar Pitti **16**
5 Ninth **5**
Florent **6**
Gray's Papaya **13**
Home **15**
John's Pizzeria **14**
Macelleria **7**

Mandoo Bar **12**
Murray's Bagels **10**
Ono **2**
Paradou **4**
Pastis **3**
Spice Market **1**
Strip House **11**
Voyage **9**

18 Ninth Ave. (at W. 13th St.). ⓒ **212/660-6766.** Reservations recommended. Rabata $3–$18; sushi/small plates $4–$16; large plates $17–$49. AE, DC, MC, V. Mon–Thurs 5pm–midnight; Fri 5pm–1am; Sat 11am–1am; Sun 11am–midnight. Subway: A, C, E to 14th St.

Dining Zone: The Meat-Packing District

The Meat-Packing District, a formerly rough-and-tumble area west of Ninth Avenue around 14th Street that was once the domain of butchers and transvestites, now attracts models, celebrities, and assorted wannabees. Why? It's the prospect of very inventive drinks in ultrahip surroundings followed by a meal at one of this tiny neighborhood's many restaurants. Here are some of the top dining choices:

Two of the Meat-Packing pioneers, who were here when the butchers in the bloody aprons (and men in makeup and high heels) were common sights on these streets, include **Florent,** 69 Gansevoort St. (ⓒ 212/989-5779; www.restaurantflorent.com), 2 blocks south of 14th Street and 1 block west of Ninth Avenue, between Greenwich and Washington streets. Open almost all day and night, Florent is French bistro dressed up as a '50s-style diner where you can combine burgers with *moules frites* (mussels and fries). For a more traditional French bistro, and one that attracts a celeb-driven crowd well into the early morning hours is **Pastis,** 9 Ninth Ave., at Little West 12th Street (ⓒ **212/929-4844;** www.pastisny.com).

In 2004, when master-chef/restaurateur Jean-Georges Vongerichten opened **Spice Market,** 403 W. 13th St., at Ninth Avenue (ⓒ **212/675-2322**), his huge, beautifully designed restaurant with a spin on East Asian street food, you knew there was no turning back. The Meat-Packing District had officially become a destination.

Right on the heels of Spice Market's opening came the arrival of the Hotel Gansevoort, just across the street, and its signature restaurant, the fun and funky Japanese effort **Ono,** 18 Ninth Ave., at West 13th Street (ⓒ **212/660-6766**). See p. 186.

For a little less glitz, but no less in stature, there's the romantic **5 Ninth,** 5 Ninth Ave., between Gansevoort and Little West 12th streets (ⓒ **212/929/9460;** www.5ninth.com). Housed in a mid-19th-century town house, this three-story charmer serves delicate variations on Asian cuisine.

While Pastis attracts the crowds (and the noise), lovely, cozy, **Paradou,** 8 Little W. 12th St., at Ninth Avenue (ⓒ **212/463-8345**), is a bistro so intimate you can actually have a conversation with your dinner date.

Finally, there is **Macelleria,** 48 Gansevoort St., between Greenwich and Washington streets (ⓒ **212/741-2555**), an Italian restaurant with a heavy emphasis on meat and steaks. Translated from Italian, "macelleria" means "butcher shop" and it's located in a former meat locker. Now what could be more apt than that for a restaurant in the Meat-Packing District?

Strip House ★★ STEAKS   With a photo gallery of semi-nude burlesque performers decorating the red velvet walls, roomy burgundy banquettes, and a steady flow of lounge music, you may, as I once did, mistakenly refer to the Strip House as the Strip Club. But despite the faux Playboy look, the only decadence here is in the titanic portions of perfectly charred and seasoned red meat, specifically, the strip steak. I had the strip on the bone that, months later, I still remember with fondness. The filet mignon is simply and impeccably prepared and the porterhouse for two, carved at your table, is in the Peter Luger league. The sides here are innovative variations on the standards: creamed spinach with black truffles, french fries with herbs and garlic, and, best of all, the crisp goose-fat potatoes. Is goose fat a good fat or a bad fat? Only your dietician knows for sure, but if you have a dietician you're probably in the wrong restaurant. Desserts are monumental, especially the multilayered chocolate cake, so have your waiter bring extra forks for sharing. With the exception of those few banquettes, seating is tight so don't expect intimacy—unless it is with your neighbor.

13 E. 12th St. (btwn University Place and Fifth Ave.). ☎ 212/328-0000. www.theglaziergroup.com. Reservations recommended. 3-course prix fixe before 6pm $49; main courses $22–$40. AE, DC, DISC, MC, V. Mon–Thurs 5–11pm; Fri–Sat 5–11:30pm; Sun 5–10pm. Subway: L, N, R, Q, 4, 5, 6 to 14th St./Union Sq.

MODERATE

Barbuto ★ COUNTRY ITALIAN   Star chef Jonathan Waxman returned to New York after 12 years away to helm the quietly elegant Washington Park (now defunct) but ended up cooking in an open kitchen in the looser, more casual environs of this West Village trattoria. The food is fresh and solid, and many of the best dishes are prepared in the blazing wood-fired oven. Start with salt cod cakes and baby greens; a good pasta choice is the Genovese-style penne rigate and pesto with haricots verts. The space has a sunny feel and gets cooking in the warm weather, when the garage-style doors are folded up and the alfresco space takes on a party atmosphere.

775 Washington St. (at W. 12th St.). ☎ 212/924-9700. www.barbutonyc.com. Reservations recommended. Main courses $14–$19. AE, DC, DISC, MC, V. Mon–Fri noon–3pm; Mon–Thurs 5:45–11pm; Fri–Sat 5:45pm–midnight; Sun 2–10pm. Subway: A, C, E to 14th St.

Home ★★ Finds CONTEMPORARY AMERICAN HOME COOKING   This cozy restaurant is the domain of a husband-and-wife team, Chef David Page and co-owner Barbara Shinn. The couple keeps things fresh, popularly priced, and welcoming; as a result, their narrow, tin-roofed dining room is always packed. The dinner menu changes regularly, but look for such signature dishes as the rich and creamy blue cheese fondue with rosemary toasts; an excellent cumin-crusted pork chop on a bed of homemade barbecue sauce; a filleted-at-your-table brook trout accompanied by sweet potatoes, apples, and sage; and perfectly moist roasted chicken with a side of spicy onion rings. For dessert, their chocolate pudding is legendary. Breakfast and weekend brunch are great times to visit, too, with fluffy pancakes and excellent egg dishes. The interesting wine list boasts a large selection of local bottles from Long Island's North Fork. Heated year-round, the lovely garden is most charming in warm weather; book an outside table well ahead.

20 Cornelia St. (btwn Bleecker and W. 4th sts.). ☎ 212/243-9579. Reservations recommended. Main courses $8–$12 at breakfast and lunch; $14–$18 at dinner; fixed-price lunch $13; 3-course dinner $28 ($48 with wines). AE, DISC, MC, V. Mon–Fri 9am–4pm and 5–11pm; Sat 10:30am–4:30pm and 5:30–11pm; Sun 10:30am–4:30pm and 5:30–10pm. Subway: A, C, E, F, B, D to W. 4th St. (use W. 3rd St. exit).

Voyage ★★ Finds GLOBAL   As its name implies, the theme of this wonderful restaurant is travel. And the food here, by just subtly touching on the spices and styles of a region, will take you to many different culinary destinations all in one sitting. The appetizer of truffled scallops combined with grits and red-eye gravy was a revelation never before sampled on my own journeys to the American South, while the phenomenal entree of roasted cod served in a bath of cilantro and coconut broth and accompanied ingeniously by samosas, was obviously inspired by India, yet like nothing I've had in an Indian restaurant. Voyage has an extensive wine list, but skip the wine and order one of the talented bartender's signature cocktails. I had an island rum punch that was as good as I've had on any island. Tables are a bit too close together but don't let that or the somewhat disconcerting black-and-white photographs on the walls of cigar-chomping Cuban men distract you from enjoying your eating expedition.

117 Perry St. (at Greenwich St.). © 212/255-9191. Reservations recommended. Main courses $14–$24. AE, MC, V. Mon–Wed 5–11pm; Thurs–Sat 5pm–midnight; Sun brunch 11am–3pm. Subway: 1, 9 to Christopher St.

INEXPENSIVE

The downtown branch of the original uptown **Gray's Papaya** is at 402 Sixth Ave., at 8th Street (© 212/260-3532). The original **John's Pizzeria** is at 278 Bleecker St., near Seventh Avenue (© 212/243-1680; see "Pizza, New York–Style," on p. 204). Also, you'll find **Murray's Bagels** at 500 Sixth Ave., between 12th and 13th streets (© 212/466-2830; see "The Hole Truth: NY's Best Bagels," on p. 198).

Also consider the new Greenwich Village outpost of the Korean dumpling house, **Mandoo Bar,** 71 University Place (© 212/358-0400).

Bar Pitti ★ Value TUSCAN ITALIAN   This indoor/outdoor trattoria is a sidewalk scene, and one of downtown's best dining bargains. Waiting for a table can be a chore, but all is forgiven once you take a seat, thanks to authentic, affordably priced cuisine and some of the friendliest waiters in town. Despite the packed seating, Bar Pitti wins you over with Italian charm—it's the kind of place where the waiter brings over the list of daily specials on a well-worn blackboard, and if you want more cheese, a block of Parmesan and a grater suddenly appear. Peruse the laminated menu, but don't get your heart set on anything until you see the board, which boasts the best of what the kitchen has to offer; on my last visit, they wowed me with fabulous veal meatballs. Winners off the regular menu, which focuses heavily on pastas and panini, include excellent beef carpaccio; grilled country bread with prosciutto, garlic, and olive oil; and spinach-and-ricotta ravioli in a creamy sage and Parmesan sauce. The all-Italian wine list is high-priced compared to the menu, but you'll find a few good-value choices.

268 Sixth Ave. (btwn Bleecker and Houston sts.). © 212/982-3300. Reservations accepted for parties of 4 or more. Main courses $7.50–$16 (some specials may be higher). No credit cards. Daily noon–midnight. Subway: A, C, E, F, V to W. 4th St. (use 3rd St. exit).

8 Chelsea

To locate the restaurants in this section, see the map on p. 192.

EXPENSIVE

The Biltmore Room ★★ ASIAN   The name Biltmore Room conjures up a retro, noirish feel, but besides the dazzling decor, much of it salvaged from the old Biltmore Hotel, there is nothing retro or noirish about the food here. Start with an original cocktail like The Way of the Dragon—vodka, lime juice, honey, mint, and a blast of hot pepper—and you know you're onto something unique. Fiery is a good word to describe much of the cuisine, especially the starter Tataki of Blue Fin Tuna; yet its tear-inducing cayenne pepper oil is thankfully balanced by cucumber-ginger sorbet. Heat-shy diners should try the crisp squash blossoms stuffed with crab in a mild mango chili dipping sauce. The mains also display Asian influence, especially the excellent Indian spiced wild king salmon and the Thai marinated free-range chicken. For dessert those passionate about chocolate will not be disappointed in the warm chocolate torte while the passion fruit souffle is worth the extra wait. Seating is a little tight and the noise can get cacophonous, but know that going in and enjoy the room's visual splendor while dining on the chef's innovatively tangy creations.

290 Eighth Ave. (btwn 24th and 25th sts.). ℂ **212/807-0111.** Reservations recommended. Main courses $27–$35. AE, MC, V. Mon–Thurs 6–10:30pm; Fri–Sat 6–11:30pm. Subway: C, E to 23rd St.

MODERATE

La Nacional ★★ *Finds* SPANISH/TAPAS   It's not easy finding the oldest Spanish restaurant in New York; in fact, the search for this unmarked restaurant on West 14th Street might get you a bit frustrated. Once you find it though, your frustration will soon be rewarded. Founded in 1868 as a gathering spot for the Benevolent Spanish Society, La Nacional, a social club, is a real hidden treat. At one time food was secondary to the company of Spanish expatriates who congregated here, filling the room with smoke and loud talk of Spanish politics and football. It was here where Gabriel Garcia Lorca spent countless hours documenting his New York City experience. The cigarette smoke has now been replaced by the smoke of the grill, which turns out extremely tasty tapas like sardines, octopus, and shrimp. There is a somewhat formal dining room in the front while in the back, next to the open kitchen, there are a few tables and TVs usually tuned to soccer matches. Come and share a bottle of Spanish wine and make a meal out of the tapas—the *albondigas* (Spanish meatballs), *boquerones* (white anchovy filets), and the aforementioned octopus are my favorites—or you can order the restaurant's excellent paella. Tapas range from $4 to $9 while no entree is more than $18. In a ballroom on the second level, the club sponsors flamenco performances and dance lessons.

239 W. 14th St. (btwn 7th and 8th aves.). ℂ **212/243-9308.** Tapas $4–$9; main courses $15–$18. No credit cards. Daily noon–11pm. Subway: A, C, E, 1, 2, 3, 9 to 14th St.

Moran's Chelsea AMERICAN   This ancient restaurant is a throwback not only because it was established in 1957 and is housed in an 1834 building, but because it also serves straight-ahead, no-nonsense seafood and chops. What isn't a throwback are the prices, which have very much kept up with the times. You won't, however, get cheated on portions, which are huge. But you don't come here for the culinary experience; the real reason to come to this far west Chelsea restaurant that features four dining rooms, each with original tin roofs, wood-burning fireplaces, and an antique bar that pours cold, refreshing pints of beer, is its cozy ambience. But the food might surprise you as it did me; the crab cakes, pan-fried and stuffed with jumbo lump crab, were some of the best I've had. The fish is very good and served with few frills, as are the steaks and chops. Service is also no-frills and sometimes slow, but be patient, you're not really in Chelsea anymore, you're in the land of Moran's.

146 Tenth Ave. (at 19th St.). ℂ **212/627-3030.** www.moranschelsea.com. Main courses $9–$20 at lunch; $17–$30 at dinner. AE, DC, DISC, MC, V. Daily noon–midnight. Subway: C, E to 23rd St.

Midtown, Chelsea, Flatiron District & Gramercy Park Dining

Abbocatto **7**

Afghan Kebab House **13**

Alain Ducasse **5**

Aquavit **50**

Atelier **54**

Becco **16**

Ben Benson's Steakhouse **11**

Beppe **32**

The Biltmore Room **24**

BLT Steak **52**

Blue Smoke **38**

Bull and Bear **46**

Burger Joint **53**

Café des Artistes **1**

Cafe Spice Express **41**

Carmine's **19**

Carnegie Deli **8**

Christer's **41**

City Bakery **28**

Cold Stone Creamery **21**

Daniel **57**

db Bistro Moderne **43**

Devi **29**

Dos Caminos **37**

Eisenberg's Coffee Shop **34**

Eleven Madison Park **36**

Ess-A-Bagel **31**

Jean-Georges **3**

John's Pizzeria **18**

Junior's **41**

Kalustyan's **39**

Knödel **41**

La Nacional **27**

Le Bernardin **48**

L'Impero **42**

Little Pie Company **41**

Mandoo Bar **40**

Marseille **17**

Masa **4**

Michael Jordan's–
The Steakhouse **41**

Mickey Mantle's **55**

Molyvos **6**

Moran's Chelsea **26**

Murray's Bagels **25**

continues on opposite page

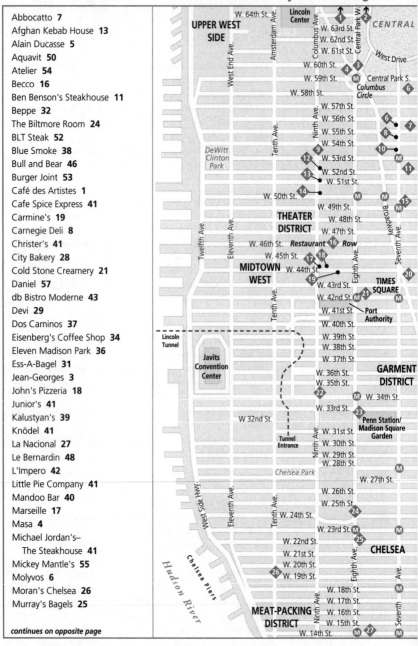

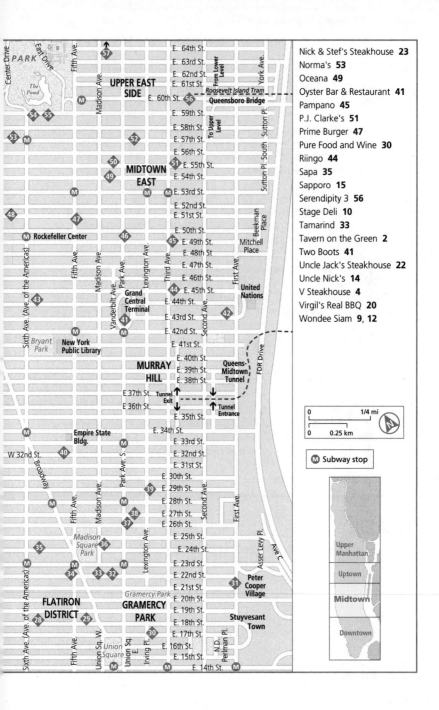

Nick & Stef's Steakhouse **23**
Norma's **53**
Oceana **49**
Oyster Bar & Restaurant **41**
Pampano **45**
P.J. Clarke's **51**
Prime Burger **47**
Pure Food and Wine **30**
Riingo **44**
Sapa **35**
Sapporo **15**
Serendipity 3 **56**
Stage Deli **10**
Tamarind **33**
Tavern on the Green **2**
Two Boots **41**
Uncle Jack's Steakhouse **22**
Uncle Nick's **14**
V Steakhouse **4**
Virgil's Real BBQ **20**
Wondee Siam **9, 12**

0   1/4 mi
0   0.25 km

Ⓜ Subway stop

Upper Manhattan

Uptown

Midtown

Downtown

The Prime Cut

Much to the delight of carnivores, this city of great steaks has undergone a big, bold chophouse explosion in recent years, virtually doubling the number of prime-cut palaces. **Peter Luger Steakhouse** ☆☆ (p. 228) has been the steakhouse standard for years, but trendy newcomer **BLT Steak** ☆☆☆ (p. 207) is now tops, with **Strip House** ☆☆ (p. 189) close behind. Two traditional and very good steakhouses with loyal followings are **Uncle Jack's Steakhouse** ☆ (p. 201) and **Ben Benson's Steakhouse** (p. 200). Here are some more meateries to try:

Don't expect an overpriced burger factory with waiters in Bulls jerseys and basketball-shaped plates from **Michael Jordan's–The Steak House** ☆☆, on the mezzanine level overlooking the main concourse at Grand Central Terminal (② **212/655-2300**; www.theglaziergroup.com). Bursting with Beaux Arts–meets–Art Deco grandeur, Michael Jordan's is wholly for grown-ups. And with a perfect view of the legendary sky ceiling, this is more than just the city's best-looking steakhouse—it's an incredible "only in New York" dining experience. The star of the classic steakhouse menu is the porterhouse for two, a whopping 44 ounces of top-quality cow, served suitably charred and salty on the outside.

MarkJoseph, 261 Water St., at Peck Slip, South Street Seaport (② **212/ 277-0020**), is the brainchild of a Peter Luger alumni. The dry-aged steaks are as terrific as those at the legendary Brooklyn joint, but the warm and well-outfitted restaurant is more comfortable, the atmosphere more relaxing, the service friendlier, and there are no throngs of tourists (yet). Great for an extra-long lunchtime break after Financial District sightseeing.

One of the best of the traditional old-world steakhouses is the clubby, fun **Bull and Bear,** in the Waldorf=Astoria, 301 Park Ave., between 49th and 50th streets (② **212/872-4900**), which serves the best New York strip I've had in the city.

Nick & Stef's Steakhouse, adjacent to Madison Square Garden at 9 Penn Plaza, at Eighth Avenue and 33rd Street (② **212/563-4444**; www.nickand stefs.com), is a comfortable contemporary steakhouse from top L.A. toque Joachim Splichal, who's finally given sports fans somewhere to eat well before the Knicks or Rangers game. The clear choice is the New York strip, dry-aged on the premises and grilled to perfection.

If you want to try the most expensive steak in New York, head to the Time Warner Center where Jean-Georges Vongerichten, of restaurant Jean-Georges fame, opened **V Steakhouse,** 10 Columbus Circle, fourth floor (② **212/823-9500**). After trying one of the organic Niman Ranch steaks for over $60 you may wonder, as I did, if you're paying extra for the privelege of dining in this lofty, rococo room with views of Central Park.

Most entrees at these steakhouses, with the exception of V Steakhouse, tend to fall in the $22 to $38 range. Always book ahead and inquire about dress codes, especially at the old-school spots.

9 Union Square, the Flatiron District & Gramercy Park

To locate the restaurants in this section, see the map on p. 192.

EXPENSIVE

Beppe ★★ TUSCAN   Many restaurants claim to serve authentic Tuscan cuisine, but dine at Beppe and you'll realize that what those restaurants offer are pale imitations. Gregarious owner/chef/host Cesare Casella whose family operated restaurants in Tuscany doesn't pander by serving typical Italian-American favorites like spaghetti and meatballs. Instead you'll get *norcino,* delicate spaghetti coated with crumbled pork sauce; *farrotto,* farro grain cooked with seasonal vegetables; or gnocchi with a wild boar ragu. Casella takes pride in his Tuscan roots and its products; all the wines are from that region and he even brought over seeds of Tuscan beans which he grows in his upstate farm. You might find those beans accompanying his incredible homemade sausage or starring in his seven-bean salad. There are many winners on Casella's menu but if you like mussels, his, pan-roasted in a fiery garlic and parsley broth, is a must. Beppe is a joyous, inviting—and loud—trattoria framed by a roaring open fire where many of the restaurant's dishes are prepared. Casella's cooking has a large and devoted following so reservations are strongly recommended.

45 E. 22nd St. (btwn Park Ave. South and Broadway). ✆ 212/982-8422. www.beppenyc.com. Reservations recommended. AE, DISC, MC, V. Main courses $17–$30. Mon–Fri noon–2:30pm; Mon–Sat 5:30–11:30pm. Subway: N, R, 6 to 23rd St.

Devi ★★ INDIAN   With the preponderance of Indian restaurants in New York City, you would think another one would be welcomed with a big yawn. But few come along like Devi, which opened in late 2004. Devi offers $55 tasting menus (vegetarian and non-vegetarian) and that's really the way to go here. The menu features nine small courses that will let you sample much of what the restaurant has to offer. Some of the highlights include tender tandoori chicken stuffed with spicy herbs, halibut coated in a cilantro rub and accompanied with mint coconut chutney and lemon rice, *zimikand koftas,* delicate yam koftas in a creamy tomato-onion sauce, and the addictive, crispy okra, the Indian equivalent of french fries. With the tasting menus, you get a choice of desserts; of them, I strongly recommend the fabulous *falooda,* an Indian sundae that's a refreshing combination of noodles with honey-soaked basil seeds, mango, and strawberry sorbet in lemongrass-infused coconut milk. Seating is comfortable and service is knowledgeable though servers regrettably don bright orange uniforms that look a bit too much like prison garb.

8 E. 18th St. (btwn Fifth Ave. and Broadway). ✆ 212/691-1300. www.devinyc.com. Reservations recommended. AE, DISC, MC, V. Main courses $14–$29; tasting menus $55. Mon–Sat noon–2:30pm and 5:30–11pm; Sun 5:30–11pm. Subway: N, R, W, Q, 4, 5, 6 to 14th St./Union Square.

Eleven Madison Park ★★★ FRENCH CONTINENTAL   Chef/restaurateur Danny Meyer's empire (Union Square Cafe, Gramercy Park Tavern, and others) is vast and impressive, yet this property, which opened several years ago in the lobby of the Art Deco Met-Life building across from Madison Square Park, is often overlooked. Maybe it's because the restaurant is unfairly compared to its famous siblings, but I think Eleven Madison Park can stand very capably on its own.

The immense, high-ceilinged restaurant is a marvel to experience, but before you have a chance to take in all that grandeur, the waitstaff, working with the efficient precision of a secret service unit, is upon you, there almost before you even have to ask.

Chef Kerry Heffernan's French-infused country cooking puts an emphasis on hearty fare, including organ meats such as the almond-crusted calf's brain; crisped pig's feet; prime-aged *cote de boeuf*; and an incredible sautéed skate wing. All the desserts are wonderful, especially the chocolate soufflé (not on the menu, but order it with your meal so it will be ready for your dessert); you might consider skipping the entrees and get right to dessert. The excellent tasting menu (choose five or seven courses) lets you sample much of what the restaurant has to offer.

11 Madison Ave. (at 24th St.). ℂ **212/889-0905.** Reservations recommended. A la carte lunch $15–$24; 3-course prix-fixe lunch $25; dinner main courses $23–$31; tasting menu (5–7 courses) $60–$80. AE, DC, DISC, MC, V. Mon–Sat 11:30am–2pm; Mon–Thurs 5:30–10:30pm; Fri–Sat 5:30–11pm; Sun 5:30–10pm. Subway: N, R, 6 to 23rd St.

Sapa 🐧🐧 FRENCH VIETNAMESE   I am usually very wary of "fusion" cuisine, but in Sapa's case, the combination of French and Vietnamese based on the two countries' respective histories is a natural one. It also helps that the food at Sapa is helmed by the immensely talented Patricia Yeo. Begin your journey in the Mediterranean, with a spectacular salad of romaine hearts, endive, and Taleggio cheese with pear fritters in a pear vinaigrette. Move quickly to Vietnam and sample one or two rolls prepared at Sapa's "roll bar"; the spiced yellowfin tartare with avocado and green papaya sprouts was my favorite. When it comes to the main courses, there is a reason Yeo's ginger-crusted ahi tuna over braised oxtail is her signature dish; the unusual mix might seem too rich, but they mesh together perfectly. The restaurant is cavernous, with high ceilings and bright white walls, and service is extremely personable and knowledgeable. The dining experience at Sapa is exotic on every level—even the restroom area, with its candle-adorned bubbling pool, Chinese screens decorating the row of bathroom doors, and soft music, is worth the trip even if you don't have to go.

43 W. 24th St. (btwn Broadway and Sixth Ave.). ℂ **212/929-1800.** www.sapanyc.com. Reservations recommended. Roll bar $8–$12; main courses $22–$32. AE, DISC, MC, V. Mon–Sat 11:30am–3:30pm; midday menu Mon–Sat 3:30–5:30pm; Mon–Thurs 5:30–11:30pm; Fri–Sat 5:30pm–12:30am; Sun 5:30–10:30pm; Sun brunch 10:30am–3:30pm. Subway: F,V to 23rd St.

Tamarind 🐧🐧 INDIAN   One of the best Indian restaurants in Manhattan, Tamarind offers innovative and flavorful variations on the old standards. The room is sleek and bleached white, giving it a gallery-like feel; in the middle of the restaurant adjacent to the bar is a glassed-in cubicle where you can watch the chefs work the tandoor ovens. And just about anything that comes out of those ovens is spectacular. But start with the *bhel poori,* assorted crisps and noodles with sweet and sour chutneys, and one of the soups. I love the she-crab soup with nutmeg, ginger juice, and saffron. Try not to fill up on the tandoor-baked breads; the nan is very hard to resist. As I said, you can't go wrong with any of the tandoor-baked entrees; the *jhinga angarey,* jumbo prawns marinated in yogurt and chiles, is my favorite. If you venture from the tandoor, try the lamb *pasanda,* apricot-filled grilled lamb in a cashew and saffron sauce or Tamarind swordfish marinated in tamarind chutney and fenugreek leaves. There are a number of vegetarian options here; the Raji vegetarian thali, an assortment of tandoori salad, lentils, vegetables, chutneys, and relishes, is a treat. Desserts are special, too; try the *gujjia,* a samosa filled with semolina, raisins, cashews, and coconut. Service is efficient and friendly and the owners will most likely stop by your table and greet you as if you are a regular.

41–43 E. 22nd St. (btwn Broadway and Park Ave.). ℂ **212/674-7400.** Reservations recommended. Main courses $11–$30. AE, DC, MC, V. Daily 11:30am–3pm and 5:30–11:30pm. Subway: N, R, 6 to 23rd St.

MODERATE

Blue Smoke ☆ BARBECUE/SOUTHERN   Leave it to Danny Meyer to have the confidence to open a restaurant where you can order a smoked bologna sandwich. For many, that would be culinary suicide; for Meyer, it is yet another triumph.

Blue Smoke is Meyer's effort to reproduce the barbecue he grew up on in St. Louis; he even had a high-tech smoker custom built for slow cooking. The ribs, which come in three varieties (Memphis baby backs, salt-and-pepper dry rubbed, and St. Louis style) were all tender to the bone, but the St. Louis variety, glazed in a mild barbecue sauce, was the clear winner. Though the meats are the attraction here, the side dishes are as good as I've tasted anywhere, especially the collard greens, speckled with bits of pork, and the slow-cooked green beans, oozing with flavor. The house Blue Smoke ale is the perfect hearty complement to the rich food. You may not find the urbane elegance so typical of Meyer's other establishments, but this heartland barbecue joint, in typical Meyer fashion, is still run to perfection.

116 E. 27th St. (btwn Park and Lexington aves.). ✆ 212/447-7733. www.bluesmoke.com. Reservations suggested. Main courses $10–$22. AE, DC, DISC, MC, V. Daily 11:30am–11pm; late-night menu Wed–Sat 11pm–1am. Subway: 6 to 28th St.

Dos Caminos MEXICAN   This upscale Mexican attracts huge after-work crowds. But do they come for the food or the incredible margaritas—try the prickly pear cactus or the tangerine margarita—and the over 100 varieties of tequila?

The guacamole here, made fresh at your table, is a show in itself. I asked for spicy, but for my taste, it lacked the bite and citrus tang of a really great guacamole. The fish tacos, made with red snapper in a soft taco with fresh coleslaw, are outstanding, as are the many ceviches, especially *pulpito* (baby octopus). The Mexican standard, chicken *mole en poblano,* is very good, though not worth the steep price (almost $20). In general, stay away from the traditional offerings and explore the more innovative dishes such as chipotle-tamarind glazed mahimahi, ancho-seared bigeye tuna, and ten-chile barbecued baby back ribs; such dishes—and those sublime tequilas—are what sets Dos Caminos apart from your local *taqueria.*

373 Park Ave. South (btwn 26th and 27th sts.). ✆ 212/294-1000. Reservations recommended. Appetizers $8–$12; entrees $17–$24. AE, DISC, MC, V. Sun 11:30am–11pm; Tues–Thurs 11:30am–midnight; Fri–Sat 11:30am–1am. Subway: 6 to 28th St.

Pure Food and Wine ☆☆ VEGAN   I admit, the prospect of dining at a vegetarian restaurant where none of the food is heated above 118°F—in other words, served raw—did not excite me. Raw foods seem to be one of the hot new trends and I'm always skeptical of new trends, but after the first few sips of my organic, unfiltered sake cocktail, my prejudices began to dissolve. And after experiencing the spicy Thai lettuce wraps with tamarind chili sauce, daikon summer rolls with coconut, green papaya in a ginger lime dipping sauce, a white corn tamale with raw cacao (chocolate) mole, and a magnificent, zucchini and green zebra tomato lasagna, I was a convert—well almost. How was it that the food I was eating could have such depths of flavor and also be so healthy? Did this mean that the excellent organic wine I was drinking was actually good for me? Who knows? The spacious restaurant, a venture by restaurateur Jeffrey Chodorow and acclaimed chef Matthew Kenney, also features a beautiful 75-seat outdoor garden.

54 Irving Place (at 17th St.). ✆ 212/477-1010. www.purefoodandwine.com. Reservations recommended. Main courses $18–$23. AE, DISC, MC, V. Sun–Wed 5:30–11pm; Thurs–Sat 5:30pm–midnight. Subway: 4, 5, 6, N, R, Q to 14th St./Union Square.

INEXPENSIVE

City Bakery ★ *Kids* ORGANIC AMERICAN   City Bakery offers comfort food that manages to be delicious, nutritious, *and* eco-friendly. Its salad bar is unlike any you'll find in the city, where the integrity of the ingredients is as important as the taste. This is health food, alright—roasted beets with walnuts, glistening sautéed greens, lavender eggplant tossed in miso—but with heart and soul, offering such classic favorites as French toast with artisanal bacon, deeply flavorful mac 'n cheese, fried chicken, tortilla pie, even smoked salmon with all the trimmings on Sunday. The "bakery" in the name refers to the plethora of sinful desserts; kids love the spinning wheel of chocolate and the homemade marshmallows. One caveat: It's a bit pricey for a salad bar, but oh, what good eats.

3 W. 18th St. (btwn Fifth and Sixth aves.). ℂ 212/366-1414. Salad bar $12 per lb.; soups $4–$7; sandwiches $5–$10. AE, MC, V. Mon–Fri 7:30am–7pm; Sat 7:30am–6:30pm; Sun 9am–6pm. Subway: N, R, Q, 4, 5, 6 to Union Square.

Eisenberg's Coffee Shop *Finds* SANDWICHES   Eisenberg's has always been, and remains, the real deal. This old-world luncheonette has been dishing up the same eggs/bacon/burgers/sandwiches since 1929, at pretty much the same prices—adjusted for inflation, of course, but still welcomingly wallet-friendly.

One of the best things about Eisenberg's is the folks who work there, some of whom have seemingly been there since the Eisenhower era. More likely than not, you'll be

---

The Hole Truth: NY's Best Bagels

There isn't much more New York than a bagel, and New Yorkers are very loyal to their favorite bagel purveyors; in fact, discussions about who makes the best bagel can lead to heated arguments. Following are the top contenders:

Absolute Bagels, 2708 Broadway, between 107th and 108th streets (ℂ 212/932-2105). A new player on the bagel scene, their egg bagels, hot out of the oven, melt in your mouth, and their whitefish salad is perfectly smoky though not overpowering.

Ess-A-Bagel, 359 First Ave., at 21st Street (ℂ 212/260-2252; www.ess-a-bagel.com). When it comes to size, Ess-a-Bagel's are the best of the biggest; plump, chewy, and oh so satisfying. Also at 831 Third Ave., between 50th and 51st streets (ℂ 212/980-1010).

H&H Bagels, 2239 Broadway, at 80th Street (ℂ 212/595-8003; www.handh bagel.com). Long reputed as the best bagel in New York—which may have resulted in the arrogant price hike to $1 a bagel. Some complain they are a bit too sweet, but I disagree. The bagels here are always fresh and warm, the bagel aficionado's prerequisite. Also at 639 W. 46th St., at Twelfth Avenue (ℂ 212/595-8000). Take out only.

Murray's Bagels, 500 Sixth Ave., between 12th and 13th streets (ℂ 212/462-2830); and 242 Eighth Ave., at 23rd Street (ℂ 646/638-1334). There's nothing like a soft, warm bagel to begin your day with, and Murray's does them beautifully. Their smoked fish goes perfectly on their bagels.

greeted with a growled "Hiya, sweetheart," or a gravelly "What'll it be, love?" Pony up to the long counter or nab one of the four or five tables and place your order. Is this the best tuna in town as often proclaimed? Decide for yourself. Or try the egg or chicken salad. Either way, you won't go wrong. Morning diners can choose from a number of egg dishes, including a Western omelet or pastrami and eggs. The egg cream—that frothy mix of milk, chocolate syrup, and real from-the-bottle seltzer—is a classic. Service is fast and efficient.

174 Fifth Ave. (at 22nd St.). ✆ 212/675-5096. Reservations not accepted. Main courses $2.25–$7.25. No credit cards. Mon–Fri 6am–5pm; Sat 7:30am–4pm. Subway: N, R to 23rd St.

10 Times Square & Midtown West

To locate the restaurants in this section, see the map on p. 192.

VERY EXPENSIVE

In addition to the choices below, consider the two *New York Times,* four-star winners **Le Bernardin,** 155 W. 51st St., between Sixth and Seventh avenues (✆ **212/489-1515;** www.le-bernardin.com), and **Alain Ducasse,** 155 W. 58th St., between Sixth and Seventh avenues (✆ **212/265-7300**). See the sidebar "Food Splurge" on p. 214.

Atelier ★★★ FRENCH   It can be tough to find a restaurant in New York City where you can actually have a quiet conversation, but Atelier, housed in the Ritz-Carlton Central Park is one such place. In fact, with quiet tones, original paintings, and glass sculptures, you'll want to tread very lightly here in fear that even a bit of heavy breathing might shatter the delicate ambience. Once seated, you'll note that the food, in both taste and preparation, matches that delicately elegant mood. Start with an item such as blue fin tuna or diver scallops tartare seasoned in Osetra caviar, then follow up with spiced venison medallions with huckleberry jus. On a final, sweet note, end with a creation of rice crispy, peanut ice cream, chocolate, and condensed milk cappuccino. From start to finish, the flavors are innovatively matched and meld perfectly together. The wine list has over 1,000 varieties and the sommelier will help pair your wine with your meal. At these prices, this is not your everyday dining experience, but the staff seems to know that by providing extra-attentive service. Atelier offers a variety of tasting menus, including the very indulgent, six-course white truffle tasting for a mere $235.

50 Central Park South (at Sixth Ave.). ✆ 212/521-6125. Reservations recommended. Jackets required for men at dinner. A la carte menus available for bruch and lunch. Dinner 3-course prix fixe $85; chef tasting menu $128; seasonal tasting menu $95. AE, MC, V. Mon–Sat noon–2pm and 6:30–10pm; Sun 6:30–8:30pm; Sun brunch 10:30am–2:30pm. Subway: N, R, W to 57th St.

EXPENSIVE

At press time, a new chef at a briefly celebrated venue was finally fashioning food to match the bewitching setting. **Mix** owners Alain Ducasse and Jeffrey Chodorow plucked Francesco Berardinelli from the kitchen of Florence's Beccofino and replaced Mix's old French-American menu with Berardinelli's seasonally changing, innovative takes on classic Tuscan dishes. **Francesco at Mix** (68 W. 58th St., btwn Fifth and Sixth aves.; ✆ **212/583-0300;** main courses $22–$29) is open Tuesday through Saturday 5:30 to 11pm. Steak lovers might also consider **Nick & Stef's Steakhouse,** 9 Penn Plaza, at Eighth Avenue and 33rd Street (✆ **212/563-4444**); see the sidebar "The Prime Cut" for more info.

Abboccato ☆☆ ITALIAN   Sometimes the anticipation of a restaurant opening can equal that of the next installment in the *Star Wars* series. That was the case for me when I heard the Livanos family, owners of **Molyvos** (p. 201) and **Oceana** (p. 218), were planning to add to their already lofty resume with their take on Italian cuisine. I wasn't first on line to try Abboccato, but when I finally did, my anticipation was justified: no ordinary Italian this. The menu is very ambitious and hearty, with offerings that include appetizers like the *affetati misti* (a platter of cured meats), *pesce crudo* (raw fish marinated in olive oil), and grilled tripe and unusual, rustic pastas such as spaghettini with razor clams and mullet roe, orecchiette with cuttlefish, plus staples like tagliatelle Bolognese and spaghetti carbonara. Rich meat mains include suckling pig cooked in milk and hazelnuts and the very intense, *vaniglia e cioccolato,* vanilla scented veal cheeks and chocolate and spice stewed wild boar. Service is good, but not up to Oceana's levels. The room is a throwback in style; its round yellow booths are reminiscent of old-school 1960s New York Italian.

136 W. 55th St. (btwn Sixth and Seventh aves.). ℂ 212/265-4000. www.abboccato.com. Reservations recommended. Pasta $20–$22; main courses $26–$30. AE, DC, MC, V. Daily 6:30am–10:30am; Mon–Sat noon–3pm; Mon–Thurs 5:30–11:30PM; Fri 5:30pm–midnight; Sat 5pm–midnight; Sun noon–11pm. Subway: N, R, Q, W to 57th St.

Ben Benson's Steakhouse STEAKHOUSE   There are better steaks to be had in New York, but there aren't many better steakhouses than Ben Benson's. Located smack in the middle of midtown, Ben Benson's is loud and large and though it's definitely a man's man's man's world at Ben's, women are treated with "respect" here. You may not be one of the regular beefy football players who frequent the restaurant, or a baseball Hall-of-Famer, like Wade Boggs, who was dining here when I last went, but the affable and hard-working host, Ben himself, will make you feel like one as he works the room. Though the prime-aged steaks are obviously the draw here, I was very pleasantly surprised by the other options including the lump crab meat cocktail with a hand-grated horseradish that will absolutely clear your sinuses. Salads are also surprisingly fresh and perfectly dressed. To complement your steak, the signature being the sirloin, don't miss the creamed spinach and the wonderful hash browns.

123 W. 52nd St. (btwn Sixth and Seventh aves.). ℂ 212/581-8888. www.benbensons.com. Reservations recommended. Main courses $23–$38. AE, DC, DISC, MC, V. Mon–Thurs 11:45am–11pm; Fri 11:45am–midnight; Sat 5pm–midnight; Sun 5–10pm. Subway: B, D, F, V to 47th–50th Sts./Rockefeller Center.

db Bistro Moderne ☆ FRENCH BISTRO   Daniel Boulud of **Café Boulud** and **Daniel** (both on p. 214) fame opened db Bistro Moderne as a casual alternative to his other two restaurants. Casual in this case means you get architect Jeffrey Beers to put a hip spin on the contemporary French bistro; the result immediately attracts a fashion-conscious crowd (meaning you can wear a T-shirt here—but make sure it's Armani). To round out the casual experience, add a hamburger to the menu. But this is not your typical $5.95 burger deluxe; no, Boulud's creation comes in at a whopping $29 and is made with minced sirloin, foie gras, preserved black truffle, and braised short ribs, served on a Parmesan onion roll. If any hamburger is worth $29—and this point is very debatable—this one is. But now Boulud has even upped the hamburger ante by offering a $69 burger with fresh shaved black truffles (fries not included). So casual might mean many things, but here it does not mean cheap. Despite the silly burger excess, the food is, like all Boulud's ventures, outstanding—especially those bistro favorites bouillabaisse, *coq au vin,* and frogs' legs.

55 W. 44th St. (btwn Fifth and Sixth aves.). ☎ **212/391-2400.** Reservations required. Lunch entrees $26–$28; pre-theater 3-course prix fixe $39; dinner entrees $27–$31. AE, DC, MC, V. Mon–Sat noon–2:30pm; daily 5:45–11pm. Subway: B, D, F, Q to 42nd St.

Molyvos ★★ GREEK   I find simple, unpretentious traditional Greek food the perfect comfort food and Molyvos does it as good as just about anyone in Manhattan. You'll find all the standards here that you might in a diner in Astoria but the Greek food in those diners never tasted as good as this. Start with the cold *mezedes,* an assortment of familiar appetizers such as the spreads *tzatziki, melitzanosalata,* and *taramosalata,* and a terrific vegetable *dolmades,* grape leaves filled with rice, raisins, and pine nuts. Move on to a sampling of hot *mezedes* like spinach pie or an appetizer of grilled octopus. You think you're done? That would be a big mistake with entrees to choose from like rabbit *stifado,* a rabbit stew that tastes even better than chicken; lamb *yuvetsi,* lamb shanks slowly baked in a clay pot with orzo, cheese, and tomatoes; or a whole fish roasted in Molyvos's wood-burning grill. The very knowledgeable sommelier will pair your choices with a comparable Greek wine, of which there are many. Or, skip the wine and sample one or two of the dozens of ouzos available, but don't skip the desserts. Sure you've had baklava before, but have you ever had chocolate baklava? Yes, it's as good as it sounds.

871 Seventh Ave. (btwn 55th and 56th sts.). ☎ **212/582-7500.** www.molyvos.com. Reservations recommended. Main courses $13–$25 at lunch (most less than $20); $20–$30 at dinner (most less than $25); fixed-price lunch $23; pre-theater 3-course dinner $35 (5:30–6:45pm). AE, DC, DISC, MC, V. Daily noon–midnight. Subway: N, R to 57th St.; B, D, E to Seventh Ave.

Uncle Jack's Steakhouse ★ STEAKS   This Queens red meat institution broke into the Manhattan market in late 2003 and immediately, and deservedly, was put onto that rarefied list of one of the top steakhouses in the city (see the sidebar "The Prime Cut," on p. 194). Like so many other steakhouses, Uncle Jack's is testosterone-fueled; portions are monstrous, decor is plush and bawdy with huge banquettes, a lively bar features a large variety of single-malt scotches, and two private party rooms are run by tuxedoed waiters who know how to treat a man with "respect." All that masculinity, however, does not, and certainly should not, deter women—especially women who like a big thick cut of meat once in a while—from visiting the restaurant. Steaks are dry-aged for 21 days and that seemed perfect for the tender 28-ounce T-bone, big enough for two big eaters, I sampled, while the 48-ounce porterhouse, Uncle Jack's signature dish, was large enough for a big family. The restaurant also features chops; the thick-cut pork chop marinated for 24-hours in Jack Daniels held its own against the steak and seafood. The baked clams appetizer was as good as I've had at many Italian restaurants. Desserts are, of course, mammoth, but find room to at least share the spectacular pecan pie.

440 Ninth Ave. (at 34th St.). ☎ **212/244-0005.** www.unclejacks.com. Reservations recommended. Main courses $37–$75 (most steaks $37). AE, DC, DISC, MC, V. Mon–Sat noon–midnight. Subway: A, C, E to 34th St.

MODERATE

The family-style Italian restaurant **Carmine's** has a Times Square branch at 200 W. 44th St., between Broadway and Eighth Avenue (☎ **212/221-3800**).

Becco ★ *Finds* ITALIAN   If you're a fan of *Lidia's Italian-American Kitchen* on PBS, you'll be happy to know you can sample Lidia Bastianich's simple, hearty Italian cooking here. Becco, on Restaurant Row, is designed to serve her meals "at a different price point" (read: cheaper) than her East Side restaurant, Felidia. The prices are not rock-bottom, but in terms of service, portions, and quality, you get tremendous bang for your buck at Becco (which means to "peck, nibble, or savor something in a discriminating way"). The main courses can head north of the $20 mark, but take a look at the prix-fixe menu for $17 at lunch, $22 at dinner, which includes either a Caesar salad or antipasto plate, followed by a "Symphony of Pasta," unlimited servings of the three fresh-made daily pastas. There's also an excellent selection of Italians wines at $20 a bottle. If you can't make up your mind about dessert, have them all: a tasting plate includes gelato, cheesecake, and whatever else the dessert chef has whipped up that day. Lidia herself does turn up at Becco and Felidia regularly; you can even "Dine with Lidia" (see website for details).

345 W. 46th St. (btwn 8th and 9th aves.). (✆) 212/387-7597. www.becconyc.com. Reservations recommended. Main courses lunch $13–$25; dinner $19–$28. AE, DC, DISC, MC, V. Mon–Tues and Thurs–Fri noon–3pm; Wed 11:30am–3pm; Sat 11:30am–2:30pm; Mon 5–10pm; Tues–Wed 4:30pm–midnight; Thurs–Fri 5pm–midnight; Sat 4pm–midnight; Sun noon–10pm. Subway: C, E to 50th St.

Marseille ✿ FRENCH   Lively and casual with open, high ceilings and a tiled floor creating a Casablanca-like ambience, this restaurant, named after the infamous port city in France, features the food of that city, including its North African influences. That means you'll find entrees like Moroccan chicken, couscous, and tangine on the menu along with Provençal specialties like bouillabaisse, which comes in three varieties (chicken, vegetarian, and traditional, made with fish—stick with the traditional), short rib daube, salad nicoise, and soup *au pistou.* You can make a meal of the *meze,* small plates, which feature a tangy grilled merguez sausage, anchovies and roasted peppers, *brandade* (whipped salt cod), tapenade, and broiled sardines wrapped in lardo (thick bacon). Located in the Film Center building on Ninth Avenue, this is a good pre-theater choice, but even better when the pre-theater rush is over.

630 Ninth Ave. (at 44th St.). (✆) 212/333-2323. www.marseillenyc.com. Meze $4–$7; main courses $16–$24. AE, DC, MC, V. Mon–Fri noon–3pm; Sat–Sun 11am–4pm; Sun–Mon 5:15–11pm; Tues–Sat 5:15pm–midnight. Subway: A, C, E, 7 to 42nd St./Times Sq.

Norma's ✿✿ *Finds* CREATIVE AMERICAN BREAKFAST   Nowhere is breakfast treated with such reverence, and decadence, as at Norma's, a soaring, ultramodern ode to the ultimate comfort food. There's something for everyone on the huge menu. Classics come in styles both simple and haute: Blueberry pancakes come piled high with fresh Maine berries and Devonshire cream, while buttermilks are topped with fresh Georgia peaches and chopped walnuts. Even oatmeal is special: genuine Irish McCann's, dressed with sautéed green apples and red pears and brûléed for a flash of sugary sweetness. Don't pass on the applewood-smoked bacon, so good that it's worth blowing any diet for. Norma's can even win over breakfast foes with creative sandwiches, a generous Cobb with seared ahi, and a terrific chicken potpie. Not cheap for breakfast, but definitely worth the splurge.

At Le Parker Meridien Hotel, 118 W. 57th St. (btwn Sixth and Seventh aves.). (✆) 212/708-7460. www.parkermeridien. com. Reservations accepted. Main courses $8–$23 (most $13–$18). AE, DC, DISC, MC, V. Mon–Fri 6:30am–3pm; Sat–Sun 7am–3pm. Subway: B, N, Q, R, W to 57th St.

Virgil's Real BBQ ✿✿ *Kids* BARBECUE/SOUTHERN   Located in the heart of the theme restaurant wasteland known as Times Square is a theme restaurant that actually has good food. The "theme" is Southern barbecue and the restaurant, sprawling with dining on two levels, is made to look and feel like a Southern roadhouse with good ol' boy decorations on the walls and blues on the soundtrack. Virgil's does a very admirable job in re-creating that authentic flavor so hard to find north of the Mason-Dixon line. The spice-rubbed ribs are slow-cooked and meaty, but it's the Owensboro Lamb, smoked slices of lamb, and the Texas beef brisket, that are the standouts. Both are melt-in-your-mouth tender; the lamb is sprinkled with a flavorful mustard sauce, while the brisket is perfect with a few dabs of Virgil's homemade spicy barbecue sauce. For starters, the corn dogs with poblano mustard are something New Yorkers rarely have the pleasure of experiencing, while the BBQ nachos—tortilla chips slathered with melted cheese and barbecued pulled pork—are a meal in themselves. Desserts are what you would expect from a restaurant emulating a Southern theme: big and sweet. Try the homemade ice-cream sandwich made with the cookie of the day. Virgil's is a great place to bring the kids; they can make as much noise as they want and no one will notice.

152 W. 44th St. (btwn Sixth and Seventh aves.). © 212/921-9494. www.virgilsbbq.com. Reservations recommended. Sandwiches $6–$11; main courses and barbecue platters $13–$26 (most less than $19). AE, DC, DISC, MC, V. Sun–Mon 11:30am–11pm; Tues–Sat 11:30am–midnight. Subway: 1, 2, 3, 7, 9, N, R to 42nd St./Times Sq.

INEXPENSIVE

If you're looking for the quintessential New York Jewish deli, you have your choice between the **Stage Deli,** 834 Seventh Ave., between 53rd and 54th streets (© 212/245-7850), known for its jaw-distending celebrity sandwiches, and the **Carnegie Deli,** 854 Seventh Ave., at 55th Street (© 800/334-5606), the place to go for the best pastrami, corned beef, and cheesecake in town. For more, see the sidebar "The New York Deli News" on p. 206.

There is a very nice outlet of **John's Pizzeria** in Times Square, 260 W. 44th St., between Broadway and Eighth avenues (© 212/391-7560; subway: 1, 2, 3, 7, A, B, C, E, N, R, W, Q, S to 42nd St-Times Square: see the box, "Pizza, New York–Style," on p. 204). Also consider the aptly named **Burger Joint** 𝒢, located discreetly in the lobby of Le Parker Meridien Hotel, 118 W. 57th St. (© 212/708-7460), for cheap yet excellent no-frills burgers.

Afghan Kebab House 𝒱𝒶𝓁𝓊𝑒 MIDDLE EASTERN You'll find Afghan Kebab Houses all over the city. Are they related? Who knows, but I like this one the best for its heaping plates of first-rate Middle Eastern fare. Kebabs are the first order of business: all are pleasing, but my favorite is the *sultani,* chunks of ground lamb marinated in aromatic spices and broiled over wood coal with green peppers and tomatoes. The *tikka kebab,* in lamb or beef, is impressive, as is the chicken korma, slow-cooked with fresh onions, tomatoes, peppers, and fresh herbs. All plates come with amazingly aromatic brown Indian basmati rice and flat Afghan bread. The room is simple and well worn but evocative, with Oriental carpets serving as table runners. Service is attentive.

764 Ninth Ave. (btwn 51st and 52nd sts.). © 212/307-1612 or 212/307-1629. Reservations accepted. Main courses $10–$16 (most less than $12). AE, DC, DISC, MC, V. Daily 11:30am–10:30pm. Subway: C, E to 50th St.

Mandoo Bar 𝒢 𝑭𝒊𝒏𝒅𝒔 KOREAN The heart of Manhattan's Koreatown is 32nd Street between Fifth and Sixth avenues—and the number of Korean restaurants on that 1 block is dizzying. You'll know you've found Mandoo Bar when you see the two women in the window lovingly rolling and stuffing fresh *mandoo* (Korean for dumpling). Because of the constant preparation, the dumplings, stuffed with a variety of ingredients, are incredibly fresh. There's the mool mandoo (basic white dumplings filled with pork and vegetables), the kimchee mandoo (steamed dumplings stuffed

Pizza, New York–Style

Once the domain of countless first-rate pizzerias, Manhattan's pizza offerings have noticeably dropped in quality. The proliferation of Domino's Pizza, Pizza Hut, and other fast-food chains into the market have lowered pizza standards. Still, there is plenty of good pizza to be found. Don't be tempted by sad imitations; when it comes to pizza, search out the real deal. Here are some of the best.

Grimaldi's Pizzeria, 19 Old Fulton St., between Front and Water streets (© **718/ 858-4300;** www.grimaldis.com). If you need incentive to walk across the Brooklyn Bridge, Grimaldi's, in Brooklyn Heights, easily provides it. In fact, the pizza is so good, made in a coal oven with a rich flavorful sauce and homemade mozzarella, you might run across the bridge to get to it. Be warned, it can get very crowded at dinnertime.

John's Pizzeria, 278 Bleecker St., near Seventh Avenue South (© **212/ 243-1680**). Since it has expanded from this original location—there are now three outlets in the city—the once-gleaming luster of John's has faded slightly, but the pizza is still a cut above all the rest. Thin-crusted, and out of a coal oven with the proper ratio of tomato sauce to cheese, John's pizza has a very loyal following. Though the quality at all of the locations is very good, the original Bleecker Street location is the most old-world romantic and my favorite. Also at 260 W. 44th St., between Broadway and Eighth Avenue (© **212/391-1560**); and 408 E. 64th St., between York and First avenues (© **212/935-2895**).

Lombardi's, 32 Spring St., between Mulberry and Mott streets (© **212/ 941-7994;** www.lombardispizza.com). Claiming to be New York's first

with potent kimchi [Korean spiced cabbage], tofu, pork, and vegetables), the green vegetable mool mandoo (boiled dumplings filled with mixed vegetables), and the goon mandoo (pan-fried dumplings filled with pork and vegetables). You really can't go wrong with any of these dumplings, so sample them all with a Combo Mandoo. Soups are also special here; try the beef noodle in a spicy, sinus-clearing broth. With seating that is nothing more than wooden benches, Mandoo Bar is better suited for quick eats rather than a lingering meal—a perfect lunch break from shopping in Herald Square or visiting the nearby Empire State Building.

2 W. 32nd St. (just west of Fifth Ave.). © **212/279-3075.** Reservations not accepted. Main courses $6–$14. AE, DC, MC, V. Daily 11:30am–11pm. Subway: B, D, F, N, Q, R, V, W to 34th St./Herald Sq. Also at 71 University Place (btwn 10th and 11th sts.). © 212/358-0400. Subway: N, R, W, Q, 4, 5, 6, L to 14th St./Union Sq.

Sapporo ★ *(Finds (Value* JAPANESE NOODLES Peruse the community bulletin board as you enter Sapporo and you might find yourself a deal on an apartment—that is, if you can read Japanese characters. Thankfully, the menu is in English in this longtime Theater District authentic Japanese noodle shop. If the mostly Japanese clientele doesn't convince you of Sapporo's authenticity, the constant din of satisfied diners slurping at huge bowls of steaming ramen (noodle soup with meat and vegetables) "licensed" pizzeria, Lombardi's opened in 1905 and still uses a generations-old Neapolitan family pizza recipe. The coal oven kicks out perfectly cooked pies, some topped with ingredients such as pancetta, homemade sausage, and even fresh-shucked clams. It's hard to go wrong here no matter what tops the pizza. A garden in the back makes it even more inviting during warm weather.

Patsy's Pizzeria, 2287 First Ave., between 117th and 118th streets (© 212/534-9783). My favorite, and also the favorite of Frank Sinatra, who liked it so much he had pies packed and flown out to Las Vegas. The coal oven here has been burning since 1932 and though the neighborhood in East Harlem where it is located has had its ups and downs, the quality of pizza at Patsy's has never wavered. Try the marinara pizza, a pie with fresh marinara sauce but no cheese that's so good you won't miss the mozzarella. Unlike the other pizzerias mentioned here, you can order by the slice at Patsy's. Don't be fooled by imitators using Patsy's name; this is the original and the best.

Totonno's Pizzeria Napolitano, 1524 Neptune Ave., between West 15th and West 16th streets, Coney Island, Brooklyn (© 718/372-8606). This unassuming little pizzeria has been at the same spot since 1924 and it makes pizzas almost exactly as it did 80 years ago—thin crust, fresh sauce, and mozzarella, and that's about it. Don't even think about asking for an exotic topping on these pies (and why would you?). Enjoy it in all its simple unadorned glory. Totonno's second branch, on the Upper East Side, 1544 Second Ave., between 80th and 81st streets (© 212/327-2800), opened about 10 years ago—go ahead and order the exotic toppings there, but for the real deal, go to Coney Island.

surely will. And though the ramen is Sapporo's well-deserved specialty, the *gyoza* (Japanese dumplings) and the *donburi* (pork or chicken over rice with soy-flavored sauce) are also terrific. Best of all, nothing on the menu is over $10 and that's not easy to accomplish in the oft-overpriced Theater District.

152 W. 49th St. (btwn Sixth and Seventh aves.). © 212/869-8972. Reservations not accepted. Main courses $6–$9. No credit cards. Mon–Sat 11am–11pm; Sun 11am–10pm. Subway: N, R to 49th St.

Uncle Nick's GREEK   For stupendous portions of surprisingly good traditional Greek food at ridiculous prices, come to Uncle Nick's. Turn off your cellphone upon entering, not because you might disturb your neighbors, but because there is no way you will be able to have a phone conversation in this very loud restaurant. But how can you talk if your mouth is filled with one or more of Nick's Greek dips like *taramosalata* or *tzatziki,* or his perfectly tender, grilled baby octopus. If you haven't filled up on his appetizers, order one of Nick's grilled specialties; the grilled lamb kabob is an absolute winner and guaranteed for leftovers while the gyro plate is a challenge for those with even the heartiest appetites. Seafood is also very good, especially the swordfish kabobs. Desserts are standard; you won't have room for them anyway. Service is

The New York Deli News

There's nothing more Noo Yawk than hunkering down over a mammoth pastrami on rye at an authentic Jewish deli, where anything you order comes with a bowl of lip-smacking sour dills and a side of attitude. Here are some of the best.

Artie's New York Delicatessen, 2290 Broadway, between 82nd and 83rd streets (© 212/579-5959; www.arties.com). This new kid on the deli block can hold its own on the playground with the big boys, thank you very much, especially in the wiener department.

Barney Greengrass, the Sturgeon King, 541 Amsterdam Ave., between 86th and 87th streets on the Upper West Side (© 212/724-4707). This unassuming, daytime-only deli has become legendary for its high-quality salmon (sable, gravlax, Nova Scotia, kippered, lox, pastrami—you choose), whitefish, and sturgeon (of course).

Carnegie Deli, 854 Seventh Ave., at 55th Street (© 800/334-5606 or 212/757-2245; www.carnegiedeli.com), where it's worth subjecting yourself to surly service, tourist-targeted overpricing, and elbow-to-elbow seating for some of the best pastrami and corned beef in town. Even big eaters may be challenged by mammoth sandwiches with names like "Fifty Ways to Love Your Liver" (chopped liver, hard-boiled egg, lettuce, tomato, and onion).

Katz's Delicatessen ★★, the city's best deli, remains fabulously old-world despite its hipster-hot Lower East Side location at 205 E. Houston St., at Ludlow Street (© 212/254-2246). For more on Katz's, see p. 182.

Second Avenue Deli, 156 Second Ave., at 10th Street (© 800/NYC-DELI or 212/677-0606), is the best kosher choice in town (for all you goyim out there, that means no milk, butter, or cheese is served). There's no bowing to tourism here—this is the real deal. The service is brusque, the decor is nondescript, and the sandwiches don't have cute names, but the dishes are true New York classics: gefilte fish, matzo-ball soup, chicken livers, potato knishes, nova lox, and eggs. What more do you want from a deli?

Stage Deli, 834 Seventh Ave., between 53rd and 54th streets (© 212/245-7850; www.stagedeli.com), is noisy and crowded and packed with tourists, but it's still as authentic as they come. The celebrity sandwiches, ostensibly created by the personalities themselves, are jaw-distending mountains of top-quality fixings: The Tom Hanks is roast beef, chopped liver, onion, and chicken fat, while the Dolly Parton is (drumroll, please) twin rolls of corned beef and pastrami.

friendly to match the rollicking atmosphere here. Next door is the slightly more intimate, Uncle Nick's Ouzeria specializing in *mezedes,* Greek small dishes like tapas. 747 Ninth Ave. (btwn 50th and 51st sts.). © 212/245-7992. Appetizers $5–$10; main courses $10–$17. Sun–Thurs 11:30am–11pm; Fri–Sat noon–11:30pm. Subway: C or E to 50th St. Nick's Ouzeria next door at 749 Ninth Ave. (© 212/397-2892).

Wondee Siam ★ *Finds* THAI   Hell's Kitchen offers countless ethnic culinary variations and one of the most prevalent is Thai—there are at least six in a 5-block radius. My favorite among these is the tiny, zero-ambience Wondee Siam. I don't need colorful decorations or a big fish tank to enjoy authentic, uncompromisingly spicy Thai food and that's what I get at Wondee Siam. Here you don't have to worry that your waiter will assume you want a milder form of Thai. If there is a little red asterisk next to your item, you can be sure it is appropriately spicy. The soups are terrific, especially the sinus-clearing Tom Yum. In fact, there is a whole section of Yum (chilis) dishes on the menu; my favorite being the Larb Gai, minced ground chicken with ground toasted rice. The curries are also first rate as are the noodles, including the mild pad Thai. This is strictly BYOB and you'll want to do so to complement the spicy food. If you want a bit more comfort, try Wondee Siam II 1 block up. But make sure you ask your waiter not to dumb down the spice and serve up the food authentic Thai style.

792 Ninth Ave. (btwn 52nd and 53rd sts.). ✆ **212/459-9057.** Reservations not accepted. Main courses $7.50–$18 (most under $10). No credit cards. Mon–Sat 11am–11pm; Sun 11am–10:30pm. Subway: C, E to 50th St. Wondee Siam II, 813 Ninth Ave. (btwn 53rd and 54th sts.). ✆ **917/286-1726.**

11 Midtown East & Murray Hill

To locate the restaurants in this section, see the map on p. 192.

EXPENSIVE

Aquavit ★★★ SCANDINAVIAN   I'll miss the waterfall and the intimate town house setting that Aquavit regrettably vacated in early 2005. Thankfully, however, the food and staff have had no trouble adjusting to the transition. Everything remains impeccably first rate. The restaurant is now housed in the bottom of a glass tower on East 55th Street, and designed in sleek Scandinavian style with modernist furniture. In the front of the restaurant is an informal and less expensive cafe while past a long bar, is the dining room.

After the move, if anything, the food has improved. The smoked fish—really all the fish—is prepared perfectly. I often daydream about the herring plate: four types of herring accompanied by a tiny glass of Aquavit, distilled liquor not unlike vodka flavored with fruit and spices, and a frosty Carlsberg beer. The hot smoked Arctic char on the main a la carte menu, served with clams and bean puree in a mustard green broth, is also a winner. Most fixed-price menus offer a well-chosen beverage accompaniment option.

65 E. 55th St. (btwn Park and Madison aves.). ✆ **212/307-7311.** www.aquavit.org. Reservations recommended. Cafe main courses $9–$20; 3-course fixed-price meal $20 at lunch, $32 at dinner. Main dining room fixed-price meal $35 at lunch, $75 at dinner ($39 for vegetarians); 3-course pre-theater dinner (5:30–6:15pm) $55; tasting menus $48 at lunch, $100 at dinner ($58 for vegetarians); supplement for paired wines $25 at lunch, $50 at dinner. AE, DC, MC, V. Daily noon–2:30pm and 5:30–10:30pm. Subway: E, F to Fifth Ave.

BLT Steak ★★★ STEAKHOUSE/BISTRO   Steakhouses are often stereotyped as bastions of male bonding; testosterone-fueled with red meat and hearty drinks. But BLT (Bistro Laurent Tourendel) Steak breaks that mold in a big way; on the night I visited, I noticed more women—slinky and model-like, chomping on thick cuts of beef than men. That doesn't mean men can't also enjoy the beef here; served in cast iron pots and finished in steak butter with a choice of sauces—béarnaise, red wine, horseradish, and blue cheese, to name a few. The signature is the Porterhouse for two (a whopping $70), but I recommend the New York strip or the succulent short ribs braised in red wine. Both dishes can be shared, which may be a good idea, especially after devouring the airy complimentary popovers and sampling an appetizer like the incredible tuna tartare or a side of onion rings, potato gratin, or creamy spinach. Even after sharing one of the meats, you might not have room for the memorable chestnut-chocolate sundae or peanut butter chocolate mousse, and that would be a shame. This is not a restaurant for intimate conversation; even the music was muffled by the cacophonous din of the diners.

106 E. 57th St. (btwn Park and Lexington aves.). ℭ **212/752-7470.** www.bltsteak.com. Reservations highly recommended. Main courses $24–$39. AE, DC, MC, V. Mon–Fri 11:45am–2:30pm; Mon–Thurs 5:30–11pm; Fri–Sat 5:30–11:30pm. Subway: 4, 5, 6, N, R, W to 59th St.

L'Impero ★★ ITALIAN   The landmark neighborhood Tudor City, situated across the street from the United Nations, is musty and old-fashioned, a classic slice of 1920s Manhattan—and until recently remained an undiscovered enclave for many longtime Manhattanites. Luckily, chef Scott Conant is drawing people to the neighborhood with his refined L'Impero, with its elegant furnishings indoors and a lovely vintage courtyard outside. The food, too, is elegant, with an emphasis on fresh, seasonal ingredients. Start with the fricassee of seasonal mushrooms. For a main course, try the rabbit risotto or seared branzino. A house specialty is the duck and foie gras agnolotti.

45 Tudor City Place (btwn 42nd and 43rd sts.). ℭ **212/599-5045.** www.limpero.com. Reservations recommended. Main courses $18–$29. AE, DC, MC, V. Mon–Thurs noon–2pm and 5:30–10:15pm; Fri–Sat 5–11:15pm. Subway: 4, 5, 6 to Grand Central.

Oceana ★★★ SEAFOOD   When you enter Oceana, the nautical themes are obvious. But this is no seafood shack; it's more like a luxury ocean liner, with its food prepared by the talented Cornelius Gallagher. Standouts among Gallagher's culinary creations include tartare of yellowfin tuna with daikon radish, black cardamom, and horseradish sorbet; striped bass wrapped in a ham croissant; and stuffed artichoke and Icelandic cod basted in butter and herbs. His dishes look so good on the plate you might not want to eat them, but that would be a big mistake. In this case the artwork is extremely edible. Oceana also features an excellent wine list and your waiter will help pair wines with your dishes if you desire. Though this is not your everyday restaurant—prices are too steep for that—the atmosphere is relaxed and the service very personable.

55 E. 54th St. (btwn Park and Madison aves.). ℭ **212/759-5941.** www.oceanarestaurant.com. Reservations recommended. AE, DISC, MC, V. 3-course prix fixe $48 lunch; $72 dinner. Mon–Fri noon–2:30pm; Mon–Sat 5:30–10:30pm. Subway: E, F to Fifth Ave.

Pampano ★★ MEXICAN SEAFOOD   I'm usually wary of overly presented and overpriced Mexican food, much preferring the working-stiff stuff I can buy from the taco trucks in East Harlem. Pampano, however, does things with Mexican ingredients, especially seafood, that no taco truck I know has ever done before—and the lovely, lush town house location is so much more comfortable. You might want to venture from the fish on the menu, but I wouldn't recommend it. Start with the ceviche tasting of either three or four ceviches; they are all spectacular, especially the mahimahi bathed in lemon juice, cilantro, chiles, and avocado. For a rare and very special treat try a lobster taco—you won't find that at your local *taqueria.* Of the entrees, it would be difficult to order anything but the fantastic *pampano adobado,* sautéed pompano with creamy black rice, roasted garlic, and chile guajillo sauce, but you won't suffer too much if you settle for the very memorable pan-fried baby red snapper in a chile de arbol sauce. Save room for chocolate flan for dessert and maybe a cleansing shot of one of the restaurant's many excellent tequilas. Pampano is a scene, but a festive one with a lively bar and a beautiful upstairs dining area.

209 E. 49th St. (at Third Ave.). ℂ **212/751-4545.** Reservations recommended. Main courses $21–$26. AE, DC, MC, V. Mon–Fri 11:30am–3pm; Sun–Tues 5–10pm; Wed–Sat 5–11pm. Subway: E, V to Lexington Ave./53rd St.; 6 to 51st St.

Riingo ⭐ JAPANESE FUSION   Marcus Samuelsson, the man mostly responsible for the wonders served at **Aquavit** (p. 207), here puts his spin on the flavors of Japan. And the results are mixed. The tuna Caesar salad with sea urchin vinaigrette is interesting yet not quite right, while the odd combination of rib-eye carpaccio with warm eel is a winner. The nori-wrapped foie gras is another, er, unique combination—this one must be an acquired taste, one I have yet to acquire. But the beef short ribs braised in beer and served with an apple puree is pure perfection. If you don't want to experiment, plenty of your standard sushi items are available, all exceptionally fresh and prepared immaculately. The sides are special here, particularly the coconut bok choy and the potato pancake. Desserts, while innovative, don't wow me. The restaurant is cramped and loud. The low-ceilinged dining room upstairs can be somewhat claustrophobic; try to snag a table in the rear dining room; or if you just want sushi, take a seat at the sushi bar. Riingo is a work in progress that, under Samuelsson, should only improve.

205 E. 45th St. (at Third Ave.). ℂ **212/867-4200.** Reservations recommended. Main courses $14–$42. AE, DISC, MC, V. Mon–Fri noon–3pm; Sun–Wed 5:30–10:30pm; Thurs–Sat 5:30–11pm. Subway: 4, 5, 6, 7 to 42nd St.

MODERATE

P.J. Clarke's ⭐ AMERICAN   Clarke's has been a New York institution for over 50 years—a late-night hangout for politicians, actors, and athletes. This is where Ray Milland went on a bender in the classic 1948 movie *The Lost Weekend.* Maybe if Milland stopped drinking and had one of P.J. Clarke's legendary hamburgers, he wouldn't have ended up in Bellevue. Clarke's hamburger, like the old wood walls, the broken telephone booth, and the hidden dining nook for two, has also been blessedly preserved. Nothing more than a slab of chopped meat cooked to order, on a bun and for the curious price of $8.10, the hamburger is a simple masterpiece. Try it with P.J's home fries or onion rings. Salads also are a good accompaniment to the beef, particularly the tomato, red onion, and blue cheese salad. If meat is not your thing, a very good raw bar was added. Beer, the drink of choice here, comes in mugs but pints are available, just ask. Amidst the steel and glass skyscrapers of Third Avenue, old P.J. Clarke's is a welcome relief.

Upstairs at P.J. Clarke's is a separate, more intimate restaurant called **Sidecar.** With its own kitchen, Sidecar features more food options than Clarke's, but don't worry, you can still get the famous hamburger here as well.

915 Third Ave. (at 55th St.). ℂ **212/317-1616.** www.pjclarkes.com. Main courses $8–$21. AE, MC, V. Daily 11:30am–4am. Sidecar daily 11:30am–1am. Subway: E, V to Lexington Ave.

INEXPENSIVE

The lower concourse of **Grand Central Terminal** ⭐⭐, 42nd Street at Park Avenue, has developed into a quick-bite bonanza that makes it an ideal choice for lunch—and the setting is an architecture-lover's delight. Head downstairs from the main concourse and choose among the many outlets, offering everything from bratwurst to sushi. Standouts among the bounty include **Junior's,** an adorable offshoot of the Brooklyn stalwart, serving deli sandwiches, terrific steak-burgers, and their world-famous cheesecake in their own waiter-serviced dining area. (With a few exceptions, most of the other outlets are takeout counters; diners can then avail themselves of the abundant and comfortable seating at the center of the concourse.) **Little Pie Company** serves up fantastic pies, plus fresh-baked morning muffins and the concourse's best coffee. **Cafe Spice Express** serves up terrific Indian fare, while countermates **Christer's** and **Knödel** specialize, respectively, in traditional batter-dipped fish and chips and terrific German-style brats, wieners, and sausages. There's also an outpost of popular pizzeria **Two Boots.** If you want beer or wine to accompany your meal, visit one of the two **bar cars,** which sit near tracks 105 and 112.

(Kids Family-Friendly Restaurants

While it's always smart to call ahead to make sure a restaurant has kids' menus and highchairs, you can count on the following to be especially accommodating. What kid doesn't love pizza? See the sidebar "Pizza, New York–Style," on p. 204 for suggestions.

Here are some other options for the whole family:

Big Nick's Burger and Pizza Joint ⚐ (p. 219) In the unlikely event that your kids can't find anything they like on the 27-page menu, they can just tune into the nonstop *Three Stooges* marathon playing on the restaurant's TVs.

Carmine's ⚐ (p. 217 and 201) This rollicking family-style Italian restaurant was created with kids in mind. You won't have to worry about them making too much noise here.

City Bakery ⚐ (p. 198) What child wouldn't be taken with the chocolate spinning wheel and homemade marshmallows? As a bonus, the organic fare is nutritious *and* delicious.

Dinosaur Bar-B-Que ⚐ (p. 223) Loud and casual, kids come away with dinosaur tattoos to go with the barbecue sauce stains that they will undoubtedly wear on their clothes.

Good Enough to Eat ⚐ (p. 221) Comfort food for kids, like macaroni and cheese, pizza, and great desserts.

Mickey Mantle's (see chapter 11) As a player, the Mick had a reputation for being testy with autograph hounds and children, but he more than made up for it in retirement when he opened his extremely kid-friendly restaurant located just across the street from Central Park.

Nick's Family-Style Restaurant and Pizzeria ⚐ (p. 222) With locations in both Queens and Manhattan, Nick's has been wowing families for over a decade with its praiseworthy pizza and Italian specialties.

Serendipity 3 (p. 223) Kids will love this whimsical restaurant and ice-cream shop, which serves up a huge menu of American favorites, followed up by colossal ice-cream treats.

Tavern on the Green (p. 215) Your kids will be wowed by the Central Park setting, and a children's menu makes them easy and affordable to feed. What's more, if the little ones get rambunctious, you just have to take them outdoors to blow off a little steam.

Virgil's Real BBQ ⚐⚐ (p. 202) This pleasing Times Square barbecue joint welcomes kids with open arms—and Junior will be more than happy, I'm sure, to be *allowed* to eat with his hands.

For a glorious meal, dining under an impressive curved and tiled ceiling, try the New York landmark **Oyster Bar & Restaurant** ᴦ ((℗ **212/490-6650;** www.oysterbarny.com). For a complete list of vendors, check out **www.grandcentralterminal.com**.

In addition to the listings below, there's also **Ess-A-Bagel** (see "The Hole Truth: NY's Best Bagels," p. 198) at 831 Third Ave., at 51st Street (℗ **212/980-1010**).

Kalustyan's ᴦ MIDDLE EASTERN/INTERNATIONAL DELI   The heady smell of spices and barrels full of nuts and other delicacies may have you lingering on the first floor, but before you start loading up with exotica, take the stairs up to the deli. A smiling little man in a white hat will likely be there to greet you. Magazine and newspaper articles plastered all over the place feature photographs of your new friend, the smiling little man with the white cap. Ask for the *mujadarra* (a traditional Arabian lentil and rice dish with caramelized onions, served as a salad or in pita bread), pay $4, and settle in at one of the little window-side tables.

123 Lexington Ave. (at 28th St.). ℗ 212/685-3451. www.kalustyans.com. AE, MC, V. Soups, salads, sandwiches under $10. Mon–Sat 10am–8pm; Sun 11am–7pm. Subway: 6 to 28 St.

Prime Burger AMERICAN/HAMBURGERS   Across the street from St. Patrick's Cathedral, this no-frills coffee shop is a heavenly find in a high-priced 'hood. The juicy burgers and well-stuffed sandwiches are tasty, the fries crispy and generous. The front seats, which might remind you of old wooden grammar-school desks, are great fun—especially when business-suited New Yorkers take their places at these oddities. A great stop during a day of Fifth Avenue shopping.

5 E. 51st St. (btwn Fifth and Madison aves.). ℗ 212/759-4729. Reservations not accepted. Main courses $3.25–$9. No credit cards. Mon–Fri 6am–6:30pm; Sat 6am–5pm. Subway: 6 to 51st St.

12 Upper West Side

To locate the restaurants in this section, see the map on p. 212.

VERY EXPENSIVE

Also consider the two four-star-rated restaurants on Columbus Circle: **Jean-Georges** ᴦᴦᴦ, in the Trump International Hotel & Tower, 1 Central Park West, at 60th Street/Columbus Circle (℗ **212/299-3900;** www.jean-georges.com) and **Masa,** in the Time Warner Center, 10 Columbus Circle (℗ **212/823-9800**). See the sidebar "Food Splurge" on p. 214.

Café des Artistes ᴦ FRENCH   One of the oldest restaurants in Manhattan, Café des Artistes was established in 1917 as a haven for artists, many whom lived in the surrounding area or upstairs at the Hotel des Artistes. One of those artists was Howard Chandler Christy, who painted the gorgeous "wood nymph" murals that still adorn the restaurant. Now, however, not many artists can afford the solid, country French food served at the Café. But this is a place to splurge—to soak in not only the history, but the romantic aura emanating from those murals. You won't find any fancy twists on French cooking here and I recommend sticking with the old favorites such as the starters, salmon five ways or snails (not escargots?), or entrées such as Dover sole with brown butter sauce, roasted duck, or the challengingly hearty *pot-au-feu,* complete with marrow bone. For dessert, the chocolate bread pudding is a treat, while the hot fudge Napoleon was truly, as described by my waiter, a "killer." The waiters here have been around the block a few times, so service is refreshingly old school. The restaurant does

Uptown Dining

Absolute Bagels **1**

Aix **5**

Artie's New York Delicatessen **11**

Barney Greengrass,
  the Sturgeon King **6**

Big Nick's Burger and Pizza Joint **16**

Café des Artistes **19**

Café Boulud **27**

Carmine's **4**

Celeste **8**

'Cesca **17**

Cold Stone Creamery **29**

Daniel **25**

El Paso Taqueria **31, 32**

Flor de Mayo **2**

Good Enough to Eat **10**

Gray's Papaya **18**

H&H Bagels **12**

Jean-Georges **23**

Kai **26**

Masa **22**

The Neptune Room **8**

Nice Matin **14**

Nick's Family-Style Restaurant
  and Pizzeria **30**

Noche Mexicana **3**

Nonna **7**

Onera **15**

Ouest **9**

Rosa Mexicano **21**

Savann **13**

Serendipity 3 **24**

Tavern on the Green **20**

Totonno's Pizzeria Napolitano **28**

V Steakhouse **22**

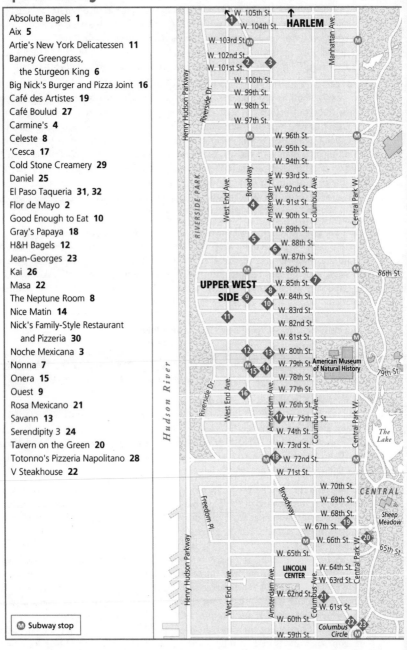

Ⓜ Subway stop

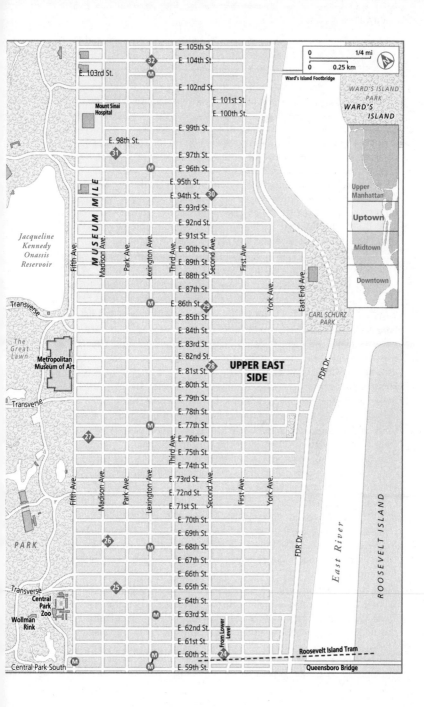

E. 105th St.
E. 104th St.
E. 103rd St.
E. 102nd St.
E. 101st St.
E. 100th St.
E. 99th St.
E. 98th St.
E. 97th St.
E. 96th St.
E. 95th St.
E. 94th St.
E. 93rd St.
E. 92nd St.
E. 91st St.
E. 90th St.
E. 89th St.
E. 88th St.
E. 87th St.
E. 86th St.
E. 85th St.
E. 84th St.
E. 83rd St.
E. 82nd St.
E. 81st St.
E. 80th St.
E. 79th St.
E. 78th St.
E. 77th St.
E. 76th St.
E. 75th St.
E. 74th St.
E. 73rd St.
E. 72nd St.
E. 71st St.
E. 70th St.
E. 69th St.
E. 68th St.
E. 67th St.
E. 66th St.
E. 65th St.
E. 64th St.
E. 63rd St.
E. 62nd St.
E. 61st St.
E. 60th St.
E. 59th St.

Mount Sinai Hospital

Jacqueline Kennedy Onassis Reservoir

MUSEUM MILE

Fifth Ave.
Madison Ave.
Park Ave.
Lexington Ave.
Third Ave.
Second Ave.
First Ave.
York Ave.
East End Ave.

Transverse

The Great Lawn

Metropolitan Museum of Art

Transverse

Third Ave.

PARK

Transverse

Central Park Zoo

Wollman Rink

Central Park South

Madison Ave.
Park Ave.
Lexington Ave.

Fifth Ave.

UPPER EAST SIDE

CARL SCHURZ PARK

FDR Dr.

FDR Dr.

East River

ROOSEVELT ISLAND

From Lower Level

Roosevelt Island Tram
Queensboro Bridge

Ward's Island Footbridge

WARD'S ISLAND PARK

WARD'S ISLAND

Upper Manhattan

Uptown

Midtown

Downtown

0   1/4 mi
0   0.25 km

Food Splurge

New York can often be silly with excess especially when it comes to food. This is, after all, the city where a restaurant offers a seasonal double-truffle burger for $99 and a breakfast joint recently pushed a caviar-stuffed frittata (that's an omelet with salty fish eggs) for $1,000. But also in this city there is never a shortage of people who are willing to fork it over just for the pleasure of eating in a four-star restaurant—the waiting lists for reservations at these places are sometimes months long. We, of course, would never waste our hard-earned money on such a frivolous thing as perfectly prepared and presented food in a memorable environment where the customer is really treated like royalty. Or would we?

Well, you only live once. So if you are going to go for it, here are five of New York's most expensive and best restaurants.

Alain Ducasse, 155 W. 58th St., between Sixth and Seventh avenues (© 212/265-7300). Ducasse is one of the renowned chefs in the world. In 2005 his New York restaurant received four stars from the *New York Times.* His tasting menu, as of this writing, consisted of seven courses for a mere $225, not including wine, while the black truffle menu was a bit higher at $265.

Daniel, 60 E. 65th St., between Madison and Park avenues (© 212/288-0033; www.danielnyc.com). Neo-Renaissance features—rich mahogany doors, elegant Corinthian columns, and a soaring terra-cotta-tiled ceiling—make an ideal setting for acclaimed chef Daniel Boulud's faultless classic-goes-country French cooking. His eight-course tasting menu goes for $168, while you can get away relatively cheap here with a three-course prix fixe for $92.

Jean-Georges, in the Trump International Hotel & Tower, 1 Central Park West, at 60th Street/Columbus Circle (© 212/299-3900; www.jean-georges.com). Another *New York Times* four-star winner, the signature restaurant of Jean-Georges Vongerichten is the ultimate special occasion restaurant. And it better be a special occasion if you are going to shell out around $100 for his tasting menu, not including wine.

Le Bernardin, 155 W. 51st St., between Sixth and Seventh avenues (© 212/489-1515; www.le-bernardin.com). Always one of the top New York restaurants in the annual *Zagat* guide, Le Bernardin also garnered four stars from the *New York Times* in 2005. So I guess it must be good. One of these days, when I save up enough money to pay for the $150 tasting menu, I hope to find out.

Masa, 10 Columbus Circle (© 212/823-9800). This sushi joint in the Time Warner Center became a major conversation piece when the *New York Times* gave it four stars in 2005. The conversation was not so much about the undoubtedly exquisite sushi prepared by the genius of chef/owner Masayoshi Takayama, but more about the price, starting at $300 and sometimes climbing to $500 per person for the chef's *omakase* lunch or dinner.

a very brisk, pre–Lincoln Center business, so if you want intimacy and romance, the main reason to come here, reserve before or after the crush.

1 W. 67th St. (at Central Park West). © **212/877-3500.** www.cafenyc.com. Reservations strongly recommended. Jackets preferred. Main courses $18–$26 for lunch; $29–$42 for dinner. AE, DC, DISC, MC, V. Mon–Fri noon–3pm; brunch Sat 11am–3pm; Sun 10am–3pm; Mon–Sat 5:30pm–12:30am; Sun 5:30–11pm. Subway: 1, 9 to 66th St.

EXPENSIVE

Also consider the legendary Central Park restaurant **Tavern on the Green,** Central Park West and West 67th Street (© **212/873-3200**). Here, food takes a back seat to dining in one of the city's prettiest settings. Views over the park are wonderful; in good weather, try for a seat in the outdoor garden, with its whimsical topiary shrubs and Japanese lanterns. It's also a great place to visit during the holidays, and there's a menu just for kids.

Aix ★★ MODERN FRENCH   This smartly designed, airy, and comfortable tri-level restaurant is helmed by chef Didier Virot, formerly the executive chef at Jean-Georges, and offers some surprisingly fresh twists on the traditional cuisine of Provence. Virot takes a classic dish like the vegetable soup, *pistou,* but adds fresh raw sardines—it not only works, it enhances the soup. Both the baked chicken with star anise, honey, mushrooms, and fingerling potatoes and the Atlantic char with a smoked salmon sauce were done to perfection. The only mistake I encountered on the menu was the bland gnocchi with Jerusalem artichoke and black truffle cream. Desserts are adventurous and may not be for everyone, but it's not often you have the chance to experience Provence salad, sugared green tomatoes, and celery topped with mint sorbet; or a licorice panna cotta. Despite the crowds, Aix's service was personable; waitresses in dowdy brown uniforms were cheerfully helpful, but the restaurant is loud, so don't expect intimacy.

2398 Broadway (at 88th St.). © **212/874-7400.** www.aixnyc.com. Reservations highly recommended. Main courses $26–$39. AE, MC, V. Sun–Thurs 5:30–10:30pm; Fri–Sat 5:30–11pm. Subway: 1, 9 to 86th St.

'Cesca ★★ ITALIAN COUNTRY   Give chef and owner Tom Valenti credit as the man most responsible for bringing first-class, innovative dining to the Upper West Side. It started a few years ago with the opening of Ouest (see below), and in 2003 he added another gem to the neighborhood when he opened 'Cesca. It's not easy to describe the Italian food served in 'Cesca; it's like nothing many New Yorkers have experienced. Where else have you had roasted sardines paired with a "soft" egg? With a roaring wood-burning oven as its centerpiece—which is used to roast everything from oysters to peppers—this is as rustic as it gets. Valenti even roasts mushrooms, which I tried with a rich creamy cheese-filled polenta. It's like you're in an Italian farmhouse where you are served slow-cooked meats like pork shank, the fat cooked off and the meat falling from the bone, or a hearty potato gnocchi with tender braised duck. The food is so intense here; a little goes a very long way. But try to save room for the equally interesting desserts like honey goat-milk gelato or fresh figs with fig gelato. Service is friendly and informal and the restaurant is spacious and comfortable, with a large bar area complete with long tables where you snack on marinated olives, fritto misto, or spicy parmigiana fritters while sipping unusual Italian wines from regions like Sicily, Puglia, or Trentino. At press time, this was the most popular restaurant on the Upper West Side, so call well ahead for reservations.

164 W. 75th St. (at Amsterdam Ave.). © **212/787-6300.** Reservations strongly recommended. Main courses $17–$30. AE, DC, MC, V. Tues–Thurs 5–11pm; Fri–Sat 5–11:30pm; Sun 5–10pm. Subway: 1, 2, 3, 9 to 72nd St.

The Neptune Room ⚓ SEAFOOD   The Upper West Side is smoked fish turf, but with the 2004 addition of the Neptune Room, the neighborhood now has its first seafood "shack." I use the word shack figuratively because the restaurant, with its aged yacht decor, is much more stylish than that. It's the Neptune Room's "Bait Bar" that gives it that seafood shack feel. Raw fresh oysters from both coasts, littleneck clams, shrimp cocktail, ceviches, cured anchovies, grilled octopus, and spicy, quickly steamed calamari come served on small plates over crushed ice and are delicious. The shack theme quickly fades when you move to the main courses and ponder Mediterranean-based items like the wonderful seafood stew, *cioppino*, Parmesan-crusted skate, or the roasted whole-fish: the branzino I had was perfectly cooked and subtly seasoned in olive oil and herbs. In between shack mode and the Mediterranean seafood tour, cleanse your palate with one of the restaurant's excellent salads; the country salad made with frisee, apples, Gorgonzola, and candied almonds was a revelation. Service is knowledgeable and the wine list, all from the Mediterranean, is impressive.

511 Amsterdam Ave. (btwn 84th and 85th sts.). ✆ 212/496-4100. www.neptuneroom.com. Reservations recommended. AE, DISC, MC, V. Bait Bar $6; main courses $19–$25. Sun–Mon 5:30–10pm; Tues–Thurs 5:30–11pm; Fri–Sat 5:30–11:30pm; Sat–Sun brunch 11:30am–3pm. Subway: 1, 9 to 86th St.

Ouest ✸✸✸ CONTEMPORARY AMERICAN   When chef/restaurateur Tom Valenti opened Ouest in 2002 it signaled a very welcome renaissance in the Upper West Side dining scene. He followed the success of Ouest up with the superb 'Cesca (p. 215) in 2003, but Ouest still remains the neighborhood's shining star. With plush red banquettes and an intimate balcony area, Ouest is both cozy and clubby. Service is personable but also efficiently professional—so good you'll need to keep reminding yourself that you are on the Upper West Side. But what really draws the crowds is Valenti's mastery in the kitchen, especially with meats like his signature braised lamb shank or his melt-in-your-mouth braised beef short ribs. The quality suffers not one iota when you switch to seafood. The sautéed skate is perfectly prepared with a simple sauce of parsley and olive oil, while the baby calamari in a spicy tomato sopressata sauce appetizer was so good I actually smiled as I ate.

2315 Broadway (at 84th St.). ✆ 212/580-8700. www.ouestny.com. Reservations required well in advance. Main courses $23–$34. AE, DC, DISC, MC, V. Tues–Thurs 5–11pm; Fri–Sat 5pm–midnight; Sun 5–10pm. Subway: 1, 2 to 86th St.

Rosa Mexicano MEXICAN   There are two branches of this popular New York Mexican eatery, but it's the spacious Lincoln Center location, designed by David Rockwell and highlighted by a 30-foot-high blue tile waterfall adorned with hundreds of sculpted divers, that is a marvel. At Rosa Mexicano they originated the now common experience of guacamole prepared tableside using the freshest ingredients. But why, when a gringo asks for it to be prepared spicy, does he always get the toned-down version? In my opinion, as long as there are those deservedly famous frozen pomegranate margaritas available to quell the heat, there will be no complaints here about the guacamole being too spicy. The ceviche starter with citrus-marinated mahimahi had the bite the guacamole was missing, but the entrees I've sampled, with the exception of the *enchiladas de jaiba* (corn tortillas filled with lump crabmeat topped with pumpkin seeds and tomatillo sauce), which are a winner, are a bit overly ambitious and as a result, bland. Desserts are decadent—especially the *tres leches de chocolate*, chocolate rum cake topped with vanilla ice cream and served with sugared bananas.

61 Columbus Ave. (at 62nd St.). ✆ 212/977-7700. www.rosamexicano.com. Reservations recommended. Main courses $13–$18 at lunch; $17–$25 at dinner. AE, DC, DISC, MC, V. Daily noon–3pm; Tues–Sat 5–11:30pm; Sun–Mon 5–10:30pm. Subway: A, B, C, D, 1, 9 to Columbus Circle.

MODERATE

Carmine's ⟨★⟩ ⟨*Kids*⟩ FAMILY-STYLE SOUTHERN ITALIAN Everything is B-I-G at this rollicking family-style mainstay with two locations, on the Upper West Side (the original) and in Times Square. In many cases big means bad, but not here. Carmine's, with a dining room vast enough to deserve its own zip code, and massive portions, remarkably turns out better pasta and entrees than most 20-table Italian restaurants. I've never had pasta here that wasn't al dente, and the marinara sauce is as good as any I've had in Manhattan. For starters, the daily salads are always fresh and the fried calamari perfectly tender. Rigatoni marinara, linguine with white-clam sauce, and ziti with broccoli are pasta standouts, while the best meat entrees include veal parmigiana, broiled porterhouse steak, shrimp scampi, and the remarkable chicken *scarpariello* (chicken pan broiled with a lemon-rosemary sauce). The tiramisu is pie-size, thick and creamy, bathed in Kahlúa and Marsala. Order half of what you think you'll need. Don't expect intimate conversation here; in fact, some earplugs might be in order. Unless you come early, expect to wait.

2450 Broadway (btwn 90th and 91st sts.). ⟨✆⟩ 212/362-2200. www.carminesnyc.com. Reservations recommended before 6pm; accepted only for 6 or more after 6pm. Family-style main courses $15–$49 (most $23 or less). AE, DC, DISC, MC, V. Tues–Sat 11:30am–midnight; Sun–Mon 11:30am–11pm. Subway: 1, 2, 3, 9 to 96th St. Also at 200 W. 44th St. (btwn Broadway and Eighth Ave.). ⟨✆⟩ 212/221-3800. Subway: A, C, E, N, R, S, 1, 2, 3, 7, 9 to 42nd St./Times Sq.

Nice Matin ⟨★⟩ FRENCH PROVENÇAL Named after Nice's major newspaper, appropriately you'll find many Provençal classics like *pistou, pissaladiere,* and *velouté* of mussels on the menu. You'll also find innovations like the creamy, delicious fava bean tortelloni, moist grilled sea bass with artichokes stewed in olive oil, and a rich daube of beef short ribs with chickpea fries. There are specials daily; and on Mondays, normally not a great day to dine out, the *aioli monstre* is featured—salt cod, shrimp, meats, and vegetables accompanied by a tangy, fresh aioli. On any day you can order the five-napkin burger, also accompanied by that pleasingly persistent aioli. If cholesterol is no problem, opt for the decadently dense, sweet-and-sour cream for dessert. Located in the Lucerne hotel, the restaurant, open for breakfast, lunch, and dinner, is loud and busy, so unless you can snare a comfortable booth, don't expect intimacy.

201 W. 79th St. (at Amsterdam Ave.). ⟨✆⟩ 212/873-NICE. Reservations recommended. Main courses $10–$20 at lunch; $16–$25 at dinner. AE, DC, MC, V. Breakfast: Mon–Fri 7–11:30am, Sat–Sun 7–11am. Lunch: Mon–Fri 11:30am–3:30pm. Dinner: Mon–Sat 5:30pm–midnight, Sun 5–11pm. Brunch: Sat 11am–3:30pm, Sun 11am–3pm. Subway: 1, 9 to 79th St.

Nonna ⟨★★⟩ ITALIAN I had a Nonna. She lived until she was 96 and for almost all her adult years, on Sundays she served pasta with a red sauce to the family. This Nonna, barely 1 year old, carries on the Italian grandmother tradition more than admirably, with excellent traditonal pastas and main courses. On the menu, you'll find excellent spaghetti carbonara (made the right way: without cream); spaghetti and meatballs, with a meatball almost as good as my late Nonna's (I've yet to find one as good); pasta fagioli; linguine with clams; pork braciole; sausage and peppers; and antipasti items like Sicilian caponata, homemade mozzarella, and spicy cherry peppers stuffed with prosciuitto and provolone. Each day there is a special; Friday is lobster fra diavolo, Tuesday is lasagna, but the best day, of course, is Sunday, when "Nonna's Sunday Feast" is offered; six courses including rigatoni with a "Brooklyn meat gravy," the Italian-American translation meaning meat-based tomato sauce. You think you've had enough of tiramisu? Think again, when at Nonna's; it's spectacular—if you have room.

520 Columbus Ave. (at 85th St.). (℃ **212/579-3194.** Reservations recommended. Main courses $10–$20. AE, MC, V. Mon–Fri 11:30am–2:30pm; Sat–Sun 10am–2pm; Mon–Thurs 5–11pm; Fri–Sat 5pm–midnight; Sun 4–10pm. Subway: B, C to 86th St.

Onera ⭐ GREEK/AMERICAN   You'll find no flaming saginaki at Onera. This is not your father's Greek restaurant. This is serious, innovative Greek-influenced cuisine as created by the ambitious chef/owner, Michael Psilakis. Here, in a cozy Upper West Side town house, you'll find nods to authentic Greek country food as evidenced by the challenging "Offal Tasting Menu." For those of you who dare, there is the jellied "head cheese" of pork, the grilled kidneys, and the braised tongue. But for all us other less adventurous diners, we just have to resort to the fresh and delicate raw "meze" like sea urchin with beets and Greek cheese fondue, yellowtail with cracked green olives, and lamb with arugula and feta cheese. Or a cooked appetizer of chilled roasted octopus drizzled with an anchovy vinaigrette. Some of the exciting entree creations include the pork two ways, grilled tenderloin and braised belly, the pan-seared John Dory with a crab orzo salad, or the pasta called Manti, a four-cheese ravioli in a sage brown butter sauce. The restaurant features an excellent Greek wine list, seating is comfortable, prices are very reasonable, and service is personable. Could this be the beginning of Nouveau Greek?

229 W. 79th St. (btwn Amsterdam Ave. and Broadway). (℃ **212/255-6717.** Reservations recommended. Appetizers $8–$11; main courses $14–$25; 4-course prix fixe $45. AE, MC, V. Mon–Thurs 5–11pm; Fri–Sat 5–11:30pm; Sun 5–10pm. Subway: 1, 9 to 79th St.

Savann ⭐ MEDITERRANEAN   The restaurant scene on Amsterdam Avenue in the low 80s is particularly volatile, but for over 8 years, Savann has survived on that very difficult stretch of real estate thanks to consistently top-notch food, very personable service, and a casual, low key atmosphere. This is a neighborhood place with regulars who swear by the food. Some favorites include the home-cured gravlax, here served over a chickpea-scallion pancake in a flying fish caviar and dill sauce; the grilled calamari; the seafood savann, a medley of seafood in a light tomato sauce served over linguini; the mixed seafood filo purse; and the perfectly cooked filet mignon. For dessert don't miss the *tarte tatine*, a homemade apple tart served with cinnamon ice cream and warm honey. In warm weather, the sidewalk cafe is a great place for people-watching.

414 Amsterdam Ave. (btwn 79th and 80th sts.). (℃ **212/580-0202.** www.savann.com. Reservations recommended. AE, MC, V. Main courses $12–$27 (most under $20). Mon–Fri noon–3:30pm and 4–11pm; Sat–Sun 11am–3:30pm and 4–11pm. Subway: 1, 9 to 79th St.

INEXPENSIVE

For breakfast or lunch, also consider **Artie's Delicatessen,** 2290 Broadway, between 82nd and 83rd streets ((℃ **212/579-5959;** www.arties.com), and **Barney Greengrass, the Sturgeon King,** 541 Amsterdam Ave., between 86th and 87th streets ((℃ **212/ 724-4707**), two of the best Jewish delis in town. See "The New York Deli News" sidebar on p. 206 for further details.

You'll find some of the best bagels in New York on the Upper West Side, including **H&H Bagels,** 2239 Broadway, at 80th Street ((℃ **212/595-8003**), and **Absolute Bagels,** 2788 Broadway, between 106th and 107th streets ((℃ **212/932-2105**). For more information, see the box "The Hole Truth: NY's Best Bagels," on p. 198.

For non-vegetarians and the non-health-minded, consider the cheapest, yet in some ways, most comforting indulgence: **Gray's Papaya,** 2090 Broadway, at 72nd Street ((℃ **212/799-0243**). This 24-hour hot-dog stand is a New York institution. Hot dogs go for 75¢, and the "Recession Special," two hot dogs and a drink, overly sweetened papaya, piña colada, or orange juice, is a whopping $2.45.

Big Nick's Burger and Pizza Joint ⚡ *Kids* AMERICAN/PIZZA A neighborhood landmark since 1962, Big Nick's has a menu that seems to have grown each year of its existence—it's now a whopping 27 pages. Trying to decide if you want the Madrid burger, with olives, feta, and pimentos, with or without buffalo meat; a slice of Hawaiian pizza; or just an order of the spinach pie can be exhausting. If reading the menu is too much for you, peruse the numerous photos of celebrities who have supposedly chowed at Big Nick's over the years, or just keep your eyes on the nonstop *Three Stooges* marathon playing on the restaurant's televisions. Whatever you do, you'll never forget your Big Nick's experience. With all those diversions, it's a great place to take the kids; they'll never be bored.

2175 Broadway (at 77th St.). © 212/362-9238. www.bignicksnyc.com. Reservations not accepted. Main courses $3.50–$19 (most less than $10). MC, V. Daily 24-hr. Subway: 1, 9 to 79th St.

Celeste ⚡⚡ *Finds* ITALIAN Like **Aix** (p. 215), this is another very welcome addition to the Upper West Side dining scene. Tiny but charming Celeste features its own wood-burning pizza oven, which churns out thin-crusted, simple but delicious pizzas. But pizza is not the only attraction here; the "fritti" (fried) course is unique; the *fritto misto de pesce* (fried mixed seafood) is delectable, but the fried zucchini blossoms, usually available in the summer and fall, are amazing. The fresh pastas are better than the dried pasta; I never thought the fresh egg noodles with cabbage, shrimp, and sheep's cheese would work, but it was delicious. Not on the menu, but usually available, are plates of rare, artisanal Italian cheeses served with homemade jams. Though the main courses are also good, stick with the pizzas, antipasto, frittis, and pastas. For dessert, try the gelato; the pistachio was the best I've ever had in New York. The restaurant has been "discovered" so go early or go late or expect a wait.

502 Amsterdam Ave. (btwn 84th and 85th sts.). © 212/874-4559. Reservations not accepted. Pizza $10–$12; antipasto $7–$10; pasta $10; main courses $14–$16. No credit cards. Mon–Sat 5–11pm; Sun noon–3:30pm. Subway: 1, 9 to 86th St.

Flor de Mayo *Finds* CUBAN/CHINESE Cuban/Chinese cuisine is a New York phenomenon that started in the late 1950s when Cubans of Chinese heritage immigrated to New York after the revolution. Most of the immigrants took up residence on the Upper West Side, and Cuban/Chinese restaurants flourished. Many have disappeared, but the best one, Flor de Mayo, still remains and is so popular that a new branch opened further south on Amsterdam Avenue. The kitchen excels at both sides of the massive menu, but the best dish is the *la brasa* half-chicken lunch special—beautifully spiced and slow-roasted until it's fork tender and falling off the bone, served with a giant pile of fried rice, bounteous with roast pork, shrimp, and veggies. Offered Monday through Saturday until 4:30pm, the whole meal is just $6.95, and it's enough to fortify you for the day. Service and atmosphere are reminiscent of Chinatown: efficient and lightning-quick. My favorite combo: the hearty, noodles-, greens-, shrimp-, and pork-laden Chinese soup with an order of yellow rice and black beans.

2651 Broadway (btwn 100th and 101st sts.). © 212/663-5520 or 212/595-2525. Reservations not accepted. Main courses $4.50–$19 (most under $10); lunch specials $5–$7 (Mon–Sat to 4:30pm). AE, MC, V ($15 minimum). Daily noon–midnight. Subway: 1, 9 to 103rd St. Also at 484 Amsterdam Ave. (btwn 83rd and 84th sts.). © 212/787-3388. Subway: 1, 9 to 86th St.

Breakfast, Not Brunch

Brunch has always been a pet peeve of mine. I mean, what is it really but a slightly fancier version of breakfast at inflated prices—and it's not served until usually after 11 in the mornings—and only on weekends. What a scam! I'll take breakfast any day over brunch—*especially* on weekends. Here are some of my favorite restaurants for breakfast, not brunch.

Big Wong King ✿, 67 Mott St., between Canal and Bayard streets (ⓒ 212/964-1452). No eggs. No coffee. No pancakes. Can this be breakfast? You bet it is. Not much is more satisfying in the morning than a hot bowl of *congee* (rice porridge with either pork, beef, or shrimp) accompanied with a fried cruller and tea served in a glass. It might sound a little unusual, but you won't be alone; Big Wong is a favorite for breakfast among the residents of Chinatown. Opens daily at 8:30am. For more on Big Wong King, see p. 178.

Bubby's Pie Company ✿, 120 Hudson St., at North Moore Street (ⓒ 212/219-0666; www.bubbys.com). I don't usually order grits north of the Mason-Dixon line, but I make an exception at Bubby's. They are the perfect complement to Bubby's Breakfast: two eggs, toast, bacon, and a cup of Joe. Open at 8am Monday through Friday and 9am Saturday and Sunday. For more on Bubby's, see p. 177.

Clinton St. Baking Company ✿, 4 Clinton St., at Houston Street (ⓒ 646/602-6263). The lines are long on weekend mornings, but you can get breakfast all day here. Meaning you can eat their unbelievable pancakes at 4 in the afternoon—if that's breakfast time for you.

Good Enough to Eat ✿, 483 Amsterdam Ave., between 83rd and 84th streets (ⓒ 212/496-0163). The wait for breakfast at this Upper West Side institution on the weekends is ridiculous, so try to go during the week when you can leisurely gorge on pumpkin French toast; a "Wall Street" omelet, baked honey-mustard-glazed ham with Vermont cheddar; or "Peter Paul" pancakes, filled with Belgian chocolate chips, coconut, and topped with roasted coconut. I'm getting hungry writing this. Opens at 8am Monday through Friday and 9am Saturday and Sunday. See p. 221.

Norma's ✿✿, at Le Parker Meridien Hotel, 118 W. 57th St., between Sixth and Seventh avenues (ⓒ 212/708-7460). A glorious ode to the ultimate comfort food. It's pricey, but worth it for classics done with style and creativity. See p. 202.

Veselka ✿, 144 Second Ave., at 9th Street (ⓒ 212/228-9682). The Greek diner might be extinct in Manhattan, but this Ukrainian diner lives on. And we are all very grateful because New York just would not be the same without Veselka's buckwheat pancakes and cheese blintzes. Open 24 hours. See p. 186.

Good Enough to Eat ⭐ *Kids* *Finds* AMERICAN HOME COOKING For 24 years the crowds have been lining up on weekends outside Good Enough to Eat to experience chef/owner Carrie Levin's incredible breakfasts (see "Breakfast, Not Brunch," p. 220); as a result, lunch and dinner have been somewhat overlooked. Too bad, because these meals can be just as great as the breakfasts. The restaurant's cow motif and farmhouse knickknacks imply hearty, home-cooked food, and that's what's done best here. Stick with the classics: meat loaf with gravy and mashed potatoes; traditional turkey dinner with cranberry relish, gravy, and cornbread stuffing; macaroni and cheese; griddled corn bread; Vermont spinach salad; and the BBQ sandwich, roasted chicken with barbecue sauce and homemade potato chips. And save room for the homemade desserts; though the selection is often overwhelming, I can never resist the coconut cake. This is food you loved as a kid, one reason why the kids will love it as well.

There are only 20 tables here, so expect a wait on weekends during the day or for dinner after six.

483 Amsterdam Ave. (btwn 83rd and 84th sts.). ℂ **212/496-0163**. www.goodenoughtoeat.com. Breakfast $4.50–$9; lunch $8.50–$15; dinner $8.50–$23 (most under $18). AE, MC, V. Breakfast Mon–Fri 8am–4pm and Sat–Sun 9am–4pm; lunch Mon–Fri 11:30am–4pm; Mon–Thurs 5:30–10:30pm; Fri–Sat 5:30–11pm; Sun 5:30pm–10pm. Subway: 1, 9 to 86th St.

Noche Mexicana ⭐ *Finds* MEXICAN This tiny Mexican restaurant serves some of the best tamales in New York. Wrapped in cornhusks, as a good tamale should be, they come in two varieties: in a red mole sauce with shredded chicken or in a green tomatillo sauce with shredded pork. There are three tamales in each order, which costs only $5, making it a cheap and almost perfect lunch. The burritos are authentic and meals unto themselves. The *tinga* burrito, shredded chicken in a tomato-and-onion chipotle sauce, is my favorite. Each is stuffed with rice, beans, and guacamole. Don't get fancy here; stick with the tamales, burritos, and soft tacos, the best being the taco *al pastor,* a taco stuffed with pork marinated with pineapple and onions.

852 Amsterdam Ave. (btwn 101st and 102nd sts.). ℂ **212/662-6900** or 212/662-7400. Burritos $6–$7.50; tacos $2; tamales $5; Mexican dishes $8.50–$9.50. AE, DISC, MC, V. Sun–Thurs 10am–11pm; Fri–Sat 10am–midnight. Subway: 1 or 9 to 103rd St.

13 Upper East Side

To locate the restaurants in this section, see the map on p. 212.

VERY EXPENSIVE

Also consider the elegant restaurant **Daniel,** 60 E. 65th St., between Madison and Park avenues (ℂ **212/288-0033;** www.danielnyc.com). See the sidebar "Food Splurge" on p. 214.

EXPENSIVE

Café Boulud ⭐ *Value* FRENCH Dying to try the stellar cuisine of Daniel Boulud, New York's best French chef, but can't quite afford **Daniel?** Then head instead to Café Boulud, Boulud's more casual playground for new ideas and culinary cross-pollinations. Daniel's high style has been pleasingly laid back and toned down here. With the food, Boulud has gone eclectic, offering four menus: *La Tradition,* featuring Boulud's signature French-country classics; *Le Potager,* a vegetarian menu; *La Saison,* seasonal dishes; and *Le Voyage,* a monthly globe-hopping menu highlighting Tuscany, Thailand, or somewhere in between. The experimental nature of the wide-ranging menu makes choosing a thrill, and even the most inventive dishes tend to dazzle the palate. But in true Boulud tradition, *La Tradition* and *La Saison* are where the kitchen really excels. The poached Dover sole with baby leeks and sauce vin blanc was truly memorable. All in all, a first-rate dining experience at more palatable prices than cuisine this memorable usually costs. Don't be in a rush, though, especially at lunch.

20 E. 76th St. (btwn Madison and Fifth aves.). ✆ 212/772-2600. www.danielnyc.com. Reservations recommended. Main courses $26–$30 at lunch; $26–$37 at dinner; 2- or 3-course prix-fixe lunch $29–$36. Daily 5:45–11pm; Tues–Sat noon–2:30pm (no Sat lunch July–Aug). Subway: 6 to 77th St.

Kai ★ JAPANESE   This calming refuge of a restaurant, located above the Ito En Tea Store in the heart of tony Madison Avenue, is inspired by *kaiseki* cuisine of Japan. Kaiseki is the multicourse food accompaniment to lavish tea ceremonies in Japan. The meal includes intricately prepared and very stylized tiny plates of the freshest ingredients—fish, meats, vegetables, and noodles. The combined plates are supposed to meld together to create a feeling of serenity, harmony, and seasonality. And in oh-so-subtle ways, Kai achieves that soothing sensation. I dined at Kai on a winter's day in the middle of the hectic Christmas season. I sampled the Chef's Lunch Tray, which included miso and baby clam soup; an appetizer tray with an assortment of tiny morsels of delicate bites: oyster, sea urchin, smoked duck, and tuna, followed by an elegant yet simple sashimi tasting plate; seared filet mignon, tender and lightly seasoned with soy, accompanied by the restaurant's homemade buckwheat soba noodles; and ended with an innovative dessert of grapefruit ice cream on top of sweet red beans. That meal took the chill and holiday stress right out of my soul. In a strange way, Kai is probably the most comfortable of comfort foods. But beware, comfort at Kai doesn't come cheap; dinner tasting menus can run up to $200. Come for lunch for a "bargain."

822 Madison Ave. (btwn 68th and 69th sts.). ✆ 212/988-7277. www.itoen.com. Reservations recommended. Lunch $18–$50; dinner/chef's tasting menus $110–$200. AE, MC, V. Tues–Sat noon–2:30 and 6–9:30pm. Subway: 6 to 68th St.

INEXPENSIVE

For better-than-average pizza, head to **Totonno's Pizzeria Napolitano,** 1544 Second Ave., between 80th and 81st streets (✆ 212/327-2800), the Manhattan branch of the more celebrated Totonno's in Coney Island (see the box "Pizza, New York–Style," p. 204).

Nick's Family-Style Restaurant and Pizzeria ★ *Kids* ITALIAN   Since 1994, Nick Angelis has wowed them in Forest Hills, Queens, with his pizza. In 2003, he took his act to Manhattan, where the pizza is garnering equally high praise. The pizza here is thin-crusted, with the proper proportions of creamy, homemade mozzarella and fresh tomato sauce. But this is much more than a pizzeria; try the light, lemony baked clams or "Josephine's" perfectly breaded eggplant parmigiana. If you dare combine pizza with a calzone, this is the place; Nick's calzone, stuffed with ricotta and mozzarella cheese, is spectacular. The orecchiette with broccoli rabe and sausage is the pasta winner, while the filet of sole oreganato Livornese with mussels is the standout main course. Save room for an extra-large cannoli for dessert; the shell is perfectly flaky and the filling ultracreamy. Full orders are enough to feed two or three and are a great bargain for a group, but half-orders are also available. The room is comfortable and far from fancy. Go early or be prepared to wait.

1814 Second Ave. (at 94th St.). ✆ 212/987-5700. Pizza $11–$13; macaroni half-orders $5–$11, full orders $11–$22; entree half-orders $7.50–$11, full orders $15–$22. AE, DC, DISC, MC, V. Sun–Thurs 11:30am–11pm; Fri–Sat 11:30am–midnight. Subway: 6 to 96th St.

Serendipity 3 *Kids* AMERICAN   You'd never guess that this whimsical place was once a top stop on Andy Warhol's agenda. Wonders never cease—and neither does the confection at this delightful restaurant and sweet shop. Tucked into a cozy brownstone a few steps from Bloomingdale's, happy people gather here at marble-topped ice-cream parlor tables for burgers and foot-long hot dogs, country meat loaf with mashed potatoes and gravy, and salads and sandwiches with cute names like "The Catcher in the Rye" (their own twist on the BLT, with chicken and Russian dressing—on rye, of course). The food isn't great, but the main courses aren't the point—they're just an excuse to get to the desserts. The restaurant's signature is Frozen Hot Chocolate, a slushie version of everybody's cold-weather favorite, but other crowd pleasers include dark double devil mousse, celestial carrot cake, lemon icebox pie, and anything with hot fudge. So cast that willpower aside and come on in—Serendipity is an irony-free charmer to be appreciated by adults and kids alike.

225 E. 60th St. (btwn Second and Third aves.). (C) **212/838-3531**. www.serendipity3.com. Reservations accepted for lunch and dinner (not dessert only). Main courses $7–$18; sweets and sundaes $5–$17 (most under $10). AE, DC, DISC, MC, V. Sun–Thurs 11:30am–midnight; Fri 11:30am–1am; Sat 11:30am–2am. Subway: N, R to Lexington Ave.; 4, 5, 6 to 59th St.

14 Harlem

To locate these restaurants, see the map on p. 225.

INEXPENSIVE

Also consider **Patsy's Pizzeria** (see "Pizza, New York–Style," on p. 204), and see the sidebar "The Soul of Harlem," on p. 226, for great, affordable soul food restaurants.

Dinosaur Bar-B-Que *Kids* BARBECUE   It's one thing for a genuine Southern barbecue joint to infiltrate Manhattan, but it's quite another when the barbecue interloper is from up north. Now that's chutzpah! The wildly popular Syracuse-originated upstate barbecue chain that built its reputation with bikers entered the New York City market in 2005 with a roadhouselike restaurant on the outskirts of west Harlem. What can Syracuse know about barbecue, you ask? Well, they know pulled pork, which is slow-cooked tender. And they know Texas brisket for the same reasons. The ribs I sampled, however, didn't fare as well, but two out of three ain't bad—especially for a northerner. Sides are standard; coleslaw, macaroni salad, collard greens, and standout barbecue beans. The restaurant is loud but if you're lucky you might be able to catch some of the good blues playing over the din. There's a lively bar and service is as down home as an upstate restaurant can be. Though its location is seemingly remote—close to the West Side Highway, it's only a 3-block walk from the number 1 train.

646 W. 131st St. (at Twelfth Ave.). (C) **212/694-1777**. www.dinosaurbarbque.com/nyc/nyc.htm. Main courses $13–$20. Tues–Thurs 11am–11pm; Fri–Sat 11am–midnight; Sun noon–9pm. AE, MC, V. Subway: 1, 9 to 125th St.

El Paso Taqueria MEXICAN   In the past decade, Spanish Harlem, predominately an enclave for Puerto Ricans, has become more a Mexican community; as a result some very authentic Mexican restaurants and groceries have emerged. El Paso Taqueria is the best of the new Mexican restaurants in the neighborhood. The menu here is extensive with tamales, *flautas,* enchiladas, *chalupas,* and tacos on the menu in many varieties including some not so familiar to the gringo palate like tripe, tongue, and salted beef. The mole poblano, the "famous Puebla stew," was chocolaty rich while the *sopes,* a thick tortilla covered with salted beef and soft cheese, ranked high on my personal spice meter. You'll eat hearty here for few pesos. If you are an early riser, come for breakfast where you can sample eggs with chorizo or eggs with cactus.

1642 Lexington Ave. (btwn 103rd and 104th sts.). ⓒ 212/831-9831. Tacos $2; poblanos $8–$11. Subway: 6 to 103rd St. Also at 64 E. 97th St. (btwn Park and Madison aves.). ⓒ 212/996-1739. Subway: 6 to 96th St.

La Fonda Boricua Ⓚ *(Value* *(Finds* PUERTO RICAN The food of Puerto Rico is vastly underrated, and the best of that cuisine can be found in the heart of El Barrio at La Fonda Boricua. Was that Marc Anthony sitting across from New York Yankee Bernie Williams? This stylish, 75-seat former diner is a hangout for leaders of the local Latino community and beyond; politicians, artists, writers, musicians, and ballplayers convene for delicious Puerto Rican staples. Excellent choices include tender, succulent octopus salad; crispy *chicharrónes* of pork; slightly smoky *arroz con pollo;* garlic-laden *lechon asado* (roasted pork shoulder); thinly pounded citrus-marinated steak smothered with onions; rice and beans in many varieties; and that artery-clogging favorite, *mofongo* (fried mashed plantains with garlic and crispy pieces of pork rind). The diverse crowd also comes for the creative vibes encouraged by the engaging owners, brothers Jorge and Roberto Ayala, who have adorned the restaurant with paintings from local artists, promote impromptu jams from visiting musicians, and foster an atmosphere of Latino sophistication. The portions are more than generous and the prices easily affordable. The only disappointment is the lack of variety for dessert; flan, though excellent, is the only option.

169 E. 106th St. (btwn Third and Lexington aves.). ⓒ 212/410-7292. Lunch $5–$8; dinner $7–$10. No credit cards. Daily 10am–10pm. Subway: 6 to 103rd St.

La Marmite Ⓚ *(Finds* AFRICAN The concentration of African restaurants in the area around 116th and Frederick Douglass Boulevard in Harlem is probably denser than anywhere outside of Dakar, with most being from West Africa—Senegal in particular. Of the ones I have sampled, La Marmite is my favorite. Though it's tiny, you'll rarely have a problem finding a table since most of the business is takeout. The wobbly television will be tuned to news from France or West African music videos will be playing—hope for the latter. The traditional West African dish, *thiebou djoun,* a combination of rice and fish in a piquant tomato-based sauce is usually available. Give it a try if it is. The *poulet braise,* baked half-chicken in a sweet brown onion sauce and the *mafe,* lamb chunks in a peanut butter sauce, are also winners. You really won't go wrong with anything here. Portions are sizable; you definitely won't leave hungry. Just don't expect typically rushed New York service; this is an authentic African experience in every way including the slow pace. No alcohol is served, but if you want a beer to accompany the spicy food, there's a bodega next door.

2264 Frederick Douglass Blvd. (at 120th St.). ⓒ 212/666-0653. Main courses $8–$11. No credit cards. Open 24 hr. (but call ahead to make sure). Subway: B, C to 116th St.

15 The Outer Boroughs

THE BRONX

MODERATE

If you are looking for old-fashioned, Italian-American food—the kind you used to get before waiters began asking if you want your water tap or sparkling—look no further than the Bronx. The best concentration of Italian-American "red sauce" restaurants can be found in the Little Italy of the Bronx, on and around **Arthur Avenue.** One of

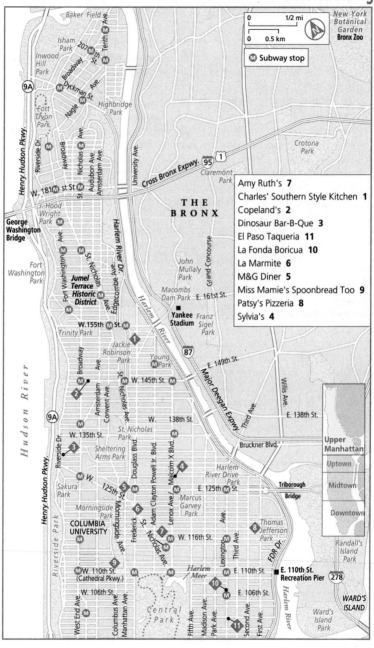

Amy Ruth's **7**

Charles' Southern Style Kitchen **1**

Copeland's **2**

Dinosaur Bar-B-Que **3**

El Paso Taqueria **11**

La Fonda Boricua **10**

La Marmite **6**

M&G Diner **5**

Miss Mamie's Spoonbread Too **9**

Patsy's Pizzeria **8**

Sylvia's **4**

The Soul of Harlem

There is much soul to go around in Manhattan, but Harlem seems to possess the mother lode—at least when it comes to food. Here is one man's primer to Harlem's soul food:

Amy Ruth's, 112 W. 116th St., between Lenox and Seventh avenues (© 212/ 280-8779). Claiming to be authentic soul, Amy Ruth's has become a mecca for Harlem celebs, with the kitschy gimmick of naming platters after some of them, such as the Rev. Al Sharpton (chicken and waffles) and the Rev. Calvin O. Butts III (chicken wings and waffles). Most of the celebrities are probably only household names in the Harlem community and that's a good thing, as are those chicken and waffles, or fried whiting and waffles, or steak and waffles. You can't go wrong with anything here as long as waffles are included.

Charles' Southern Style Kitchen ⭐, 2841 Eighth Ave., between 151st and 152nd streets (© 877/813-2920 or 212/926-4313). Nothing fancy about this place, just a brightly lit, 25-seater on a not very attractive block in upper Harlem. But you don't come here for fancy, you come for soul food at its simplest and freshest. And you better come hungry. The $11 all-you-can-eat buffet features crunchy, incredibly moist, pan-fried chicken; ribs in a tangy sauce, with meat falling off the bone; smoky stewed oxtails in a thick brown onion gravy; macaroni and cheese; collard greens with bits of smoked turkey; black-eyed peas; and corn bread, warm and not overly sweet. Hours can be erratic, so call ahead before you make the trek.

Copeland's, 547 W. 145th St., between Broadway and Amsterdam Avenue (© 212/234-2357; www.copelands-ny.com). With food almost as good as Charles', but in a much more elegant setting (you'll find tables adorned with china and white tablecloths), Copeland's has been dishing out excellent soul food for 40 years. Fried chicken is their trademark, but I favor the braised

my favorites is **Mario's Restaurant,** 2342 Arthur Ave., between Crescent Avenue and East 187th Street (© 718/584-1188), where the Neapolitan pizza is magnificent and the ziti with broccoli unforgettable. Reservations are accepted, as are American Express, Discover, Diners Club, MasterCard, and Visa. Wonderful **Dominick's,** on the same block at 2335 Arthur Ave. (© 718/733-2807), is the inspiration behind family-style recreations like Carmine's. There's no menu here, but trust your waiter to ramble off what is on the day's menu, which almost always includes tender calamari marinara and luscious veal francese. There's always a crowd so go early or expect to wait for a communal table. Reservations are not accepted and please, cash only.

To get to Arthur Avenue, take the 4 or D train to Fordham Road and then the 12 bus East; the 2 or 5 train to Pelham Parkway, and the 12 bus West; or the Metro-North Harlem line to Fordham Road, and the shuttle bus to Belmont and Bronx Zoo.

A few miles east of Arthur Avenue you'll find another classic Italian "red sauce" restaurant. This one, **Frankie and Johnnie's Pine Restaurant,** 1913 Bronxdale Ave., short ribs. The jazz buffet on Tuesday, Wednesday, and Thursday nights is a double treat.

M&G Diner, 383 W. 125th St., at St. Nicholas Avenue (© 212/864-7325). All the soul food joints I've listed here serve top-notch fried chicken, but the best I've had is the perfectly pan-fried, super moist bird at the M&G. This small, no-frills diner, open 24 hours, is a treat any time of day. Start your day here with a soul breakfast of eggs with salmon croquettes or eggs with grits or finish it with the celebrated chicken, chitterlings, or meat loaf. All the sides are freshly made and the desserts, especially the sweet-potato pie, are phenomenal. There's also a great jukebox loaded with soul to complement the food.

Miss Mamie's Spoonbread Too, 366 W. 110th St., between Columbus and Manhattan avenues (© 212/865-6744). Entering this bright, strawberry-curtained charmer is like stepping straight into South Carolina. But you are in Harlem, or at least the southern fringe of Harlem, and you won't be paying South Carolina soul prices, or Harlem soul prices, either. Still, despite the somewhat inflated prices, Miss Mamie's is the real deal, especially their barbecued ribs, falling off the bone and smothered in a sweet peppery sauce, and the smothered chicken, fried and then covered with thick pan gravy.

Sylvia's, 328 Lenox Ave., between 126th and 127th streets (© 212/996-0660; www.sylviassoulfood.com). Sylvia is the self-proclaimed queen of not only Harlem soul food but all soul food. In reality, Sylvia is queen of self-promotion. Sylvia's now has become a franchise, with canned food products, beauty and hair products, and fragrances and colognes. With all that attention to merchandising, the food at her original Harlem restaurant has suffered and now has regressed into a tourist trap. If you plan to go, however, make it on Sunday for the gospel brunch, which is an absolute joy.

between Matthews and Muliner avenues (© 718/792-5956), has been around so long, I remember watching the Times Square ball drop on a black-and-white television in the dining room while devouring a big bowl of *zuppa di pesce* one lonely New Year's Eve many years ago. I remember that New Year's, though lonely, very fondly mainly because of that *zuppa di pesce.* Now the Pine, as it's known, has become very popular as a hangout for New York Yankees who crave pasta after their games at Yankee Stadium. As a result, you'll find plenty of baseball memorabilia on the walls. No reservations accepted, cash only. To get there, take the 2 or 5 train to Bronx Park East.

BROOKLYN
VERY EXPENSIVE
Located at the foot of the Brooklyn Bridge, with spectacular views of the New York skyline, the **River Café,** 1 Water St. (© 718/522-5200), could possibly be the most romantic, special-occasion restaurant in New York. Service is good, prices are steep, the contemporary continental cuisine more than adequate, but nothing can top that view.

EXPENSIVE

Peter Luger Steakhouse ★★ STEAKS   If you love steak, then book a table here and hop a cab to Williamsburg. Expect loads of attitude and nothing in the way of decor or atmosphere (beer hall is the theme)—but this 114-year-old institution is porterhouse heaven. The first-rate cuts—the only ones they serve—are dry-aged on the premises and come off the grill dripping with fat and butter, crusty on the outside and tender pink within. It's the best steak in the five boroughs, bar none. Nonbelievers can order sole or lamb chops, but don't bother if you're not coming for the cow. The $5.95 Peter Luger burger is a little-known treasure. As sides go, the German fried potatoes are crisp and delicious, and the creamed spinach is everything it should be. Bring wads of cash because this place is expensive, but doesn't take credit cards (other than their own house account).

178 Broadway (at Driggs Ave.), Williamsburg, Brooklyn. ✆ 718/387-7400. www.peterluger.com. Reservations essential; call a month in advance for weekend bookings. Main courses $5–$20 at lunch; $20–$32 at dinner. No credit cards (Peter Luger accounts only). Mon–Thurs 11:45am–9:45pm; Fri–Sat 11:45am–10:45pm; Sun 12:45–9:45pm. Subway: J, M, Z to Marcy Ave. (Or take a cab.)

MODERATE

Consider the DUMBO outpost of the comforting, comfort-food legend Bubby's Pie Company (p. 177), **Bubby's Brooklyn,** 1 Main St., at Water Street (✆ **718/222-0666**).

INEXPENSIVE

The fabulous **Grimaldi's Pizza** is located at 19 Old Fulton St., between Front and Water streets (✆ **718/858-4300**); and out in Coney Island, the 1924-established and little-changed **Totonno's** is at 1524 Neptune Ave., between West 15th and West 16th streets (✆ **718/372-8606**). See "Pizza, New York–Style," on p. 204, for more information.

Also in Coney Island is the famous **Nathan's Famous,** 1310 Surf Ave., at Stillwell Avenue (✆ **718/946-2202**), for hot dogs by the beach. See how many you can eat.

If you are traveling to BAM to see a show, you'll be tempted to have either your pre- or post-theater meal at **Junior's,** 386 Flatbush Ave., at DeKalb Avenue (✆ **718/852-5257**). Everyone knows about Junior's world-famous cheesecake, the epitome of New York cheesecake; but don't miss the opportunity to experience the authentic Brooklyn atmosphere here, complete with old-school waiters you'll not soon forget. Don't expect anything fancy, but do expect great cheesecake.

Ferdinando's Focacceria ★ SICILIAN   You might think that focaccia, that wonderful Italian bread coated with olive oil, herbs, and tomato sauce is a recent culinary innovation. Think again. They've been making focaccia at Ferdinando's since 1904. But the focaccia they make at this Sicilian restaurant, in the increasingly trendy neighborhood of Cobble Hill, is nothing like the focaccia you've tasted. Here the specialty focaccia is panelle, a deep-fried pancake made of chickpea flour. You can have your panelle plain, or you can have it topped with ricotta and grated cheese. Trust me, any way you have it is good. The restaurant also features Sicilian specials like marinated octopus, stuffed calamari, tripe in tomato sauce, and a magnificent *caponatina,* or eggplant salad.

151 Union St. (btwn Columbia and Hicks sts.), Cobble Hill. ✆ 718/855-1545. Panelle $3; main courses $10–$13. No credit cards. Mon–Thurs 10:30am–6pm; Fri–Sat 10:30am–9pm. Subway: F, G to Carroll St.

QUEENS
INEXPENSIVE

The no. 7 train is sometimes known as the International Express. Take it out of Manhattan and through the borough of Queens and you will pass one ethnic neighborhood after another. You could write a book on all the different restaurants located around the no. 7 train in Queens. Here are a few of my favorites:

Get off at the 69th Street stop in Woodside, walk 1 block north, and you might begin to detect the aroma of barbecued meats. That smell is coming from **Ihawan,** 40–06 70th St. (© **718/205-1480**), which claims to be home of the best barbecue in town. But unless you've been to the Philippines, Ihawan's country of origin, this is barbecue unlike any you've tasted before. Here you can sample barbecue pork on bamboo skewers, grilled marinated pork chops, and the local favorite, grilled marinated pork belly. The menu here also includes other Filipino specialties such as *dinuguan,* pork stewed in pork-blood gravy, and *lapu-lapu,* a whitefish, served in tamarind soup.

If you get off the train at the 82nd Street/Jackson Heights stop, just a few steps from the elevated tracks, you'll find **Arunee Thai,** 37–68 79th St., off Roosevelt Avenue (© **718/205-5559**). Here, the Thai food is so authentic (and the clientele mostly Thai) that the menus are written in both Thai and English. Everything is delicious, and thankfully the spice level is not toned down to appease those with delicate palates. The fish, served whole on the bone, with chili, garlic, and hot-and-sour sauce, will either take the chill off a cold winter's day or, if it's summer, the chiles will cool down your overheated body and soul.

Further down the no. 7 line, get off at 103rd Street and Corona Plaza and take the Q23 bus to Northern Boulevard. You are in Corona now and it is here where you will find the marvelous Peruvian restaurant **La Pollada de Laura,** 102–03 Northern Blvd. (© **718/426-7818**). If you like ceviche, you've come to the right place. The restaurant makes over 15 varieties, including the mythical *leche de tigre,* also known as Peruvian Viagra, a few pieces of raw shrimp and crab smothered in coconut milk, lime juice, and hot chiles and served in a wine glass. If you prefer your fish cooked, the *jalea,* a gigantic platter of fried fish, squid, and shrimp served with salsa criolla, is unforgettable. *Note:* La Pollada de Laura is within walking distance of the **Louis Armstrong House Museum** (see chapter 9), and combining the two will make a memorable excursion to Queens.

Exploring New York City

If this is your first trip to New York, face the facts: It will be impossible to take in the entire city. Because New York is almost unfathomably big and constantly changing, you could live your whole life here and still make fascinating daily discoveries—we New Yorkers do. This chapter is designed to give you an overview of what's available in this multifaceted place so you can narrow your choices to an itinerary that's digestible for the amount of time you'll be here—be it a day, a week, or something in between.

So don't try to tame New York—you can't. Decide on a few must-see attractions, and then let the city take you on its own ride. See chapter 5 for my suggestions on what to see and how to cram it all in 1, 2, or 3 days. But inevitably, as you make your way around the city, you'll be blown off course by unplanned diversions that are just as much fun as what you meant to see. After all, the true New York is in the details. As you dash from sight to sight, take time to admire a lovely cornice on a prewar building, linger over a cup of coffee at a sidewalk cafe, or just idle away a few minutes on a bench watching New Yorkers parade through their daily lives.

1 Sights & Attractions by Neighborhood

MANHATTAN

CHELSEA
Bateaux New York (p. 286)
Chelsea Piers Sports & Entertainment Complex (p. 285)
Spirit Cruises (p. 287)

EAST VILLAGE & NOHO
Merchant's House Museum (p. 270)

THE FLATIRON DISTRICT/UNION SQUARE
Center for Jewish History (p. 252)
Flatiron Building (p. 268)
Union Square Greenmarket (p. 284)
Union Square Park (p. 284)

GREENWICH VILLAGE
Washington Square Park (p. 284)

HARLEM
Abyssinian Baptist Church (p. 272)
Astor Row Houses (p. 267)

Jumel Terrace Historic District (p. 267)
Morris-Jumel Mansion (p. 270)
Mother A.M.E. Zion Church (p. 273)
Schomburg Center for Research in Black Culture (p. 263)
Strivers' Row (p. 267)
Studio Museum in Harlem (p. 266)
Sylvan Terrace (p. 267)
Sugar Hill (p. 267)

LOWER EAST SIDE
Lower East Side Tenement Museum (p. 256)
Museum of Chinese in the Americas (p. 269)

LOWER MANHATTAN/THE FINANCIAL DISTRICT/NEW YORK HARBOR
Battery Park (p. 282)
Brooklyn Bridge (p. 241)

> *Tips* **Subway Access Alert**
>
> On almost every weekend, and throughout the year, changes in normal subway service tend to occur. I strongly recommend you check with the **Metropolitan Transit Authority** at ⓒ **718/330-1234** or **www.mta.nyc.ny.us** before you plan your travel routes; your hotel concierge or any token booth clerk should also be able to assist you.

Castle Clinton National Monument (p. 271)

Ellis Island (p. 242)

Federal Hall National Memorial (p. 271)

Fraunces Tavern Museum (p. 271)

Museum of Jewish Heritage—A Living Memorial to the Holocaust (p. 260)

National Museum of the American Indian, George Gustav Heye Center (p. 261)

New York City Police Museum (p. 269)

New York Stock Exchange (p. 250)

St. Paul's Chapel (p. 271 and 275)

Skyscraper Museum (p. 263)

South Street Seaport & Museum (p. 263)

Staten Island Ferry (p. 248)

Statue of Liberty (p. 249)

Trinity Church (p. 274)

U.S. Customs House (p. 271)

Wall Street (p. 250)

Woolworth Building (p. 272)

World Trade Center Site (Ground Zero; p. 251)

MIDTOWN EAST

Chrysler Building (p. 268)

Dahesh Museum of Art (p. 254)

Empire State Building (p. 242)

Grand Central Terminal (p. 244)

Lever House (p. 267)

Morgan Library (p. 257; closed until late 2006)

Museum of Sex (p. 260)

New York Public Library (p. 268)

New York Skyride (p. 296)

St. Patrick's Cathedral (p. 274)

Scandinavia House: The Nordic Center in America (p. 262)

Seagram Building (p. 267)

Sony Building (p. 267)

Sony Wonder Technology Lab (p. 296)

United Nations (p. 270)

Whitney Museum of American Art at Altria (p. 266)

SOHO

Children's Museum of the Arts (p. 295)

New Museum of Contemporary Art (p. 261)

New York City Fire Museum (p. 262)

TIMES SQUARE & MIDTOWN WEST

American Folk Art Museum (p. 252)

Broadway City (p. 296)

Bryant Park (p. 283)

Circle Line Sightseeing Cruises (p. 286)

Gray Line New York Tours (p. 286)

International Center of Photography (p. 255)

Intrepid Sea-Air-Space Museum (p. 255)

Lazer Park (p. 296)

Liberty Helicopters (p. 288)

Madame Tussauds New York (p. 257)

Madison Square Garden (p. 307)

Museum of Arts and Design (formerly American Craft Museum) (p. 257)

Museum of Modern Art (p. 245)

Museum of Television & Radio (p. 261)

New York Waterway (p. 287)

Downtown Attractions

GREENWICH VILLAGE

Washington Square Park

NOHO

SOHO

NOLITA

LITTLE ITALY

TRIBECA

Holland Tunnel

CHINATOWN

City Hall Park

World Financial Center

World Trade Center site

Battery Park City

FINANCIAL DISTRICT

Vietnam Veterans Plaza

Pier 17

Pier 16

Pier 6

South Gardens

Battery Park

Brooklyn-Battery Tunnel

Hudson River

Upper Manhattan

Uptown

Midtown

Downtown

Ⓜ Subway stop
Ⓜ Closed indefinitely

0   1/4 mi
0   0.25 km

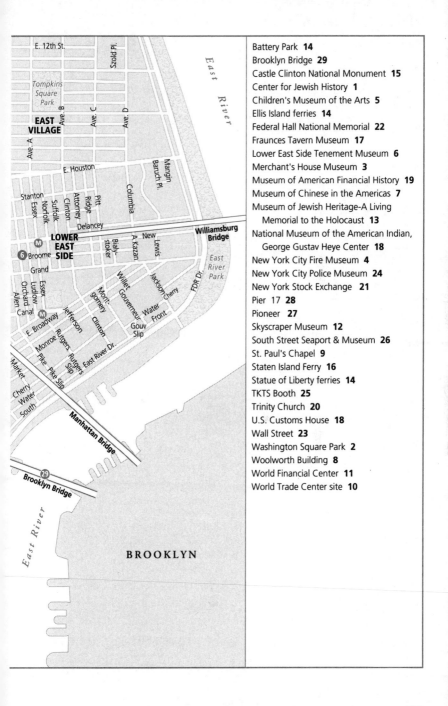

Battery Park **14**
Brooklyn Bridge **29**
Castle Clinton National Monument **15**
Center for Jewish History **1**
Children's Museum of the Arts **5**
Ellis Island ferries **14**
Federal Hall National Memorial **22**
Fraunces Tavern Museum **17**
Lower East Side Tenement Museum **6**
Merchant's House Museum **3**
Museum of American Financial History **19**
Museum of Chinese in the Americas **7**
Museum of Jewish Heritage-A Living
   Memorial to the Holocaust **13**
National Museum of the American Indian,
   George Gustav Heye Center **18**
New York City Fire Museum **4**
New York City Police Museum **24**
New York Stock Exchange **21**
Pier 17 **28**
Pioneer **27**
Skyscraper Museum **12**
South Street Seaport & Museum **26**
St. Paul's Chapel **9**
Staten Island Ferry **16**
Statue of Liberty ferries **14**
TKTS Booth **25**
Trinity Church **20**
U.S. Customs House **18**
Wall Street **23**
Washington Square Park **2**
Woolworth Building **8**
World Financial Center **11**
World Trade Center site **10**

Midtown Attractions

American Folk Art Museum **34**
Bateaux New York **12**
Broadway City **6**
Bryant Park **27**
Carnegie Hall **2**
Center for Jewish History **15**
Central Park Zoo **41**
Chelsea Piers Sports &
    Entertainment Complex **14**
Chrysler Building **23**
Circle Line Sightseeing Cruises **8**
Dahesh Museum of Art **39**
Empire State Building **19**
Flatiron Building **17**
Grand Central Terminal **24**
Gray Line Tours **3**
International Center of
    Photography **28**
Intrepid Sea-Air-Space Museum **5**
Lazer Park **4**
Lever House **36**
Liberty Helicopters **10**
Lincoln Center **1**
Madame Tussauds New York **7**
Madison Square Garden **11**
Morgan Library
    (closed until late 2006) **20**
Museum of Arts and Design **33**
Museum of Modern Art **35**
Museum of Sex **18**
Museum of Television & Radio **32**
New Museum of Contemporary
    Art **13**
New York Public Library **26**
New York Skyride **19**
New York Transit Museum **24**
New York Waterway **9**
Radio City Music Hall **29**
Rockefeller Center **30**
Roosevelt Island Tram **40**
Scandinavia House:
    The Nordic Center in America **21**
Seagram Building **37**
Sony Building **38**
Spirit Cruises **12**
St. Patrick's Cathedral **31**
Temple Emanu-El **42**
Tisch Children's Zoo **41**
Union Square Park **16**
United Nations **22**
Whitney Museum of American Art
    at Altria **25**

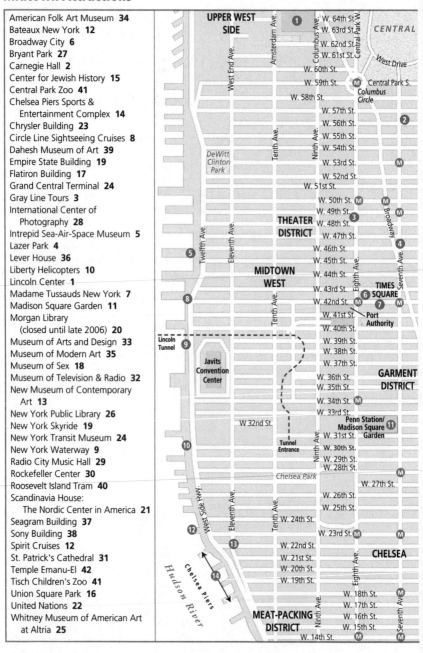

Uptown Attractions

American Museum
  of Natural History **22**

The Ansonia **20**

Asia Society **14**

Cathedral of St. John the Divine **1**

Central Park Zoo **16**

Children's Museum
  of Manhattan **23**

Cooper–Hewitt
  National Design Museum **7**

The Dakota **19**

El Museo del Barrio **3**

The Frick Collection **13**

Gracie Mansion **10**

Guggenheim Museum **8**

Jewish Museum **5**

Lasker Rink **2**

Lincoln Center **18**

Metropolitan Museum of Art **11**

Museum of the
  City of New York **4**

Neue Galerie **9**

New-York Historical Society **21**

92nd Street Y **6**

Rose Center for
  Earth and Space **22**

Temple Emanu-El **15**

Tisch Children's Zoo **16**

Whitney Museum
  of American Art **12**

Wollman Rink **17**

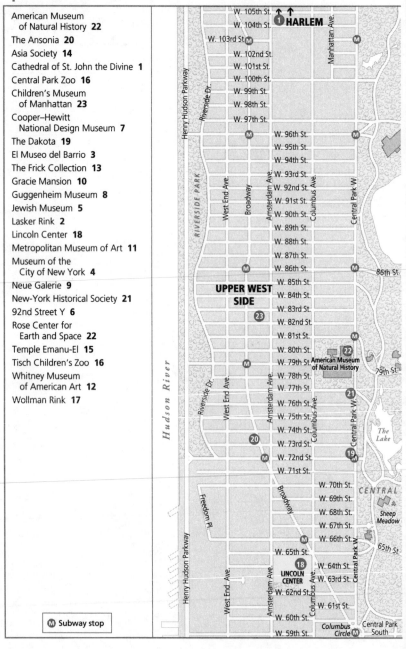

Ⓜ Subway stop

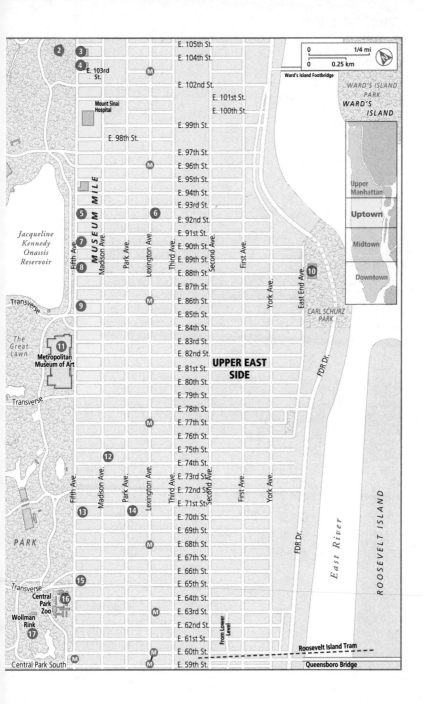

2 **3**
4 E. 103rd
St.

E. 105th St.
E. 104th St.
E. 102nd St.
E. 101st St.
E. 100th St.

Ⓜ

Mount Sinai
Hospital

Ward's Island Footbridge

*WARD'S ISLAND
PARK*

**WARD'S
ISLAND**

E. 98th St.

E. 99th St.

Jacqueline
Kennedy
Onassis
Reservoir

MUSEUM MILE

Ⓜ

E. 97th St.
E. 96th St.
E. 95th St.
E. 94th St.
E. 93rd St.

Upper
Manhattan

Uptown

Midtown

5 **6**

E. 92nd St.
E. 91st St.

Downtown

7

Fifth Ave.

Madison Ave.

Park Ave.

Lexington Ave.

Third Ave.

Second Ave.

First Ave.

York Ave.

East End Ave.

10

E. 90th St.
E. 89th St.
E. 88th St.

8

Transverse

9

Ⓜ

E. 87th St.
E. 86th St.
E. 85th St.
E. 84th St.
E. 83rd St.

*CARL SCHURZ
PARK*

*The
Great
Lawn*

11

Metropolitan
Museum of Art

E. 82nd St.

**UPPER EAST
SIDE**

Transverse

E. 81st St.
E. 80th St.
E. 79th St.
E. 78th St.
E. 77th St.
E. 76th St.
E. 75th St.

Ⓜ

12

E. 74th St.
E. 73rd St.
E. 72nd St.
E. 71st St.
E. 70th St.

ROOSEVELT ISLAND

Madison Ave.

Park Ave.

Lexington Ave.

Third Ave.

Second Ave.

First Ave.

York Ave.

13

Fifth Ave.

14

E. 69th St.
E. 68th St.
E. 67th St.
E. 66th St.
E. 65th St.

Ⓜ

East River

PARK

15

Transverse

Central
Park
Zoo

16

Wollman
Rink

17

Ⓜ

E. 64th St.
E. 63rd St.
E. 62nd St.
E. 61st St.
E. 60th St.

From Lower
Level

Ⓜ
Ⓜ

Roosevelt Island Tram

E. 59th St.

Queensboro Bridge

Central Park South

0   1/4 mi
0   0.25 km

237

Harlem Attractions

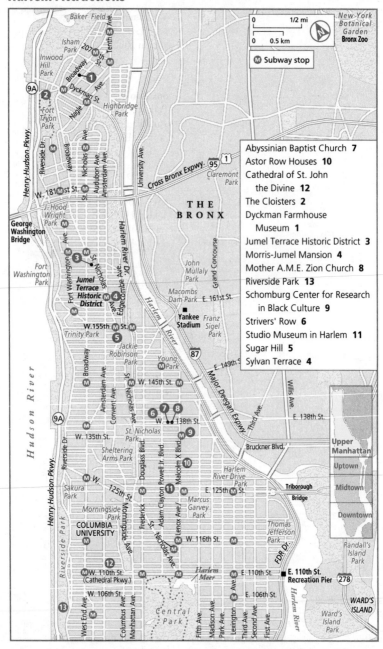

Abyssinian Baptist Church **7**
Astor Row Houses **10**
Cathedral of St. John
  the Divine **12**
The Cloisters **2**
Dyckman Farmhouse
  Museum **1**
Jumel Terrace Historic District **3**
Morris-Jumel Mansion **4**
Mother A.M.E. Zion Church **8**
Riverside Park **13**
Schomburg Center for Research
  in Black Culture **9**
Strivers' Row **6**
Studio Museum in Harlem **11**
Sugar Hill **5**
Sylvan Terrace **4**

Radio City Music Hall (p. 247)
Rockefeller Center (p. 246)
Times Square (p. 249)

UPPER EAST SIDE
Asia Society (p. 252)
Central Park (p. 275)
Central Park Zoo (p. 280)
Cooper-Hewitt National Design
  Museum (p. 253)
El Museo del Barrio (p. 254)
The Frick Collection (p. 254)
Graffiti Hall of Fame (p. 269)
The Jewish Museum (p. 256)
Metropolitan Museum of Art (p. 244)
Museum of the City of New York
  (p. 260)
Neue Gallerie New York (p. 261)
Solomon R. Guggenheim Museum
  (p. 247)
Temple Emanu-El (p. 274)
Tisch Children's Zoo (p. 280)
Whitney Museum of American Art
  (p. 250)

UPPER MANHATTAN
The Cloisters (p. 253)
Dyckman Farmhouse Museum
  (p. 270)

UPPER WEST SIDE
American Museum of Natural History
  (p. 239)
The Ansonia (p. 267)
Cathedral of St. John the Divine
  (p. 273)
Central Park (p. 275)
Children's Museum of Manhattan
  (p. 295)
The Dakota (p. 268)
New-York Historical Society (p. 262)
Riverside Park (p. 283)

Rose Center for Earth and Space
  (p. 239)
Wollman Rink (p. 281)

OUTER BOROUGHS
THE BRONX
Bronx Zoo Wildlife Conservation
  Park (p. 297)
Edgar Allan Poe Cottage (p. 270)
New York Botanical Garden (p. 297)
Wave Hill (p. 298)
Yankee Stadium (p. 251)

BROOKLYN
Brooklyn Botanic Garden (p. 299)
Brooklyn Heights Historic District
  (p. 302)
Brooklyn Museum of Art (p. 299)
Brooklyn Tabernacle (p. 300)
Coney Island (p. 300)
Coney Island Museum (p. 269)
Grand Army Plaza (p. 239)
New York Aquarium (p. 300)
New York Transit Museum (p. 301)
Prospect Park (p. 301)

QUEENS
American Museum of the Moving
  Image (p. 303)
Flushing Meadows–Corona Park
  (p. 295)
Isamu Noguchi Garden Museum
  (p. 304)
Louis Armstrong House Museum
  (p. 304)
Museum for African Art (p. 304)
New York Hall of Science (p. 295)
P.S. 1 Contemporary Art Center
  (p. 305)
Queens Museum of Art (p. 305)
Shea Stadium (p. 306)
Socrates Sculpture Park (p. 305)

2 The Top Attractions

In addition to the choices below, don't forget about **Central Park** ✶✶✶, the great green swath that is, just by virtue of its existence, New York City's greatest marvel. Central Park is so big and multifaceted that it earns its own dedicated section, starting on p. 275.

American Museum of Natural History ✶✶✶ *Kids*   This is one of the hottest museum tickets in town, thanks to the **Rose Center for Earth and Space** ✶, whose four-story-tall planetarium sphere hosts the excellent Harrison Ford–narrated Space Show "Are We Alone?," the most technologically advanced sky show on the planet. Prepare to be blown away. The show is short—less than a half-hour from start to finish—but phenomenal. (*New York* magazine has called it "the world's largest, most powerful virtual-reality simulator.")

Buy your tickets in advance for the Space Show in order to guarantee admission (they're available online); I also recommend buying tickets in advance for a specific IMAX film or special exhibition, such as the Butterfly Conservatory (see below), especially during peak seasons (summer, autumn, holiday time) and for weekend visits; otherwise, you might miss out.

Other must-sees include the Big Bang Theater, which re-creates the theoretical birth of the universe; the main Hall of the Universe, with its very own 16-ton meteorite; and the terrific Hall of Planet Earth, which focuses on the geologic processes of our home planet (great volcano display!). All in all, you'll need a minimum of 2 hours to fully explore the Rose Center. *Tip:* Friday night is a great time to plan your visit, as the center isn't overcrowded, live jazz and food fill the Hall of the Universe, and, bathed in blue light, the sphere looks magical.

The rest of the 4-square-block museum is nothing to sneeze at, either. Founded in 1869, it houses the world's greatest natural science collection in a square-block group of buildings made of towers and turrets, pink granite and red brick. The diversity of the holdings is astounding: some 36 million specimens, ranging from microscopic organisms to the world's largest cut gem, the Brazilian Princess Topaz (21,005 carats). Rose Center aside, it would take you all day to see the entire museum, and then you *still* wouldn't get to everything. If you don't have a lot of time, you can see the best of the best on free **highlights tours** offered daily every hour at 15 minutes after the hour

---

⌐Value⌐ A Money- & Time-Saving Tip

CityPass just may be New York's best sightseeing deal. Pay one price ($53, or $41 for kids 12–17) for admission to six major Big Apple attractions: The American Museum of Natural History (admission only; does not include Space Show); the Solomon R. Guggenheim Museum; the Empire State Building; the *Intrepid* Sea-Air-Space Museum; the Museum of Modern Art; and a 2-hour Circle Line harbor cruise. Purchased individually, you'd spend more than twice as much.

More important, CityPass is not a coupon book. It contains actual admission tickets, so you can bypass lengthy ticket lines. This can literally save you hours, since popular sights such as the Empire State Building often have ticket lines of an hour or more.

CityPass is good for 9 days from the first time you use it. It's sold at all participating attractions and online at http://citypass.com. To avoid online service and shipping fees, you may buy the pass at your first attraction (start at an attraction that's likely to have the shortest admission line, such as the Guggenheim, or arrive before opening to avoid a wait at such spots as the Empire State Building). However, if you begin your sightseeing on a weekend or during holidays, when lines are longest, online purchase may be worthwhile.

For more information call CityPass at ☎ **208/787-4300** (note, however, that CityPass is not sold over the phone).

from 10:15am to 3:15pm. Free daily **spotlight tours,** thematic tours that change monthly, are also offered; stop by an information desk for the day's schedule. **Audio Expeditions,** high-tech audio tours that allow you to access narration in the order you choose, are also available to help you make sense of it all.

If you only see one exhibit, see the **dinosaurs** ⚔, which take up the entire fourth floor.

The **Hall of Biodiversity** is an impressive multimedia exhibit, but its doom-and-gloom story about the future of rainforests and other natural habitats might be too much for the little ones. Kids 5 and up should head to the **Discovery Room,** with lots of hands-on exhibits and experiments. (*Parents, be prepared:* There seems to be a gift shop overflowing with fuzzy stuffed animals at every turn.)

The museum excels at **special exhibitions,** so check to see what will be on while you're in town in case any advance planning is required. The magical **Butterfly Conservatory** ⚔, a walk-in enclosure housing nearly 500 free-flying tropical butterflies, has developed into a can't-miss fixture from October through May; check to see if it's in the house while you're in town.

Central Park West (btwn 77th and 81 sts.). © 212/769-5100 for information, or 212/769-5200 for tickets (tickets can also be ordered online). www.amnh.org. Suggested admission $13 adults, $10 seniors and students, $7.50 children 2–12; Space Show and museum admission $22 adults, $17 seniors and students, $13 children under 12. Additional charges for IMAX movies and some special exhibitions. Daily 10am–5:45pm; Rose Center open Fri to 8:45pm. Subway: B, C to 81st St.; 1, 9 to 79th St.

Brooklyn Bridge ⚔⚔ *(Moments)*   Its Gothic-inspired stone pylons and intricate steel-cable webs have moved poets like Walt Whitman and Hart Crane to sing the praises of this great span, the first to cross the East River and connect Manhattan to Brooklyn. Begun in 1867 and ultimately completed in 1883, the beautiful Brooklyn Bridge is now the city's best-known symbol of the age of growth that seized the city during the late 19th cen-

> **Impressions**
> If you're bored in New York, it's your own fault.
> —Myrna Loy

tury. Walk across the bridge and imagine the awe that New Yorkers of that age felt at seeing two boroughs joined by this monumental span. It's still astounding.

Walking the Bridge: Walking the Brooklyn Bridge is one of my all-time favorite New York activities, although there's no doubt that the Lower Manhattan views from the bridge now have a painful resonance as well as a joyous spirit. A wide wood-plank pedestrian walkway is elevated above the traffic, making it a relatively peaceful, and popular, walk. It's a great vantage point from which to contemplate the New York skyline and the East River.

There's a sidewalk entrance on Park Row, just across from City Hall Park (take the 4, 5, or 6 train to Brooklyn Bridge/City Hall). But why do this walk *away* from Manhattan, toward the far less impressive Brooklyn skyline? Instead, for Manhattan skyline views, take an A or C train to High Street, one stop into Brooklyn. From there, you'll be on the bridge in no time: Come above ground, then walk through the little park to Cadman Plaza East and head downslope (left) to the stairwell that will take you up to the footpath. (Following Prospect Place under the bridge, turning right onto Cadman Plaza E., will also take you directly to the stairwell.) It's a 20- to 40-minute stroll over the bridge to Manhattan, depending on your pace, the amount of foot traffic, and the number of stops you make to behold the spectacular views (there are benches along the way). The footpath will deposit you right at City Hall Park.

Tasty tips: The perfect complement to your stroll over the Brooklyn Bridge is a stop for pizza at **Grimaldi's** (see "Pizza, New York–Style," on p. 204), followed by delicious homemade ice cream at the **Brooklyn Ice Cream Factory** (© **718/246-3963**), located at the Fulton Ferry Fire Boat House on the river and in the shadow of the bridge. The pizza and ice cream will fortify you for your return stroll into Manhattan.
Subway: A, C to High St.; 4, 5, 6 to Brooklyn Bridge–City Hall.

Ellis Island ⭐⭐   One of New York's most moving sights, the restored Ellis Island opened in 1990, slightly north of Liberty Island. Roughly 40% of Americans (myself included) can trace their heritage back to an ancestor who came through here. For the 62 years when it was America's main entry point for immigrants (1892–1954), Ellis Island processed some 12 million people. The greeting was often brusque—especially in the early years of the century (until 1924), when as many as 12,000 came through in a single day. The statistics can be overwhelming, but the **Immigration Museum** skillfully relates the story of Ellis Island and immigration in America by placing the emphasis on personal experience.

It's difficult to leave the museum unmoved. Today you enter the Main Building's baggage room, just as the immigrants did, and then climb the stairs to the **Registry Room,** with its dramatic vaulted tiled ceiling, where millions waited anxiously for medical and legal processing. A step-by-step account of the immigrants' voyage is detailed in the exhibit, with haunting photos and touching oral histories. What might be the most poignant exhibit is *Treasures from Home,* 1,000 objects and photos donated by descendants of immigrants, including family heirlooms, religious articles, and rare clothing and jewelry. Outside, the **American Immigrant Wall of Honor** commemorates the names of more than 500,000 immigrants and their families, from Myles Standish and George Washington's great-grandfather to the forefathers of John F. Kennedy, Jay Leno, and Barbra Streisand. You can even research your own family's history at the interactive **American Family Immigration History Center.** You might also make time to see the award-winning short film *Island of Hope, Island of Tears,* which plays on a continuous loop in two theaters. Short live theatrical performances depicting the immigrant experience are also often part of the day's events.

Touring tip: Ferries run daily to Ellis Island and Liberty Island from Battery Park and Liberty State Park at frequent intervals; see the Statue of Liberty listing (p. 249) for details.
In New York Harbor. © **212/363-3200** (general info), or 212/269-5755 (ticket/ferry info). www.nps.gov/elis or www.ellisisland.org. Free admission (ferry ticket charge). Daily 9:30am–5:15pm (last ferry departs around 3:30pm). For subway and ferry details, see the Statue of Liberty listing on p. 249 (ferry trip includes stops at both sights).

Empire State Building ⭐⭐⭐   It took 60,000 tons of steel, 10 million bricks, 2.5 million feet of electrical wire, 120 miles of pipe, and 7 million man-hours to build.

Impressions

It's the nearest thing to heaven we have in New York.

—Deborah Kerr to Cary Grant in *An Affair to Remember,* on the Empire State Building

---

King Kong climbed it in 1933. A plane slammed into it in 1945. The World Trade Center superseded it in 1970 as the island's tallest building. And in 1997, a gunman ascended it to stage a deadly shooting. On that horrific day of September 11, 2001, it once again regained its status as New York City's tallest building, after 31 years of taking second place.

And through it all, the Empire State Building has remained one of the city's favorite landmarks, and its signature high-rise. Completed in 1931, the limestone-and–stainless

---

(Tips **Empire State Building Ticket-Buying**

Lines can be horrible at the concourse-level ticket booth, so be prepared to wait—or consider purchasing **advance tickets** online using a credit card at **www.esbnyc.com**. You'll pay slightly more—tickets were priced $1 higher on the website at press time—but it's well worth it, especially if you're visiting during busy seasons, when the line can be shockingly long. You're not required to choose a time or date for your tickets in advance; they can be used on any regular open day. However, order them well before you leave home, because only regular mail is free. Expect them to take 7 to 10 days to reach you (longer if you live out of the country). Overnight delivery adds $15 to your total order. With tickets in hand, you're allowed to proceed directly to the second floor—past everyone who didn't plan as well as you did!

Now you can call in advance to get an estimate of your wait in line along with the visibility from the observatory. Dial ℂ **877/692-8439** for the service.

Remember: Advance purchase of a CityPass (see the box on p. 240), will get you admission to the Empire State Building, plus five other major attractions.

---

steel streamline deco dazzler climbs 102 stories (1,454 ft.) and now harbors the offices of fashion firms, and, in its upper reaches, a jumble of high-tech broadcast equipment.

Always a conversation piece, the Empire State Building glows every night, bathed in colored floodlights to commemorate events of significance—red, white, and blue for Independence Day; green for St. Patrick's Day; red, black, and green for Martin Luther King Day; blue and white for Hanukkah; even lavender and white for Gay Pride Day (you can find a complete lighting schedule online). The familiar silver spire can be seen from all over the city.

The best views, and what keeps the nearly three million visitors coming every year, are the ones from the 86th- and 102nd-floor **observatories.** The lower one is best—you can walk out on a windy deck and look through coin-operated viewers (bring quarters!) over what, on a clear day, can be as much as an 80-mile visible radius. The citywide panorama is magnificent. One surprise is the flurry of rooftop activity, an aspect of city life that thrives unnoticed from our everyday sidewalk vantage point. The higher observation deck is glass-enclosed and cramped.

Light fog can create an admirably moody effect, but it goes without saying that a clear day is best. Dusk brings the most remarkable views and the biggest crowds. Consider going in the morning, when the light is still low on the horizon, keeping glare to a minimum. Starry nights are pure magic.

In your haste to go up, don't rush through the beautiful three-story-high marble **lobby** without pausing to admire its features, which include a wonderful streamline mural.

At press time, it was announced that the Empire State Building will make waiting to get to the observation deck more visitor-friendly. While you wait you will be treated to a filmed visual history of the construction of the building and in 2006 the 80th and 86th floors will be remodeled.

350 Fifth Ave. (at 34th St.). ℂ **212/736-3100.** www.esbnyc.com. Observatory admission $12 adults, $11 seniors and children 12–17, $7 children 6–11, free for children under 6. Mon–Fri 10am–midnight; Sat–Sun 9:30am–midnight; last elevator at 11:15pm. Subway: B, D, F, N, R, Q, V, W to 34th St.; 6 to 33rd St.

Grand Central Terminal ★★ Even if you're not catching one of the subway lines or Metro-North commuter trains that rumble through Grand Central Terminal, come for a visit; it's one of the most magnificent public places in the country. And even if you arrive and leave by subway, be sure to exit the station, walking a couple of blocks south, to about 40th Street, before you turn around to admire Jules-Alexis Coutan's neoclassical sculpture *Transportation* hovering over the south entrance, with a majestically buff Mercury, the Roman god of commerce and travel, as its central figure.

The greatest visual impact comes when you enter the vast majestic **main concourse.** The high windows allow sunlight to penetrate the space, glinting off the half-acre Tennessee marble floor. The brass clock over the central kiosk gleams, as do the gold- and nickel-plated chandeliers piercing the side archways. The masterful **sky ceiling,** a brilliant greenish blue, depicts the constellations of the winter sky above New York. They're lit with 59 stars, surrounded by dazzling 24-carat gold and emitting light fed through fiber-optic cables, their intensities roughly replicating the magnitude of the actual stars as seen from Earth. Look carefully and you'll see a patch near one corner left unrestored as a reminder of the neglect once visited on this splendid overhead masterpiece. On the east end of the main concourse is a grand **marble staircase.**

This dramatic Beaux Arts splendor serves as a hub of social activity as well. Excellent-quality retail shops and restaurants have taken over the mezzanine and lower levels. The highlights of the west mezzanine are **Michael Jordan's–The Steak House,** a gorgeous Art Deco space that allows you to dine within view of the sky ceiling (see "The Prime Cut," on p. 194) as well as the gorgeously restored The **Campbell Apartment** (p. 379), which serves cocktails. Off the main concourse at street level, there's a nice mix of specialty shops and national retailers, as well as the truly grand **Grand Central Market** for gourmet foods. The **New York Transit Museum Store** (p. 338), in the shuttle passage, houses city transit-related exhibitions and a terrific gift shop that's worth a look for transit buffs. The **lower dining concourse** ★ houses a stellar food court and the famous **Oyster Bar & Restaurant** (see chapter 8 for details on both).

The **Municipal Art Society** (© 212/935-3960; www.mas.org) offers a free walking tour of Grand Central Terminal on Wednesday at 12:30pm, which meets at the information booth on the Grand Concourse.

42nd St. at Park Ave. © 212/340-2210 (events hot line). www.grandcentralterminal.com. Subway: S, 4, 5, 6, or 7 to 42nd St./Grand Central.

Metropolitan Museum of Art ★★★ Home of blockbuster after blockbuster exhibition, the Metropolitan Museum of Art attracts some five million people a year, more than any other spot in New York City. And it's no wonder—this place is magnificent. At 1.6 million square feet, this is the largest museum in the western hemisphere. Nearly all the world's cultures are on display through the ages—from Egyptian mummies to ancient Greek statuary to Islamic carvings to Renaissance paintings to Native American masks to 20th-century decorative arts—and masterpieces are the rule. You could go once a week for a lifetime and still find something new on each visit.

So unless you plan on spending your entire vacation in the museum (some people do), you cannot see the entire collection. My recommendation is to give it a good day—or better yet, 2 half days so you don't burn out. One good way to get an overview is to take advantage of the little-known **Museum Highlights Tour,** offered every day at various times throughout the day (usually between 10:15am and 3:15pm; tours also offered in Spanish, Italian, German, and Korean). Even some New Yorkers

> **(** *Moments* **Evenings at the Met**
>
> On **Friday and Saturday evenings,** the Met remains open late not only for art viewing but also for cocktails in the Great Hall Balcony Bar (5–8pm) and classical music from a string ensemble. A slate of after-hours programs (gallery talks, walking tours, family programs) changes by the week; call for the current schedule. The restaurant stays open until 10pm (last reservation at 8:30pm), and dinner is usually accompanied by piano music.

who've spent many hours in the museum could profit from this once-over. Visit the museum's website for a schedule of this and subject-specific walking tours (Old Master Paintings, American Period Rooms, Arts of China, Islamic Art, and so on); you can also get a schedule of the day's tours at the Visitor Services desk when you arrive. A daily schedule of **Gallery Talks** is available as well.

The least overwhelming way to see the Met on your own is to pick up a map at the round desk in the entry hall and choose to concentrate on what you like, whether it's 17th-century paintings, American furniture, or the art of the South Pacific. Highlights include the American Wing's **Garden Court,** with its 19th-century sculpture; the terrific ground-level **Costume Hall;** and the **Frank Lloyd Wright room.** The beautifully renovated **Roman and Greek galleries** are overwhelming, but in a marvelous way, as are the collections of **Byzantine Art** and later **Chinese art.** The highlight of the astounding **Egyptian collection** is the **Temple of Dendur,** in a dramatic, purpose-built glass-walled gallery with Central Park views. The **Greek Galleries,** which at last fully realize McKim, Mead & White's grand neoclassical plans of 1917, and the **Ancient Near East Galleries,** are particularly of note. But it all depends on what your interests are. **Special exhibitions** can range from *Orazio and Artemisia Gentileschi: Father and Daughter Painters in Baroque Italy* to *Earthly Bodies: Irving Penn's Nudes, 1949–50.*

In a response to the huge crowds the Met now opens on "Holiday Mondays." On those Mondays, such as Memorial Day or Labor Day, the museum is open from 9:30am to 5:30pm.

To purchase tickets for concerts and lectures, call **(** **212/570-3949** (Mon–Sat 9:30am–5pm). The museum contains several dining facilities, including a **full-service restaurant** serving Continental cuisine (**(** **212/570-3964** for reservations). The roof garden is worth visiting if you're here from spring to autumn, offering peaceful views over Central Park and the city.

The Met's medieval collections are housed in Upper Manhattan at the **Cloisters;** see the full listing on p. 253.

Fifth Ave. at 82nd St. **(** 212/535-7710. www.metmuseum.org. Admission (includes same-day entrance to the Cloisters) $12 adults, $7 seniors and students, free for children under 12 when accompanied by an adult. Sun, Holiday Mon (Labor Day, Memorial Day, and so forth), and Tues–Thurs 9:30am–5:30pm; Fri–Sat 9:30am–9pm. No strollers allowed Sun (back carriers available at 81st St. entrance coat-check area). Subway: 4, 5, 6 to 86th St.

Museum of Modern Art After two years of being temporarily ensconced in Queens, MoMA returned to its original Manhattan location in late 2004. And though the address is the same, the building is now, with over 630,000 square feet, almost twice the size of the original. The renovation, designed by Yoshio Taniguchi, highlights space and light, with open rooms, high ceilings, and gardens—a beautiful work of architecture and a perfect complement to the art that resides within. This is where you'll find van Gogh's *Starry Night,* Cezanne's *Bather,* Picasso's *Les Demoiselles d'Avignon,* and the amazing sculpture by Rodin, *Monument to Balzac.* Whenever I visit, I like to browse the fun "Architecture and Design" department, with examples of design for modern appliances, furniture, and even sports cars. MoMA also features edgy new exhibits and a celebrated film series that attracts serious cinephiles. But the heart of the museum, as it was before the renovation, remains the **Abby Aldrich Rockefeller Sculpture Garden,** which has been enlarged; the museum's new design affords additional views of this lovely space from other parts of the museum. My only complaint with the new MoMA is its very high ($20) admission charge for adults.

11 W. 53rd St. (btwn Fifth and Sixth aves.). ⒸⒸ 212/708-9400. www.moma.org. Admission $20 adults, $16 seniors, $12 students, children under 16 free accompanied by an adult. Sat–Mon and Wed–Thurs 10:30am–5:30pm; Fri 10:30am–8pm. Subway: E, V to Fifth Ave.; B, D, E to Seventh Ave.

Rockefeller Center ⭐⭐   A streamline moderne masterpiece, Rockefeller Center is one of New York's central gathering spots for visitors and New Yorkers alike. A prime example of the city's skyscraper spirit and historic sense of optimism, it was erected mainly in the 1930s, when the city was deep in the Depression as well as its most passionate Art Deco phase. Designated a National Historic Landmark in 1988, it's now the world's largest privately owned business-and-entertainment center, with 18 buildings on 21 acres.

For a dramatic approach to the entire complex, start at Fifth Avenue between 49th and 50th streets. The builders purposely created the gentle slope of the Promenade, known here as the **Channel Gardens** because it's flanked to the south by La Maison Française and to the north by the British Building (the Channel, get it?). You'll also find a number of attractive shops along here, including a big branch of the **Metropolitan Museum of Art Store,** a good stop for elegant gifts. The Promenade leads to the **Lower Plaza,** home to the famous ice-skating rink in winter (see next paragraph) and alfresco dining in summer in the shadow of Paul Manship's freshly gilded bronze statue *Prometheus.* All around, the flags of the United Nations' member countries flap in the breeze. Just behind *Prometheus,* in December and early January, towers the city's official and majestic Christmas tree.

The **Rink at Rockefeller Center** ⭐ (Ⓒ 212/332-7654; www.rockefellercenter.com) is tiny but positively romantic, especially during the holidays, when the giant Christmas tree's multicolored lights twinkle from above. The rink is open from mid-October to mid-March, and you'll skate under the magnificent tree for the month of December. Overlooking the rink, and with a terrific view of *Prometheus,* is the excellent **Sea Grill** restaurant.

The focal point of this "city within a city" is the building at **30 Rockefeller Plaza** ⭐, a 70-story showpiece towering over the plaza. It's still one of the city's most impressive buildings; walk through for a look at the granite and marble lobby, lined with monumental sepia-toned murals by José Maria Sert. You can pick up a walking tour brochure highlighting the center's art and architecture at the main information desk in this building. On the 65th floor, the legendary **Rainbow Room** is once again open to the public on a limited basis (see chapter 11). At press time, the six-level, 55,000-square-foot observation deck, **Top of the Rock,** was scheduled to reopen, fully renovated, October 2005 on the 67th to 70th floors after being closed for nearly 20 years. The observatory will be open daily from 8:30am to midnight; admission is $14 for adults, $12 for seniors, $9 for ages 6 to 11, and free for children under 6. For more information call Ⓒ **877/NYC-ROCK** (877-692-7625) or 212/698-2000 or visit www.topoftherocknyc.com.

NBC television maintains studios throughout the complex. *Saturday Night Live* and *Late Night with Conan O'Brien* originate at 30 Rock (see "Talk of the Town: TV Tapings," on p. 292, for tips on getting tickets). NBC's *Today* show is broadcast live on weekdays from 7 to 10am from the glass-enclosed studio on the southwest corner of 49th Street and Rockefeller Plaza; come early if you want a visible spot, and bring your HI MOM! sign.

The 70-minute **NBC Studio Tour** (© 212/664-3700; www.nbcsuperstore.com) will take you behind the scenes at the Peacock network. The tour changes daily, but may include the *Today* show, *NBC Nightly News, Dateline NBC,* and/or *Saturday Night Live* sets. Who knows? You may even run into Tom Brokaw or Stone Phillips in the hall. Tours run every 15 minutes Monday through Saturday from 8:30am to 5:30pm, Sunday from 9:30am to 4:30pm (later on certain summer days); of course, you'll have a better chance of encountering some real live action on a weekday. Tickets are $18 for adults, $15 for seniors and children 6 to 16. You can reserve your tickets for either tour in advance (reservations are recommended) or buy them right up to tour time at the **NBC Experience** store, on Rockefeller Plaza at 49th Street. They also offer a 75-minute **Rockefeller Center Tour** hourly every day between 10am and 4pm. Tickets are $10 for adults, $8 for seniors and children 6 to 16; two-tour combination packages are available for $21.

Other notable buildings throughout the complex include the **International Building,** on Fifth Avenue between 50th and 51st streets, worth a look for its Atlas statue out front; and the **McGraw-Hill Building,** on Sixth Avenue between 48th and 49th streets, with its 50-foot sun triangle on the plaza.

The restored **Radio City Music Hall** ⭐, 1260 Sixth Ave., at 50th Street (© 212/247-4777; www.radiocity.com), is perhaps the most impressive architectural feat of the complex. Designed by Donald Deskey and opened in 1932, it's one of the largest indoor theaters, with 6,200 seats. But its true grandeur derives from its magnificent Art Deco appointments. The crowning touch is the stage's great proscenium arch, which from the distant seats evokes a faraway sun setting on the horizon of the sea. The men's and women's lounges are also splendid. The theater hosts the annual **Christmas Spectacular,** starring the Rockettes. The illuminating 1-hour **Stage Door Tour** is offered Monday through Saturday from 10am to 5pm, Sunday from 11am to 5pm; tickets are $16 for adults, $10 for children under 12.

Between 48th and 50th sts., from Fifth to Sixth aves. © 212/332-6868. www.rockefellercenter.com. Subway: B, D, F, V to 47th–50th sts./Rockefeller Center.

Solomon R. Guggenheim Museum ⭐

It's been called a bun, a snail, a concrete tornado, and even a giant wedding cake; bring your kids, and they'll probably see it as New York's coolest opportunity for skateboarding. Whatever description you choose to apply, Frank Lloyd Wright's only New York building, completed in 1959, is best summed up as a brilliant work of architecture—so consistently brilliant that it competes with the art for your attention. If you're looking for the city's best modern art, head to MoMA or the Whitney first; come to the Guggenheim to see the house.

It's easy to see the bulk of what's on display in 2 to 4 hours. Inside, a spiraling rotunda circles over a slowly inclined ramp that leads you past changing exhibits that, in the past, have ranged from *Matthew Barney: The Cremaster Cycle* to *Norman Rockwell: Pictures for the American People,* said to be the most comprehensive exhibit ever of the beloved painter's works. Usually the progression is counterintuitive: from the first floor up, rather than from the sixth floor down. If you're not sure, ask a guard before you begin. Permanent exhibits of 19th- and 20th-century art, including strong holdings of Kandinsky, Klee, Picasso, and French Impressionists, occupy a stark annex called the **Tower Galleries,** an addition (accessible at every level) that some critics claimed made the entire structure look like a toilet bowl backed by a water tank (judge for yourself—I think there may be something to that view).

The Guggenheim runs some interesting special programs, including free docent tours daily, a limited schedule of lectures, free family films, avant-garde screenings for grown-ups, curator-led guided gallery tours on select Friday afternoons, and the **World Beat Jazz Series,** which resounds through the rotunda on Friday and Saturday from 5 to 8pm.

1071 Fifth Ave. (at 89th St.). ℂ 212/423-3500. www.guggenheim.org. Admission $15 adults, $10 seniors and students, free for children under 12, pay what you wish Fri 6–8pm. Sat–Wed 10am–5:45pm; Fri 10am–8pm. Subway: 4, 5, 6 to 86th St.

Staten Island Ferry 🌟 (Value)   Here's New York's best freebie—especially if you just want to glimpse the Statue of Liberty and not climb her steps. You get an enthralling hour-long excursion (round-trip) into the world's biggest harbor. This is not strictly a sightseeing ride but commuter transportation to and from Staten Island. As a result, during business hours, you'll share the boat with working stiffs reading papers and drinking coffee inside, blissfully unaware of the sights outside.

You, however, should go on deck and enjoy the busy harbor traffic. The old orange-and-green boats usually have open decks along the sides or at the bow and stern; try to catch one of these boats if you can, since the newer white boats don't have decks. Grab a seat on the right side of the boat for the best view. On the way out of Manhattan, you'll pass the Statue of Liberty (the boat comes closest to Lady Liberty on the way to Staten Island), Ellis Island, and from the left side of the boat, Governor's Island; you'll see the Verrazano Narrows Bridge spanning the distance from Brooklyn to Staten Island in the distance.

When the boat arrives at St. George, Staten Island, if you are required to disembark, follow the boat-loading sign on your right as you get off; you'll circle around to the

---

(Moments Roosevelt Island Tram

Want to impress your family and friends with a little known, but spectacular view of the New York skyline? Take them for a ride on the Roosevelt Island Tram (ℂ 212/832-4543, ext. 1). This is the same tram that King Kong "attacks" in the Universal Studio Theme Park in Florida. The same tram you have probably seen in countless movies, most recently *Spiderman*. The tram originates at 59th Street and Second Avenue, costs $2 each way ($2 round-trip for seniors), and takes 4 minutes to traverse the East River to Roosevelt Island, where there are a series of apartment complexes and parks. During those 4 minutes you will be treated to a gorgeous view down the East River and the East Side skyline, with views of the United Nations and four bridges: the Queensboro, Williamsburg, Manhattan, and Brooklyn bridges. On a clear day you might even spot Lady Liberty. And don't worry, despite what you've seen in the movies, the tram is safe, the Green Goblin is dead, and your friendly neighborhood Spiderman has everything under control. The tram operates daily from 6am until 2:30am and until 3:30am on weekends.

next loading dock, where there's usually another boat waiting to depart for Manhattan. The skyline views are simply awesome on the return trip. Well worth the time spent.

Departs from the Whitehall Ferry Terminal at the southern tip of Manhattan. ℂ **718/815-BOAT.** www. ci.nyc.ny.us/html/dot. Free admission ($3 for car transport on select ferries). 24 hr.; every 20–30 min. weekdays, less frequently during off-peak and weekend hours. Subway: N, R to Whitehall St.; 4, 5 to Bowling Green; 1, 9 to South Ferry (ride in the 1st 5 cars).

Statue of Liberty 🎯🎯🎯 *Kids*   For the millions who first came by ship to America in the last century—either as privileged tourists or needy, hopeful immigrants—Lady Liberty, standing in the Upper Bay, was their first glimpse of America. No monument so embodies the nation's, and the world's, notion of political freedom and economic potential. Even if you don't make it out to Liberty Island, you can get a spine-tingling glimpse from Battery Park, from the New Jersey side of the bay, or during a free ride on the Staten Island Ferry (see above). It's always reassuring to see her torch lighting the way.

Proposed by French statesman Edouard de Laboulaye as a gift from France to the United States, commemorating the two nations' friendship and joint notions of liberty, the statue was designed by sculptor Frédéric-Auguste Bartholdi with the engineering help of Alexandre-Gustave Eiffel (who was responsible for the famed Paris tower) and unveiled on October 28, 1886. *Touring tips:* Ferries leave daily every half-hour to 45 minutes from 9am to about 3:30pm, with more frequent ferries in the morning and extended hours in summer. Try to go early on a weekday to avoid the crowds that swarm in the afternoon, on weekends, and on holidays.

A stop at **Ellis Island** (p. 242) is included in the fare, but if you catch the last ferry, you can only visit the statue or Ellis Island, not both.

Note that you can **buy ferry tickets in advance** via **www.statuereservations.com**, which will allow you to board the boat without standing in the sometimes-long ticket line; however, there is an additional service charge attached. Even if you've already purchased tickets, arrive as much as 30 minutes before your desired ferry time to allow for increased security procedures prior to boarding the ferry. The ferry ride takes about 20 minutes.

Once on Liberty Island, you'll start to get an idea of the statue's immensity: She weighs 225 tons and measures 152 feet from foot to flame. Her nose alone is 4½ feet long, and her index finger is 8 feet long.

After September 11, 2001, access to the base of the statue was prohibited, but in the summer of 2004, access, albeit still somewhat limited (you can't climb to the Statue's crown), was once again allowed. Now you can explore the Statue of Liberty Museum, peer into the inner structure through a glass ceiling near the base of the Statue, and enjoy views from the observation deck on top a 16-story pedestal.

On Liberty Island in New York Harbor. ℂ **212/363-3200** (general info), or 212/269-5755 (ticket/ferry info). www.nps. gov/stli or www.statueoflibertyferry.com. Free admission; ferry ticket to Statue of Liberty and Ellis Island $10 adults, $8 seniors, $4 children 3–17. Daily 9am–5pm (last ferry departs around 4pm); extended hours in summer. Subway: 4, 5 to Bowling Green; 1, 9 to South Ferry. Walk south through Battery Park to Castle Clinton, the fort housing the ferry ticket booth.

Times Square *Overrated*   There's no doubting that Times Square has evolved into something much different than it was over a decade ago when it had a deservedly sleazy reputation. Yet there is much debate among New Yorkers about which incarnation was better. For New Yorkers, Times Square is a place we go out of our way to avoid. The crowds, even by New York standards, are stifling; the restaurants, mostly national chains, aren't very good; the shops, also mostly national chains, are unimaginative; and the attractions, like **Madame Tussauds New York** wax museum (p. 257), are kitschy. I suppose it's a little too Vegas for us. Still, you've come all this way; you've got to at least take a peek, if only for the amazing neon spectacle of it.

Most of the Broadway shows are centered around Times Square, so plan your visit around your show tickets. For your pre-dinner meal, walk 2 blocks west to Ninth Avenue where you'll find a number of relatively inexpensive, good restaurants. If you are with the kids, the Ferris wheel in the **Toys "R" Us** store makes a visit to Times Square worthwhile.

1, 2, 3, 7, S, A, C, E, N, R, W to Times Sq.

Wall Street & the New York Stock Exchange

Wall Street—it's an iconic name, and the world's prime hub for bulls and bears everywhere. This narrow 18th-century lane (you'll be surprised at how little it is) is appropriately monumental, lined with neoclassical towers that reach as far skyward as the dreams and greed of investors who built it into the world's most famous financial market.

At the heart of the action is the **New York Stock Exchange (NYSE),** the world's largest securities trader, where billions change hands. The NYSE came into being in 1792, when merchants met daily under a nearby buttonwood tree to try and pass off to each other the U.S. bonds that had been sold to fund the Revolutionary War. By 1903, they were trading stocks of publicly held companies in this Corinthian-columned Beaux Arts "temple" designed by George Post. About 3,000 companies are now listed on the exchange, trading nearly 314 billion shares valued at about $16 trillion. Unfortunately, the NYSE is no longer open to the public for tours.

20 Broad St. (between Wall St. and Exchange Place). © 212/656-3000. www.nyse.com. Subway: J, M, Z to Broad St.; 2, 3, 4, 5 to Wall St.

Whitney Museum of American Art

What is arguably the finest collection of 20th-century American art in the world belongs to the Whitney thanks to the efforts of Gertrude Vanderbilt Whitney. A sculptor herself, Whitney organized exhibitions by American artists shunned by traditional academies, assembled a sizable personal collection, and founded the museum in 1930 in Greenwich Village.

Today's museum is an imposing presence on Madison Avenue—an inverted three-tiered pyramid of concrete and gray granite with seven seemingly random windows designed by Marcel Breuer, a leader of the Bauhaus movement. The rotating permanent collection consists of an intelligent selection of major works by Edward Hopper, George Bellows, Georgia O'Keeffe, Roy Lichtenstein, Jasper Johns, and other significant artists. A pleasing second-floor exhibit space is devoted exclusively to works from its permanent collection from 1900 to 1950, while the rest of the space is dedicated to rotating exhibits.

Shows are usually all well curated and more edgy than what you'd see at the MoMA or the Guggenheim (though not as left-of-mainstream as what you'll find at the New Museum). Topics range from topical surveys, such as *American Art in the Age of Technology* and *The Warhol Look: Glamour Style Fashion* to in-depth retrospectives of famous or lesser-known movements (such as Fluxus, the movement that spawned Yoko Ono, among others) and artists (Mark Rothko, Keith Haring, Duane Hanson, Bob Thompson). Free **gallery tours** are offered daily, and music, screenings, and lectures fill the calendar. The Whitney is also notable for having the best museum restaurant in town: **Sarabeth's at the Whitney,** worth a visit in its own right.

World Trade Center Site (Ground Zero)

Do you call a place where over 3,000 people lost their lives an "attraction"? Or do you now call it a shrine? This is the quandary of the World Trade Center site. As you read this book it is still just a site, and though ground was broken for rebuilding in the summer of 2004, there is still controversy over what actually will be built on the site. So don't expect to see much more than a big open hole for years to come.

In the mean time, you can see the site through a viewing wall on the Church Street side of the site; on that "Wall of Heroes" are the names of those who lost their lives that day along with the history of the site, including photos of the construction of the World Trade Center in the late 1960s and how, after it opened in 1972, it changed the New York skyline and downtown. A walk along the Wall of Heroes remains a painfully moving experience.

The site is bounded by Church, Barclay, Liberty, and West streets. Call ✆ 212/484-1222, or go to www.nycvisit.com or www.southstseaport.org for viewing information; go to www.downtownny.com for Lower Manhattan area information and rebuilding updates.

For details on the **Whitney Museum of American Art at Altria,** the petite Midtown annex, see p. 266.

945 Madison Ave. (at 75th St.). ✆ 877/WHITNEY or 212/570-3676. www.whitney.org. Admission $12 adults, $9.50 seniors and students, free for children under 12, pay what you wish Fri 6–9pm. Mon–Tues, Thurs, and Sat–Sun 11am–6pm; Fri 1–9pm. Subway: 6 to 77th St.

Yankee Stadium ★★   Next to the Colosseum in Rome, there aren't many more famous sports' arenas in the world than the House That Ruth Built. The Yankees play from April until October (and, since they seem to be in the playoff most years, mostly through October). Depending on who's in town, tickets, which range in price from $8 to $80, can be tough to score. But if you plan in advance, and even if you don't, you should be able to purchase a seat by going through a broker or scalping (be careful of forgeries) the day of a game. If you are not visiting during the baseball season, tours of the Stadium, including Monument Park, are held year-round. For more information see the section "Spectator Sports" later in this chapter.

161st St. and River Ave., Bronx. ✆ 718/293-6000. www.yankees.com. Tickets: $8–$80. Subway: 4, B, C to 161st St.

3 More Manhattan Museums

For the **Brooklyn Museum of Art,** the **New York Transit Museum,** the **American Museum of the Moving Image,** the **Queens Museum of Art,** the **Isamu Noguchi Garden Museum,** the **P.S. 1 Contemporary Art Center,** and the **Louis Armstrong House Museum,** see "Highlights of the Outer Boroughs," later in this chapter.

If you're traveling with the kids, also consider the museums listed under "Especially for Kids," on p. 294, which include the **Children's Museum of Manhattan,** the **Sony Wonder Technology Lab,** and the **New York Hall of Science.**

If you're interested in historic house museums, see the box called "In Search of Historic Homes," on p. 270.

Also, don't forget to see what's on at the monumental **New York Public Library,** which regularly holds excellent exhibitions; see p. 268.

American Folk Art Museum ★★   This gorgeous, ultramodern boutique museum is not only a stunning structure, but it also heralds American folk art's entry into the top echelon of museum-worthy art.

The modified open-plan interior features an extraordinary collection of traditional works from the 18th century to the self-taught artists and craftspeople of the present, reflecting the breadth and vitality of the American folk-art tradition. A splendid variety of quilts, in particular, makes the textiles collection the museum's most popular. The book- and gift shop is outstanding, filled with one-of-a-kind objects.

45 W. 53rd St. (btwn Fifth and Sixth aves.). ✆ 212/265-1040. www.folkartmuseum.org. Admission $9 adults, $7 seniors and students, free for children under 12, free to all Fri 6–8pm. Tues–Thurs and Sat–Sun 10:30am–5:30pm; Fri 10:30am–7:30pm. Subway: E, V to Fifth Ave.

Asia Society   The Asia Society was founded in 1956 by John D. Rockefeller III with the goal of increasing understanding between Americans and Asians through art exhibits, lectures, films, performances, and international conferences. The society is a leader in presenting contemporary Asian and Asian-American art. After a $30-million renovation that doubled the exhibition space, the society's headquarters is bigger, smarter, and better than ever. Never has so much of the core collection, which comprises Rockefeller's Pan-Asian acquisitions dating from 2000 B.C. to the 19th century, been on display before. Well-curated temporary exhibits run the gamut from *The New Way of Tea,* exploring Japan's elaborate tea ceremony, to *Through Afghan Eyes: A Culture in Conflict, 1987–1995,* a study in photographs and video. Additionally, the mammoth calendar of events ranges from film screenings to arts lectures to discussion panels featuring experts in Pan-Asian and global politics, business, and more; call or check the website for a current schedule.

725 Park Ave. (at 70th St.). ✆ 212/327-9276. www.asiasociety.org. Gallery admission $10 adults, $7 seniors, $5 students with ID, free for children under 16, free to all Fri 6–9pm. Tues–Sun 11am–6pm (Fri to 9pm; except July 4–Labor Day). Subway: 6 to 68th St./Hunter College.

Center for Jewish History *Finds*   This 125,000-square-foot complex is the largest repository of Jewish history, art, and literature in the Diaspora. It unites five of America's leading institutions of Jewish scholarship: the **American Jewish Historical Society** (www.ajhs.org), the national archives of the Jewish people in the Americas; the **Leo Baeck Institute** (www.lbi.org), documenting the robust history of German-speaking Jewry from the 17th century until annihilation under the Nazis; the **Yeshiva**

Tips **Be an Early Bird**

New York is the city that never sleeps, and you shouldn't either—at least not too much. My advice is to get an early start on your day. Check opening times for museums and other attractions and plan to be there very soon after they open to avoid the crowds. Believe me, it's no fun waiting on lines or peering over throngs of people to view exhibits. So bring your portable alarm clock or have your hotel give you a wake-up call.

University Museum (www.yumuseum.org), general-interest exhibits, plus a renowned collection of Judaica objects confiscated by the Nazis; the **YIVO Institute for Jewish Research** (www.yivoinstitute.org), focusing on exhibits exploring the diversity of the Jewish experience; and the **American Sephardi Federation** (www.asfonline.org), representing the spiritual, cultural, and social traditions of the American Sephardic communities (Jews from Southern Europe, North Africa, and the Middle East). Together, this union represents about 100 million archival documents, 500,000 books, and tens of thousands of objects of art and ephemera, ranging from Thomas Jefferson's letter denouncing anti-Semitism to memorabilia of famous Jewish athletes.

The main gallery space is the Yeshiva Museum, which comprises four galleries, an outdoor sculpture garden, and a children's workshop; a range of exhibits also showcase various holdings belonging to the other institutions as well. A central feature is the **Reading Room,** home to open stacks accessible by serious researchers and lay historians like, as well as the **Center Genealogy Institute,** which offers assistance in family history research. Another huge component of the Center is its 250-seat state-of-the-art auditorium, home to a packed schedule of lectures, music, and film presentations. If you get hungry, a kosher cafe is on site.

15 W. 16th St. (btwn Fifth and Sixth aves.). ✆ 212/294-8301. www.cjh.org. Admission to Yeshiva University Museum $6 adults, $4 seniors and students; free admission to all other facilities. Yeshiva University Museum Sun and Tues–Wed 11am–5pm; Thurs 11am–8pm. Reading Room and Genealogy Institute Mon–Thurs 9:30am–5pm; Fri by appt. All other exhibition galleries Mon–Thurs 9am–5pm; Fri 9am–4pm. Subway: L, N, R, 4, 5, 6 to 14th St./Union Sq.; F, V to 14th St.

The Cloisters ★★   If it weren't for this branch of the Metropolitan Museum of Art, many New Yorkers would never get to this northernmost point in Manhattan. This remote yet lovely spot is devoted to the art and architecture of medieval Europe. Atop a magnificent cliff overlooking the Hudson River, you'll find a 12th-century chapter house, parts of five cloisters from medieval monasteries, a Romanesque chapel, and a 12th-century Spanish apse brought intact from Europe. Surrounded by peaceful gardens, this is the one place on the island that can even approximate the kind of solitude suitable to such a collection. Inside you'll find extraordinary works that include the famed Unicorn tapestries, sculpture, illuminated manuscripts, stained glass, ivory, and precious metal work.

Despite its remoteness, the Cloisters are extremely popular, especially in fine weather, so try to schedule your visit during the week rather than on a crowded weekend afternoon. A free guided **Highlights Tour** is offered Tuesday through Friday at 3pm and Sunday at noon; gallery talks are also a regular feature. Additionally, **Garden Tours** are offered Tuesday through Sunday at 1pm in May, June, September, and October; lectures and other special programming are always on Sunday from noon to 2pm; and medieval music concerts are regularly held in the stunning 12th-century Spanish chapel. For an extra-special experience, you may want to plan your visit around one.

At the north end of Fort Tryon Park. ✆ 212/923-3700. www.metmuseum.org. Suggested admission (includes same-day entrance to the Metropolitan Museum of Art) $15 adults, $10 seniors, $7 students, free for children under 12. Nov–Feb Tues–Sun 9:30am–4:45pm; Mar–Oct Tues–Sun 9:30am–5:15pm. Subway: A to 190th St., then a 10-min. walk north along Margaret Corbin Dr., or pick up the M4 bus at the station (1 stop to Cloisters). Bus: M4 Madison Ave. (Fort Tryon Park–The Cloisters).

Cooper-Hewitt National Design Museum ★   Part of the Smithsonian Institution, the Cooper-Hewitt is housed in the Carnegie Mansion, built by steel magnate

Andrew Carnegie in 1901 and renovated to the tune of $20 million in 1996. Some 11,000 square feet of gallery space is devoted to changing exhibits that are invariably well conceived, engaging, and educational. Shows are both historic and contemporary in nature, and topics range from *The Work of Charles and Ray Eames: A Legacy of Invention* to *Russell Wright: Creating American Lifestyle* to *The Architecture of Reassurance: Designing the Disney Theme Parks.* Many installations are drawn from the museum's own vast collection of industrial design, drawings, textiles, wall coverings, books, and prints.

On your way in, note the fabulous Art Nouveau–style copper-and-glass canopy above the entrance. And be sure to visit the garden, ringed with Central Park benches from various eras.

2 E. 91st St. (at Fifth Ave.). ℂ 212/849-8400. www.si.edu/ndm. Admission $10 adults, $7 seniors and students, free for children under 12, free to all Fri 5–9pm. Tues–Thurs 10am–5pm; Fri 10am–9pm; Sat 10am–6pm; Sun noon–5pm. Subway: 4, 5, 6 to 86th St.

Dahesh Museum of Art   If you consider yourself a classicist, this small museum is for you. It's dedicated to 19th- and early-20th-century European academic art, a continuation of Renaissance, baroque, and rococo traditions that were overshadowed by the arrival of Impressionism on the art scene. (If you're not familiar with this academic school, expect lots of painstaking renditions of historical subjects and pastoral life.) Artists represented include Jean-Léon Gérôme, Lord Leighton, and Edwin Long, whose *Love's Labour Lost* is a conerstone of the permanent collection.

580 Madison Ave. (btwn 56th and 57th sts.). ℂ 212/759-0606. www.daheshmuseum.org. Admission $9 adults, $4 seniors and students, free for children under 12 and to all first Thurs of the month, 6–9pm. Tues–Sun 11am–6pm; first Thurs until 9pm. Subway: F, N, R, Q, W to 57th St.; 4, 5, 6 to 59th St.

El Museo del Barrio   What started in 1969 with a small display in a local school classroom in East Harlem is today the only museum in America dedicated to Puerto Rican, Caribbean, and Latin American art. The northernmost Museum Mile institution has a permanent exhibit ranging from pre-Columbian artifacts to photographic art and video. The display of *santos de palo* (wood-carved religious figurines) is especially worth noting, as is *Taíno, Ancient Voyagers of the Caribbean,* dedicated to the active, highly developed cultures that Columbus encountered when he landed in the "New World." The well-curated changing exhibitions tend to focus on 20th-century artists and contemporary subjects.

1230 Fifth Ave. (at 104th St.). ℂ 212/831-7272. www.elmuseo.org. Suggested admission $6 adults, $4 seniors (free on Thurs), and students, free for children under 12. Wed–Sun 11am–5pm. Subway: 6 to 103rd St.

The Frick Collection ★★   Henry Clay Frick could afford to be an avid collector of European art after amassing a fortune as a pioneer in the coke and steel industries at the turn of the 20th century. To house his treasures and himself, he hired architects Carrère & Hastings to build this 18th-century French-style mansion (1914), one of the most beautiful remaining on Fifth Avenue.

Most appealing about the Frick is its intimate size and setting. This is a living testament to New York's vanished Gilded Age—the interior still feels like a private home (albeit a really, really rich guy's home) graced with beautiful paintings, rather than a museum. Come here to see the classics by some of the world's most famous painters: Titian, Bellini, Rembrandt, Turner, Vermeer, El Greco, and Goya, to name only a few. A highlight of the collection is the **Fragonard Room,** graced with the sensual rococo series *The Progress of Love.* The portrait of Montesquieu by Whistler is also stunning.

Included in the price of admission, the AcousticGuide audio tour is particularly useful because it allows you to follow your own path rather than a proscribed route. A free 22-minute video presentation is screened in the Music Room every half-hour from 10am to 4:30pm (from 1:30 on Sun); starting with this helps to set the tone for what you'll see.

In addition, free **chamber music concerts** are held twice a month, generally every other Sunday at 5pm in fall and winter and select Thursdays at 5:45pm in warm weather, and once-a-month **lectures** are offered select Wednesdays at 5:30pm; call or visit the website for the current schedule and ticket information.

1 E. 70th St. (at Fifth Ave.). (© 212/288-0700. www.frick.org. Admission $12 adults, $8 seniors, $5 students. Children under 10 not admitted; children under 16 must be accompanied by an adult. Tues–Sat 10am–6pm; Sun 1–6pm. Closed all major holidays. Subway: 6 to 68th St./Hunter College.

International Center of Photography 🕊 *Finds* The ICP is one of the world's premier educators, collectors, and exhibitors of photographic art. The state-of-the-art gallery space is ideal for viewing rotating exhibitions of the museum's 50,000-plus prints as well as visiting shows. The emphasis is on contemporary photographic works, but historically important photographers aren't ignored. A must on any photography buff's list.

1133 Sixth Ave. (at 43rd St.). (© 212/857-0000. www.icp.org. Admission $10 adults, $7 seniors and students. Tues–Thurs and Sat–Sun 10am–6pm; Fri 10am–8pm. Subway: B, D, F, V to 42nd St.

Intrepid Sea-Air-Space Museum 🕊🕊 *Kids* The most astonishing thing about the aircraft carrier USS *Intrepid* is how it can be simultaneously so big and so small. It's a few football fields long, weighs 40,000 tons, holds 40 aircraft, and sometimes doubles as a ballroom for society functions. But stand there and think about landing an A-12 jet on the deck and suddenly it's minuscule. Furthermore, in the narrow passageways below, you'll find it isn't quite the roomiest of vessels. Now a National Historic Landmark, the exhibit also includes the naval destroyer USS *Edson,* and the submarine USS *Growler,* the only intact strategic missile submarine open to the public anywhere in the world, as well as a collection of vintage and modern aircraft, including the A-12 Blackbird, the world's fastest spy plane, and the newest addition to the museum, a retired British Airways Concorde jet.

Kids just love this place. They, and you, can climb inside a replica Revolutionary War submarine, sit in an A-6 Intruder cockpit, and follow the progress of America's astronauts as they work in space. There are even navy flight simulators—including a "Fly with the Blue Angels" program—for educational thrill rides in the Technologies Hall. Look for family-oriented activities and events at least 1 Saturday a month.

The program "All Hands on Deck" teaches both children and adults how things work on ships, plus there's a new AH-1 Cobra attack helicopter. The action-packed *Intrepid Wings* shows aircraft carrier take-offs and recoveries in the new Allison and Howard Lutnick Theater; the film runs continuously throughout the day. The exhibit *Remembering 9-11* recalls those lost, both civilians and rescuers. The grand visitor center makes for an impressive entrance, and the massive museum store is well stocked; goods include NYPD and FDNY logo gear. Dress warmly for a winter visit—it's almost impossible to heat an aircraft carrier.

Pier 86 (W. 46th St. at Twelfth Ave.). (© 212/245-0072. www.intrepidmuseum.org. Admission $17 adults, $13 veterans, seniors, and college students, $12 children 6–17, $4.50 children 2–5. $5 extra for flight simulator rides. Apr–Sept Mon–Fri 10am–5pm, Sat–Sun 10am–6pm; Oct–Mar Tues–Sun 10am–5pm. Last admission 1 hr. before closing. Subway: A, C, E to 42nd St./Port Authority. Bus: M42 crosstown.

The Jewish Museum   Housed in a Gothic-style mansion renovated in 1993 by AIA Gold Medal winner Kevin Roche, this wonderful museum now has the world-class space it deserves to showcase its remarkable collections, which chronicle 4,000 years of Jewish history. The two-floor permanent exhibit, *Culture and Continuity: The Jewish Journey,* tells the story of the Jewish experience from ancient times through today, and is the museum's centerpiece. Artifacts include daily objects that might have served the authors of the books of Genesis, Psalms, and Job, and a great assemblage of intricate Torahs. A wonderful collection of classic TV and radio programs is available for viewing through the Goodkind Resource Center (as any fan of television's Golden Age knows, its finest comic moments were Jewish comedy). The scope of the exhibit is phenomenal, and its story an enlightening—and intense—one. A random-access audio guide is geared to families (free with admission). In addition to the in-house shop, don't miss the Jewish Museum Design Shop, housed in the adjacent brownstone.

1109 Fifth Ave. (at 92nd St.). ✆ **212/423-3200.** www.thejewishmuseum.org. Admission $10 adults, $7.50 seniors and students, free for children under 12, pay what you wish Thurs 5–8pm. Check website for special online admission discounts (50% off at press time). Sun–Wed 11am–5:45pm; Thurs 11am–8pm; Fri 11am–3pm. Subway: 4, 5 to 86th St.; 6 to 96th St.

Lower East Side Tenement Museum ⭐ *Kids*   This museum is the first-ever National Trust for Historic Preservation site that was not the home of someone rich or famous. It's something quite different: a five-story tenement that 10,000 people from 25 countries called home between 1863 and 1935—people who had come to the United States looking for the American dream and made 97 Orchard St. their first stop. The tenement museum tells the story of the great immigration boom of the late 19th and early 20th centuries, when the Lower East Side was considered the "Gateway to America." A visit here makes a good follow-up to an Ellis Island trip—what happened to all the people who passed through that famous way station?

The only way to see the museum is by guided tour. Two primary tenement tours, held on all open days and lasting an hour, offer a satisfying exploration of the museum: **Piecing It Together: Immigrants in the Garment Industry,** which focuses on the restored apartment and the lives of its turn-of-the-20th-century tenants, an immigrant Jewish family named Levine from Poland; and **Getting By: Weathering the Great Depressions of 1873 and 1929,** featuring the homes of the German-Jewish Gumpertz family and the Sicilian-Catholic Baldizzi family, respectively. A knowledgeable guide leads you into each dingy urban time capsule, where several apartments have been faithfully restored to their lived-in condition, and recounts the real-life stories of the families who occupied them in fascinating detail. You can pair them for an in-depth look at the museum, since the apartments and stories are so different; however, one tour serves as an excellent introduction if you don't want to invest an entire afternoon here.

These tours are not really for kids, however, who won't enjoy the serious tone and "don't touch" policy. Much better for them is the 45-minute, weekends-only **Confino Family Apartment** tour, an interactive living history program geared to families, which allows kids to converse with an interpreter who plays teenage immigrant Victoria Confino (ca. 1916); kids can also handle whatever they like in the apartment and even try on period clothes.

The hour-long **Streets Where We Lived** neighborhood heritage walking tour is also offered on weekends from April through December. Small permanent and rotating exhibits, including photos, videos, and a model tenement, are housed in the Visitors'

Center and exhibition space in the tenement building at 97 Orchard St. Special tours and programs are sometimes on the schedule.

Tours are limited in number and sell out quickly, so it pays to buy tickets in advance, which you can do online, or over the phone by calling Ticketweb at ℂ **800/ 965-4827.** Note that the potential acquisition of a neighboring tenement at 99 Orchard St. may change programming, so confirm schedules.

Visitors' Center at 90 Orchard St. (at Broome St.). ℂ **212/431-0233.** www.tenement.org. Tenement and walking tours $9 adults, $7 seniors and students; Confino Apt. $9 adults, $7 seniors and students. Tenement tours depart Tues–Fri every 40 min. 1–4pm; Sat–Sun every half-hour 11am–4:45pm. Confino Apt. tour Sat–Sun hourly noon–3pm. Walking tour Apr–Dec Sat–Sun 1 and 2:30pm. Subway: F to Delancey St.; J, M, Z to Essex St.

Madame Tussauds New York *(Overrated)*   A branch of the famously garish London institution, this wax museum is just plain *overpriced*. Considering that you can get in to the Met for 12 bucks, admission to Madame Tussauds should be $6 or $7, not $30—especially since you'll be in and out of here inside of 2 hours. Museum folks tout the five floors and 85,000 square feet of space, but there's not a heckuva lot here; the collection of high-profile wax figures is relatively small.

That said, not everybody wants to go to the Met, and if you don't mind shelling out, you'll likely enjoy yourself. Don't forget your camera, because fully half the fun is having yourself photographed along eerily lifelike replicas of famous figures ranging from Joan Rivers to Gandhi. (Whoopi Goldberg has deadpanned, "My wax portrait is so close to the real me that one of my husbands asked it for alimony.") Best is the "Opening Night Party," the first room you'll enter, in which a wide range of contemporary stars are arranged in such candid poses that it's sometimes hard to distinguish the real folks from the fakes. While most of the figures are excellent likenesses, a few are clearly off target (the wax Beatles win the "What Were They Thinking?" award). Despite the wealth of John Travoltas, Lenny Kravitzes, and Woody Allens, I found my favorite figure to be Napoléon; the rest of the bloody "Madame Tussauds Story" exhibit is downright gruesome, however (she was a French Revolution–era death mask sculptor), so skip it if you have little ones in tow.

234 W. 42nd St. (btwn Seventh and Eighth aves.) ℂ **212/512-9600.** www.madame-tussauds.com. Admission $30 adults, $27 seniors, $24 children 4–12, free for children under 4. Daily 10am–8pm (last ticket sold). Subway: 1, 2, 3, 7, A, C, E, N, R, S, W to Times Sq.

Morgan Library ★★ *(Finds)*   This New York treasure, boasting one of the world's most important collections of original manuscripts, rare books and bindings, master drawings, and personal writings will be closed for a major renovation until late in 2006. Renovations will include a welcoming entrance on Madison Avenue; new and renovated galleries, so that more of the library's holdings can be exhibited; a modern auditorium; and a new Reading Room with greater capacity and electronic resources and substantially expanded space for collections storage.

29 E. 36th St. (at Madison Ave.). ℂ **212/685-0610.** www.morganlibrary.org.

Museum of Arts and Design ★ *(Finds)*   Formerly called the American Craft Museum, this small but aesthetically pleasing museum is the nation's top showcase for contemporary crafts. The collection focuses on objects that are prime examples of form and function, ranging from jewelry to baskets to vessels to furniture. You'll see a strong emphasis on material as well as craft, whether it be fiber, ceramics, or metal. Special exhibitions can range from expressionist clay sculpture to fine bookbinding, and can celebrate movements or single artisans. Or just take your chances and stop

Art for Art's Sake: The Gallery Scene

Manhattan has more than 500 private art galleries, selling everything from old masters to tomorrow's news. Galleries are open free to the public, generally Tuesday through Saturday from 10am to 6pm. Saturday afternoon gallery hopping, in particular, is a favorite pastime—nobody will expect you to buy, so don't worry.

The best way to winnow down your choices is by perusing the "Art Guide" in the Friday weekend section of the *New York Times,* or in the back of the Sunday "Arts & Leisure" section; the listings section at the back of the weekly *New York* magazine, which I find to be particularly descriptive and user-friendly; the Art section in the weekly *Time Out New York;* or the *New Yorker*'s weekly "Goings on About Town" section. You can also find the latest exhibition listings online at **www.nymetro.com**, whose "Arts" page gives you full access to *New York* magazine's listings; **www.newyorkmetro.com** (click on "Attractions"), **www.artnet.com**, and **www.galleryguide.org**. An excellent source—more for practicals on the galleries and the artists and genres they represent rather than current shows—is **www.artincontext.org**. The *Gallery Guide* is available at most galleries around town.

I suggest picking a gallery or a show in a neighborhood that seems to suit your taste, and just start browsing from there. Be aware that my list below doesn't even begin to scratch the surface. There are many, many more galleries in each neighborhood, as well as smaller concentrations of galleries in areas like the East Village, TriBeCa, and Brooklyn (check the Art in Context site).

Keep in mind that uptown galleries tend to be more traditional and exclusive-feeling, downtown galleries more high-ticket contemporary, and far west Chelsea galleries the most cutting edge. Museum-quality works dominate uptown, while raw talent and emerging artists are most common in west Chelsea. But there are constant surprises in all neighborhoods.

UPTOWN Uptown galleries are clustered in and around the glamorous crossroads of Fifth Avenue and 57th Street as well as on and off stylish Madison Avenue in the 60s, 70s, and 80s. Unlike their upstart Chelsea and SoHo counterparts, these blue-chip galleries maintain a quiet white-glove demeanor. They include art-world powerhouses **Gagosian Gallery,** 980 Madison Ave. (✆ 212/744-2313; www.gagosian.com), and **PaceWildenstein,** 32 E. 57th St. (✆ 212/421-3292; www.pacewildenstein.com), whose focus is on classic modernism, representing such artists as Jim Dine, Barbara Hepworth, and Claes Oldenburg; **Richard Gray Gallery,** 1018 Madison Ave., fourth floor (✆ 212/472-8787; www.richardgraygallery.com), featuring American and European contemporary works, with artists ranging from Joan Miró to David Hockney; the **Margo Feiden Galleries,** 699 Madison Ave. (✆ 212/677-5330; www.alhirschfeld.com), the sole authorized representative of the works of the late master ink caricaturist Al Hirschfeld; the **Mary Boone Gallery,** 745 Fifth Ave. (✆ 212/752-2929; www.maryboonegallery.com), known for success with such artists as Ross Bleckner and Nancy Ellison; and **Wildenstein & Co, Inc,** the classical big brother of **PaceWildenstein,** 19 E. 64th St. (© 212/879-0500; www.wildenstein.com), both specializing in big-ticket works: old masters, Impressionism, and Renaissance paintings and drawings.

CHELSEA The area in the West 20s between Tenth and Eleventh avenues is home to the avant-garde of today's New York art scene, with West 26th serving as the unofficial "gallery row." Most galleries are not in storefronts but in the large spaces of multistory former garages and warehouses. Galleries worth seeking out include **Paula Cooper,** 534 W. 21st St. (© 212/255-1105), a heavyweight in the modern art world, specializing in conceptual and minimal art; **George Billis Gallery,** 511 W. 25th St., 9F (© 212/645-2621; www.georgebillis.com), who shows works by talented emerging artists; **Barbara Gladstone Gallery,** 515 W. 24th St. (© 212/206-9300; www.gladstone gallery.com); uptown powerhouse **Gagosian Gallery,** 555 W. 24th St. (© 212/741-1111; www.gagosian.com), which shows such major modern artists as Richard Serra and Julian Schnabel; **Feigen Contemporary,** 535 W. 20th St. (© 212/929-0500), the modern counterpart to the uptown Old Masters gallery; **Cheim & Read,** 547 W. 25th St. (© 212/242-7727), which often shows works by such high-profile pop artists as Diane Arbus and Robert Mapplethorpe; **DCA Gallery,** 525 W. 22nd St. (© 212/255-5511; www.dcagallery. com), specializing in contemporary Danish artists; **Alexander and Bonin,** 132 Tenth Ave. (© 212/367-7474; www.alexanderandbonin.com), which mounts excellent solo exhibitions; **James Cohan Gallery,** 533 W. 26th St. (© 212/714-9500; www.jamescohan.com), particularly strong in modern photography; and **Lehmann Maupin,** 540 W. 26th St. (© 212/255-2923; www.lehmannmaupin. com), whose roster runs the gamut from young unknowns to contemporary masters like Ross Bleckner.

DOWNTOWN SoHo remains colorful, if less edgy than it used to be, with the action centered around West Broadway and encroaching onto the edge of Chinatown of late. Start with **Bronwyn Keenan,** 3 Crosby St. (© 212/431-5083), who's known for a keen eye for spotting emerging talent; **Peter Blum Gallery,** 99 Wooster St. (© 212/343-0441), who showcased the divine Kim Sooja, a Korean artist who uses traditional Korean bedcovers to comment on the promise of wedded bliss; **O. K. Harris,** 383 W. Broadway (© 212/431-3600; www.okharris.com), which shows a wide and fascinating variety of contemporary painting, sculpture, and photography; and **Louis K. Meisel,** 141 Prince St. (© 212/677-1340; www.meiselgallery.com), specializing in photorealism and American pinup art (yep, Petty and Vargas girls). In TriBeCa, try **Cheryl Hazan Arts Gallery,** 35 N. Moore St. (© 212/343-8964; www.cheryl hazanarts.com), or **DFN Gallery,** 176 Franklin St. (© 212/334-3400; www.dfn gallery.com), both of which focus on fresh and distinctive contemporary art.

in—you're unlikely to be disappointed. Stop into the gorgeous **shop** even if you don't make it into the museum.

40 W. 53rd St. (btwn Fifth and Sixth aves.). ℂ **212/956-3535**. www.americancraftmuseum.org. Admission $9 adults, $6 students and seniors, free for children under 12, pay what you wish Thurs 6–8pm. Fri–Wed 10am–6pm; Thurs 10am–8pm. Subway: E, V to Fifth Ave.

Museum of the City of New York A wide variety of objects—costumes, photographs, prints, maps, dioramas, and memorabilia—trace the history of New York City from its beginnings as a humble Dutch colony in the 16th century to its present-day prominence. Two outstanding permanent exhibits are the re-creation of John D. Rockefeller's master bedroom and dressing room, and the space devoted to *Broadway!*, a history of New York theater. Kids will love *New York Toy Stories*, a permanent exhibit showcasing toys and dolls owned and adored by centuries of New York children. The permanent *Painting the Town: Cityscapes of New York* explores the changing cityscape from 1809 to 1997, and carries new profundity in the wake of the September 11, 2001, terrorist attacks.

1220 Fifth Ave. (at 103rd St.). ℂ **212/534-1672**. www.mcny.org. Suggested admission $7 adults, $5 seniors, students, and children, $12 families. Tues–Sun 10am–5pm. Subway: 6 to 103rd St.

Museum of Jewish Heritage—A Living Memorial to the Holocaust Located in the south end of Battery Park City, the Museum of Jewish Heritage occupies a strikingly spare six-sided building designed by award-winning architect Kevin Roche, with a six-tier roof alluding to the Star of David and the six million murdered in the Holocaust. The permanent exhibits—*Jewish Life a Century Ago, The War Against the Jews,* and *Jewish Renewal*—recount the daily prewar lives, the unforgettable horror that destroyed them, and the tenacious renewal experienced by European and immigrant Jews in the years from the late 19th century to the present. The museum's power derives from the way it tells that story: through the objects, photographs, documents, and, most poignantly, through the videotaped testimonies of Holocaust victims, survivors, and their families, all chronicled by Steven Spielberg's Survivors of the Shoah Visual History Foundation. Thursday evenings are dedicated to panel discussions, performances, and music, while Sundays are dedicated to family programs and workshops; a film series is also a regular part of the calendar

While advance tickets are not usually necessary, you may want to purchase them to guarantee admission; call ℂ **212/945-0039.** Audio tours narrated by Meryl Streep and Itzhak Perlman are available at the museum for an additional $5.

36 Battery Place (at First Place), Battery Park City. ℂ **212/968-1800**. www.mjhnyc.org. Admission $10 adults, $7 seniors, $5 students, free for children under 12 and for everyone Wed 4–8pm. Check website for $2-off admission coupon (available at press time). Sun–Tues and Thurs 10am–5:45pm; Wed 10am–8pm; Fri and eves of Jewish holidays 10am–3pm. Subway: 4, 5 to Bowling Green.

Museum of Sex *Finds* How many cities can claim their own Museum of Sex? This one debuted in 2002 and despite its provocative title, offers a studied, historical look at the history of sex in our culture. In 2005, "*Stags, Smokers & Blue Movies:* The origin of American Pornographic Film" was the main exhibit. Don't miss a trip through the gift shop—definitely not your typical museum shop. How about a $1,375 snakeskin souvenir to show your friends back home? *Note:* Many of the displays are very graphic, so the museum may not be for everyone.

233 Fifth Ave. (at 27th St.). 𝄐 866/MOSEX NYC. www.museumofsex.com. Admission $15 adults, $14 students and seniors. No one under 18 admitted. Sun–Fri 11am–6:30pm; Sat 11am–8pm. Last ticket sold 45 min. before museum closing. Subway: N, R to 28th St.

Museum of Television & Radio   If you can resist the allure of this museum, I'd wager you've spent the last 70 years in a bubble. You can watch and hear all the great personalities of TV and radio—from Uncle Miltie to Johnny Carson to Jerry Seinfeld—at a private console (available for 2 hr.). You can also conduct computer searches to pick out the great moments of history, viewing almost anything that made its way onto the airwaves, from the Beatles' first appearance on *The Ed Sullivan Show* to the crumbling of the Berlin Wall (the collection consists of 75,000 programs and commercials). Selected programs are also presented in two theaters and two screening rooms, which can range from "Barbra Streisand: The Television Performances" to little-seen Monty Python episodes.

25 W. 52nd St. (btwn Fifth and Sixth aves.). 𝄐 212/621-6600. www.mtr.org. Admission $10 adults, $8 seniors and students, $5 children under 14. Tues–Sun noon–6pm (Thurs until 8pm, Fri theater programs until 9pm). Subway: B, D, F, V to 47–50th sts./Rockefeller Center; E, V to 53rd St.

National Museum of the American Indian, George Gustav Heye Center
This impressive collection represents the Smithsonian Institution. The collection spans more than 10,000 years of native heritage, gathered a century ago mainly by New York banking millionaire George Gustav Heye. About 70% of the collection is dedicated to the natives of North America and Hawaii; the rest represents the cultures of Mexico and Central and South America. There's a wealth of material here, but it's not as well organized as it could be. The museum also hosts temporary themed exhibitions and interpretive programs, plus free storytelling, music, and dance presentations.

The museum is housed in the beautiful 1907 Beaux Arts **U.S. Customs House** ⚶, designed by Cass Gilbert and a National Historic Landmark that's worth a look in its own right (see the box "Downtown Relics," on p. 271).

1 Bowling Green (btwn State and Whitehall sts.). 𝄐 212/514-3700. www.nmai.si.edu. Free admission. Daily 10am–5pm (Thurs until 8pm). Subway: 4, 5 to Bowling Green; N, R to Whitehall.

Neue Gallerie New York *Finds*   This museum is dedicated to German and Austrian art and design, with a particular focus on the early 20th century. Displayed on two floors, the collection features painting, works on paper, decorative arts, and other media from such artists as Klimt, Kokoschka, Kandinsky, Klee, and leaders of the Wiener Werkstätte decorative arts and Bauhaus applied arts movements, such as Adolf Loos and Mies van der Rohe, respectively. Once occupied by Mrs. Cornelius Vanderbilt III, the impeccably restored, landmark-designated 1914 Carrère & Hastings building (they built the New York Public Library as well) is worth a look in itself. Cafe Sabarsky is modeled on a Viennese cafe, so museumgoers in need of a snack break can expect a fine Linzer torte.

1048 Fifth Ave. (at 86th St.). 𝄐 212/628-6200. www.neuegalerie.org. Admission $10 adults, $7 seniors and students. Fri 11am–9pm; Sat–Mon 11am–6pm. Subway: 4, 5, 6 to 86th St.

New Museum of Contemporary Art ⚶   This contemporary arts museum has moved closer to the mainstream in recent years, but it's only a safety margin in from the edge as far as most of us are concerned. Expect adventurous and well-curated exhibitions. The 2006 exhibition calendar had not been announced at press time, but previous schedules have included *Portrait of the Lost Boys,* New Zealander Jacqueline Fraser's moving narrative made of sumptuous fabric and fragile wire sculptures that examines the high incidence of suicide among teenage boys in New Zealand, and *John Waters: Change of Life,* photographs by the filmmaker who brought us *Pink Flamingos* and *Hairspray.* In 2006, the museum will move to a new 60,000-square-foot, $35-million home on the Bowery at Prince Street. It will be the first new art museum ever constructed from the ground up below 14th Street.

556 W. 22nd St. (at Eleventh Ave.). (f) 212/219-1222. www.newmuseum.org. Admission $6 adults, $3 seniors and students, free to visitors 18 and under, $3 Thurs after 6pm. Tues–Wed and Fri–Sat noon–6pm; Thurs noon–8pm (Zenith Media Lounge to 6:30pm). Subway: C,E to 23rd St.

New York City Fire Museum ⚡ *Kids*   Housed in a real three-story 1904 firehouse, the former quarters of FDNY Engine Co. 30, this museum houses one of the country's most extensive collections of fire-service memorabilia from the 18th century to the present. It is also the best place to pay tribute to the 343 heroic firefighters who lost their lives just blocks away in the World Trade Center disaster. Expect ongoing changing exhibits relating to the September 11, 2001, terrorist attack. Other displays range from vintage fire marks to firetrucks (including the last-known example of a 1921 pumper) to the gear and tools of modern firefighters. Also look for leather hoses, fireboats, and Currier & Ives prints, plus a new exhibit on fire safety and burn prevention especially geared to families. Best of all, real firefighters are almost always on hand to share stories and fire-safety information with kids. The retail store sells authorized FDNY logo wear and souvenirs. Call ahead for details on scheduling a guided tour.

278 Spring St. (btwn Varick and Hudson sts.). (f) 212/691-1303. www.nycfiremuseum.org. Suggested admission $5 adults, $2 seniors and students, $1 children under 12. Tues–Sat 10am–5pm; Sun 10am–4pm. Subway: C, E to Spring St.

New-York Historical Society ⚡   Launched in 1804, the New-York Historical Society is a major repository of American history, culture, and art, with a special focus on New York and its broader cultural significance. The grand neoclassical edifice near the Museum of Natural History is finally emerged from the renovation tent. Now open on the fourth floor is the Henry Luce III Center for the Study of American Culture, a state-of-the-art study facility and gallery of fine and decorative arts, which displays more than 40,000 objects amassed over 200 years—including paintings, sculpture, Tiffany lamps, textiles, furniture, even carriages—that had previously been in storage for decades. Also look for paintings from Hudson River School artists Thomas Cole, Asher Durand, and Frederic Church, including Cole's five-part masterpiece, *The Course of Empire.* Of particular interest to scholars and ephemera buffs are the extensive Library Collections, which include books, manuscripts, maps, newspapers, photographs, and more documents chronicling the American experience. (An appointment may be necessary to view some or all of the Library Collections, so call ahead.)

An extensive, top-quality calendar of public programs runs the gamut from family story hours to Irving Berlin music nights to lectures by such luminaries as Ric Burns to expert-led walks through various Manhattan neighborhoods; call or check the website for the schedule.

2 W. 77th St. (at Central Park West). (f) 212/873-3400. www.nyhistory.org. Admission $10 adults, $5 seniors and students, free for children 12 and under. Tues–Sun 10am–6pm. Subway: B, C to 81st St.; 1, 9 to 79th St.

Scandinavia House: The Nordic Center in America *Finds*   Dedicated to both the shared and unique cultures of Denmark, Finland, Iceland, Norway, and Sweden, Scandinavia House features two floors of galleries and an outdoor sculpture terrace displaying rotating art and design exhibits that can range from *Scandia: Important Early Maps of the Northern Regions* to *Strictly Swedish: An Exhibition of Contemporary Design.* The rest of the space, including the 168-seat Victor Borge Hall, is dedicated to a chock-full calendar of lectures, film screenings, music and drama performances, and scholarly presentations, all of a Nordic ilk. The exquisite modern building—sleekly designed to showcase Scandinavian materials and aesthetics—is worth a look in itself, especially if you're a modern architecture buff. Guided tours are offered Tuesdays and Thursdays at 2pm, and last a half-hour; they're free, but reservations are recommended.

The shop is a riot of fine Scandinavian design, and the excellent AQ Cafe—an offshoot of the terrific Midtown restaurant **Aquavit** (p. 207)—serves up Swedish meatballs and other Scandinavian delicacies.

58 Park Ave. (btwn 37th and 38th sts.). ✆ 212/879-9779. www.scandinaviahouse.org. Suggested admission to 3rd- and 4th-floor galleries $3, $2 seniors and students; free admission to other spaces. Exhibitions Tues–Sat noon–6pm; cafe Mon–Sat 10am–5pm; store Mon–Sat 10am–6pm. Subway: 6 to 33rd St.; 4, 5, 6, 7, S to 42nd St./Grand Central.

Schomburg Center for Research in Black Culture   Arturo Alfonso Schomburg, a black Puerto Rican, set himself to accumulating materials about blacks in America, and his massive collection—one of the largest collections of African-American materials in the world—is now housed and preserved at this research branch of the New York Public Library. The Exhibition Hall, the Latimer/Edison Gallery, and the Reading Room host changing exhibits related to black culture, such as *Lest We Forget: The Triumph over Slavery* and *Masterpieces of African Motherhood.* A rich calendar of talks and performing arts events is also part of the continuing program. Make an appointment for a guided tour so you can see the 1930s murals by Harlem Renaissance artist Aaron Douglas; it'll be worth your while. Academics and others interested in a more complete look at the center's holdings can preview what's available online. Call to inquire about current exhibitions and information on tours and public programs.

515 Malcolm X Blvd. (Lenox Ave., btwn 135th and 136th sts.). ✆ 212/491-2200. www.nypl.org. Free admission. Gallery Tues–Sat 10am–6pm; Sun 1–5pm. Subway: 2, 3 to 135th St.

Skyscraper Museum   Wowed by the sheer verticality in this town? Awed by the architectural marvel that is the high-rise? You're not alone. If you'd like to learn more about the technology, culture, and sheer muscle behind it all, seek out this formerly itinerant museum, which moved into its first permanent home in 2004 in the 38-story Skidmore, Owings & Merrill tower that also houses the Ritz-Carlton New York, Battery Park. The new space comprises two galleries, one housing a permanent exhibition dedication to the evolution of Manhattan's commercial skyline, the other for changing shows.

39 Battery Place (Little West St. and 1st Place). ✆ 212/968-1961. www.skyscraper.org. Admission: $5 adults; $2.50 seniors and students. Wed–Sun noon–6pm. Subway: 4, 5 to Bowling Green.

South Street Seaport & Museum *(Kids)*   Dating back to the 17th century, this landmark historic district on the East River encompasses 11 square blocks of historic buildings, a maritime museum, several piers, shops, and restaurants.

You can explore most of the Seaport on your own. It's a beautiful but somewhat odd place. The mainly 18th- and 19th-century buildings lining the cobbled streets and alleyways are impeccably restored but nevertheless have a theme-park air about them, no doubt due to the mall-familiar shops housed within. The Seaport's biggest tourist attraction is Pier 17, a historic barge converted into a mall, complete with food court and cheap jewelry kiosks.

Get Set: New York's Best Movie Locations

New York has been the backdrop for so many films that it really is a character in itself. What follows are my favorite New York City movie locations and the movies that best represent them.

Times Square: You can watch the evolution of Times Square in two distinct and very gritty movies. When I say gritty, you should know immediately that neither of these movies were made in and around the cleaned-up Times Square of today. The Times Square of the 1950s is best illustrated in the great film, *Sweet Smell of Success* (1957) starring Burt Lancaster and Tony Curtis. The film's setting is a time when Times Square's the place where those who aspired to celebrity come to be discovered. It's tough, but not as tough as the Times Square depicted in *Taxi Driver* (1976). Directed by Martin Scorsese, the Times Square of the 1970s is a literal hell where Robert DeNiro's Travis Bickle says: "Someday a real rain will come and wash all this scum off the streets."

Empire State Building: Something about that view from the 86th-story observatory ignites romance. Here, Tom Hanks woos Meg Ryan in *Sleepless in Seattle* (1993), and Cary Grant waits for his love Deborah Kerr in *An Affair to Remember* (1957). But the greatest love story of all meets its tragic ending at the Empire State Building when King Kong woos Fay Wray in the 1933 masterpiece, *King Kong.* Remember, ". . . it wasn't the airplanes. It was beauty that killed the beast."

Little Italy: Not much of Little Italy is left today, especially compared with what is depicted in two movie classics. In *The Godfather: Part II* (1974), the neighborhood of the early 20th century is a teeming, vibrant place with its own social strata. Who can forget the great scene where young Vito Corleone (played by Robert DeNiro) stalks the local mafia don during the Feast of San Gennaro—when the Feast was truly a feast. We return to the Feast of San Gennaro and Little Italy in the 1970s, this time in Scorsese's *Mean Streets* (1973), where the neighborhood is beginning to disintegrate, as are the proud Vito Corleone–like Mafiosos who are replaced by young small-time thugs.

New York Delis: Woody Allen films all of his movies in New York, not so much because it's such a colorful place, but because he says he likes to sleep at home when he works. His movies have countless memorable New York scenes and one of my favorites, *Broadway Danny Rose* (1984), is no exception. The story of Broadway Danny Rose is told by a group of standup comedians who convene at none other than the Carnegie Deli (p. 206) where, it's said, there's a sandwich named after him. New York's best deli is Katz's (p. 182) on the Lower East Side, famous for its salami and kosher hot dogs. Katz's is also famous for Meg Ryan's pretend orgasm in the Rob Reiner film *When Harry Met Sally* (1989).

Central Park Reservoir: I'm a regular jogger at the Central Park Reservoir, now known as the Jacqueline Kennedy Onassis Reservoir, where the views of the New York skyline are spectacular. I'm not sure if Dustin Hoffman cares about the skyline views when he runs the track in the thriller, *Marathon Man* (1976).

And Keanu Reeves, I think, is more interested in selling his soul than getting a good workout when he hits the track in the movie *The Devil's Advocate* (1997).

Roosevelt Island Tram: What is it about this tram that attracts evildoers? In the Sylvester Stallone movie *Nighthawks* (1981), Stallone plays a New York cop who saves a packed tram from a terrorist. And in *Spider-Man* (2002), Peter Parker (a.k.a. Spiderman) rescues a group of young tram riders from the clutches of the diabolical Green Goblin.

New York Subways: Today, New York's subways are cleaner, safer, and cooler than they ever were. But one of the best movies about the bad days on New York subways is *The Taking of Pelham One Two Three* (1974), in which a subway car is hijacked by Robert Shaw, and it's up to transit cop Walter Matthau to crack the crime. The best New York subway movie of all time actually has very little actual inside-the-subway footage. Most of the action is below the subway, the elevated train to be precise, where Gene Hackman, in a car, is in mad pursuit of a suave heroin dealer on the train above him in *The French Connection* (1971).

Statue of Liberty: Poor Lady Liberty carries a heavy burden as the symbol of democratic society. Who can forget the eyes of the immigrants on the boat carrying Vito Corleone to the New World in *The Godfather: Part II* (1974)? But it's because she's such a symbol that Hollywood likes to trash her. It's their unsubtle way of showing how fragile our society is, but it usually takes unusual force to do so, like a tsunami in *The Day After Tomorrow* (2004). Or what happens in my favorite Statue of Liberty scene, in the original *Planet of the Apes* (1968), when Charlton Heston spots her torch coming out of the sand and screams: "You maniacs! You blew it up. Damn you! God damn you all to hell!"

Central Park West: One of the most filmed streets in the whole city. All five (yes, five!) versions of *Miracle on 34th Street* feature the street. Central Park West is the street the giant Stay Puft Marshmallow Man lurches up in *Ghost Busters* (1984), on his way to Sigourney Weaver's building at 55 Central Park West (at 66th St.). A few blocks up, at the stately Dakota apartment building at 72nd Street, Mia Farrow discovers some devilish neighbors in *Rosemary's Baby* (1968).

New York City Apartments: Not much irks me more than seeing those palatial digs that television seems to think represent New York apartments. Most of us live in closets, and some filmmakers actually understand this. Sure, Audrey Hepburn dressed like a rich fashion model in the wonderful *Breakfast at Tiffany's* (1961), but she lived in a small studio walk-up. That didn't stop her from entertaining, and the party scene in that movie, where the revelers were practically on top of each other, is a classic. Maybe even more realistic is the heatless, cockroach-swarming hovel that Dustin (Ratso Rizzo) Hoffman inhabits and offers to share with country boy Jon Voight in another tough New York movie, *Midnight Cowboy* (1969).

Despite its rampant commercialism, the Seaport is well worth a look. There's a good amount of history to be discovered here, most of it around the **South Street Seaport Museum,** a fitting tribute to the sea commerce that once thrived here.

In addition to the galleries—which house paintings and prints, ship models, scrimshaw, and nautical designs, as well as frequently changing exhibitions—there are a number of historic ships berthed at the pier to explore, including the 1911 four-masted *Peking* and the 1893 Gloucester fishing schooner *Lettie G. Howard.* A few of the boats are living museums and restoration works in progress; the 1885 cargo schooner *Pioneer* (© 212/748-8786) offers 2-hour public sails daily from early May through September. Tickets are $25 for adults, $15 for children 12 and under. If you'd rather keep those sea legs on dry land, the museum offers a number of guided walking tours; call or check **www.southstseaport.org** for details.

Even **Pier 17** has its merits. Head up to the third-level deck overlooking the East River, where the long wooden chairs will have you thinking about what it was like to cross the Atlantic on the *Normandie.* From this level you can see south to the Statue of Liberty, north to the Gothic majesty of the Brooklyn Bridge, and Brooklyn Heights on the opposite shore.

At the gateway to the Seaport, at Fulton and Water streets, is the *Titanic* **Memorial Lighthouse,** a monument to those who lost their lives when the ocean liner sank on April 15, 1912. It was erected overlooking the East River in 1913 and moved to this spot in 1968, just after the historic district was so designated.

A variety of events take place year-round, ranging from street performers to concerts to fireworks; check the website or dial © 212/SEA-PORT.

At Water and South sts.; museum visitor center is at 12 Fulton St. © 212/748-8600 or 212/SEA-PORT. www.southst seaport.org. Museum admission $5. Museum Apr–Sept Fri–Wed 10am–6pm, Thurs 10am–8pm; Oct–Mar Wed–Mon 10am–5pm. Subway: 2, 3, 4, 5 to Fulton St. (walk east, or downslope, on Fulton St. to Water St.).

Studio Museum in Harlem This small but lovely museum is devoted to presenting 19th- and 20th-century African-American art as well as 20th-century African and Caribbean art and traditional African art and artifacts. Rotating exhibitions are a big part of the museum's focus, such as *Smithsonian African-American Photography: The First 100 Years, 1842–1942;* the silkscreens and lithographs of Jacob Lawrence; and an annual exhibition of works by emerging artists as part of its Artists-in-Residence program. There's also a small sculpture garden, a good gift shop, and a full calendar of special events.

144 W. 125th St. (btwn Lenox Ave. and Adam Clayton Powell Blvd.). © 212/864-4500. www.studiomuseuminharlem. org. Admission $7 adults, $3 seniors, $1 children under 12, free to all 1st Sat of the month. Wed–Thurs noon–6pm; Fri noon–8pm; Sat–Sun 10am–6pm. Subway: 2, 3 to 125th St.

Whitney Museum of American Art at Altria This Midtown branch of the **Whitney Museum of American Art** (p. 250) features an airy sculpture court and a petite gallery that hosts changing exhibits, usually the works of living contemporary artists. Well worth peeking into if you happen to be in the neighborhood. Free gallery talks are offered Wednesdays and Fridays at 1pm.

120 Park Ave. (at 42nd St., opposite Grand Central Terminal). © 917/663-2453. www.whitney.org. Free admission. Gallery Mon–Wed and Fri 11am–6pm; Thurs 11am–7:30pm. Sculpture Court Mon–Sat 7:30am–9:30pm; Sun 11am–7pm. Subway: S, 4, 5, 6, 7 to 42nd St./Grand Central.

4 Skyscrapers & Other Architectural Highlights

For details on the **Empire State Building,** see p. 242; for **Grand Central Terminal,** p. 244; for **Rockefeller Center,** p. 246; for the **U.S. Customs House,** p. 271; and for the **Brooklyn Bridge,** p. 241. You might also wish to check out "Places of Worship," later in this chapter, for treasures like **St. Patrick's Cathedral, Temple Emanu-El,** and the **Cathedral of St. John the Divine.** See also chapter 2, "A Traveler's Guide to New York's Architecture," for a look at the city's evolving architecture.

In addition to checking out the landmarks below, architecture buffs may also want to seek out these notable buildings: The **Lever House,** built in 1952 at 390 Park Ave., between 53rd and 54th streets, and the neighboring **Seagram Building** (1958), at 375 Park Ave., are the city's best examples of the form-follows-function, glass-and-steel International style, with the latter designed by master architect Mies van der Rohe. Also in Midtown East is the **Sony Building,** at 550 Madison Ave., designed in 1984 by Philip Johnson, with a pretty rose-granite facade and a playful Chippendale-style top that puts it a cut above the rest on the block.

The Upper West Side is home to two of the city's prime examples of residential architecture. On Broadway, taking up the block between 73rd and 74th streets, is the **Ansonia,** looking for all the world like a flamboyant architectural wedding cake. This splendid Beaux Arts building has been home to the likes of Stravinsky, Toscanini, and Caruso, thanks to its virtually soundproof apartments. (It was also the spot where members of the Chicago White Sox plotted to throw the 1919 World Series, a year

Harlem's Architectural Treasures

Originally conceived as a bucolic suburbia for 19th-century Manhattan's monied set, Harlem has always had more than its share of historic treasures. To find them, pay a call on the **Astor Row Houses,** 130th Street between Fifth and Lenox avenues, a fabulous series of 28 red-brick town houses built in the early 1880s by the Astor family and graced with wooden porches, generous yards, and ornamental ironwork.

Equally impressive is **Strivers' Row,** West 139th Street between Adam Clayton Powell Jr. and Frederick Douglass boulevards, where hardly a brick has changed among the gorgeous McKim, Mead & White neo-Italian Renaissance town houses since they were built in 1890. Once the original white owners had moved out, these lovely houses attracted the cream of Harlem, "strivers" like Eubie Blake and W. C. Handy.

Handsome brownstones, limestone town houses, and row houses are sprinkled atop **Sugar Hill,** 145th to 155th streets, between St. Nicholas and Edgecombe avenues, named for the "sweet life" enjoyed by its residents. In the early 20th century, such prominent blacks as W. E. B. DuBois, Thurgood Marshall, and Roy Wilkins lived in the now-landmark building at 409 Edgecombe Ave.

And if you're venturing uptown this far, don't miss the **Jumel Terrace Historic District,** west of St. Nicholas Avenue between 160th and 162nd streets. Of particular note is **Sylvan Terrace,** which feels more like an upstate Hudson River town than a part of Harlem—well worth seeking out for architecture lovers. A walk along it will lead you directly to the grand **Morris-Jumel Mansion,** which is open to the public for tours (see "In Search of Historic Homes," below).

before Babe Ruth moved in after donning the New York Yankees' pinstripes.) Even more notable is the **Dakota,** at 72nd Street and Central Park West. Legend has it that the angular 1884 apartment house—accented with gables, dormers, and oriel windows that give it a brooding appeal—earned its name when its forward-thinking developer, Edward S. Clark, was teased by friends that he was building so far north of the city that he might as well be building in the Dakotas. The building's most famous resident, John Lennon, was gunned down outside the 72nd Street entrance on December 8, 1980; Yoko Ono still lives inside.

Chrysler Building ★★ Built as Chrysler Corporation headquarters in 1930 (they moved out decades ago), this is perhaps the 20th century's most romantic architectural achievement, especially at night, when the lights in its triangular openings play off its steely crown. As you admire its facade, be sure to note the gargoyles reaching out from the upper floors, looking for all the world like streamline–Gothic hood ornaments.

There's a fascinating tale behind this building. While it was under construction, its architect, William Van Alen, hid his final plans for the spire that now tops it. Working at a furious pace in the last days of construction, the workers assembled in secrecy the elegant pointy top—and then they raised it right through what people had assumed was going to be the roof, and for a brief moment it was the world's tallest building (a distinction stolen by the Empire State Building only a few months later). Its exterior chrome sculptures are magnificent and spooky. The observation deck closed long ago, but you can visit its lavish ground-floor interior, which is Art Deco to the max. The ceiling mural depicting airplanes and other early marvels of the first decades of the 20th century evince the bright promise of technology. The elevators are works of art, masterfully covered in exotic woods (especially note the lotus-shaped marquetry on the doors).

405 Lexington Ave. (at 42nd St.). Subway: S, 4, 5, 6, 7 to 42nd St./Grand Central.

Flatiron Building This triangular masterpiece was one of the first skyscrapers. Its knife-blade wedge shape is the only way the building could fill the triangular property created by the intersection of Fifth Avenue and Broadway, and that happy coincidence created one of the city's most distinctive buildings. Built in 1902 and fronted with limestone and terra cotta (not iron), the Flatiron measures only 6 feet across at its narrow end. So called for its resemblance to the laundry appliance, it was originally named the Fuller Building, then later "Burnham's Folly" (since folks were certain that architect Daniel Burnham's 21-story structure would fall down). It didn't. There's no observation deck, and the building mainly houses publishing offices, but there are a few shops on the ground floor. The building's existence has served to name the neighborhood around it—the Flatiron District, home to a bevy of smart restaurants and shops.

175 Fifth Ave. (at 23rd St.). Subway: R to 23rd St.

New York Public Library ★★ The New York Public Library, adjacent to **Bryant Park** (p. 283) and designed by Carrère & Hastings (1911), is one of the country's finest examples of Beaux Arts architecture, a majestic structure of white Vermont marble with Corinthian columns and allegorical statues. Before climbing the broad flight of steps to the Fifth Avenue entrance, take note of the famous lion sculptures—*Fortitude* on the right, and *Patience* on the left—so dubbed by whip-smart former mayor Fiorello LaGuardia. At Christmastime they don natty wreaths to keep warm.

This library is actually the **Humanities and Social Sciences Library,** only one of the research libraries in the New York Public Library system. The interior is one of the

Finds Not Your Ordinary Attractions

If you have a little extra time after covering all your must-sees—or would just rather eschew the crowds and discover the unusual and obscure for awhile—here are a few sights you might not find in other guide books:

When in Chinatown, before or after dim sum or *congee,* venture to 70 Mulberry St., to the second floor where the **Museum of Chinese in the Americas** is located (*©* **212/619-4785;** www.chinatownweb.com/MOCA). Here you'll find a celebration of the Chinese immigrant experience in New York and throughout the country. In 2005, I found the exhibit "Have You Eaten Yet: The Chinese Restaurant in America," particularly fascinating. An upcoming exhibit will be a presentation of family Chinese recipes.

Heading further downtown, you might find the **New York City Police Museum,** 100 Old Slip (*©* **212/480-3100;** www.nycpolicemuseum.org), of interest. Located in New York's first precinct station house built in 1901, the museum exhibits police equipment throughout the years such as pistols, uniforms, and vehicles along with really fun stuff like master burglar Willie Sutton's lock picks and a machine gun used by Al Capone.

If you are here in the summer, or even if you are not, I recommend a visit to Coney Island in Brooklyn (p. 300). After the beach, or during a break from the rides, take a walk to the nearby **Coney Island Museum,** 1208 Surf Ave. (*©* **718/372-5159;** www.coneyisland.com). Here you will find relics from Coney Island's heyday as the premier amusement park in the world. Check out an original "steeplechase horse" or vintage bumper cars, or funhouse distortion mirrors. And for a mere 99¢, even if all you want to do is use the clean bathroom, the museum is a bargain.

I've recommended El Museo del Barrio on page 254, but to see another "art" form of del barrio, make your way to 106th Street and Park Avenue. There you will see a schoolyard with a playground wall covered in graffiti. That wall is also known as the **Graffiti Hall of Fame** where some of the street greats have made their mark.

finest in the city and features **Astor Hall,** with high arched marble ceilings and grand staircases. Thanks to massive restoration and modernization, the stupendous **Main Reading Rooms** have been returned to their stately glory and moved into the computer age (goodbye, card catalogs!).

Even if you don't stop in to peruse the periodicals, you may want to check out one of the excellent rotating **exhibitions.** Call or check the website to see what's on while you're in town. There's also a full calendar of **lecture programs,** with past speakers ranging from Tom Stoppard to Cokie Roberts; popular speakers often sell out, so it's a good idea to purchase tickets in advance.

Fifth Ave. and 42nd St. *©* 212/869-8089 (exhibits and events), or 212/661-7220 (library hours). www.nypl.org. Free admission to all exhibitions. Thurs–Sat 10am–6pm; Tues–Wed 11am–7:30pm. Subway: B, D, F, V to 42nd St.; S, 4, 5, 6, 7 to Grand Central/42nd St.

United Nations   In the midst of New York City is this working monument to world peace. The U.N. headquarters occupies 18 acres of international territory—neither the city nor the United States has jurisdiction here—along the East River from 42nd to 48th streets. Designed by an international team of architects (led by American Wallace K. Harrison and including Le Corbusier) and finished in 1952, the complex along the East River weds the 39-story glass slab Secretariat with the free-form General Assembly on beautifully landscaped grounds donated by John D. Rockefeller, Jr. One hundred eighty nations use the facilities to arbitrate worldwide disputes.

Guided tours leave every half-hour or so and last 45 minutes to an hour. Your guide will take you to the General Assembly Hall and the Security Council Chamber and introduce the history and activities of the United Nations and its related organizations. Along the tour you'll see donated objects and artwork, including charred artifacts that survived the atomic bombs at Hiroshima and Nagasaki, stained-glass windows by Chagall, a replica of the first *Sputnik*, and a colorful mosaic called *The*

In Search of Historic Homes

The **Historic House Trust of New York City** preserves 19 houses, located in city parks in all five boroughs. Those particularly worth seeking out include the **Morris-Jumel Mansion** ⊛, in Harlem at 65 Jumel Terrace, at 160th Street, east of St. Nicholas Avenue (✆ 212/923-8008; www.morrisjumel.org; Wed–Sun 10am–4pm), a grand Colonial mansion built in the Palladian style (ca. 1765) and now Manhattan's oldest surviving residential house.

Built around 1764, the **Dyckman Farmhouse Museum,** farther uptown at 4881 Broadway, at 204th Street (✆ 212/304-9422; www.historichousetrust. org; Tues–Sun 11am–4pm), is the only Dutch Colonial farmhouse remaining in Manhattan, stoically and stylishly surviving the urban development that grew up around it.

The simple **Edgar Allan Poe Cottage,** 2460 Grand Concourse, at East Kingsbridge Road in the Bronx (✆ 718/881-8900; www.bronxhistoricalsociety. org; Sat 10am–4pm, Sun 1–5pm), was the last home (1846–49) of the brilliant but troubled poet and author, who moved his wife here because he thought the "country air" would be good for her tuberculosis. The house is outfitted as a memorial to the writer, with period furnishings and exhibits on his life and times.

The **Merchant's House Museum** ⊛, 29 E. 4th St., between Lafayette Street and Bowery in NoHo (✆ 212/777-1089; www.merchantshouse.com; Thurs–Mon 1–5pm), is a rare jewel: a perfectly preserved 19th-century home, complete with intact interiors, whose last resident is said to be the inspiration for Catherine Sloper in Henry James's *Washington Square*.

Each of the 15 other houses also has a fascinating story to tell. A brochure listing the locations and touring details of all 19 of the historic homes is available by calling ✆ 212/360-8282; recorded information is available at ✆ 212/360-3448. You'll also find information online at www.preserve.org/hht. Admission to each house is generally no more than $3 ($5 at Merchant's House).

Downtown Relics

New York is neither Rome nor Athens, yet the city can boast a few old structures, at least New World old. To find a good sampling of "ancient" New York, head downtown, where it all began.

You might want to first stop at the southern tip of the island at Battery Park where an old fort called **Castle Clinton National Monument** (© 212/344-7220; www.nps.gov/cacl) still stands. The fort, or what remains of it, was built between 1808 and 1811 to defend New York Harbor against the British. In the mid–19th century the fort was the city's first immigration center. A small museum was added to the monument in 1986, with exhibits that follow the evolution of the fort.

Not far from Castle Clinton at 1 Bowling Green is the relatively modern 1907-built **U.S. Customs House** 🎭, which houses the National Museum of the American Indian, George Gustav Heye Center (p. 261). Designed by Cass Gilbert and now a National Historic Landmark, the granite structure features giant statues carved by Daniel Chester French (of Lincoln Memorial fame) lining the front that personify Asia (pondering philosophically), America (bright-eyed and bushy-tailed), Europe (decadent, whose time has passed), and Africa (sleeping). Inside, the airy oval rotunda designed by Spanish engineer Raphael Guastavino was frescoed by Reginald Marsh to glorify the shipping industry (and, by extension, the Customs office once housed here).

One of Wall Street's most recognizable sights is the imposing, majestic **Federal Hall National Memorial,** 26 Wall St. (© 212/825-6888; www.nps.gov/feha). Built in 1842, the Memorial, with the 1883-built statue of George Washington on the steps, and directly across from the New York Stock Exchange, was erected on the site of New York's first City Hall. Inside it's now a museum, with exhibits that elucidate the events surrounding the Memorial and other aspects of American history. The infrastructure of the Memorial suffered from the massive shock of the nearby attack on the World Trade Center; as a result, the Memorial is undergoing a $16-million rehabilitation. Call to see if the museum's reopened in time for your visit.

George Washington was a very visible presence in 18th-century New York and he worshiped at the still standing **St. Paul's Chapel,** built in 1766 and part of the Trinity Church (p. 274) at 74 Trinity Place (© 212/602-0800). The Chapel now serves as a memorial to the victims of 9/11.

So now we know where Washington worshiped, but where did he eat? The answer is at **Fraunces Tavern,** the same place where Washington bade farewell to his officers at the end of the American Revolution. This 1907-built tavern is an exact replica of the original 1717 tavern. It's now a museum, 54 Pearl St., near Broad Street (© 212/425-1778; www.fraunces tavernmuseum.org), and an actual restaurant.

Golden Rule, based on a Norman Rockwell drawing, which was a gift from the United States in 1985.

If you take the time to wander the beautifully landscaped **grounds,** you'll be rewarded with lovely views and some surprises. The mammoth monument *Good Defeats Evil,* donated by the Soviet Union in 1990, fashioned a contemporary St. George slaying a dragon from parts of a Russian ballistic missile and an American Pershing missile.

For an unusual treat try a multi-ethnic meal while visiting the UN at the **Delegates' Dining Room** (**$\textcircled{C}$ 212/963-7625**).

At First Ave. and 46th St. $\textcircled{C}$ **212/963-8687.** www.un.org/tours. Guided tours $12 adults, $8.50 seniors, $7.50 high school and college students, $6.50 children 5–14. Children under 5 not permitted. Daily tours every half-hour 9:30am–4:45pm; closed weekends Jan–Feb; limited schedule may be in effect during the general debate (late Sept to mid-Oct). Subway: S, 4, 5, 6, 7 to 42nd St./Grand Central.

Woolworth Building ⭑ This soaring "Cathedral of Commerce" cost Frank W. Woolworth $14 million worth of nickels and dimes in 1913. Designed by Cass Gilbert, it was the world's tallest edifice until 1930, when it was surpassed by the Chrysler Building. At its opening, Pres. Woodrow Wilson pressed a button from the White House that illuminated the building's 80,000 electric light bulbs. The neo-Gothic architecture is rife with spires, gargoyles, flying buttresses, vaulted ceilings, 16th-century-style stone-as-lace traceries, castle-like turrets, and a churchlike interior. Housing financial institutions and high-tech companies, the grand tower is still dedicated to the almighty dollar.

Step into the lofty marble entrance arcade to view the gleaming mosaic Byzantine-style ceiling and gold-leafed neo-Gothic cornices. The corbels (carved figures under the crossbeams) in the lobby include whimsical portraits of the building's engineer Gunwald Aus measuring a girder (above the staircase to the left of the main door), Gilbert holding a miniature model of the building, and Woolworth counting coins (both above the left-hand corridor of elevators). Stand near the security guard's central podium and crane your neck for a glimpse at Paul Jennewein's murals of *Commerce* and *Labor,* half hidden up on the mezzanine. Cross Broadway for the best overview of the exterior.

233 Broadway (at Park Place, near City Hall Park). Subway: 2, 3 to Park Place; N, R to City Hall.

5 Places of Worship

New York has an incredible range of renowned religious institutions, notable for their history, architecture, and/or inspirational music. I've listed two of Harlem's premier gospel institutions below; if you would rather go to one of these gospel services in the company of a knowledgeable guide, see "Organized Sightseeing Tours," on p. 286 of this chapter. Additionally, if you would like to hear the rousing gospel of the four-time Grammy Award–winning **Brooklyn Tabernacle Choir** ⭑, see p. 300.

If you do plan to attend a gospel service, be prepared to stay for the entire 1½- to 2-hour service. It is impolite to exit early. (Services are extremely popular, so you'll find it just plain difficult to leave before the end, anyway.)

Abyssinian Baptist Church ⭑ The most famous of Harlem's more than 400 houses of worship is this Baptist church, founded downtown in 1808 by African-American and Ethiopian merchants. It was moved uptown to Harlem back in the 1920s by Adam Clayton Powell, Sr., who built it into the largest Protestant congregation—white or black—in America. His son, Adam Clayton Powell, Jr. (for whom the adjoining boulevard was named), carried on his tradition, and also became the first-ever black U.S. congressman. Abyssinian is now the domain of the fiery, activist-minded Rev. Calvin O. Butts, whom the chamber of commerce has declared a "Living Treasure." The Sunday morning services—at 9 and 11am—offer a wonderful opportunity to experience the Harlem gospel tradition.

132 Odell Clark Place (W. 138th St., btwn Adam Clayton Powell Blvd. and Lenox Ave.). (*) **212/862-7474.** www. abyssinian.org. Subway: 2, 3, B, C to 135th St.

Cathedral of St. John the Divine ★

The world's largest Gothic cathedral, St. John the Divine has been a work in progress since 1892. Its sheer size is amazing enough—a nave that stretches two football fields and a seating capacity of 5,000—but keep in mind that there is no steel structural support. The church is being built using traditional Gothic engineering—blocks of granite and limestone are carved out by master masons and their apprentices—which may explain why construction is still ongoing, more than 100 years after it began, with no end in sight. In fact, a December 2001 fire destroyed the north transept, which housed the gift shop. But this phoenix rose from the ashes quickly; the cathedral was reopened to visitors within a month, even though the scent of charred wood was still in the air and restoration will not be complete for months to come. That's precisely what makes this place so wonderful: Finishing isn't necessarily the point.

Though the seat of the Episcopal Diocese of New York, St. John's embraces an interfaith tradition. Internationalism is a theme found throughout the cathedral's iconography. Each chapel is dedicated to a different national, ethnic, or social group. The genocide memorial in the Missionary chapel—dedicated to the victims of the Ottoman Empire in Armenia (1915–23), of the Holocaust (1939–45), and in Bosnia-Herzegovina since 1992—moved me to tears, as did the FDNY memorial in the Labor chapel. Although it was originally conceived to honor 12 firefighters killed in 1966, hundreds of personal notecards and trinkets of remembrance have evolved it into a moving tribute to the 343 firefighting heroes killed on September 11, 2001.

You can explore the cathedral on your own, or on the **Public Tour,** offered 6 days a week; also inquire about the periodic (usually twice monthly) **Vertical Tour,** which takes you on a hike up the 11-flight circular staircase to the top, for spectacular views. At press time, these were still suspended due to the fire. Check the website for updates. St. John the Divine is also known for presenting outstanding workshops, musical events, and important speakers. The free **New Year's Eve concert** draws thousands of New Yorkers; so, too, does its annual **Feast of St. Francis** (Blessing of the Animals), held in early October (see the "New York City Calendar of Events," in chapter 3). Call for event information and tickets. To hear the incredible pipe organ in action, attend the weekly **Choral Evensong and Organ Meditation** service, which highlights one of the nation's most treasured pipe organs, Sundays at 6pm.

1047 Amsterdam Ave. (at 112th St.). (*) **212/316-7540,** 212/932-7347 for tour information and reservations, 212/662-2133 for event information and tickets. www.stjohndivine.org. Suggested admission $2; tour $5; vertical tour $10. Mon–Sat 7am–6pm; Sun 7am–7pm. Tours offered Tues–Sat 11am; Sun 1pm. Worship services Mon–Sat 8 and 8:30am (morning prayer and holy Eucharist), 12:15pm, and 5:30pm (1st Thurs service 7:15am); Sun 8, 9, and 11am and 6pm; AIDS memorial service 4th Sat of the month at 1pm. Subway: B, C, 1, 9 to Cathedral Pkwy.

Mother A.M.E. Zion Church

Another of Harlem's great gospel churches is this African Methodist Episcopal house of worship, the first black church to be founded in New York State. Established on John Street in Lower Manhattan in 1796, Mother

A.M.E. was known as the "Freedom Church" for the central role it played in the Underground Railroad. Among the escaped slaves the church hid was Frederick Douglass; other famous congregants have included Sojourner Truth and Paul Robeson. Mother A.M.E. relocated to Harlem in 1914, and moved into this grand edifice in 1925. Rousing Sunday services are at 11am.

140–7 W. 137th St. (btwn Adam Clayton Powell Blvd. and Lenox Ave.). ℂ 212/234-1544. www.motherafrican methodistezchurch.com. Subway: 2, 3 or B, C to 135th St.

St. Patrick's Cathedral   This incredible Gothic white-marble-and-stone structure is the largest Roman Catholic cathedral in the United States, as well as the seat of the Archdiocese of New York. Designed by James Renwick, begun in 1859, and consecrated in 1879, St. Patrick's wasn't completed until 1906. Strangely, Irish Catholics picked one of the city's WASPiest neighborhoods for St. Patrick's. After the death of the beloved John Cardinal O'Connor in 2000, Pope John Paul II installed Bishop Edward Egan, whom he elevated to cardinal in 2001. The vast cathedral sits a congregation of 2,200; if you don't want to come for Mass, you can pop in between services to get a look at the impressive interior. The St. Michael and St. Louis altar came from Tiffany & Co. (also located here on Fifth Ave.), while the St. Elizabeth altar—honoring Mother Elizabeth Ann Seton, the first American-born saint—was designed by Paolo Medici of Rome.

Fifth Ave. (btwn 50th and 51st sts.). ℂ 212/753-2261. www.ny-archdiocese.org/pastoral/cathedral_about.html. Free admission. Sun–Fri 7am–8:30pm; Sat 8am–8:30pm. Mass Mon–Fri 7, 7:30, 8, and 8:30am, noon, and 12:30, 1, and 5:30pm; Sat 8 and 8:30am, noon, and 12:30 and 5:30pm; Sun 7, 8, 9, and 10:15am (Cardinal's mass), noon, and 1, 4, and 5:30pm; holy days 7, 7:30, 8, 8:30, 9, 11, and 11:30am, noon, and 12:30, 1, and 5:30 and 6:30pm. Subway: B, D, F, V to 47–50th sts./Rockefeller Center.

Temple Emanu-El   Many of New York's most prominent and wealthy families are members of this Reform congregation—the first to be established in New York City—housed in the city's most famous synagogue. The largest house of Jewish worship in the world is a majestic blend of Moorish and Romanesque styles, symbolizing the mingling of Eastern and Western cultures. The temple houses a small but remarkable collection of Judaica in the Herbert & Eileen Bernard Museum, including a collection of Hanukkah lamps with examples ranging from the 14th to the 20th centuries. Three galleries also tell the story of the congregation Emanu-El from 1845 to the present. Tours are given after morning services Saturdays at noon. Inquire for a schedule of lectures, films, music, symposiums, and other events.

1 E. 65th St. (at Fifth Ave.). ℂ 212/744-1400. www.emanuelnyc.org. Free admission. Daily 10am–5pm. Services Sun–Thurs 5:30pm; Fri 5:15pm; Sat 10:30am. Subway: N, R to Fifth Ave.; 6 to 68th St.

Trinity Church   Serving God and mammon, this Wall Street house of worship—with neo-Gothic flying buttresses, beautiful stained-glass windows, and vaulted ceilings—was designed by Richard Upjohn and consecrated in 1846. At that time, its 280-foot spire dominated the skyline. Its main doors, embellished with biblical scenes, were inspired in part by Ghiberti's famed doors on Florence's Baptistry. The historic Episcopal church stood strong while office towers crumbled around it on September 11, 2001; however, an electronic organ has temporarily replaced the historic pipe organ, which was severely damaged by dust and debris. The gates to the historic church currently serve as an impromptu memorial to the victims of 9/11, with countless tokens of remembrance left by both locals and visitors alike.

The church runs a brief tour daily at 2pm (a second Sun tour follows the 11:15am Eucharist); groups of five or more should call ℂ **212/602-0872** to reserve. There's a small museum at the end of the left aisle displaying documents (including the 1697 church charter from King William III), photographs, replicas of the Hamilton-Burr duel pistols, and other items. Surrounding the church is a churchyard whose monuments read like an American history book: a tribute to martyrs of the American Revolution, Alexander Hamilton, Robert Fulton, and many more. Lined with benches, this makes a wonderful picnic spot on warm days.

Also part of Trinity Church is **St. Paul's Chapel,** at Broadway and Fulton Street, New York's only surviving pre-Revolutionary church, and a transition shelter for homeless men until it was transformed into a relief center after September 11; it returned to its former duties in mid-2002. Built by Thomas McBean, with a temple-like portico and fluted Ionic columns supporting a massive pediment, the chapel resembles London's St. Martin-in-the-Fields. In the small graveyard, 18th- and early-19th-century notables rest in peace and modern businesspeople sit for lunch.

Trinity holds its renowned **Noonday Concert series** of chamber music and orchestral concerts Mondays and Thursdays at 1pm; call ℂ **212/602-0747** or visit the website for the full schedule, and to see if concert programming has resumed at St. Paul's.

At Broadway and Wall St. ℂ **212/602-0800,** 212/602-0872, or 212/602-0747 for concert information. www.trinity wallstreet.org. Free admission and free tours; $2 suggested donation for noonday concerts. Museum Mon–Fri 9–11:45am; Sun–Fri 1–3:45pm; Sat 10am–3:45pm. Services Mon–Fri 8:15am, 12:05, and 5:15pm (additional Healing Service Thurs at 12:30pm); Sat 8:45am; Sun 9 and 11:15am (also 8am Eucharist service at St. Paul's Chapel, btwn Vesey and Fulton sts.). Subway: 4, 5 to Wall St.

6 Central Park & Other Places to Play

CENTRAL PARK

Without the miracle of civic planning that is **Central Park** ★★★, Manhattan would be a virtual unbroken block of buildings. Instead, smack in the middle of Gotham, an 843-acre natural retreat provides a daily escape valve and tranquilizer for millions of New Yorkers.

While you're in the city, be sure to take advantage of the park's many charms—not the least of which is its sublime layout. Frederick Law Olmsted and Calvert Vaux won a competition with a plan that marries flowing paths with sinewy bridges, integrating them into the natural rolling landscape with its rocky outcroppings, man-made lakes, and wooded pockets. Construction concluded in 1870 and designers predicted the hustle and bustle to come, and tactfully hid traffic from the eyes and ears of parkgoers by building roads that are largely hidden from the bucolic view.

On just about any day, Central Park is crowded with New Yorkers and visitors alike. On nice days, especially weekend days, it's the city's party central. Families come to play in the snow or the sun, depending on the season; in-line skaters come to fly through the crisp air and twirl in front of the band shell; couples come to stroll or paddle the lake; dog owners come to hike and throw Frisbees to Bowser; and just about everybody comes to sunbathe at the first sign of summer. On beautiful days, the crowds are part of the appeal—folks come here to peel off their urban armor and relax, and the common goal puts a general feeling of camaraderie in the air. On these days, the people-watching is more compelling than anywhere else in the city. But even on the most crowded days, there's always somewhere to get away from it all, if you just want a little peace and quiet, and a moment to commune with nature.

Central Park

Alice in Wonderland Statue **15**
Balto Statue **21**
The Bandshell **19**
Belvedere Castle **7**
Bethesda Terrace &
  Bethesda Fountain **17**
Boathouse Cafe **12**
Bow Bridge **9**
Carousel **27**
Central Park Zoo **24**
Charles A. Dana
  Discovery Center **1**
Cleopatra's Needle
  (The Obelisk) **10**
Conservatory **14**
Conservatory Garden **1**
The Dairy Information Center **26**
Delacorte Clock **23**
Delacorte Theater **8**
Diana Ross Playground **5**
Hans Christian Andersen Statue **13**
Harlem Meer **1**
Hecksher Ball Fields **29**
Hecksher Playground **30**
Henry Luce
  Nature Observatory **7**
Imagine Mosaic **18**
Jacqueline Kennedy Onassis
  Reservoir **3**
Lasker Rink and Pool **1**
Loeb Boathouse **16**
The Mall **20**
North Meadow Ball Fields **2**
Pat Hoffman Friedman
  Playground **11**
The Pool **2**
Rustic Playground **22**
Shakespeare Garden **9**
Spector Playground **4**
Swedish Cottage
  Marionette Theatre **6**
Tavern on the Green **28**
Tisch Children's Zoo **24**
Wollman Rink **25**

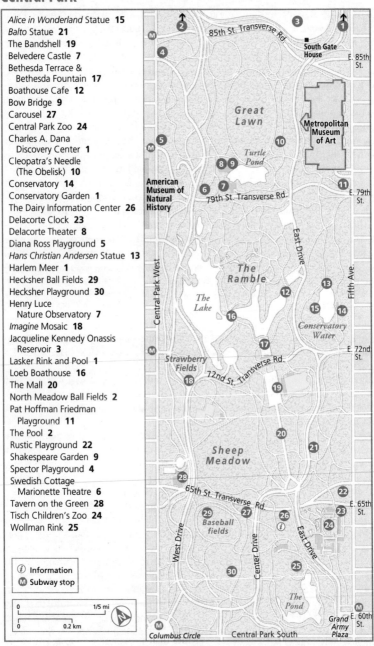

i Information
Ⓜ Subway stop

0   1/5 mi
0   0.2 km

ORIENTATION & GETTING THERE Look at your map—that great green swath in the center of Manhattan is Central Park. It runs from 59th Street (also known as Central Park South) at the south end to 110th Street at the north end, and from Fifth Avenue on the east side to Central Park West (the equivalent of Eighth Ave.) on the west side. A 6-mile rolling road, **Central Park Drive,** circles the park, and has a lane set aside for bikers, joggers, and in-line skaters. A number of **transverse (crosstown) roads** cross the park at major points—at 65th, 79th, 86th, and 97th streets—but they're built down a level, largely out of view, to minimize intrusion on the bucolic nature of the park.

A number of subway stops and lines serve the park, and which one you take depends on where you want to go. To reach the southernmost entrance on the west side, take an A, B, C, D, 1, or 9 to 59th Street/Columbus Circle. To reach the southeast corner entrance, take the N, R to Fifth Avenue; from this stop, it's an easy walk into the park to the Information Center in the **Dairy** (© 212/794-6564; daily 11am–5pm, to 4pm in winter), midpark at about 65th Street. Here you can ask questions, pick up park information, and purchase a good park map.

If your time for exploring is limited, I suggest entering the park at 72nd or 79th streets for maximum exposure (subway: B, C to 72nd St. or 81st St./Museum of Natural History). From here, you can pick up park information at the visitor center at **Belvedere Castle** (© 212/772-0210; Tues–Sun 10am–5pm, to 4pm in winter), midpark at 79th Street. There's also a third visitor center at the **Charles A. Dana Discovery Center** (© 212/860-1370; daily 11am–5pm, to 4pm in winter), at the northeast corner of the park at Harlem Meer, at 110th Street between Fifth and Lenox avenues (subway: 2, 3 to Central Park N./110th St.). The Dana Center is also an environmental education center hosting workshops, exhibits, music programs, and park tours, and lends fishing poles for fishing in Harlem Meer (park policy is catch-and-release).

Food carts and vendors are set up at all of the park's main gathering points, selling hot dogs, pretzels, and ice cream, so finding a bite to eat is never a problem. You'll also find a fixed food counter at the **Conservatory,** on the east side of the park north of the 72nd Street entrance, and both casual snacks and more sophisticated New American dining at **The Boat House,** on the lake near 72nd Street and Park Drive North (© 212/517-2233).

GUIDED WALKS The **Central Park Conservancy** offers a slate of free walking tours of the park; call © 212/360-2726 or check **www.centralparknyc.org** for the current schedule (click on the "Walking Tours" button on the left). The Dana Center hosts ranger-guided tours on occasion (call © 212/860-1370, or 800/201-PARK for a schedule). Also consider a private walking tour; many of the companies listed in "Organized Sightseeing Tours," later in this chapter, offer guided tours of the park.

FOR FURTHER INFORMATION Call the main number at © 212/310-6600 for recorded information, or 212/310-6600 or 212/628-1036 to speak to a live person. Call © 888/NY-PARKS for special events information. The park also has two comprehensive websites that are worth checking out before you go: the city parks department's site at **www.centralpark.org**, and the Central Park Conservancy's site at **www.centralparknyc.org**, both of which feature excellent maps and a far more complete rundown of park attractions and activities than I have room to include here. If you have an **emergency** in the park, dial © 800/201-PARK, which will link you directly to the park rangers.

SAFETY TIP Even though the park has the lowest crime rate of any of the city's precincts, keep your wits about you, especially in the more remote northern end. It's a good idea to avoid the park entirely after dark, unless you're heading to one of the restaurants for dinner or to a **Summerstage** or **Shakespeare in the Park** event (see "Park It! Shakespeare, Music & Other Free Fun," p. 360), when you should stick with the crowds. For more safety tips, see "Playing It Safe," in chapter 6.

EXPLORING THE PARK

The best way to see Central Park is to wander along the park's 58 miles of winding pedestrian paths, keeping in mind the following highlights.

Before starting your stroll, stop by the **Information Center** in the Dairy (© 212/794-6464; daily 11am–5pm, to 4pm in winter), midpark in a 19th-century-style building overlooking Wollman Rink at about 65th Street, to get a good park map and other information on sights and events, and to peruse the kid-friendly exhibit on the park's history and design.

The southern part of Central Park is more formally designed and heavily visited than the relatively rugged and remote northern end. Not far from the Dairy is the **Carousel,** with 58 hand-carved horses (© 212/879-0244; daily Apr–Nov 10am–6pm, to 4:30pm in winter; rides are $1); the zoo (see below); and the Wollman Rink for roller- or ice-skating (see "Activities," below).

The **Mall,** a long formal walkway lined with elms shading benches and sculptures of sometimes forgotten writers, leads to the focal point of Central Park, **Bethesda Fountain** (along the 72nd St. transverse road). **Bethesda Terrace** and its grandly sculpted entryway border a large **lake** where dogs fetch sticks, rowboaters glide by, and dedicated early morning anglers try their luck at catching carp, perch, catfish, and bass. You can rent a rowboat at or take a gondola ride from **Loeb Boathouse,** on the eastern end of the lake (see "Activities," below). Boats of another kind are at **Conservatory Water** (on the east side at 73rd St.), a stone-walled pond flanked by statues of both **Hans Christian Andersen** and **Alice in Wonderland.** On Saturday at 10am, die-hard yachtsmen race remote-controlled sailboats in fierce competitions that follow Olympic regulations. (Sorry, model boats aren't for rent.)

If the action there is too intense, **Sheep Meadow** on the southwestern side of the park is a designated quiet zone, where Frisbee throwing and kite flying are as energetic as things get. Another respite is **Strawberry Fields** , at 72nd Street on the West Side. This memorial to John Lennon, who was murdered across the street at the Dakota apartment building (72nd St. and Central Park West, northwest corner), is a gorgeous garden centered around an Italian mosaic bearing the title of the lead Beatle's most famous solo song, and his lifelong message: IMAGINE. In keeping with its goal of promoting world peace, the garden has 161 varieties of plants, donated by each of the 161 nations in existence when it was designed in 1985. This is a wonderful place for peaceful contemplation.

Bow Bridge, a graceful lacework of cast iron, designed by Calvert Vaux, crosses over the lake and leads to the most bucolic area of Central Park, the **Ramble.** This dense 38-acre woodland with spiraling paths, rocky outcroppings, and a stream is the best spot for bird-watching and feeling as if you've discovered an unimaginably leafy forest right in the middle of the city.

North of the Ramble, **Belvedere Castle** is home to the **Henry Luce Nature Observatory** (© 212/772-0210), worth a visit if you're with children. From the castle, set on Vista Rock (the park's highest point at 135 ft.), you can look down on the **Great**

Tips **Softball for the Stars**

Every spring and summer, Central Park is home to dozens of softball leagues. One of the oldest and most celebrated is the **Broadway Show League** (© 212/ **944-3849;** www.broadwayshowleague.com), which plays at Hecksher Fields, around 63rd Street on the west side of the park (check the website for a schedule). The league features representatives from all the major Broadway productions; in 2004, **The Producers** beat out the team from **Beauty and the Beast** to capture their third league championship. The co-ed games, which are open for all to watch, can get pretty intense, and you might be surprised who you see out there shagging flies; Al Pacino, Matthew Broderick, and Robert Redford have all played in the league. I once witnessed Edie Falco slide headfirst into second base. And yes, she was safe.

Lawn, where softball players and sun worshipers compete for coveted greenery, and the **Delacorte Theater,** home to Shakespeare in the Park (see chapter 11). The small **Shakespeare Garden** south of the theater is scruffy, but it does have plants, herbs, trees, and other bits of greenery mentioned by the playwright. Behind the Belvedere Castle is the **Swedish Cottage Marionette Theatre** 𝒻 (© **212/988-9093**), hosting various marionette plays for children throughout the year; call to see what's on.

Continue north along the east side of the Great Lawn, parallel to East Drive. Near the glass-enclosed back of the **Metropolitan Museum of Art** (p. 244) is **Cleopatra's Needle,** a 69-foot obelisk originally erected in Heliopolis around 1475 B.C. It was given to the city as a gift from the khedive of Egypt in 1880. (The khedive bestowed to the city of London a similar obelisk, which now sits on the embankment of the Thames.)

North of the 86th Street Transverse Road is the **Jacqueline Kennedy Onassis Reservoir,** so named following the death of the beloved first lady, who lived nearby and often enjoyed a run along the 1½-mile jogging track that circles the reservoir.

North of the reservoir is my favorite part of the park. It's much less traversed and in some areas, absolutely tranquil. The **North Meadow** (at 96th St.) features 12 baseball and softball fields. Sadly, the North Meadow is circled by a not very attractive fence, and 6 months of the year that fence is locked and the Meadow closed. An unfortunate recent trend in Central Park has been the proliferation of fences. They have become so prevalent, that at times you get the feeling you are not really in a park, but a museum.

North of the North Meadow at the northeast end of the park is the **Conservatory Garden** 𝒻 (at 105th St. and Fifth Ave.), Central Park's only formal garden, with a magnificent display of flowers and trees reflected in calm pools of water. (The gates to the garden once fronted the Fifth Ave. mansion of Cornelius Vanderbilt II.) **The Lasker Rink and Pool** (© 212/534-7639) is the only swimming pool in Central Park, and in the winter it's converted to a skating rink that offers a less hectic alternative to Wollman Rink (see "Activities," below). **Harlem Meer** and its boathouse were recently renovated and look beautiful. The boathouse now berths the **Charles A. Dana Discovery Center,** near 110th Street between Fifth and Lenox avenues (© **212/ 860-1370**), where children learn about the environment and borrow fishing poles for catch-and-release at no charge. **The Pool** (at W. 100th St.), possibly the most idyllic spot in all of Central Park, was recently renovated and features willows, grassy banks, and a small pond populated by some very well-fed ducks. You might even spot an egret and a hawk or two lurking around here.

GOING TO THE ZOO

Central Park Zoo/Tisch Children's Zoo ★ *Kids*   Here is a pleasant refuge within a refuge where lithe sea lions frolic in the central pool area with beguiling style, gigantic but graceful polar bears glide back and forth across a watery pool that has glass walls through which you can observe very large paws doing very smooth strokes, monkeys seem to regard those on the other side of the fence with knowing disdain, and in the hot and humid Tropic Zone, large colorful birds swoop around in freedom, sometimes landing next to nonplused visitors.

Fun Fact Going to the Dog

The people at Central Park say that the question they're asked almost more than any other these days is "Where is the statue of Balto?" The heroic dog is just northwest of the zoo, midpark, just above 66th Street.

Because of its small size, the zoo is at its best with its displays of smaller animals. The indoor multilevel Tropic Zone is a real highlight, its steamy rainforest home to everything from black-and-white colobus monkeys to Emerald tree boa constrictors to a leaf-cutter ant farm; look for the new dart poison frog exhibit, which is very cool. So is the large penguin enclosure in the Polar Circle, which is better than the one at San Diego's SeaWorld. In the Temperate Territory, look for the Asian red pandas (cousins to the big black-and-white ones), which look like the world's most beautiful raccoons. Despite their pool and piles of ice, however, the polar bears still look sad.

The entire zoo is good for short attention spans; you can cover the whole thing in 1½ to 3 hours, depending on the size of the crowds and how long you like to linger. It's also very kid-friendly, with lots of well-written and -illustrated placards that older kids can understand. For the littlest ones, there's the $6-million **Tisch Children's Zoo.** With pigs, llamas, potbellied pigs, and more, this petting zoo and playground is a real blast for the 5-and-under set.

830 Fifth Ave. (at 64th St., just inside Central Park). ℭ 212/861-6030. www.wcs.org/zoos. Admission $6 adults, $1.25 seniors, $1 children 3–12, free for children under 3. Summer hours (Apr–Oct) weekdays 10am–5pm, weekends 10am–5:30pm; Winter hours (Nov–Mar) daily 10am–4:30pm. Last entrance 30 min. before close. Subway: N, R to Fifth Ave.

ACTIVITIES

The 6-mile rolling road circling the park, **Central Park Drive,** has a lane set aside for bikers, joggers, and in-line skaters. The best time to use it is when the park is closed to traffic: Monday to Friday 10am to 3pm (except Thanksgiving to New Year's) and 7 to 10pm. It's also closed from 7pm Friday to 6am Monday, but when the weather is nice, the crowds can be hellish.

BIKING   Off-road mountain biking isn't permitted; stay on Central Park Drive or your bike may be confiscated by park police.

You can rent 3- and 10-speed bikes as well as tandems in Central Park at the **Loeb Boathouse,** midpark near 72nd Street and Park Drive North, just in from Fifth Avenue (ℭ 212/517-2233 or 212/517-3623), for $9 to $15 an hour, with a complete selection of kids' bikes, cruisers, tandems, and the like ($200 deposit required); at

Metro Bicycles, 1311 Lexington Ave., at 88th Street (☎ **212/427-4450**), for about $7 an hour, or $35 a day; and at **Toga Bike Shop,** 110 W. End Ave., at 64th Street (☎ **212/799-9625;** www.togabikes.com), for $30 a day. No matter where you rent, be prepared to leave a credit card deposit.

BOATING   From March through November, gondola rides and rowboat rentals are available at the **Loeb Boathouse,** midpark near 74th Street and Park Drive North, just in from Fifth Avenue (☎ **212/517-2233** or 212/517-3623). Rowboats are $10 for the first hour, $2.50 for every 15 minutes thereafter, and a $30 deposit is required; reservations are accepted. (Note that rates were not set for the summer season at press time, so these may change.)

HORSE-DRAWN CARRIAGE RIDES *(Overrated* At the entrance to the park at 59th Street and Central Park South, you'll see a line of **horse-drawn carriages** waiting to take passengers on a ride through the park or along certain of the city's streets. Horses belong on city streets as much as chamber pots belong in our homes. You won't need me to tell you how forlorn most of these horses look; if you insist, a ride is about $50 for two for a half-hour, but I suggest skipping it.

ICE-SKATING   Central Park's **Wollman Rink** ⍟, on the east side of the park between 62nd and 63rd streets (☎ **212/439-6900;** www.wollmanskatingrink.com), is the city's best outdoor skating spot, more spacious than the tiny rink at Rockefeller Center. It's open for skating generally from mid-October to mid-April, depending on the weather. Rates are $8.50 for adults, $4.50 for seniors and kids under 12, and skate rental is $4.75; lockers are available (locks are $6.75). **Lasker Rink** ☎ **212/534-7639,** on the east side around 106th street, is a less expensive alternative to the much more crowded Wollman Rink. Open November through March. Rates are $4.50 for adults, $2.25 for kids under 12, and skate rental is $4.75.

IN-LINE SKATING   Central Park is the city's most popular place for blading. See the beginning of this section for details on Central Park Drive, the main drag for skaters. On weekends, head to West Drive at 67th Street, behind Tavern on the Green, where you'll find trick skaters weaving through a New York Roller Skating Association (NYRSA) slalom course at full speed, or to the Mall in front of the band shell (above Bethesda Fountain) for twirling to tunes. In summer, **Wollman Rink** converts to a hotshot roller rink, with half-pipes and lessons available (see "Ice-Skating," above).

You can rent skates for $20 a day from **Blades Board and Skate,** 120 W. 72nd St., between Broadway and Columbus Avenue (☎ **212/787-3911;** www.blades.com). Wollman Rink (see above) also rents in-line skates for park use at similar rates.

PLAYGROUNDS   Nineteen Adventure Playgrounds are scattered throughout the park, perfect for jumping, sliding, tottering, swinging, and digging. At Central Park West and 81st Street is the **Diana Ross Playground** ⍟, voted the city's best by *New York* magazine. Also on the west side is the **Spector Playground,** at 85th Street and Central Park West, and, a little farther north, the **Wild West Playground** at 93rd Street. On the east side is the **Rustic Playground,** at 67th Street and Fifth Avenue, a delightfully landscaped space rife with islands, bridges, and big slides; and the **Pat Hoffman Friedman Playground,** right behind the Metropolitan Museum of Art at East 79th Street, is geared toward older toddlers.

RUNNING   Marathoners and wannabes regularly run in Central Park along the 6-mile **Central Park Drive,** which circles the park (please run toward traffic to avoid being mowed down by wayward cyclists and in-line skaters). The **New York Road**

Tips   Running the City

Here are the **New York Road Runners'** top picks for running routes in Manhattan.

Jacqueline Kennedy Onassis Reservoir: Possibly the most famous running route in the world; presidential candidates have run this 1½-mile route as well as the famous former first lady for whom it is now named.

The Loop in Central Park: I used to run past Madonna and her male bodyguards when she was a frequenter of the 6-mile loop. Now I see Howard Stern jogging, no bodyguards in sight, but usually with a female companion or two.

East River: Entering on 63rd Street and York Avenue and running up to 125th Street and back is a 6-mile jog where you will pass Gracie Mansion, high-rises overlooking the river, and fishermen testing the river waters.

Hudson River South: Enter at Chelsea Piers at West 23rd Street and continue down to Battery Park City and back for this approximately 5-mile run. In the warm months it's a carnival downtown, with in-line skaters, kayakers, musicians, and cyclists crowding the slim downtown park.

Hudson River North: This approximately 6-mile run starts at Riverbank State Park at 145th Street on the Hudson River and continues through lovely Riverside Park, passing the 79th Street Boat Basin, and ending at the *Intrepid* Sea-Air-Space Museum.

Runners (© 212/860-4455; www.nyrrc.org), organizers of the New York City Marathon, schedules group runs 7 days a week at 6am and 6pm, leaving from the entrance to the Park at 90th Street and Fifth Avenue. (For the NYRRC's list of the suggested running routes, see the box titled "Running the City," below.)

SWIMMING   The only pool in Central Park, **Lasker Pool** (on the east side at around 106th St.; © 212/534-7639), is open July 1 through Labor Day weekend. Rates are $4 for adults, $2 for kids under 12. Bring a towel.

OTHER PARKS

For parks in Brooklyn and Queens, see "Highlights of the Outer Boroughs," later in this chapter. For more information on these and other city parks, go online to **www.nycgovparks.org**.

Battery Park 🎔🎔   As you traverse Manhattan's concrete canyons, it's sometimes easy to forget that you're actually on an island. But here, at Manhattan's southernmost tip, you get the very real sense that just out past Liberty, Ellis, and Staten islands is the vast Atlantic Ocean.

The 21-acre park is named for the cannons built to defend residents after the American Revolution. **Castle Clinton National Monument** (the place to purchase tickets for the Statue of Liberty and Ellis Island ferry; see listings earlier in this chapter) was built as a fort before the War of 1812, though it was never used as such. The 22-ton **bronze sphere** by Fritz Koenig that was recovered from the rubble of the World Trade Center, where it stood on the plaza between the two Twin Towers as a symbol of global peace, now stands here—severely damaged but still whole. This may be the finest place in the city to pay tribute to those who were lost.

Besides the requisite T-shirt vendors and hot-dog carts, you'll find several statues and memorials scattered throughout the park. This is quite the civilized park, with lots of STAY OFF THE GRASS! signs and Wall Streeters eating deli sandwiches on the many park benches. Pull up your own bench for a good view out across the harbor.

From State St. to New York Harbor. Subway: N, R to Whitehall St.; 1, 9 to South Ferry; 4, 5 to Bowling Green.

Bryant Park ✦   Another success story in the push for urban redevelopment, Bryant Park is the latest incarnation of a 4-acre site that was, at various times in its history, a graveyard and a reservoir. Named for poet and *New York Evening Post* editor William Cullen Bryant (look for his statue on the east end), the park actually rests atop the New York Public Library's many miles of underground stacks. Another statue is also notable: a squat and evocative stone portrait of Gertrude Stein, one of the few outdoor sculptures of women in the city.

This simple green swath, just east of Times Square, is welcome relief from Midtown's concrete, taxi-choked jungle, and good weather attracts brown-baggers from neighboring office buildings. Just behind the library is **Bryant Park Grill** (𝒞 212/840-6500), a gorgeous, airy bistro with spectacular views but merely decent New American food. Still, brunch is a good bet, and the grill's two summer alfresco restaurants—**The Terrace,** on the Grill's roof, and the casual **Cafe,** with small tables beneath a canopy of trees—are extremely pleasant on a nice day.

Le Carrousel complements the park's French classical style. It's not as big as the Central Park Carousel, but utterly charming, with 14 different animals that revolve to the sounds of French cabaret music. Le Carrousel is open all year, weather permitting, 11am to 7pm, and costs $1.50 to ride.

Additionally, the park plays host to New York's **Seventh on Sixth** fashion shows, set up in billowy white tents (open to the trade only) in the spring and fall.

Behind the New York Public Library, at Sixth Ave., btwn 40th and 42nd sts. Subway: B, D, F, Q to 42nd St.; 7 to Fifth Ave.

⟮Finds A Park with a View

I acknowledge that Central Park is the king of New York parks, but if I can't have Central Park, I'll take **Riverside Park** ✦✦—any day. I spent much of my early years in New York in Riverside Park (𝒞 212/408-0264; www.nycgovparks.org) staring at the New Jersey skyline, jogging along the windswept Hudson river, playing hoops at the courts on 77th Street (when I still could jump), taking strolls along the promenade on hot summer nights, and watching the comings or goings of the unusual community that lives in the boats at the 79th Street Boat Basin. This underrated beauty designed by Frederick Law Olmsted, the same man who designed Central Park, stretches 4 miles from 72nd Street to 158th Street. The serpentine route along the Hudson River offers a variety of lovely river vistas, 14 playgrounds, two tennis courts, softball and soccer fields, a skate park, beach volleyball, the aforementioned Boat Basin, two cafes—the **Boat Basin Café** at 79th Street (𝒞 212/496-5542) and **Hurley's Hudson Beach Café** at 105th Street (𝒞 917/370-3448), open April through September only—and monuments such as the Eleanor Roosevelt statue at 72nd Street, the Soldiers and Sailors Monument at 90th Street, and Grant's Tomb at 122nd Street (𝒞 212/666-1640).

But here's the best part: On a hot summer day, when Central Park is teeming with joggers, sunbathers, and in-line skaters, Riverside Park, just a few blocks from Central Park's western fringe, is comparatively serene.

Tips   The Greening of New York

Whenever I travel to a city anywhere around the world, I make it a priority to visit that city's greenmarket, or farmer's market. I've been to some great ones, and I might be a tad bit prejudiced, but I haven't been to many better than the **Union Square Greenmarket** 👉👉 here in New York City. New York has green-markets throughout the city on different days of the week, but the biggest and the best is at Union Square every Monday, Wednesday, Friday, and Saturday. You'll find pickings from upstate and New Jersey farms, fresh fish from Long Island, homemade cheese and other dairy products, baked goods, plants, and organic herbs and spices. It's a true New York scene with everyone from models to celebrated chefs poring through the bounty. The Union Square Green-market is open year-round, but is at its peak August through October when the local harvest—tomatoes, corn, greens, grapes, peppers, and apples—flourishes. If you are lucky enough to be in the city during this period, don't miss the bonanza and do pick up some apples or grapes for your travels around the city—but even if you're not, check it out no matter what the season. For more information and locations and schedules, refer to the Council on the Environ-ment of New York City website at www.cenyc.org or call ✆ **212/477-3220.**

Union Square Park   Here's a delightful place to spend an afternoon. Reclaimed from drug dealers and abject ruin in the late '80s, Union Square Park is now one of the city's best assets and home of the New York's most famous **Greenmarket** (see box below). The seemingly endless subway work should no longer be disturbing the peace by the time you're here. This patch of green remains, with or without the construc-tion, the focal point of the newly fashionable Flatiron and Gramercy Park neighbor-hoods. Don't miss the grand equestrian statue of George Washington at the south end or the bronze statue (by Bartholdi, the sculptor of the Statue of Liberty) of the Mar-quis de Lafayette at the eastern end, gracefully glancing toward France. A **cafe** is open at the north end of the park in warm weather.

From 14th to 17th sts., btwn Park Ave. South and Broadway. Subway: 4, 5, 6, L, N, or R to 14th St./Union Sq.

Washington Square Park   You'll be hard-pressed to find much "park" in this mainly concrete square—a burial ground in the late 18th century—but it's undeni-ably the focal point of Greenwich Village. Chess players, skateboarders, street musi-cians, New York University students, gay and straight couples, the occasional film crew, and not a few homeless people compete for attention throughout the day and most of the night. (If anyone issues a friendly challenge to play you in the ancient and complex Chinese game of Go, don't take them up on it—you'll lose money.)

In the 1830s, elegant Greek Revival town houses on **Washington Square North,** known as "The Row" (note especially nos. 21–26), attracted the elite. Stanford White designed Washington Arch (1891–92) to commemorate the centenary of George Washington's inauguration as first president. The arch was refurbished in 2004 and now features exterior lighting.

At the southern end of Fifth Ave. (where it intersects Waverly Place btwn MacDougal and Wooster sts.). Subway: A, C, E, F, V to W. 4th St. (use 3rd St. exit).

CHELSEA PIERS

One of the city's biggest—and most successful—private urban development projects is the 30-acre **Chelsea Piers Sports & Entertainment Complex** (℃ **212/336-6666; www.chelseapiers.com**). Jutting out into the Hudson River on four huge piers between 17th and 23rd streets, it's a terrific multifunctional recreational facility.

The **Sports Center** (℃ **212/336-6000**), a three-football-fields-long megafacility, does health clubs one better. It offers not only the usual cardiovascular training, weights, and aerobics but also a four-lane quarter-mile indoor running track, a boxing ring, basketball courts, a sand volleyball court, a gorgeous 25-yard indoor pool with a whirlpool and sun deck, the world's most challenging rock-climbing wall plus a bouldering wall, and the **Spa at Chelsea Piers,** which offers massage, reflexology, facials, and the like. Day passes to the Sports Center are $50 for nonmembers; spa treatments are extra, of course.

The **Golf Club** (℃ **212/336-6400**) has 52 all-weather fully automated hitting stalls on four levels and a 200-yard, net-enclosed, artificial-turf fairway jutting out over the water, making it the best place in the city to hit a few. Prices start at $20 for 80 balls (118 balls during off-peak hours), and club rentals are available.

The **Sky Rink** (℃ **212/336-6100**) has twin around-the-clock indoor rinks for recreational skating and pickup hockey games with Hudson River views. General skating is $16 for adults, $14 for seniors and kids 12 and under; skate rental is $5.75. Due to organized skating activities, general skating is limited, so call ahead to find out schedules of availability.

If wheels are your thing, there are two outdoor **Roller Rinks** (℃ **212/336-6200**) for seasonal in-line skating and roller hockey games. Expect to pay about $8 for adults, $7 for kids for general skating; equipment rentals are available. The general skating schedule can change from month to month and is sometimes limited to weekends, so call ahead. The **Skating School** offers instruction if you would like to learn.

The **Field House** (℃ **212/336-6500**) is mainly for team sports, but young rock climbers will enjoy the 30-foot indoor **climbing wall,** designed for kids as well as grown-ups. Open climbs are $15, with climbs limited to 2½ hours on weekdays, 90 minutes on weekends; they start taking same-day climb reservations at 9am, and weekends can book up quickly. Children's lessons are available. **Batting cages** are $2 per 10 pitches.

Feeling like a little 10-pin tonight? State-of-the-art **AMF Chelsea Piers Lanes** (℃ **212/835-BOWL; www.chelseapiersbowl.com**) offers 40 lanes of fun. Games are $7.50 per person, and shoe rental is $4.50.

Beyond its athletics, the complex is a destination in and of itself. The 1¼-mile esplanade has benches and picnic tables with terrific river views; they serve as the perfect vantage point for watching the *QEII* head out to sea, or the navy and Coast Guard ships sailing in for Fleet Week each May.

Getting there: Chelsea Piers is accessible by taxi and the M23 or M14 crosstown buses. The nearest subway is the C and E at 23rd Street and Eighth Avenue, then pick up the M23 or walk 4 long blocks west. Another option is to take the A, C, E to 14th Street or the L train to Eighth Avenue, walk to the river, then follow the walking/riding/running path along the river north.

7 Organized Sightseeing Tours

Reservations are required for some of the tours listed below, but even if they're not, it's always best to call ahead to confirm prices, times, and meeting places.

DOUBLE-DECKER BUS TOURS

Taking a narrated bus tour is one of the best ways to see and learn quickly about New York's major sights and neighborhoods. However, keep in mind that the commentary is only as good as the guide, who is seldom an expert. Tour guides tend toward hyperbole and might get a few of the facts wrong. The *New York Times* once found tour-bus guides spouting the following inaccuracies: New York has the oldest subway system in the world (third, behind London's—41 years before New York—and Boston's, which was the first in the U.S.); Frank Sinatra was born in Jersey City (it was Hoboken); and Herald Square was named after the founder of the *New York Herald Tribune* (there was no Mr. Herald). But the idea is to see the highlights, not write a dissertation from this stuff. So enjoy the ride—and take the "facts" you hear along the way with a grain of salt.

Gray Line New York Tours   Gray Line offers just about every sightseeing tour option and combination you could want. There are bus tours by day and by night that run uptown, downtown, and all around the town, as well as bus combos with Circle Line cruises, helicopter flights, museum admittance, and guided visits of sights. There's no real point to purchasing some combination tours—you don't need a guide to take you to the Statue of Liberty, and you don't save any money on admission by buying the combo ticket. I've found Gray Line to put a higher premium on accuracy than the other big tour-bus operators, so this is your best bet among the biggies.

777 Eighth Ave. (btwn 47th and 48th sts.). Tours depart from additional Manhattan locations. © 800/669-0051 or 212/445-0848. www.graylinenewyork.com. Hop-on, hop-off bus tours from $37 adults, $20 children 5–11.

HARBOR CRUISES

If you'd like to sail the New York Harbor aboard the 1885 cargo schooner *Pioneer*, see the listing for South Street Seaport & Museum on p. 263.

Note that some of the lines below may have limited schedules in winter, especially for evening cruises. Call ahead or check online for current offerings.

Bateaux New York   The most elegant and romantic of New York's evening dinner cruises. Cruises are aboard the *Celestial*, designed to accommodate 300 guests with two suites, one dance floor, two outdoor strolling decks, a state-of-the-art sound system, and windows galore. Dinner is a three-course sit-down affair, with jackets and ties suggested for men, evening dresses for women. The food isn't what you'd get at Jean-Georges, but Bateaux (sister to egalitarian Spirit Cruises, below) offers a very nice supper club–style night on the town, and the views are fabulous. A live quartet entertains with jazz standards and pop vocal tunes.

Departing from Pier 62, Chelsea Piers, W. 23rd St. and Twelfth Ave. © 212/727-7735. www.bateauxnewyork.com. 2-hr. lunch cruises $46; 3-hr. dinner cruises $88–$117. Subway: C, E to 23rd St.

Circle Line Sightseeing Cruises 🌟🌟   A New York institution, the Circle Line is famous for its 3-hour tour around the entire 35 miles of Manhattan. This **Full Island** cruise passes by the Statue of Liberty, Ellis Island, the Brooklyn Bridge, the United Nations, Yankee Stadium, the George Washington Bridge, and more, including Manhattan's wild northern tip. The panorama is riveting, and the commentary isn't bad.

Transportation Alternatives

You really don't want to burden that nag with a carriage ride through Central Park in the middle of the summer, do you? Better you should hire a real beast of burden—a driver of a pedicab who probably really needs the money. Pedicabs are becoming very common sights on the streets of New York. The drivers are friendly, informative, and don't litter the streets. **Manhattan Pedicab, Inc. (© 212/ 586-9486;** www.ajnfineart.com), one of the two primary pedicab companies, charges $35 for a half hour, $65 for a full hour, and $10 for an impromptu street pick-up. Tours are also available, including Upper East and Upper West Side Bar and Restaurant Tours, and a Central Park–Rockefeller Center Tour. Another option is the **Manhattan Rickshaw Company (© 212/604-4724;** www.manhattan rickshaw.com), where fares range from $8 to $15 for a pick-up to $50 for an hourly ride.

The big boats are basic but fine, with lots of deck room for everybody to enjoy the view. Snacks, soft drinks, coffee, and beer are available onboard for purchase.

If 3 hours is more than you or the kids can handle, go for either the 2-hour **Semi-Circle** or the **Sunset/Harbor Lights** cruise, both of which show you the highlights of the skyline. There's also a 1-hour **Seaport Liberty** version that sticks close to the south end of the island. But of all the tours, the kids might like **The Beast** best, a thrill-a-minute speedboat ride offered in summer only.

In addition, a number of adults-only **Live Music and DJ Cruises** sail regularly from the seaport from May through September ($20–$40 per person). Depending on the night of the week, you can groove to the sounds of jazz, Latin, gospel, dance tunes, or blues as you sail along the skyline.

Departing from Pier 83, at W. 42nd St. and Twelfth Ave. Also departing from Pier 16 at South St. Seaport, 207 Front St. © 212/563-3200. www.circleline42.com. and www.seaportmusiccruises.com. Sightseeing cruises $18–$28 adults, $15–$23 seniors, $10–$15 children 12 and under. Subway to Pier 83: A, C, E to 42nd St. Subway to Pier 16: J, M, Z, 2, 3, 4, 5 to Fulton St.

New York Waterway ★★   New York Waterway, the nation's largest privately held ferry service and cruise operator, like Circle Line, also does the 35-mile trip around Manhattan, but does it in 2 hours, taking in all the same sights. They also offer a staggering amount of different sightseeing options, including a very good 90-minute New York Harbor Cruise, a Romantic Twilight Cruise, a Friday Dance Party Cruise, and Baseball Cruises to Yankee games.

Departing from 38th St. Ferry Terminal, at W. 38th St. and Twelfth Ave. © 800/533-3779. www.nywaterway.com. Sightseeing cruises $14–$25 adults, $13–$20 seniors, $7–$12 children. Free bus transportation from 57th, 49th, 42nd, and 34th sts. to 38th St. Terminal; you can flag down any of the big red buses labeled NY WATERWAY or wait at any of the bus stops along those streets.

Spirit Cruises   Spirit Cruises' modern ships are floating cabarets that combine sightseeing in New York Harbor with freshly prepared meals, musical revues, and dancing to live bands. The atmosphere is festive, fun, and relaxed. The buffet meals are nothing special, but they're fine.

Departing from Pier 61 at Chelsea Piers, W. 23rd St. and Twelfth Ave. © 866/211-3805. www.spiritcruises.com. 2-hr. lunch cruises $30–$39; 3-hr. dinner cruises $55–$95. Inquire about children's rates. Subway: C, E to 23rd St.

AIR TOURS

Liberty Helicopters　How about a bird's-eye view of Manhattan? These flight-seeing trips offer a quick thrill—literally. Five-minute tours from Midtown take in the USS *Intrepid*, Midtown skyscrapers, and Central Park, while longer tours last 10 or 15 minutes and take in a wider view that includes Lower Manhattan and the Statue of Liberty. If you opt for the longest tour, you'll also fly far enough uptown to take in the George Washington Bridge and Yankee Stadium. Flights leave every 15 minutes daily from 9am to 9pm, but note that reservations are required for two or more.

Departing 1 block north of VIP Heliport, W. 30th St. and Twelfth Ave. ℂ 212/967-6464. www.libertyhelicopters.com. Pilot-narrated tours $63–$169. Subway: A, C, E to 34th St.

SPECIALTY TOURS

In addition to the options below, those interested in touring the Financial District with a knowledgeable guide should also consider the **World of Finance Walking Tour** offered Fridays at 10am by the Museum of American Financial History, 28 Broadway (just north of Bowling Green) (ℂ **877/FINANCE** or 212/908-4601). Also, both the Municipal Art Society (directly below) and the Grand Central Partnership offer free walking tours of **Grand Central Terminal,** Wednesdays at 12:30pm and Fridays at 12:30pm, respectively; see p. 244.

　The Alliance for Downtown New York, the Business Improvement District in charge of Lower Manhattan, offers a free, 90-minute **Wall Street Walking Tour** 🏛 every Thursday and Saturday at noon, rain or shine. This guided tour explores the vivid history and amazing architecture of the nation's first capital and the world center of finance. Stops include the New York Stock Exchange, Trinity Church, Federal Hall National Monument, and many other sites of historic and cultural importance. Tours meet on the steps of Cass Gilbert's gorgeous **U.S. Customs House** (p. 271), at 1 Bowling Green (subway: 4, 5 to Bowling Green). Reservations are not required (unless you're a group), but you can call ℂ **212/606-4064** or visit **www.downtown ny.com** to confirm the schedule.

CULTURAL ORGANIZATIONS

The **Municipal Art Society** 🏛 (ℂ **212/439-1049** or 212/935-3960; www.mas.org) offers excellent historical and architectural walking tours aimed at intelligent, individualistic travelers, not the mass market. Each is led by a highly qualified guide who offers insights into the significance of buildings, neighborhoods, and history. Topics range from the urban history of Greenwich Village to "Williamsburg: Beyond the Bridge," to an examination of the "new" Times Square. Weekday walking tours are $12; weekend tours are $15. Reservations may be required depending on the tour, so it's best to call ahead. A full schedule is available online or by calling ℂ **212/439-1049.**

　The **92nd Street Y** 🏛 (ℂ **212/415-5500** or 212/415-5628; www.92ndsty.org) offers a wonderful variety of walking and bus tours, many featuring funky themes or behind-the-scenes visits. Subjects can range from "Diplomat for a Day at the U.N." to "Secrets of the Chelsea Hotel," or from "Artists of the Meat-Packing District" to "Jewish Harlem." Prices range from $20 to $60 (sometimes more for bus tours), but many include ferry rides, afternoon tea, dinner, or whatever suits the program. Guides are well-chosen experts on their subjects, ranging from highly respected historians to an East Village poet, mystic, and art critic (for "Allen Ginsberg's New York" and "East Village Night Spots"), and many routes travel into the outer boroughs; some day trips even reach beyond the city. Advance registration is required for all walking and bus tours. Schedules are planned a few months in advance, so check the website for tours that might interest you.

INDEPENDENT OPERATORS

NYC Discovery Tours (© 212/465-3331) offers more than 70 tours of the Big Apple divided into five categories: neighborhood (including "Central Park" and "Brooklyn Bridge and Heights"); theme (such as "Gotham City Ghost Tour" and "Art History NYC"); biography ("John Lennon's New York"); tavern/food tasting; and American history and literature ("The Charles Dickens Tours"). Tours are about 2 hours long and cost $13 per person (more for food tastings).

All tours from **Joyce Gold History Tours of New York** ★★ (© 212/242-5762; www.nyctours.com) are offered by Joyce Gold herself, an instructor of Manhattan history at New York University and the New School for Social Research, who has been conducting history walks around New York since 1975. Her tours can really cut to the core of this town; Joyce is full of fascinating stories about Manhattan and its people. Tours are arranged around themes like "The Colonial Settlers of Wall Street," "The Genius and Elegance of Gramercy Park," "Downtown Graveyards," "The Old Jewish Lower East Side," "Historic Harlem," and "TriBeCa: The Creative Explosion." Tours are offered most weekends March to December and last from 2 to 4 hours, and the price is $12 per person; no reservations are required. Private tours can be arranged year-round, either for individuals or groups.

Myra Alperson, founder and lead tour guide for **NoshWalks** (© 212/222-2243; www.noshwalks.com), knows food in New York City and knows where to find it. For the past 6 years, Alperson has been leading adventurous, hungry walkers to some of the city's most delicious neighborhoods. From the Uzbek, Tadjik, and Russian markets of Rego Park, Queens, to the Dominican coffee shops of Washington Heights in upper Manhattan, Alperson has left no ethnic neighborhood unexplored. Tours are conducted on Saturday and Sunday, leaving around 11:30am. The preferred means of transportation is subway and the tours generally last around 3 hours and cost $20 ($30 for Bronx Bites), not including the food you will undoubtedly buy on the tour. Space is limited, so book well in advance.

On Location Tours (© 212/209-3370; www.sceneontv.com) offers narrated minibus tours through TV history on their Manhattan TV Tour; tickets are $30 for adults. Or, if you want to see Carrie Bradshaw's Big Apple, cut right to the chase and take the company's 2½-hour **Sex and the City Tour,** which includes over 40 show-related sights; tickets are $35. Most tours take place on Saturdays and depart from the Times Square Visitors Center (see "Orientation," in chapter 6), usually at noon and 2:30pm, respectively. There's also a 3-hour **Sopranos Tour** that will take you over to New Jersey for an afternoon of sights that range from Satriale's Pork Store to the Bada-Bing! club; this tour leaves from Bryant Park on Sundays at 2pm and costs $40. Reservations are strongly suggested for all tours, as most sell out in advance; it also makes sense to confirm days and times and check for any additional offerings.

Harlem Spirituals (© 800/660-2166 or 212/391-0900; www.harlemspirituals. com) specializes in gospel and jazz tours of Harlem that can be combined with a traditional soul-food meal. A variety of options are available, including a tour of Harlem sights with gospel service, and a soul-food lunch or brunch as an optional add-on. The Harlem jazz tour includes a neighborhood tour, dinner at a family-style soul-food restaurant, and a visit to a local jazz club; there's also an Apollo Theater variation on

Offbeat New York Tours

So maybe you've taken a harbor cruise or the double-decker bus tour, but you just don't feel you got a taste of the gritty, quirky, neurotic elements that make New York so unique. You want to see those sights that even many native New Yorkers have never seen. Here are a few alternatives to the conventional tours that might satisfy that need.

Soundwalk (www.soundwalk.com): This innovative company behind the audio self-guided tour CDs debuted in 2003, with audio tours offering insider's peeks at Chinatown, the Lower East Side, Times Square, DUMBO, and the Meat-Packing District. All of these are great fun and will take you places no double-decker bus ever will, but my favorite is the three-CD set **"Bronx Soundwalk."** The CD set includes *Baseball,* a tour of Yankee Stadium and environs, narrated by longtime employee Tony Morante; *Graffiti,* a tour of Hunts Point and the trail of some of the legendary graffiti artists, narrated by BG183 (aka Sotero Ortiz), founding member of the TATS Cru and Mural Kings of the Bronx; and *Hip Hop,* a Bronx River tour narrated by hip-hop DJ, the Original Jazzy Jay, which takes you to the birthplace of hip-hop and the haunts of rap pioneers like Afrika Bambaataa and Cool Herc. These tours are so authentic; on the Bronx tour you'll even visit the G&R Pastry Shop where Mr. Steinbrenner, we learn, is a big fan of the shop's cheese Danish. CDs range from $13 to $19; all you need is a portable CD player, map, MetroCard, walking shoes, and an adventurous spirit. You can purchase CDs on the website, or at retailers listed on the site.

Wildman Steve Brill (www.wildmanstevebrill.com): If you ever get stranded in Central Park, a tour with Wildman Steve Brill might help you survive. I've seen him in the park, raggedy beard, shorts, hiking boots, and pith helmet, leading groups of eager-eyed followers while instructing them on what flora and fauna they can forage—breaking off a stick of some edible tree and gnawing on it as an example. Brill's Central Park tours occur twice monthly and are not only hilarious, they actually are educational. If you're lucky, maybe he'll regale you with his tale of his arrest by a park ranger for eating a dandelion. Reservations must be made in advance; call ✆ **914/835-2153.** Suggested donation is $10.

this tour. Bronx and Brooklyn tours are also an option for those who want a taste of the outer boroughs. Prices start at $30, $23 for children, for a Harlem Heritage tour, and go up from there based on length and inclusions (tours that include food and entertainment are pay-one-price). All tours leave from Harlem Spirituals' Midtown office (690 Eighth Ave., between 43rd and 44th sts.), and transportation is included.

Active visitors with an adventurous spirit can hook up with **Tours by Bike: Bike the Big Apple** (✆ **201/837-1133;** www.bikethebigapple.com). Tours by Bike offers guided half-day, full-day, and customized tours through a variety of city neighborhoods,

Hidden Jazz Haunts (www.bigapplejazz.com): This tour hosted by New York Jazz expert Gordon Polatnick is the real deal for jazz buffs. Polatnick's tours are small (2 to 10 people) and are tailor-made to the jazz interests of his clients. If you're into bebop, he'll show you Minton's Playhouse, the still standing but now defunct jazz club that was the supposed birthplace of bop. From there he'll take you to other active Harlem clubs that he feels embody that Minton's bebop spirit. If you're into the Bohemian Village scene, he'll take you to clubs that represent that era. The tour lasts 5 hours and costs $100, including transportation, music charges, two drinks, and guide service. For reservations call ✆ **718/606-8442.**

Radical Walking Tours: Led by self-proclaimed "radical historian" Bruce Kayton, these are unconventional tours of conventional tourist sights. A tour to Harlem covers the Black Panthers, Malcolm X, and the Communist party in addition to the Apollo Theater and the Schomburg Center. My favorite is the Non-Jerry Seinfeld Upper West Side Tour, which stops at the home of Fidel Castro when he lived in the neighborhood in the late 1940s, the site of the shootout with Black Panther H. Rap Brown and police, and Lincoln Center and how it destroyed what once was a thriving Puerto Rican community. Call ✆ **718/492-0069** or visit www.he.net/~radtours for more information. Tours are $10 and no reservations are necessary.

Adventures on a Shoestring: One of the earliest entrants into the now booming walking tour market, host Howard Goldberg has provided unique views of New York since 1963, exploring New York with a breezy, man-of-the-people style. Tours, which go behind the scenes of neighborhoods, range from a variety of Greenwich Village tours—haunted, picturesque, historic—to Historic Roosevelt Island, which includes taking the Roosevelt Island Tram. He even does theme walks such as "Marilyn Monroe's Manhattan" and a "Salute to Katharine Hepburn." Tours are a bargain at $5 for 90 minutes and are conducted year-round, rain or shine. Call ✆ **212/265-2663** for more info.

including the fascinating but little-explored Upper Manhattan and Harlem; an ethnic tour that takes you over the legendary Brooklyn Bridge, through Chinatown and Little Italy, and to Ground Zero; and around Flushing, Queens, where you'll feel like you're biking around Hong Kong. You don't have to be an Ironman candidate to participate; tours are designed for the average rider, with an emphasis on safety and fun; shorter (approximately 2½ hr.) and longer versions (around 5 hr.) are available. Tours are offered year-round; prices run $69 to $89, and include all gear, including bike.

8 Talk of the Town: TV Tapings

The trick to getting tickets for TV tapings in this city is to be from out of town. You visitors have a much better chance than we New Yorkers; producers are gun-shy about filling their audiences with obnoxious locals and see everybody who's not from New York as being from the heartland—and therefore their target TV audience.

If your heart's set on getting tickets to a show, request them as early as possible—6 months ahead isn't too early, and even earlier is better for the most popular shows. You're usually asked to send a postcard. Always include the number of tickets you want, your preferred dates of attendance (be as flexible as you can), and your address *and* phone number. Tickets are always free. The shows tend to be pretty good about trying to meet your specific date requests, but don't be surprised if Ricki is far more responsive than, say, Dave. And even if you send in your request early, don't be surprised if tickets don't arrive at your house until 1 or 2 weeks before tape date.

If you come to town without any tickets, all hope is not lost. Because they know that every ticket holder won't make it, many studios give out a limited number of standby tickets on the day of taping. If you can just get up a little early and don't mind standing in line for a couple (or a few) hours, you have a good chance of getting one. Now, the bad news: Only one standby ticket per person is allowed, so everybody who wants to get in has to get up at the crack of dawn and stand in line. And even if you get your hands on a standby ticket, it doesn't guarantee admission; they usually only start seating standbys after the regular ticket holders are in. Still, chances are good.

For additional information on getting tickets to tapings, call the NYCVB at ✆ **212/484-1222.** And remember—you don't need a ticket to be on the *Today* show.

If you do attend a taping, be sure to bring a sweater, even in summer. As anybody who watches Letterman knows, it's an icebox in those studios. And bring ID, as proof of age may be required.

The Daily Show with Jon Stewart Comedy Central's boldly irreverent, often hilarious mock newscast tapes every Monday through Thursday at 5:45pm, at 513 W. 54th St. Make your advance ticket requests by phone at ✆ **212/586-2477,** or check with them for any cancellation tickets for the upcoming week; the line is open Monday through Thursday from 10:30am to 4pm for tickets.

The Jane Pauley Show What goes around comes around . . . and around . . . and around. The former Today and Dateline host is back with her own morning gabfest. If you are interested in attending one of the shows, call ✆ **212/664-3056.** For standby tickets, arrive at the NBC Studios marquee (on the 50th St. side of 30 Rockefeller Plaza) no later than 9am on the morning of the taping. You may choose standby tickets for either the 11:30am or 3:30pm show. The show tapes twice a day Tuesday to Friday. Only one ticket will be issued per person. Audience members must bring photo ID and a reservation confirmation, and are advised not to bring any unnecessary electronic devices.

Last Call with Carson Daly Tapings of the MTV heartthrob's NBC late-night gabfest is much like a grown-up TRL, without the countdown or screaming sweet 16s. Tapings are on select weeknights at 7 and/or 9pm. You can reserve up to four tickets in advance by calling ✆ **212/664-3056.** Standby tickets are distributed on the day of taping at 9am outside 30 Rockefeller Plaza, on the 49th Street side of the building, on a first-come, first-served basis (read: come early if you actually want to get one). Note that a standby ticket does not guarantee admission.

Late Night with Conan O'Brien   Conan tix might not have the cachet of a Dave ticket, but they're a very hot commodity nevertheless—so start planning now. Tapings are Tuesday through Friday at 5:30pm (plan on arriving by 4:45pm if you have tickets), and you must be 16 or older to attend. You can reserve up to four tickets in advance by calling ℂ **212/664-3056.** Standby tickets are distributed on the day of taping at 9am outside 30 Rockefeller Plaza, on the 49th Street side of the building (under the NBC Studios awning), on a first-come, first-served basis (read: come early if you actually want to get one).

The Late Show with David Letterman   Here's the most in-demand TV ticket in town. Tapings are Monday through Thursday at 5:30pm (arrive by 4:15pm), with a second taping Thursday at 8pm (arrive by 6:45pm). You must be 18 or older to attend. Send your postcard at least 6 to 9 months in advance (two tickets max; one request only, or all will be disregarded), to *Late Show* Tickets, Ed Sullivan Theater, 1697 Broadway, New York, NY 10019. You can also register at **www.cbs.com/latenight/lateshow** (click on "Get Tickets") to be notified of tickets that may become available for specific dates you select over the next 3 months. On tape days, there are no standby lines anymore; call ℂ **212/247-6497** at 11am for up to two standby tickets; start dialing early, because the machine will kick in as soon as all standbys are gone. If you do get through, you may have to answer a trivia question about the show to score tickets.

Live! with Regis and Kelly   Tapings with Regis Philbin and Kelly Ripa are Monday through Friday at 9am at the ABC Studios at 7 Lincoln Square (Columbus Ave. and W. 67th St.) on the Upper West Side. You must be 10 or older to attend (under 18s must be accompanied by a parent). Send your postcard (four tickets max) at least a *full year* in advance to *Live!* Tickets, Ansonia Station, P.O. Box 230777, New York, NY 10023-0777 (ℂ **212/456-3054**). Standby tickets are sometimes available. Arrive at the studio no later than 7am and request a standby number; standby tickets are handed out on a first-come, first-served basis, so earlier is better.

Saturday Night Live   SNL tapings are Saturday at 11:30pm (arrival time 10pm); there's also a full dress rehearsal at 8pm (arrival time 7pm). You must be 16 or older to attend. Here's the catch: Written requests are taken only in August and the odds are always long. However, you can try for standby tickets on the day of the taping, which are distributed at 7am outside 30 Rockefeller Plaza, on the 49th Street side of the building (under the NBC Studios awning), on a first-come, first-served basis; only one ticket per person will be issued. If you want to try your luck with advance tickets, call ℂ **212/664-3056** *as far in advance of your arrival in New York as possible* to determine the current ticket-request procedure.

The *Today* Show   Anybody can be on TV with Katie, Matt, and cuddly weatherman Al Roker. All you have to do is show up outside *Today*'s glass-walled studio at Rockefeller Center, on the southwest corner of 49th Street and Rockefeller Plaza, with your very own HI, MOM! sign. Tapings are Monday through Friday from 7 to 10am, but come at the crack of dawn if your heart's set on being in front. Who knows? If it's a nice day, you may even get to chat with Katie, Matt, or Al in a segment. Come extra early to attend a Friday Summer Concert Series show.

The Tony Danza Show   The Brooklyn native and star of *Who's the Boss?* comes home to host his own talk show. For tickets to attend the live show, send a request in a SASE to *The Tony Danza Show*, Ansonia Station, P.O. Box 234095, New York, NY

10023-9426 or call ✆ **212/479-8422.** The show is taped Monday through Thursday at 10am at ABC Studios, 30 W. 67th St. (between Central Park West and Amsterdam Ave.).

Total Request Live The countdown show that made Carson Daly a household name is broadcast live from MTV's second-floor glass-walled studio at 1515 Broadway, at 44th Street in Times Square, weekdays at 3:30pm. Crowds start gathering below at all hours, depending on the drawing power of the day's guest. Audience tickets can sometimes be reserved in advance by calling the **TRL Ticket Reservation Hot Line** at ✆ **212/398-8549;** you must be between the ages of 16 and 24 to attend. If you're not able to score reservations, arrive by 2pm (preferably earlier) if you want a prayer of making it into the in-studio audience; a producer usually roams the crowd asking music trivia questions like "What's Britney Spears's middle name?" and "Who's the lead singer of Linkin Park?", giving away standby tickets for correct answers. And don't forget to make your WE LOVE YOU, CARSON! signs large enough to be captured on camera. You may also be able to watch or participate in other MTV tapings; stop into the MTV Store on the corner of 44th and Broadway, where flyers for tapings and events are sometimes stacked next to the register.

The View ABC's hugely popular girl-power gabfest tapes live Monday through Friday at 11am (ticket holders must arrive by 9:30am). Requests, which should be made 12 to 16 weeks in advance, can be submitted online (**www.abc.go.com/theview**) or via postcard to Tickets, *The View,* 320 W. 66th St., New York, NY 10023. Since exact date requests are not usually accommodated, try standby: Arrive at the studio before 10am and put your name on the standby list; earlier is better, since tickets are handed out on a first-come, first-served basis. You must be 18 or older to attend.

Who Wants to Be a Millionaire The trivia show is filmed at ABC's Upper West Side studios. To request tickets to be an audience member, send a postcard to *Who Wants to Be a Millionaire,* Columbia University Station, P.O. Box 250225, New York, NY 10025. Ticket requests are limited to four, and you must be 18 or older to attend. You can also request tickets online at www.millionairetv.com or call ✆ **212/479-7755.**

9 Especially for Kids

Some of New York's sights and attractions are designed specifically with kids in mind, and I've listed those below. But many of those I've discussed in the rest of this chapter are terrific for kids as well as adults; I've also included cross-references to the best of them.

Probably the best place of all to entertain the kids is in **Central Park** ★★★, which has kid-friendly diversions galore (see the section beginning on p. 275). For kid-friendly theatrical performances, see the "Kids Take the Stage: Family-Friendly Theater" box, on p. 348.

For general tips and additional resources, see "For Families" under "Tips for Travelers with Special Needs," in chapter 3.

MUSEUMS

In addition to the museums designed specifically for kids below, also consider the following, discussed elsewhere in this chapter: The **American Museum of Natural History** (p. 239), whose dinosaur displays are guaranteed to wow both you and the kids;

the *Intrepid* Sea-Air-Space Museum (p. 255), on a real battleship with an amazing collection of vintage and high-tech airplanes; the New York City Fire Museum (p. 262), housed in a real firehouse; the American Museum of the Moving Image (p. 303), where you and the kids can learn how movies are actually made; the Lower East Side Tenement Museum (p. 256), whose weekend living-history program really intrigues school-age kids; the New York Transit Museum (p. 301), where kids can explore vintage subway cars and other hands-on exhibits; and the South Street Seaport & Museum (p. 263), which little ones will love for its theme park–like atmosphere and old boats bobbing in the harbor.

Children's Museum of the Arts *(Kids* Interactive workshop programs for children ages 1 to 12 and their families are the attraction here. Kids dabble in puppet making and computer drawing or join in singalongs and live performances. Also look for rotating exhibitions of the museum's permanent collection featuring WPA work. Call or check the website for the current exhibition and activities schedule.

182 Lafayette St. (btwn Broome and Grand sts.). (C) **212/941-9198** or 212/274-0986. www.cmany.org. Admission $8 for everyone 65 and under, pay what you wish Thurs 4–6pm. Wed–Sun noon–5pm (Thurs to 6pm). Subway: 6 to Spring St.

Children's Museum of Manhattan ★ *(Kids* Here's a great place to take the kids when they're tired of being told not to touch. Designed for ages 2 to 12, this museum is strictly hands-on. Interactive exhibits and activity centers encourage self-discovery—and a recent expansion means that there's now even more to keep the kids busy and learning. The Time Warner Media Center takes children through the world of animation and helps them produce their own videos. The Body Odyssey is a zany, scientific journey through the human body. This isn't just a museum for the 5-and-up set—there are exhibits especially designed for babies and toddlers, too. The busy schedule also includes daily art classes and storytellers, and a full slate of entertainment on weekends.

212 W. 83rd St. (btwn Broadway and Amsterdam Ave.). (C) **212/721-1234.** www.cmom.org. Admission $8 children and adults, $5 seniors. School season Wed–Sun and school holidays 10am–5pm; summer Tues–Sun 10am–5pm. Subway: 1, 9 to 86th St.

New York Hall of Science ★ *(Kids* Children of all ages will love this huge hands-on museum, which bills itself as "New York's Only Science Playground." This place is amazing for school-age kids—it's just like *Beakman's World* come to life. Exhibits let them be engulfed by a giant soap bubble (shades of Veruca Salt, Mom and Dad?), float on air in an antigravity mirror, compose music by dancing in front of light beams, and explore the more-than-miniature world of microbes. There are even video machines that kids can use to retrieve astronomical images, including pictures taken by the *Galileo* in orbit around Jupiter. There's a Preschool Discovery Place for the really little ones. But probably best of all is the summertime Outdoor Science Playground for kids 6 and older—ostensibly lessons in physics, but really just a great excuse to laugh, jump, and play on jungle gyms, slides, seesaws, spinners, and more.

The museum is located in **Flushing Meadows–Corona Park,** where kids can enjoy even more fun beyond the Hall of Science. Not only are there more than 1,200 acres of park and playgrounds, but there's also a zoo, a carousel, an indoor ice-skating rink, an outdoor pool, and bike and boat rentals. Kids and grown-ups alike will love getting an up-close look at the Unisphere steel globe, which was not really destroyed in

Men in Black. The park is also home to the **Queens Museum of Art** (p. 305) as well as Shea Stadium and the U.S. Open Tennis Center.

4701 111th St., in Flushing Meadows–Corona Park, Queens. (C) 718/699-0005. www.nyhallsci.org. Admission $11 adults, $8 seniors and children 4–17, $2.50 preschoolers, free on Fridays 2–5pm. Additional $3 for Science Playground. Mon–Wed 9:30am–2pm (Tues–Wed to 5pm in summer); Thurs–Sun 9:30am–5pm. Subway: 7 to 111th St.

Sony Wonder Technology Lab *Kids*   Not as much of an infomercial as you'd expect. Both kids and adults love this four-level high-tech science and technology center, which explores communications and information technology. You can experiment with robotics, explore the human body through medical imaging, edit a music video, mix a hit song, design a video game, and save the day at an environmental command center. The lab also features the first high-definition interactive theater in the United States. Admission is absolutely free; this place is extremely popular, however, so it's wise to make reservations in advance. Reservations can be made up to 2 weeks in advance by calling (C) **212/833-5414** on Monday, Wednesday, or Friday between 11am and 4pm. Otherwise, you may not get in, or you may get tickets that require you to return at a different time.

Sony Plaza, 550 Madison Ave. (at 56th St.). (C) 212/833-8100, or 212/833-5414 for reservations. www.sonywonder techlab.com. Free admission. Sun noon–6pm; Tues–Sat 10am–5pm; last entrance 30 min. before closing. Subway: E, V or N, R to Fifth Ave.; 4, 5, 6 to 59th St.

OTHER KID-FRIENDLY DIVERSIONS

ARCADES   **Lazer Park,** in Times Square at 1560 Broadway (entrance around the corner at 163 W. 46th St.; (C) **212/398-3060;** www.lazerpark.com), has amusements ranging from good old-fashioned pinball to virtual-reality games and a full-on laser tag arena. Even better is the **Broadway City** *,* 241 W. 42nd St., between Seventh and Eighth avenues ((C) **212/997-9797;** a neon-bright, multilevel interactive game center designed on a Big Apple theme where you could lose your kids (and a year's supply of quarters) for an entire day.

SHOPPING   Everybody loves to shop in New York—even kids. Don't forget to take them to **Books of Wonder;** that temple of sneakerdom, **Niketown;** the **NBA Store; Dylan's Candy Bar,** for a real Willy Wonka experience; and **Toys "R" Us** in Times Square, with its very own indoor Ferris wheel. See chapter 10 for details.

SKY-HIGH VIEWS   Kids of all ages can't help but turn dizzy with delight at incredible views from atop the **Empire State Building** (p. 242). The Empire State Building also has the **New York Skyride** ((C) **212/279-9777;** www.skyride.com), which offers a short motion-flight simulation sightseeing tour of New York, just in case the real one isn't enough for your kids. Open daily 10am to 10pm; tickets are $17 for adults, $16 for kids 5 to 11, and $15 for seniors and kids 4 to 12; combination Empire State observation deck/New York Skyride tickets are available at a discount.

SPECIAL EVENTS   Children's eyes grow wide at the yearlong march of **parades** (especially Macy's Thanksgiving Day Parade), **circuses** (Big Apple, and Ringling Bros. and Barnum & Bailey), and **holiday shows** (the Rockettes' Christmas and Easter performances). See the "New York City Calendar of Events," in chapter 3, for details.

ZOOS & AQUARIUMS   Bigger kids will love the legendary **Bronx Zoo** (p. 297), while the **Central Park Zoo,** with its Tisch Children's Zoo (p. 280), is particularly suitable for younger kids. At the **New York Aquarium** at Coney Island (p. 300), kids can touch starfish and sea urchins and watch bottle-nosed dolphins and California sea lions stunt-swim in the outdoor aqua theater. Brooklyn's **Prospect Park** (p. 301) also boasts a wonderful little zoo.

10 Highlights of the Outer Boroughs

IN THE BRONX

In addition to the options below, literary buffs might also want to visit the **Edgar Allan Poe Cottage,** the final home for the brilliant but troubled author of *The Raven, The Tell-Tale Heart,* and other masterworks. See the sidebar "In Search of Historic Homes" on p. 270.

Bronx Zoo Wildlife Conservation Park ★★★ *Kids*   Founded in 1899, the Bronx Zoo is the largest metropolitan animal park in the United States, with more than 4,000 animals living on 265 acres, and one of the city's best attractions.

One of the most impressive exhibits is the **Wild Asia Complex.** This zoo-within-a-zoo comprises the **Wild Asia Plaza** education center; **Jungle World,** an indoor re-creation of Asian forests, with birds, lizards, gibbons, and leopards; and the **Bengali Express Monorail** (open May–Oct), which takes you on a narrated ride high above free-roaming Siberian tigers, Asian elephants, Indian rhinoceroses, and other nonnative New Yorkers (keep your eyes peeled—the animals aren't as interested in seeing you). The **Himalayan Highlands** is home to some 17 extremely rare snow leopards, as well as red pandas and white-naped cranes. The 6½-acre **Congo Gorilla Forest** is home to Western lowland gorillas, okapi, red river hogs, and other African rainforest animals.

The **Children's Zoo** (open Apr–Oct) allows young humans to learn about their wildlife counterparts. Kids can compare their leaps to those of a bullfrog, slide into a turtle shell, climb into a heron's nest, see with the eyes of an owl, and hear with the acute ears of a fox. There's also a petting zoo. Camel rides are another part of the summertime picture, as is the **Butterfly Zone** and the **Skyfari** aerial tram (each an extra $3 charge).

If the natural settings and breeding programs aren't enough to keep zoo residents entertained, they can always choose to ogle the two million annual visitors. But there are ways to beat the crowds. Try to visit on a weekday or on a nice winter's day. In summer, come early in the day, before the heat of the day sends the animals back into their enclosures. Expect to spend an entire day here—you'll need it.

Getting there: Liberty Lines' BxM11 express bus, which makes various stops on Madison Avenue, will take you directly to the zoo; call ⓒ **718/652-8400.** By subway, take the 2 train to Pelham Parkway and then walk west to the Bronxdale entrance.

Fordham Rd. and Bronx River Pkwy., the Bronx. ⓒ 718/367-1010. www.wcs.org/zoos. Admission $11 adults, $8 seniors and children 2–12; discounted admission Nov–Mar; free Wed year-round. There may be nominal additional charges for some exhibits. Nov–Mar daily 10am–4:30pm (extended hours for Holiday Lights late Nov to early Jan); Apr–Oct Mon–Fri 10am–5pm, Sat–Sun 10am–5:30pm. Transportation: See "Getting there," above.

New York Botanical Garden ★   A National Historic Landmark, the 250-acre New York Botanical Garden was founded in 1891 and today is one of America's foremost public gardens. The setting is spectacular—a natural terrain of rock outcroppings, a river with cascading waterfalls, hills, ponds, and wetlands.

Highlights of the Botanical Garden include the 27 **specialty gardens,** an exceptional **orchid collection,** and 40 acres of **uncut forest,** as close as New York gets to its virgin state before the arrival of Europeans. The **Enid A. Haupt Conservatory,** a stunning series of Victorian glass pavilions that recall London's former Crystal Palace, shelters a rich collection of tropical, subtropical, and desert plants as well as seasonal flower shows. There's also a **Children's Adventure Garden.** Natural exhibits are augmented by year-round educational programs, musical events, bird-watching excursions, lectures, special family programs, and many more activities. Best of all is the annual **Holiday Train Show** (late Nov–early Jan; call for exact dates), where railway trains and trolleys wind their way through more than 100 replicas of historic New York buildings and attractions—such as the Statue of Liberty, the Metropolitan Museum of Art, and the Garden's own Enid A. Haupt Conservatory—all made from plant parts and other natural materials. There are so many ways to see the garden—tram, golf cart, walking tours—that it's best to call or check the website for more information.

Getting there: Take Metro-North (© **800/METRO-INFO** or 212/532-4900; www.mta.nyc.ny.us/mnr) from Grand Central Terminal to the New York Botanical Garden station; the easy ride takes about 20 minutes. By subway, take the D or 4 train to Bedford Park, then take bus Bx26 or walk southeast on Bedford Park Boulevard for 8 long blocks. The garden operates a shuttle to and from Manhattan April through October on Fridays and weekends, Saturdays only in November and December. Round-trip shuttle and garden tickets are $15 for adults, $12 for seniors and students, $9 for children 2 to 12; call © **718/817-8779** for reservations.

200th St. and Southern Blvd., the Bronx. © 718/817-8700. www.nybg.org. Admission $3 adults, $2 seniors and students, $1 children 2–12. Extra charges for Everett Children's Adventure Garden, Enid A. Haupt Conservatory, T. H. Everett Rock Garden, Native Plant Garden, and narrated tram tour; entire Garden Passport package $13 adults, $11 seniors and students, $5 children 2–12. Apr–Oct Tues–Sun and Mon holidays 10am–6pm; Nov–Mar Tues–Sun and Mon holidays 10am–5pm. Transportation: See "Getting there," above.

Wave Hill ★ *Finds* Formerly a private estate with panoramic views of the Hudson River and the Palisades, Wave Hill has, at various times in its history, been home to a British U.N. ambassador as well as Mark Twain and Theodore Roosevelt. Set in a stunningly bucolic neighborhood that doesn't look anything like you'd expect from the Bronx, its 28 gorgeous acres were bequeathed to the city of New York for use as a public garden that is now one of the most beautiful spots in the city. It's a wonderful place to commune with nature, both along wooded paths and in beautifully manicured herb and flower gardens, where all of the plants are clearly labeled by careful horticulturists. Benches are positioned throughout the property for quiet contemplation and spectacular views. A great spot for taking in the Hudson River vibe without having to rent a car and travel to Westchester to visit the Rockefeller estate; in 2004 a 28-acre public garden and cultural center opened making it even more attractive and accessible. Programs range from horticulture and environmental education, landscape history, and forestry to dance performances and concerts.

Getting there: Take the 1 or 9 subway to 231st St., then take the Bx7 or Bx10 bus to the 252nd Street stop; or take the A subway to 207th Street and pick up the Bx7 to 252nd Street. From the 252nd Street stop, walk west across the parkway bridge and turn left; at 249th Street, turn right. Metro North trains (© **212/532-4900**) travel from Grand Central to the Riverdale station; from there, it's a pleasant 5-block uphill walk to Wave Hill.

675 W. 252nd St. (at Independence Ave.), Bronx. © 718/549-3200. www.wavehill.org. Admission $4 adults, $2 seniors and students, free admission in winter, and Sat mornings and Tues in summer. Tues–Sun 9am–4:30pm; extended hours in summer (check ahead). Transportation: See "Getting there," above.

IN BROOKLYN

For details on walking the **Brooklyn Bridge,** see p. 241.

It's easy to link visits to the Brooklyn Botanic Garden, the Brooklyn Museum of Art, and Prospect Park, since they're all an easy walk from one another, just off **Grand Army Plaza.** Designed by Frederick Law Olmsted and Calvert Vaux as a suitably grand entrance to their Prospect Park, it boasts a grand Civil War memorial arch designed by John H. Duncan (1892–1901) and the main **Brooklyn Public Library,** an Art Deco masterpiece completed in 1941 (the garden and museum are just on the other side of the library, down Eastern Pkwy.). The entire area is a half-hour subway ride from Midtown Manhattan.

Brooklyn Botanic Garden ⟲ Just down the street from the Brooklyn Museum of Art (below) is the most popular botanic garden in the city. This peaceful 52-acre sanctuary is at its most spectacular in May, when thousands of deep pink blossoms of cherry trees are abloom. Well worth seeing is the spectacular **Cranford Rose Garden,** one of the largest and finest in the country; the **Shakespeare Garden,** an English garden featuring plants mentioned in his writings; a **Children's Garden;** the **Osborne Garden,** a 3-acre formal garden; the **Fragrance Garden,** designed for the blind but appreciated by all noses; and the extraordinary **Japanese Hill-and-Pond Garden.** The renowned **C. V. Starr Bonsai Museum** is home to the world's oldest and largest collection of bonsai, while the impressive $2.5-million Steinhardt Conservatory holds the garden's extensive indoor plant collection.

1000 Washington Ave. (at Eastern Pkwy.), Brooklyn. ℂ **718/623-7200.** www.bbg.org. Admission $5 adults, $3 seniors and students, free for children under 16, free to all Tues and Sat 10am–noon year-round, plus Wed–Fri from mid-Nov to mid-Mar. Apr–Sept Tues–Fri 8am–6pm, Sat–Sun 10am–6pm; Oct–Mar Tues–Fri 8am–4:30pm, Sat–Sun 10am–4:30pm. Subway: Q to Prospect Park; 2, 3 to Eastern Pkwy./Brooklyn Museum.

Brooklyn Museum of Art ⟲⟲ One of the nation's premier art institutions, the Brooklyn Museum of Art rocketed back into public consciousness in 1999 with the hugely controversial *Sensation: Young British Artists from the Saatchi Collection,* which drew international media attention and record crowds who came to see just what an artist—and a few conservative politicians—could make out of a little elephant dung.

Indeed, the museum is best known for its consistently remarkable temporary exhibitions as well as its excellent permanent collection. The museum's grand Beaux Arts building, designed by McKim, Mead & White (1897), befits its outstanding holdings,

---

⟨ *Moments* An Arts Party Grows in Brooklyn

First Saturday is the Brooklyn Museum of Art's ambitious and popular program that takes place on, you guessed it, the first Saturday of each month. It runs from 5 to 11pm and includes free admission and a slate of live music, films, dancing, curator talks, and other entertainment that can get pretty esoteric— think karaoke, lesbian poetry, silent film, experimental jazz, and disco. On a recent Saturday, events included a traditional Irish dance performance, a panel discussion on contemporary black photographers, a screening of *Hair,* and a dance party featuring a funk-and-soul deejay from Brooklyn Underground. As "only in New York" events go, First Saturday is a good one—you can always count on a full slate of cool.

most notably the Egyptian, Classical, and Ancient Middle Eastern collection of sculpture, wall reliefs, and mummies. The distinguished decorative arts collection includes 28 American period rooms from 1675 to 1928 (the extravagant Moorish-style smoking room from John D. Rockefeller's 54th St. mansion is my favorite). Other highlights are the African and Asian arts galleries, dozens of works by Rodin, a good costumes and textiles collection, and a diverse collection of both American and European painting and sculpture that includes works by Homer, O'Keeffe, Monet, Cézanne, and Degas. Look for more terrific exhibits on the 2005–06 calendar.

200 Eastern Pkwy. (at Washington Ave.), Brooklyn. © 718/638-5000. www.brooklynmuseum.org. Suggested admission $8 adults, $4 seniors and students, free for children under 12, free to all 1st Sat of the month 11am–11pm. Wed–Fri 10am–5pm; 1st Sat of the month 11am–11pm, each Sat thereafter 11am–6pm; Sun 11am–6pm. Subway: 2, 3 to Eastern Pkwy./Brooklyn Museum.

Brooklyn Tabernacle ✦ Under the direction of passionate orator Pastor Jim Cymbala and his choral-director wife, Carol, this nondenominational Christian revival church has grown into one of the largest—with a congregation of nearly 10,000 from all walks of city life—and most renowned inner-city churches in the nation. Folks come from all over the world to see the 275-voice, four-time Grammy Award–winning **Brooklyn Tabernacle Choir,** one of the nation's most celebrated gospel choirs.

Brooklyn Tabernacle relocated from Flatbush Avenue to 392 Fulton St., on Fulton Mall in the heart of downtown Brooklyn, in mid-2002. The gloriously renovated 1918 building is the fourth-largest theatrical space in the five boroughs, and seats nearly 4,000 for each service. Still, come early for a prime seat, especially when the choir sings (at the noon and 4pm Sun services).

17 Smith St. (btwn Fulton and Livingston sts.), downtown Brooklyn. © 718/290-2000. www.brooklyntabernacle.org. Services Sun 9am, noon, and 4pm; Tues 7pm. Subway: A, C, F to Jay St./Borough Hall; 2, 3 to Hoyt St.; 4, 5 to Borough Hall; M, N, R to Lawrence St.

Coney Island ✦✦ Sure, Coney Island is just a shell of what it once was in its heyday in the early 20th century. But it's that shell and what remains that make it such an intriguing attraction. The almost mythical Parachute Jump, recently refurbished though long inoperable, stands as a monument to Coney Island. But this is not a dead amusement park; **Astroland,** home of the famed **Cyclone** roller coaster, has some great rides for children and adults. The best amusement of all, however, is the people-watching. Maybe because it is at the extreme edge of New York City, but Coney Island attracts more than its share of the odd, freaky, and funky. It's here where **Nathan's Famous Hot Dogs** holds its annual hot dog eating contest on July 4 at noon; where the wholly entertaining **Mermaid Parade** spoofs the old bathing beauty parades (late June); and where members of the **Polar Bear Swim Club** show their masochistic gusto by taking a plunge into the icy ocean on January 1. There is also the small **Coney Island Museum,** 1208 Surf Ave., near West 12th Street (© 718/372-5158); see page 269. The best time to visit is from Memorial Day until mid-September, when the rides and amusement park are open. Bring your bathing suit and test the waters.

Subway: D to Coney Island–Stillwell Ave., Brooklyn.

New York Aquarium *Kids* Because of the long subway ride (about an hour from Midtown Manhattan) and its proximity to Coney Island, it's best to combine the two attractions, preferably in the summer. This surprisingly good aquarium is home to hundreds of sea creatures. Taking center stage are Atlantic bottle-nosed dolphins and California sea lions that perform daily during summer at the **Aquatheater.** Also basking in the spotlight are gangly Pacific octopuses, sharks, and a brand-new sea horse exhibit. Black-footed penguins, California sea otters, and a variety of seals live at the **Sea Cliffs exhibit,** a re-creation of a Pacific coastal habitat. But my absolute favorites are the beautiful white Beluga whales, which exude buckets of aquatic charm. Children love the hands-on exhibits at **Discovery Cove.** There's an indoor oceanview cafeteria and an outdoor snack bar, plus picnic tables.

502 Surf Ave. (at W. 8th St.), Coney Island, Brooklyn. ℂ 718/265-3400. www.nyaquarium.com. Admission $11 adults, $7 seniors and children 2–12. Daily 10am–4:30pm. Subway: D to Coney Island–Stillwell Ave., Brooklyn.

New York Transit Museum *Kids*   Housed in a real (decommissioned) subway station, this recently renovated underground museum is a wonderful place to spend an hour or so. The museum is small but very well done, with good multimedia exhibits exploring the history of the subway from the first shovelful of dirt scooped up at groundbreaking (Mar 24, 1900) to the present. Kids and parents alike will enjoy the interactive elements and the vintage subway cars, old wooden turnstiles, and beautiful station mosaics of yesteryear. A new exhibit dedicated to surface transportation is *On the Streets: New York's Trolleys and Buses.* All in all, a minor but remarkable tribute to an important development in the city's history.

The even smaller **Gallery Annex & Store at Grand Central Station** also houses rotating exhibitions and a terrific transit-themed gift shop (see "Museum Stores," in chapter 10). A second museum store, along with a travel information kiosk, is at the **Times Square Visitors Center;** see chapter 6.

Boerum Place and Schermerhorn St., Brooklyn. ℂ 718/694-5100. http://mta.info/mta/museum/index.html. Admission $3 adults, $1.50 seniors and children 3–17, free for seniors Tues noon–4pm. Mon–Fri 10am–4pm; Sat–Sun noon–5pm. Subway: A, C, to Hoyt St.; F to Jay St.; M, R to Court St.; 2, 3, 4, 5 to Borough Hall. Gallery Annex: In Grand Central Terminal (on the main level, in the shuttle passage next to the Station Masters' office), 42nd St. and Lexington Ave. ℂ 212/878-0106. Subway: 4, 5, 6, 7, S to 42nd St./Grand Central.

Prospect Park *★★*   Designed by Frederick Law Olmsted and Calvert Vaux after their great success with Central Park, this 562 acres of woodland, meadows, bluffs, and ponds is considered by many to be their masterpiece and the *pièce de résistance* of Brooklyn.

The best approach is from Grand Army Plaza, presided over by the monumental **Soldiers' and Sailors' Memorial Arch** (1892) honoring Union veterans. For the best view of the lush landscape, follow the path to Meadowport Arch, and proceed through to the Long Meadow, following the path that loops around it (it's about an hour's walk). Other park highlights include the 1857 Italianate mansion **Litchfield Villa** on Prospect Park West; the **Friends' Cemetery** Quaker burial ground (where Montgomery Clift is eternally prone—sorry, it's fenced off to browsers); the wonderful 1906 Beaux Arts **boathouse;** the 1912 **carousel,** with white wooden horses salvaged from a famous Coney Island merry-go-round (open Apr–Oct; rides 50¢); and **Lefferts Homestead Children's Historic House Museum** (ℂ 718/789-2822), a 1783 Dutch farmhouse with a museum of period furniture and exhibits geared to kids (open Apr–Nov Fri–Sun 1–4pm). There's a map at the park entrance that you can use to get your bearings.

On the east side of the park is the **Prospect Park Zoo** (ℂ **718/399-7339**). This is a thoroughly modern children's zoo where kids can walk among wallabies, explore a prairie-dog town, and much more. Admission is $5 for adults, $1.25 for seniors, $1 for children 3 to 12. April through October, open Monday through Friday 10am to 5pm, to 5:30pm weekends and holidays; November through March, open daily from 10am to 4:30pm.

At Grand Army Plaza, bounded by Prospect Park W., Parkside Ave., and Flatbush Ave., Brooklyn. © **718/965-8951,** or 718/965-8999 for events information. www.prospectpark.org. Subway: 2, 3 to Grand Army Plaza (walk down Plaza St. W. 3 blocks to Prospect Park W. and the entrance) or Eastern Pkwy./Brooklyn Museum.

BROOKLYN HEIGHTS HISTORIC DISTRICT

Just across the Brooklyn Bridge is **Brooklyn Heights** ⚓, a peaceful neighborhood of tree-lined streets, more than 600 historic houses built before 1860, landmark churches, and restaurants. Even with its magnificent promenade providing sweeping views of Lower Manhattan's ragged skyline, it feels more like its own village than part of the larger urban expanse.

This is where Walt Whitman lived and wrote *Leaves of Grass,* one of the great accomplishments in American literature. And in the 19th century, fiery abolitionist Henry Ward Beecher railed against slavery at **Plymouth Church of the Pilgrims** on Orange Street between Henry and Hicks streets (his sister wrote *Uncle Tom's Cabin*). If you walk down **Willow Street** between Clark and Pierrepont, you'll see three houses (nos. 108–112) in the Queen Anne style that was fashionable in the late 19th century, as well as an attractive trio of Federal-style houses (nos. 155–159) built before 1829. Also visit lively **Montague Street,** the main drag of Brooklyn Heights and full of cafes and shops. On Water Street, under the Brooklyn Bridge, is the **River Café** (© **718/ 522-5200;** www.rivercafe.com) where a drink or dinner at twilight, as the lights of Manhattan begin to flicker on, will offer an unforgettable view.

GETTING THERE   Bounded by the East River, Fulton Street, Court Street, and Atlantic Avenue, the Brooklyn Heights Historic District is one of the most outstanding and easily accessible sights beyond Manhattan. The neighborhood is reachable via a number of subway trains: the A, C, F to Jay St.; the 2, 3, 4, 5 to Clark Street or Borough Hall; or the N, R to Court Street.

It's easy to link a walk around Brooklyn Heights and along its Promenade with a walk over the **Brooklyn Bridge** (p. 241), a tour that makes for a lovely afternoon on a nice day. Take a 2 or 3 train to **Clark Street** (the first stop in Brooklyn). Turn right out of the station and walk toward the water, where you'll see the start of the waterfront **Brooklyn Promenade.** Stroll along the promenade admiring both the stellar views of lower Manhattan to the left and the gorgeous multimillion-dollar brownstones to the right, or park yourself on a bench for a while to contemplate the scene.

The promenade ends at Columbia Heights and Orange Street. To head to the bridge from here, turn left and walk toward the Watchtower Building. Before heading downslope, turn right immediately after the playground onto Middagh Street. After 4 or 5 blocks, you'll reach a busy thoroughfare, Cadman Plaza West. Cross the street and follow the walkway through little **Cadman Plaza Park;** veer left at the fork in the walkway. At Cadman Plaza East, turn left (downslope) toward the underpass, where you'll find the stairwell up to the Brooklyn Bridge footpath on your left.

Brooklyn Heights

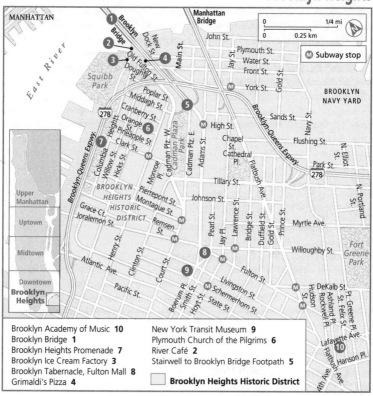

Brooklyn Academy of Music **10**
Brooklyn Bridge **1**
Brooklyn Heights Promenade **7**
Brooklyn Ice Cream Factory **3**
Brooklyn Tabernacle, Fulton Mall **8**
Grimaldi's Pizza **4**

New York Transit Museum **9**
Plymouth Church of the Pilgrims **6**
River Café **2**
Stairwell to Brooklyn Bridge Footpath **5**

Brooklyn Heights Historic District

IN QUEENS

For details on the **New York Hall of Science** and **Flushing Meadows–Corona Park** (also home to the Queens Museum of Art, below), see p. 295.

American Museum of the Moving Image ★ *Kids* Head here if you truly love movies. Unlike Manhattan's Museum of Television & Radio (p. 261), which is more of a library, this is a thought-provoking museum examining how moving images—film, video, and digital—are made, marketed, and shown; it encourages you to consider their impact on society as well. It's housed in part of the Kaufman Astoria Studios, which once were host to W. C. Fields and the Marx Brothers, and more recently have been used by Martin Scorsese *(The Age of Innocence)*, Woody Allen *(Radio Days)*, Bill Cosby (his *Cosby* TV series), and *Sesame Street.*

The museum's core exhibit, **Behind the Screen,** is a thoroughly engaging two-floor installation that takes you step-by-step through the process of making, marketing, and exhibiting moving images. There are more than 1,000 artifacts on hand, from technological gadgetry to costumes, and interactive exhibits where you can try your own hand at sound effects editing or create your own animated shorts, among other simulations.

Special-effects benchmarks—from the mechanical mouth of *Jaws* to the blending of past and present in *Forrest Gump*—are explored and explained. And in a nod to Hollywood nostalgia, memorabilia that wasn't swept up by the Planet Hollywood chain is displayed, including a Hopalong Cassidy lunch box, an E. T. doll, celebrity coloring books, and Dean Martin and Jerry Lewis hand puppets. Also on display are sets from *Seinfeld.* Even better are the daily hands-on demonstrations, where you can watch film editors, animators, and the like at work.

"Insiders' Hour" tours are offered every day at 2pm. Additionally, the museum hosts free **film and video screenings,** often accompanied by artist appearances, lectures, or panel discussions. Seminars often feature renowned film and TV pros discussing their craft; past guests have included Spike Lee, Terry Gilliam, Chuck Jones, and Atom Egoyan, so it's definitely worth seeing if someone's on while you're in town.

35th Ave. at 36th St., Astoria, Queens. ✆ **718/784-0077.** www.ammi.org. Admission $10 adults, $7.50 seniors and college students, $5 children 5–18, free for children under 5. Tues–Fri noon–5pm; Sat–Sun 11am–6pm (evening screenings Sat–Sun 6:30pm). Subway: R to Steinway St.; N to Broadway.

Isamu Noguchi Garden Museum 🌟 *(Finds)*   No place in the city is more Zen than this marvelous indoor/outdoor garden museum showcasing the work of Japanese American sculptor Isamu Noguchi (1904–88). In 2004, after a 2½-year renovation, the museum returned to its original site and will once again showcase the beautifully curated collection of the artist's masterworks in stone, metal, wood, and clay; you'll even see theater sets, furniture, and models for public gardens and playgrounds that Noguchi designed. A new gallery highlights the artist's work in interior design.

9-01 33rd Rd. (at Vernon Blvd.), Long Island City, Queens. ✆ **718/545-8842.** www.noguchi.org. Suggested admission $5 adults, $2.50 seniors and students. Wed–Fri 10am–5pm; Sat–Sun 11am–6pm. Subway: N to Broadway. Walk west on Broadway toward Manhattan until Broadway ends at Vernon Blvd.; turn left on Vernon and go 2 blocks.

Louis Armstrong House Museum 🌟 *(Finds)*   What is it about celebrities' homes that we find so fascinating? Is it that we get to see how they lived away from the glare of the cameras; how they functioned on a daily basis just like the rest of us? Armstrong was an international celebrity and could have lived anywhere, yet this unassuming, bi-level house in the working-class neighborhood of Corona, Queens, was the great Satchmo's home from 1943 until his death in 1971. It was bought and designed by his fourth wife, Lucille, who lived in it until her death in 1983. No one has lived in the house since and in 2003, the house, a National Historic Landmark and a New York City landmark, opened its doors to the public as a museum. The 40-minute tour takes you through the small, impeccably preserved home and explains the significance of each room to both Louis and Lucille. My favorite is Armstrong's den, where he kept his reel-to-reel tape recordings, cataloging everything he taped—music, conversations, and compositions, some of which are displayed on his desk. The house also includes a small exhibit with some of his memorabilia, including two of his trumpets, and a gift shop, where many of his CDs are for sale along with other Satchmo-centric items. If you have any interest in jazz and in Armstrong, this is a must see.

34–56 107th St., Corona, Queens. ✆ **718/478-8274.** www.satchmo.net. $8 adults, $6 seniors, students, and children. Tues–Fri 10am–5pm; Sat–Sun noon–5pm; last tour at 4pm. Subway: 7 to 103rd St.–Corona Plaza. Walk north on 103rd St., turn right on 37th Ave., turn left onto 107th St., and the house is a half-block north of 37th Ave.

Museum for African Art *(Finds)*   This captivating museum is a leading organizer of temporary—and usually excellent—exhibits dedicated to historic and contemporary African art and culture. In September 2002, the museum moved out of its old SoHo space and into a long-term temporary home in Long Island City (the same building where the Isamu Noguchi Museum is temporarily housed), which it will occupy until its new Museum Mile home is ready on Fifth Avenue between 109th and 110th streets. Weekend and evening programs include music and dance performances, art-making workshops, family events, and more; call or check the website for the current schedule.

36–01 43rd Ave. (at 36th St.), Long Island City, Queens. ☎ 212/784-7700. www.africanart.org. Admission $6 adults, $3 seniors, students, and children. Mon and Thurs–Fri 10am–5pm; Sat–Sun 11am–5pm. Subway: 7 to 33rd St. Walk north to 36th St., turn left and go 1 block to 43rd Ave.

P.S. 1 Contemporary Art Center

If you're interested in contemporary art that's too cutting-edge for most museums, don't miss this MoMA affiliate museum. Originally a public school (hence the name), this is the world's largest institution exhibiting contemporary art from America and abroad. You can expect to see a kaleidoscopic array of works from artists ranging from Jack Smith to Julian Schnabel; the museum is particularly well known for large-scale exhibitions by artists such as James Turrell. In 2005 the museum featured a very well received and popular exhibit, *Greater New York*, featuring works by more than 160 New York–based artists who have come into prominence since the year 2000.

22–25 Jackson Ave. (at 46th Ave.), Long Island City, Queens. ☎ 718/784-2084. www.ps1.org. Suggested admission $5 adults, $2 seniors and students. Thurs–Mon noon–6pm. Subway: E, V to 23rd St./Ely Ave. (walk 2 blocks south on Jackson Ave. to 46th Ave.); 7 to 45th Rd./Court House Sq. (walk 1 block south on Jackson Ave.).

Queens Museum of Art

One way to see New York in the shortest time (albeit without the street life) is to visit the Panorama, created for the 1939 World's Fair, an enormous building-for-building architectural model of New York City complete with an airplane that takes off from LaGuardia Airport. The 9,335-square-foot Gotham City is the largest model of its kind in the world, with 895,000 individual structures built on a scale of 1 inch = 100 feet. A red-white-and-blue ribbon is draped mournfully over the Twin Towers, which still stand in this Big Apple.

Also on permanent display is a collection of Tiffany glass manufactured at Tiffany Studios in Queens between 1893 and 1938. The *Contemporary Currents* series features rotating exhibits focusing on the works of a single artist, often with an international theme (suitable to New York's most diverse borough). History buffs should take note of the museum's NYC Building, which housed the United Nation's General Assembly from 1946 to 1952. Rotating art exhibitions, tours, lectures, films, and performances are part of the program, making this a very strong museum on all fronts.

Next to the Unisphere in Flushing Meadows–Corona Park, Queens. ☎ 718/592-9700. www.queensmuseum.org. Suggested admission $5 adults, $2.50 seniors and students, free for children under 5. Tues–Fri 10am–5pm; Sat–Sun noon–5pm. Subway: 7 to Willets Point/Shea Stadium (follow the yellow signs for the 10-min. walk through the park to the museum, which sits next to the Unisphere).

Socrates Sculpture Park

This former riverside landfill is now the best exhibition space for large-scale outdoor sculpture in the city. No velvet ropes and motion sensors here—interaction with the artwork is encouraged. Well worth a look, especially on a lovely day. Check the website for the current exhibition schedule—or just let yourself be happily surprised.

Broadway at Vernon Blvd., Long Island City, Queens. ☎ 718/956-1819. www.socratessculpturepark.org. Free admission. Daily 10am–sunset. Subway: N or W to Broadway; walk 8 blocks along Broadway toward the East River.

11 Spectator Sports

For details on the **New York City Marathon** and the **U.S. Open Tennis Championships,** see the "New York City Calendar of Events," in chapter 3.

BASEBALL   With two baseball teams in town, you can catch a game almost any day from opening day in April to the beginning of the playoffs in October. (Don't bother trying to get subway series tix, though—they're the hottest seats in town. Ditto for Opening Day or any playoff game.)

Pedro Martinez, Carlos Beltran, Mike Piazza, and the rest of the Amazin' **Mets** play at **Shea Stadium** in Queens (subway: 7 to Willets Point/Shea Stadium). For tickets (which ran $12–$45 for regular-season games in the 2005 season) and information, call the **Mets Ticket Office** at ✆ **718/507-TIXX,** or visit **www.mets.com**. Also keep in mind that you can buy game tickets (as well as logo wear and souvenirs, if you want to dress appropriately for the big game) at the **Mets Clubhouse Shop,** which has two Midtown Manhattan locations; see p. 336.

So the **Yankees** haven't won a World Series in 5 years—that only means they are overdue to win their 27th championship in 2005. The Yanks play at the House That Ruth Built, otherwise known as Yankee Stadium (subway: C, D, 4 to 161st St./Yankee Stadium); NY Waterway (p. 287) offers baseball cruises to games. Call ✆ **800/533-3779** or visit www.nywaterway.com for more info). For tickets ($10–$80 in 2005), contact **Ticketmaster** (✆ **212/307-1212** or 212/307-7171; www.ticketmaster.com) or **Yankee Stadium** (✆ **718/293-6000;** www.yankees.com). Serious baseball fans might check the schedule well in advance and try to catch **Old Timers' Day,** usually held in July, when pinstriped stars of years past return to the stadium to take a bow.

At Yankee Stadium, upper tier box seats (which run about $35), especially those behind home plate, give you a great view of all the action. Upper tier reserve seats are directly behind the box seats and are significantly cheaper ($17). Bleacher seats are even cheaper, and the rowdy commentary from that section's roughneck bleacher creatures is absolutely free. Most of the expensive seats (field boxes) are sold out in advance to season ticket holders. You can often purchase these very same seats from scalpers, but you'll pay a premium for them. Tickets can be purchased at the team's **clubhouse shop** in Manhattan; see p. 337.

Minor-league baseball ⚡ made a Big Apple splash in summer 2001 when the **Brooklyn Cyclones,** the New York Mets' A-level farm team, and the **Staten Island Yankees,** the Yanks' junior leaguers, came to town. Boasting their very own waterfront stadium, the Brooklyn Cyclones have been a major factor in the revitalization of Coney Island; the new Keyspan Park sits right off the legendary boardwalk (subway: F, N, Q, W to Stillwell Ave./Coney Island). The SI Yanks also have their own shiny new playing field, the Richmond County Bank Ballpark, just a 5-minute walk from the Staten Island Ferry terminal (subway: N, R to Whitehall St.; 4, 5 to Bowling Green; 1, 9 to S. Ferry). What's more, with bargain-basement ticket prices (which topped out at $12 for the Cyclones, $11 for the Yanks in the 2005 season), this is a great way to experience baseball in the city for a fraction of the major-league hassle and cost. Both teams have already developed a rabidly loyal fan base, so it's a good idea to buy your tickets for the 2006 summer season—which will run from June through September—in advance. For the Cyclones, call ✆ **718/449-8497** or visit **www.brooklyncyclones.com**; to reach the SI Yanks, call ✆ **718/720-9200** or go online to **www.siyanks.com**.

Moments Year-Round Yankee Tour

For a taste of Yankee glory at any time of year, take the **Insider's Tour of Yankee Stadium** (© **718/579-4531**). This official tour of the House That Ruth Built will take you onto the field, to Monument Park, and into the dugout. You'll even visit the press box and take a peek inside the clubhouse. The guide peppers the tour with lots of Yankee history and anecdotes as you go. And who knows? You might even spot a certain gorgeous green-eyed multimillionaire shortstop as you make the rounds.

Tours are offered daily at 10am except New Year's Day, during Opening Day preparations (usually the 3 weeks prior), and on weekends when the team is at home and weekdays when there is a home day game; plan to arrive by 9:40am. Tickets for the 1-hour basic **Classic Tour** are $12 for adults, $6 for kids 14 and under. No reservations are required; all you need to do is show up at the ballpark's press gate just before tour time, but it's still a good idea to call and confirm. (Groups of 12 or more require reservations and can book the 80-min. **Champions Tour,** which includes a short film on Yankee history screened in the Adidas Hall of Fame Suite, on a more varied schedule; prices are $17 for adults, $12 for seniors and kids.) The **Champions Plus Tour** adds a 15-minute tour of the club level ($25 adults, $17 kids). Check the Yankee website (**www.yankees. com**; click on "Yankee Stadium") for more info.

BASKETBALL   Though the New Jersey Nets are rumored to be moving (possibly) to Brooklyn, there are now two pro teams that play in New York at **Madison Square Garden,** Seventh Avenue between 31st and 33rd streets (© **212/465-6741** or www.thegarden.com; **212/307-7171** or www.ticketmaster.com for tickets; subway: A, C, E, 1, 2, 3, 9 to 34th St.), home court: Stephon Marbury, Allen Houston, and Penny Hardaway, and the rest of the **New York Knicks** (© **877/NYK-DUNK** or 212/465-JUMP; www.nyknicks.com). The **New York Liberty** (© **212/465-6080;** www.wnba.com/liberty), who electrify fans with their tough defense and WNBA All-Stars like Becky Hammon and Elena Baranova, occupy MSG from late May through the fall. Tickets start at $8, and go up to about $65 for courtside, with plenty of good seats available ranging from $14 to $24.

ICE HOCKEY   As of this writing the NHL and the **New York Rangers** had canceled their season and there is no guarantee that the sport will return.

Shopping

For many, shopping is their raison d'être—an uncontrollable urge, almost an addiction. What a perfect place New York, to satisfy that urge. No city in the world has the breadth and variety of stores that New York has; it's a shopper's paradise.

In this chapter, I've done my best to point out the city's shopping highlights; it's certainly enough to get you started. For much, much more on the New York shopping scene, check out *Suzy Gershman's Born to Shop New York* (Wiley Publishing, Inc.).

1 The Top Shopping Streets & Neighborhoods

Here's a rundown of New York's most interesting shopping areas, with some highlights of each to give you a feel for the neighborhood. If location is not given here, refer to the store's expanded listing under the appropriate category in "Shopping A to Z," later in this chapter.

DOWNTOWN

LOWER MANHATTAN & THE FINANCIAL DISTRICT

South Street Seaport (© 212/732-8257; subway: 2, 3, 4, 5 to Fulton St.) carries the neighborhood's torch. Familiar names like Abercrombie & Fitch, Ann Taylor, and the Sunglass Hut line Fulton Street, the Seaport's main cobbled drag; several tiers of largely nondescript shops and a large food court fill the levels at Pier 17, a waterfront barge–turned–shopping mall. There's nothing here you can't get anywhere else in Manhattan; come for the historic ambience and the wonderful harbor views. For a store list, visit **www.southstreetseaport.com**.

Century 21, the king of discount department stores, is across the street from the World Trade Center site. Electronics megamart **J&R** is still going strong, now occupying a full city block, with great prices on everything from cameras and computers to CDs and software.

CHINATOWN

Don't expect to find the purchase of a lifetime on Chinatown's often very crowded streets, but there's some quality browsing to be had. The fish and herbal markets along Canal, Mott, Mulberry, and Elizabeth streets are fun for their bustle and exotica. Dispersed among them (especially along **Canal St.**), you'll find a mind-boggling collection of knock-off sunglasses and watches, cheap backpacks, discount leather goods, and exotic souvenirs. It's a fun daytime browse, but don't expect quality—and be sure to bargain before you buy. (Also, skip the bootleg CDs, videos, and software—these are stolen goods, and you *will* be disappointed with the product.) **Mott Street,** between Pell Street and Chatham Square, boasts the most interesting of Chinatown's off-Canal shopping,

---

Tips **Sales Tax**

New York City sales tax is 8.65%, but it is not added to clothing and footwear items under $110. If you're visiting from out of state, consider having your purchases shipped directly home to avoid paying sales tax.

---

with an antiques shop or two dispersed among the tiny storefronts selling blue-and-white Chinese dinnerware. Just around the corner, peek into **Ting's Gift Shop** (18 Doyer St.; © **212/962-1081**), one of the oldest operating businesses in Chinatown. Under a vintage pressed-tin ceiling, it sells good-quality Chinese toys, kits, and lanterns.

THE LOWER EAST SIDE

The bargains aren't quite what they used to be in the **Historic Orchard Street Shopping District**—which basically runs from Houston to Canal along Allen, Orchard, and Ludlow streets, spreading outward along both sides of Delancey Street—but prices on leather bags, shoes, luggage, linens, and fabrics on the bolt are still quite good. Be aware, though, that the hard sell on Orchard Street can be pretty hard to take. Still, the district is a nice place to discover a part of New York that's disappearing. Come during the week; many stores are Jewish-owned and therefore close Friday afternoon and all day Saturday. Sunday tends to be a madhouse.

The artists and other trendsetters who have been turning this neighborhood into a bastion of hip have also added a cutting edge to its shopping scene in recent years. You'll find a growing—and increasingly upscale—crop of alterna-shops south of Houston and north of Grand Street, between Allen and Clinton streets to the east and west, specializing in up-to-the-minute fashions and edgy club clothes for 20-somethings, plus funky retro furnishings, Japanese toys, and other offbeat items. Before you browse, stop in at the **Lower East Side Visitor Center,** 261 Broome St., between Orchard and Allen streets (© **866/224-0206** or 212/226-9010; subway: F to Delancey St.), for a shopping guide that includes vendors both Old World and new. Or you can preview the list online at **www.lowereastsideny.com**.

SOHO

People love to complain about superfashionable SoHo—it's become too trendy, too tony, too Mall of America. True, **J. Crew** is only one of many big names that have supplanted many of the artists' lofts that used to inhabit its historic buildings. But SoHo is still one of the best shopping 'hoods in the city—and few are more fun to browse. The elegant cast-iron architecture, the cobblestone streets, the distinct rich-artist vibe: SoHo has a look and feel unlike any other Manhattan neighborhood.

SoHo's shopping grid runs from Broadway west to Sixth Avenue, and Houston Street south to Canal Street. **Broadway** is the most commercial strip, with such recognizable names as **Pottery Barn, Banana Republic, Sephora,** and **A/X Armani Exchange. H&M,** the popular Swedish department store with cutting-edge fashions sold at unbelievably low prices, has two stores that face one another on Broadway. **Bloomingdale's** has opened up a downtown branch in the old Canal Street Jeans space. **Prada**'s flagship store, also on Broadway, is worth visiting for its spacious, almost soothing design alone (by Dutch architect Rem Koolhaus). A definite highlight is the two-story **Pearl River** Chinese emporium (see "Gifts" in "Shopping A to Z," later in this chapter), which offers everything from silk cheongsam (traditional Chinese high-necked dress) to teaware.

The big names in avant-garde fashion (see "Clothing" in "Shopping A to Z," later in this chapter) have landed in SoHo, but you'll also find one-of-a-kind boutiques, such as the **Hat Shop,** 120 Thompson St., between Prince and Spring (© **212/219-1445**), a full-service milliner for women that also features plenty of off-the-rack toppers, plus shoe stores galore and high-end home design and housewares boutiques.

NOLITA

Not so long ago, **Elizabeth Street** was a quiet adjunct to Little Italy. Today it's one of the hottest shopping strips in the neighborhood known as Nolita. Elizabeth and neighboring **Mott** and **Mulberry streets** are dotted with an increasing number of shops between Houston Street and the Bowery. It's an easy walk from the Broadway/Lafayette stop on the F, V line to the neighborhood, since it starts just east of Lafayette Street; you can also take the 6 to Spring Street, or the N, R to Prince Street and walk east from there.

Nolita is clearly the stepchild of SoHo—meaning don't expect cheap. Its wall-to-wall boutiques are largely the province of sophisticated shopkeepers specializing in high-quality fashion-forward products and design. More and more, it's become a beacon of ethnic designs from around the world. **Indomix** (232 Mulberry St.; © **212/334-6356;** www.indomix.com) offers beautiful beaded tunics and other colorful South Asian styles by five top designers in India. **Sol** (6 Prince St.; © **212/966-0002;** www.solnewyork.com) sells everything Brazilian, from the über flip-flop, Havianas, to teeny-weeny bikinis. Texan-born designer and skateboarder **Tracy Feith** (209 Mulberry St.; © **212/334-3097**) creates irresistibly pretty slip dresses, skirts, and tops in eye-popping colors and light-as-air Indian silk in his eponymous store on Mulberry Street.

(Tips Additional Sources for Serious Shoppers

If you're looking for specific items, check the shopping listings at **www.new york.citysearch.com**, **www.timeoutny.com**, and **www.nymetro.com** before you leave home.

For an online guide to sample sales/designer bargains, you can't do better than the free registration site **www.nysale.com**, which will let you in on unadvertised sales taking place throughout the city.

Hard information about current sales, new shops, sample and close-out sales, and special art, craft, and antiques shows is best found in the "Check Out" section of *Time Out New York* or the "Sales & Bargains," "Best Bets," and "Smart City" sections of *New York* magazine. *New York* also runs daily updates of these features at **www.nymetro.com**, and *Time Out* usually publishes a twice-yearly shopping guide that's usually available on newsstands for about 6 bucks.

Other Web sources include **www.dailycandy.com**, a daily online newsletter highlighting store openings and where to find the day's sales, and **www.girl shop.com**, a website dedicated to New York insider fashion news. Now, Girlshop aficionados have more than just the website to shop from: In 2005, the flagship **Girlshop Boutique** opened in the Meat-Packing District (819 Washington St., between Little W. 12th and Gansevoort sts.; © **212/255-4985**).

Nolita is also an accessories bonanza; stop in at **Sigerson Morrison** for great shoes or **Push** for eye-catching jewelry. You'll find more standouts in the listings in "Shopping A to Z," later in this chapter, but just cruising the blocks will do the trick.

THE EAST VILLAGE

The East Village personifies bohemian hip. The easiest subway access is the 6 train to Astor Place, which lets you right out at **Astor Wines & Spirits;** from here, it's just a couple blocks east to the prime hunting grounds.

East 9th Street between Second Avenue and Avenue A is lined with an increasingly smart collection of boutiques, proof that the East Village isn't just for kids anymore. Designers, including **Jill Anderson** and **Huminska,** sell excellent-quality and original fashions for women along here.

If it's strange, illegal, or funky, it's probably available on **St. Marks Place,** which takes over for 8th Street, running east from Third Avenue to Avenue A. This strip is a permanent street market, with countless T-shirt and boho jewelry stands. The height of the action is between Second and Third avenues, which is prime hunting grounds for used-record collectors (see "Music," in "Shopping A to Z," later in this chapter).

LAFAYETTE STREET FROM SOHO TO NOHO

Lafayette Street has a retail character all its own, distinct from the rest of SoHo. It has grown into something of an Antiques Row, especially strong in mid-century furniture. Prices are high, but so is quality. The stretch to stroll is between 8th Street to the north and Spring Street to the south. Either take the 6 train to Astor Place and work your way south, get off at Spring Street and walk north, or take the F or V to Broadway–Lafayette and get dropped off in the heart of the action. Highlights include **Guéridon,** at no. 359, between Bleecker and Bond streets (✆ **212/677-7740;** www.gueridon.com), for sophisticated 20th-century European pieces, mainly French, plus some original designs in the same vein.

Dispersed among the furniture and design stores are a number of clothiers, including **Ghost** (28 Bond St.; ✆ **646-602-2891**), featuring upscale bohemian designs for women—no girl stuff, thank you very much.

GREENWICH VILLAGE

The West Village is great for browsing and gift shopping. Specialty bookstores and record stores, antiques and crafts shops, and gourmet food markets dominate. On 8th Street—NYU territory between Broadway and Sixth Avenue—you can find trendy footwear and affordable fashions.

But the biggest shopping boom of late has happened on **Bleecker Street** west of Sixth Avenue. Between Carmine Street and Seventh Avenue, foodies will delight in the strip of boutique food shops, including **Amy's Bread, Wild Edibles,** and **Murray's Cheese** (in a large new space). In between are record stores, guitar shops, and a sprinkling of artsy boutiques. Past narrow **Christopher Street,** the center of gay Village life, Bleecker becomes boutique alley, where one jewel box of a shop follows still another. Among them: **Intermix, Olive & Bette, Ralph Lauren, Lulu Guinness,** and **Marc Jacobs.**

Those who really love to browse should also wander **west of Seventh Avenue** and along **Hudson Street,** where charming shops like **House of Cards and Curiosities,** 23 Eighth Ave., between Jane and 12th streets (✆ **212/675-6178**), the Village's own funky take on an old-fashioned nickel-and-dime, are tucked among the brownstones.

CHELSEA/MEAT-PACKING DISTRICT

Almost overnight, it seems, West Chelsea has been transformed into the **Chelsea Art District,** where more than 200 galleries have sprouted up in a once-moribund enclave of repair shops and warehouses. The district unofficially stretches from 14th to 29th streets and the West Side Highway and Seventh Avenue, but the high-density area lies between 20th and 26th streets between Tenth and Eleventh avenues.

The Meat-Packing District has also zoomed from quaint to hot (and some say over) in no time, with such big-name designers as **Stella McCartney** (429 W. 14th St.; ✆ **212/ 929-7180**), **Christian Louboutin** (59 Horatio St.; ✆ **212/255-1910**), and **Alexander McQueen** (417 W. 14th St.; ✆ **212/645-1797**) in residence. **Jeffrey New York,** an offshoot of the Atlanta department store, has pricey designer clothes, an amazing shoe collection, and the friendliest staff in New York.

UNION SQUARE/THE FLATIRON DISTRICT

The hottest shopping/eating/hanging-out neighborhood in the city may be Union Square. The long-forlorn south side of the square is now a mega shopping area with **Whole Foods, Filene's Basement,** and **DSW (Designer Shoe Warehouse).** Just to the right is a **Virgin Megastore.** On the north side of the park, **Barnes & Noble** is situated in a beautifully restored 1880 cast-iron building. Of course, the beating heart of Union Square is the 4-days-a-week **Greenmarket,** the biggest farmer's market in the city.

On Broadway, just a few blocks north of Union Square, is the amazing shopping emporium **ABC Carpet & Home,** where the loft-size floors hold brilliantly decadent displays of furniture, housewares, linens (thread counts off the charts), and tchotchkes of all size and shape.

Upscale retailers who have rediscovered the architectural majesty of **lower Fifth Avenue** include **Banana Republic, Victoria's Secret,** and **Kenneth Cole.** You won't find much that's new along here, but it's a pleasing stretch nonetheless.

When 23rd Street was the epitome of New York uptown fashion more than 100 years ago, the major department stores stretched along **Sixth Avenue** for about a mile from 14th Street up. These elegant stores stood in huge cast-iron buildings that were long ago abandoned and left to rust. In the last several years, however, the area has become the city's discount shopping center, with superstores and off-pricers filling up the renovated spaces: **Filene's Basement, TJ Maxx,** and **Bed Bath & Beyond** are all at 620 Sixth Ave., while **Old Navy** is next door, and **Barnes & Noble** is just a couple of blocks away at Sixth Avenue near 22nd Street.

MIDTOWN
HERALD SQUARE & THE GARMENT DISTRICT

Herald Square—where 34th Street, Sixth Avenue, and Broadway converge—is dominated by **Macy's,** the self-proclaimed world's biggest department store. At Sixth Avenue and 33rd Street is the **Manhattan Mall** (✆ **212/465-0500;** www.manhattan mallny.com), home to mall standards like LensCrafters and Radio Shack.

A long block over on Seventh Avenue, not much goes on in the grimy, heavily industrial Garment District. This is, however, where you'll find that quintessential New York experience called the **sample sale** (the box titled "Additional Sources for Serious Shoppers," on p. 310, explains how to find out about upcoming sample sales).

TIMES SQUARE & THE THEATER DISTRICT

You won't find much to entice the serious shopper here, since you can find most of the goods that are sold here back home. The best of the Times Square stores is Richard

---

> ## _Tips_ Open Hours
>
> Open hours can vary significantly from store to store—even different branches of the Gap can keep different schedules depending on location and management. Generally, stores open at 10 or 11am on Monday through Saturday, and 7pm is the most common closing hour (although sometimes it's 6pm). Both opening and closing hours tend to get later as you move downtown; stores in the East Village often don't open until 1 or 2pm, and they stay open until 8pm or later.
>
> All of the big department stores are open 7 days a week. However, unlike department stores in suburban malls, most of these stores don't keep a regular 10am to 9pm schedule. The department stores, and shops along major strips like Fifth Avenue, usually stay open later 1 night a week (often Thurs), although not all shops may comply. Sunday hours are usually noon to 5 or 6pm. Most shops are open 7 days a week, but smaller boutiques may close 1 day a week; in addition, some neighborhoods virtually shut down on a particular day—namely the Lower East Side on Saturday, the East Village on Monday, and most of the Financial District for the weekend. But at holiday time, anything goes: Macy's often stays open until midnight for the last couple of weeks before Christmas!
>
> Your best bet is to **call ahead** if your heart's set on visiting a particular store.

Branson's rollicking **Virgin Megastore,** and the fabulous **Toys "R" Us** flagship on Broadway and 44th Street, which even has its own full-scale Ferris wheel.

West 47th Street between Fifth and Sixth avenues is the city's famous **Diamond District;** see "Jewelry & Accessories" in "Shopping A to Z," later in this chapter.

You'll also notice a wealth of **electronics stores** throughout the neighborhood, many suspiciously trumpeting GOING OUT OF BUSINESS sales. These guys have been going out of business since the Stone Age. That's the bait and switch; pretty soon you've spent too much money for not enough stereo. If you want to check out what they have to offer, go in knowing the going price on that PDA or digital camera you're interested in. You can make a good deal if you know exactly what the market is, but these guys will be happy to suck you dry given half a chance.

FIFTH AVENUE & 57TH STREET
The heart of Manhattan retail ranges up Fifth Avenue to 57th Street and across. Time was, only the very rich could shop these sacred crossroads. Such is not the case anymore, now that **Tiffany & Co.,** which has long reigned supreme here, sits a stone's throw from **Niketown** and the **NBA Store** and the huge **Louis Vuitton** flagship store at the corner of 57th Street and Fifth Avenue. In addition, a good number of mainstream retailers, like **Banana Republic,** have flagships along Fifth, further democratizing the avenue. Still, you will find a number of big-name, big-ticket designers radiating from the crossroads, including **Versace, Chanel, Dior,** and **Cartier.** You'll also find big-name jewelers along here, as well as chi-chi department stores like **Bergdorf Goodman, Henri Bendel,** and **Saks Fifth Avenue,** all of which help the avenue maintain its classy cachet.

UPTOWN

MADISON AVENUE

Madison Avenue from 57th to 79th streets has usurped Fifth Avenue as *the* tony shopping street in the city; in fact, it boasts the most expensive retail real estate in the world. Bring lots of plastic. This ultradeluxe strip—particularly in the high 60s—is home to *the* most luxurious designer boutiques, with **Barneys New York** as the anchor. For a sampling of local designers, see "Clothing" in "Shopping A to Z," later in this chapter.

For those of us without unlimited budgets, the good news is that stores like **Crate & Barrel** and the **Ann Taylor** flagship make the untouchable Madison Avenue seem approachable and affordable.

UPPER WEST SIDE

The Upper West Side's best shopping street is **Columbus Avenue.** Small shops catering to the neighborhood's white-collar mix of young hipsters and families line both sides of the pleasant avenue from 66th Street (where you'll find an excellent branch of **Barnes & Noble**) to about 86th Street. Highlights include **Maxilla & Mandible** for museum-quality natural science–based gifts, and **Harry's Shoes** (see "Museum Stores" and "Shoes" in "Shopping A to Z," later in this chapter), but you won't lack for good browsing along here. **The Shops at Columbus Circle** also offers a world of upscale choices for shopping (see the box "Mall with a View," below).

Boutiques also dot Amsterdam Avenue, but main-drag **Broadway** is most notable for its terrific gourmet edibles at **Zabar's** and **Fairway** markets (see "Edibles" in "Shopping A to Z," later in this chapter).

THE OUTER BOROUGHS

Brooklyn is becoming a shopping destination in its own right, and the best can be found in **Williamsburg.** To get to the prime shopping in Williamsburg, take the L train, which runs across 14th Street, and get off at the first stop in Brooklyn, Bedford Avenue. Walk out of the subway towards Bedford (not Driggs). Most of the shops in Williamsburg are on Bedford, including the vintage music and clothing store **Beacon's Closet,** 88 N. 11th St. (© 718/486-0816); **Metaphors,** 195 Bedford Ave. (© 718/ 782-0917), a New-Age gift shop that also carries women's clothing and lingerie; and **Crypto,** 154 Bedford Ave. (© 718/486-6779), for ultrahip clothing and accessories. The Bedford Avenue **Mini Mall,** 218 Bedford Ave. (© 718/302-9337; www.mini minimarket.com), has a conglomerate of stores, including **Spoonbill & Sugartown**

Mall with a View

The Shops at Columbus Circle mall, located in the Time Warner Center, features not only some of the biggest (and most expensive) names in retail, it also offers shopping with a view of Central Park. Located just off the southwest corner of Central Park, the mall is 2 city blocks long and four stories high. But does the picturesque view really matter to the shoppers who set their sights on the goods at retailers like **Williams Sonoma, A/X Armani Exchange, Coach, Hugo Boss, Joseph Abboud, Eileen Fisher, Thomas Pink, Border's Books,** and the massive 59,000-square-foot **Whole Foods Supermarket?** For more information, and a complete list of stores, check the mall's website at www.shopsatcolumbus.com or call © 212/823-6300.

Shopping One Two Five Street

Maybe it was the arrival of Bill Clinton on the block. Or maybe it's just part of a Harlem renaissance. Whatever the reason, 125th Street is more vibrant than ever; a true shopping thoroughfare, especially on the blocks between St. Nicholas Avenue and Fifth Avenue. Big chains like **Old Navy, The Children's Store, H&M, The Body Shop, Starbucks,** and **Modell's** have recently set up franchises on 125th. Not everyone is happy with this retail gentrification, believing that Harlem might be losing its identity. But sprinkled among the big names are still plenty of stores that represent that unique Harlem character. Hip-hop boutiques like **Jimmy Jazz,** 239 West 125th St., near Frederick Douglass Boulevard (© 212/664-2877), and **Dr. Jay's** at 256 W. 125th St., between Lenox and Seventh avenues (© 212/665-7795), and **Jersey Man Cap, USA** 112 W. 125th St., between Lenox and Fifth avenues (© 212/222-7942), where you can get anything from a Kangol cap to Girbaud Femme are mainstays on The Street. Since 1979, the **125th St. Record Shack** at 274 W. 125th St., between Lenox Avenue and Adam Clayton Powell Jr. Boulevard, has been selling jazz, gospel, R&B, doo-wop, and hip-hop, the music usually carrying well out into the already loud street.

At the West African importer **African Paradise,** 27 W. 125th St., at Lenox Avenue (© 212/410-5294), you'll find all the supplies you'll ever need for ancestral worship.

On your shopping tour, you might get hungry—and there is no shortage of places to eat. Skip the usual fast-food options and try the local grub at places like the **M&G Diner,** 383 W. 125th St., at St. Nicholas Avenue (© 212/864-7325), where you'll get some of the best fried chicken in the city (see chapter 7 for more). For coffee, some fine pie, and even a martini, don't miss **Wimp's Southern-Style Bakery, Skye Café and Martini Bar,** 29 W. 125th St., between Fifth and Lenox avenues (© 212/410-2296). For a cultural diversion, stop in at the **Studio Museum in Harlem,** 144 W. 125 St., between Lenox Avenue and Adam Clayton Powell Jr. Boulevard (© 212/864-4500), which also features an interesting gift shop (for more, see chapter 9).

Booksellers (© 718/387-7332), purveyors of art and architecture books, and **Otte** (© 718/302-3007), where you can find Juicy Couture and Cosa Bella underwear.

The other burgeoning area in Brooklyn is **DUMBO** (that's **D**own **U**nder the **M**anhattan **B**ridge **O**verpass), and high-end stores are beginning to move in, including **Jacques Torres Chocolates** (see the sidebar "Chocolate City," later in this chapter), and a warehouse outlet of **ABC Carpet,** 20 Jay St. (© **718/643-7400;** www.abc home.com).

There is not much fine shopping in any of the other boroughs, with the very notable exception of the **Arthur Avenue Retail Market** (see "Edibles" in "Shopping A to Z," later in this chapter) located in the Little Italy of the **Bronx.**

2 The Big Department Stores

ABC Carpet & Home ★★   Shopping ABC has often been compared to taking a fantasy tour of your very rich and very well-traveled ancestor's attic. This two-building emporium is legendary and deserves to be: It's the ultimate home-fashions and furnishings department store. On the west side of the street is the stunning 10-floor home emporium. The goods run the gamut from Moroccan mosaic-tile end tables to hand-painted Tuscan pottery to Tiffany-style lamps to distressed bed frames sporting meltingly soft Italian linens to much, much more, all exquisitely displayed. A whole floor of on-the-bolt upholstery fabrics is to die for. These are high-end goods, but sales can produce substantial bargains. The Parlor floor boasts an eclectic collection of beautiful gift items and housewares, and some of the smaller items are quite affordable. Across the street is the multifloor carpet store, which boasts a stunning collection of area rugs. 881 & 888 Broadway (at 19th St.). ✆ **212/473-3000.** http://abchome.com. Subway: L, N, R, 4, 5, 6 to 14th St./Union Sq.

Barneys New York ✪ After financial woes forced the closure of the original Chelsea store a few years back, New York's self-made temple of chic is back on top. The Madison Avenue store exudes impeccable high style—and a frostiness that's hard to overcome, but designer-fashion fans probably won't mind. While the store focuses on hot-off-the-runway women's wear, its menswear runs the gamut from classic to cutting edge. The fragrance department works hard to offer offbeat and unusual scents as well as the classics. Bring your platinum card, because nothing comes cheap here, although house brands are solidly made and aren't off-the-chart expensive.

Both the downtown (in two locations) and uptown **Barneys Co-Op**s have blossomed into real fashion hot spots, sisterly but separate from the chic Barneys New York Madison Avenue headquarters. At Barneys Co-Op, more downtown-casual fashions for men and women—from such designer names as Diane von Furstenberg, Juicy Couture, and Rebecca Taylor—set the tone. Prices are more reasonable than at the flagship but not cheap by any means.

Tip: Twice a year, Barneys hosts its famous warehouse sale in Chelsea. Prices are changed daily, but markdowns are 50% to 80% off the original retail prices on all clothing and gifts. So if you are planning a shopping trip to the city, keep your eyes open for when the sales will occur. 660 Madison Ave. (at 61st St.). ✆ **212/826-8900.** www.barneys.com. Subway: N, R to Fifth Ave. Barneys Co-Op: 116 Wooster St. (btwn. Prince and Spring sts.). ✆ **212/965-9964.** Subway: N/R to Prince St. 236 W. 18th St. (btwn Seventh and Eighth aves.). ✆ **212/593-7800.** Subway: 1, 9 to 18th St. 2151 Broadway (between 75th and 76th sts.). ✆ **646/335=0978.** Subway 1, 9 to 79th St. Barneys Warehouse: 255 W. 17th St. (btwn Seventh and Eighth aves.). No phone.

Bergdorf Goodman ✪✪ Bergdorf's is a museum of haute couture. The store is designed on an intimate scale and lacks the kicky nouveau riche feel of Bendel's. Although the customer base is primarily composed of ladies who lunch and businesswomen with gobs of money but little time for nonsense, fashionistas in the know appreciate Bergdorf's little secret: Sales can garner fantastic bargains, with designer clothing prices slashed to the bone. Finely tuned designer salons represent both couture powerhouses and downtown darlings. The fifth floor is an open space filled with fashions at more reasonable prices. The jewelry on the main floor and unparalleled gift and tabletop floor are worth a browse alone. The store has two ladies' shoe departments, one tops for one-stop designer shopping in the $300-and-up range, and the less-expensive fifth-floor salon. Just across the street is **Bergdorf Goodman Man,** a palace of fine men's fashion. 754 Fifth Ave. (at 57th St.). ✆ **212/753-7300.** www.bergdorfgoodman. com. Subway: E, F to Fifth Ave.

Bloomingdale's ✪ More accessible than Barneys and more affordable than Saks, Bloomingdale's has a certain New York pizazz. Taking up the space of a city block, Bloomie's stocks just about anything you could want, from clothing (both designer and everyday basics) and fragrances to housewares and furniture—not necessarily a good thing, because sometimes it feels too stuffed full of merchandise for comfort. It pays to make a reconnaissance trip to get the overview, then move in for the kill. The main entrance is on Third Avenue, but pop up to street level from the 59th Street station and you'll be right at the Lexington Avenue entrance. A smaller, downtown branch opened in 2004 offering pricier and edgier items. 1000 Third Ave. (Lexington Ave. at 59th St.). ℂ 212/705-2000. www.bloomingdales.com. Subway: 4, 5, 6 to 59th St. 504 Broadway (at Broome St.). ℂ 212/729-5900. Subway: N, R to Prince St.

Century 21 *(Value)*   Prices here on designer goods are 40% to 70% off what you would pay at a department store or designer boutique. Don't think that $250 Armani blazer is a bargain? Look again at the tag—the retail price is upward of $800. This is the place to find $5 Liz Claiborne tees, $20 Todd Oldham pants, or the $50 Bally loafers you've been dreaming of—not to mention underwear, hosiery, and ties so cheap that they're almost free. Kids' clothes, linens, and housewares are also part of the extensive stock. Expect big crowds and avoid the weekday lunch hour and Saturdays, if you can help it. 22 Cortlandt St. (btwn Broadway and Church St.). ℂ 212/227-9092. www.c21stores.com. Subway: 1, 2, 3, 4, 5, M to Fulton St.; A, C to Broadway/Nassau St.; E to Chambers St.

Henri Bendel *(Finds)*   This gorgeous Fifth Avenue store is a lot of fun to browse. It feels like you're shopping in the town house of a slightly offbeat, moneyed lady, who doesn't think twice about throwing on a little something by Anna Sui and an outrageously wide-brimmed hat to go out shopping for the day—she's got the panache to pull it off. It's a superstylish, high-ticket collection for ladies with a flair for the funky and frilly—but sales are good, and there are always some one-of-a-kind accessories that make affordable souvenirs (and earn you one of the black-and-white-striped shopping bags, the best in town). The makeup department is always on the cutting edge. The pretty tearoom looks out on Fifth Avenue through Lalique windows. 712 Fifth Ave. (btwn 55th and 56th sts.). ℂ 212/247-1100. Subway: N, R to Fifth Ave.

Lord & Taylor   Okay, so maybe Lord & Taylor isn't the first place you'd go for a vinyl miniskirt, but this New York institution has an understated, elegant mien. It now operates under the May Company banner but maintains its own sensibility. Long known as an excellent source for women's dresses and coats, L&T stocks all the major labels for men and women, with a special emphasis on American designers. Their house-brand clothes (khakis, blazers, turtlenecks, and summer sportswear) are well made and a great bargain. Sales, especially around holidays, can be stellar. The store is big enough to have a good selection (especially for petites), but doesn't overwhelm. The Christmas window displays are an annual delight. 424 Fifth Ave. (at 39th St.). ℂ 212/391-3344. www.lordandtaylor.com. Subway: F, V to 42nd St.

Macy's *(Overrated)*   A four-story sign on the side of the building trumpets MACY'S, THE WORLD'S LARGEST STORE—a hard fact to dispute, since the 10-story behemoth covers an entire city block, even dwarfing Bloomie's on the other side of town. Macy's is a hard place to shop: The size is unmanageable, the service is dreadful, and the incessant din from the crowds on the ground floor alone will kick your migraine into action. But they do sell *everything*. Massive renovation over the past few years has redesigned many departments into more manageable "ministores"—there's a Metropolitan Museum Gift Shop, a Swatch boutique, and cafes and makeup counters on several floors—but the store's one-of-a-kind flair that I remember so well from my childhood is just a memory now. Still, sales run constantly, holiday or no (1-day sales are popular on Wed and Sat), so bargains are guaranteed. And because so many feel adrift in this retail sea, the store provides personal guides/shoppers at no charge. My advice: Get the floor plan, and consult it often to avoid wandering off into the sportswear netherworld. At Christmastime, come as late as you can manage (the store is usually open until midnight in the final shopping days). At Herald Square, W. 34th St. and Broadway. ✆ 212/695-4400. www.macys.com. Subway: B, D, F, N, Q, R, 1, 2, 3, 9 to 34th St.

Saks Fifth Avenue 🌟🌟 There are branches of Saks all over the country now, but this is it: Saks *Fifth Avenue*. No other store better typifies the Big Apple these days than this legendary flagship store, which is well worth your time—and the smaller-than-most size makes it quite manageable. There's something for everyone here. Saks carries a wide range of clothing; departments err on the pricey designer side (stay out of the lingerie department if you're looking for affordable basics), but run the gamut to affordable house-brand basics. The men's department is the finest in the city. The cosmetics and fragrance departments on the main floor are justifiably noteworthy—they carry many hard-to-find and brand-new brands, including Laura Mercier, the Big Apple's own Kiehl's, and more—as are the extensive fine and costume jewelry counters. And the location, right across from Rockefeller Center, makes it a convenient stop for those on the sightseeing circuit. And the holiday windows are often the city's best. 611 Fifth Ave. (btwn 49th and 50th sts.). ✆ 212/753-4000. www.saksfifthavenue.com. Subway: B, D, F, Q to 47th–50th sts./Rockefeller Center; E, F to Fifth Ave.

Takashimaya 🌟 *Finds* This petite branch of Japan's most famous department store chain exudes an appealingly austere, Japanese-tinged French country charm. Come to see some of the city's most beautiful displays of tableware and boudoir fashions. Paris's most famous florist, Christian Tortu, has a main-floor boutique that's a work of art in its own right. The cosmetics department on the top floor is a must for fans of high-end designer brands looking for something special. The serenely elegant Tea Box specializes in delicate bento lunches and beautiful sweets. Aesthetes shouldn't miss this place; it's a wonderful spot for delicate, elegant gifts. 693 Fifth Ave. (btwn 54th and 55th sts.). ✆ 212/350-0100. Subway: E, F to Fifth Ave.

3 Shopping A to Z

ANTIQUES & COLLECTIBLES

Antiques hounds will dazzle at the bounty that New York has to offer, from Louis XIV settees to vintage DeFranco Family lunchboxes. Be prepared, however—you will pay top dollar for everything.

Traditionalists will love the blocks off **Broadway near 10th and 11th streets,** where the bounty includes Kentshire Galleries (see below); and **East 59th, 60th, and 61st streets** around Second Avenue, not far from the Manhattan Art and Antiques Center (1050 Second Ave., between 55th and 56th streets; ✆ 212/355-4400), where about two dozen high-end dealers line the street and spill over onto surrounding blocks. Fans of mid-century furniture and Americana with a twist should browse **Lafayette Street** in SoHo/NoHo. Just about any dealer you visit will have the current issue of the free *Greyrock Antiques Guide* and/or *Antiques New York,* which will lead you to specialty dealers around the city.

Most call it the 26th Street flea market: The famous **Annex Antiques Fair and Flea Market** (✆ 212/243-5343; www.annexantiques.citysearch.com) is an outdoor emporium of nostalgia, filling a few parking lots along Sixth Avenue between 24th and 27th streets on weekends year-round. The assemblage is hit or miss—some days you'll find treasures galore, and others it seems like there's nothing but junk. A few quality vendors are almost always on hand, though, making it well worth the $1 admission fee. The truly dedicated arrive at 6:30am, but the browsing is still plenty good as late as 4pm. Sunday is always best, since there's double the booty on hand. The website will also link you to other flea markets around the city.

Also check out "Jewelry & Accessories," below, if that's what you're in the market for.

Alphaville   This gallery specializes in 1940s, 1950s, and 1960s toys and movie posters, all in mint condition and beautifully displayed. Space toys are an emphasis. Well worth a look for nostalgic baby boomers, even if you have no intention of buying. 226 W. Houston St. (btwn Sixth Ave. and Varick St.). ✆ **212/675-6850**. www.alphaville.com. Subway: 1, 9 to Houston St.

Chelsea Antiques Building   Right around the corner from New York's best flea market (see Annex Antiques Fair and Flea Market, above), this 12-floor building houses more than 100 dealers and is open daily. The permanent stalls run the gamut from 18th-century antiques to rare books to early-20th-century radios, jewelry, and toys. Prices are so good that it's known as a dealer's source, and shoppers are the type who love to prowl, touch everything, and sniff out a bargain. 110 W. 25th St. (btwn Sixth and Seventh aves.). ✆ **212/929-0909**. Subway: F to 23rd St.

Kentshire Galleries   Still going strong after a half-century, this large and lovely gallery is the city's prime stop for 18th- and 19th-century English antiques, ranging from jewelry and tabletop items to formal furnishings. Furniture is displayed in richly appointed rooms that make for great browsing. 37 E. 12th St. (btwn University Place and Broadway). ✆ **212/673-6644**. www.kentshire.com. Subway: N, R, L, 4, 5, 6 to 14th St./Union Sq.

Lost City Arts   Lost City features vintage modern furnishings and a quirky selection of accessories (station signs, 3-D photos, and the like), plus their own new mid-century–inspired furniture and accessories, including one inspired by the otherwise forbiddingly expensive custom designs of Machine Age genius Warren MacArthur. A real treat. 18 Cooper Sq. (Third Ave. at 5th St.). ✆ **212/375-0500**. www.lostcityarts.com. Subway: N, R to 8th St.

Mood Indigo   This dandy of a shop is the city's top dealer in glassware, dishware, and kitchen accessories from the 1930s through the 1950s. The charming shopkeepers also specialize in Bakelite jewelry and 1939 World's Fair memorabilia and boast a whopping collection of '50s novelty salt-and-pepper shakers and even Stork Club cologne (now what could that smell like?). Everything is pristine, so expect to pay accordingly. 181 Prince St. (btwn Sullivan and Thompson sts.). ✆ **212/254-1176**. www.mood indigonewyork.com. Subway: C, E to Spring St.; N, R to Prince St.

ART

See the box titled "Art for Art's Sake: The Gallery Scene," on p. 258.

BEAUTY

In addition to the choices below, consider the French beauty superstore **Sephora**, 597 Fifth Ave. (between 48th and 49th sts.; ✆ **212/980-6354;** www.sephora.com). There are outlets all over the city, but this midtown branch is a real beauty.

C. O. Bigelow   Who'd think that a 166-year-old apothecary would carry the city's most eclectic, enjoyable, and international collection of healthy skin and personal care products? The goodies run the gamut from Kusco-Murphy hair creams to French Elgydium toothpaste, a bestseller. And now, taking a page from Kiehl's (see below), Bigelow has beautifully packaged its own house-brand line of soaps, salves, essential oils, and beauty treatments. 414 Sixth Ave. (btwn 8th and 9th sts.). ℂ 212/533-2700. www. bigelowchemists.com. Subway: A, C, E, F, V to W. 4th St.

Kiehl's   Kiehl's is more than a store: It's a virtual cult. Models, stockbrokers, foreign visitors, and just about everyone else stops by this always packed, old-time apothecary for its simply packaged, wonderfully formulated products for women and men. Kiehl's now has counters in several department stores (evidence of how they've really moved up in the world), but stop into the original if you can. Love the free samples! 109 Third Ave. (btwn 13th and 14th sts.). ℂ 212/677-3171. www.kiehls.com. Subway: L, N, R, 4, 5, 6 to 14th St./ Union Sq.

Ricky's ⊛   This chain of funky drugstores also features a wide range of beauty products. It's a haven for make-up mavens, with multicolored wigs, rainbow-colored lipstick, glitter galore, green nail polish, over 80 kinds of hairbrushes, and even edible undies. Try going into Ricky's and coming out with just a pack of gum. 44 E. 8th St. (at Greene St.). ℂ 212/254-5247. Subway: N, R to 8th St. Also at 466 Sixth Ave. (at 11th St.). ℂ 212/924-3401. Subway: A,C, E, B, D, F to W. 4th St. 112 W. 72nd St. (btwn Columbus–Broadway). ℂ 212/769-3670. Subway: 1, 2, 3, 9 to 72nd St. 988 Eighth Ave. (at 58th St.). ℂ 212/957-8343. Subway: A, B, C, D, 1, 9 to Columbus Circle.

Zitomer's ⊛⊛   This three-story drugstore is more a mini department store than a pharmacy. You'll find everything from electronics to pet supplies here. But the first floor is where you'll spend most of your time if you're looking for beauty products. They have their own very good line of cosmetics called Z New York. Big Apple lip gloss will make a wonderful souvenir; something you won't find in your local Walgreens. 969 Madison Ave. (at 76th St.). ℂ 212/737-2016. www.zitomer.com. Subway: 6 to 77th St.

BOOKS

In addition to the choices below, there are the big chains: **Barnes & Noble,** with my favorite outlet opposite Union Square, 33 E. 17th St. (ℂ 212/253-0810; www.bn. com); and **Borders,** which has four stores in Manhattan, including one in the Time Warner Center, 10 Columbus Circle (ℂ 212/823-9775; www.bordersstores.com).

Argosy Books   Antiquarian-book hounds should check out this stately 77-year-old store, with high ceilings, packed shelves, a quietly intellectual air, and an outstanding collection of rarities, including 18th- and 19th-century prints, maps, and autographs. 116 E. 59th St. (btwn Park and Lexington aves.). ℂ 212/753-4455. www.argosybooks.com. Subway: 4, 5, 6 to 59th St.

Bauman Rare Books   Dealing strictly in highly prized volumes in topics ranging from philosophy and science to children's classics, Bauman's is one of the foremost resources for serious collectors willing to spend big money for pristine first editions, ranging from Milton's *Paradise Lost* (1669) to Harper Lee's *To Kill a Mockingbird* (1960), signed by the author. 535 Madison Ave. (btwn 54th and 55th sts.). ℂ 800/99-BAUMAN or 212/751-0011. www.baumanrarebooks.com. Subway: 6 to 51st St. Smaller location at the Waldorf=Astoria Hotel, 301 Park Ave. (btwn 49th and 50th sts.). ℂ 212/759-8300. Subway: 6 to 51st St.

Books of Wonder *Kids*   You don't have to be a kid to fall in love with this charming bookstore, which served as the model for Meg Ryan's shop in *You've Got Mail.* (Meg even worked here for a spell to train for the role.) Kids will love BOW's story readings; call or check the website for the latest schedule. 16 W. 18th St. (btwn Fifth and Sixth aves.). ℭ 212/989-3270. www.booksofwonder.net. Subway: L, N, R, 4, 5, 6 to 14th St./Union Sq.

Coliseum Books ★★ *(Finds)*   Before there were book-selling superstores, there was Coliseum Books. This independent bookstore was my favorite haunt for years when it was located on 57th Street. Intense competition from the big hitters forced it to close, but happily, after a 2-year absence, it has found a new home on 42nd Street just opposite Bryant Park. Though not quite as big as the original, the store still has that same independent spirit, and many of the original, very helpful, knowledgeable staff have returned. 11 W. 42nd St. (btwn Fifth and Sixth aves.). ℭ 212/803-5890. www.coliseumbooks. com. Subway: B, D, F, V to 42nd St.

Complete Traveller   Whether your destination is Texas or Tibet, you'll find what you need in this, possibly the world's best, travel bookstore. There are travel accessories as well, plus a rare collection of antiquarian travel books whose facts may be outdated but whose writers' perceptions continue to shine. The staff is attentive. 199 Madison Ave. (at 35th St.). ℭ 212/685-9007. www.completetravellerbooks.com. Subway: 6 to 33rd St.

Drama Book Shop   This store has a resident theater company and in-house performance space. It also hosts discussions and book signings with members of the theater community, ranging from playwright Tina Howe to critic Mel Gussow. Offering thousands of plays, from translations of Greek classics to this season's biggest hits, the shop also sells books, magazines, and newspapers on the craft and business of the performing arts. 250 W. 40th St. (btwn Eighth and Ninth aves.). ℭ 212/944-0595. www.dramabook shop.com. Subway: A, C, E to 42nd St.

Eichler's   *The* Jewish bookstore of New York City, covering everything from cookbooks to Kaballah. The Brooklyn outlet is even bigger, and features all manner of Judaica, including silver items, garments, music, gifts, and more. 62 W. 45th St. (btwn Fifth and Sixth aves.). ℭ 877/EICHLERS or 212/719-1918. www.eichlers.com. Subway: B, D, F, V to 42nd St. Also at 1401 Coney Island Ave. (btwn aves. J and K). ℭ 888/EICHLERS or 718/258-7643. Subway: D, Q to Ave. J.

Forbidden Planet   Here is the city's largest collection of sci-fi, comics, and graphic-illustration books. The proudly geeky staff really knows what's what. Great sci-fi-themed toys, too. 840 Broadway (at 13th St.). ℭ 212/473-1576. Subway: L, N, R, 4, 5, 6 to 14th St./Union Sq.

Gotham Book Mart   Paris may have had its Sylvia Beach, but New York was lucky enough to have Frances Steloff. She opened Gotham Book Mart in 1920, and quickly became a defender of the First Amendment rights of authors. She championed such once-banned works as Henry Miller's *Tropic of Cancer*, and numbered among her admirers Ezra Pound, Saul Bellow, and Jackie Kennedy Onassis. Frances has since passed on, but her aura lives, now in a new location. As always, the emphasis is on poetry, literature, and the arts. 16 E. 46th St. (btwn Fifth and Madison aves.). ℭ 212/719-4448. Subway: B, D, F, V to 47th–50th sts./Rockefeller Center.

Housing Works Used Books Cafe *(Finds)*   Here's a way to do something good for yourself and others at the same time: Buy your reading material at this spacious yet quietly cozy used bookshop, sporting 45,000 books and records to browse. It's part of Housing Works, a not-for-profit organization that provides housing, services, and advocacy for homeless people living with HIV and AIDS. The collection is terrific and well organized, with lots of well-priced paperbacks, hardbacks, advance copies,

Murder, They Wrote

New York–based mystery writer Lawrence Block once wrote a book titled *Eight Million Ways to Die,* starring his famed detective creation, Matthew Scudder. The title was a spin on the famous line "there are eight million stories in the naked city," culled from the old film *Naked City.* The naked city of the movie was New York, and many of those eight million stories were about crime. That's one reason why New York was and still is fertile fodder for crime writers.

A number of New York's bookstores celebrate the city's reputation as the crime writer's capital. Though you can find many of the same books at chains like Barnes & Noble, these small, independent stores live and breathe mysteries. My favorite of the lot, and one of the oldest in the country, is **The Mysterious Bookshop** ⚐, 129 W. 56th St., between Sixth and Seventh avenues (② **212/765-0900;** www.mysteriousbookshop.com). This two-level shop, where the second floor is reached via a spiral staircase, is owned by mystery publisher Otto Penzler, and is a great source for rare and collectable titles, along with signed first editions. Who knows, that might be Ed McBain next to you perusing the paperbacks . . . or is it Evan Hunter?

Another great mystery bookstore is **Murder Ink,** 2486 Broadway, between 92nd and 93rd streets (② **212/362-8905;** www.murderink.com), which claims to be one of the oldest crime bookstores in the *world*. The store, a gathering ground for crime-writing aficionados, also hosts numerous author readings.

As fun as a good thriller is the West Village shop **Partners & Crime,** 44 Greenwich Ave., at Christopher Street (② **212/243-0440;** www.crimepays.com). Like the other stores, this one also features a good selection of new and used collections and signed first editions, but the real thrill is the in-store live performance of a 1940s mystery radio show, complete with an organist and sound effects, performed on the first Saturday of the month.

Representing literary murder on the Upper East Side is **Black Orchid Books,** 303 E. 81st St., between First and Second avenues (② **212/734-5980**), where in-store readings and signings are a regular feature.

and coffee-table books. There's a comfortable cafe in back that serves coffee and tea as well as freshly prepared sandwiches, sweets, and other light bites, plus beer and wine. The bookstore often hosts readings by well-known writers as well as occasional music performances on Wednesday and Thursday evenings; call or check the website for the current calendar. 126 Crosby St. (south of Houston St.). ② 212/334-3324. www.housingworksubc.com. Subway: F, V to Broadway/Lafayette St.; 6 to Spring St.

Hue-Man Bookstore   One of the nation's largest black-owned bookstores, providing the area's largest selection of African-American literature and books. Lines snaked around the block in 2004 when local homeboy, Bill Clinton, staged a signing of his memoirs. 2319 Frederick Douglass Blvd. (at Eighth Ave.). ② 212/665-7400. www.huemanbookstore.com. Subway: A, B, C, D to 125th St.

Kitchen Arts & Letters   Foodies, take note: Here's the ultimate cook's and food-lover's bookstore. You'll be wowed by the depth of the selection, which includes rare, out-of-print, and foreign-language titles focusing on food and wine. The staff will conduct free searches for hard-to-find titles. The shop is an overstuffed jumble, but if this is your bag, you'll be browsing for hours. 1435 Lexington Ave. (btwn 93rd and 94th sts.). ✆ 212/876-5550. Subway: 6 to 96th St.

Oscar Wilde Bookshop   The world's oldest gay and lesbian bookstore was on the brink of extinction until it was thankfully saved by the Lambda Rising chain. The nice staff makes browsing in this landmark a pleasure. 15 Christopher St. (btwn Sixth and Seventh aves.). ✆ 212/255-8097. www.oscarwildebooks.com. Subway: 1, 9 to Christopher St.

Rizzoli   This clubby Italian bookstore is the classiest—and most relaxing—spot in town to browse for visual art and design books, plus quality fiction, gourmet cookbooks, and other upscale reading. There's a decent selection of foreign-language, music, and dance titles as well. 31 W. 57th St. (btwn Fifth and Sixth aves.). ✆ 212/759-2424. Subway: N, R to Fifth Ave.

The Scholastic Store (Kids)   This mammoth store is located at the ground level of the headquarters for children's book publisher Scholastic (which also introduced a boy named Harry Potter to America). The 6,200-foot retail space is a veritable interactive playground for kids. Books, toys, and software products feature Scholastic's top-selling brands, from Clifford the Big Red Dog to Captain Underpants. Needless to say, Hogwarts is well represented. A full slate of in-store events, from author signings to crafts workshops, also keeps kids busy; check the website or call for the current schedule. 557 Broadway (btwn Prince and Spring sts.). ✆ 212/343-6166. www.scholastic.com/sohostore. Subway: N, R to Prince St.

The Strand (Value)   Something of a New York legend, The Strand is worth a visit for its staggering "eight miles of books" as well as its extensive inventory of review copies and bargain titles at up to 85% off list price. It's unquestionably the city's best book deal—there's almost nothing marked at list price—and the selection is phenomenal in all categories (there's even a rare book department on the third floor). Still, you'll work for it: The narrow aisles mean you're always getting bumped; the books are only roughly alphabetized; and there's no air-conditioning in summer. Nevertheless, it's a used-book-lover's paradise. Note that the Lower Manhattan location is significantly smaller. 828 Broadway (at 12th St.). ✆ 212/473-1452. www.strandbooks.com. Subway: L, N, R, 4, 5, 6 to 14th St./Union Sq. Strand Annex: 95 Fulton St. (btwn William and Gold sts.). ✆ 212/732-6070. Subway: 4, 5, 6 to Fulton St.

Urban Center Books   Housed in an architectural landmark, McKim, Mead & White's 1882 Villard Houses, the Municipal Art Society's bookstore boasts a terrific selection of new books on architecture, urban planning, and landscape design. In the Villard Houses, 457 Madison Ave. (at 51st St.). ✆ 800/352-1880 or 212/935-3592. www.urbancenter books.com. Subway: 6 to 51st St.

CLOTHING
RETAIL FASHIONS
The Top Designers

The legendary locale for the classic designer names has always been Fifth Avenue and 57th Street. There's been some exodus to Madison Avenue (see below), but the opening of the **Gianni Versace** shop at 647 Fifth Ave., between 51st and 52nd streets

(© **212/317-0224;** www.versace.com), just before the designer's death, heralded a new era of respect for the avenue. Other deluxe designer tenants from Italy's haute couture world are **Prada** (see "For Men & Women," below); **Salvatore Ferragamo,** no. 661, between 52nd and 53rd streets (© **212/759-3822;** www.ferragamo.com). Tom Ford's stellar **Gucci** is at Fifth Avenue and 54th Street (© **212/826-2600;** www. gucci.com), while classic **Chanel** is at 15 E. 57th St., between Fifth and Madison avenues (© **212/355-5050**), with the freshly hip tartans of **Burberry** just down the block at 9 W. 57th St. (© **212/371-5010;** www.burberry.com).

The Upper East Side's Madison Avenue is the heartland of haute couture these days. The biggest names in clean-lined modern design line up along the platinum-coated boulevard; between 59th and 80th streets, you'll find **Calvin Klein, Giorgio Armani, Valentino, Bottega Veneta, Dolce & Gabbana, Emmanuel Ungaro, Givenchy, Hermès, Issey Miyake, Krizia, Max Mara, Prada** (see below), **Polo/Ralph Lauren** (see below), **Roberto Cavalli, Versace** (see above), and many more; the density is greatest in the high 60s.

Established avant-garde designers hang out in SoHo. Highlights include **Anna Sui,** 113 Greene St., just south of Prince Street (© **212/941-8406;** www.annasui.com), who specializes in boho fashions with a glam edge. **Marc Jacobs,** 163 Mercer St., between Houston and Prince (© **212/343-1490;** www.marcjacobs.com), excels at modern takes on classic cuts. Girlish designs are the specialty of **Cynthia Rowley,** 376 Bleecker St., at Perry St. (© **212/242-3803**), while **Vivienne Tam,** 99 Greene St., between Prince and Spring streets (© **212/966-2398**), specializes in pretty and playful Asian motifs. SoHo has become so designer hot that plenty of established names have moved in as well, including **Louis Vuitton,** 116 Greene St., between Prince and Spring streets (© **212/274-9090;** www.vuitton.com); always-avant **Helmut Lang,** 80 Greene St., near Spring Street (© **212/925-7214**); **Burberry,** 131 Spring St., between Greene and Wooster streets (© **212/925-9300;** www.burberry.com), and, in the same block, **Chanel,** 139 Spring St. (© **212/334-0055**).

Talented up-and-comers have set up shop on and around **Bond Street** in NoHo; on **Elizabeth, Mott,** and **Mulberry streets** in Nolita; along **East 9th Street** in the East Village (see "For Men & Women," below); and on the **Lower East Side,** in the blocks south of Houston Street.

Fashion Flagships

Some New York flagship stores of the major brands are an experience you won't catch in your nearest mall. These stores are display cases for the complete line of fashions, so you'll often find much more to choose from than in your at-home branch. You'll find other locations throughout the city, but these are meant to be the biggest and best: Check out **Ann Taylor** at 645 Madison Ave., at 60th Street (© **212/832-2010;** www.anntaylor.com); the **Banana Republic** flagship at Rockefeller Center, 626 Fifth Ave., at 50th Street (© **212/974-2350;** www.bananarepublic.com); **Eddie Bauer,** 1960 Broadway, at 67th Street (© **212/877-7629;** www.eddiebauer.com), which also carries the AKA Eddie Bauer line and the sports and mountaineering line; **Liz Claiborne,** 650 Fifth Ave., at 52nd Street (© **212/965-6505;** www.lizclaiborne.com), which carries all of Liz's lines; and **DKNY,** 655 Madison Ave., at 60th Street (© **212/ 223-DKNY;** www.dkny.com). **J. Crew** has a big bi-level SoHo store at 100 Prince St., between Mercer and Greene streets (© **212/966-2739;** www.jcrew.com), as well as a large store on Rockefeller Plaza at 50th Street (© 212/765-4227). **Old Navy** has a huge flagship featuring its affordable basics and signature sense of humor at 610 Sixth Ave., at 18th Street (© **212/645-0663;** www.oldnavy.com).

For Men & Women

Brooks Brothers   The perfect definition of all that is preppy lies behind this clubby storefront. The label is synonymous with quality, quiet taste, and classic tailoring. The cut of the man's suit is a tad boxy, making it great for the full American body. 346 Madison Ave. (at 44th St.). © **212/682-8800.** www.brooksbrothers.com. Subway: S, 4, 5, 6, 7 to 42nd St./Grand Central. Also at 666 Fifth Ave. (btwn 52nd and 53rd sts.). © 212/261-9440. Subway: 6 to 51st St. 1 Church St. © 212/267-2400. Subway: A, C, E to Chambers St.

H&M _Value_   The Swedish superdiscounter Hennes & Mauritz has sprouted all over New York the past 5 years. The loud, bustling stores are mammoth, but the departments are better organized than those at most full-retail department stores. The men's and women's clothing is ultrachic, and the prices are low, low, low. A real fave with teens, in particular. The main Herald Square store carries all lines, including babies, children's, and maternity wear. 1328 Broadway (at 34th St.). © **212/564-9922.** www.hm.com. Subway: B, D, F, N, R, V, W to 34th St./Herald Sq. Also at 640 Fifth Ave. (at 51st St.). © 212/489-0390. Subway: E, F to Fifth Ave. Smaller location at 558 Broadway (btwn Prince and Spring sts.). © 212/343-0220. Subway: N, R to Prince St.

Jeffrey New York ★   At the end of a deserted street in the still-industrial Meat-Packing District is this oasis of cutting-edge haute couture. Jeffrey New York caters to the Barneys crowd, but this outpost of the famed Atlanta megaboutique is much more accessible and user-friendly. Great accessories and shoes galore. The collection is mostly geared to women, but there's a notable men's department, too. A worthy schlep for style hounds. 449 W. 14th St. (near Tenth Ave.). © **212/206-1272.** Subway: A, C, E, L to 14th St.

Paul Stuart   Paul Stuart is a touch more hip and a touch more expensive than Brooks Brothers. Stuart is the classic New York haberdasher—gorgeous fabrics, impeccable tailoring, high price tags on everything from suits to weekend wear; there's women's wear, too, but Paul Stuart is more about men. This is a way-of-life store for those who subscribe. Madison Ave. at 45th St. © **212/682-0320.** www.paulstuart.com. Subway: 4, 5, 6, 7, S to 42nd St./Grand Central.

Polo/Ralph Lauren   Among all the high-ticket designers whose shops line Madison Avenue, Ralph Lauren deserves special mention for the stunning beauty of his flagship store, housed in a landmark Rhinelander mansion. One of New York's first important freestanding American designer shops, it has continued to wear as well as the classics Ralph churns out. Housewares and infants' clothing as well as women's and men's clothes are for sale. The active wear and sporty country looks are at Polo Sport. 867 & 888 Madison Ave. (at 72nd St.). © **212/606-2100.** www.ralphlauren.com. Subway: 6 to 68th St.

Prada   Few designer labels are more body-conscious, cachet-laden, and downright chic than this sleek Italian line, which reaches beyond clothing to embrace shoes, accessories, and the hippest handbags on the globe (yes, still). SoHo's **Prada Sport** and **Miu Miu** are the destinations for under-30 fashionistas with platinum cards. 841 Madison Ave. (at 70th St.). © **212/327-4200.** Subway: 6 to 68th St. **Prada Sport** at 116 Wooster St. (btwn Prince and Spring sts.). © **212/925-2221.** Subway: C, E to Spring St. **Miu Miu** at 100 Prince St. (btwn Mercer and Greene sts.). © **212/334-5156.** www.miumiu.com. Subway: C, E to Spring St.

Sean John   P. Diddy has come a long way from his Harlem roots. In 2004 he opened a flagship on Fifth Avenue and 41st Street featuring his signature hip-hop duds. But the store looks more like a refined library (maybe inspired by the big one across the street—the New York Public Library) than any gangsta club, uptown *or* downtown. Still, if you don't feel like making your way up to 125th Street, you'll find similar street style here in the heart of corporate brand-name midtown. 475 Fifth Ave. (at 41st St.). ☎ 212/220-2633. Subway: B, D, F, V, 7 to 42nd Street.

Seize sur Vingt *Finds* This smart Nolita shop custom-tailors Egyptian cotton shirts in bright colors and bold patterns for men and women—perfect for adding a bit of individual flair to your corporate threads. They've also reinvented the bespoke suit in clean, slim, contemporary lines. 243 Elizabeth St. (btwn Houston and Prince sts.). ☎ 212/343-0476. www.16sur20.com. Subway: F, V to Broadway/Lafayette St; 6 to Spring St.

Ted Baker London This hip Brit import, housed in a store that feels like an old-school country club, is a more-than-welcome addition to the men's clothing options in Manhattan. I like their sloppy-chic button-down shirts, which bring back memories of the post-Beatles British invasion. 107 Grand St. (at Mercer St.). ☎ 212/343-8989. www.tedbaker.co.uk. Subway: J, M, N, R, Z, 6 to Canal St.

Just Women

Anthropologie Funky, slightly exotic, and affordable wearables and accessories mix with fun gifts, furniture, and home decorating items. Geared to funky-chic post-collegiate young women who've outgrown Urban Outfitters. 375 W. Broadway (btwn Spring and Broome sts.). ☎ 212/343-7070. www.anthropologie.com. Subway: C, E to Spring St. Also at 85 Fifth Ave. (at 15th St.). ☎ 212/627-5885. Subway: L, N, R, 4, 5, 6 to Union Sq.

Eileen Fisher ★★ Making their way around the nation in her own shops and through outlets like Saks and the Garnet Hill catalog, Eileen Fisher's separates are a dream come true for stylish women looking for easy-to-wear classic pieces that transcend the latest fads. She designs fluid clothes in a pleasing neutral palette and uses natural fibers that don't sacrifice comfort for chic. The A-line styles look a bit droopy on shorter women, but otherwise suit all figure types well. The superior quality, fabrics, and style make these clothes worth every penny. The beautifully austere SoHo location is Fisher's prime showcase. The semiannual consolidation sales, in March and August, are a bargain hunter's delight. Note that only the SoHo flagship sells the complete line, including both the petite and women's collections. The closet-size East 9th Street location basically functions as an outlet store, with lots of sale merchandise and seconds on hand. 395 W. Broadway (btwn Spring and Broome sts.). ☎ 212/431-4567. www.eileen fisher.com. Subway: C, E to Spring St. Also at 521 Madison Ave. (at 53rd St.). ☎ 212/759-9888. Subway: 6 to 51st St. 341 Columbus Ave. (near 76th St.). ☎ 212/362-3000. Subway: B, C to 81st St. 1039 Madison Ave. (btwn 79th and 80th sts.). ☎ 212/879-7799. Subway: 6 to 77th St. 314 E. 9th St. (btwn First and Second aves.). ☎ 212/529-5715. Subway: 6 to Astor Place. 166 Fifth Ave. (at 22nd St.). ☎ 212/924-4777. Subway: N, R to 23rd St.

Huminska If you're addicted to colorful, flirty dresses and shapely swirl skirts, make a beeline for this shop. The offerings change with the whims of the designer, but the current collection of dresses seems to be inspired by the 1950s and the wonder that is polka dots. 315 E. 9th St. (btwn First and Second aves.). ☎ 212/677-3458. www.huminska.com. Subway: 6 to Astor Place.

Intermix The place to dress and accessorize in style, at not-too-expensive prices. The Flatiron location is the original, and remains the best. 125 Fifth Ave. (btwn 19th and 20th sts.). ☎ 212/533-9720. www.intermix-ny.com. Subway: N, R to 23rd St. Also at 210 Columbus Ave.

(btwn 69th and 70th sts.). ℭ 212/769-9116. Subway: B, C to 72nd St. 365 Bleecker St. ℭ 212/929-7189. Subway: 1, 9 to Christopher St.

Jill Anderson *Finds*   Finally, a New York designer who designs affordable clothes for real women to wear for real life—not just for 22-year-old size-2s to match with a pair of Pradas and wear out club-hopping. This narrow, peaceful shop and studio is lined on both sides with Jill's simple, clean-lined designs, which drape beautifully and accentuate a woman's form without clinging. They're wearable for all ages and many figure types. (Her small sizes are small enough to fit petites, and her larges generally fit a full-figured size 14.) Her clothes are feminine without being frilly, retro-reminiscent but completely modern, understated, and utterly stylish. 331 E. 9th St. (btwn First and Second aves.). ℭ 212/253-1747. www.jillanderson.com. Subway: 6 to Astor Place.

Searle ★★   If you're looking for a winter coat or jacket, there aren't many better choices than Searle. But the stores are not only known for their jackets, they also feature great clothes, period, in beautiful colors and fabrics. 156 Fifth Ave. (btwn 20th and 21st sts.). ℭ 212/924-4330. www.searlenyc.com. Subway: N, R to 23rd St. Also at 609 Madison Ave. (at 58th St.). ℭ 212/753-9021. Subway: N, R, 4, 5, 6 to 59th St. 1035 Madison Ave. (at 79th St.). ℭ 212/717-4022. Subway: 6 to 77th St.

Vera Wang   The petite powerhouse is still the hottest name in bridal fashions. Vera clothes scads of top stars (particularly petite ones with great figures) on their big day or for the Oscars in her simple, elegant designs. Vera's studio is open by appointment only, so brides-to-be looking for the best should call ahead. There's also a Vera Wang salon on the third floor at **Bergdorf's** (p. 316). Ask about the annual warehouse sale, usually in September. 991 Madison Ave. (at 77th St.). ℭ 212/628-3400. www.verawang.com. Subway: 6 to 77th St. **Bridesmaids' store** at 980 Madison Ave. (btwn 76th and 77th sts., 3rd floor). ℭ 212/628-9898. Subway: 6 to 77th St.

Just Men

Frank Stella   This refined shop sells casually elegant clothes for the well-dressed 21st-century man, including clean-lined blazers, quality knits, and beautifully cut trousers. 440 Columbus Ave. (at 81st St.). ℭ 212/877-5566. Subway: B, C to 81st St. Also at 921 Seventh Ave. (at 58th St.). ℭ 212/957-1600. Subway: A, B, C, D, 1, 9 to 59th St./Columbus Circle.

Paul Smith   This temple of new English fashion is a can't miss. When it comes to menswear that's at once fashion forward and undisputedly classic, Paul Smith wins the prize, with jackets, suits, pants, shoes, sportswear, and accessories that are superpricey but worth every cent. 108 Fifth Ave. (at 16th St.). ℭ 212/627-9770. www.paulsmith.co.uk. Subway: F to 14th St.

Saint Laurie Merchant Tailors *Finds*   Family-owned since 1913, this custom tailor offers a huge selection of fabrics, from Scottish worsted wools to Italian silks, and offers you a selection of styles to choose from. The custom job is about $1,000 for a suit (less when sales are going), substantially less for a blazer. 22 W. 32nd St. (at Fifth Ave.). ℭ 212/643-1916. www.saintlaurie.com. Subway: 6 to 51st St.

Just Kids

If you need the basics, you'll find branches of **Gap Kids, Baby Gap,** and **The Children's Place** all over town—it's harder to avoid one than to find one. The department stores are also great sources, of course.

Bu & the Duck *Finds*   This divine shop sells its own unique vintage-inspired clothing and shoes that your kids can really wear. Delightful sock puppets and other vintage-inspired toys are also in the mix. 106 Franklin St. (btwn Church St. and W. Broadway). ℂ 212/431-9226. www.buandtheduck.com. Subway: 1, 9 to Franklin St.

rockstarbaby Here's the place to clad your kid in the coolest glad rags around. This new line of newborn and infant clothing is a collaboration between rocker Tico Torres (Bon Jovi) and designer Cinzia Spinetti. Despite the pedigree and attitude (how 'bout a bib that says BORN TO ROCK for your favorite newborn?), these are gorgeous, practical, and moderately priced wearables. 298 Elizabeth St. (just north of Houston St.). ℂ 212/ 226-2771. www.rockstarbaby.com. Subway: 6 to Bleecker St.

Shoofly Top-quality clothing, footwear, and accessories for kids from newborns through teens. You'll find lots of distinctive stuff here, including imported lines. The shoe selection, in particular, is terrific, and not too pricey. The downtown store also sells toys and infant gifts. 465 Amsterdam Ave. (at 82nd St.). ℂ 212/580-4390. www.shooflynyc. com. Subway: 1, 9 to 79th St. Also at 42 Hudson St. (btwn Duane and Thomas sts.). ℂ 212/406-3270. Subway: 1, 2, 3, 9 to Chambers St.

Space Kiddets *Finds* This sleeper in the Flatiron district has been around for 23 years and features solid children's clothing in refreshing styles—a cut above chains like the Children's Place. But the prices are also a cut above. Sales are frequent. 46 E. 21st St. (at Broadway). ℂ 212/420-9878. Subway: N, R to 23rd St.

Vintage & Consignment Clothing

Allan & Suzi *Finds* Make it past the freaky windows and inside you'll find one of the best consignment shops in the city. Allan and Suzi have specialized in gently worn 20th-century designer wear for well over a decade now, and their selection is marvelous. Their extensive vintage and contemporary couture collection—which ranges from conservative Chanel to over-the-top Halston, Mackie, and Versace—is so well priced that it's well within reach of the average shopper looking for something extra-glamorous to wear. 416 Amsterdam Ave. (at 80th St.). ℂ 212/724-7445. Subway: 1, 9 to 79th St.

Michael's *Value* This consignment boutique boasts top-drawer designer wear for women—including such names as Chanel, YSL, Prada, Gucci, Richard Tyler, and Escada—at a fraction of the original cost. The bridal salon is an unbeatable find for engaged gals looking for a top-quality dress at an off-the-rack price. 1041 Madison Ave. (btwn 79th and 80th sts., 2nd floor). ℂ 212/737-7273. www.michaelsconsignment.com. Subway: 6 to 77th St.

Screaming Mimi's *Value* Think you hate vintage shopping? Think again: Screaming Mimi's is as neat and well organized as any high-priced boutique—yet prices are surprisingly reasonable, especially given the pricey vintage shops that have popped up around the city in recent years. The vintage housewares department is a wonderful cornucopia of kitsch, and includes a selection of New York memorabilia; prices start under $10. 382 Lafayette St. (btwn E. 4th and Great Jones sts.). ℂ 212/677-6464. www.screaming mimis.com. Subway: 6 to Astor Place.

EDIBLES

Arthur Avenue Retail Market ★★ This colorful, enclosed market opened in the heart of the Bronx's Little Italy in 1940 and is my absolute favorite. The market, like the Bronx, has had its ups and downs, but now is thriving. You'll find fresh produce purveyors like the **Biano** fruits and vegetables and **Joe Liberatore's Garden of Plenty,** where I buy the best tomato plants for my terrace. There is **Peter's Market** for homemade sausages and braciole, **Mike's Deli** for freshly made mozzarella and sandwiches, the **Arthur Avenue Baking Company** for loaves of *pane di casa* and Parmesan bread-sticks, and even **La Casa Grande Tobacco Company,** where they roll their own cigars. 2344 Arthur Ave., Bronx. No phone. www.arthuravenuebronx.com. Subway: B, D to Fordham Rd.

Chelsea Market   Located in an old Nabisco factory, this big, dazzling food mall is the city's largest. Come for both raw and ready-to-eat foods, including divinely inspired baked goods and cappuccino from **Amy's Bread;** yummy soups from **Hale**

Chocolate City

The Big Apple is fast becoming a city consumed by a near-feverish craving for chocolate. Many sweet shops around the city now are turning out homemade chocolates in every variety that are so good, the stores, like four-star restaurants, are destinations in their own right. The best of these can be found just over the Brooklyn Bridge in DUMBO at **Jacques Torres Chocolate** ✸✸, 60 Water St., Brooklyn (✆ **718/875-9772;** www.mrchocolate. com). Torres, the former celebrated pastry chef at Le Cirque, ventured out on his own a few years ago and opened this mecca to chocolate where your mouth will water as you watch chocolate being made. The variations here are staggering and include chocolate peanut brittle, chocolate-covered corn flakes, champagne truffles, and some of the best hot chocolate you've ever tasted. Take home a tin of the "wicked" hot chocolate, which features all-spice, cinnamon, sweet ancho chile peppers, and hot chipotle peppers. In 2004, another outlet of **Jacques Torres Chocolate** opened at 350 Hudson St., at King Street, in TriBeCa. The new store is the first chocolate manufactur-ing facility open to the public in New York City.

In Manhattan, in the middle of one of the toniest stretches of Madison Avenue, is the Paris import **La Maison du Chocolat,** 1018 Madison Ave., at 78th Street (✆ **212/744-7117;** www.lamaisonduchocolat.com). This bou-tique takes its chocolate very seriously. You won't find any of the foolish-ness here, like adding chile peppers or coating corn flakes with the stuff. What you will find is possibly the best pure chocolate you've ever tasted. They abhor any bitterness in their chocolate and make it a point to claim that they use nothing stronger than 65% cocoa. Now that's taking your chocolate seriously.

One of the oldest chocolate shops in the city is the 1923-established **Li-Lac Chocolates,** 120 Christopher St., between Bleecker and Hudson streets (✆ **800/624-4784** or 212/242-7374). This West Village shop makes their sweets by hand and whips up batches of chocolate fudge daily. In fact, they do chocolate fudge like no one else in the city.

Also in the village is a newcomer to the chocolate scene, **The Chocolate Bar,** 48 Eighth Ave., between Jane and Horatio streets (✆ **212/366-1541;** www.chocolatebarnyc.com). Their homemade chocolate bars are worthy of their name. I love the mocha, with its flecks of coffee. For those who wor-ship the cocoa gods, go for the super dark 72%, so dark and rich you might speak in tongues after a few bites.

and Hearty; Manhattan's best brownie at **Fat Witch Bakery;** and much more, including the wonderful **Chelsea Wine Vault. Chelsea Market Baskets** is a great place to pick up gifts for home. 75 Ninth Ave. (btwn 15th and 16th sts.). www.chelseamarket.com. Subway: A, C, E, L to 14th St.

Dean & DeLuca   This bright, clean-lined store offers premier quality across the board: In addition to the excellent butcher, fish, cheese, and dessert counters (check out the stunning cakes and the great character cookies) and beautiful fruits and veggies, you'll find a dried fruit and nut bar, a huge coffee bean selection, a gorgeous cut-flower selection, lots of imported waters and beers in the refrigerator case, and a limited but quality selection of kitchenware in back. A small cafe up front makes a great stop for a cappuccino break from SoHo shopping. 560 Broadway (at Prince St.). © 212/226-6800. www.dean-deluca.com. Subway: N, R to Prince St.

Fairway ★★ (Value)   There is no better all-in-one market in Manhattan than Fairway. Here you will find the best and most modestly priced vegetables in the city. Cheeses are top of the line and well organized. The fish counter is excellent and, again, very modestly priced. The second floor of the Broadway store features hard to find health foods and a wide array of organic fruits and vegetables. Fairway also carries the gourmet items you might find at Dean & Deluca but at a fraction of the cost. The Harlem store is huge and features a walk-in freezer, complete with down jackets provided for customers' use. 2127 Broadway (btwn 74th and 75th sts.). © 212/595-1888. www.fairwaymarket. com. Subway: 1, 2, 3, 9 to 72nd St. Also at 2328 Twelfth Ave. (at 132nd St.). © 212/234-3883. Subway: 1, 9 to 125th St.

Zabar's ★   More than any other of New York's gourmet food stores, Zabar's is an institution. This giant deli sells prepared foods, packaged goods from around the world, coffee beans, excellent fresh breads, and much more (no fresh veggies, though). This is the place for lox, and the rice pudding is the best I've ever tasted. You'll also find an excellent—and well-priced—collection of housewares and restaurant-quality cookware on the second floor. Prepare yourself for serious crowds. The attached cafe serves terrific sandwiches and takeout—ideal for a Central Park picnic. 2245 Broadway (at 80th St.). © 212/787-2000. www.zabars.com. Subway: 1, 9 to 79th St.

COFFEE & TEA

Ito En (Finds)   You want green tea? You want black tea? Herbal tea? White tea? No problem. There are so many varieties of teas here you need a catalog to peruse the selections. Located in a Madison Avenue town house, Ito En is like an art gallery of teas; everything is neatly displayed and there is a calming, serene feel to the store. There is a *sencha* bar (tea bar) where you can sample some of their teas and get tea advice from the experts working there. They also sell green-tea-dusted chocolate-covered almonds that are an addictive, and very expensive, munchie. 822 Madison Ave. (at 69th St.). © 212/988-7111. www.itoen.com. Subway: 6 to 68th St.

McNulty's Tea & Coffee Company ★   McNulty's has been around since 1895, making it one of the oldest coffee purveyors in the country. And it still has that old-time feel, with overflowing sacks of coffees and rare teas cluttering the quaint West Village store—and they roast their own coffees right there. The Colombia Supremo is as perfect as it gets, and I can't leave the store without my monthly fix of Italian roast espresso. 109 Christopher St. (btwn Bleecker and Hudson sts.). © 212/242-5351. www.mcnultys.com. Subway: 1, 9 to Christopher St.

A Taste of New York

Do you want to bring back a *real* New York souvenir—something that evokes the genuine flavor of New York more than an I ♥ NEW YORK T-shirt or an Empire State Building figurine? Give your friends and family some real New York edibles. Possibly the best place to pick up food "souvenirs" is the Lower East Side. This neighborhood, home to so many immigrants over the years, is where a number of traditional New York foods originated. Do you have a friend who craves pickles, pregnant or not? Then venture to **Guss's Pickles** at 85 Orchard Street (© **917/701-4000**). Bring home a gallon of half or full sour, a mix of both, or pickled green tomatoes. If you can't lug it back home, have them ship it for you for about $49 a gallon.

If anyone can really explain what a bialy is exactly, I'm all ears. But whatever it really is doesn't matter as long as it tastes good. You'll find the oldest (over 65 years) bialy makers and the best in New York at **Kossar's Bialys,** 367 Grand St., between Norfolk and Essex streets (© **212/473-4810**). A dozen go for around $9 and come in different flavors like sesame, poppy, and garlic.

East Houston Street features two New York food souvenir choices worth bringing home. Start with knishes from the 1910-established **Yonah Schimmel Knishes** at 137 E. Houston St., between First and Second avenues (© **212/477-2858**). The choices range from potato to spinach to mushroom; a box of 12 goes for about $34. At 179 E. Houston St., between Allen and Orchard streets, the remarkable **Russ & Daughters** (© **212/475-4880**; www.russanddaughters.com) has incomparable smoked fish and nova. A medley of smoked salmon goes for about $70, and, in my humble opinion, is worth every penny.

SWEETS

Dylan's Candy Bar *(Finds)* Dylan (daughter of Ralph) Lauren is one of the co-owners of this bazaar for sugar addicts. Located across the street from Bloomingdale's, you'll find all the candy classics, such as Necco wafers, Charleston Chews, and both of my favorite childhood chewing gums, Black Jack and Gold Mine. Dylan's also makes signature chocolates, candy creations, candy spa products like hot chocolate bath beads, and custom-made ice-cream flavors. 1011 Third Ave. (at 60th St.). © **646/735-0078.** www.dylanscandybar.com. Subway: 4, 5, 6, N, R to 59th St.

Fauchon This Parisian chocolatier operates a large, elegant boutique featuring an ultracharming tea salon (at the larger Park Ave. location only), and sparkling glass cases display a gorgeous array of chocolates and sweet treats flown in daily; the candied fruits are among the most gorgeous foods I've ever seen. Afternoon tea is served daily from noon to 6pm (to 5pm on Sun); you can choose between a two-course tea ($30) or a lovely array of salads, quiches, and so forth. Beautifully packaged candies, biscuits, preserves, and the like make elegant and pretty take-home treats. 442 Park Ave. (at 56th St.). © **212/308-5919.** www.fauchon.com. Subway: 4, 5, 6 to 59th St.

ELECTRONICS

The Apple Store ⭐ Most any time or day of the week, this bi-level store with huge glass windows contains mobs of people happily playing with futuristic-looking computers and accessories. It's almost impossible to walk by without popping in to see what the fuss is all about. I'm not sure anyone actually buys all the Apple gadgets sold here, but it sure is fun to try out the floor samples. Or better yet, take an Apple tech lesson in the store's own theater. 103 Prince St. (at Greene St.). ✆ **212/226-3126.** www.apple. com. Subway: N, R to Prince St.

B&H Photo & Video ✿ *Value*   Looking for a digital camera at a good price? You really won't do any better than B&H, the largest camera store in the country. This camera superstore has everything from lenses to darkroom equipment. If you are a B&H virgin, the store can be somewhat intimidating, but service is helpful. Just follow the signs and they will direct you to whatever you are seeking. 420 Ninth Ave. (at 34th St.). ✆ **800/606-6969** or 212/444-6615. www.bhphotovideo.com. Subway: A, C, E to 34th St.

J&R Music & Computer World ✿   This block-long Financial District emporium is the city's top discount computer, electronics, small appliance, and office equipment retailer. The sales staff is knowledgeable but can get pushy if you don't buy at once or know exactly what you want. Don't succumb—take your time and find exactly what you need. Or better yet, peruse the store's copious catalog or extensive website, both of which make advance research, and mail order and comparison-shopping, easy. Park Row (at Ann St., opposite City Hall Park). ✆ **800/426-6027** or 212/238-9000. www.jandr.com. Subway: 2, 3 to Park Place; 4, 5, 6 to Brooklyn Bridge/City Hall.

GIFTS

For first-rate Fifth Avenue gifts, don't forget **Tiffany & Co.,** whose upper level boasts wonderful small gifts, all crafted in signature Tiffany silver or crystal and wrapped in the unmistakable blue box (see "Jewelry & Accessories," below).

For additional suggestions, see "Antiques & Collectibles," earlier in this chapter, and "Home Design & Housewares," below.

auto.   If a Lucite tic-tac-toe set sounds like a good idea to you, don't miss this witty Meat-Packing District boutique. The mod and minimalist home accessories and gift items—mostly original designs by Brooklyn-based artists—are both well conceived and good-humored. 805 Washington St. (btwn Gansevoort and Horatio sts.). ✆ **212/229-2292.** www.thisisauto.com. Subway: A, C, E, L to 14th St.

Jack Spade   Looking for a gift for the man who has everything? Then head to Jack Spade, which specializes in vintage and new "guy toys." The inventory changes constantly, but expect goodies along the lines of vintage phonographs and microscopes, old maps and globes, cool desk accessories, and the like. This shop was launched by the husband of Kate Spade (she of chic handbags and paper goods fame), so you can expect a smart, upmarket collection. 56 Greene St. (btwn Spring and Broome sts.). ✆ **212/625-1820.** Subway: C, E to Spring St.; N, R to Prince St.

Pearl River *Value*   Even after moving from tight quarters on Canal Street to a more spacious location, this Chinese mall still overflows with affordable Asian exotica. You need vials of ginseng? They got it. How about a pair of Mandarin-collared silk pajamas or a mah-jongg set? They got it. While you're perusing the goods, enjoy a cup of tea at the cafe and meditate to the sound of the store's bubbling waterfall. 477 Broadway (at Grand St.). ✆ **212/431-4770.** www.pearlriver.com. Subway: N, R to Canal St. Also at 200 Grand St. (btwn Mott and Mulberry sts.). ✆ 212/966-1010. Subway: B, D, Q to Grand St.

Steuben Glass   This is the flagship store for America's premier manufacturer of fine glass and crystal, said to be the world's purest. The store is gorgeous, and the pieces— which run the gamut from fruit bowls to elaborate sculptures—are spectacularly crafted and refract light beautifully. Prices start around $200 for a "hand cooler" (a small collectible, often animal-shaped, that fits in your palm) and run into the five figures. The Corning Gallery, on the lower level, hosts rotating art exhibits. 667 Madison Ave. (at 61st St.). ✆ 212/752-1441. www.steuben.com. Subway: N, R to Fifth Ave.

HANDBAGS & LEATHER GOODS

Jutta Neumann *(Finds)* If you stop into this studio-like shop, you're likely to find the artist herself behind the counter, cutting and stitching her geometric, bold-hued leather goods—bags, wallets, boots, and more. Her mules and strappy sandals are also popular. 158 Allen St. (btwn Stanton and Rivington sts.). ✆ 212/982-7048. www.juttaneumann-new york.com. Subway: F to Delancey/Essex sts.

kate spade Kate Spade revolutionized the high-end handbag market with her practical yet chic rectangular handbags, which have seemingly taken over the planet. They come in a wide range of fabrics and sizes, from pretty seersuckers to groovy prints to fashionable flannel to basic black, plus a wide range of solids. The daintier evening line is charming, particularly the grosgrain silks. The line has expanded to include chic baby bags, luggage, sexy shoes, and comfy pajamas. You can also find the signature bags at Saks, Barneys, Bergdorf Goodman, and Bloomingdale's. 454 Broome St. (at Mercer St.). ✆ 212/274-1991. www.katespade.com. Subway: N, R to Prince St. **kate spade travel** at 59 Thompson St. (btwn Spring and Broome sts.). ✆ 212/965-8654. Subway: C, E to Spring St.

Manhattan Portage Ltd. Store Come here for the hippest nylon and canvas carryalls in town. True to its name, Manhattan Portage manufactures all its bags right in the city, and they're made from hard-wearing materials that can stand up to an urban lifestyle. Popular styles include all-purpose messenger bags, deejay bags, and backpacks (in both standard and nouveau one-shoulder styles) in a range of colors from iridescent yellow to camouflage. Manhattan Portage bags are also sold through other outlets, but you'll find the most complete selection here. 333 E. 9th St. (btwn First and Second aves.). ✆ 212/995-5490. www.manhattanportageltd.com. Subway: 6 to Astor Place. Also at 301 West Broadway. ✆ 212/226-4557. Subway: N, R to Prince St.

HOME DESIGN & HOUSEWARES

Attention, Oriental rug and cilium fans: Dealers line **Broadway** around the queen of home furnishings department stores, **ABC Carpet & Home** (see "The Big Department Stores," earlier in this chapter). The second floor of **Zabar's** (see "Edibles," earlier in this chapter) is another excellent source for high-end kitchenware.

Broadway Panhandler If you're looking for restaurant-quality cookware and kitchen tools, you've found your place. The best combination of selection, prices, and service in town. 477 Broome St. (btwn Greene and Wooster sts.). ✆ 212/966-3434. Subway: C, E to Spring St.

Fishs Eddy *(Value)* What a great idea—selling remainders of kitschy, custom-designed china left over from yesteryear. Ever wanted a dish that *really* says "Blue Plate Special"? Or how about a coffee mug with the terse logo "Cup o' Joe to Go"? The store is Browse Heaven, and prices on its American industrial china are low enough. The store's own designs are equally wonderful, especially its series with the New York skyline. Other items for sale include basic vintage and retro-inspired flatware, heavy crockery bowls, and classic restaurant-supply glassware that can be hard to find in regular stores, like soda-fountain and pint glasses. 889 Broadway (at 19th St.). ✆ 212/420-9020.

www.fishseddy.com. Subway: L, N, R, 4, 5, 6 to 14th St./Union Sq. Also at 2176 Broadway (at 77th St.). ⓒ 212/873-8819. Subway: 1, 9 to 79th St. 1388 Third Ave. (at 79th St.). ⓒ 212/873-8819. Subway: 6 to 77th St.

Frette This Italian linen maker has taken the hotel world by storm with its silky cotton sheets and ultraplush terry towels and robes. If you've slept on some and now you want your own, head to this dedicated boutique or ABC Carpet & Home (p. 315) for the best selections. Also at Saks, Bloomingdale's, and Bergdorf's. 799 Madison Ave. (btwn 67th and 68th sts.). ⓒ 212/988-5221. www.frette.it. Subway: 6 to 68th St.

Jonathan Adler Anybody who has been reading shelter magazines over the last couple of years will recognize this hot potter's bold vases and lamps instantly. His style merges organic shapes, geometric patterns, natural hues, and mod ideas into a one-of-a-kind style that works in almost any decor—really. Good throw pillows, too. A new uptown branch is scheduled to open on Madison Avenue late in 2005. 47 Green St. (at Broome St.). ⓒ 212/941-8950. www.jonathanadler.com. Subway: N, R to Canal St.

kar'ikter *(Finds)* New York's biggest collection of sleek and playful Alessi housewares from Italy (including Michael Graves's iconic teakettle with bird whistle), as well as European animation cells and toys starring Tintin, Babar, and Asterix. 19 Prince St. (btwn Elizabeth and Mott sts.). ⓒ 212/274-1966. www.karikter.com. Subway: 6 to Spring St.

Leader Restaurant Equipment & Supplies *(Value)* The Bowery is the place to find restaurant-supply-quality kitchenware, and Leader is the best dealer on the block. This big, bustling, friendly shop is a particularly good source for Chinese and Japanese wares—chopsticks, rice and noodle bowls, sushi plates, sake cups, and the like. You'll see a lot of the same styles you'd find at the high-end home stores in SoHo or the Village but at a fraction of the prices (this is where they buy, too). 191 Bowery (btwn Spring and Delancey sts.). ⓒ 800/666-6888 or 212/677-1982. Subway: 6 to Spring St.

Moss *(Finds)* If you have any interest in modern industrial design, don't miss this sleek, brightly lit store. All kinds of everyday objects are reinvented by cutting-edge European designers, from staplers to flatware to shelving units. The products were designed with 21st-century homes in mind, so they're surprisingly utilitarian and space-efficient—not to mention pricey. 146 Greene St. (btwn Houston and Prince sts.). ⓒ 212/204-7100. www.mossonline.com. Subway: N, R to Prince St.

Royal Hut After traveling the globe with her husband, Island Records founder Chris Blackwell, Mary Vinson merged her design degree and her world-travel experience to create her own line of cross-cultural home furnishings. Her own gorgeous line of textiles has been handcrafted by weavers and dyers in Europe, Africa, and Asia. Also expect a stunning collection of dishware, glassware, vessels, and accessories in a riot of Asian- and African-inspired color and texture—ideal for the global home. 328 E. 59th St. (btwn First and Second aves.). ⓒ 212/207-3027. www.royalhut.com. Subway: 4, 5, 6 to 59th St.

Terence Conran Shop Sir Terence Conran rules the London design and restaurant world, and now he's looking to make inroads in America with this bold sleek home shop. It's like an upscale—and, frankly, overpriced—version of IKEA, with lots of sleek contemporary lines, lightweight materials (chrome, blond woods, colorful plastic), and fun twists on standard household goods. Still, he set the tone for affordable contemporary design, and that alone makes this bright, browsable multilevel shop well worth a look. 407 E. 59th St. (at First Ave.). ⓒ 212/755-9079. www.conran.com. Subway: 4, 5, 6 to 59th St.

Waterworks   The place to give that most sacred of rooms, the bath, a whole new, luxurious look. Half the store displays top-quality, hard-to-find designer hardware and fixtures, while the other half is dedicated to thick Egyptian terry towels, robes, and bathmats, plus stylish accessories for easy reinvention. 469 Broome St. (at Greene St.). ✆ 212/966-0605. www.waterworks.com. Subway: 6 to Canal St.; N, R to Prince St. Also at 225 E. 57th St. (btwn Second and Third aves.). ✆ 212/371-9266. Subway: 4, 5, 6 to 59th St.

JEWELRY & ACCESSORIES

Every big-name international jewelry merchant has a shop on Fifth Avenue in the 50s: glam Italian jeweler **Bulgari,** 730 Fifth Ave., at 57th Street (✆ **212/315-9000;** www.bulgari.com); royal jeweler **Asprey & Garrard,** no. 725, at 56th Street (✆ **212/688-1811**); ultraglamorous **Harry Winston,** no. 718, also at 56th Street (✆ **212/245-2000;** www.harrywinston.com); **Cartier,** housed in a stunningly restored mansion at 653 Fifth Ave., at 52nd Street (✆ **212/753-0111;** www.cartier.com); and, best of all, **Van Cleef & Arpels,** 744 Fifth Ave., at 57th Street (✆ **212/644-9500**), which also has a boutique at Bergdorf's.

Some of the smaller boutique names are on Madison Avenue in the 60s; **Fred Leighton,** 773 Madison Ave., at 66th Street (✆ **212/288-1872**), specializes in magnificent estate jewelry.

Boucher *(Finds* This jewel box of a store sparkles on a gentrifying corner of the Meat-Packing District. Designer Laura Mady and her staff meticulously handcraft feminine, nature-inspired necklaces, earrings, and other jewelry using unusual gemstones in organic shapes and freshwater pearls in soft ice-cream hues. Affordable, and ideal for dressing up or everyday wear. 9 Ninth Ave. (near Little W. 12th St., next to Pastis). ✆ 212/206-3775. www.boucherjewelry.com. Subway: A, C, E, L to 14th St.

Doyle & Doyle *(Finds* Elizabeth Doyle's lovely antiques boutique offers further evidence of the transformation of the Lower East Side from old-world cheap to exceptionally chic. Doyle & Doyle specializes in fine antique and estate jewelry, from the Georgian period to contemporary items. Pieces are all carefully chosen and beautifully displayed. 189 Orchard St. (btwn Houston and Stanton sts.). ✆ 212/677-9991. www.doyledoyle.com. Subway: F to Second Ave. (exit at the front of the train and walk 1 block east).

Value The Diamond District

West 47th Street between Fifth and Sixth avenues is the city's famous Diamond District. Apparently more than 90% of the diamonds sold in the United States come through this neighborhood first, so there are some great deals to be had if you're in the market for a nice rock or another piece of fine jewelry. The street is lined shoulder-to-shoulder with showrooms; and you'll be wheeling and dealing with the largely Hasidic dealers, who offer quite a juxtaposition to the crowds. For a complete introduction to the district, including smart buying tips, point your Web browser to **www.diamonddistrict.org**. If you're in the market for wedding rings, there's only one place to go: Herman Rotenberg's **1,873 Unusual Wedding Rings,** 4 W. 47th St., booth 86 (✆ **800/877-3874** or 212/944-1713; www.unusualweddingrings.com). For semiprecious stones, head 1 block over to the **New York Jewelry Mart,** 26 W. 46th St. (✆ **212/575-9701**). Virtually all of these dealers are open Monday through Friday only.

Fortunoff *(Value)*   Despite the high-ticket facade, Fortunoff is a good resource for Swatch watches and a nice place to start pricing classic pieces: gold earrings, necklaces, bracelets, and the like. The styles aren't innovative, but the store tries to keep up an image as a discounter, and prices are low. Great for silver and wedding gifts, too. 681 Fifth Ave. (btwn 53rd and 54th sts.). **© 800/FORTUNOFF or 212/758-6660. www.fortunoff.com. Subway: E, F to Fifth Ave.**

Jill Platner *(Finds)*   Platner's aborigine- and nature-inspired silver pieces are bold enough to look great on both men and women. Many are strung on brightly colored Tenara (a Gore-Tex-like thread) for a prehistoric-meets-21st-century feel. Prices are quite reasonable; it's easy to find a cool pair of earrings or a groovy ring for just a little more than $100. 113 Crosby St. (btwn Houston and Prince sts.). **© 212/324-1298. www.jill platner.com. Subway: N, R to Prince St.**

Push   Often featuring rough-hewn finishes and asymmetrical gems and stones, Karen Karch's eye-catching jewelry has attracted an A-list clientele to her atmospheric Nolita shop. Six degrees of separation moment: If you buy one of her pieces, you'll take home a work of art from the designer who worked with Ethan Hawke to design Uma Thurman's wedding ring. Wonder whatever became of that ring? 240 Mulberry St. (btwn Prince and Spring sts.). **© 212/965-9699. Subway: 6 to Spring St.**

Tiffany & Co.   The most famous jewelry store in New York—and maybe the world—deserves all the kudos. This wonderful multilevel store offers a breathtaking selection of jewelry, signature watches, tableware and stemware, and a handful of surprisingly affordable gift items. The store is so full of tourists that it's easy to browse without having any intention of buying. Believe it or not, it's not hard to find a lovely wearable piece in silver (Tiffany's best color, in my opinion) for around $200. If you do indulge, anything you buy—even a $50 silver bookmark or key chain—comes wrapped in that unmistakable blue box with a classic white ribbon tied just so. 727 Fifth Ave. (at 57th St.). **© 212/755-8000. www.tiffany.com. Subway: N, R to Fifth Ave.**

Tourneau Time Machine   The snazzy three-floor emporium on E. 57th Street is the world's largest watch store, carrying more than 90 brands and 8,000 different styles. The mind-boggling selection runs the gamut from Swatch to Rolex; Swiss Army knives, too. 12 E. 57th St. (btwn Fifth and Madison aves.). **© 212/758-7300. www.tourneau.com. Subway: N, R to Fifth Ave.** Also at 500 Madison Ave. (at 52nd St.). **© 212/758-6098. Subway: 6 to 51st St.** 200 W. 34th St. (at Seventh Ave.). **© 212/563-6880. Subway: 1, 2, 3 to 34th St.** 10 Columbus Circle (The Shops at Columbus Circle). **© 212/823-9425. Subway: A, B, C, D, 1 to Columbus Circle.**

LOGO STORES

Mets Clubhouse Shop   Stop in for goods galore—baseball caps, T-shirts, posters, Piazza jerseys, '69 Miracle Mets memorabilia, and much more amazin' merchandise. You can buy regular season game tix here, too. 143 E. 54th St. (btwn Lexington and Third aves.). **© 212/888-7508. www.mets.com. Subway: E, F to Lexington Ave.**

The MTV Store   This petite boutique sits street side, just below the MTV studio. There's not much here—but your kids will surely find something they want. Celebrity Deathmatch T-shirt, anyone? Flyers are sometimes on hand at the register, advertising for audience members for MTV shows—yet another reason for your teen to drag you in. 1515 Broadway (at 44th St.). **© 212/846-5655. Subway: 1, 2, 3, 7, 9, N, R, S to 42nd St./Times Sq.**

NBA Store *(★)*   For all things NBA and WNBA, head to this three-level megastore, a multimedia celebration of pro hoops, complete with a bleacher-seated arena for player appearances and signings. 666 Fifth Ave. (at 52nd St.). © 212/515-6221. www.nbastore. com. Subway: B, D, F, V to 47th–50th sts./Rockefeller Center.

NBC Experience   This mammoth, neon-lit store sits directly across from the *Today* show studio and sells all manner of NBC-themed merchandise, from Matt and Katie's favorite mugs to *ER* scrubs to *Frasier* umbrellas to *West Wing* T-shirts to . . . you get the picture. Your kids will enjoy the silly interactive features, like the virtual-reality "Conan O'Brien's Wild Desk Ride," as well as the second-level candy shop. NBC Studio Tours also leave from here; call for details. 30 Rockefeller Plaza (at 49th St.). © 212/664-3700. www.nbcsuperstore.com. Subway: B, D, F, V to 47th–50th sts./Rockefeller Center.

New York Firefighter's Friend *(Finds*   What better way to spend your souvenir budget than by saluting New York's bravest? Here's the place to purchase FDNY logo wear, including T-shirts, sweatshirts, hats, and more. The goods are all top-quality, and a portion of profits support the widows and children of the 343 firefighter victims lost in the September 11, 2001, terrorist attacks. 263 Lafayette St. (btwn Prince and Spring sts.). © 212/226-3142. www.nyfirestore.com. Subway: 6 to Spring St.

New York 911 *(Finds*   Adjacent to Firefighter's Friend (above) is the place to shop for not only NYPD logo wear, but also EMT, FBI, and NYC coroner gear. The bounty includes shirts, caps, badge pins, patches, logo toys, and much more. (Not all of the products are licensed by the city, however; I suggest trying to stick with those that are.) The store is well stocked and fun to browse, making it a great place to buy souvenirs and gifts for the folks back home. A portion of the proceeds goes to NYPD-related charities. 263 Lafayette St. (btwn Prince and Spring sts.). © 888/723-3907 or 212/219-3907. www. ny911.com. Subway: 6 to Spring St.

Niketown   More multimedia advertorial than sportswear store, Niketown is surprisingly low key and attractive, with five floors of shoes and athletic wear displayed in stark Lucite and polished metal surroundings. "Museum" cases display Sneakers of the Rich and Famous, and everywhere you're assailed by images of celebrity pitchmen and women. No sales or bargains here—plan on paying top dollar for the high-style athletic wear. Somebody's gotta pay for this place! 6 E. 57th St. (btwn Fifth and Madison aves.). © 212/891-6453. www.niketown.com. Subway: N, R to Fifth Ave.

The Pop Shop *(Finds*   For affordable and wearable art that makes supercool souvenirs, come to the Pop Shop. This groovy store is chock-full of items based on designs by artist Keith Haring, who died in 1990. T-shirts, posters, calendars, stationery, toys, notebooks, and neat transparent backpacks all sport the vivid primary colors and loopy stick-figure drawings that Haring made famous. Best of all, the Pop Shop is a nonprofit organization, offering continued support to the AIDS-related and children's charities that the young artist championed in life. 292 Lafayette St. (btwn Houston and Prince sts.). © 212/219-2784. www.haring.com. Subway: F, V to Broadway/Lafayette St.

Yankees Clubhouse Shop   For all your Bronx Bombers needs—hats, jerseys, jackets, and so on. Tickets for regular-season home games are also for sale, and there's a limited selection of other New York team jerseys. 245 W. 42nd St. (btwn Seventh and Eighth aves.). © 212/768-9555. www.yankeesmerchandise.com. Subway: A, C, E to 42nd St./Port Authority. Also at 393 Fifth Ave. (btwn 36th and 37th sts.). © 212/685-4693. Subway: 6 to 33rd St. 110 E. 59th St. (btwn Park and Lexington aves.). © 212/758-7844. Subway: 4, 5, 6 to 59th St. 8 Fulton St. (in the South St. Seaport). © 212/514-7182. Subway: 2, 3, 4, 5 to Fulton St.

MUSEUM STORES

In addition to these standouts, other noteworthy museum shops worth seeking out include the **New York Public Library,** the **Museum for African Art, The Jewish Museum,** and the **American Folk Art Museum** (see chapter 9).

Maxilla & Mandible *Finds*   This shop is not affiliated with the American Museum of Natural History, but a visit here makes a good adjunct to your trip to the museum (which is right around the corner). It may look like a freak shop at first glance, but it's really a fascinating natural history emporium. Inside you'll find unusual rocks and shells from around the world, luminescent butterflies in display boxes, even surprisingly affordable real fossils containing prehistoric fish and insects that come with details on their history and where they were excavated. There's also a good variety of natural history–themed toys for the kids. 451 Columbus Ave. (btwn 81st and 82nd sts.). ✆ 212/ 724-6173. www.maxillaandmandible.com. Subway: B, C to 81st St.

Metropolitan Museum of Art Store   Given the scope of the museum itself, it's no wonder that the gift shop is outstanding. Many treasures from the museum's collection have been reproduced as jewelry, china, and other objets d'art. The range of art books is dizzying, and upstairs is an equally comprehensive selection of posters and inventive children's toys. 1000 Fifth Ave. (at 82nd St.). ✆ 212/570-3894. www.metmuseum.org/ store. Subway: 4, 5, 6 to 86th St. Also at Rockefeller Center, 15 W. 49th St. ✆ 212/332-1360. Subway: B, D, F, V to 47th–50th sts./Rockefeller Center. 113 Prince St. (at Greene St.). ✆ 212/614-3000. Subway: N, R to Prince St. On the mezzanine level at Macy's, 34th St. and Sixth Ave. ✆ 212/268-7266. Subway: B, D, F, N, R, Q to 34th St./Herald Sq.

MoMA Design Store   Across the street from the Museum of Modern Art is this terrific shop, whose stock ranges from museum posters and clever toys for kids to fully licensed reproductions of many of the classics of modern design, including free-form Alvar Aalto vases, Frank Lloyd Wright chairs, and Eames recliners. If these high-design items are out of your reach, choose from plenty of more affordable outré home accessories. The SoHo store is equally fabulous. 44 W. 53rd St. (btwn Fifth and Sixth aves.). ✆ 212/ 767-1050. www.momastore.org. Subway: E, F to Fifth Ave.; B, D, F, Q to 47th–50th sts./Rockefeller Center. Also at 81 Spring St. (at Crosby St.). ✆ 646/613-1367. Subway: 6 to Spring St.

New York Transit Museum Store   Lots of nifty transportation-themed gifts—the cufflinks made out of vintage subway tokens are just great. With all this train stuff, my 4-year-old son could spend hours here. Grand Central Terminal (on the main level, in the shuttle passage next to the Station Masters' office), 42nd St. and Lexington Ave. ✆ 212/878-0106. Subway: 4, 5, 6, 7, S to 42nd St./Grand Central. Also at 1560 Broadway (at 47th St.). ✆ 212/230-4901. Subway: 1, 9 to 50th St. Boerum Place (at Schermerhorn St.), Brooklyn. ✆ 718/694-5100. Subway: 4, 5 to Borough Hall.

MUSIC
AUDIO & VIDEO

Academy Records & CDs   This Flatiron District shop has a cool intellectual air that's more reminiscent of a good used-book store than your average used-record store. Academy is always filled with classical, opera, and jazz junkies perusing the extensive and well-priced collection of used CDs and vinyl. In addition to the extensive classical and jazz collection is a variety of other audiophile favorites, from rare '60s pop songsters to spoken word. 12 W. 18th St. (btwn Fifth and Sixth aves.). ✆ 212/242-3000. www. academy-records.com. Subway: L, N, R, 4, 5, 6 to 14th St./Union Sq.

Colony Music Center ⭐   This long-lived Theater District shop ("since 1948") is housed in the legendary Brill Building, the Tin Pan Alley of '50s and '60s pop, where legendary songwriters like Leiber and Stoller and producers like Don Kirschner and Phil Spector crafted the soundtrack for a generation. It's the perfect home for Colony, a nostalgia emporium filled with a pricey but excellent collection of vintage vinyl and new CDs. You'll find a great collection of Broadway scores and cast recordings; decades worth of recordings by pop song stylists both legendary and obscure; the city's best collection of sheet music (including some hard-to-find international stuff); and a great selection of original theater and movie posters. 1619 Broadway (at 49th St.). ℂ 212/265-2050. www.colonymusic.com. Subway: N, R to 49th St.; 1, 9 to 50th St.

Footlight ⭐ *Finds*   If you like Colony (see above), also check out this dreamy collection of vintage vinyl, strong in jazz and pop vocalists, soundtracks, and show tunes. 113 E. 12th St. (btwn Third and Fourth aves.). ℂ 212/533-1572. www.footlight.com. Subway: L, N, R, 4, 5, 6 to 14th St./Union Sq.

Generation Records *Value*   This tidy little store sells mostly CDs and is an excellent source for "import" live recordings. Originally specializing in hard-core, punk, and heavy metal, the new collection upstairs still has a heavy edge but has since diversified appreciably. Downstairs is a well-organized and well-priced used CD selection that's not as picked over as most and runs the genre gamut; there's also a good selection of used LPs. Despite the help's tough look, they're actually quite friendly and helpful. 210 Thompson St. (btwn Bleecker and 3rd sts.). ℂ 212/254-1100. Subway: A, B, C, D, E, F, V to W. 4th St.

House of Oldies ⭐   I skipped many a high school class to spend time in this musty old store searching for doo-wop. I think it was here that I bought a mint "Woo Woo Train," by the Valentines on Rama Records for less than $5. That same record now probably costs over $60 and you can probably still find it at the House of Oldies. The store has over one million vinyl records in stock in everything from R&B to surf music. If vinyl oldies are your thing, there's no better place to go. 35 Carmine St. (at Bleecker St.). ℂ 212/243-0500. www.houseofoldies.com. Subway: A, B, C, D, F, V to W. 4th St.

Jazz Record Center   I have a friend from Paris who lives jazz and this is the first place he hits whenever he visits New York. It's *the* place to find rare and out-of-print jazz records. In addition to the extensive selection of CDs and vinyl (including 78s), videos, books, posters, magazines, photos, and other memorabilia are available. Prices start at $5 for vinyl, $10 for CDs, and soar from there, befitting the rarity of the stock. Owner Frederick Cohen is extremely knowledgeable, so come here if you're trying to track down something obscure. (Cohen does mail-order business as well.) 236 W. 26th St. (btwn Seventh and Eighth aves., 8th floor). ℂ 212/675-4480. www.jazzrecordcenter.com. Subway: 1, 9 to 28th St.

Other Music *Finds*   Head to Other Music for the wildest sounds in town. You won't find a major label here (that's what Tower, across the street, is for). This shop focuses exclusively on small international labels, especially those on the cutting edge. The bizarro runs the gamut from underground Japanese spin doctors to obscure Irish folk; needless to say, the world music selection is terrific—fascinating and bound to be filled with music you've never heard of. The sales staff really knows their stuff, so ask away. 15 E. 4th St. (btwn Broadway and Lafayette St.). ℂ 212/477-8150. www.othermusic.com. Subway: F, V to Broadway/Lafayette St.; 6 to Astor Place.

Tower Records   Long my favorite music superstore, both main locations are huge multimedia superstores brimming with an encyclopedic collection of music—classical, jazz, rock, world, you name it. The Village location also stocks a very good selection of indie and alternative labels. Just behind it at West 4th and Lafayette is **Tower Books and Video** (✆ 212/228-5100), where you'll find videos, books, and magazines (although the video selection isn't as good as you might expect). Look for in-store appearances by big names in music, usually advertised in *Time Out New York* and the *Village Voice*. 692 Broadway (at W. 4th St.). ✆ 212/505-1500. www.towerrecords.com. Subway: N, R to 8th St.; 6 to Astor Place. Also at 1961 Broadway (at 66th St.). ✆ 212/799-2500. Subway: 1, 9 to 66th St.

Virgin Megastore   Right in the heart of Times Square, this superstore bustles day and night. For the size of it, the selection isn't as wide as you'd think; still, you're likely to find what you're looking for among the two levels of domestic and imported CDs and cassettes. Other pluses are an extensive singles department, a phenomenal number of listening posts, plus a huge video department. There's also a bookstore, a cafe, and a multiplex movie theater, and you can even arrange airfare on Virgin Atlantic with the on-site travel agent. As at Tower, look for a busy schedule of in-store appearances at both locations. 1540 Broadway (at 45th St.). ✆ 212/921-1020. www.virginmega.com. Subway: N, R, 1, 2, 3, 7, 9 to Times Sq./42nd St. Also at 52 E. 14th St. (at Broadway). ✆ 212/598-4666. Subway: 4, 5, 6, N, R, L to 14th St./Union Sq.

PAPER & STATIONERY

Kate's Paperie ⭐   Three cheers to Kate's for keeping the art of letter writing alive in our computer age. You could browse for hours among this delightful shop's handmade stationery and wrap, innovative invitations and thank-yous, imported notebooks, writing tools, and other creative paper products, including cool paper lampshades. Lovely art cards, too—perfect for writing the folks back home—a joy! The SoHo location is best. 561 Broadway (btwn Prince and Spring sts.). ✆ 212/941-9816. www.katespaperie.com. Subway: N, R to Prince St. Also at 8 W. 13th St. (btwn Fifth and Sixth aves.). ✆ 212/633-0570. Subway: F to 14th St. 1282 Third Ave. (btwn 73rd and 74th sts.). ✆ 212/396-3670. Subway: 6 to 77th St. 140 W. 37th St. (btwn Sixth and Seventh aves.). ✆ 212/459-0700. Subway: 1, 2, 3, 9 to 34th St.

SHOES

Designer shoe shops start on **East 57th Street** and amble up **Madison Avenue,** becoming pricier as you move uptown. **SoHo** is an excellent place to search for the latest styles; the streets are overrun with terrific shoe stores. Cheaper copies of the trendiest styles are sold along **8th Street** between Broadway and Sixth Avenue in the Village, which some people call Shoe Row.

Most department stores have two sizable shoe departments—one for designer stuff and one for daily wearables. See "The Top Shopping Streets & Neighborhoods" and "The Big Department Stores," earlier in this chapter. For **Prada** and **Polo/Ralph Laren,** see "Clothing," and for **Niketown,** see "Logo Stores," both earlier in this section.

Camper   This Big Apple outpost features the full line of made-in-Spain Camper footwear for men and women. These are the hippest walking shoes and boots on the planet, hands down—ideal for those with an eye for style and a craving for comfort. 125 Prince St. (at Wooster St.). ✆ 212/358-1842. www.camper.com. Subway: N, R to Prince St.; C, E to Spring St.

Giraudon New York   This French designer makes fashionable, well-made street shoes for hip men and women who want something clean-lined and stylish but not too chunky or trendy. Not cheap, but not overpriced—these shoes last forever. Prices run $115 to $200, and sales are excellent. 152 Eighth Ave. (btwn 17th and 18th sts.). ℂ 212/633-0999. www.giraudonnewyork.com. Subway: A, C, E, L to 14th St.

Harry's Shoes ✍   This shoe store was an Upper West Side institution even before gentrification hit the neighborhood over 20 years ago. They were one of the first shoe stores to carry New Balance in the city and now their selection of brands range from Bruno Magli to retro Keds. With a huge selection of children's brands, Harry's is the place for kids' shoes, which is why you might want to stay away, unless you don't mind parental hysteria, during the back-to-school frenzy of late August as well as the pre-summer camp throngs that descend in late June. 2299 Broadway (at 83rd St.). ℂ 212/874-2035. www.harrys-shoes.com. Subway: 1, 9 to 86th St.

Jimmy Choo   *The* boutique for *sexy* stilettos. The shoe display is gorgeous at this sophisticated three-floor emporium. 645 Fifth Ave. (at 51st St.). ℂ 212/524-6600. www.jimmy choo.com. Subway: E, F to Fifth Ave. Also at 716 Madison Ave. (at 63rd St.). ℂ 212/759-7078. Subway: F, V to Lexington Avenue.

Manolo Blahnik   These wildly sexy women's shoes are notorious for their cut and sway, and the way they shape the leg. Most famous are the catch-me-if-you-can high heels, but there are plenty of flats and low heels, too. Custom shoes in your own fabric are also a possibility. 31 W. 54th St. (btwn Fifth and Sixth aves.). ℂ 212/582-3007. Subway: E, F to Fifth Ave.

Sacco   These mostly Italian-made women's shoes and wonderful boots combine style with supreme comfort. Good prices and sales, too. 94 Seventh Ave. (btwn 15th and 16th sts.). ℂ 212/675-5180. www.saccoshoes.com. Subway: 1, 9 to 18th St. Also at 14 E. 17th St. (btwn Fifth Ave. and Broadway). ℂ 212/243-2070. Subway: L, N, R, S, 4, 5, 6 to 14th St./Union Sq. 111 Thompson St. (btwn Prince and Spring sts.). ℂ 212/925-8010. Subway: C, E to Spring St. 324 Columbus Ave. (btwn 75th and 76th sts.). ℂ 212/799-5229. Subway: B, C to 81st St. 2355 Broadway (at 86th St.). ℂ 212/874-8362. Subway: 1, 9 to 86th St.

Sigerson Morrison *Finds*   Women who love shoes and are willing to pay in the neighborhood of $200 to $300 for something really special should make a beeline for this Nolita shop. These fashion-forward originals wow with their immaculate details, bright color palette, and sexy, strappy retro appeal—worth every penny. You'll also find some of their styles at Bergdorf Goodman and Saks if you don't want to go downtown. Attention, bargain-hunters: Check out the January winter and August summer sales; prices drop to less than half of retail as the sales wind down. 28 Prince St. (btwn Mott and Elizabeth sts.). ℂ 212/219-3893. www.sigersonmorrison.com. Subway: B, D, F, Q to Broadway/Lafayette St.; N, R to Prince St.; 6 to Spring St.

SPORTING GOODS

Modell's ✍   I confess, like the annoying ad, I often "go to Mo's." And I have my reasons. The best is the very reasonable prices, especially for sneakers and other footwear. Another is the excellent selection of team apparel; I can get my retro New York Giant football cap at half the price they sell it at Giants' Stadium. And there are stores in practically every neighborhood, making it very convenient to go to Mo's. 1293 Broadway (at 33rd St.). ℂ 212/244-4544. www.modells.com. Subway: B, D, F, N, R, V to 34th St. Also at

300 W. 125th St. (at Frederick Douglass Blvd.). ℂ 212/280-9100. Subway: A, B, C, D to 125th St. 51 E. 42nd St. (at Vanderbilt Ave.). ℂ 212/661-4242. Subway: 4, 5, 6, 7, S to Grand Central. 55 Chambers St. (at Broadway). ℂ 212/732-8484. Subway: E to Chambers St.

Paragon Sporting Goods The emphasis at this excellent all-purpose sporting goods store—New York's best—is on equipment and athletic wear for virtually every sport, from tennis to biking to mountain climbing. End-of-the-season sales, especially on sneakers and outdoor clothing, bring serious discounts. 867 Broadway (at 18th St.). ℂ 800/961-3030 or 212/255-8036. www.paragonsports.com. Subway: L, N, R, 4, 5, 6 to 14th St./ Union Sq.

Patagonia Expensive though it may be, Patagonia deserves kudos for its commitment to producing efficient and eco-friendly sports and adventure wear—fleece pullovers made from recycled plastic soda bottles, shell jackets in ultralight weatherproof materials, and organic cotton T-shirts. 101 Wooster St. (btwn Prince and Spring sts.). ℂ 212/343-1776. www.patagonia.com. Subway: N, R to Prince St.; C, E to Spring St. Also at 426 Columbus Ave. (btwn 80th and 81st sts.). ℂ 917/441-0011. Subway: B, C to 81st St.

TOYS

If your kids love to read, don't miss **Books of Wonder** (p. 320). For vintage toys, check out **Alphaville** (p. 319).

American Girl Place ⭐ Your princess will never forgive you if you don't take her to this gargantuan, 43,000-square-foot emporium for little girls featuring a cafe, a bookstore, and a theater. If you come, don't forget to bring her favorite doll so it can get a makeover at the store's own doll salon. Birthday parties at the store are extremely popular, so if you want to plan one for your visit to New York, make sure to book well in advance. 609 Fifth Ave. (at 49th St.). ℂ 800/845-0005 (for reservations) or 212/371-2220. www. americangirl.com. Subway: B, D, F, V to 47th-50th-Rockefeller Center.

FAO Schwarz After a year closed due to bankruptcy, this venerable toy institution reopened with little fanfare just before Christmas 2004. After eliminating products carried by the big discounters, FAO Schwarz now just carries those hard-to-find and oh-so-expensive items like Vespa scooters for older children, mini luxury cars like Hummers and Jaguars, and serious karaoke machines. There's also a soda fountain where the kids can load up on sugar to fuel their romp through the magical store. The giant piano keys made famous in the movie *Big* thankfully still remain. 767 Fifth Ave. (at 58th St.). ℂ 212/644-9400. www.faoschwarz.com. Subway: N, R to Fifth Ave.

Kidding Around This boutique stocks pricey, high-quality toys, many imported from Europe. The emphasis is on the old-fashioned—low-tech goodies like puzzles, rocking horses, and tops. One wall is devoted exclusively to tub toys, windups, and other stocking stuffers. 60 W. 15th St. (btwn Fifth and Sixth aves.). ℂ 212/645-6337. www.kidding aroundnyc.com. Subway: F to 14th St. Also at 68 Bleecker St. (btwn Broadway and Lafayette St.). ℂ 212/ 598-0228. Subway: 6 to Bleecker St.

Toys "R" Us Geoffrey the Giraffe must be mighty pleased with this multi-level, high-tech home. It occupies almost an entire city block in the heart of Times Square, and even boasts its own full-scale Ferris wheel, which kids can ride for free. The huge collection is very well organized, and the store's "ambassadors" are abundant and very helpful; they'll even point you to restaurants and kid-friendly attractions in the neighborhood. Don't miss it if you're traveling with kids. 1514 Broadway (at 44th St.).

© 800/869-7787. Subway: 1, 2, 3, 7, 9 to 42nd St. Also at 24–30 Union Sq. © 212/674-8697. Subway: 4, 5, 6, N, R, L, S to 14th St./Union Sq.

WINE & SPIRITS

Acker Merrall & Condit Co.   In business since 1820—which makes Acker America's oldest wine shop—this attractive little store is the Upper West Side's best wine source. There are no bad bottles here. The careful selection is well displayed, with opinionated cards attached to each bin to help you choose. A supremely knowledgeable staff is on hand for additional assistance. 160 W. 72nd St. (btwn Broadway and Columbus aves.). © 212/787-1700. www.ackerwines.com. Subway: 1, 2, 3, 9 to 72nd St.

Astor Wines & Spirits *Value*   This large store is the source for excellent values on liquor and wine; their stock is deep and diverse. The staff is always willing to recommend a vintage. Astor hosts excellent wine tastings 2 to 3 afternoons a week, often paired with edibles from local restaurants and gourmet shops; call or check the website for the schedule. 12 Astor Place (at Lafayette St.). © 212/674-7500. www.astoruncorked.com. Subway: 6 to Astor Place.

Morrell & Company   One of the leading retailers in America boasts a friendly, helpful staff, and has a Fine Wine Division that hosts high-profile auctions. Adjacent is the **Morrell Wine Bar & Cafe** (© 212/262-7700; www.morrellwinebar.com), an ideal place to sample the goods in comfort. 1 Rockefeller Plaza (at 49th St.). © 212/688-9370. www.morrellwine.com. Subway: B, D, F, V to 47th–50th sts./Rockefeller Center.

Sherry-Lehmann ★   Zagat's has called Sherry-Lehmann "the Rolls-Royce" of wine shops, and the readers of *Decanter* magazine just named it best wine merchant in the United States. Their vast inventory is mind-boggling and includes ritzy gift baskets that make luxurious gifts. Service is excellent and free wine tastings are often on hand. Although expensive, this is the place to come if you're looking for a special bottle. 679 Madison Ave. (btwn 61st and 62nd sts.). © 212/838-7500. www.sherry-lehmann.com. Subway: N, R to Lexington Ave.; 4, 5, 6 to 59th St.

Union Square Wines and Spirits ★ *Finds*   This small, cozy wine store squeezes in over 4,000 varieties of wines. There are numerous wine tastings throughout the week and recommendations by sommeliers from local restaurants. The store is well located across from the Union Square Greenmarket. If you have loaded up with fresh produce for a picnic, have the very personable clerks pair a wine with your food. 33 Union Sq. W. (btwn 15th and 16th sts.). © 212/675-8100. www.unionsquarewines.com. Subway: L, N, R, 4, 5, 6 to Union Sq.

11

New York City After Dark

New York's nightlife scene is an embarrassment of riches. There's so much to see and do in this city after the sun goes down that your biggest problem is probably going to be choosing among the many temptations.

There's no way that I can tell you in these pages what's going to be on the calendar while you're in town. For the latest, most comprehensive nightlife listings, from theater and performing arts to live rock, jazz, and dance club coverage, *Time Out New York* (www.timeoutny.com) is my favorite weekly source; a new issue hits newsstands every Thursday. The free weekly *Village Voice* (www.villagevoice.com), the city's legendary alterna-paper, is available late Tuesday downtown and early Wednesday in the rest of the city. The arts and entertainment coverage couldn't be more extensive, and just about every live music venue advertises its shows here. The *New York Times* (www.nytoday.com) features terrific entertainment coverage, particularly in the two-part Friday "Weekend" section. The cabaret, classical music, and theater guides are particularly useful. Other great weekly sources are the *New Yorker* (www.newyorker.com), in its "Goings on About

Town" section; and *New York* magazine (www.nymetro.com) features the latest happenings in "The Week" section. *New York's* **www.nymetro.com** site is an excellent online source.

Barhoppers shouldn't pass up the comprehensive *Shecky's New York Bar, Club & Lounge Guide,* printed annually. The website (**www.sheckys.com**) is even more current, as is **Shecky's Bar Phone** at ✆ 212/777-BARS, which offers up-to-the-minute nightlife news for the cost of a phone call.

Another good online bar source is **www.murphguide.com**. This website has all the latest happy hour information and is a particularly good source if you are seeking out an Irish pub, of which there are many in New York.

NYC/Onstage (✆ 212/768-1818; www.tdf.org) is a recorded service providing complete schedules, descriptions, and other details on theater and the performing arts. The bias is toward plays, but NYC/Onstage is a good source for chamber and orchestral music (including all Lincoln Center events), dance, opera, cabaret, and family entertainment, too.

1 All the City's a Stage: The Theater Scene

Nobody does theater better than New York. No other city—not even London—has a theater scene with so much breadth and depth, with so many wide-open alternatives. Broadway, of course, gets the most ink and the most airplay, and deservedly so. It's where you'll find the big stage productions, from crowd-pleasing warhorses like *The Lion King* to phenomenally successful shows like *The Producers*. But today's scene is thriving beyond the bounds of just Broadway—smaller, "alternative" theater has taken

Broadway Theaters

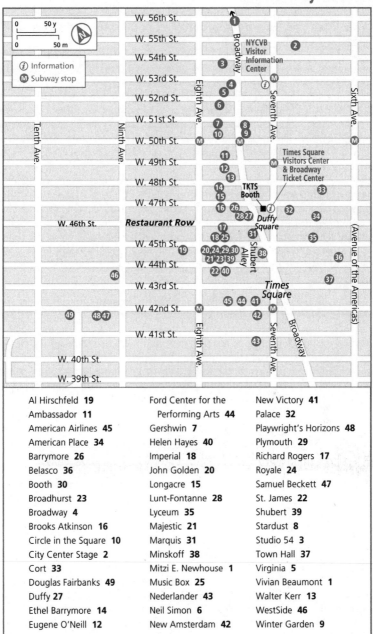

W. 56th St.
W. 55th St.
W. 54th St.
W. 53rd St.
W. 52nd St.
W. 51st St.
W. 50th St.
W. 49th St.
W. 48th St.
W. 47th St.
W. 46th St.
W. 45th St.
W. 44th St.
W. 43rd St.
W. 42nd St.
W. 41st St.
W. 40th St.
W. 39th St.

Broadway
Eighth Ave.
Seventh Ave.
Sixth Ave.
Tenth Ave.
Ninth Ave.
(Avenue of the Americas)

0   50 y
0   50 m

ⓘ Information
Ⓜ Subway stop

NYCVB Visitor Information Center
Times Square Visitors Center & Broadway Ticket Center
TKTS Booth
Duffy Square
Restaurant Row
Shubert Alley
Times Square

Al Hirschfeld **19**	Ford Center for the Performing Arts **44**	New Victory **41**
Ambassador **11**	Gershwin **7**	Palace **32**
American Airlines **45**	Helen Hayes **40**	Playwright's Horizons **48**
American Place **34**	Imperial **18**	Plymouth **29**
Barrymore **26**	John Golden **20**	Richard Rogers **17**
Belasco **36**	Longacre **15**	Royale **24**
Booth **30**	Lunt-Fontanne **28**	Samuel Beckett **47**
Broadhurst **23**	Lyceum **35**	St. James **22**
Broadway **4**	Majestic **21**	Shubert **39**
Brooks Atkinson **16**	Marquis **31**	Stardust **8**
Circle in the Square **10**	Minskoff **38**	Studio 54 **3**
City Center Stage **2**	Mitzi E. Newhouse **1**	Town Hall **37**
Cort **33**	Music Box **25**	Virginia **5**
Douglas Fairbanks **49**	Nederlander **43**	Vivian Beaumont **1**
Duffy **27**	Neil Simon **6**	Walter Kerr **13**
Ethel Barrymore **14**	New Amsterdam **42**	WestSide **46**
Eugene O'Neill **12**		Winter Garden **9**

hold of the popular imagination, too. With bankable stars on stage, crowds lining up for hot tickets, and hits popular enough to generate major-label cast albums, Off-Broadway isn't just for culture vultures anymore.

I can't tell you precisely what will be on while you're in town, so check the publications listed at the start of this chapter or the websites listed in "Online Sources for Theatergoers & Performing Arts Fans," below, to get an idea of what you might like to see. Another useful source is the **Broadway Line** (© **888/BROADWAY** or 212/302-4111; www.broadway.org), where you can get details and descriptions on current Broadway shows, hear about special offers and discounts, and choose to be transferred to TeleCharge or Ticketmaster to buy tickets. The recorded service **NYC/Onstage** (© **212/768-1818;** www.tdf.org) provides the same kind of service for both Broadway and Off-Broadway productions.

Helping to ensure the recent success of the New York theater scene has been the presence of Hollywood stars like Kevin Spacey, Glenn Close, Patrick Stewart, Molly Ringwald, Brooke Shields, Kevin Bacon, Liam Neeson, and Dame Judi Dench. But keep in mind that stars' runs are often very short, and tickets tend to sell out fast. If you hear that there's a celeb you'd like to see coming to the New York stage, don't put off your travel and ticket-buying plans. (The box office can tell you how long a star is contracted for a role.)

THE BASICS

The terms **Broadway, Off-Broadway,** and **Off-Off-Broadway** refer to theater size, pay scales, and other arcane details, not location—or, these days, even star wattage. Most of the Broadway theaters are in Times Square, huddled around the thoroughfare the scene is named for, but not directly on it: Instead, you'll find them dotting the side streets that intersect Broadway, mostly in the mid-40s between Sixth and Eighth avenues (44th and 45th sts. in particular) but running north as far as 53rd Street. There's even a Broadway theater outside Times Square: the Vivian Beaumont in Lincoln Center, on the Upper West Side at Broadway and 65th Street.

Off-Broadway, on the other hand, is not that exacting an expression. With the increasing popularization of off-the-beaten-track productions, the distinction between Off- and Off-Off-Broadway productions has become fuzzier. Off-Off-Broadway shows tend to be more avant-garde, experimental, and/or nomadic. Off- and Off-Off-Broadway productions tend to be based downtown, but pockets show up in Midtown and on the Upper West Side. Broadway shows tend to keep pretty regular **schedules.** There are usually eight performances a week: evening shows Tuesday through Saturday, plus matinees on Wednesday, Saturday, and Sunday. Evening shows are usually at 8pm, while matinees are usually at 2pm on Wednesday and Saturday, and 3pm on Sunday, but schedules can vary, especially Off-Broadway. Shows usually start on the dot, or within a few minutes of starting time; if you arrive late, you may have to wait until after the first act to take your seat.

Ticket prices for Broadway shows vary dramatically. Expect to pay for good seats; the high end for any given show is likely to be between $60 and $100. The cheapest end of the price range can be as low as $20 or as high as $50, depending on the theater configuration. If you're buying tickets at the very low end of a wide available range, be aware that you may be buying obstructed-view seats. If all tickets are the same price or the range is small, you can pretty much count on all of the seats being pretty good. Otherwise, price is your barometer. Note that legroom can be tight in these old theaters, and you'll usually get more in the orchestra seats.

Off-Broadway and Off-Off-Broadway shows tend to be cheaper, with tickets often as low as $10 or $15. However, seats for the most established shows and those with star power can command prices as high as $50.

Don't let price be a deterrent to enjoying the theater. There are ways to pay less if you're willing to make the effort and be flexible, with a few choices at hand as to what you'd like to see. Read on.

TOP TICKET-BUYING TIPS
BEFORE YOU LEAVE HOME

Phone ahead or go online for tickets to the most successful or popular shows as far in advance as you can—in the case of shows like *The Lion King,* it's never too early.

Buying tickets can be simple, if the show you want to see isn't sold out. You need only call such general numbers as **TeleCharge** (© **212/239-6200;** www.telecharge. com), which handles most Broadway and Off-Broadway shows and some concerts; or **Ticketmaster** (© **212/307-4100;** www.ticketmaster.com), which also handles Broadway and Off-Broadway shows and most concerts.

Theatre Direct International (TDI) is a ticket broker that sells tickets to select Broadway and Off-Broadway shows—including some of the most popular crowd-pleasers, like *Oklahoma!* and *Cabaret*—directly to individuals and travel agents. Check to see if they have seats to the shows you're interested in by calling © **800/BROAD-WAY** or 212/541-8457; you can also order tickets through TDI via their commercial website, **www.broadway.com**. (Disregard the discounted prices, unless you're buying for a group of 20 or more.) Because there's a minimum service charge of $15 per ticket, you'll definitely do better by trying Ticketmaster or TeleCharge first; but because they act as a consolidator, TDI may have tickets left for a specific show even if the major outlets don't.

Other reputable ticket brokers include **Keith Prowse & Co.** (© **800/669-8687;** www.keithprowse.com) and **Global Tickets Edwards & Edwards** (© **800/223-6108**). For a list of other licensed ticket brokers recommended by the New York Convention & Visitors Bureau (NYCVB), get a copy of the Official NYC Visitor Kit (see "Visitor Information," in chapter 3, for details). All kinds of ticket brokers list ads in the Sunday *New York Times* and other publications, but don't take the risk. Stick with a licensed broker recommended by the NYCVB.

You may have heard about a new development on the Broadway ticket scene: **Broadway Inner Circle** (© **212/391-9621;** www.broadwayinnercircle.com), the ticket agency that, in a supposed effort to circumvent scalpers, has arranged with select in-demand shows to sell select premium seats for prices close to $500 a ticket. If price is no object, you might want to try this service.

If you don't want to pay even a service charge, try calling the **box office** directly. Broadway theaters don't sell tickets over the telephone—the one major exception, the **Roundabout Theatre Company** (© **212/719-1300;** www.roundabouttheatre.org), charges a $5-per-ticket "convenience" fee—but a good number of Off-Broadway theaters do.

Also, before you resort to calling broker after broker to snag tickets to a hot show, consider calling the **concierge** at the hotel where you'll be staying. If you've chosen a hotel with a well-connected concierge, he or she may be able to have tickets waiting for you when you check in—for a premium, of course. For more on this, see "When You Arrive," below.

Kids Take the Stage: Family-Friendly Theater

The family-friendly theater scene is flourishing these days. There's so much going on that it's best to check *New York* magazine, *Time Out New York,* or the Friday *New York Times* for current listings. Besides larger-than-life general-audience Broadway shows, the following offer some dependable kid-targeted entertainment options.

The stunningly renovated **New Victory Theater,** 229 W. 42nd St., between Seventh and Eighth avenues (✆ 646/223-3020; www.newvictory.org), reopened in 1995 as the city's first full-time family-oriented performing arts center, and has hosted companies ranging from the Trinity Irish Dance Company to the astounding Flaming Idiots, who juggle everything from fire and swords to beanbag chairs.

The **Paper Bag Players** (✆ 212/663-0390; www.paperbagplayers.org), called "the best children's theater in the country" by *Newsweek,* perform funny tales for children 4 to 9 in a set made from bags and boxes, in winter only, at Hunter College's Sylvia and Danny Kaye Playhouse, 68th Street between Park and Lexington avenues (✆ 212/772-4448). If you can't make it to the Kaye, call the Players to inquire whether they'll be staging other performances about town.

TADA! Youth Theater, 15 W. 28th St., between Fifth Avenue and Broadway (✆ 212/252-1619; www.tadatheater.com), is a terrific youth ensemble that performs musicals and plays with a multiethnic perspective for kids, teens, and their families.

The **Swedish Cottage Marionette Theatre** (✆ 212/988-9093; www.central park.org) puts on marionette shows for kids at its 19th-century Central Park theater throughout the year. Reservations are a must.

For details on how to obtain advance-purchase theater tickets at a discount, see "Reduced-Price Ticket Deals," below.

Online Sources for Theatergoers & Performing Arts Fans

Some of your best, most comprehensive, and up-to-date information sources for what's going on about town are in cyberspace.

Three competing commercial sites—**Broadway.com (www.broadway.com), Playbill Online (www.playbill.com** or www.playbillclub.com), and **TheaterMania (www.theatermania.com)**—offer complete information on Broadway and Off-Broadway shows, with links to the ticket-buying agencies once you've selected your show. Each offers an **online theater club** that's free to join and can yield substantial savings—as much as 50%—on advance-purchase theater tickets for select Broadway and Off-Broadway shows. All you have to do is register, and you'll have access to discounts that can range from a few dollars to as much as 50% off regular ticket prices. You can sign up to be notified by e-mail as offers change. By far, I like the *Playbill Club* best; it was the first of the bunch, and its discount offers tend to be the most

The "World Voices Club" of the **New Perspectives Theatre,** 750 Eighth Ave., between 46th and 47th streets (℃ 212/730-2030; www.new perspectivestheatre.org), has a different puppet show based on fables from different world cultures each month.

While David Mamet hardly seems like a playwright for the kiddies, the "Atlantic for Kids" series is making a go of it at the **Atlantic Theater Company,** 336 W. 20th St., between Eighth and Ninth avenues (℃ **212/645-8015;** www.atlantictheater.org), which Mamet cofounded with Academy Award–nominated actor William H. Macy.

Another excellent troupe that excels at children's theater is the **Vital Theatre Company,** 432 W. 42nd St., between Ninth and Tenth avenues (℃ **212/ 579-0528;** www.vitaltheatre.org); it's well worth seeing what's on.

If you want to introduce your kids to the magic of live opera, check out the "Opera in Brief" program, which runs most Saturdays at 11:30am, at **Amato Opera Theatre** (p. 353). For kid-friendly classical music, see what's on at **Bargemusic** (p. 354), which presents chamber-music concerts for kids throughout their regular season. Look for Young People's Concerts and Kidzone Live!, in which kids get to interact with orchestra members prior to curtain time, at the **New York Philharmonic** (p. 355). Also check to see what's on for the entire family at **Carnegie Hall** (p. 357), which offers family concerts for a bargain-basement ticket price of just $5, plus the CarnegieKids program, which introduces kids ages 3 to 6 to basic musical concepts through a 45-minute music and storytelling performance. And don't forget "Jazz for Young People," Wynton Marsalis's stellar family concert series at **Jazz at Lincoln Center** (p. 358) and the new "Jazz for Kids" program at the **Jazz Standard** (p. 367), 116 E. 27th St., between Park and Lexington avenues (℃ **212/576-2232;** www. jazzstandard.net), which takes place every Sunday afternoon.

wide-ranging, often including the best Broadway and Off-Broadway shows. Theater-Mania's **TM Insider** is the runner-up; the Broadway.com site wants a bit too much personal information for my taste. Nothing prevents you from signing up with all of them and taking advantage of the best deals.

As an information source, you can't beat **LiveBroadway.com (www.livebroadway. com),** the official website of Broadway, sponsored by the League of American Theatres and Producers. Theater buffs will also enjoy perusing the **Internet Broadway Database (www.ibdb.com),** the official archival database for Broadway theater information, past and present.

WHEN YOU ARRIVE

Once you arrive in the city, getting your hands on tickets can take some street smarts—and failing those, cold hard cash. Even if it seems unlikely that seats are available, always **call the box office** before attempting any other route. Single seats are often easiest to obtain, so people willing to sit apart may find themselves in luck.

Tips More Dramatics Venues Worth Seeking Out

When you want a spectacle, there's no place like Broadway: For helicopters, dozens of tap dancing chorines, and collapsing chandeliers, Broadway is your ticket (and a very high-priced one it is, too!). But you can see some amazing work at prices ranging from just-below-Broadway to less than $20 if you know where to look. For Off-Broadway, expect to pay $20 to $60 or so for tickets; Off-Off-Broadway rarely charges more than $20, and you can sometimes get in for $12 or less (so you don't feel quite as bad leaving at intermission if the show's a stinker!).

Where do you find the hidden gems? The *Village Voice* (which sponsors the annual Obies, or Off-Broadway Awards) is a good source. *Timeout New York* has excellent listings and capsule descriptions for major Off-Broadway productions. For Off-Off-Broadway, check the reviews on Theatermania.com (which also lets you purchase tickets and offers regular discounts) and the Off-Off Broadway Review (www.oobr.com), which also gives awards to the best productions each season.

Three resident theaters in New York—**Lincoln Center Theater** (p. 358), the **Roundabout Theatre** (p. 347), and Manhattan Theatre Club (www.mtc-nyc. org)—present work in Broadway houses, as well as in smaller venues Off-Broadway. You'll pay Broadway prices (or whatever discount you can get on TKTS) for the best seats in the big houses, but you can also usually find special, lower prices for students or seniors; or last-minute rush tickets. In their smaller spaces (MTC's Stage II; the Roundabout's Laura Pels Theatre; Lincoln Center's Mitzi Newhouse) you can find good seats for less than $50 to see new plays and revivals by the likes of Terence McNally and John Patrick Shanley. These theater often offer extra events like play readings, "talk-backs" with the cast and production team, and so on—sometimes free, sometimes for a small charge. Following are a few other notable Off-Broadway venues, but really, these are just the tip of the iceberg; check out the sources listed above for many, many more options.

You should also try the **Broadway Ticket Center,** run by the League of American Theatres and Producers (the same people behind the LiveBroadway.com, above) at the Times Square Visitors Center, 1560 Broadway, between 46th and 47th streets (open Mon–Sat 9am–7pm, Sun 10am–6pm). They often have tickets available for otherwise sold-out shows, both for advance and same-day purchase, and only charge about $5 extra per ticket.

Even if saving money isn't an issue for you, check the boards at the **TKTS Booth** in Times Square; more on that can be found under "Reduced-Price Ticket Deals," below.

In addition, your **hotel concierge** may be able to arrange tickets for you. These are usually purchased through a broker and a premium will be attached, but they're usually good seats and you can count on them being legitimate. (A $20 tip to the concierge for this service is reasonable—perhaps even more if the tickets are for an extremely hot show. By the time you've paid this tip, you might come out better by

- **Joseph Papp Public Theater** 🕭, 425 Lafayette St. (📞 212/539-8900; www. publictheater.org). Legendary among Off-Broadway theaters, this is the legacy of the late visionary theater producer Joseph Papp. Now under the direction of George C. Wolfe, the Public always draws top talent to the stage with its groundbreaking stagings of Shakespeare's plays as well as new plays, classical dramas, and solo performances. The Public also produces Broadway shows rather regularly, such as *Bring in 'Da Noise, Bring in 'Da Funk*, and hosts New York's best annual alfresco event, Shakespeare in the Park, each summer (see the box "Park It! Shakespeare, Music & Other Free Fun," on p. 360). If that's not enough, it's also home to Joe's Pub (p. 369).

- **Atlantic Theater Company**, 336 W. 20th St. (📞 212/645-8015; www. atlantictheater.com), "produces great plays simply and truthfully, utilizing an artistic ensemble," according to its mission statement. It has recently presented new work by Woody Allen, David Mamet, and Tina Howe's Ionesco translations. It also accepts volunteer ushers.

- **Signature Theatre Company**, 555 W. 42nd St. (📞 212/244-PLAY; www. signaturetheatre.org), presents season-long explorations of a living playwright's body of work. You can also volunteer usher here.

- **New York Theater Workshop (NYTW)**, 79 E. 4th St. (📞 212/460-5475; www.nytw.org), has been around since 1979, but it was *Rent* (and later, *Dirty Blonde*) that put it on the map. NYTW specializes in new work, rethought revivals, and collaborations. All Sunday evening performances are $20; there are discounts for students and opportunities to usher.

- **Keen Company**, 520 Eighth Ave. (📞 212/216-0963; www.keencompany. org) has a mandate to produce "sincere plays" under the direction of Artistic Director Carl Forsman, who has an eye for old pieces that gleam anew with a heartfelt production.

—Kathleen Warnock

contacting a broker or ticket agency yourself.) If you want to deal with a licensed broker directly, **Keith Prowse & Co.** has a local office that accommodates drop-ins at 234 W. 44th St., between Seventh and Eighth avenues, Suite 1000 (📞 **800/223-6108;** open Mon–Sat 9am–6pm).

If you buy from one of the **scalpers** selling tickets in front of the theater doors, you're taking a risk. They may be perfectly legitimate—a couple from the 'burbs whose companions couldn't make it for the evening, say—but they could be swindlers passing off fakes for big money. It's a risk that's not worth taking.

One preferred **insiders' trick** is to make the rounds of Broadway theaters at about 6pm, when unclaimed house seats are made available to the public. These tickets—reserved for VIPs, friends of the cast, the press, or other hangers-on—offer great locations and are sold at face value.

Also, note that **Monday** is often a good day to cop big-name show tickets. Though most theaters are dark on that day, some of the most sought-after choices aren't. Locals are at home on the first night of the workweek, so all the odds are in your favor. Your chances will always be better on weeknights, or for Wednesday matinees, rather than weekends.

REDUCED-PRICE TICKET DEALS

Your best bet is to try before you go. You may be able to purchase **reduced-price theater tickets** in advance over the phone (or in person at the box office) by joining one or more of the online theater clubs. Membership is free and can garner you discounts of up to 50% on select Broadway and Off-Broadway shows. For further details, see "Online Sources for Theatergoers & Performing Arts Fans," above.

Broadway shows—even blockbusters—sometimes have a limited number of cheaper tickets set aside for students and seniors, and they may even be available at the last minute; call the box office direct to inquire. *Rent* has offered all kinds of bargains to keep younger theatergoers coming.

The best deal in town on same-day tickets for both Broadway and Off-Broadway shows is at the **Times Square Theatre Centre,** better known as the **TKTS** booth run by the nonprofit Theatre Development Fund in the heart of the Theater District at Duffy Square, 47th Street and Broadway (open 3–8pm for evening performances, 10am–2pm for Wed and Sat matinees, from 11am–8pm on Sun for all performances). Tickets for that day's performances are usually offered at half price, with a few reduced only 25%, plus a $2.50 per ticket service charge. Boards outside the ticket windows list available shows; you're unlikely to find certain perennial or out-size smashes, but most other shows turn up. Only cash and traveler's checks are accepted (no credit cards). There's often a huge line, so show up early for the best availability and be prepared to wait—but frankly, the crowd is all part of the fun. If you don't care much what you see and you'd just like to go to a show, you can walk right up to the window later in the day and something's always available.

Run by the same group and offering the same discounts is the **TKTS Lower Manhattan Theatre Centre,** at South Street Seaport, located at the corner of Front and John streets at 199 Water St. (open Mon–Fri 11am–6pm, Sat 11am–4pm; subway: 2, 3, 4, 5 to Fulton St.). All the same policies apply. The advantages to coming down here are that the lines are generally shorter, and matinee tickets are available the day before, so you can plan ahead.

Visit **www.tdf.org** or call **NYC/Onstage** at © **212/768-1818** and press "8" for the latest TKTS information.

2 Opera, Classical Music & Dance

While Broadway is the Big Apple's greatest hit, many other performing arts also flourish in this culturally rich and entertainment-hungry town.

In addition to the listings below, see what's happening at **Carnegie Hall** and the **Brooklyn Academy of Music,** two of the most respected—and enjoyable—multifunctional performing arts venues in the city. The marvelous **92nd Street Y** also regularly hosts events that are worth considering. I've listed the operatic and symphonic companies housed at **Lincoln Center** below; also check the center's full calendar for all offerings. See "Major Concert Halls & Landmark Venues," below.

OPERA

New York has grown into one of the world's major opera centers. The season generally runs September through May, but there's usually something going on at any time of year.

Amato Opera Theatre *(Finds)*   This cozy, off-the-beaten-track venue functions as a showcase for talented young American singers. The intimate 100-plus-seat house celebrates its 59th season in 2006 amid a rising reputation and increasing ticket sales. The staple is full productions of Italian classics—Verdi's *La Traviata,* Puccini's *Madame Butterfly,* Bizet's *Carmen,* with an occasional Mozart tossed in—at great prices for regular performances ($30, $25 for seniors and kids). Performances, usually held on Saturday and Sunday, now regularly sell out, so it's a good idea to reserve 3 weeks in advance.

Note for adults: On 1 Saturday a month, "Opera in Brief" offers fully costumed, kid-length versions of the classics interwoven with narration so chaperones have a palatable forum in which to introduce the little ones to opera. At $15 or so per ticket, these matinee performances are wallet-friendly, too. 319 Bowery (at 2nd St.). © 212/228-8200. www.amato.org. Subway: F to Second Ave.; 6 to Bleecker St.

Metropolitan Opera   Tickets can cost a small fortune—anywhere from $25 to $295. But for its full productions of the classic repertory and a schedule packed with world-class grand sopranos and tenors, the Metropolitan Opera ranks first in the world. Millions are spent on fabulous stagings, and the venue itself is a wonder of acoustics. The 2005–06 season had not been announced at press time, but whatever is on the schedule, the quality will be second to none.

To guarantee that its audience understands the words, the Met has outfitted the back of each row of seats with screens for subtitles—translation help for those who want it, minimum intrusion for those who don't. James Levine continues his role as the brilliant and popular conductor of the orchestra. At the Metropolitan Opera House, Lincoln Center, Broadway and 64th St. © 212/362-6000. www.metopera.org. Subway: 1, 9 to 66th St.

New York City Opera   The New York City Opera is a superb company, with a delightful duality to its approach: It not only attempts to reach a wider audience than the Met with its more "human" scale and significantly lower prices ($32–$115), but it's also committed to adventurous premieres, newly composed operas, the occasional avant-garde work, American musicals *(Porgy and Bess)* and novels *(Of Mice and Men)* presented as fresh, innovative operettas, and even obscure works by mainstream or lesser-known composers. Its mix stretches from the "easy" works of Puccini, Verdi, and Gilbert and Sullivan to the more challenging oeuvres of the likes of Arnold Schönberg and Philip Glass. At the New York State Theater, Lincoln Center, Broadway and 64th St. © 212/870-5570 (information or box office), or 212/307-4100 for Ticketmaster. www.nycopera.com or www.ticketmaster.com. Subway: 1, 9 to 66th St.

New York Gilbert and Sullivan Players   If you're in the mood for light-hearted operetta, try this lively company, which specializes in Gilbert and Sullivan's 19th-century English comic works. Tickets are affordable, usually in the $40 to $65 range (exact prices for the 2005–06 season were not yet determined at press time). The annual calendar generally runs from October through April and includes four shows a year, with some performances held at **City Center** (p. 355). At Symphony Space, Broadway and 95th St. © 212/864-5400 or 212/769-1000. www.nygasp.org. Subway: 1, 2, 3, 9 to 96th St.

CLASSICAL MUSIC

Bargemusic *(Finds)*   Many thought Olga Bloom peculiar, if not deranged, when she transformed a 40-year-old barge into a chamber music concert hall. More than 20 years later, Bargemusic is an internationally renowned recital room boasting more than 100 first-rate chamber music performances a year. Visiting musicians love the chance to play in such an intimate setting, so the roster regularly includes highly respected international musicians as well as local stars like violinist Cynthia Phelps.

There are three shows per week, on Thursday and Friday evenings at 7:30pm and Sunday afternoon at 4pm. The musicians perform on a small stage in a cherry-paneled, fireplace-lit room accommodating 130. The barge may creak a bit and an occasional boat may speed by, but the music rivals what you'll find in almost any other New York concert hall—and the panoramic view through the glass wall behind the stage can't be beat. Neither can the price: Tickets are just $35 ($25 for students), or $40 for performances by larger ensembles. Reserve well in advance. At Fulton Ferry Landing (just south of the Brooklyn Bridge), Brooklyn. © **718/624-2083** or 718/624-4061. www.bargemusic. org. Subway: 2, 3 to Clark St.; A, C to High St.

The Juilliard School *(Value)*   During its school year, the nation's premier music education institution sponsors about 550 performances of the highest quality—at the lowest prices. With most concerts free and $20 as a maximum ticket price, Juilliard is one of New York's greatest cultural bargains. Though most would assume that the school presents only classical music concerts, Juilliard also offers other music as well

---

Tips Last-Minute Ticket-Buying Tips

Most seats at New York Philharmonic performances are sold to subscribers, with just a few left for the rest of us. But there are still ways to get tickets. Periodically, a number of same-day orchestra tickets are made available at the Philharmonic, and sold first thing in the morning for $25 a pop (two-ticket maximum). They usually go on sale at 10am weekdays, 1pm Saturday (noon if there's a matinee). And when subscribers can't attend, they may turn their tickets back to the theaters, which then resell them at the last moment. These can be in the most coveted rows of the orchestra. Ticket holders can donate unwanted tickets until curtain time, so tickets that are not available first thing in the morning may become available later in the day. The hopeful form "cancellation lines" 2 hours or more before curtain time for a crack at returned tickets on a first-come, first-served basis. Senior/student/disability rush tickets may be available for $10 (two-ticket max) on concert day, but never at Friday matinees or Saturday evening performances. To check availability for any of these programs at all performances, call Audience Services at © **212/875-5656** before you head to the box office.

Note that Lincoln Center's **Alice Tully Hall** (where the Chamber Music Society performs and other concerts are held), the **Metropolitan Opera,** the **New York City Opera,** and **Carnegie Hall** offer similar last-minute and discount programs (the **New York City Ballet** offers Student Rush tickets only). It makes sense to call the box office first to check on same-day availability before heading to the theater—or, if you're willing to risk coming away empty-handed, be there at opening time for first crack.

as drama, dance, opera, and interdisciplinary works. The best way to find out about the wide array of productions is to call, visit the school's website (click on "Calendar of Events"), or consult the bulletin board in the building's lobby. Note that tickets are sometimes required even for free performances. Watch for master classes and discussions open to the public featuring celebrity guest teachers. 60 Lincoln Center Plaza (Broadway at 65th St.). © 212/799-5000, or 212/721-0965 for charge tickets. www.juilliard.edu. Subway: 1, 9 to 66th St.

New York Philharmonic   Symphony-wise, you'd be hard-pressed to do better than the New York Philharmonic. The country's oldest orchestra is now under the guidance of distinguished conductor Lorin Maazel, formerly of the Bavarian Radio Symphony Orchestra. Don't expect quality to falter one bit. There's a summer season in July, when themed classics brighten the hall, as well as free summer concerts in Central Park that are worth checking into.

Tickets range from $36 to $68; opt for a rush-hour concert or a matinee for the lowest across-the-board prices. If you can afford it—and if the tickets are available—it's well worth it to pay for prime seats. The acoustics of the hall are such that, at the midrange price points, I prefer the second tier (especially the boxes) over the more expensive rear orchestra seats. Go cheap if you have to; you're sure to enjoy the program from any vantage. At Avery Fisher Hall, Lincoln Center, Broadway at 65th St. © 212/875-5656 for audience services, 212/875-5030 for box office information, or Center Charge at 212/721-6500 for tickets. www.newyorkphilharmonic.org. Subway: 1, 9 to 66th St.

DANCE

In general, dance seasons run September through February and then March through June, but there's almost always something going on. In addition to the major venues and troupes below, some other names to keep in mind are the **Brooklyn Academy of Music,** the **92nd Street Y, Radio City Music Hall,** and **Town Hall** (see "Major Concert Halls & Landmark Venues," below). For particularly innovative works, see what's on at the **Dance Theater Workshop,** in the Bessie Schönberg Theater, 219 W. 19th St., between Seventh and Eighth avenues (© 212/691-6500 or 212/924-0077; www.dtw.org), a first-rate launching pad for nearly a quarter-century.

In addition to regular appearances at City Center (below), the **American Ballet Theatre** (www.abt.org) takes up residence at Lincoln Center's Metropolitan Opera House (© 212/477-3030) for 8 weeks each spring. The same venue also hosts such visiting companies as the Kirov, Royal, and Paris Opéra ballets.

The weekly *Time Out New York,* available on newsstands around town, maintains a section dedicated to dance events around town that's an invaluable resource to fans.

City Center   Modern dance usually takes center stage in this Moorish dome-topped performing arts palace. The companies of Merce Cunningham, Martha Graham, Paul Taylor, Alvin Ailey, Twyla Tharp, the Dance Theatre of Harlem, and the American Ballet Theatre are often on the calendar. Don't expect cutting edge—but do expect excellence. Sightlines are terrific from all corners, and a new acoustical shell means the sound is pitch-perfect. Ticket prices range from $25 to $100. 131 W. 55th St. (btwn Sixth and Seventh aves.). © 877/247-0430 or 212/581-1212. www.citycenter.org. Subway: F, N, Q, R, W to 57th St.; B, D, E to Seventh Ave.

Joyce Theater   Housed in an old Art Deco movie house, the Joyce has grown into one of the world's greatest modern dance institutions. You can see everything from

Native American ceremonial dance to Maria Benites Teatro Flamenco to the innovative works of Pilobolus to the Martha Graham Dance Company. In residence annually is Eliot Feld's ballet company, Ballet Tech, which WQXR radio's Francis Mason called "better than a whole month of namby-pamby classical ballets." The Joyce has a second space, **Joyce SoHo,** where you can see rising young dancers and experimental works in the intimacy of a 70-seat performance space. In either space, seats go for $35 to $45. 175 Eighth Ave. (at 19th St.). ℂ 212/242-0800. www.joyce.org. Subway: C, E to 23rd St.; 1, 9 to 18th St. **Joyce SoHo** at 155 Mercer St. (btwn Houston and Prince sts.). ℂ 212/431-9233. Subway: N, R to Prince St.

New York City Ballet   Highly regarded for its unsurpassed technique, the New York City Ballet is the world's best. The company renders with happy regularity the works of two of America's most important choreographers: George Balanchine, its founder, and Jerome Robbins. Under the direction of Ballet Master in Chief Peter Martins, the troupe continues to expand its repertoire and performs to a wide variety of classical and modern music. The cornerstone of the annual season is the Christmastime production of *The Nutcracker,* for which tickets usually become available in early October. Ticket prices for most events run $28 to $66. At the New York State Theater at Lincoln Center, Broadway and 64th St. ℂ 212/870-5570. www.nycballet.com. Subway: 1, 9 to 66th St.

3 Major Concert Halls & Landmark Venues

Apollo Theater ⊛   Built in 1914, this legendary Harlem theater launched or abetted the careers of countless musical icons—including Bessie Smith, Billie Holiday, Dinah Washington, Duke Ellington, Ella Fitzgerald, Sarah Vaughan, Count Basie, Aretha Franklin, and James Brown—and is in large part responsible for the development and worldwide popularization of black music in America. By the 1970s, it had fallen on hard times, but a 1986 restoration breathed new life into the landmark. Today the Apollo is internationally renowned for its African-American acts of all musical genres, from hip-hop acts to Wynton Marsalis's "Jazz for Young People" events. Wednesday's "Amateur Night at the Apollo" is a loud, fun-filled night that draws in young talents from all over the country with high hopes of making it big (a very young Lauryn Hill started out here—and didn't win!). 253 W. 125th St. (btwn Adam Clayton Powell and Frederick Douglass boulevards). ℂ 212/531-5300 or 212/531-5301. www.apollo theater.com. Subway: 1, 9 to 125th St.

Brooklyn Academy of Music *Finds*   BAM is the city's most renowned contemporary arts institution, presenting cutting-edge theater, opera, dance, and music. Offerings have included historically informed presentations of baroque opera by William Christie and Les Arts Florissants; pop opera from Lou Reed; Marianne Faithfull singing the music of Kurt Weill; dance by Mark Morris and Mikhail Baryshnikov; the Philip Glass ensemble accompanying screenings of *Koyannisqatsi* and Lugosi's original *Dracula;* the Royal Dramatic Theater of Sweden directed by Ingmar Bergman; and many more experimental works by both renowned and lesser-known international artists as well as visiting companies from all over the world.

Of particular note is the **Next Wave Festival,** September through December, this country's foremost showcase for new experimental works (see the "New York City Calendar of Events," in chapter 3). The **BAM Rose Cinemas** show first-run independent films, and there's free live music every Thursday, Friday, and Saturday night at **BAMcafé,** which can range from atmospheric electronica from cornetist Graham

Lincoln Center

W. 66th St.

The Rose Building

Walter Reade Theater

The Juilliard School

Alice Tully Hall

Broadway

W. 65th St.

NY Public Library for the Performing Arts
Vivian Beaumont/ Mitzi E. Newhouse Theaters

Avery Fisher Hall

Amsterdam Avenue

Columbus Avenue

W. 64th St.

Metropolitan Opera House

W. 63rd St.

DAMROSCH PARK

Guggenheim Bandshell

New York State Theater

W. 62nd St.

0   100 y
0   100 m
N
M Subway stop

Haynes to radical jazz from the Harold Rubin Trio to the tango band Tanguardia! ($10 food minimum). Inquire about the gospel brunch on select Sundays from 2 to 4pm. 30 Lafayette Ave. (off Flatbush Ave.), Brooklyn. © 718/636-4100. www.bam.org. Subway: 2, 3, 4, 5, M, N, Q, R, W to Pacific St./Atlantic Ave.

Carnegie Hall 🎭🎭 Perhaps the world's most famous performance space, Carnegie Hall offers everything from grand classics to the music of Ravi Shankar. The **Isaac Stern Auditorium,** the 2,804-seat main hall, welcomes visiting orchestras from across the country and the world. Many of the world's premier soloists and ensembles give recitals. The legendary hall is both visually and acoustically brilliant; don't miss an opportunity to experience it if there's something on that interests you.

There's also the intimate 268-seat **Weill Recital Hall,** usually used to showcase chamber music and vocal and instrumental recitals. Carnegie Hall has also, after being occupied by a movie theater for 38 years, reclaimed the ornate underground 650-seat **Zankel Concert Hall.** For last-minute ticket-buying tips, see the box on p. 354. 881 Seventh Ave. (at 57th St.). © 212/247-7800. www.carnegiehall.org. Subway: B, N, Q, R to 57th St.

Lincoln Center for the Performing Arts New York is the world's premier performing arts city, and Lincoln Center is its premier institution. Whenever you're planning an evening's entertainment, check the offerings here—which can include opera,

Jazz at Lincoln Center Not at Lincoln Center

I'm usually a stickler for accuracy, but I'll make an exception for **Jazz at Lincoln Center,** which can no longer be found at Lincoln Center. As of the fall of 2004, JALC moved a few blocks south to the Time Warner Center at Broadway and 60th Street on Columbus Circle (© **212/258-9800;** www.jalc.org). Though the move was slightly downtown, this was definitely a move up. Its complex on the fourth floor of Time Warner's northern tower features two amazing performance spaces, a jazz club, a mini jazz hall of fame, and a 7,000-square-foot atrium with views of Central Park.

The largest of the three venues is the **Rose Theater,** where you might see the Lincoln Center Jazz Orchestra, led by Wynton Marsalis, performing the swing music of Thad Jones. Acoustics are perfect and seating is spacious. The glittering jewel of the Center, however, is the **Allen Room** with its 4,500-square-foot glass backdrop behind the main stage offering glittering views of Central Park and the Manhattan night sky. Hard to believe that what was once played in smoky basements is now presented in venues as spectacular and opulent as these.

Also at Jazz at Lincoln Center is **Dizzy's Club Coca-Cola** (© **212/258-9598;** p. 367), a stylish, intimate jazz club open every day.

---

dance, symphonies, jazz, theater, film, and more, from the classics to the contemporary. Lincoln Center's many buildings serve as permanent homes to their own companies as well as major stops for world-class performance troupes from around the globe.

Resident companies include the following: The **Chamber Music Society of Lincoln Center** (© **212/875-5788;** www.chambermusicsociety.org) performs at Alice Tully Hall or the Daniel and Joanna S. Rose Rehearsal Studio, often in the company of such high-caliber guests as Anne Sofie von Otter and Midori. The **Film Society of Lincoln Center** (© **212/875-5600;** www.filmlinc.com) screens a daily schedule of movies at the Walter Reade Theater, and hosts a number of important annual film and video festivals as well as the Reel to Real program for kids, pairing silent screen classics with live performance. **Lincoln Center Theater** (© **212/362-7600;** www.lct.org) consists of the Vivian Beaumont Theater, a modern and comfortable venue with great sightlines that has been home to much good Broadway drama, and the Mitzi E. Newhouse Theater, a well-respected Off-Broadway house that has also boasted numerous theatrical triumphs. Past seasons have included excellent productions of Tom Stoppard's *Arcadia, Carousel* in revival, and David Hare's one-man show, *Via Dolorosa.*

For details on the **Metropolitan Opera,** the **New York City Opera,** the **New York City Ballet,** the **Juilliard School,** the phenomenal **New York Philharmonic,** and the **American Ballet Theatre,** which takes up residence here every spring, see "Opera, Classical Music & Dance," earlier in this chapter.

Most of the companies' **major seasons** run from about September or October to April, May, or June. **Special series** like Great Performers and the new American Songbook, showcasing classic American show tunes, help round out the calendar. Indoor and outdoor events are held in warmer months: Summer kicks off with the **JVC Jazz Festival** in June; July sees **Midsummer Night's Swing,** with partner dancing, lessons, and music on the plaza; August's **Mostly Mozart** attracts talents like Alicia de Larrocha and André Watts; **Lincoln Center Festival** celebrates the best of the performing arts; **Lincoln Center Out-of-Doors** is a series of free alfresco music and dance performances; there's also the **New York Film Festival,** and more. Check the "New York City Calendar of Events" section, in chapter 3, or Lincoln Center's website to see what special events will be on while you're in town.

Tickets for all performances at Avery Fisher and Alice Tully halls can be purchased through **CenterCharge** (© **212/721-6500**) or online at www.lincolncenter.org (click on "Event Calendar"). Tickets for all Lincoln Center Theater performances can be purchased thorough **TeleCharge** (© **212/239-6200;** www.telecharge.com). Tickets for New York State Theater productions (New York City Opera and Ballet companies) are available through **Ticketmaster** (© **212/307-4100;** www.ticketmaster.com), while tickets for films showing at the Walter Reade Theater can be bought up to 7 days in advance by calling © **212/496-3809.** For last-minute ticket-buying tips, see the box on p. 354.

Lincoln Center is also home to the **New York Public Library for the Performing Arts** (© **212/870-1630;** www.nypl.org), which is now reopened after a major renovation.

Offered daily, 1-hour **guided tours** of Lincoln Center tell the story of the great performing arts complex, and even offer glimpses of rehearsals; call © **212/875-5350.** 70 Lincoln Center Plaza (at Broadway and 64th St.). © **212/546-2656** or 212/875-5456. www.lincoln center.org. Subway: 1, 9 to 66th St.

Madison Square Garden U2, Springsteen, The Stones, Lauryn Hill, and other monsters of rock and pop regularly fill this 20,000-seat arena, which is also home to the Knicks, the Rangers, and the WNBA's Liberty. A cavernous concrete hulk, it's better suited to sports than to concerts, or in-the-round events such as the Ice Capades,

---

Moments Music Under New York

The noise of honking horns, car alarms, and sirens are not the only sounds you will hear in your travels around Manhattan. Music is everywhere. In the warm weather, a trumpet player or violinist will set up at a busy corner and play for hours. In the winter musicians head into subway stations, where, legally, they are not allowed to play, but I've rarely seen the law enforced. Many are very good, while others, well, are just trying to make a few bucks. Some of the very good ones, who actually audition for the opportunity, perform under a program sponsored by the New York Metropolitan Transit Authority (MTA) called "Music Under New York." If selected, they can perform legally at designated subway stations, including Times Square/42nd Street, 34th Street/Sixth Avenue, 14th Street/Union Square, and 59th Street/Columbus Circle. In the summer, there is a Music Under New York festival at Grand Central Station and Bowling Green Park. The variety of music is amazing and the quality as good as you might see at some of New York's clubs. In subway stations I've heard gospel, blues, Cajun, Dixieland jazz, Andean, Brazilian drumming, rumba, and my favorite, doo-wop, the original sound of the New York subways. So take a few moments before boarding your train and listen to the music. For more information, visit the MTA website (www.mta.nyc.ny.us/mta/aft/muny.htm).

Park It! Shakespeare, Music & Other Free Fun

As the weather warms, New York culture comes outdoors to play in the city's parks.

Shakespeare in the Park, a New York institution since 1957, is as much a part of a New York summer as fireworks on the Fourth of July. The outdoor free event at the open-air Delacorte Theater in Central Park was the brainchild of the late Joseph Papp, former director of the Public Theater. Budget cuts in the last few years have reduced the number of shows offered to one, usually a revival of a Shakespeare play featuring a large company, including at least one or more "names" from film or television. The production runs from the end of June to early August. Depending on the star power of the cast, tickets can be quite scarce. In years past, *Much Ado About Nothing* featured Jimmy Smits, Sam Waterston, and Kristen Johnston; Morgan Freeman and Tracey Ullman starred in *Taming of the Shrew;* and Patrick Stewart starred in *The Tempest,* which later graduated to a successful Broadway run.

Summer 2004 brought a new program to the Delacorte, with 2 weeks of musical performances, called **Joe's Pub in the Park,** an outdoor version of the shows at Joe's Pub, the intimate musical venue at the Public Theater.

The Delacorte Theater itself, next to Belvedere Castle near 79th Street and West Drive, is a dream—on a starry night, there's no better stage in town. Tickets are distributed at the theater free on a first-come, first-served basis (two per person), at 1pm on the day of the performance. The Delacorte might have 1,881 seats, but each is a hot commodity; whatever the show, people line up next to the theater 2 to 3 hours in advance (even earlier if a big name is involved). You can also pick up same-day tickets between 1 and 3pm at the Public Theater, at 425 Lafayette St. For more information, call the Public Theater at ✆ **212/539-8750** or the Delacorte at ✆ **212/861-7277,** or visit www.publictheater.org.

Ringling Bros. and Barnum & Bailey Circus, or the International Cat Show. If you end up with seats in the back, you better have binoculars.

You'll find far better sightlines at the **Theater at Madison Square Garden,** an amphitheater-style auditorium with 5,600 seats that has also played host to some major pop stars, from Barbra Streisand to Bob Dylan. Watch for annual stagings of *The Wizard of Oz; A Christmas Carol;* and family shows such as *Sesame Street Live.* Newest at MSG is the **Comedy Garden** (www.comedygarden.com), the Garden's own comedy club at the Theater, where talent runs the gamut from well-known local comics to Robin Williams and Joan Rivers.

The box office is located at Seventh Avenue and 32nd Street. Or you can purchase tickets through **Ticketmaster** (✆ 212/307-7171; www.ticketmaster.com). On Seventh Ave. from 31st to 33rd sts. ✆ 212/465-MSG1. www.thegarden.com. Subway: A, C, E, 1, 2, 3, 9 to 34th St.

92nd Street Y Tisch Center for the Arts *(Value)* This generously endowed community center offers a phenomenal slate of top-rated cultural happenings, from classical to folk to jazz to world music to cabaret to lyric theater and literary readings. Just

Free concerts by the **New York Philharmonic** and the **Metropolitan Opera** are held beneath the stars on Central Park's Great Lawn and in parks throughout the five boroughs. For schedules, call the Philharmonic at ℂ **212/ 875-5656** or the Metropolitan Opera at ℂ **212/362-6000.** The Philharmonic maintains a list of their upcoming gigs at www.newyorkphilharmonic.org; look under "Attend Concerts."

The most active music stage in Central Park, however, is **SummerStage,** at Rumsey Playfield, midpark around 72nd Street. SummerStage has featured everyone from James Brown to Patti Smith; recent offerings have included concerts by Hugh Masekela, the Jon Spencer Blues Explosion, and Marianne Faithfull; "Viva, Verdi!" festival performances by the New York Grand Opera; cabaret nights; and more. The season usually lasts from mid-June to August. While some big-name shows charge admission, tickets aren't usually required but donations are always accepted. Call the hot line at ℂ **212/ 360-2777** or visit www.summerstage.org.

Beyond Central Park, more free outdoor fun includes the **Bryant Park Summer Film Festival,** held in Bryant Park, just behind the main branch of the New York Public Library, at Sixth Avenue between 41st and 42nd streets. Every Monday night a classic film—think *Dr. Zhivago* or *Viva Las Vegas*—is shown on a large screen under the stars. The lawn is open at 5pm for blankets and picnicking; the movie starts at dusk (about 8 or 9pm). Rain dates are Tuesdays. For the schedule and more information, call ℂ **212/512-5700.**

The calendar of free events heats up throughout the city's parks in summertime. You can find out what's happening by calling the **Parks and Recreation Special Events Hot Line** at ℂ **888/NY-PARKS** or 212/360-3456, or pointing your browser to **www.nycgovparks.org.**

because it's the "Y," don't think this place is small potatoes: Great classical performers—Isaac Stern, Janos Starker, Nadja Salerno-Sonnenberg—give recitals here. In addition, the full concert calendar often includes luminaries such as Max Roach, John Williams, and Judy Collins; Jazz at the Y from Dick Hyman and guests; the long-standing Chamber Music at the Y series; the classical Music from the Jewish Spirit series; and regular cabaret programs. The lectures and literary readings calendar is unparalleled, with featured speakers ranging from Lorne Michaels to David Halberstam to Ralph Nader to Katie Couric to Erica Jong to Ken Burns to Elie Wiesel to Alan Dershowitz to A. S. Byatt to . . . the list goes on and on. There's a regular schedule of modern dance, too, through the Harkness Dance Project. Best of all, readings and lectures are usually priced between $20 and $30 for nonmembers, dance is usually $20, and concert tickets generally go for $15 to $50—half or a third of what you'd pay at comparable venues. Additionally, a full calendar of entertainment targeted to the culturally aware in their 20s and 30s—from poetry readings to film screenings to live music, including the debut of a very young Norah Jones—is offered at the Upper

West Side community center **Makor.** 1395 Lexington Ave. (at 92nd St.). ℭ 212/415-5500. www.92ndsty.org. Subway: 4, 5, 6 to 86th St.; 6 to 96th St. **Makor:** 35 W. 67th St. ℭ 212/601-1000. www.makor.org. Subway: 1, 9 to 66th St.

Radio City Music Hall   This stunning 6,200-seat Art Deco theater, with interior design by Donald Deskey, opened in 1932, and legendary Radio City continues to be a choice venue, where the theater alone adds a dash of panache to any performance. Star of the Christmas season is the **Radio City Music Hall Christmas Spectacular,** starring the legendary Rockettes. Visiting pop chart-toppers, from Neil Young to the Gipsy Kings, also perform here. Thanks to perfect acoustics and uninterrupted sight-lines, there's hardly a bad seat in the house. The theater also hosts dance performances; family entertainment; a number of annual awards shows, such as the Essence Awards, the GQ Man of the Year Awards, and anything MTV is holding in town; and in 2004, the WNBA New York Liberty played a few select games here. 1260 Sixth Ave. (at 50th St.). ℭ **212/247-4777,** or 212/307-7171 for Ticketmaster. www.radiocity.com or www.ticketmaster.com. Subway: B, D, F, V to 49th–50th sts./Rockefeller Center.

Symphony Space ℟ *Finds*   An eclectic mix of culture can be found at this Upper West Side institution that was renovated in 2002. The variety of shows at the **Peter Jay Sharp Theater** include music, with series by the World Music Institute as well as classical, rock, and blues; dance, with marathon tributes to choreographers like George Balanchine to original creations of Israeli Zvi Gotheiner; literature, such as the selected shorts series introduced by writers such as Susan Orleans, Edwidge Danticant, and Walter Mosely; and family, with performances by folk singer Tom Chapin, and the Putuyamo Kids. Adjacent to the Sharp Theater is the **Leonard Nimoy Thalia Theater;** the film revival house that was known for its quirky sightlines was rescued by none other than Mr. Spock and has now been totally renovated. Though I'm sure it is much more comfortable now, I'll miss having to peer around a pole to watch a movie like *Plan Nine from Outer Space.* 2537 Broadway (at 95th St.). ℭ **212/864-1414.** www.symphonyspace.org. Subway: 1, 2, 3, 9 to 96th St.

Town Hall   This intimate landmark theater—a National Historic Site designed by McKim, Mead & White—is blessed with outstanding acoustics, making it an ideal place to enjoy many kinds of performances, including theater, dance, lectures, drama, comedy, film, and pop and world music. The calendar regularly includes such offerings as American tap and Brazilian tango exhibitions; Native American music and global rhythms; comedy from the *Kids in the Hall* Reunion Tour or Eddie Izzard; live tapings of "A Prairie Home Companion" with Garrison Keillor or spoken word from Al Franken; lectures by luminaries such as Marianne Williamson and Frank Gehry; concerts by the likes of David Sanborn or the reunited Blondie; symphony, opera, and ballet companies from around the world; and much more. The grade is extremely steep, so unless Yao Ming sits in front of you, fellow audience members shouldn't block your view. 123 W. 43rd St. (btwn Sixth and Seventh aves.). ℭ **212/840-2824,** or 212/307-4100 for Ticketmaster. www.the-townhall-nyc.org or www.ticketmaster.com. Subway: N, Q, R, S, W, 1, 2, 3, 7, 9 to 42nd St./Times Sq.; B, D, F, V to 42nd St.

4 Live Rock, Jazz, Blues & More

I discuss the top venues, both large and small, below. But there are far more than these, and new ones are popping up all the time. For the latest, be sure to check the

Tips   Ticket-Buying Tips

Tickets for events at all larger theaters as well as at Hammerstein Ballroom, Roseland, Irving Plaza, B.B. King's, and S.O.B.'s can be purchased through **Ticketmaster** (© **212/307-7171;** www.ticketmaster.com).

Advance tickets for an increasing number of shows at smaller venues—including CBGB, Bowery Ballroom, Mercury Lounge, and Village Underground—can be purchased through **Ticketweb** (© **866/468-7619;** www.ticketweb.com). Do note, however, that Ticketweb can sell out in advance of actual ticket availability. Just because Ticketweb doesn't have tickets left for an event doesn't mean it's completely sold out, so be sure to check with the venue directly.

Even a sold-out show doesn't mean you're out of luck. There are usually a number of people hanging around at show time trying to get rid of extra tickets for friends who didn't show, and they're usually happy to pass them off for face value. You'll also see professional scalpers, who often peddle forgeries and are best avoided—it doesn't take a rocket scientist to tell the difference. Be aware, of course, that all forms of resale are illegal.

---

publications discussed in the introduction to this chapter as well as the online sources outlined in "Online Sources for Live Music Fans," below.

LARGER VENUES

For coverage of **Madison Square Garden,** the **Theater at MSG,** and **Town Hall,** see "Major Concert Halls & Landmark Venues," earlier in this chapter.

Beacon Theatre   This pleasing midsize Upper West Side venue—a 1928 Art Deco movie palace with an impressive lobby, stairway, and auditorium seating about 2,700—hosts mainly pop music performances, usually for the over-30 crowd. Featured acts have ranged from street-smart pop diva Sheryl Crow to handsome-as-ever Bryan Ferry to befuddled Beach Boy Brian Wilson to Grateful Dead heirs apparent Phish to not-yet-deads the Allman Brothers. You'll also find such special events as the bodybuilding "Night of Champions" on the mix-and-match calendar. 2124 Broadway (at 74th St.). © 212/496-7070. www.livetonight.com. Subway: 1, 2, 3, 9 to 72nd St.

Roseland   This old warhorse of a venue, a 1919 ballroom gone to seed, has been under threat of the wrecking ball for years now. Everybody has played at this too-huge-for-its-own-good 2,500-capacity general-admission hall, from Marc Anthony to Fiona Apple to Busta Rhymes to Smashmouth to Rage Against the Machine to Jeff Beck. Bands who tend to inspire mosh pits like to book here (think Nine Inch Nails, The Offspring) because there's plenty of space for slamming and surfing at the front of the stage. Thankfully, there's also lots of room to steer clear and still enjoy the show. Advance tickets can be purchased at the **Irving Plaza** box office (p. 364) without the service fee that Ticketmaster charges. Take a moment on your way through the lobby to check out the cases memorializing Roseland's postwar heydays as the city's premier dance hall. Ballroom dancing still takes place Sundays from 2:30 to 10pm; admission is $10. 239 W. 52nd St. (btwn Broadway and Eighth Ave.). © 212/247-0200, or 212/307-7171 for Ticketmaster. www.roselandballroom.com or www.livetonight.com. Subway: C, E, 1, 9 to 50th St.

MIDSIZE & MULTIGENRE VENUES

Also see what's on at the stellar **Joe's Pub** (p. 369), a top-flight cabaret that hosts intimate shows by pop acts.

B.B. King Blues Club & Grill   This 550-seat venue is one of the prime anchors of Times Square's "new" 42nd Street. Despite its name, B.B. King's seldom sticks to the blues; instead, what you're likely to find is a bill full of familiar pop, funk, and rock names, mainly from the past. The big-ticket talent runs the gamut from the George Clinton and the P. Funk All Stars, and John Mayall and the Bluesbreakers to Tower of Power to Jimmy Cliff and Delbert McClinton. A few more (relatively) esoteric acts take the stage on occasion, such as "An Intimate Evening with Donny Osmond" and surf guitarist Dick Dale. Tourist-targeted pricing makes for a very expensive night on the town, word is that the food isn't as good as it was in the beginning, and seating policies can be terribly convoluted, but there's no arguing with the quality of the talent. The Sunday gospel lunch is a genuine slice of joy. 237 W. 42nd St. (btwn Seventh and Eighth aves.). ✆ **212/997-4144**, or 212/307-7171 for tickets. www.bbkingblues.com. Subway: A, C, E, Q, W, 1, 2, 3, 7, 9 to 42nd St.

Bowery Ballroom   Run by the same people behind the **Mercury Lounge** (see below), the Bowery space is bigger, accommodating a crowd of 500 or so, and even better. The stage is big and raised to allow good sightlines from every corner. The sound couldn't be better, and Art Deco details give the place a sophistication that doesn't come easy to general-admission halls. The balcony has its own bar and seating alcoves. This place is a favorite with alt-rockers like Vic Chesnutt, Travis, Steve Earle, Rinocerose, The Delgados, and the marvelous Toshi Reagon, as well as more established acts (Neil Finn, Patti Smith), who thrive in an intimate setting. Save on the service charge by buying advance tickets at Mercury's box office. 6 Delancey St. (at Bowery). ✆ **212/533-2111**. www.boweryballroom.com. Subway: F, J, M, Z to Delancey St.

Irving Plaza   This high-profile midsize music hall is the prime stop for national-name rock bands that aren't quite big enough yet (or anymore) to sell out Hammerstein, Roseland, or the Beacon. Think Five for Fighting, the Eels, Jars of Clay, Badly Drawn Boy, the Reverend Horton Heat, the resurrected Television, Kenny Wayne Shepherd, Cowboy Junkies, and Cheap Trick. From time to time, big-name artists also perform—Bob Dylan, Trent Reznor, and A. J. McLean of the Backstreet Boys have all played "secret" shows here. All in all, a very nice place to see a show, with a well-elevated stage and lots of open space even on sold-out nights. There's an upstairs balcony

---

Online Sources for Live Music Fans

These websites are your top online sources for live music schedules:

- **Live Tonight:** www.livetonight.com
- **Metropolitan Concert Hot Line:** www.concerthotline.com
- **Clear Channel Entertainment:** www.cc.com
- **Ticketmaster:** www.ticketmaster.com

   Additionally, Web sources **Citysearch (www.citysearch.com),** *Time Out New York* **(www.timeoutny.com),** and all of the hard-copy resources (and their corresponding websites) listed at the start of this chapter offer a wealth of live-music listings.

that offers unparalleled views, but come early for a spot. 17 Irving Place (1 block west of Third Ave. at 15th St.). ✆ **212/777-1224** or 212/777-6800. www.irvingplaza.com. Subway: L, N, R, 4, 5, 6 to 14th St./Union Sq.

The Knitting Factory   New York's premier avant-garde music venue has four separate spaces, each showcasing performances ranging from experimental jazz and acoustic folk to spoken-word and poetry readings to out-there multimedia works. Regulars who use the Knitting Factory as their lab of choice include former Lounge Lizard John Lurie; around-the-bend experimentalist John Zorn; guitar gods Vernon Reid, Eliot Sharp, and David Torn; innovative sideman (to Tom Waits and Elvis Costello, among others) Marc Ribot; and Television's Richard Lloyd. (If these names mean nothing to you, chances are good that The Knitting Factory is not for you.) The schedule is peppered with edgy star turns from the likes of Yoko Ono, Taj Mahal, Faith No More's Mike Patton, and Lou Reed. There are often two show times a night in the remarkably pleasing main performance space, so it's easy to work a show around other activities. The Old Office Lounge offers an extensive list of microbrews and free live entertainment. 74 Leonard St. (btwn Broadway and Church St.). ✆ **212/219-3132.** www.knitting factory.com. Subway: 1, 9 to Franklin St.

(MOSTLY) ROCK CLUBS

Live music at rock clubs usually begins around 9pm, but check the sources listed at the beginning of this chapter for up-to-date starting times and prices.

In addition to the choices below, rock fans on the hunt for diamonds in the rough might also want to see what's on at folk rock's legendary **Bitter End,** 147 Bleecker St., between Thompson and LaGuardia streets in the heart of the Village (✆ **212/673-7030;** www.bitterend.com).

Arlene Grocery   This casual Lower East Side club boasts a friendly bar and a good sound system; unfortunately, music isn't always free anymore, but the quality of the artists is usually pretty high, and the cover usually tops out at $7. Arlene Grocery primarily serves as a showcase for hot bands looking for a deal or promoting their self-pressed record. The crowd is an easygoing mix of club-hoppers, rock fans looking for a new fix, and industry scouts looking for new blood. 95 Stanton St. (btwn Ludlow and Orchard sts.). ✆ **212/995-1652.** Subway: F to Second Ave.

The Baggot Inn *Value*   This easygoing pub has become one of the best showcases in the city for unknown acts, especially if you like quality acoustic and folk-rock music. Blues, Irish music, poetry, acoustic jams, and open-mic nights also regularly pop up on the calendar. The cover is always bargain-priced; happy hour until 7pm and nightly drink specials round out the entertainment value. 82 W. 3rd St. (btwn Thompson and Sullivan sts., below the Boston Comedy Club). ✆ **212/477-0622.** www.thebaggotinn.com. Cover free to $5. Subway: A, C, E, F, or V to W. 4th St.

Mercury Lounge   The Merc is everything a top-notch live music venue should be: unpretentious, extremely civilized, and outfitted with a killer sound system. The rooms themselves are nothing special: a front bar and an intimate back-room performance space with a low stage and a few tables along the wall. The calendar is filled with a mix of accomplished local rockers and national acts like Fat Possum, the Mekons, and Sleepy Jackson. The crowd is grown-up and easygoing. The only downside is that it's consistently packed thanks to the high quality of the entertainment and all-around pleasing nature of the experience. 217 E. Houston St. (at Essex St./Ave. A). ✆ **212/ 260-4700.** www.mercuryloungenyc.com. Subway: F to Second Ave.

Rodeo Bar *(Value* Here's New York's oldest—and finest—honky-tonk. Hike up your Wranglers and head those Fryes inside, where you'll find longhorns on the walls, peanut shells underfoot, first-class margaritas at the bar, and Tex-Mex on the menu. But this place is really about the music: urban-tinged country, foot-stompin' bluegrass, swinging rockabilly, Southern-flavored rock. Bigger names like Brian Setzer and up-and-comers on the tour circuit like Hank Williams III occasionally grace the stage, but regular acts like the Dixieland Swingers, the Flying Neutrinos, cowpunk goddess Rosie Flores, and the good-time BBQ Bob and the Spareribs usually supply free music, keeping the urban cowboys plenty happy. A 10-gallon hat full o' fun. It's happy hour until 7pm; the music starts around 9:30pm nightly, and goes till at least 3am. 375 Third Ave. (at 27th St.). © 212/683-6500. www.rodeobar.com. Subway: 6 to 28th St.

Tonic *(Finds* This intimate, Lower East Side, loftlike space attracts seekers of the alternative in both jazz and rock. But as of this writing, its survival was in peril and money was being raised to keep it alive. If it does survive and if you like your music challenging, to say the least, this is the Tonic for you. Most of the performers are far from household names, but avant-garde artists such as John Zorn, Marc Ribot, Sonic Youth, and Ravi Coltrane occasionally appear on the calendar. Cover is only $8 to $10. 107 Norfolk St. (btwn Rivington and Delancey sts.). © 212/358-7501. www.tonicnyc.com. Subway: F, J to Delancey St.

JAZZ, BLUES, LATIN & WORLD MUSIC

Be aware that a night at a top-flight jazz club can be expensive. Cover charges can vary dramatically—from as little as $10 to as high as $65, depending on who's taking the stage—and there is likely to be an additional two-drink minimum (or a dinner requirement, if you choose an early show). Call ahead so you know what you're getting into; reservations are also an excellent idea at top spots.

For those of you who like your jazz with an edge, see what's on at **The Knitting Factory** (p. 365). Swingsters should consider **Swing 46** (p. 385). Weekends at **Carnegie Club** (p. 377) are ideal for Sinatra fans looking to relive the moment.

Despite its name, **B.B. King Blues Club & Grill** extends well beyond the blues genre to embrace over-the-hill acts of just about any ilk, from Morris Day and the Time to Blue Oyster Cult. Still, the venerable bluesman does take the stage from time to time, so you might want to see what's on; turn to p. 364.

You might also consider **Jazz at the Kitano,** in the mezzanine of the Kitano Hotel, 66 Park Ave., at 38th Street (© 212/885-7119; www.kitano.com), for some first-rate jazz in a casual, comfortable setting. **The Kitchen,** 512 W. 19th St., between Tenth and Eleventh avenues (© 212/255-5793; www.thekitchen.org), has a full slate of live music and performance art. In association with the 92nd Street Y, **Makor** (p. 362) offers a similarly eclectic mix, as does **Joe's Pub** (p. 369), which adds a cabaret spin.

There's also world-beat jazz every Friday and Saturday from 5 to 8pm in the rotunda at the **Guggenheim Museum;** see chapter 9. And don't forget **Jazz at Lincoln Center,** the nation's premier forum for the traditional and developing jazz canon; see p. 358.

Birdland This legendary club abandoned its distant uptown roost in 1996 for a more convenient Midtown nest, where it has established itself once again as one of the city's premier jazz spots. While the legend of Parker, Monk, Gillespie, and other bebop pioneers still holds sway, this isn't a crowded, smoky joint of yesteryear. The big room is spacious, comfy, and classy, with an excellent sound system and a top-notch talent roster any night of the week. Expect lots of accomplished big bands and jazz trios, plus occasional appearances by stars like Pat Metheny and Dave Brubeck. You can't go wrong with the regular Sunday night show, starring Chico O'Farrell's smokin' Afro-Cuban Jazz Big Band. At press time, Tuesday was the domain of the Duke Ellington Orchestra, led by Duke's grandson Paul Ellington every other week. 315 W. 44th St. (btwn Eighth and Ninth aves.). © 212/581-3080. www.birdlandjazz.com. Subway: A, C, E to 42nd St.

Blue Note   The Blue Note has attracted some of the biggest names in jazz to its intimate setting. Those who've played here include just about everyone of note: Dave Brubeck, Ray Charles, B. B. King, Manhattan Transfer, Dr. John, George Duke, Chick Corea, David Sanborn, Arturo Sandoval, Gato Barbieri, and the superb Oscar Peterson. The sound system is excellent, and every seat in the house has a sightline to the stage, however, in recent years, the hard edge that once was the Blue Note has faded. Softer, smoother jazz is the domain now so if that's your thing, enjoy. But be warned: Prices are astronomical. There are two shows per night, and dinner is served. 131 W. 3rd St. (at Sixth Ave.). © 212/475-8592. www.bluenote.net. Subway: A, B, C, D, E, F, V to W. 4th St.

Dizzy's Club Coca-Cola ♣   This beautiful, cozy new jazz club is part of the Jazz at Lincoln Center complex in the Time Warner Center on Columbus Circle. Acoustics and sightlines are excellent and, though not nearly as dramatic as the window in the complex's Allen Room, there is a window behind the stage with views of Central Park and the city. The club attracts an interesting mix of both up-and-coming and established bands. Every Monday the club features the Upstarts, a student showcase from local schools including Juilliard and the Manhattan School of Music. My only complaint is the high $30 cover every day of the week—even for the Upstarts. Time Warner Center, 60th Street and Broadway. © 212/258-9598. www.jalc.org. Subway: A, B, C, D, 1, 9 to Columbus Circle.

Iridium   This well-respected and snazzily designed jazz club has relocated from its longtime perch across from Lincoln Center to an even better heart-of-the–Theater District location. Everything else remains the same, including the accomplished talent and big-name acts that always take the stage. Like the Energizer bunny, Les Paul keeps on going, still playing every Monday night while the very popular Mingus Big Band makes Iridium their home each Tuesday. Other top-notch performers who often appear include Jackie McLean, Mose Allison, McCoy Tyner, and saxophonist Houston Person. A full, rather sophisticated dinner menu is served. 1650 Broadway (at 51st St.). © 212/582-2121. www.iridiumjazzclub.com. Subway: 1, 9 to 50th St.

Jazz at the Cajun   This cozy, rather casual New Orleans–themed supper club is the best venue in town for genuine prewar big band and Dixieland jazz—think Jelly Roll Morton, Scott Joplin, early Duke. The fanatical crowd comes from all walks of life, united in their love of the old school. The place jumps no matter what top-notch crew takes the stage. The food is affordable and just fine; be sure to reserve in advance. 129 Eighth Ave. (btwn 16th and 17th sts.). © 212/691-6174. www.jazzatthecajun.com. Subway: A, C, E, L to 14th St.

Jazz Standard ♣   Kudos to the Jazz Standard, where both the food and music meet all expectations. Boasting a sophisticated retro-speakeasy vibe, the Jazz Standard is one of the city's largest jazz clubs, with well-spaced tables seating 150 and a reasonable $15 to $25 cover. The rule is straightforward, mainstream jazz by new and established musicians, including such stars as Branford Marsalis. On Sunday afternoons, the club features a Jazz for Kids program. A limited menu from Danny Meyer's barbecue joint, **Blue Smoke** (p. 197), located upstairs, is available. Jazz, blues, and barbecue—hard to go wrong with that. 116 E. 27th St. (btwn Park Ave. South and Lexington Ave.). ℂ 212/576-2232. www.jazzstandard.net. Subway: 6 to 28th St.

Lenox Lounge This beautifully renovated classic is a symbol of Harlem's current renaissance. The intimate, Art Deco–cool back room—complete with zebra stripes on the walls and built-in banquettes—hosts top-flight live jazz vocalists, trios, and quartets for a crowd that comes to listen and be wowed. Blues and R&B are the province of Thursday. The cover never goes higher than $15, which makes Lenox Lounge a good value to boot. There's a warm, cozy, and immensely popular bar up front. Good soul food is served. Well worth the trip uptown for those who want a genuine Harlem jazz experience. 288 Malcolm X Blvd. (Lenox Ave.; btwn 124th and 125th sts.). ℂ 212/427-0253. www.lenoxlounge.com. Subway: 2, 3 to 125th St.

St. Nick's Pub 🖈 *Finds* As unpretentious a club as you'll find, St. Nick's in Harlem's Sugar Hill district is the real deal, with live entertainment every night and never a cover. On Tuesday, it's Oldies but Goodies provided by Sexy Charles and Poetry on the Hill, hosted by Chance & Lilah; all the other nights are devoted to jazz, straight up and rarely with a chaser. 773 St. Nicholas Ave. (at 149th St.). ℂ 212/283-9728. Subway: A, C, D, B to 145th St.

Satalla 🖈 *Finds* Satalla was a hit the moment it opened in late 2003. Intimate and innovative, Satalla does a great job of finding hidden (at least hidden from most U.S. audiences) talent from across the globe. The diversity of music that can be heard on any given night is staggering. Flamenco, Klezmer, Celtic, Middle-Eastern jazz, Afro-Cuban, and Quebecois are examples of just some of the music you might hear at the club. The room is cozy and sometimes the performers can get cheerily up close and personal with the crowd—and vice versa. Most nights there is no admission charge but there is always a $10 drink or food minimum. 37 W. 26th St. (btwn Sixth Ave. and Broadway). ℂ 212/576-1155. www.satalla.com. Subway: F to 23rd St.

Smoke 🖈🖈 *Value* A rising star in the New York jazz scene and the best place to hear it on the Upper West Side, Smoke is a welcome throwback to the informal, intimate clubs of the past—the kind of place that on most nights you can just walk in and experience some solid jazz. And though it seats only 65, for no more than a $25 cover, Smoke still manages to attract big names like the Steve Turre Quartet, Ron Carter, Eddie Henderson, and John Hicks. On Sunday through Thursday there is no cover and each night has a theme, including funk on Wednesdays with the rocking Hot Pants Funk Sextet, Latin jazz on Sundays, and my favorite, Hammond organ grooves on Tuesday with Mike LeDonne on the organ and the incomparable Eric Alexander on sax. There are three sets nightly and a very popular happy hour. 2751 Broadway (btwn 105th and 106th sts.). ℂ 212/864-6662. www.smokejazz.com. Subway: 1 to 103rd St.

S.O.B.'s If you like your music hot, hot, hot, visit S.O.B.'s, the city's top world-music venue, specializing in Brazilian, Caribbean, and Latin sounds. The packed house dances and sings along nightly to calypso, samba, mambo, African drums, reggae, or other global grooves, united in the high-energy, feel-good vibe. Bookings include top-flight performers from around the globe; Astrud Gilberto, Mighty Sparrow, King Sunny Ade, Eddie Palmieri, Buckwheat Zydeco, Beausoleil, and Baaba Maal are only a few of the names who have graced this lively stage. The room's Tropicana Club style has island pizazz that carries through to the Caribbean-influenced cooking and extensive tropical drinks menu. This place is so popular that it's an excellent idea to book in advance, especially if you'd like table seating. Monday is dedicated to Latin sounds, Tuesday to reggae; Friday features a late-night French Caribbean dance party, while Saturday is reserved for samba. 204 Varick St. (at Houston St.). © 212/243-4940. www.sobs.com. Subway: 1, 9 to Houston St.

The Village Vanguard ★★ What CBGB is to rock, the Village Vanguard is to jazz. One look at the photos on the walls will show you who's been through since 1935, from Coltrane, Miles, and Monk to recent appearances by Bill Charlap and Roy Hargrove. Expect a mix of established names and high-quality local talent, including the Vanguard's own jazz orchestra on Monday nights. The sound is great, but sightlines aren't, so come early for a front table. If you are looking for serious jazz, this is the place. 178 Seventh Ave. S. (just below 11th St.). © 212/255-4037. www.villagevanguard.net. Subway: 1, 2, 3, 9 to 14th St.

5 Cabaret

An evening spent at a sophisticated cabaret just might be the quintessential New York night on the town. It isn't cheap: Covers can range from $10 to $60, depending on the showroom and the act, and also require two-drink or dinner-check minimums. Always reserve ahead, and get the complete lowdown when you do.

Cafe Carlyle ★ Cabaret doesn't get any better than this. This is where the great Bobby Short, who passed away in 2005, held court for over 35 years. Without him, there will be a temporary void, but the club still attracts rarefied talents like Betty Buckley and Barbara Cook. The room is intimate and as swanky as they come. Expect a high tab—admission is $65 to $75 with a $30 per-person minimum; with dinner, two people could easily spend $300—but if you're looking for the best of the best, look no further. Value-minded cabaret fans can save by reserving standing room (which usually results in a spot at the bar) for just $35. On most Mondays, Woody Allen joins the Eddy Davis New Orleans Jazz Band on clarinet to swing Dixie style ($85 cover). At the Carlyle Hotel, 781 Madison Ave. (at 76th St.). © 212/744-1600. Closed July–Aug. Subway: 6 to 77th St.

Feinstein's at The Regency *Finds* This intimate and elegant cabaret-style nightclub is the first from Grammy-winning song impresario Michael Feinstein. Cover charges can soar, but you can count on a memorable night of first-quality dining and song, and no other cabaret merges old-school cool and hipster appeal so well. Recent high-wattage talent has included Keely Smith, Patti LuPone, and the man himself. Call ahead to reserve; you can also purchase tickets through Ticketmaster. At the Regency Hotel, 540 Park Ave. (at 61st St.). © 212/339-4095, or 212/307-4100 for Ticketmaster. www.feinsteins attheregency.com or www.ticketmaster.com. Subway: 4, 5, 6 to 59th St.

Joe's Pub Joe's Pub isn't exactly your daddy's cabaret. Still, this beautiful—and hugely popular—cabaret and supper club, eloquently named for the legendary Joseph Papp, is everything a New York cabaret should be. The multilevel space serves up an American menu and top-notch entertainment from a more eclectic mix of talent than you'll find on any other cabaret calendar. The sophisticated crowd comes for music and spoken word that ranges from operatic diva Diamanda Galas to solo shows from Broadway stars like Daphne Rubin-Vega *(Rent)* and Tom Wopat *(Annie Get Your Gun)* to first-class pop from husband-and-wife singer/songwriters Michael Penn and Aimee

Mann to modern rumba masters Los Munequitos de Matanzas. There's always jazz on the calendar, and don't be surprised if Broadway actors show up on off-nights to exercise their substantial chops. Deejays take over during the late-night hours. At the Joseph Papp Public Theater, 425 Lafayette St. (btwn Astor Place and 4th St.). (✆ 212/539-8777, or TeleCharge at 212/239-6200 (for advance tickets). www.joespub.com. Subway: 6 to Astor Place.

The Oak Room   Recently refurbished to recall its glory days, the Oak Room is one of the city's most intimate, elegant, and sophisticated spots for cabaret. Headliners include such first-rate talents as Andrea Marcovicci, Steve Ross, Dave Frishberg, the marvelous Julie Wilson, and cool-cat jazz guitarist John Pizzarelli, plus occasional lesser names that are destined for greatness. At the Algonquin Hotel, 59 W. 44th St. (btwn Fifth and Sixth aves.). (✆ 212/840-6800. Closed July–Aug. Subway: B, D, F, V to 42nd St.

6 Stand-Up Comedy

Cover charges are generally in the $8 to $20 range, with all-star Carolines going as high as $30 on occasion. Many clubs also have a two-drink minimum. Be sure to ask about the night's cover when you make reservations, which are strongly recommended, *especially* on weekends.

You might also see who's taking the stage at Madison Square Garden's laugh-a-minute offshoot, **Comedy Garden** (p. 360), where even Robin Williams books in to hone his stand-up chops every once in a while.

Carolines on Broadway   Caroline Hirsch presents today's hottest headliners in her upscale Theater District showroom, which doesn't have a bad seat in the house. You're bound to recognize at least one or two of the established names and hot up-and-comers on the bill in any given week, like Dave Chapelle, Janeane Garofalo, Colin Quinn, Bill Bellamy, Kathy Griffin, Robert Wuhl, Jimmie Walker ("Dyn-o-mite!"), Pauly Shore, or Jay Mohr. Monday is usually New Talent Night, while HOT97 radio hosts up-and-coming black comedians on select Tuesdays. 1626 Broadway (btwn 49th and 50th sts.). (✆ 212/757-4100. www.carolines.com. Subway: N, R to 49th St.; 1, 9 to 50th St.

Comedy Cellar *(Finds)*   This intimate subterranean club is the club of choice for stand-up fans in the know, thanks to the best, most consistently impressive lineups in the business. I'll always love the Comedy Cellar for introducing an uproariously funny unknown comic named Ray Romano to me some years back. 117 MacDougal St. (btwn Bleecker and W. 3rd sts.). (✆ 212/254-3480. www.comedycellar.com. Subway: A, B, C, D, E, F, S, V to W. 4th St. (use 3rd St. exit).

Dangerfield's   Dangerfield's is the nightclub version of the comedy club, with a mature crowd and a straight-outta-Vegas atmosphere. The comedians are all veterans of the comedy-club and late-night talk-show circuit. 1118 First Ave. (btwn 61st and 62nd sts.). (✆ 212/593-1650. www.dangerfieldscomedyclub.com. Subway: N, R to Lexington Ave.; 4, 5, 6 to 59th St.

Gotham Comedy Club *(Finds)*   Here's the city's trendiest, most comfortable, and most sophisticated comedy club. The young talent—Tom Rhodes, Sue Costello, Mitch Fatel, Lewis Black of the *Daily Show*—is red hot. Jerry Seinfeld has also been exercising his chops here of late. Look for theme nights like "Comedy Salsa" and "A Very Jewish Christmas." Tuesday is set aside for new talent. 34 W. 22nd St. (btwn Fifth and Sixth aves.). (✆ 212/367-9000. www.gothamcomedyclub.com. Subway: F, N, R to 23rd St.

Stand-Up New York   The Upper West Side's premier stand-up comedy club hosts some of the brightest young comics in the business, plus frequent drop-ins like Dennis

Leary, Caroline Rhea, Robin Williams, and Mr. Upper West Side himself, Jerry Sein-feld. 236 W. 78th St. (at Broadway). ℭ 212/595-0850. www.standupny.com. Subway: 1, 9 to 79th St.

Upright Citizens Brigade Theatre *Value* You've seen their twisted, highly original sketch comedy on Comedy Central—now you can see the Upright Citizens Brigade, New York's premier alternative comedy troupe, live. The best of the nonstop hilarity is ASSSSCAT 3000, the troupe's extremely popular long-form improv show, which often sells out in advance. The company has supplied a few members of the Not-Ready-For-Prime-Time Players in recent years, including Amy Poehler. Reservations are a must and tickets are a cheap 8 bucks or less. 307 W. 26th St. (btwn Eighth and Ninth aves.). ℭ 212/366-9176. www.ucbtheatre.com. Tickets $8 or less. Subway: 1 or 9 to 23rd St.

7 Bars & Cocktail Lounges

Remember: Smoking is prohibited in bars but allowed in outdoor spaces.

TRIBECA

Bubble Lounge From the first cork that popped, this wine bar dedicated to the bubbly was an effervescent hit. More than 300 champagnes and sparkling wines are served in this glamorous living-room setting, more than 30 of them by the glass, to pair with caviar, foie gras, cheese, and elegant sweets. No jeans, sneakers, or baseball caps. There' s live bluesy jazz on Monday and Tuesday. 228 W. Broadway (btwn Franklin and White sts.). ℭ 212/431-3443. www.bubblelounge.com. Subway: 1, 9 to Franklin St.

Church Lounge The big, superstylish Larry Bogdanow–designed atrium lobby bar and restaurant at the **Tribeca Grand Hotel** (p. 128) is a great place to enjoy a top-flight cocktail and rub elbows with the neighborhood's chic locals (which include just about anybody who has business with Miramax). Dress well and call ahead to see what's on tap that eveningif you want to experience the height of the action—around 11pm. 2 Sixth Ave. (at White and Church sts.). ℭ 212/519-6600. Subway: 1, 9 to Franklin St.; A, C, E to Canal St.

Walker's *Finds* Walker's is an old holdout from prefabulous TriBeCa. It's got some charm, with a tin ceiling, a long wooden bar, oldies on the sound system, and cozy tables where you can dine on good, affordable meat-and-potatoes fare. Don't get fancy with your drink orders; stick with Guinness or one of the other drafts. 16 N. Moore St. (at Varick St.). ℭ 212/941-0142. Subway: 1, 9 to Franklin St.

CHINATOWN

Double Happiness *Finds* The only indicator to the subterranean entrance is a ver-tical WATCH YOUR STEP sign. Once through the door, you'll find a beautifully designed speakeasyish lounge with artistic nods to the neighborhood throughout, plus a won-derfully low-key vibe. The space is large, but a low ceiling and intimate nooks add a hint of romance. The fabulous food is from the upstairs restaurant, Wyanoka, so this is a great place to satisfy the munchies, too. Don't miss the green tea martini, an inspired house creation. 173 Mott St. (btwn Grand and Broome sts.). ℭ 212/941-1282. Subway: 6 to Spring St.

Winnie's I usually abhor karaoke bars, but I make an exception for Winnie's. Maybe it's because I'm a sucker for Asian pop tunes or perhaps it's the "Hawaiian Punch," a sickly sweet drink that, after a couple, will have you crooning in Cantonese. Even if you don't partake in the Chinatown version of *American Idol*, you will enjoy

Cocktails Alfresco

One of my favorite moments in the movie *The Producers* is when Max Bialy-stock (played by Zero Mostel) tries to woo Leo Bloom (Gene Wilder) into helping him carry out his theater scam. Bialystock tells Bloom that he will treat him to dinner and they will dine "alfresco." The next shot is Bialystock buying a hot dog for Bloom from a street vendor near Central Park.

But food and drink always *do* taste better alfresco. Here are some of my favorite places for cocktails out of doors.

The outdoor space at rowdy **Jeremy's Ale House,** 228 Front St. (© 212/964-3537; www.jeremysalehouse.com), near the South Street Seaport, is no fairy tale, but it does have one of the best views of the Brooklyn Bridge. Maybe that's because the bar is practically under the Bridge (on the Man-hattan side). Jeremy's is so close to the river you may think you smell the sea, but what you are really smelling is an endless supply of calamari and clams sizzling in the deep fryers and gallons of Coors beer, served in 32-ounce Styrofoam cups.

Some of the best outdoor drinking can be found at a few select hotels. The best of the best, way downtown at the southern tip of Manhattan, is the **Rise Bar** at the Ritz-Carlton New York, Battery Park, 2 West St., just north of Battery Place (© 212/344-0800). Located on the 14th floor of the hotel, the bar boasts incomparable views of Lady Liberty and busy New York Harbor from the massive waterfront terrace.

For the more trendy set, where the eye candy is not just the spectacular views, take the elevator up to the top of the Hotel Gansevoort, 18 Ninth Ave., at 13th Street (© 212/206-6700) to **Plunge,** where the you can gaze out at New Jersey, inhale the chlorine fumes from the hotel's pool (which only guests can use) all the while sipping pricey cocktails. A few blocks north at the Maritime Hotel, 366 W. 17th St., at Ninth Avenue, the scene on the roof at **Cabanas** (© 212/242-4300) is like something out of Hollywood. In fact, you'll probably recognize a few Hollywood denizens sunning them-selves with colorful drinks, umbrella stirrers and all, balanced on their abnormally firm abs. Uptown, in the heart of Midtown, the **Pen-Top Bar** at the classic "grand dame," the Peninsula Hotel, 700 Fifth Ave., at 55th Street (© 212/956-2888), offers views of the glittering neighboring spires and the bustle of Fifth Avenue below that are not only calming, but romantic if that is actually possible.

One of my favorite parks is Riverside Park (see chapter 9), and two of the reasons why I love this park are the **79th Street Boat Basin Café,** 79th Street, at the Hudson River (© 212/496-5542; www.boatbasincafe.com), where you can sip a drink and watch the boats bob on the river as the sun sets, and **Hurley's Hudson Beach Café,** Riverside Park and 103rd Street (© 917/370-3448), where beach volleyball games and stunning sunsets are the enter-tainment, marred only by the constant automobile buzz of nearby West Side Highway.

others as they drunkenly embarrass themselves in the spotlight. 104 Bayard St. (btwn Baxter and Mulberry sts.). © 212/732-2384. Subway: N, R, W, W, 6 to Canal St.

THE LOWER EAST SIDE

Abaya *(Finds)*   A flight of cool new hangouts continues to energize the bar scene, and the best of the bunch is Abaya. The *Clockwork Orange*–inspired '70s-chic club offers both style and substance: The design is futuristic but comfortable, the Mediterranean finger-foods menu is *Zagat*-worthy, the deejay talent spinning eclectic house music is first-rate, and the one-of-a-kind cocktails include the tasty Tang martini. 244 E. Houston St. (btwn aves. A and B). © 212/777-7467. Subway: F to 2nd Ave.

Barramundi   This lounge has a friendly staff, and a settled-in feel in a neighborhood overrun by hipster copycats. Come on a weeknight to snare a table in the little corner of heaven out back. A fireplace makes Barramundi almost as appealing on cool nights. 147 Ludlow St. (btwn Stanton and Rivington sts.). © 212/569-6900. Subway: F to Second Ave.

Punch & Judy *(Finds)*   This unpretentious, cozy wine bar on the Lower East Side is a godsend in the land of the terminally hip. With a list that is constantly changing, you'll find many more than the usual suspects here. There are over 32 varieties offered by the glass, and each month the bar promotes wines from different regions to encourage sampling of new wines. A very good small-bites menu complements the wines. 26 Clinton St. (btwn Houston and Stanton sts.). © 212/982-1116. Subway: F to Second Ave.

Whiskey Ward *(Finds)*   Here's the second-best bar in town for serious whiskey fans (only behind the East Village's dba): first-class single malts and bourbons to choose from, and absolutely no pretensions. Nice on-tap and bottled beer selection, too. 121 Essex St. (btwn Rivington and Delancey sts.). © 212/477-2998. Subway: F to Delancey St.

SOHO

Ear Inn *(Value)*   There are many debates about which is the oldest bar in New York, and with its 1870s origins, Ear Inn is a serious contender for that crown. In super-chic SoHo, this pub is a welcome cranky relief. They pull an excellent draft of Guinness and make a surprisingly good margarita as well. On Saturday afternoon, the poetry readings just might make you cry into your beer. In warm weather, tables are set up outside within exhaust distance of the nearby UPS depot. *Note:* Respect the no-cellphone policy or suffer the consequences. 326 Spring St. (btwn Greenwich and Washington sts.). © 212/226-9060. Subway: C, E to Spring St.

Merc Bar   Notable for its long tenure in the fickle world of beautiful-people bars, the upscale Merc Bar has mellowed nicely. The decor bespeaks civilized rusticity with warm woods, a canoe over the bar, copper-top tables, and butter-leather banquettes—think SoHo goes to Yosemite. The European martini (Stoli raspberry and Chambord) is divine. Look carefully, because there's no sign. 151 Mercer St. (btwn Prince and Houston sts.). © 212/966-2727. www.mercbar.com. Subway: N, R to Prince St.

Pravda   This Bolshevik-chic lounge (which careful watchers might recognize from *Sex and the City*) makes pricey but perfect martinis for a classy crowd drawn in by the romantic pre-Gorbachev revolutionary vibe. More than 70 vodkas are on hand from 18 countries, and plenty of Russian caviar to wash down with those pricey cocktails. There's no sign, so look for the light that says "281" on the east side of the street and walk down the stairwell. 281 Lafayette St. (btwn Houston and Prince sts.). © 212/226-4944 or 212/334-5015. Subway: N, R to Prince St.

Tips Whiling Away the Happy Hours

Many of the city's best bars suddenly become more affordable from 4 to 8pm or thereabouts, when it's definitely a happy hour if you can snag one of those signature cocktails ($10 martinis, anyone?) at half-price or two-for-one; or maybe there's some free bar food, or another value-saving offer. Happy hour is a great time to experience those pricey places you've heard so much about. For information on happy hour at many of the city's watering holes, check online at www.sheckys.com or **Murph's NYC Bar Guide** at www.murphguide.com, which is updated daily.

Puck Fair *(Finds)* This gleaming pub looks as if it could have been lifted wholesale out of an equally stylish corner of London and plunked down on this side of the pond. It's genuine through and through, but a young crowd and a hip soundtrack make it feel fresh rather than old man–neighborhoody (like Fanelli's). Twenty beers are on tap (including Guinness, of course). If you can snare a table, the petite mezzanine makes a great spot to sit down and dig into the surprisingly good pub grub. 298 Lafayette St. (just south of Houston St.). ℂ 212/431-1200. Subway: F to Broadway/Lafayette St.

THE EAST VILLAGE & NOHO

dba *(Finds)* dba has completely bucked the loungey trend that has taken over the city, instead remaining firmly and resolutely an unpretentious neighborhood bar. It's a beer- and scotch-lover's paradise, with a massive drink menu on giant chalkboards. Owner Ray Deter specializes in British-style cask-conditioned ales (the kind that you pump by hand) and stocks a phenomenal collection of single-malt scotches. Ray has enclosed the back garden, transforming it into a cozy East Village beer garden. Excellent jukebox, too. Look for daily specials like Sunday Bloody Marys with free lox and bagels from Russ & Daughters. 41 First Ave. (btwn 2nd and 3rd sts.). ℂ 212/475-5097. www.drinkgoodstuff.com. Subway: F to Second Ave.

KGB Bar This former Ukrainian social club still boasts its Soviet-themed decor, but it now draws creative types who like the low-key boho vibe. There's also free entertainment almost every night of the week, thanks to KGB's excellent reading series, where a talented pack of up-and-coming and established writers read their prose in various genres (fiction, science fiction, poetry, and so on) to a receptive crowd starting at 7pm. Past readers have included playwright Tina Howe *(Painting Churches),* Rick Moody *(The Ice Storm),* and Kathryn Harrison *(The Kiss).* 85 E. 4th St. (btwn Second and Third aves.). ℂ 212/505-3360. www.kgbbar.com. Subway: 6 to Astor Place.

McSorley's Old Ale House In business for more than 140 years, McSorley's window proudly claims WE WERE HERE BEFORE YOU WERE BORN. Only McSorley's Ale is served, light or dark, and two at a time. This is an ale-sodden frat-boy madhouse most nights and an Irish Armageddon on St. Patrick's Day, but everybody seems to love it. Although it's also a McSorley's tradition to urinate on the wall outside, they prefer you honor that one in the breach, not in the commission. Weekday afternoons are the best time to go to avoid the crowds. 15 E. 7th St. (btwn Second and Third aves.). ℂ 212/473-9148. Subway: 6 to Astor Place.

Temple Bar One of the first comers to New York's lounge scene, Temple Bar is still a gorgeous deco hangout, with a long L-shaped bar leading to a lovely seating area with velvet drapes, romantic backlighting, and Sinatra crooning in the background. Cocktails simply don't get any better than the classic martini (with just a kiss of vermouth) or the smooth-as-peignoir-silk Manhattan (Johnnie Walker Black, sweet vermouth, bitters). Bring a date—and feel free to invite me along anytime. Look for the petroglyph-like lizards on the otherwise-unmarked facade. 332 Lafayette St. (just north of Houston St., on the west side of the street). ✆ 212/925-4242. Subway: 6 to Bleecker St.

Tom & Jerry's (288 Bar)   Here's an extremely pleasing neighborhood bar minus the grunge factor that usually plagues such joints. The place has an authentic local vibe, and the youngish, artsy crowd is unpretentious and chatty. The beer selection is very good and the mixed drinks are better than average. Flea-market hounds will enjoy the vintage collection of "Tom & Jerry" punchbowl sets behind the bar, and creative types will enjoy the rotating collection of works from local artists, which changes monthly. There's no sign, but you'll spy the action through the plate-glass window on the east side of Elizabeth Street just north of Houston. 288 Elizabeth St. ✆ 212/260-5045. Subway: 6 to Bleecker St.

Zum Schneider *Finds*   You know New York has just about everything when you can find an authentic indoor German beer garden in the heart of Alphabet City. With long tables and bench seating, this is a fun place for a group. There are more than a dozen varieties of German beer on tap here, and all are served in sturdy steins. To complement those hearty beers you can sample equally hearty German fare such as Bavarian blood sausage and rolled beef filled with pickle, bacon, and mustard. If that seems a bit much, you can just munch on the homemade pretzels. 107 Ave. C (at 7th St.). ✆ 212/598-1098. www.zumschneider.com. Subway: F to Second Ave.; L to First Ave.

GREENWICH VILLAGE & THE MEAT-PACKING DISTRICT

Bowlmor/Pressure   Super-cool Bowlmor isn't your daddy's bowling alley: deejays spin, martinis flow, candy-colored balls knock down Day-Glo pins, and strikes and spares are automatically tallied into the wee hours. Frankly, Bowlmor is a blast. Once you're finished with your 10-pin—or while you're waiting for your lane—head upstairs to the palatial rooftop lounge, Pressure, housed in a 16,000-square-foot inflated bubble and boasting designer-mod furnishings, a sexy cocktail menu that includes a luscious chocolate martini (infused with Godiva chocolate liqueur), a fleet of pool tables, and always-on movie screens adding an arty-party flair. 110 University Place (btwn 12th and 13th sts.). ✆ 212/255-8188 (Bowlmor), or 212/352-1161 (Pressure). www.bowlmor.com or www.pressurenyc.com. Subway: 4, 5, 6, L, N, R to 14th St./Union Sq.

Chumley's   Many bars in New York date their beginnings to Prohibition, but Chumley's still has the vibe. The crowd doesn't date back nearly as far, however. Come to warm yourself by the fire and indulge in a once-forbidden pleasure: beer. There is a good selection of on-taps and microbrews. The door is unmarked, with a metal grille on the small window; another entrance is at 58 Barrow St., which takes you in through a back courtyard. 86 Bedford St. (at Barrow St.). ✆ 212/675-4449. Subway: 1, 9 to Christopher St.

Hudson Bar & Books   This former exclusive gentleman's club maintains a similar appeal as an elegant bar. Among the draws are cool jazz, a magnificent copper-topped marble bar, good lighting, comfortable seating, and an extensive—and expensive—champagne, cocktails, cognacs, and malts menu. Pleasantly, the crowd comprises more at-home locals than preening tourists. A great date place. 636 Hudson St. (btwn Horatio and Jane sts.). ✆ 212/229-2642. Subway: A, C, E, L to 14th St.

White Horse Tavern Poets and literary buffs pop into this 1880 pub to pay their respects to Dylan Thomas, who tipped his last jar here before shuffling off this mortal coil. Best enjoyed in the warm weather when there's outdoor drinking, or at happy hour for the cheap drafts that draw in a big frat-boy and post-frat yuppie crowd. 567 Hudson St. (at 11th St.). (C) 212/243-9260. Subway: 1, 9 to Christopher St.

CHELSEA

Bongo (Value) This casual, comfortable mid-century-modern lounge is the place to come for cocktails that are well made and a great value considering their bathtub size. Don't miss the French martini, made with Vox vodka and Lillet—yum! Even better: Bongo boasts a full raw-bar menu—a half dozen varieties of oysters, cherrystones, and littlenecks, even lobster and caviar—and an excellent lobster roll. The crowd is hip, but, happily, not too trendy. Come early if you want to have space to sit and eat. 299 Tenth Ave. (btwn 27th and 28th sts.). (C) 212/947-3654. Subway: C, E to 23rd St.

Kanvas Apropos to its location, just a stone's throw from west Chelsea's clutch of cutting-edge art galleries, this sleek Chelsea lounge doubles as an art gallery itself, so it makes a great place to commune with an artsy crowd. It's a plush designer space, with a classic, long wood bar up front, cozy banquettes in back, and artwork that rotates monthly. The martini menu boasts two dozen varieties, including a mint chocolate-chip version. Monday through Wednesday, $20 pitchers of mojitos and sangria are the draw. 219 Ninth Ave. (btwn 23rd and 24th sts.). (C) 212/727-2616. Subway: C, E to 23rd St.

Late-Night Bites

I have fond, but now distant, memories of barhopping until the early hours, rounded off by a meal in one of Chinatown's 24-hour restaurants only to emerge as the sun was rising the next day. Throughout the city, but especially downtown, are some great late-night eats. Here's a sampling:

Open until 4am nightly, **Blue Ribbon**, 97 Sullivan St., between Prince and Spring streets in SoHo ((C) 212/274-0404), is where the city's top chefs come to unwind after they close their own kitchens for the night. Thanks to a top-drawer oyster bar and excellent comfort food, this cozy bistro is always packed, so expect a wait.

Other great choices for after-hours eats include the funky Francophile diner **Florent** (p. 188), and authentic bistro **Pastis** (p. 188), both in the red-hot Meat-Packing District. TriBeCa has **The Odeon** (p. 177), an attractive and affordable Art Deco bistro that's one of the top after-hours eateries in town. In SoHo, consider sexy siren **Balthazar** (p. 183), the Claudette Colbert of bistros, which serves until 1:30am weeknights, until 2:30am weekends.

In the East Village, head to **Veselka** (p. 186), a comfortable and appealing diner offering authentic Eastern European fare at rock-bottom prices; **Katz's Delicatessen** (p. 182) for first-class Jewish deli eats Friday and Saturday until 2:30am. In Chinatown, many restaurants are open late or even all night.

In the Theater District feast on first-class pastrami and cheesecake until 3:45am at **Carnegie Deli** (p. 206), until 2am at the **Stage Deli** (p. 206).

Serena   Done in deep, sexy reds, Serena is as hip as can be—I've even spotted mix-master Moby here. It's relatively unpretentious considering its hot-spot status; still, dress the part if you want to make it past the doorman, especially on weekends. The crowd is young and pretty, and the schizophrenic music mix is a blast—think Fatboy Slim meets ABBA meets Foghat, and you'll get the picture. In the basement level of the Hotel Chelsea, 222 W. 23rd St. (btwn Seventh and Eighth aves.). ✆ 212/255-4646. Subway: C, E, 1, 9 to 23rd St.

THE FLATIRON DISTRICT, UNION SQUARE & GRAMERCY PARK

Dusk *(Finds*   This casual, artsy lounge is a great choice for a cocktail. There's a fab mir-rored mosaic wall, cozy banquettes, a friendly bar serving affordable drinks, a pool table, and mostly U.K. tunes—from drum-and-bass to Super Furry Animals to Blur to Enya—on the sound system. Expect an easygoing, youngish crowd that stays relaxed and unpretentious into the evening. No sign, but look for the three blue lights attached to a dark storefront. 147 W. 24th St. (btwn Sixth and Seventh aves.). ✆ 212/924-4490. Subway: F to 23rd St.

Old Town Bar & Restaurant   If you've watched TV at all over the last couple of decades, this place should look familiar: It was featured in the old *Late Night with David Letterman* intro, starred as Riff's Bar in *Mad About You*, and appeared in such movies as *The Devil's Own, Bullets Over Broadway,* and *The Last Days of Disco.* But this is no stage set—it's a genuine tin-ceilinged 19th-century bar serving up good pub grub, lots of beers on tap, and a sense of history. 45 E. 18th St. (btwn Broadway and Park Ave. S.). ✆ 212/529-6732. Subway: L, N, R, Q, W, 4, 5, or 6 to 14th St./Union Sq.

Pete's Tavern   The oldest continually operating establishment in the city, Pete's opened while Lincoln was still president. It reeks of genuine history—this is where O. Henry wrote the Christmas tale "Gift of the Magi." Pete's is the kind of place where you go to warm up on a cold winter's night with a dark creamy comforting Guinness. And that Guinness doesn't taste too bad in the summer when Pete's sidewalk cafe is open. 129 E. 18th St. (at Irving Place). ✆ 212/473-7676. www.petestavern.com. Subway: L, N, R, 4, 5, 6 to 14th St./Union Sq.

TIMES SQUARE & MIDTOWN WEST

Don't forget those dives—you can find **Jimmy's Corner** and **Rudy's Bar & Grill** in the neighborhood (see the box "The New York Dive Experience," above).

Carnegie Club *(Finds*   Like sister lounge **The Campbell Apartment** (p. 379), this swellegant lounge is another architecturally magnificent space, with soaring ceilings and an intimate mezzanine, plus a grand stone fireplace—a Gothic mood warmed up with plush, contemporary furnishings and a romantic vibe. "Weekends with Sinatra" stars Cary Hoffman and the Stan Rubin Orchestra in a wonderfully evocative—and surprisingly exact—cabaret show featuring the music of Frank Sinatra (two shows nightly on Sat; cover $30, plus $15 minimum). There's also live swing on Friday. Reservations are recommended on live music nights. 156 W. 56th St. (btwn Sixth and Seventh aves.). ✆ 212/957-9676. Subway: B, Q to 57th St.

Hudson Bar   Outfitted like a futuristic canteen, Hudson Bar, in the Hudson Hotel, glows from below with an underlit floor, while the low ceiling wears a Crayola-like fresco by Francesco Clemente. In between you'll find a tony, older-than-you'd-expect crowd. The one-of-a-kind cocktail menu is terrific, too. Enter at street level, on the

The New York Dive Experience

Not all of New York nightlife means bars and clubs with cover charges, outrageously expensive cocktails, elegant finger food, beautiful people, and velvet ropes to keep you waiting in the cold. There are places here that you should be rewarded for braving; old dark places where the drinks are cheap and the characters colorful. These are the dive bars and they are just as much New York as their hot, trendy counterparts. Here are some of my favorites; stop in one for a real New York experience.

Jimmy's Corner, 140 W. 44th St., between Broadway and Sixth Avenue (✆ 212/221-9510). Owned by a former boxing trainer, Jimmy's is a tough guy's joint that has been around for more than 30 years and survived the Disneyfication of Times Square. Pictures of boxers adorn the walls, and the jukebox plays lots of R&B and '70s disco. In the pre–smoking ban days, the smoke would get so thick in Jimmy's you needed night goggles to see through the haze. Beer is cheap and drinks aren't fancy. Skip the theme bars and restaurants in the area and go for an after-theater pop at Jimmy's instead.

Rudy's Bar & Grill, 627 Ninth Ave., between 44th and 45th streets (✆ 212/974-9169). This Hell's Kitchen establishment is no secret; its happy hour is legendary and the small place is usually packed with slackers sucking up cheap beer, including the house brand, Rudy's Red, a weak watery brew served in a huge plastic cup for $3. My advice is to get there before happy hour, grab a seat on one of the few broken banquettes and keep your eyes open for the hot dog guy who gives out free hot dogs. You'll need one to

Ninth Avenue side of the hotel's main entrance; dress well to avoid attitude. 356 W. 58th St. (btwn Eighth and Ninth aves.). ✆ 212/554-6000. Subway: A, B, C, D, 1, 9 to 59th St./Columbus Circle.

Mickey Mantle's   Before Mickey Mantle's officially opened years ago, I was walking past the restaurant, peered into the window, and there was my boyhood idol, the Mick, sitting at the bar by himself. Through the window I waved—and he waved back. It made my day. And though the food's not very good and the drinks are overpriced, I still have a soft spot for Mickey Mantle's and always will. With plenty of Yankee memorabilia on the walls and sports on all the televisions, it's an ideal place to watch a game, but stick with the basics: beer and burgers. 42 Central Park South (btwn Fifth and Sixth aves.). ✆ 212/688-7777. www.thesearingens.com/mick/mmrest.htm. Subway: F to 57th St.

Morrell Wine Bar & Cafe   One of the leading wine purveyors in America has created the ideal place to sample the first-rate collection of vintages in comfort. Situated at the heart of Rockefeller Center, just across the alley from the plaza, the bi-level space is contemporary and comfortable and attended by an extremely knowledgeable waitstaff. In addition to the extensive bar and lounge space, a nice New American menu is also served; make reservations for dinner. 1 Rockefeller Plaza (at 49th St.). ✆ 212/262-7700. www.morrellwinebar.com. Subway: B, D, F, V to 47th–50th sts./Rockefeller Center.

balance out a bucket of Rudy's Red. In the summer, Rudy's opens its cement garden for drinks "alfresco."

Subway Inn, 143 E. 60th St., at Lexington Avenue (℃ 212/223-9829). My all-time favorite dive, the Subway has been around for over 60 years and I believe some of the regulars have been on their stools the whole time. The red neon sign beckons from outside while inside, no matter what time of day, it's midnight dark. The bartender is ancient and until recently served Schaeffer on tap. The demise of Schaeffer was troubling, but thankfully not much else has changed. The booths are still wobbly and the models of Godzilla and E.T. along with assorted other dusty junk continue to decorate the shelves behind the bar. The last time I visited, I was barred from entering the men's room by police who were shaking down one of the regulars during a drug bust. You might find workers from the upscale stores in the neighborhood and writers searching for "material" slumming at the Subway, but this joint remains the pinnacle of divedom.

Tap a Keg, 2731 Broadway, between 103rd and 104th streets (℃ 212/749-1734). Tap a Keg calls itself a "Hell of a Joint." And hell can mean two things here: very good fun or a nightmare. That's the happy contradiction of the Tap a Keg and all dives really. There are a few wooden tables and televisions, a great jukebox with jazz, reggae, and R&B, and a very popular pool table. But it's the 7-hour happy hour with pints of beer for about 3 bucks and the regular gathering of wizened, disheveled characters that give the Tap a Keg its well-deserved dive status.

Rainbow Room Skip eating here, but come to this legendary bar, sip a too-expensive cocktail and soak in the ambience, views, and live piano music. No jeans or sneakers, please. 30 Rockefeller Plaza (entrance on 49th St., btwn Fifth and Sixth aves., 64th floor). ℃ 212/632-5000. www.rainbowroom.com. Subway: B, D, F, V to 47th–50th sts./Rockefeller Center.

Russian Vodka Room *(Finds* This terrific old-school lounge is a real Theater District find. It's not going to win any style awards, but it's extremely comfortable and knows what's what when it comes to vodkas. There are more than 50 on hand, plus the RVR's own miraculous infusions; you can order an iced rack of six if you can't decide between such yummy flavors as cranberry, apple cinnamon, ginger, horseradish, and more (the raspberry makes a perfect Cosmo). The 30-something-and-up crowd is peopled with post-Soviet imports as well as New Yorkers in the know about this best-kept secret. Come early if you want to snag a bar table. 265 W. 52nd St. (btwn Broadway and Eighth Ave.). ℃ 212/307-5835. Subway: C, E, 1, 9 to 50th St.

MIDTOWN EAST & MURRAY HILL

The Campbell Apartment This swank lounge on the mezzanine level at Grand Central Terminal has been created out of the former business office of prewar businessman John W. Campbell, who transformed the space into a pre-Renaissance palace worthy of a Medici. The high-ceilinged room has been restored to its full Florentine

Checking into Hotel Bars

A hotel bar should provide comfort and hospitality to the out-of-town visitor; it should be the kind of place where you can unwind after a day seeing the sights, have a leisurely drink before heading out to dinner or a show, or enjoy a quiet nightcap before retiring. When the bar becomes a nighttime destination unto itself, and hotel guests have to fight their way through a throng of locals just to get a drink, well, I'd say that hotel bar has defeated its purpose. Thankfully, New York has plenty of hotel bars that draw outsiders but keep their own guests happy, too. Here are my top picks:

Bemelmans Bar, in the Carlyle Hotel, 35 E. 76th St., at Madison Avenue (© 212/744-1600). This is my choice as New York's best hotel bar. It has everything you want from a hotel bar: white-coated service; lush seating with many dark romantic corners to sink into; a nice mix of locals and guests; and incredible cocktails, like the Old Cuban, a *mojito* topped with champagne, created by mixologist and self-proclaimed cocktail geek Audrey Saunders. The bar is named after children's book illustrator Ludwig Bemelmans, who created the *Madeline* books after he painted the whimsical mural here.

Bull and Bear, in the Waldorf=Astoria, 301 Park Ave., between 49th and 50th streets (© 212/872-4900). The Bull and Bear is like a gentlemen's pub, with brass-studded red leather chairs, a waistcoated staff, and a grand troika-shaped mahogany bar polished to a high sheen at the center of the room. Still, it's plenty comfy for casual drinkers. Ask Oscar, who's been here for more than 30 years, or one of the other accomplished bartenders to blend you a classic cocktail like The Bronx, a combination of gin, orange juice, and fresh pineapple juice. An ideal place to kick back after a hard day of sightseeing.

glory, and serves wines and champagnes by the glass, single-malt scotches, and haute noshies to a well-heeled commuting crowd. Try to snag a seat in the little-used upstairs room if you want some quiet. Call ahead before heading over, as the space tends to be closed for private parties on a rather frequent basis. No sneakers, baseball caps, athletic wear, or ripped jeans. In Grand Central Terminal, 15 Vanderbilt Ave. © 212/953-0409. Subway: S, 4, 5, 6, 7 to 42nd St./Grand Central.

The Ginger Man   The big bait at this appealing upscale beer bar is the 66 gleaming tap handles lining the wood-and-brass bar, dispensing everything from Sierra Nevada and Hoegaarden to cask-conditioned ales. The cavernous space has a clubby feel. The Cohiba fumes were ripe here before the smoking ban but the new non-smoking laws have not stopped the crowds coming to this popular Murray Hill hangout. 11 E. 36th St. (btwn Fifth and Madison aves.). © 212/532-3740. Subway: 6 to 33rd St.

Monkey Bar   This legendary bar and restaurant has experienced quite a resurgence since Carrie and Mr. Big hooked up here on *Sex and the City.* It definitely deserved the attention: The swanky space is dolled up like a Hollywood supper club from the 1930s, the drinks are faultless, and the legendary monkey murals are worth a look

King Cole Bar, in the St. Regis, 2 E. 55th St., at Fifth Avenue (© **212/744-4300**). The birthplace of the Bloody Mary, this theatrical spot may just be New York's most historic hotel bar. The Maxfield Parrish mural alone is worth the price of a classic cocktail (ask the bartender to tell you about the "hidden" meaning of the painting). The one drawback is the bar's small size; after-work hours and holiday times, the bar is jammed.

Mark's Bar, in the Mark, 25 E. 77th St., at Madison Avenue (© **212/744-4300**). Outfitted like an elegant living room with a romantic flair, Mark's is small but cozy. There's a European feel to the atmosphere, with first-class service and perfectly mixed drinks. The crowd tends to be older and in some ways mysterious. Sophisticated nibbles are also served.

M Bar, in the Mansfield Hotel, 12 W. 44th St., between Fifth and Sixth avenues (© **212/944-6050**). This library-style lounge more than holds its own on a block where the hotel bar competition is intense; The **Oak Room** at the Algonquin (see below) is just a few doors away, as is the very hip Royalton. M Bar features a lovely circular bar, a first-rate cocktail menu, comfortable seating, and a dark and romantic Art Deco mood.

Oak Room at the Algonquin, in the Algonquin Hotel, 59 W. 44th St., between Fifth and Sixth avenues (© **212/840-6800**). The splendid oak-paneled lobby of this venerable literati-favored hotel is the comfiest and most welcoming in the city, made to linger over pre- or post-theater cocktails. You'll feel the spirit of Dorothy Parker and the legendary Algonquin Round Table that pervades the room. Try the Matilda, a light, refreshing blend of orange juice, Absolut Mandarin, triple sec, and champagne, named after the Algonquin's legendary feline in residence.

alone. Skip the dining room and head directly to the piano bar for the ultimate Monkey Bar experience. At the Hotel Elysee, 60 E. 54th St. (btwn Madison and Park aves.). © **212/838-2600**. Subway: 6 to 51st St.

Under the Volcano *(Finds)*   If you've been shopping crowded Macy's or braving the lines at the Empire State Building and want (need?) a drink, one of the few choices in the area, but a good one, is this Mexican-themed tequila bar. The decor is Mexican folk with Frida Kahlo undertones throughout, but the main attractions are the 16 varieties of tequila and the very smooth, subtly potent margaritas. The bar also features an excellent selection of aged rums. 12 E. 36th St. (btwn Fifth and Madison aves.). © **212/213-0093**. Subway: B, D, F, N, R to 34th St.

Villard Bar & Lounge   This decadent two-floor lounge is a sumptuous place to celebrate over a cocktail and enjoy the opulent McKim, Mead & White architecture of the Villard Houses. Word is the sage and pineapple martini is a real treat. Be sure to dress well to fit in with the Prada-suited, Manolo-heeled crowd. In the New York Palace Hotel, 24 E. 51st St. (at Madison Ave.). © **212/303-7757**. Subway: E, F to Fifth Ave.; 6 to 51st St.

UPPER WEST SIDE

All State Cafe *Finds* This subterranean pub is one of Manhattan's undiscovered treasures—the quintessential neighborhood "snugger." It's easy to miss from the street, and the regulars like it that way. The All State attracts a grown-up neighborhood crowd drawn in by the casual ambience, the great burgers, and an outstanding jukebox. If you're lucky, you'll get the round table by the fire. 250 W. 72nd St. (btwn Broadway and West End Ave.). ℂ 212/874-1883. Subway: 1, 2, 3, 9 to 72nd St.

Café del Bar *Finds* This casual reggae lounge in the northern hinterlands of Columbus Avenue is so small, everyone will surely know your name. African and Jamaican roots music adds to the exotic vibe here while the $4 Red Stripes and the special of the house, Mango Mimosas, will have you fantasizing about beautiful sandy beaches. 945 Columbus Ave. (at 106th St.). ℂ 212/531-1643. Subway: C or B to 103rd St.

Dublin House For years, like a welcoming beacon, the Dublin House's neon harp has blinked invitingly. This very old pub is a no-frills Irish saloon and the perfect spot for a drink after visiting the nearby Museum of Natural History or Central Park. There's a long, narrow barroom up front and a bigger room in the back that's good for groups. Original wood veneer detail remains, adding to the pub's charm. The Guinness is cheap and drawn perfectly by the very able and sometimes crusty bartenders. Best enjoyed in the late afternoon or early evening when the regulars populate the bar. Stay away on weekend nights and St. Patrick's Day when the place is overrun with amateurs: frat boys and sorority girls on pub crawls. 225 W. 79th St. (btwn Broadway and Amsterdam Ave.). ℂ 212/874-9528. Subway: 1, 9 to 79th St.

Eden *Finds* A sleek downtown cocktail lounge has finally found its way uptown. This French-owned lounge features a sleek granite-topped bar, a dark comfy back room with couches, and plush chairs. Happy hour here lasts 4 hours, from 5 to 9pm, 7 days a week. The deejay comes on after happy hour and spontaneous dancing has been known to occasionally take place. There is live blues on Wednesday and reggae on Thursday. A belly dancer entertains late on weekends. Light bites like quesadillas and croque-monsieur are available. A fashionable refuge in an unfashionable neighborhood. 2728 Broadway (btwn 104th and 105th sts.). ℂ 212/865-5565. Subway: 1, 9 to 103rd St.

UPPER EAST SIDE

There's also an outpost of the Meat-Packing District *Coyote Ugly* roadhouse **Hogs & Heifers** at 1843 First Ave., between 95th and 96th streets (ℂ 212/722-8635; subway: 6 to 96th St.). Despite its offshoot status, this one's slightly more laid-back and boasts more genuine saloon style than the original.

Elaine's *The Big Chill* claimed that Elaine's was over and done with way back when. They were dreaming. Glittering literati still come here for dinner and book parties. Look for regulars such as Woody Allen and other A-list types. If you can't get a table, you can always scan the room from the upfront bar. 1703 Second Ave. (btwn 88th and 89th sts.). ℂ 212/534-8103. Subway: 4, 5, 6 to 86th St.

Great Hall Balcony Bar *Moments* One of Manhattan's best cocktail bars is only open on Friday and Saturday—and only from 4 to 8:30pm, to boot. The Metropolitan Museum of Art transforms the lobby's mezzanine level into a cocktail-and–classical music lounge twice weekly, offering a marvelous only-in–New York experience. The music is usually provided by a grand piano and string quartet. You'll have to pay the $10 admission, but the galleries are open until 9pm. At the Metropolitan Museum of Art, Fifth Ave. at 82nd St. Ⓒ 212/535-7710. www.metmuseum.org. Subway: 4, 5, 6 to 86th St.

8 Dance Clubs & Party Scenes

Nothing in New York nightlife is as mutable as the club scene. In this world, hot spots don't even get 15 minutes of fame—their time in the limelight is usually more like a commercial break.

First things first: Finding and going to the latest hot spot is not worth agonizing over. Clubbers spend their lives obsessing over the scene. My rule of thumb is that if I know about a place, it must not be hip anymore. Even if I could tell you where the hippest club kids hang out today, they'll have moved on by the time you arrive in town.

"Clubs" as actual, physical spaces don't mean much anymore. The hungry-for-nightlife crowd now follows events of certain party "producers" who switch venues and times each week. A number of bars and lounges listed in the previous section host "club" scenes on various nights of the week.

The tracking game is best left to the perennial party crowd who know the rest of the crowd as well as the guy at the door (who lets them in for free) and someone at the bar (who comps them drinks). You're not likely to get that well connected in your week of vacation. Just find someplace that amuses you, and enjoy the crowd that enjoys it with you.

I've concentrated on a wide variety of club scenes below, from performance artsy to perennially popular discos, most of which are generally easy to make your way into. You can find listings for the most current hot spots and movable parties in the **publications and online sources** listed at the start of this chapter. Additional online sources that might score you discount admissions to select clubs include **www.promony.com**. You can also check **www.sheckys.com** for VIP guest list access.

⟨Tips⟩ Getting Beyond the Velvet Rope

If you are somewhat masochistic, enjoy humiliation and ridicule, and are determined to get into that oh-so-trendy club you heard about back home, here are a few pointers that may help tip the scale in your favor:

- **Dress well and fashionably.** Like it or not, the doorman is sizing you up to decide if you're hip enough to make the scene. If you want to get in, you have to play along.
- **Arrive early.** Frankly, the bouncers are just not as vigilant at 9pm, when the place is half empty, as they are at 11pm—and once you're inside, you're in for the night. Weeknights are also a better bet. Clubbers may tell you that eager beavers are disdained for arriving too early, but I find earlier to almost always be more successful than later.
- **Be polite.** No matter how obnoxious the doorman may be, giving attitude back won't help. And who knows? You might just charm him with your winning personality.
- **Don't try to talk your way in.** Don't drop names or make up some story to get in the door. These guys have heard it all. If you're not wanted, why bother? Take your business to a friendlier establishment, where you'll be happier in the long run.

No matter what, **always call ahead,** because schedules change constantly and can do so at the last minute. Even better: You also may be able to put your name on a guest list that will save you a few bucks at the door.

New York nightlife starts late. With the exception of places that have scheduled performances, clubs stay almost empty until about 11pm. Don't depend on plastic—bring cash, and plan on dropping a wad at most places. Cover charges run anywhere from $7 to $30, and often get more expensive as the night wears on.

Avalon Housed in the old former church where dance club legend Limelight once reigned supreme, Avalon opened with a big splash in late 2003. The interior has been updated with VIP balconies that overlook the dance floor. Off the dance floor are many small rooms for commingling, if you are tired of dancing. 660 Sixth Ave. (at 20th St.). ℂ 212/807-7780. Subway: F to 23rd St.

Baktun This club has been hot, hot, hot since the word go. Sleek Baktun was conceived in 2000 as a multimedia lounge, and as such incorporates avant-garde video projections (shown on a clever double-sided video screen) into its raging dance parties as well as live cybercasts. The music tends toward electronica, with some live acts in the mix. At press time, Saturday's Direct Drive was the key drum 'n' bass party in town. 418 W. 14th St. (btwn Ninth Ave. and Washington St.). ℂ 212/206-1590. www.baktun.com. Subway: A, C, E, L to 14th St.

Black Formerly known as Exit, this space has been aptly called the "supermall of nightclubs," and for good reason—it covers 45,000 square feet and is able to accommodate more than 5,000 partiers. Any velvet rope scene is pure posturing. The main floor is a mammoth atrium with a deejay booth—usually housing the top talent of the moment spinning tunes—suspended above. The space was made for crazy carnival acts like Antigravity, a bizarre clubland take on the Flying Wallendas. Upstairs is a warren of ultraplush VIP rooms, each with its own deejay. With capacity this big, expect clubgoers of all stripes to show up on any given night. 610 W. 56th St. (btwn Eleventh and Twelfth aves.). ℂ 212/582-8282. www.exitnyc.com. Subway: A, B, C, D, 1, 9 to 59th St./Columbus Circle.

Cafe Wha? You'll find a carefree crowd dancing in the aisles of this casual basement club just about any night of the week. From Wednesday through Sunday, the stage features the house's own Wha Band, which does an excellent job of cranking out crowd-pleasing covers of familiar rock-'n'-roll hits from the '70s, '80s, and '90s. Monday night is the hugely popular Brazilian Dance Party, while Tuesday night is Classic Funk Night. Expect to be surrounded by lots of Jersey kids and out-of-towners on the weekends, but so what? Reservations are a good idea. The cover runs from free to $10. 115 MacDougal St. (btwn Bleecker and W. 3rd sts.). ℂ 212/254-3706. www.cafewha.com. Subway: A, B, C, D, E, F, V to W. 4th St.

Club Shelter House-heads flock to this old-school disco. The big draw is the "Saturday Night Shelter Party," when late '80s house music takes over. The crowd is racially and sexually diverse and dress is not fancy; wear whatever is comfortable for doing some heavy sweating on the dance floor. 20 W. 39th St. (btwn Fifth and Sixth aves.). ℂ 212/719-9867. www.clubshelter.com. Subway: B, D, F, Q, V, 7 to 42nd St.

crobar With over 25,000 square feet—room enough for 3,000—this is one place where your odds of getting in are very good. The excellent sound system and deejays from around the world—like Paul Van Dyk and Tiesto of Holland—will have you sweating in no time. If you lose your friends or lovers in the crowd, don't worry, you'll find new ones. 530 W. 28th St. (btwn 10th and 11th aves.). ℂ 212/629-9000. www.crobar.com. Subway: C or E to 23rd St.

Decade Finally—somewhere to dance until nearly dawn for the baby boomers. This upscale hybrid supper/dance club attracts a well-dressed, well-heeled crowd who lounge in the cigar and champagne bars in between dancing to a fun mix of tunes from the '70s, '80s, and '90s. The food is quite tasty and the service is top-notch, too. Nights can sell out, so it pays to reserve ahead. 1117 First Ave. (at 61st St.). ℂ 212/835-5979. Subway: N, R to Lexington Ave.; 4, 5, 6 to 59th St.

Don Hill's This long-lived, eccentric, divey club draws a heavily integrated gay, lesbian, and straight crowd that comes for rock, glam, and punk some nights, campy parties on others. Röck Cändy is a fun neo-glam resurrection on Wednesday nights, featuring live hair-metal bands (for whom there is still a scene in New York). Drinks are affordable. 511 Greenwich St. (at Spring St.). ℂ 212/334-1390. www.donhills.com. Subway: 1 or 9 to Canal St.

Spirit Mind, Body, and Soul is the theme here. Start with the Body, the 10,000-square-foot dance floor where you'll try to compete with acrobats, aerialists, and professional dancers. The effort will wear you out and you'll need to retreat to the Mind, the club's holistic healing center where you can get a massage or have your palm read, among other New-Agey amenities. Finally, you don't want to leave hungry, so sample Soul, the club's organic vegetarian restaurant. 530 W. 27th St. (btwn 10th and 11th aves.). ℂ 212/268-9477. Subway: C, E to 23rd St.

Swing 46 *(Finds)* Swing is a nightly affair at this Theater District jazz and supper club (supper not required). Music is live nightly except Monday, when a deejay takes over, and runs the gamut from big band to boogie-woogie to jump blues. Do not miss Vince Giordano and His Nighthawks if they're on the bill, especially if sharp-dressed Casey McGill is singing and strumming his ukulele too. The Harlem Renaissance Orchestra is another great choice. Even first-timers can join in the fun, as free swing lessons are offered Wednesday through Saturday at 9:15pm. No jeans or sneakers. 349 W. 46th St. (btwn Eighth and Ninth aves.). ℂ 212/262-9554. www.swing46.com. Subway: C, E to 50th St.

13 *(Value)* This little lounge is a great place to dance the night away. It's stylish but unpretentious, with a steady roster of fun weekly parties. Sunday night's Britpop fest Shout! lives on, as popular as ever—and with no cover, to boot. The rest of the week runs the gamut from '70s and '80s New Wave and glam nights to progressive house and trance to poetry slams and performance art. If there's a cover, it's usually $5, occasionally $7 or $10. Happy hour offers two-for-one drinks (and no cover) from 4 to 8pm. 35 E. 13th St. (btwn Broadway and University Place), 2nd floor. ℂ 212/979-6677. www.bar13. com. Subway: 4, 5, 6, L, N, R, Q, W to 14th St./Union Sq.

9 The Gay & Lesbian Scene

To get a thorough, up-to-date take on what's happening in gay and lesbian nightlife, pick up copies of *HX* (www.hx.com), the *New York Blade* (www.nyblade.com), or *Next.* They're available for free in bars and clubs all around town or at the **Lesbian and Gay Community Center,** at 208 W. 13th St., between Seventh and Eighth avenues (ℂ 212/620-7310; www.gaycenter.org). The interdisciplinary weekly *Time Out New York* boasts a terrific gay and lesbian section that some consider to be the city's best source; another great source is the legendary free weekly *Village Voice.* Always remember that asking people in one bar can lead you to discover another that fits your tastes.

These days, many bars, clubs, cabarets, and cocktail lounges are neither gay nor straight but a bit of both, either catering to a mixed crowd or to varying orientations on different nights of the week. In addition to the choices below, most of the clubs listed in "Dance Clubs & Party Scenes," above, cater to a gay crowd, some predominantly so.

Barracuda   Chelsea is central to gay life—and gay bars. This trendy, loungey place is a continuing favorite, regularly voted "Best Bar" by *HX* and *New York Press* magazines, while *Paper* singles out the hunky bartenders. There's a sexy bar for cruising out front and a comfy lounge in back. Look for the regular drag shows. 275 W. 22nd St. (btwn Seventh and Eighth aves.). © **212/645-8613.** Subway: C, E, 1, 9 to 23rd St.

Big Cup   Big Cup isn't a bar but a coffeehouse—a really great one. Still, you'd be hard-pressed to find a cooler, comfier pickup joint, or a more preening crowd. This is where all the Chelsea boys hang. 228 Eighth Ave. (btwn 21st and 22nd sts.). © **212/206-0059.** Subway: C, E to 23rd St.

Boiler Room   This down-to-earth East Village bar is everybody's favorite gay dive. Despite the mixed guy-girl crowd, it's a serious cruising scene for well-sculpted beautiful boys and a perfectly fine hangout for those who'd rather play pool. 86 E. 4th St. (btwn First and Second aves.). © **212/254-7536.** Subway: F to Second Ave.

Brandy's Piano Bar   Though gay, this intimate, old-school piano bar attracts a mixed crowd for the friendly atmosphere and nightly entertainment. The talented waitstaff does most of the singing while waiting for their big break, but enthusiastic patrons regularly join in. 235 E. 84th St. (btwn Second and Third aves.). © **212/650-1944.** Subway: 4, 5, 6 to 86th St.

The Cock *(Finds*   This gleefully seedy East Village joint is the most envelope-pushing gay club in town. A self-proclaimed "rock and sleaze fag bar," it's dedicated to goodnatured depravity. Head elsewhere if you're the retiring type. 188 Ave. A (at 12th St.). © **212/777-6254.** Subway: L to First Ave.

Duplex Cabaret   The heart of the gay cabaret and piano-bar scene. Expect a high camp factor and lots of good-natured fun that runs the gamut from minimusicals to drag revues to stand-up comedy. 61 Christopher St. (at Seventh Ave.). © **212/255-5438.** Subway: 1, 9 to Christopher St.

Hell   This glamorous lounge is a sexy haven for a predominantly gay weekend crowd in the hipper-than-hell Meat-Packing District. The cocktails are well mixed, and plenty of comfy sofas are on hand for getting cozy. 59 Gansevoort St. (btwn Washington and Greenwich sts.). © **212/727-1666.** Subway: A, C, E to 14th St.

Henrietta Hudson *(Finds*   This friendly and extremely popular women's bar/lounge is known for drawing in an attractive, upmarket lipstick lesbian crowd that comes for the great jukebox and videos as well as the pleasingly low-key atmosphere. There's a $5 to $7 cover when deejays spin tunes on Fridays and Saturdays, and when live bands are in the house on Sundays. 438–444 Hudson St. (at Morton St.). © **212/924-3347.** www.henriettahudsons.com. Subway: 1, 9 to Houston St.

Splash/SBNY   Beautiful bartenders, video screens playing campy scenes, New York's best drag queens—Splash has it all. Theme nights are a big deal. The best of the bunch is Musical Mondays, dedicated to Broadway video clips and music. Musical Mondays' now-famous singalongs are such a blast that they regularly draw a crossover gay/straight mixed crowd as well as celebs like Nathan Lane and the cast of the ABBA musical, *Mamma Mia!* 50 W. 17th St. (btwn Fifth and Sixth aves.). © 212/691-0073. www.splashbar.com. Subway: F, V to 14th St.; 4, 5, 6, L, N, R, Q, W to 14th St./Union Sq.

Stonewall Bar   The spot where it all started. A mixed gay and lesbian crowd—old and young, beautiful and great personalities—makes this an easy place to begin. At least pop in to relive a defining moment in queer history. 53 Christopher St. (east of Seventh Ave.). © 212/463-0950. Subway: 1, 9 to Christopher St.

View Bar *(Finds)*   Up front is a very attractive and comfortable lounge, in back is a pool room with the name-worthy view; throughout you'll find friendly bartenders, affordable drinks, and Kenneth Cole–dressed boys who could pass on either side of bi. A welcome addition to the scene. 232 Eighth Ave. (btwn 21st and 22nd sts.). © 212/929-2243. Subway: C, E to 23rd St.

Appendix A:
A Brief History of New York City

The area that became New York City was the home to many Native Americans before Giovanni da Verrazano arrived in 1524. Even though Verrazano didn't stay, a bridge was named after him. And it wasn't until 1609, when Henry Hudson, while searching for the Northwest Passage, claimed it for the Dutch East India Company, that New York was recognized as a potential, profitable settlement in the New World.

Hudson (the river that separates Manhattan from the mainland is named after him) said of New York, "It is as beautiful a land as one can hope to tread upon." The treading didn't really start until years later, but by 1625, Dutch settlers established a fur trade with the locals and called their colony New Amsterdam. A year later, Peter Minuit of the Dutch West India Company made that famous deal for the island. He bought New Amsterdam from the Lenape Tribe for what has widely been reported as $24.

New Amsterdam became a British colony in the 1670s, and during the Revolutionary War it was occupied by British troops. England controlled New York until 1783 when it withdrew from the city two full years after the end of the American Revolution. Two years after *that*, New York was named the first capital of the United States. The first Congress was held at Federal Hall on Wall Street in 1789 with George Washington inaugurated as president. But New York's tenure as the capital didn't last long. A year later, the government headed south to the newly created District of Columbia.

By 1825, New York City's population swelled to 250,000 and rose again to a half-million by mid-century. The city was a hotbed of Union recruitment during the Civil War; in the 1863 draft riots, Irish immigrants violently protested the draft and lynched 11 African Americans.

The late 19th century, with industry booming, was termed the "Gilded Age." New York City was an example of this label in action; millionaires built mansions on Fifth Avenue, while rows of

Dateline

- **1524** Giovanni da Verrazano sails into New York Harbor.
- **1609** Henry Hudson sails up the Hudson River.
- **1621** The Dutch West India Company begins trading from New York City.
- **1626** The Dutch pay 60 Guilders ($24) to the Lenape Tribe for the island of New Amsterdam.
- **1664** The Dutch surrender New Amsterdam to the British and the island is renamed after the brother of King Charles II, The Duke of York.
- **1765** The Sons of Liberty burn the British Governor in effigy.
- **1776** Independence from England is declared.
- **1789** The first Congress is held at Federal Hall on Wall Street, and George Washington is inaugurated.
- **1792** The first stock exchange is established on Wall Street.
- **1820** New York City is the nation's largest city with a population of 124,000.
- **1863** The draft riots rage throughout New York; 125 people die.
- **1883** The Brooklyn Bridge opens.
- **1886** The Statue of Liberty is completed.
- **1892** Ellis Island opens and begins processing over a million immigrants yearly.

tenements teeming with families (made up of the cheap, mostly immigrant laborers who were employed by the industrial barons) filled the city's districts. In 1880, the city's population boomed to 1.1 million.

More European immigrants poured into the city between 1900 and 1930, arriving at Ellis Island and then fanning out into neighborhoods like the Lower East Side, Greenwich Village, Little Italy, and Harlem. With the city population in 1930 at 7 million and a Depression raging, New York turned to a feisty mayor named Fiorello La Guardia to help turn things around. With the help of civic planner Robert Moses, who masterminded a huge public works program, the city was remade. Moses did some things well, but his highway, bridge, tunnel, and housing projects ran through (and sometimes destroyed) many vibrant neighborhoods.

While most of the country prospered after World War II, New York, with those Moses-built highways and a newly forming car culture, endured an exodus to the suburbs. By 1958, the Dodgers had left Brooklyn and the Giants had left the Polo Grounds in Upper Manhattan. This economic slide climaxed in the late 1970s with the city's declaration of bankruptcy.

As Wall Street rallied during the Reagan years of the 1980s, New York's fortunes also improved. In the 1990s, with Rudolph Giuliani—whom they haven't named anything after yet—as the mayor, the city rode a wave of prosperity that left it safer, cleaner, and more populated. The flip side of this boom was that Manhattan became more homogenized. Witness the Disneyfication of Times Square—the ultimate symbol of New York's homogenization—and the growing gap between the rich and poor.

Everything changed on September 11, 2001, when terrorists took down the Twin Towers of the World Trade Center. But New York's grit and verve showed itself once more, as the city immediately began to rebound emotionally and financially from that terrible tragedy. As you read this book, however, the World Trade Center is still just a site, and though ground was broken for rebuilding in the summer of 2004, there is still controversy over what actually will be built on the site.

- **1904** The first subway departs from City Hall.
- **1920** Babe Ruth joins the New York Yankees.
- **1929** The stock market crashes.
- **1931** The Empire State Building opens and is the tallest building in the world.
- **1939** The New York World's Fair opens in Flushing Meadows, Queens.
- **1947** The Brooklyn Dodgers sign Jackie Robinson, the first African American to play in the Major Leagues.
- **1957** Elvis Presley performs on *The Ed Sullivan Show*.
- **1969** The Gay Rights movement begins with the Stonewall Rebellion in Greenwich Village.
- **1990** David Dinkins is elected as the first African American mayor of New York City.
- **2000** The New York Yankees beat the New York Mets in the first Subway Series in 44 years.
- **2001** Terrorists use hijacked planes to crash into the Twin Towers of the World Trade Center, which brings both towers down and kills more than 3,000 people.
- **2003** Smoking is banned in all restaurants and bars.
- **2004** Ground breaks for rebuilding on the site of the World Trade Center.

Appendix B:
Useful Toll-Free Numbers
& Websites

AIRLINES

Air Canada
℃ 888/247-2262
www.aircanada.ca

Air Jamaica
℃ 800/523-5585 in U.S.
℃ 888/359-2475 in Jamaica
www.airjamaica.com

Air New Zealand
℃ 800/423-5494 (reservations/
flight info) or -2468 in the U.S.
(travel agent hotline)
℃ 800/663-5494 in
Canada
℃ 0800/737-767 in
New Zealand
www.airnewzealand.com

Airtran Airlines
℃ 800/247-8726
www.airtran.com

Alaska Airlines
℃ 800/252-7522
www.alaskaair.com

American Airlines
℃ 800/433-7300
www.aa.com

ATA Airlines
℃ 800/1-FLY-ATA
www.ata.com

America West Airlines
℃ 800/235-9292
www.americawest.com

British Airways
℃ 800/247-9297 in. U.S.
℃ 0345/222-111 or
0845/77-333-77 in Britain
www.british-airways.com

BWIA
℃ 800/538-2942
www.bwee.com

Continental Airlines
℃ 800/525-0280
www.continental.com

Delta Air Lines
℃ 800/221-1212
www.delta.com

Easy Jet/Go Fly
www.easyjet.com

Frontier Airlines
℃ 800/432-1359
www.frontierairlines.com

Jet Blue Airlines
℃ 800/538-2583
www.jetblue.com

Mexicana
℃ 800/531-7921 in U.S.
℃ 01800/502-2000 in Mexico
www.mexicana.com

Midwest Airlines
℃ 800/452-2022
www.midwestairlines.com

North American Airlines
℃ 800/371-6297
www.northamericanair.com

Northwest Airlines
© 800/225-2525
www.nwa.com

Olympic Airways
© 800/223-1226 in U.S.
© 80/111-44444 in Greece
www.olympicairlines.com

Qantas
© 800/227-4500 (in U.S.)
© 13 13 13 (in Australia)
www.qantas.com

Ryanair
No U.S. number
© 0818 30 30 30 (in Ireland)
© 0871 246 0000 (in U.K.)
www.ryanair.com

Song
© 800/359-7664
www.flysong.com

Southwest Airlines
© 800/435-9792
www.southwest.com

Spirit Airlines
© 800/772-7117
www.spiritair.com

TACA
© 800/535-8780 in U.S.
© 503/267-8222 in El Salvador
www.taca.com

United Airlines
© 800/241-6522
www.united.com

US Airways
© 800/428-4322
www.usairways.com

Virgin Atlantic Airways
© 800/862-8621 in
    Continental U.S.
© 0870 380 2007 in
    Britain
www.virgin-atlantic.com

MAJOR HOTEL & MOTEL CHAINS

Best Western International
© 800/528-1234 or 800/780-7234
www.bestwestern.com

Clarion Hotels
© 800/CLARION or 877/424-6423
www.clarionhotel.com or
    www.hotelchoice.com

Comfort Inns
© 800/228-5150
www.hotelchoice.com

Courtyard by Marriott
© 800/321-2211
www.courtyard.com or
    www.marriott.com

Crowne Plaza Hotels
© 888/303-1746
www.crowneplaza.com

Days Inn
© 800/325-2525
www.daysinn.com

Doubletree Hotels
© 800/222-TREE
www.doubletree.com

Econo Lodges
© 800/55-ECONO
www.hotelchoice.com

Embassy Suites
© 800/EMBASSY
www.embassysuites.com

Fairfield Inn by Marriott
© 800/228-2800
www.marriott.com

Four Seasons
© 800/819-5053
www.fourseasons.com

Hampton Inn
© 800/HAMPTON
www.hamptoninn.com

Hilton Hotels
© 800/HILTONS
www.hilton.com

Holiday Inn
℃ 800/HOLIDAY
http://www.ichotelsgroup.com

Howard Johnson
℃ 800/654-2000
www.hojo.com

Hyatt Hotels & Resorts
℃ 800/228-9000
www.hyatt.com

Inter-Continental
Hotels & Resorts
℃ 888/567-8725
http://www.ichotelsgroup.com

ITT Sheraton
℃ 800/325-3535
www.starwood.com or
    www.sheraton.com

La Quinta Inns
℃ 800/531-5900 or 866/725-1661
www.laquinta.com

Loews Hotels
℃ 800/23LOEWS
www.loewshotels.com

Marriott Hotels
℃ 800/228-9290
www.marriott.com

Motel 6
℃ 800/4-MOTEL6
(800/466-8356)
www.motel6.com

Omni
℃ 800/THEOMNI
www.omnihotels.com

Quality
℃ 877/424-6423
www.hotelchoice.com

Radisson Hotels International
℃ 800/333-3333
www.radisson.com

Ramada
℃ 800/2-RAMADA
www.ramada.com

Red Carpet Inns
℃ 800/251-1962
www.bookroomsnow.com

Red Lion Hotels & Inns
℃ 800/RED-LION
www.redlion.com

Red Roof Inns
℃ 800/REDROOF
www.redroof.com

Renaissance
℃ 800/228-9290
www.renaissancehotels.com or
    www.marriott.com

Residence Inn by Marriott
℃ 800/331-3131
www.marriott.com

Ritz-Carlton
℃ 800/241-3333
www.ritzcarlton.com

Rodeway Inns
℃ 800/228-2000
www.hotelchoice.com

Sheraton Hotels & Resorts
℃ 800/325-3535
www.sheraton.com

Super 8 Motels
℃ 800/800-8000
www.super8.com

Travelodge
℃ 800/255-3050 or 800/578-7878
www.travelodge.com

Vagabond Inns
℃ 800/522-1555
www.vagabondinn.com

Westin Hotels & Resorts
℃ 800/937-8461
www.westin.com

Wyndham Hotels and Resorts
℃ 800/822-4200 in
    Continental U.S. and
    Canada
www.wyndham.com

Index

See also Accommodations and Restaurant indexes, below.

GENERAL INDEX

A
AA (American Automobile Association), 74
AARP, 42–43
Abaya, 373
ABC Carpet & Home, 315–316
Above and Beyond Tours, 43
Abyssinian Baptist Church, 272–273
Academy Records & CDs, 338
Accommodations, 122–167.
See also Accommodations Index
best, 9–11
chains, 124
Chelsea, 134
family-friendly, 149
Greenwich Village and the Meatpacking District, 131–133
landing the best room, 126
Midtown East and Murray Hill, 150–160
pet policies, 122
price categories and rack rates, 122
seasonal guidelines, 29–30
senior discounts, 42
SoHo, 129–131
South Street Seaport and Financial District, 129–131
surfing for, 45–47
Times Square and Midtown West, 139–150
tipping, 78–79
tips for saving on, 122–126
TriBeCa and the Lower East Side, 128–129
Union Square, the Flatiron District, and Gramercy Park, 135–139
Upper East Side, 165–167
Upper West Side, 160–165
what's new in, 1
Acker Merrall & Condit Co., 343

Address locator, Manhattan, 102
Adventures on a Shoestring, 291
Airfares
discounts for international visitors, 72
surfing for, 44
tips for getting the best, 58–60
Airlines, 51–52, 73
bankrupt, 59
international, 72
Airporter, 57
Airports, 51–52
security procedures, 57–58
transportation to and from, 52–57
Air-Ride, 52
Air Tickets Direct, 59
Air tours, 288
AirTrains, 54–55
Alexander and Bonin, 259
Allan & Suzi, 328
All State Cafe, 382
Allstate limousines, 53
Alphabet City, 97
Alphaville, 319
Amato Opera Theatre, 349, 353
American Airlines Vacations, 61
American Automobile Association (AAA), 74
American Ballet Theatre, 355
American Express, 28, 118
American Family Immigration History Center, 242
American Folk Art Museum, 252
American Girl Place, 342
American Immigrant Wall of Honor, 242
American Jewish Historical Society, 252
American Museum of Natural History, 6, 86, 239–241
American Museum of the Moving Image (Queens), 303–304

American Sephardi Federation, 253
American Surety Company, 22
Amtrak, 61
Anna Sui, 324
Annex Antiques Fair and Flea Market, 318–319
The Ansonia, 267
Anthropologie, 326
Antiques and collectibles, 318–319
Apartment rentals, 125–126
Apollo Theater, 356
The Apple Store, 331–332
Aquarium, New York (Brooklyn), 300–301
Arcades, 296
Architecture, 15–26
Art Deco, 25
art moderne, 25–26
Beaux Arts, 23–24
best structures, 7
Federal, 16, 18
Georgian, 15–16
Gothic Revival, 19–20
Greek Revival, 18–19
International style, 24–25
Italianate, 20–22
Second Renaissance Revival, 22–23
skyscrapers, 22
Area codes, 118
Argosy Books, 320
Arlene Grocery, 365
Armstrong, Louis, House Museum (Queens), 304
Art Deco architecture, 25
Art galleries, 258–259
Art moderne buildings, 25–26
Asia Society, 252
Astor Hall, 269
Astor Row Houses, 267
Astor Wines & Spirits, 343
Atlantic Theater Company, 349, 351
ATMs (automated teller machines), 28, 70

Auto., 332
Avalon, 384

Babysitting services, 42
Bagels, 198
The Baggot Inn, 365
Baktun, 384
Ballet, 355, 356
Balto, statue of, 280
BAM (Brooklyn Academy
  of Music), 356–357
BAM Next Wave Festival
  (Brooklyn), 34–35
B&H Photo & Video, 332
Barbara Gladstone Gallery, 259
Bargemusic, 349, 354
Barnes & Noble, 320
Barney's Co-op, 3, 316
Barneys New York, 13, 316
Barracuda, 386
Barramundi, 373
Bars and cocktail lounges,
  371–383
Baseball, 306
Basketball, 307
Bateaux New York, 286
Bath and beauty products,
  319–320
Battery Park, 92, 282–283
Bauman Rare Books, 320
B.B. King Blues Club & Grill,
  364, 366
Beacon Theatre, 363
Beaux Arts architecture, 23–24
Bed & breakfasts (B&Bs),
  125–126
Belmont Stakes, 32
Belvedere Castle, 277, 278
Bemelmans Bar, 11, 165, 380
Bergdorf Goodman, 316
Bergdorf Goodman Man, 316
Bethesda Fountain, 278
Bethesda Terrace, 278
Bicycling
  in Central Park, 280–281
  along the Hudson River, 8
  tours, 290
Big Apple Circus, 36
Big Apple Greeter, 41
Big Cup, 386
Bike New York: The Great Five
  Boro Bike Tour, 32
Birdland, 366–367
Bitter End, 365
Black, 384
Black Orchid Books, 322
Bloomingdale's, 3, 316–317
Blue Note, 367

The Boat House, 277
Boating, Central Park, 281
Boiler Room, 386
Boingo, 48
Bongo, 376
Books, recommended, 63
Books of Wonder, 320–321
Bookstores, 320–323
Borders, 320
Botanic Garden, Brooklyn, 299
Botanical Garden, New York
  (the Bronx), 297–298
Boucher, 335
Bow Bridge, 278
Bowery Ballroom, 364
Bowling, 285
Bowlmor/Pressure, 375
Brandy's Piano Bar, 386
Brill, Wildman Steve, 290
Broadway City, 296
Broadway Line, 346
Broadway on Broadway, 34
Broadway Panhandler, 333
Broadway Show League, 279
Broadway Ticket Center, 350
Bronwyn Keenan, 259
The Bronx
  best way to spend a day in, 9
  brief description of, 108
  restaurants, 224, 226–227
  sights and attractions,
    297–298
Bronx Zoo Wildlife Conserva-
  tion Park, 7, 297
Brooklyn
  best way to spend a day in, 9
  brief description of, 105–108
  restaurants, 227–228
  shopping, 314–315
  sights and attractions,
    299–303
Brooklyn Academy of Music
  (BAM), 356–357
Brooklyn Botanic Garden, 299
Brooklyn Bridge, 4, 6, 84,
  241–242
Brooklyn Cyclones, 306
Brooklyn Heights, 105, 302
Brooklyn Ice Cream Factory, 180
Brooklyn Museum of Art,
  299–300
Brooklyn Promenade, 302
Brooklyn Public Library, 299
Brooklyn Tabernacle, 300
Brooks Brothers, 325
Bryant Park, 283
Bryant Park Summer Film
  Festival, 361
Bu & the Duck, 327–328

Bubble Lounge, 371
Bucket shops, 59
Bull and Bear, 380
Burberry, 324
Buses, 73, 113–114
  to/from airports, 54–57
  for disabled travelers, 41
Business hours, 74, 118–119
Bus tours, double-decker, 286
Butterfly Conservatory, 241

Cabanas, 372
Cabaret, 369–370
Cabs, 115–116
  to/from airports, 52–53
  for disabled travelers, 41
Cafe Carlyle, 369
Café del Bar, 382
Cafe Wha?, 384
Caffè Roma, 178
Calendar of events, 30–37
Cameras, digital, 49, 60
The Campbell Apartment, 379
Camper, 340
Carmel, 53
Carnegie Club, 377
Carnegie Hall, 14, 349, 357
Carolines on Broadway, 370
Car rentals, 27, 116
  for disabled travelers, 40
Car travel, 73–74, 107, 116
Castle Clinton National
  Monument, 271
Cathedral of St. John the
  Divine, 7, 35, 88, 273
  New Year's Eve Concert for
    Peace, 37
Cellphones, 49–51
Center for Jewish History,
  252–253
Central Park, 7, 86, 239,
  275–282
  activities, 280–282
  entertainment, 360–361
  exploring, 278–280
  guided walks, 277
  orientation, 277
  safety tip, 278
  traveling to, 277
  visitor information, 277, 278
The Central Park Conservancy,
  277
Central Park Drive, 277, 280
Central Park Reservoir,
  6, 264–265
Central Park West, movie
  locations on, 265
Central Park Zoo, 280

Century 21, 317
Chamber Music Society of
    Lincoln Center, 358
Chanel, 324
Channel Gardens, 246
Charles A. Dana Discovery
    Center, 277, 279
Cheap Tickets, 59
Cheim & Read, 259
Chelsea, 43–44
    accommodations, 134
    art galleries, 259
    bars and lounges, 376–377
    brief description of, 98–99
    restaurants, 190–191
    shopping, 312
Chelsea Antiques Building, 319
Chelsea Art District, 312
Chelsea Market, 329–330
Chelsea Piers, 98–99, 285
Cheryl Hazan Arts Gallery, 259
Children, families with
    accommodations, 149
    best places to take the kids, 7
    information and resources,
        41–42
    restaurants, 210
    shopping
        clothing, 327–328
        toys, 342–343
    sights and activities, 294–297
    theater, 348
Children's Museum of
    Manhattan, 295
Children's Museum of the Arts,
    295
Children's Zoo (the Bronx), 297
Chinatown, 8
    bars and lounges, 371, 373
    brief description of, 94–95
    restaurants, 178–179
    shopping, 308–309
Chinatown Ice Cream Factory,
    180
Chinese New Year, 30–31
Chocolate, 329
The Chocolate Bar, 329
The Chocolate Show, 35
Christmas traditions, 36–37
Christmas tree, Rockefeller
    Center, 36
Chrysler Building, 7, 25,
    82, 268
Chumley's, 375
Church Lounge, 371
Circle Line Sightseeing Cruises,
    80, 286–287
City Center, 355
City Hall, 94

CityPass, 240
Classical music, 354–355
Classic Transportation, 56, 57
Cleopatra's Needle, 279
Climate, 30
The Cloisters, 253
Clothing, 323–328
Club Shelter, 384
C. O. Bigelow, 319–320
The Cock, 386
Coffee, 330
Cold Stone Creamery, 180
Coliseum Books, 13, 321
Colonial Transportation, 56
Colony Music Center, 339
Comedy Cellar, 370
Comedy clubs, 370–371
Complete Traveller, 321
Coney Island (Brooklyn),
    108, 300
Coney Island Museum, 269
Connecticut Limousine, 57
The Conservatory, 277
Conservatory Garden, 279
Conservatory Water, 278
Consolidators, 59
Consulates, 75
Continental Airlines
    Vacations, 61
Cooper-Hewitt National Design
    Museum, 253–254
Council Travel, 59
Credit cards, 29, 70
Crime, 117–118
Crobar, 384–385
Currency and currency
    exchange, 69
Custard Beach, 180
Customs regulations, 67–68
CyberCafe, 48
Cynthia Rowley, 324

Dahesh Museum of Art, 254
The Daily Show with
    Jon Stewart, 292
The Dairy, 277
The Dakota, 86, 268
Dance clubs and party scenes,
    383–385
Dance performances, 355–356
Dangerfield's, 370
Dba, 374
DCA Gallery, 259
Dean & DeLuca, 330
Decade, 385
Deep vein thrombosis, 39
Delacorte Theater, 279, 360
Delis, Jewish, 203, 206, 264

Delta Vacations, 61
Department stores, 315–318
DFN Gallery, 259
Diamond District, 335
Digital cameras, 49, 60
Disabilities, travelers with,
    40–41
Dive bars, 378–379
Dizzy's Club Coca-Cola, 367
Doctors, 119
Don Hill's, 385
Double-decker bus tours, 286
Double Happiness, 371
Downtown (Manhattan)
    art galleries, 259
    neighborhoods, 92–98
    shopping, 308
Downtown Brooklyn, 107–108
Doyle & Doyle, 335
Drama Book Shop, 321
Drinking laws, 74–75
Driver's licenses, foreign, 66
Dublin House, 382
DUMBO (Brooklyn), 105–106
Duplex Cabaret, 386
Dusk, 377
Dyckman Farmhouse Museum,
    270
Dylan's Candy Bar, 331

Ear Inn, 14, 373
Easter Parade, 31
East River, running along the,
    282
The East Village
    bars and lounges, 374–375
    brief description of, 96–97
    restaurants, 185–186
    shopping, 311
EasyInternetCafé, 48
Economy class syndrome, 39
Eden, 382
Edgar Allan Poe Cottage, 270
Eichler's, 321
Eileen Fisher, 326
Elaine's, 382
Elderhostel, 43
ElderTreks, 43
Electricity, 75
Electronics, 313, 331–332
Electronics stores, 107
Ellis Island, 83, 242, 249
El Museo del Barrio, 254
ELTExpress, 59
Embassies and consulates, 75
Emergencies, 75–76, 119
Empire State Building, 2, 4, 25,
    82, 242–243, 264, 296

Enid A. Haupt Conservatory (the Bronx), 298
Entry requirements, 65–67
Escorted tours, 62–63
ETS Air Service, 57

Fairway, 330
Families with children
 accommodations, 149
 best places to take the kids, 7
 information and resources, 41–42
 restaurants, 210
 shopping
  clothing, 327–328
  toys, 342–343
 sights and activities, 294–297
 theater, 348
Familyhostel, 42
Family Travel Files, 42
Family Travel Forum, 42
Family Travel Network, 42
FAO Schwarz, 342
Fauchon, 331
Fax machines, 78
Feast of St. Francis, 35, 273
Feast of San Gennaro, 107
Federal architectural style, 16, 18
Federal Hall National Memorial, 19, 271
FedEx Kinko's, 48
Feigen Contemporary, 259
Feinstein's at The Regency, 369
Ferrara, 178
Festivals and special events, 30–37
Field House (Chelsea Piers), 285
Fifth Avenue, 82, 103
 and 57th Street, shopping on, 313
Film, flying with, 60
Film festivals
 New York Film Festival, 34
 Tribeca Film Festival, 32
Films, recommended, 63–64
Film Society of Lincoln Center, 358
The Financial District, 92
 accommodations, 126–128
 restaurants, 174–178
 shopping, 308
First Saturday (Brooklyn), 299
Fishs Eddy, 333–334
Flatiron Building, 22, 268
The Flatiron District
 accommodations, 135–139
 bars and lounges, 377

brief description of, 99
 restaurants, 195–199
 shopping, 312
Fleet Week, 32
Flights.com, 59
Flushing Meadows–Corona Park, 295–296
FlyCheap, 59
Food Festival, Ninth Avenue International, 6, 32
Food stores and markets, 328–331
Footlight, 339
Forbidden Planet, 321
Foreign visitors, 65–79
 entry requirements, 65–67
 health insurance, 68–69
 immigration and customs clearance, 72–73
 money matters, 69–70
 safety, 70–72
 traveling around the U.S., 73–74
 traveling to the U.S., 72–73
Fortunoff, 336
Fourth of July Fireworks Spectacular, 33
Frank Stella, 327
Fraunces Tavern, 16, 271
Free or almost free activities, 8
Frequent-flier clubs, 60
Frette, 334
The Frick Collection, 254–255
Frommers.com, 46

Gagosian Gallery, 258, 259
Garment District, 101
 shopping, 312
Gasoline, 76
Gay & Lesbian National Hot Line, 44
Gay and lesbian travelers
 accommodations, 132
 bookstore, 323
 information and resources, 43
 nightlife, 385–387
Gay Men's Health Crisis (GMHC), 44
Generation Records, 339
George Billis Gallery, 259
Georgian architecture, 15–16
Gianni Versace, 323
Gifts, 332–333
The Ginger Man, 380
Giraudon New York, 341
Golf at the Chelsea Piers, 285
Gospel services, 8
Gotham Book Mart, 321

Gotham Comedy Club, 14, 370
Gothic Revival architecture, 19–20
Graffiti Hall of Fame, 269
Gramercy Park
 accommodations, 135–139
 bars and lounges, 377
 brief description of, 100
 restaurants, 195–199
Grand Army Plaza, 299
Grand Central Terminal, 7, 24, 80, 82, 244
 take-out food and restaurants, 209–210
Gray Line New York Tours, 286
Great Hall Balcony Bar, 382–383
Great Lawn (Central Park), 278–279
Greek Revival architecture, 18–19
Greenmarket, Union Square, 284
Greenwich Village, 7–8
 accommodations, 131–133
 bars and lounges, 375–376
 restaurants, 186–190
 shopping, 311
 Treebdo, 97–98
Greenwich Village Halloween Parade, 35–36
Greyhound/Trailways, 73
Ground Zero (World Trade Center site), 251
Gucci, 324
Guéridon, 311
Guggenheim Museum, 86, 88, 247–248
Gunther Building, 22
Guss's Pickles, 331

HAI Hot Line, 41
Halloween Parade, Greenwich Village, 35–36
Hampton Jitney, 56
Handbags, 333
H&M, 325
Hanukkah Menorah, lighting of the (Brooklyn), 37
Harbor cruises, 286–287
Harlem
 architectural treasures, 267
 brief description of, 104–105
 restaurants, 223–224, 226–227
 shopping, 315
Harlem Meer (Central Park), 279

Harlem Spirituals, 289–290
Harlem Week, 33
Harry's Shoes, 341
Haughwout Store, 22
Health concerns, 38–39
Health insurance, 38
for international visitors,
68–69
Hell, 386
Hell's Kitchen, 101
Henri Bendel, 317
Henrietta Hudson, 386
Henry Luce Nature Observatory, 278
Herald Square, 101–102
shopping, 312
Hidden Jazz Haunts, 291
Historic homes, 270
Historic Orchard Street
Shopping District, 309
HIV-positive visitors, 66
Hogs & Heifers, 382
Holidays, 76
Holiday Trimmings, 36
Home design and housewares,
333–335
Horse-drawn carriage rides,
106, 281
Hospital Audiences, Inc., 40–41
Hospitals, 38, 119
Hot lines, 119
Hotwire, 45–47
House of Oldies, 339
Housing Works Used Books
Cafe, 321–322
Hudson Bar, 377–378
Hudson Bar & Books, 375
Hudson River, running along
the, 282
Hue-Man Bookstore, 322
Humanities and Social Sciences
Library, 268–269
Huminska, 326
Hurley's Hudson Beach Café,
372

Ice-cream, 180
Ice hockey, 307
Ice-skating, 35
Central Park, 281
Il Laboratorio del Gelato,
84, 180
Immigration Museum, 242
Independence Day Harbor
Festival, 33
In-line skating, Central Park,
281
Intermix, 326–327

International Ameripass, 73
International Building, 247
International Center of
Photography, 255
International Gay and Lesbian
Travel Association (IGLTA), 43
International style, 24–25
International visitors, 65–79
entry requirements, 65–67
health insurance, 68–69
immigration and customs
clearance, 72–73
money matters, 69–70
safety, 70–72
traveling around the U.S.,
73–74
traveling to the U.S., 72–73
Internet access, 47–49
InTouch USA, 50
INTRAV, 43
Intrepid Sea-Air-Space
Museum, 7, 255
Inwood, 105
IPass network, 49
Iridium, 367
Irving Plaza, 364–365
Isamu Noguchi Garden
Museum (Queens), 304
Islip Airport (Long Island), 56
Italianate architecture, 20–22
Itineraries, suggested, 80–88
Ito En, 330
i2roam, 49

Jack Spade, 332
Jacqueline Kennedy Onassis
Reservoir, 279, 282
Jacques Torres Chocolate,
329
James Cohan Gallery, 259
J&R Music & Computer World,
332
The Jane Pauley Show, 292
Jazz, 358
tour, 291
Jazz at Lincoln Center, 3, 349,
358
Jazz at the Cajun, 367
Jazz at the Kitano, 366
Jazz Record Center, 339
Jazz Standard, 349, 367–368
Jefferson Market Library, 20
Jeffrey New York, 325
Jeremy's Ale House, 372
Jewelry and accessories,
335–336
Jewish delis, 203, 206, 264
The Jewish Museum, 256

JFK (John F. Kennedy International Airport), 51
transportation to/from, 52–56
JFK Flyer, 57
Jill Anderson, 327
Jill Platner, 336
Jimmy Choo, 341
Jimmy's Corner, 378
Joe's Pub, 369–370
Jogging, 6
Jonathan Adler, 334
Joseph Papp Public Theater, 351
Joyce Gold History Tours of
New York, 289
Joyce SoHo, 356
Joyce Theater, 355–356
The Juilliard School, 354–355
Jumel Terrace Historic District,
267
Jutta Neumann, 333

Kanvas, 376
Kar'ikter, 334
Kate spade, 333
Kate's Paperie, 340
Keen Company, 351
Kentshire Galleries, 319
KGB Bar, 374
Kidding Around, 342
Kiehl's, 320
King Cole Bar, 381
The Kitchen, 366
Kitchen Arts & Letters, 323
The Knitting Factory, 365
Kossar's Bialys, 331

Lafayette Street, shopping,
311
LaGuardia Airport, 51
transportation to/from, 52–56
La Maison du Chocolat, 329
The Lasker Rink and Pool,
35, 279, 281, 282
Last Call with Carson Daly, 292
Late Night with Conan O'Brien,
293
The Late Show with David
Letterman, 293
Layout of New York City, 90–91
Lazer Park, 296
Leader Restaurant Equipment
& Supplies, 334
Leather goods, 333
Le Carrousel, 283
Lefferts Homestead Children's
Historic House Museum
(Brooklyn), 301

Legal aid, 76
Legends, 53, 56
Lehmann Maupin, 259
Lenox Lounge, 368
Leo Baeck Institute, 252
Leonard Nimoy Thalia Theater, 362
Lesbian and Gay Community Services Center, 44, 385
Lesbian and Gay Pride Week and March, 32
Lever House, 24, 267
Liberty Helicopters, 288
Li-Lac Chocolates, 329
Limousine services, 53–54
Lincoln Center Festival 2006, 33
Lincoln Center for the Performing Arts, 357–359
Lincoln Center Theater, 350, 358
Liquor laws, 120
Little Italy, 264
    brief description of, 95
Little Italy (the Bronx), 8
Live! with Regis and Kelly, 293
Loeb Boathouse, 278, 280, 281
Logo stores, 336–337
Long Island City (Queens), 108–109
Long Island Rail Road (LIRR), 117
The Loop in Central Park, 282
Lord & Taylor, 317
Lost City Arts, 319
Lost-luggage insurance, 38
Louis Armstrong House Museum (Queens), 7, 304
Louis K. Meisel, 259
The Lower East Side
    accommodations, 128–129
    bars and lounges, 373
    brief description of, 95–96
    restaurants, 179–182
    shopping, 309
Lower East Side Business Improvement District, 96
Lower East Side Tenement Museum, 84, 256–257
Lower Manhattan, 92
    shopping, 308
Luggage, shipping your, 58
Luggage Express, 58

Macy's, 317–318
Macy's Thanksgiving Day Parade, 36
Madame Tussauds New York, 257

Madison Avenue, shopping on, 314
Madison Square, 100
Madison Square Garden, 307, 359–360
Mail, 76
Majestic Apartments, 26
The Mall (Central Park), 278
Manhattan Pedicab, 287
Manhattan Portage Ltd. Store, 333
Manhattan Rickshaw Company, 287
Manolo Blahnik, 341
Maps, street, 91–92
Marathon, New York City, 35
Marc Jacobs, 324
Margo Feiden Galleries, 258
Mark's Bar, 381
Mary Boone Gallery, 258–259
MasterCard traveler's checks, 28
Maxilla & Mandible, 338
M Bar, 381
McGraw-Hill Building, 247
McNulty's Tea & Coffee Company, 330
McSorley's Old Ale House, 374
Meat-Packing District, 99
    accommodations, 131–133
    bars and lounges, 375–376
    restaurants, 2, 186–190
    shopping, 312
Medical insurance, 38
    for international visitors, 68–69
Medical requirements for entry, 66
Merc Bar, 373
Merchant's House Museum, 270
Mercury Lounge, 14, 365
Messiah, singalong perform-ances of, 37
MetroCard, 1, 111–113
Metro-North Railroad, 117
Metropolitan Club, 23
Metropolitan Museum of Art, 6, 86, 244–245
Metropolitan Museum of Art Store, 246, 338
Metropolitan Opera, 353, 361
Mets, 306
Mets Clubhouse Shop, 306, 336
Michael's, 328
Mickey Mantle's, 378
Midsummer Night's Swing, 33
Midtown
    brief description of, 98–103
    shopping, 312–313

Midtown East
    accommodations, 150–160
    bars and lounges, 379–381
    brief description of, 102–103
Midtown West
    bars and lounges, 377–379
    brief description of, 100–102
    restaurants, 199–207
Mies van der Rohe, Ludwig, 24
Miu Miu, 325
Modell's, 341–342
MoMA Design Store, 338
Money matters, 28–29
Monkey Bar, 380
Mood Indigo, 319
Morgan Bank Headquarters, 26
Morgan Library, 257
Morrell & Company, 343
Morrell Wine Bar & Cafe, 343, 378
Morris-Jumel Mansion, 267, 270
Moss, 334
Mostly Mozart, 33
Mother A.M.E. Zion Church, 273–274
Movie locations, 264
The MTV Store, 336
Municipal Art Society, 288
Murder Ink, 322
Murray Hill, 103
    accommodations, 150–160
    bars and lounges, 379–381
Museum for African Art (Queens), 304–305
Museum Mile Festival, 32
Museum of Arts and Design, 257, 260
Museum of Chinese in the Americas, 269
Museum of Jewish Heritage—A Living Memorial to the Holocaust, 260
Museum of Modern Art (MoMA), 2, 7, 82, 245–246
    Design Store, 338
Museum of Sex, 8, 260–261
Museum of Television & Radio, 261
Museum of the City of New York, 260
Museums
    best, 6–7
    free, 8
    for kids, 294–296
Museum stores, 338
Music
    classical, 354–355
    live (rock, jazz, blues, and Latin), 362–369

Music stores, 338–340
The Mysterious Bookshop, 322

National Museum of the American Indian, George Gustav Heye Center, 261
Natural History, American Museum of, 86, 239–241
NBA Store, 336–337
NBC Experience, 337
NBC Studio Tour, 247
NBC television studios, 247
Neighborhoods in brief, 92–109
    the Bronx, 108
    Brooklyn, 105–108
    Manhattan, 92–109
    Queens, 108–109
    Staten Island, 109
Neue Gallerie New York, 261
Newark International Airport, 51
    for disabled travelers, 41
    transportation to/from, 52–57
New Jersey Transit, 117
New Museum of Contemporary Art, 261–262
New Perspectives Theatre, 349
Newspapers and magazines, 77, 120
New Victory Theater, 348
New Year's Day, 6
New Year's Eve, 37, 106
    Brooklyn's fireworks celebration, 37
    Concert for Peace, 37
New York 911, 337
New York Airport Service, 54–57
New York Aquarium (Brooklyn), 300–301
New York Botanical Garden (the Bronx), 297–298
New York City Ballet, 356
New York City Fire Museum, 262
New York City Gay Men's Chorus, 44
New York City Marathon, 35
New York City Opera, 353
New York City Police Museum, 269
New Yorker, 90, 344
New York Film Festival, 34
New York Firefighter's Friend, 337
New York Gilbert and Sullivan Players, 353

New York Hall of Science, 295
New-York Historical Society, 262
New York International Auto Show, 31
New York International Fringe Festival, 34
New York Knicks, 307
New York Liberty, 307
New York magazine, 90, 344
New York National Boat Show, 30
New York Philharmonic, 349, 355, 361
New York Public Library, 24, 80, 120, 268
New York Public Library for the Performing Arts, 359
New York Skyride, 296
New York Stock Exchange (NYSE), 250
New York Theater Workshop (NYTW), 351
New York Times, 89–90, 344
New York Transit Museum (Brooklyn), 301
New York Transit Museum Store, 338
New York Waterway, 287
Nightlife, 344–387
    bars and cocktail lounges, 371–383
    best, 14
    cabaret, 369–370
    comedy clubs, 370–371
    dance clubs and party scenes, 383–385
    gay and lesbian, 385–387
    live music (rock, jazz, blues, and Latin), 362–369
    major concert halls and landmark venues, 356–362
    opera, classical music, and dance, 352–356
    theater, 344–352
Niketown, 337
92nd Street Y Tisch Center for the Arts, 288–289, 360–362
Ninth Avenue International Food Festival, 6, 32
NoHo, 97
    bars and lounges, 374–375
    restaurants, 185–186
Nolita
    brief description of, 96
    restaurants, 182–185
    shopping, 310–311
The North Meadow, 279

NoshWalks, 289
Now, Voyager, 43
The Nutcracker, 36
NYC & Company, 27
NYC Discovery Tours, 289
NYCVB Visitor Information Center, 89
NYCVB Visitor Information Center (London), 27

Oak Room at the Algonquin, The, 370, 381
Official NYC Visitor Kit, 27
O. K. Harris, 259
Old Town Bar & Restaurant, 377
Olivia Cruises & Resorts, 43
Olympia Airport Express, 56
Olympia Trails and Express Shuttle USA, 54
Olympic Limousine, 57
On Location Tours, 289
Opera, 353
Oscar Wilde Bookshop, 44, 323
Other Music, 339

PaceWildenstein, 258
Package tours, 61–62
Paper and stationery, 340
Paper Bag Players, 14, 348
Parades, summer, 32
Paragon Sporting Goods, 342
Parks, 282–284. *See also* Central Park
    best, 7
    Prospect Park (Brooklyn), 301–302
Park Slope (Brooklyn), 108
Partners & Crime, 322
Passports, 66–67
Patagonia, 342
PATH system, 116
Paula Cooper, 259
Paul Smith, 327
Paul Stuart, 325
Pearl River, 332
Pedicabs, 287
Penn Station, 61, 101
Pen-Top Bar, 372
Peter Blum Gallery, 259
Peter Jay Sharp Theater, 362
Pete's Tavern, 377
Petrol, 76
Pharmacies, 120
Pier 17, 266
Pizzerias, 204–205
Playbill Online, 348

Playgrounds, Central Park, 281
Plunge, 372
Plymouth Church of the
    Pilgrims (Brooklyn), 302
Poe, Edgar Allan, Cottage
    (the Bronx), 270
Police, 120
Polo/Ralph Lauren, 325
The Pool (Central Park), 279–280
The Pop Shop, 337
Postmodern architecture, 26
Prada, 324, 325
Pravda, 373
Priceline, 45–47
Prime Time Shuttle of
    Connecticut, 57
Private car and limousine
    services, 53–54
Prospect Park (Brooklyn),
    301–302
Prospect Park Zoo (Brooklyn),
    301–302
P.S. 1 Contemporary Art Center
    (Queens), 305
Public Theater, Joseph Papp, 351
Puck Fair, 374
Punch & Judy, 373
Push, 336

Queens
    best way to spend a day in, 9
    brief description of, 108–109
    restaurants, 229
    sights and attractions,
        303–305
Queens Museum of Art, 305

Racquet and Tennis Club, 23
Radical Walking Tours, 291
Radio City Music Hall, 26,
    247, 362
Radio City Music Hall Christ-
    mas Spectacular, 35, 362
Rainbow Room, 246, 379
Rainfall, average, 30
The Ramble, 278
Religious institutions, 272–275
Restaurants, 168–229. See also
    Restaurants Index
        best, 11–13
        breakfast, 220
        Brooklyn, 227–228
        Chelsea, 190–191
        Chinatown, 178–179
        by cuisine, 170–174
        the East Village and NoHo,
            185–186

family-friendly, 210
Financial District, South Street
    Seaport, and TriBeCa,
    174–178
Greenwich Village and the
    Meat-Packing District,
    186–190
Harlem, 223–224, 226–227
Jewish delis, 206
late-night, 376
the Lower East Side, 179–182
Midtown East and Murray
    Hill, 207–211
pizzerias, 204–205
Queens, 229
reservations, 168–169
smoking, 169
SoHo and Nolita, 182–185
sources for serious foodies,
    169–170
splurge, 214
steakhouses, 194
Times Square and Midtown
    West, 199–207
tipping, 79, 169
Union Square, the Flatiron
    District, and Gramercy Park,
    195–199
Upper East Side, 221–223
Upper West Side, 211–221
what's new in, 2
Restaurant Week, 31, 33
Restrooms, 79, 120
Richard Gray Gallery, 258
Ricky's, 320
Rise Bar, 14, 372
Riverside Park, 7, 283, 372
Rizzoli, 323
RoadPost, 50
Rock clubs, 365–366
Rockefeller Center, 25, 82,
    101, 246
    ice-skating rink, 35
    lighting of the Christmas
        tree, 36
    Rink at, 246
Rockefeller Center Tour, 247
Rockstarbaby, 328
Rodeo Bar, 366
Roller Rinks (Chelsea Piers),
    285
Roosevelt Island Tram, 8,
    248, 265
Rose Center for Earth and
    Space, 239–240
Roseland, 363
Rose Theater, 358
Roundabout Theatre Company,
    347, 350

The Row, 19
Royal Hut, 334
Rudy's Bar & Grill, 378–379
Runner's World Midnight
    Run, 37
Running, 281–282
Russ & Daughters, 331
Russian Vodka Room, 379

Sacco, 341
Safety, 39, 117–118
    for international visitors,
        70–72
St. John the Divine, Cathedral
    of, 7, 35, 88, 273
    New Year's Eve Concert for
        Peace, 37
Saint Laurie Merchant
    Tailors, 327
St. Nick's Pub, 368
St. Patrick's Cathedral, 274
St. Patrick's Day Parade, 31
St. Paul's Chapel, 16, 271, 275
Saks Fifth Avenue, 13, 318
Sales tax, 121, 309
Salon services, 120–121
Salvatore Ferragamo, 324
Satalla, 368
Saturday Night Live, 293
Scandinavia House: The Nordic
    Center in America, 262–263
The Scholastic Store, 323
Schomburg Center for
    Research in Black
    Culture, 263
Screaming Mimi's, 328
Seagram Building, 24, 267
Sean John, 325–326
Searle, 327
Seasons, 29–30
Second Renaissance Revival
    architecture, 22–23
Seize sur Vingt, 326
Senior travel, 42–43
Sephora, 319
Serena, 377
79th Street Boat Basin Café, 372
Sex and the City Tour, 289
Shakespeare Garden, 279
Shakespeare in the Park, 14,
    33, 360
Shea Stadium, 306
Shecky's New York Bar, Club &
    Lounge Guide, 344
Sheep Meadow, 278
Sherry-Lehmann, 343
Shipping your luggage, 58
Shoes, 340–341

Shoofly, 328
Shopping, 308–343
    best, 13
    department stores, 315–318
    for kids, 296
    open hours, 313
    sources for serious
        shoppers, 310
    top streets and neighbor-
        hoods for, 308–315
    what's new in, 2–3
The Shops at Columbus
    Circle, 314
Shuttle services, to/from
    airports, 54–57
SideStep, 45
Sigerson Morrison, 341
Sights and attractions,
    230–305
    the Bronx, 297–298
    Brooklyn, 299–303
    for kids, 294–297
    by neighborhood, 230–231,
        239
    organized tours, 286–291
    parks, 282–284 (See also
        Central Park)
    Queens, 303–305
    skyscrapers and other archi-
        tectural highlights, 267–272
    subway stops for, 110
    TV tapings, 292–294
    what's new in, 2
Signature Theatre Company, 351
SkyCap International, 58
Sky Rink (Chelsea Piers), 285
Skyscraper Museum, 263
Skyscrapers, 22, 267–272
Smoke, 368
Smoking, 121
S.O.B.'s, 368–369
Socrates Sculpture Park
    (Queens), 305
Softball leagues (Central
    Park), 279
SoHo
    accommodations, 129–131
    art galleries, 259
    bars and lounges, 373–374
    brief description of, 96
    restaurants, 182–185
    shopping, 309–310
SoHo–Cast Iron Historic
    District, 22
Solomon R. Guggenheim
    Museum, 86, 88, 247–248
Sony Building, 26, 267
Sony Wonder Technology
    Lab, 296

Sopranos Tour, 289
Soundwalk, 290
South Street Seaport, 84, 92,
    263, 266, 308
    accommodations, 126–128
    restaurants, 174–178
South Street Seaport Museum,
    266
Space Kiddets, 328
Special events and festivals,
    30–37
Spectator sports, 306–307
Spirit, 385
Spirit Cruises, 287
Splash/SBNY, 386–387
Sports Express, 58
Stand-Up New York, 370–371
Staten Island, 109
Staten Island Ferry, 8, 248–249
Staten Island Yankees, 306
State Shuttle, 57
STA Travel, 59
Statue of Liberty, 4, 83, 249
    movie locations, 265
Steakhouses, 194
Steuben Glass, 332–333
Stonewall Bar, 387
The Strand, 323
Strawberry Fields, 278
Street maps, 91–92
Strivers' Row, 267
Studio Museum in Harlem,
    266
Subway, 109–113
    for disabled travelers, 41
    the International Express
        (7 train), 8–9
    to/from JFK airport, 52
    movie locations, 265
    music in the, 359
    service interruption notes,
        112
Subway Inn, 14, 379
Sugar Hill, 267
Summer, 6, 29
SummerStage, 33, 361
Super Shuttle, 54–55
Swedish Cottage Marionette
    Theatre, 279, 348
Swimming, Central Park, 282
Swing 46, 385
Sylvan Terrace, 267
Symphony Space, 362

TADA! Youth Theater, 348
Takashimaya, 318
Tap a Keg, 379
Taxes, 77, 121

Taxis, 115–116
    to/from airports, 52–53
    for disabled travelers, 41
TDI (Theatre Direct Interna-
    tional), 347
Tea, 330
Ted Baker London, 326
Telegraph and telex services, 78
Telephone, 77–78
    area codes, 118
    cellphones, 49–51
Temperature, average, 30
Temple Bar, 374–375
Temple Emanu-El, 274
Tennis, U.S. Open Tennis
    Championships, 34
Terence Conran Shop, 334
TFI Tours, 59
Thanksgiving Day Parade,
    Macy's, 36
Theater, 344–352
Theater at Madison Square
    Garden, 360
Theater District, 101
    shopping, 312–313
TheaterMania, 348
Theatre Direct International
    (TDI), 347
30 Rockefeller Plaza, 246
Ticketmaster, 363
Ticketweb, 363
Tiffany & Co., 336
Time Out New York, 90, 344
Time Out New York: Eating &
    Drinking, 169–170
Times Square, 83, 100–101,
    249–250
    bars and lounges, 377–379
    movie locations, 264
    New Year's Eve in, 106
    restaurants, 199–207
    shopping, 312–313
Times Square Visitors Center,
    48, 89
Time zones, 78
Tipping, 78–79
Tisch Children's Zoo, 280
Titanic Memorial Lighthouse,
    266
TKTS Booth, 350, 352
T-Mobile Hotspot, 48
The Today Show, 293
Toilets, 79
Tom & Jerry's (288 Bar), 375
Tonic, 366
The Tony Danza Show,
    293–294
Top of the Rock, 246
Total Request Live, 294

Tourist information, 27, 89–90
Tourneau Time Machine, 336
Tours
    escorted, 62–63
    organized, 286–291
    package, 61–62
    walking. See Walking tours
    Yankee Stadium, 307
Tower Books and Video, 340
Tower Records, 13, 340
Town Hall, 362
Toys, 342–343
Toys "R" Us, 342–343
Train travel, 73
Transit information, 121
Transportation, 109–117
    to/from airports, 52–57
    by bus, 113–114
    by car, 116
    to the suburbs, 116–117
    by subway, 109–113
    by taxi, 115–116
Traveler's assistance, 121
Traveler's checks, 28, 69–70
The TravelHub, 59
Traveling
    around the U.S., 73–74
    to New York City, 51–61
        by car, 60–61
        by plane, 51
        by train, 61
    to the U.S., 72–73
Traveling Internationally with
    Your Kids, 42
Travel insurance, 37–38
TriBeCa
    accommodations, 128–129
    bars and lounges, 371
    brief description of, 94
    restaurants, 174–178
Tribeca Film Festival, 32
Trinity Church, 20, 274
Trip-cancellation insurance,
    37–38
Triple Pier Antiques Show,
    31, 36
TV tapings, 292–294

Under the Volcano, 381
Union Square, 100
    accommodations, 135–139
    bars and lounges, 377
    restaurants, 195–199
    shopping, 312
Union Square Greenmarket, 284
Union Square Park, 84, 284
Union Square Wines and
    Spirits, 343

United Nations, 25, 270–272
United Vacations, 61
Upper East Side
    accommodations, 165–167
    art galleries, 258–259
    bars and lounges, 382–383
    brief description of, 104
    restaurants, 221–223
Upper West Side, 7
    accommodations, 160–165
    bars and lounges, 382
    brief description of, 103–104
    restaurants, 211–221
    shopping, 314
Upright Citizens Brigade
    Theatre, 371
Uptown, brief description of,
    103–105
Urban Center Books, 323
USA Rail Pass, 73
U.S. Customs House, 24,
    261, 271
U.S. Open Tennis Champi-
    onships, 34

Vera Wang, 327
Victorian Gothic, 20
Video, flying with, 60
The View, 294
View Bar, 387
The Village Vanguard, 14, 369
Village Voice, 90, 344
Villard Bar & Lounge, 381
Virgin Megastore, 340
Virtual Bellhop, 58
Visas for international visitors,
    65–66
Visa traveler's checks, 28
Visitor information, 27, 89–90
Visitors, international, customs
    regulations, 67–68
Vital Theatre Company, 349
Vivienne Tam, 324

Walker's, 371
Walking, 109
Walking tours
    guided, 288–291
        Central Park, 277
        Grand Central Terminal,
            244
        Streets Where We Lived,
            256
Wall Street, 83, 250
Washington Heights, 105
Washington Square North,
    284

Washington Square Park,
    84, 284
Waterworks, 335
Wave Hill (the Bronx), 298
Wayport, 48
Weather, 30
Weather conditions and
    forecasts, 121
Websites
    for live music fans, 364
    traveler's toolbox, 50
    travel-planning and booking,
        44–47
Weill Recital Hall, 357
West 4th Street Basketball
    Courts, 8
West Indian–American Day
    Carnival and Parade, 6, 34
Westminster Kennel Club Dog
    Show, 31
West Village, 43
    Federal-style houses, 18
Wheelchair accessibility, 40
Whiskey Ward, 373
White Horse Tavern, 376
Whitney Museum of American
    Art, 250–251
Whitney Museum of American
    Art at Altria, 266
Who Wants to Be a Millionaire,
    294
Wi-Fi, 47–49
Wildenstein & Co, 259
Willow Street (Brooklyn),
    302
Wines and spirits, 343
Winnie's, 371
Wollman Rink, 35, 281
Woolworth Building, 22, 272
World Trade Center site
    (Ground Zero), 251

Yankees, 306
Yankees Clubhouse Shop,
    337
Yankee Stadium, 6, 88, 251,
    306, 307
Yeshiva University Museum,
    252–253
YIVO Institute for Jewish
    Research, 253
Yonah Schimmel Knishes, 331

Zabar's, 330
Zagat Survey, 169
Zankel Concert Hall, 357
Zitomer's, 320

Zoos, 296–297
  Bronx Zoo Wildlife
    Conservation Park, 297
  Central Park, 280
  Prospect Park Zoo (Brooklyn),
    301–302
Zum Schneider, 375

ACCOMMODATIONS

Affinia Dumont, 150
Akwaaba Mansion, 133
The Alex, 153
The Algonquin, 139–140, 144
Americana Inn, 147–148
The Bed and Breakfast Mont
  Morris, 133
Bed & Breakfast on the
  Park, 133
Belvedere Hotel, 143–144, 149
The Benjamin, 150–151
The Blakely New York, 1, 140
Broadway Inn, 144–146
The Carlyle: A Rosewood Hotel,
  9, 165
Casablanca Hotel, 146
Chelsea Lodge, 134
City Club, 144
Colonial House Inn, 132, 134
Country Inn the City, 132–133,
  161
Doubletree Guest Suites–Times
  Square, 10, 140–141, 149
Doubletree Metropolitan Hotel,
  2, 158
The Dream, 1–2
Excelsior Hotel, 161
Four Seasons Hotel New York,
  151
Gershwin Hotel, 138, 149
Gramercy Park Hotel, 1
Habitat Hotel, 158–159
Hotel Beacon, 10, 149,
  162–163
Hotel Belleclaire, 164
Hotel Chandler, 153–154
Hotel Elysée, 11, 154
Hotel Gansevoort, 1, 131
Hotel Giraffe, 135
Hotel Grand Union, 159
Hotel Metro, 10, 146, 149
Hotel Newton, 164–165
Hotel on Rivington, 1
Hotel Plaza Athénée, 165–166
Inn at Irving Place, 132, 135
Inn on 23rd Street, 10,
  132, 134
Iroquois Hotel, 144–145
The Kimberly, 154

The Kitano New York, 10, 155
La Quinta Inn Manhattan, 148
Larchmont Hotel, 131–132
Le Parker Meridien, 141, 149
The Library Hotel, 155–156
The Lowell, 10, 149, 166
The Lucerne, 10, 164
The Mansfield, 145
The Marcel, 138
The Mark, 166–167
The Melrose Hotel, 167
The Mercer, 9, 129–130
The Michelangelo, 141–142
Murray Hill Inn, 159
The Muse, 142
Novotel New York, 147, 149
The Peninsula-New York,
  9, 151–152
The Phillips Club, 161
Red Roof Inn, 148
The Regency, 149, 156
Ritz-Carlton New York, Battery
  Park, 126
Ritz-Carlton New York, Central
  Park, 9, 139, 149
The Roger, 156
Royalton, 145
St. Regis, 9, 152–153
San Carlos Hotel, 156–157
70 Park Avenue, 1, 157
The Sherry-Netherland, 152
Skyline Hotel, 148–149
Sofitel New York, 10, 142, 145
Thirty Thirty, 159–160
Travel Inn, 149, 150
Trump International Hotel &
  Tower, 9, 160
Union Square Inn, 138–139
Waldorf=Astoria and the
  Waldorf Towers, 157–158
Wall Street District Hotel by
  Holiday Inn, 128
The Wall Street Inn, 128
Washington Square Hotel,
  132–133
The Westin New York at Times
  Square, 142–143
WJ Hotel, 147
W Times Square, 143
W Union Square, 138

RESTAURANTS

Abboccato, 12, 200
Absolute Bagels, 13, 198, 218
Afghan Kebab House, 203
Aix, 215
Alain Ducasse, 199, 214
Amy Ruth's, 226
Aquavit, 2, 11, 207

Artie's New York Delicatessen,
  206, 218
Arunee Thai, 229
Atelier, 11, 199
Balthazar, 183–184, 376
Barbuto, 189
Barney Greengrass, the
  Sturgeon King, 206, 218
Bar Pitti, 190
Becco, 201–202
Ben Benson's Steakhouse, 200
Beppe, 12, 195
Big Nick's Burger and Pizza
  Joint, 210, 219
Big Wong King, 11, 178, 220
The Biltmore Room, 190–191
BLT Steak, 11, 207–208
Blue Ribbon, 376
Blue Smoke, 197
Bread, 185
Bread Tribeca, 177
Brick Lane Curry House,
  185–186
Brooklyn Ice Cream Factory, 13
Bryant Park Grill, 283
Bubby's Brooklyn (Brooklyn),
  228
Bubby's Pie Company, 177, 220
Bull and Bear, 194
Burger Joint, 10, 12, 141, 203
Café Boulud, 221–222
Café des Artistes, 211, 215
Capsouto Frères, 174, 176
Carmine's, 201, 210, 217
Carnegie Deli, 203, 206, 376
Celeste, 219
'Cesca, 215
Chanterelle, 11
Charles' Southern Style
  Kitchen, 13, 226
City Bakery, 198, 210
Clinton St. Baking Company,
  182, 220
Copeland's, 226–227
Cosmopolitan Hotel–Tribeca,
  129
Cub Room, 182
Daniel, 214, 221
db Bistro Moderne, 12, 200–201
Devi, 2, 12, 195
Dinosaur Bar-B-Que, 210, 223
Dos Caminos, 197
Dos Caminos Soho, 183
Eisenberg's Coffee Shop,
  198–199
Eleven Madison Park,
  11, 195–196
El Paso Taqueria, 223–224
Ess-A-Bagel, 198, 211

Ferdinando's Focacceria (Brooklyn), 228
Fiamma Osteria, 12, 182–183
5 Ninth, 188
Flor de Mayo, 219
Florent, 188
Francesco at Mix, 199
Good Enough to Eat, 12, 210, 220, 221
Gray's Papaya, 13, 190, 218–219
Grimaldi's Pizza (Brooklyn), 228
Grimaldi's Pizzeria, 84, 204
H&H Bagels, 198, 218
Holiday Inn Downtown/SoHo, 130–131
Home, 189
Ihawan, 229
Jean-Georges, 211, 214
John's Pizzeria, 190, 203, 204
Junior's (Brooklyn), 228
Kai, 222
Kalustyan's, 211
Katz's Delicatessen, 12, 182, 206, 376
King Cole Bar, 83
Kittichai, 2, 183
La Fonda Boricua, 224
La Marmite, 224
La Nacional, 191
Landmarc, 176
La Pollada de Laura, 229
Le Bernardin, 199, 214
L'Impero, 208
Lombardi's Pizza, 185, 204–205
Lupa, 184
Lure Fishbar, 183
Macelleria, 188
M&G Diner, 88, 227

Mandoo Bar, 190, 203–204
MarkJoseph, 174, 194
Marseille, 202
Masa, 2, 211, 214
Michael Jordan's–The Steak House, 194
Mickey Mantle's, 210
Miss Mamie's Spoonbread Too, 227
Molyvos, 201
Moran's Chelsea, 191
Murray's Bagels, 190, 198
Nathan's Famous (Brooklyn), 228, 300
The Neptune Room, 216
New York Noodletown, 178–179
Nice Matin, 217
Nick & Stef's Steakhouse, 194, 199
Nick's Family-Style Restaurant and Pizzeria, 210, 222
Noche Mexicana, 221
Nonna, 217–218
Norma's, 12, 202, 220
Nyonya, 179
Oceana, 12–13, 208
The Odeon, 177–178, 376
Onera, 218
Ono, 186, 188
Ouest, 216
Oyster Bar & Restaurant, 211
Pampano, 208–209
Pao!, 184
Paradou, 188
Pastis, 188
Patsy's Pizzeria, 12, 205, 223
Per Se, 2
Peter Luger Steakhouse (Brooklyn), 194, 228

Pete's Tavern, 84
Pho Viet Huong, 179
P.J. Clarke's, 209
PlateNYC, 184–185
Prime Burger, 211
Pure Food and Wine, 197
Riingo, 209
River Café (Brooklyn), 227, 302
The River Café, 11
Rosa Mexicano, 216
Sapa, 2, 13, 196
Savann, 218
Second Avenue Deli, 186, 206
Serendipity 3, 210, 223
60 Thompson, 130
Soho Grand, 130
Spice Market, 2, 188
Stage Deli, 203, 206, 376
Strip House, 13, 189
Suba, 179–180
Sylvia's, 227
Tamarind, 196
Tavern on the Green, 210, 215
Thalassa, 176
Totonno's (Brooklyn), 228
Totonno's Pizzeria Napolitano, 205, 222
Tribeca Grand Hotel, 128–129
Uncle Jack's Steakhouse, 201
Uncle Nick's, 205–206
Veselka, 186, 220, 376
Virgil's Real BBQ, 13, 202–203, 210
Voyage, 190
V Steakhouse, 2, 194
Walker's, 178
Wondee Siam, 207

FROMMER'S® COMPLETE TRAVEL GUIDES

Alaska
Alaska Cruises & Ports of Call
American Southwest
Amsterdam
Argentina & Chile
Arizona
Atlanta
Australia
Austria
Bahamas
Barcelona
Beijing
Belgium, Holland & Luxembourg
Bermuda
Boston
Brazil
British Columbia & the Canadian
  Rockies
Brussels & Bruges
Budapest & the Best of Hungary
Calgary
California
Canada
Cancún, Cozumel & the Yucatán
Cape Cod, Nantucket & Martha's
  Vineyard
Caribbean
Caribbean Ports of Call
Carolinas & Georgia
Chicago
China
Colorado
Costa Rica
Cruises & Ports of Call
Cuba
Denmark
Denver, Boulder & Colorado Springs
Edinburgh & Glasgow
England
Europe
Europe by Rail
European Cruises & Ports of Call
Florence, Tuscany & Umbria

Florida
France
Germany
Great Britain
Greece
Greek Islands
Halifax
Hawaii
Hong Kong
Honolulu, Waikiki & Oahu
India
Ireland
Italy
Jamaica
Japan
Kauai
Las Vegas
London
Los Angeles
Madrid
Maine Coast
Maryland & Delaware
Maui
Mexico
Montana & Wyoming
Montréal & Québec City
Munich & the Bavarian Alps
Nashville & Memphis
New England
Newfoundland & Labrador
New Mexico
New Orleans
New York City
New York State
New Zealand
Northern Italy
Norway
Nova Scotia, New Brunswick &
  Prince Edward Island
Oregon
Ottawa
Paris
Peru

Philadelphia & the Amish Country
Portugal
Prague & the Best of the Czech
  Republic
Provence & the Riviera
Puerto Rico
Rome
San Antonio & Austin
San Diego
San Francisco
Santa Fe, Taos & Albuquerque
Scandinavia
Scotland
Seattle
Seville, Granada & the Best of
  Andalusia
Shanghai
Sicily
Singapore & Malaysia
South Africa
South America
South Florida
South Pacific
Southeast Asia
Spain
Sweden
Switzerland
Texas
Thailand
Tokyo
Toronto
Turkey
USA
Utah
Vancouver & Victoria
Vermont, New Hampshire & Maine
Vienna & the Danube Valley
Virgin Islands
Virginia
Walt Disney World® & Orlando
Washington, D.C.
Washington State

FROMMER'S® DOLLAR-A-DAY GUIDES

Australia from $50 a Day
California from $70 a Day
England from $75 a Day
Europe from $85 a Day
Florida from $70 a Day
Hawaii from $80 a Day

Ireland from $80 a Day
Italy from $70 a Day
London from $90 a Day
New York City from $90 a Day
Paris from $90 a Day
San Francisco from $70 a Day

Washington, D.C. from $80 a Day
Portable London from $90 a Day
Portable New York City from $90
  a Day
Portable Paris from $90 a Day

FROMMER'S® PORTABLE GUIDES

Acapulco, Ixtapa & Zihuatanejo
Amsterdam
Aruba
Australia's Great Barrier Reef
Bahamas
Berlin
Big Island of Hawaii
Boston
California Wine Country
Cancún
Cayman Islands
Charleston
Chicago
Disneyland®
Dominican Republic

Dublin
Florence
Frankfurt
Hong Kong
Las Vegas
Las Vegas for Non-Gamblers
London
Los Angeles
Los Cabos & Baja
Maui
Miami
Nantucket & Martha's Vineyard
New Orleans
New York City
Paris

Phoenix & Scottsdale
Portland
Puerto Rico
Puerto Vallarta, Manzanillo &
  Guadalajara
Rio de Janeiro
San Diego
San Francisco
Savannah
Vancouver Island
Venice
Virgin Islands
Washington, D.C.
Whistler

FROMMER'S® NATIONAL PARK GUIDES

Algonquin Provincial Park
Banff & Jasper
Family Vacations in the National
  Parks

Grand Canyon
National Parks of the American West
Rocky Mountain

Yellowstone & Grand Teton
Yosemite & Sequoia/Kings Canyon
Zion & Bryce Canyon

FROMMER'S® MEMORABLE WALKS

Chicago
London

New York
Paris

San Francisco

FROMMER'S® WITH KIDS GUIDES

Chicago
Hawaii
Las Vegas
New York City

Ottawa
San Francisco
Toronto

Vancouver
Walt Disney World® & Orlando
Washington, D.C.

SUZY GERSHMAN'S BORN TO SHOP GUIDES

Born to Shop: France
Born to Shop: Hong Kong, Shanghai
  & Beijing

Born to Shop: Italy
Born to Shop: London

Born to Shop: New York
Born to Shop: Paris

FROMMER'S® IRREVERENT GUIDES

Amsterdam
Boston
Chicago
Las Vegas
London

Los Angeles
Manhattan
New Orleans
Paris
Rome

San Francisco
Seattle & Portland
Vancouver
Walt Disney World®
Washington, D.C.

FROMMER'S® BEST-LOVED DRIVING TOURS

Austria
Britain
California
France

Germany
Ireland
Italy
New England

Northern Italy
Scotland
Spain
Tuscany & Umbria

THE UNOFFICIAL GUIDES®

Beyond Disney
California with Kids
Central Italy
Chicago
Cruises
Disneyland®
England
Florida
Florida with Kids
Inside Disney

Hawaii
Las Vegas
London
Maui
Mexico's Best Beach Resorts
Mini Las Vegas
Mini Mickey
New Orleans
New York City
Paris

San Francisco
Skiing & Snowboarding in the West
South Florida including Miami &
  the Keys
Walt Disney World®
Walt Disney World® for
  Grown-ups
Walt Disney World® with Kids
Washington, D.C.

SPECIAL-INTEREST TITLES

Athens Past & Present
Cities Ranked & Rated
Frommer's Best Day Trips from London
Frommer's Best RV & Tent Campgrounds
  in the U.S.A.
Frommer's Caribbean Hideaways
Frommer's China: The 50 Most Memorable Trips
Frommer's Exploring America by RV
Frommer's Gay & Lesbian Europe

Frommer's NYC Free & Dirt Cheap
Frommer's Road Atlas Europe
Frommer's Road Atlas France
Frommer's Road Atlas Ireland
Frommer's Wonderful Weekends from
  New York City
Retirement Places Rated
Rome Past & Present

THE NEW TRAVELOCITY GUARANTEE

**EVERYTHING YOU BOOK WILL BE RIGHT, OR WE'LL WORK
WITH OUR TRAVEL PARTNERS TO MAKE IT RIGHT, RIGHT AWAY.**

*To drive home the point,
we're going to use the word "right" in every single sentence.*

Let's get right to it. Right to the meat! Only Travelocity guarantees everything about your booking will be right, or we'll work with our travel partners to make it right, right away. Right on!

Here's a picture taken smack dab right in the middle of Antigua, where the guarantee also covers you.

The guarantee covers all but one of the items pictured to the right.

Now, you may be thinking, "Yeah, right, I'm so sure." That's OK; you have the right to remain skeptical. That is until we mention help is always right around the corner. Call us right off the bat, knowing that our customer service reps are there for you 24/7. Righting wrongs. Left and right.

For example, what if the ocean view you booked actually looks out at a downright ugly parking lot? You'd be right to call – we're there for you. And no one in their right mind would be pleased to learn the rental car place has closed and left them stranded. Call Travelocity and we'll help get you back on the right track.

Now if you're guessing there are some things we can't control, like the weather, well you're right. But we can help you with most things – to get all the details in righting,* visit **travelocity.com/guarantee**.

*Sorry, spelling things right is one of the few things not covered under the guarantee.

I'd give my right arm for a guarantee like this, although I'm glad I don't have to.

travelocity
You'll never roam alone.